CW00968401

Victorian Turkish Baths

For Devra
Many waters cannot quench love,
Neither can the floods drown it;
(Song of Songs 8:7)

Victorian Turkish Baths

Malcolm Shifrin

Published by Historic England, The Engine House, Fire Fly Avenue, Swindon SN2 2EH
www.HistoricEngland.org.uk

Historic England is a Government service championing England's heritage and giving expert, constructive advice, and, the English Heritage Trust is a charity caring for the National Heritage Collection of more than 400 historic properties and their collections.

The views expressed in this book are those of the author and not necessarily those of Historic England.

The author has no medical qualifications. Any suggestion that the Victorian Turkish, or any other type of hot-air bath, could be used as a therapy for a medical condition is to be understood only as reporting and discussing historical views. Anyone with a medical condition should always seek a doctor's advice before taking a hot-air bath for the first time.

First published 2015

ISBN 978-1-84802-230-0

British Library Cataloguing in Publication data
A CIP catalogue record for this book is available from the British Library.

Historic England holds an unparalleled archive of 12 million photographs, drawings, reports and publications on England's places. It is one of the largest archives in the UK, the biggest dedicated to the historic environment, and a priceless resource for anyone interested in England's buildings, archaeology, landscape and social history. Viewed collectively, its photographic collections document the changing face of England from the 1850s to the present day. It is a treasure trove that helps us understand and interpret the past, informs the present and assists with future management and appreciation of the historic environment.

For more information about images from the Archive, contact Archives Services Team, Historic England, The Engine House, Fire Fly Avenue, Swindon SN2 2EH; telephone (01793) 414600.

Brought to publication by Robin Taylor, Publishing, Historic England

Typeset in Charter ITC Std/9.5pt

Edited by John Duggan
Page layout by Sparks—www.sparkspublishing.com
Indexed by the author

Printed in the UK by Bell & Bain Ltd

CONTENTS

PREFACE

One day towards the end of 1990, I was chatting with some friends in the front room of a health club in the city of Bath. Looking round, I noticed that the door leading into the changing rooms had a stained glass panel decorated with a series of small stars and crescents. There were also a few panes with a monogram in the form of a highly decorated letter B (Fig 0.1).

I asked if anyone knew the significance of the symbols or the strange initial. I learned that about 30 years earlier part of the building had been occupied by Bartholomew's Turkish Baths, and that their original owner, Charles Bartholomew, had built the first Turkish baths in the country in nearby Bristol.

I was intrigued and, as any recently retired librarian would, I dashed down to the local library to see what I could find. I soon discovered that there was very little, and left the library even more intrigued.

I decided to do some serious research and visited the British Library. There was more material there, but not nearly as much as I had expected. In due course, I discovered that the first of these baths was built not by Charles Bartholomew in Bristol, but near Cork in Ireland, by a somewhat eccentric but brilliant ex-diplomat by the name of David Urquhart, and a hydropathic physician named Richard Barter. By now I was totally hooked.

As a teenager, too many decades ago, I occasionally visited the unique Turkish baths at London's Imperial Hotel—sadly long demolished. Unfortunately, although I *enjoyed* Turkish baths, I was not then *interested* in them. By the time that happened there were relatively few left.

Discovering that the last book on Turkish baths in Britain had been published almost 100 years ago—and that it had been written specifically for architects—I decided that researching the history of this rapidly disappearing phenomenon would be a satisfying way to spend my retirement.

This book is the result of over 20 years of enquiry during which time I have visited all the remaining Turkish baths, and innumerable libraries and archives.

One of the most interesting things I discovered was the manner in which the baths spread across the world so quickly, even arriving in Australia before it reached London. This is shown throughout the book by a series of maps which, taken together, immediately give the reader a quick insight into its progress (Table 0.1).

Fig 0.1
Charles Bartholomew's monogram. Part of a stained glass panel in an internal door at 2 Edgar Buildings, Bath, in 1990.
(© Malcolm Shifrin)

At the end of 1999 I started a website, *Victorian Turkish baths: their origin, development, & gradual decline*. This was well received and became an information exchange enabling historians, postgraduate students, writers, TV researchers, and journalists to discover the bath. Some local historians asked about those in their own locality and family historians asked about establishments which were owned, worked in, or used by their ancestors. With these two groups it was often a two-way process, the website sometimes receiving valuable information or images, often with details and dates which had been impossible to find elsewhere.

The website virtually shaped itself into the form of an encyclopædia, partly as a result of the manner in which the information was discovered, and partly because the internet is particularly hospitable to this type of publication. Arranged in broad sections dealing with the baths, the

Table 0.1 Maps showing the spread of the Victorian Turkish bath

companies and people who ran them, together with other areas of general and historical interest, it seems to help those trying to discover answers to specific questions. But a website is not necessarily the easiest or most enjoyable way to read about something and get a balanced picture.

This book, then, is designed to relate the history of the Victorian Turkish bath, as it happened. And because books have a finite length, the website can often provide additional examples, or further detail for the specialist, without holding up the story. It also provides space for any corrections, and for information sent in by readers.

Whenever the website provides extra information, the following symbol§ appears in the text, so that only one URL, http://www.victorianturkishbath.org/thebook.htm needs to be remembered. This links to a screen with a hyperlinked list of all additional material arranged in order of the book's pages; all you need to do is click on the item you want.

I have written as much for the general reader as for the academic, and the few technical terms used are indicated on their first appearance by an asterisk* and have been defined in the glossary.

I hope the book will be found enjoyable by those who enjoy any type of spa or hot-air bath—not only the Victorian Turkish bath, but also the Islamic *hammam*, Russian steam baths, and the Finnish sauna—for it tells the story of the Victorian institution which led directly to the popularity in the British Isles of our 21st-century baths and spas.

It should also appeal to anyone who is interested in architecture, the development of the leisure and tourism industry, public health and the sanitary movement, social attitudes to medicine, pressure groups and the Turkish Bath Movement, gendered spaces, and much else besides.

Some parts of the story will be of special interest to those in the United States, Canada, Australia and New Zealand, as well as to those in our European neighbours in Scandinavia, Germany, the Netherlands, France and Hungary.

Because the book is not intended solely as an academic work, it includes little theorising. But it does have the full scholarly apparatus of endnotes and bibliography, and I hope that it will be useful to students and academics who wish to do further research on the many topics treated here.

There is a limit to what can be achieved by an individual researcher, and this is a frustrating time for what is politely called the independent scholar. On the one hand, digitisation brings to light previously unimaginable quantities of historically important information on subjects of concern. On the other hand, it has never been so difficult for those of us outside academia to access this information so tantalisingly dangled before us; we are not entitled to use the necessary institutional subscriptions.

Furthermore, the printed scholarly journal is rapidly being replaced by digital versions no longer accessible to those visiting their nearest university library. Digital resources are becoming the 21st century's chained library—restricted to the privileged.

So it would be particularly gratifying if the book, as well as being an enjoyable read, were to act as a trigger for academic research on a wide-ranging and interesting subject which has so far been almost entirely neglected.[1]

Malcolm Shifrin
Leatherhead
October 2014

GLOSSARY

The glossary is divided into three alphabetical sections: (A) The Victorian Turkish bath; (B) Other hydropathic baths and treatments; (C) Architecture. Words appearing in **bold type** within a definition are themselves defined in the glossary. Within the book, an asterisk * precedes at least the first mention of a term defined in the glossary.

A The Victorian Turkish bath

I have based these definitions of the Latin terms relating to the Roman bath on the explanations given in 'Individual elements of the baths', the appendix to the first volume of Inge Nielsen's standard work *Thermae et balnea: the architecture and cultural history of Roman public baths.*[1]

apodyterium

The changing room, or dressing-room. Smaller establishments substituted cubicles, sometimes furnished with couches and lockers, placed around the walls of the ***frigidarium***.

balnea

A public bath without sports facilities, usually smaller than ***thermae.***

cal(i)darium

Usually the larger of two hot rooms, or the second of three. Lewis and Short's standard *Latin Dictionary*, the *Oxford English Dictionary*, and Nielsen all prefer to omit the additional letter 'i', though Lewis and Short allows it as an option.

chibouk

A Turkish tobacco-pipe (*chibouque,* in French) with an extremely long stem and not to be confused with the ***narghile***. The mouthpieces and bowls can be varied.

This rare silver encrusted pipe is in the collection of Arjan de Haan.

© *Arjan de Haan (www.the-curiosity-shop.nl/itempages/index_private.htm)*

dureta

When used in a Victorian Turkish bath, a wooden couch shaped like three-quarters of a letter 'w'. Probably from the Spanish *dureza* meaning hard, though according to David Urquhart, 'in reality forming a most pleasant and agreeable couch, as the angles of the couch correspond with the joints of the body when in a reclining position.'

Lewis and Short quotes Seutonius, but suggests his meaning was 'a wooden bathing-tub.'

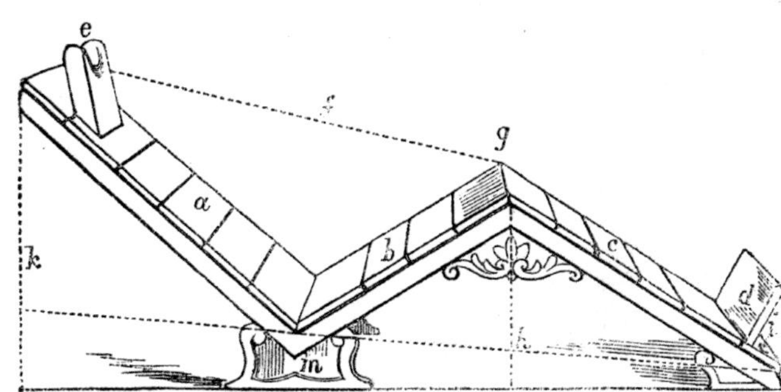

Source: Eastern, or Turkish bath *Erasmus Wilson (Churchill, 1861) p.xxxi*

frigidarium

The cooling-room of the Victorian Turkish bath.

In the Roman bath this room often had cold water pools, but in the Victorian bath it became the acclimatising area between outdoors and the first hot room. Often with a fountain and a plunge pool, its main use now is for relaxation after the bath.

hammam

The Islamic hot-air bath, often called 'Turkish bath' by non-Muslims, adapted from the baths of the Ancient Romans. (See Chapter 2, page 11)

hypocaust

The Roman heating system by means of which hot air circulated beneath the floor and between double walls.

© Urban

The floor was raised above the ground, supported by stacks of tiles, or *pilae*.

laconicum
The hottest, and usually the smallest, of the hot rooms, derived from Laconian (the Romanised form of Spartan).

lavatorium
The washing room, sometimes called the *labrum*.

lavatory
Until the word became a euphemism for toilet, water closet or, more recently, loo, lavatory simply meant a room for washing in.

narghile
A pipe consisting of one or more flexible stems connected to a container of water or other liquid through which smoke is drawn and cooled.

© Kelisi

From the Persian *nargileh*, by way of the French *narguil*, also known as the *hookah* or *shisha*.

pattens
Wooden clogs or sandals designed to insulate and protect a bather's feet from burns when the floor is heated by a ***hypocaust***. They also help to keep the feet dry and stop bathers slipping on floors which, in an Islamic ***hammam***, are often wet. In the Victorian Turkish bath they were more usually simple wooden sandals.

© Jean-Etienne Liotard

shampoo
'To shampoo' originally meant to give a person, or part of that person's body, a massage. According to the *Oxford English Dictionary*, the word—probably from the Hindi, to press—is now used in this sense only in the context of a Turkish bath. The modern use referring to washing one's hair is not much older than 1860.

sudatorium
Sometimes used by Victorians as a synonym for **laconicum**. In Roman baths, water was sometimes thrown onto the floor to give an effect similar to that in a Finnish sauna.

tepidarium
The first (and coolest) of the hot rooms.

thermae
Authors quoted in this book are using *thermae* loosely to indicate ancient Roman hot-air baths but, as Nielsen explains, 'there is no clear ancient definition' of either of the terms *thermae* or ***balnea*** which she uses in the title of her own book. (*Balnea* always appears, in its plural form.)

B Other hydropathic baths and treatments

Aeratone™ bath
A patented deep circular bath with jets of compressed air which massage the body. The bath, normally used by one bather at a time, is filled by an attendant with hot water at the correct temperature and at the right depth for that particular bather. The time spent in the bath can be as long as an hour. It was invented by Professor William Oliver and was manufactured from about 1938 until the early 1950s.

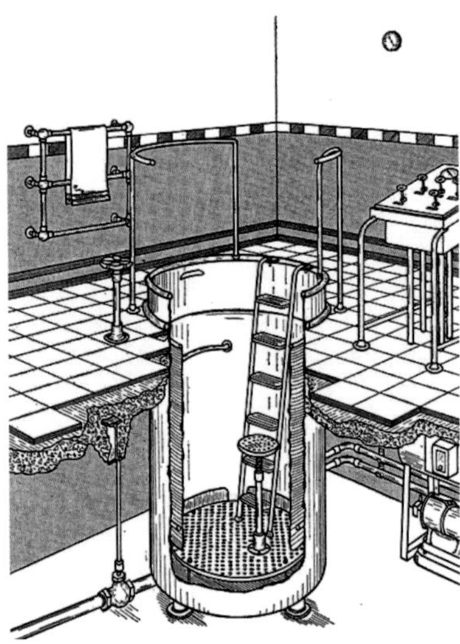

Courtesy of Victoria Baths History Archive

blanket pack *See:* wet sheet packing

cold water cure *See:* hydropathy

diathermy
Localised heating of the body tissues with an electric current for medical purposes. This was on offer at, for example, Bartholomew's Turkish baths in Bristol, but it is not known if it was widely used.

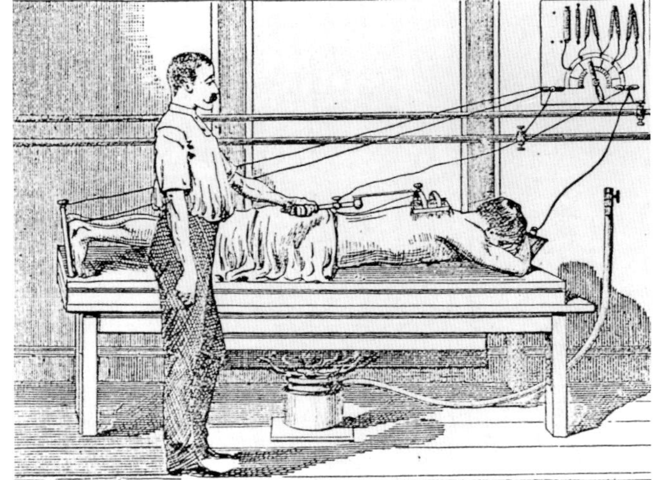

Source: Illustrated guide to the Turkish baths… *Charles Bartholomew (Marshall, 1887)*

douche
A stream of water directed onto the body, or into a body cavity, for cleansing (or medical) purposes. Often used to mean a shower, but in this context it usually indicates that the water is directed from an open pipe or hose rather than through a shower rose.

Source: Hydropathy; or, the cold water cure… *3 edn R T Claridge (Madden, 1842) frontis. (Wellcome Library, London)*

electric baths and electric lamp baths
There were two types of electric baths which some establishments occasionally provided as an additional facility.

In the earlier one, the bather sat in a normal water-filled bath while a very mild electric current was passed through wires placed in the water.

Source: The hydro-electric method in medicine *W S Hedley (Lewis, 1892) (Wellcome Library, London)*

The other one (sometimes called the lamp bath) was an early type of sunbed in which the bather was warmed by the heat of the surrounding electric lamps.

In this bath from the *RMS Olympic*, the bather would lie on the bed with the lid shut so that the whole body was enclosed apart from the head. Additional side lamps were then fitted before they were all switched on for a pre-determined time.

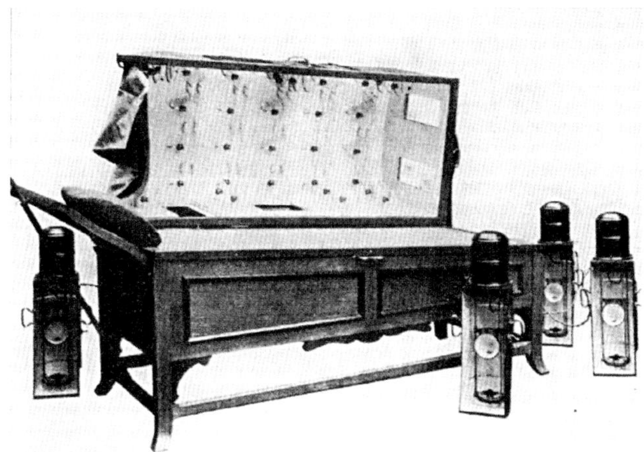

Source: 'White Star liners Olympic *and* Titanic' Shipbuilder *(1911, Special no.) p.108 (Bruce Beveridge Collection)*

needle shower

Directs fine jets of water all round the body. Also called the *needle bath* or *needle douche*, it is usually fitted with an overhead spray and often also, as in this illustration, with an upward spray from the floor.

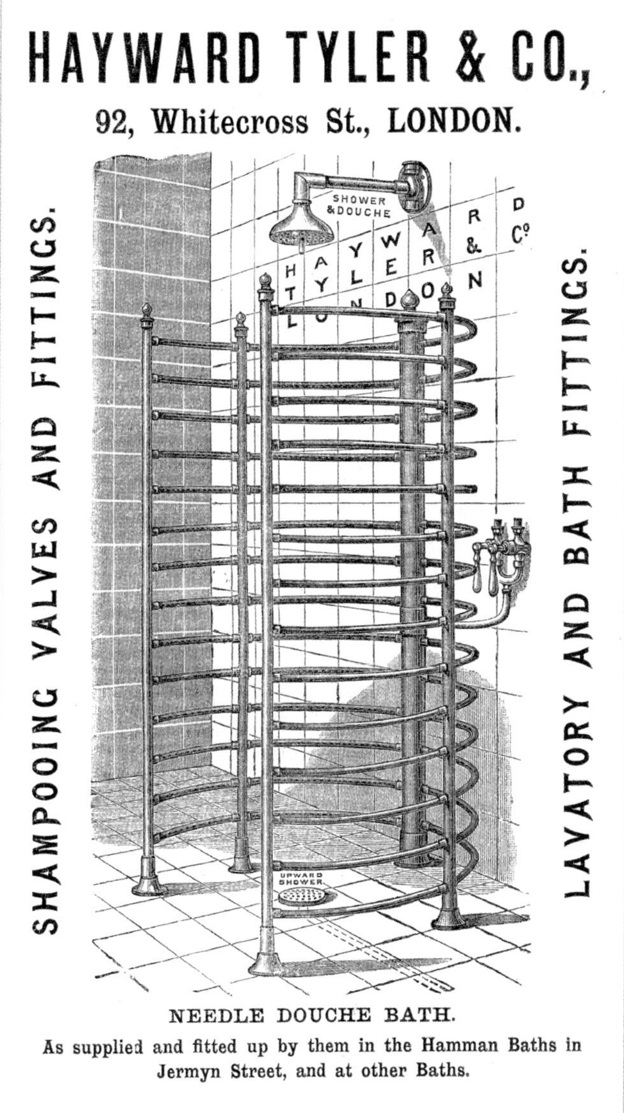

Source: The Turkish bath *Robert Owen Allsop (Spon, 1890) endpaper*

hydropathy

The application of water, internally and externally, as a therapy. There were three components of the (cold) water cure: drinking mineralised water; **wet sheet packing**; and specialised showers and **douches**.

mikveh

A pool of running water used by religious Jews for ritual cleansing. Sometimes spelled *mikvah,* plural *mikvaoth*.

rain bath, rain shower

Other names for a standard shower where the bather stands under a shower rose.

schmeissing

Scrubbing and whisking with a raffia brush, usually after a Russian steam bath. Introduced to Britain by Russian Jewish immigrants at the end of the 19th century, *schmeissing* is rather similar to the Finnish *vihta,* with raffia being more accessible in London's East End than birch twigs.

sitz bath

A bath with a seat. The bather sits so that the water level is just above the abdomen, and with the shoulders covered by a blanket. From the German *sitzen*, to sit.

Source: Practical hydropathy *John Smedley (Kent, 1870) p.69a*

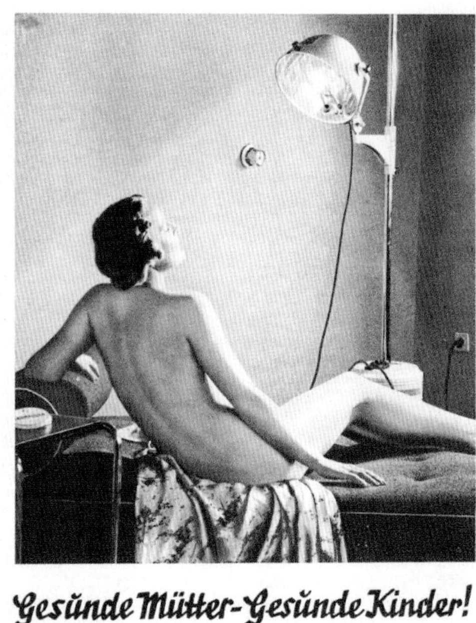

German postcard. Author's collection

slipper baths

An establishment where members of the public could take a bath for a small fee. Named after the slipper-shaped baths which were used. Initially, they were provided for wealthier patrons by commercial concerns, and later, after the Baths and Wash-houses Acts, by local authorities at low prices stipulated in the acts.

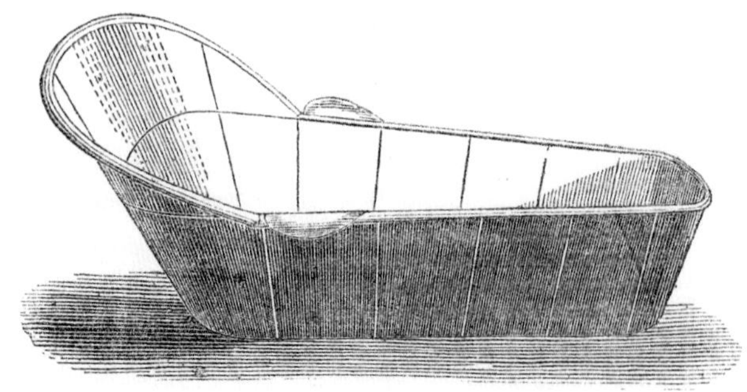

Source: Practical hydropathy *John Smedley (Kent, 1870) p.70*

sun bath

Usually, prior to the invention of the **sun-ray lamp**, a sun lounge on the roof.

sun-ray lamp

A lamp producing ultraviolet rays utilised for artificial sun-tanning and muscular therapy. First produced in Germany in the 1920s, sun-ray lamps were superseded in the mid-1970s by the sunbed, now considered unsafe by the World Health Organisation since over-exposure to ultraviolet radiation is known to cause skin cancer.

Vichy douche

A four-handed massage under a continuous spray of water at around 70°F (21°C). Originating at the French spa town in the latter part of the 19th century, the Vichy douche has become popular again at modern-day spas.

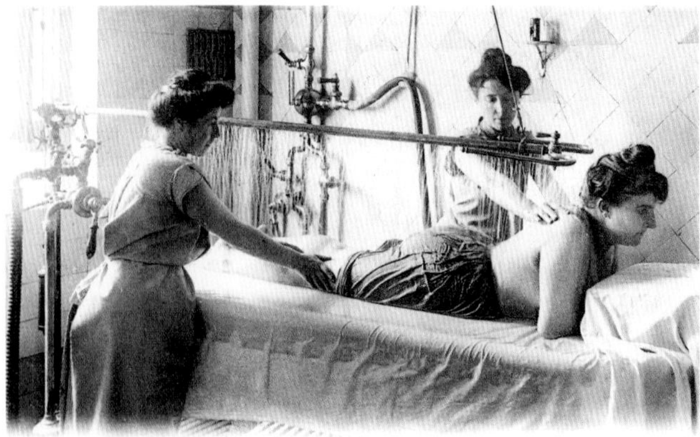

French postcard. Author's collection

water cure *See:* hydropathy

wave douche

A horizontal 'gush' of water like a small cascade, before which a bather stands and turns according to preference.

wet sheet packing

Patients were wrapped in wet sheets, within a dry blanket, for a prescribed time. Initially they felt decidedly cold, then merely cool, and finally extremely warm until they broke out in a sweat (the 'crisis') rather akin to a fever.

Dr Richard Barter deduced that it was the feverish perspiration which was responsible for any improvement in the patient's condition, and realised that the Turkish bath was a more comfortable way of inducing a sweat.

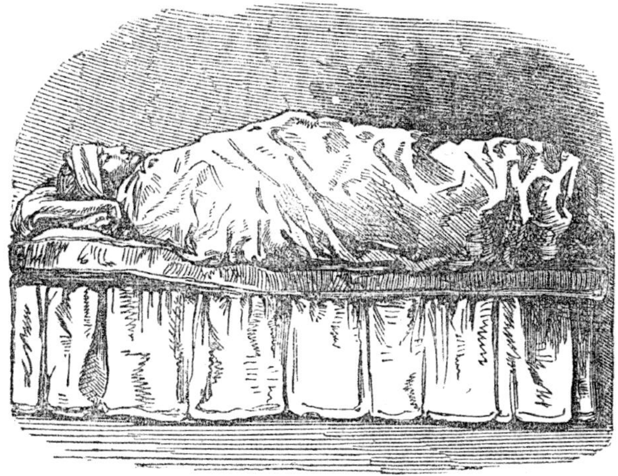

Source: Practical hydropathy *John Smedley (Kent, 1870) p.69a*

Zotofoam™ bath

Patients bathed in an ordinary slipper bath in which bubbles were produced by pumping compressed air or oxygen through a distributor placed on the bottom of the bath. This was covered by hot water at around 105°F to which had been added an ounce of Zotofoam extract. The foam acted as insulation preventing the heat from escaping so that the body temperature increased and the bather sweated profusely.

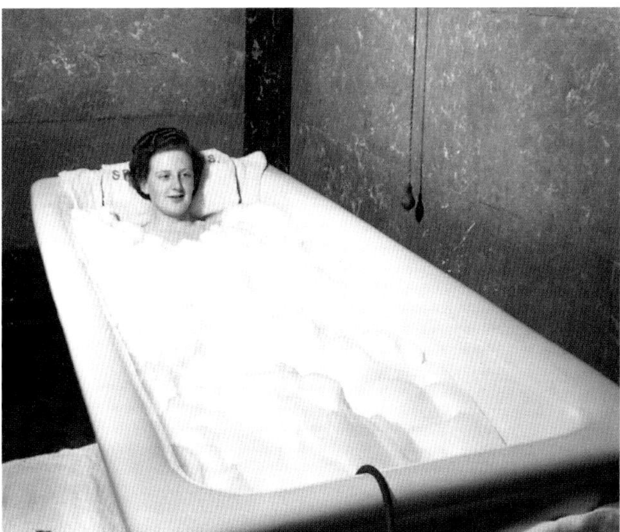

Courtesy of Leamington Spa Art Gallery & Museum (Warwick District Council)

C Architecture

arabesque

Surface decoration of intricately patterned foliage, scrolls, bands, spirals, etc.

Its probable derivation from Islamic ornamentation accounts for the exclusion of any human forms in the design.

© Pentocelo

boss

An ornamental projection placed at the intersection of the ribs of a **vault**, or sometimes of the beams in a wooden ceiling.

These bosses can be seen in Hereford Cathedral.

© Mattana

corbel
A structural support projecting from the face of a wall, often carved or moulded.

This ***faïence*** corbel is one of several which support arches in the ***frigidarium*** of the Edwardian Turkish baths at Carlisle.

© *Malcolm Shifrin*

cupola
A small decorative form of dome.

Doric columns

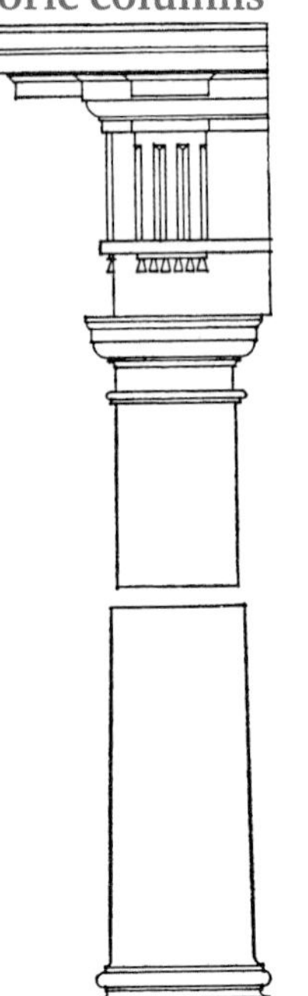

Author's rendering

The Roman Doric is the simplest type of classical column.

Its design and proportions follow, as do all Greek and Roman columns, the rules of its particular type, or *order*. The special characteristics of each order were considered to make them suitable for certain types of buildings, the Doric order being associated with strength.

dumbwaiter
A small lift used for transferring food and waste between floors.

In a 19th-century Turkish bath it would also, typically, be used for carrying clean towels, and be moved from floor to floor by means of a hand-held rope. Soiled towels would usually be sent down a chute when not carried by hand.

encaustic
Encaustic, or inlaid tiles, have their design impressed in the surface of the body of the tile and then filled with clay of a different colour or colours.

At first they were mainly used in churches but in the second half of the 19th century they became increasingly popular in other buildings.

Tile by Robert Minton Taylor, c 1872. Courtesy Hans van Lemmen

faïence
Tin-glazed earthenware used structurally or decoratively.

The glaze hides the colour of the clay allowing brightly coloured internal and external surfaces to be used decoratively to great effect.

© *Malcolm Shifrin*

groin

The angled edge where two **vaults** of semicircular section meet at right angles.

In the illustration, the barrel vault is divided into bays, the groins being formed by arches intersecting at right angles as part of a framework supporting the roof above.

© Anxanum

horseshoe arch

An arch which is greater than a semicircle and so appears to be horseshoe shaped.

Here the roof of the 12th century Ibn Shushan synagogue in Toledo is supported by a series of such arches following the local Moorish style of the day. Also known as the keyhole arch.

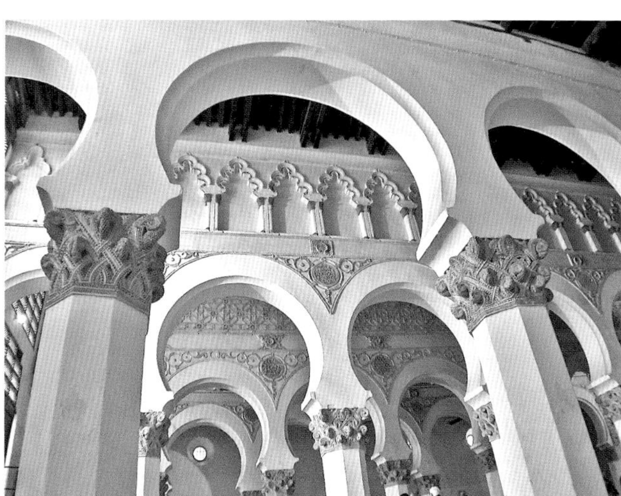

Photo © Adrian Fletcher (www.paradoxplace.com)

lantern

A small circular or polygonal structure with windows, raised on a dome or roof in order to admit light. This one is from the Roman Baths in Cambridge.

© Malcolm Shifrin

ogee

An ogee arch is formed by two mirrored flattened 'S' shapes meeting at a point.

No ogee arches have so far been found in any Victorian Turkish baths, though the Lincoln Place baths in Dublin had an ogee shaped dome. These are the gilded domes of the Cathedral of the Annunciation, Moscow, built between 1884 and 1889.

© Петар Милошевић (Petar Milošević)

ottoman

An upholstered seat, usually without back or arms.

Sometimes the seat formed the lid of a storage chest. In the late 19th century they could also be circular or octagonal with a central surface designed to hold a plant or statue.

Source: Victorian catalogue of household furnishings *Studio Editions (1994) No.321*

pediment

The triangular gable above a classical **portico**.

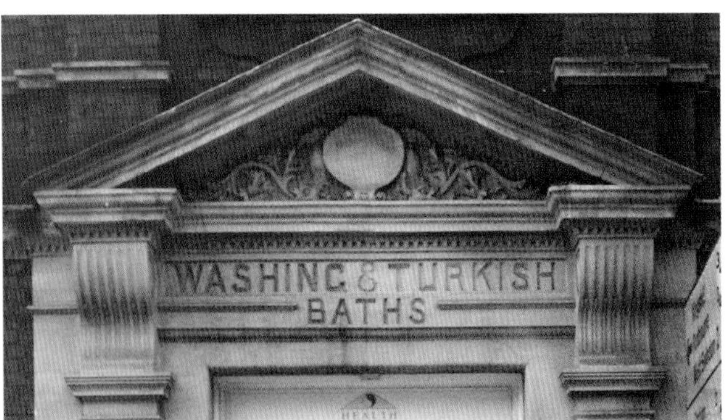

© *Malcolm Shifrin*

portico

A porch with the roof supported by columns or pillars. When, as shown here at Avery Hill, it is wide enough for a carriage to shelter while passengers alight, it is known as a porte-cochere.

Photograph by Colonel North. Courtesy University of Greenwich (Proctor Collection)

Saracenic (style)

Saracenic is 'a catch-all description of Islamic architecture from different periods and different places.'[2]

Although no longer used by architects or architectural historians, it was widely used in 19th-century newspapers and professional journals such as *The Builder* from which I frequently quote and on which I often comment.

I have, therefore, used the term for convenience throughout the book, just as I have also retained imperial measurements and pre-decimalisation money. The term is further discussed in Chapter 3.

soffit

The underneath surface of a building component such as a lintel, overhang, stair or window sill.

© *Malcolm Shifrin*

stalactite cornice

Three-dimensional decoration, here at Nevill's New Broad Street Turkish bath, is based on *muqarnas,* the Islamic device in which niche-like features are projected over those below, suggesting, when used *en masse,* stalactites.

Nevill's Turkish Baths, Ltd., London.
View of a Cooling Room.

Postcard. Author's collection

sunburners

A Sugg ventilating light of the type used in the House of Commons and probably used within the hot rooms at the London Hamman. These were called 'sunburners' in the *Building News* description of the baths.

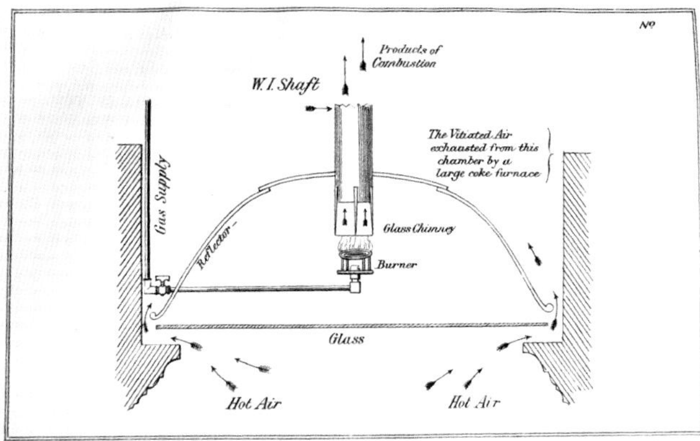

Chris Sugg (http://williamsugghistory.co.uk/)

terracotta

Unglazed fired clay bricks or decorative facings retaining the colour of the clay used. It could be moulded and mass produced, as here at the Miller Arcade in Preston, but it could also be sculpted by artists.

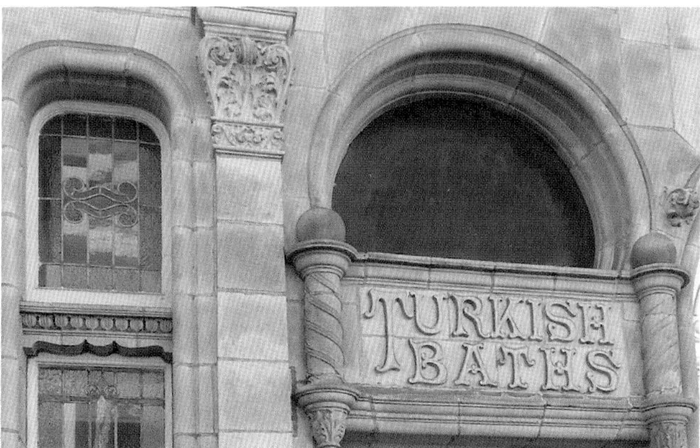

© Joanne Burke

terrazzo

Cement with chips of coloured stone embedded and polished, frequently used for floors.

© Richard Mayer

vault

An arched ceiling, or roof—here, a series of barrel vaults in one of the hot rooms at the Victoria Baths, Hathersage Road, Manchester.

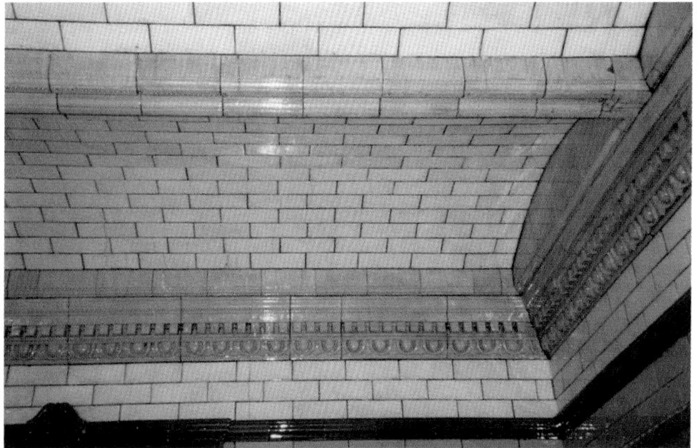

© Malcolm Shifrin

Dating the baths: a cautionary note

The data used in the book

The history of the Victorian Turkish bath, as told in this book and its ongoing complementary website, is derived from a much larger database relating to as many baths as I could discover. In the book, I have tried, in the space available, to give as rounded a picture as possible. Inevitably much has been omitted and it is hoped that baths which have been left out—and those only mentioned in passing—will gradually be added to the website.

I hope some readers will be encouraged to explore the subject more deeply and I feel it is important, therefore, to indicate what type of information I tried to find, where it came from, and how accurate it is likely to be.

The baths included

My main target has been Victorian-style Turkish baths, which were open to the general public in Ireland and Great Britain from 1856 until the present time. I have tried to find as many of these as possible. In addition, I have looked at baths for several types of special user, for example, patients and staff in hospitals. Here I have discussed some of those encountered—without necessarily specifically seeking them out. Finally, I have researched the first Victorian Turkish baths to open in a number of other countries, mainly in the 19th-century British Empire. Every bath in the main database is listed in the §directory section of the website.

The use of local directories as an information source

For most of the establishments in Ireland and Great Britain, local directories have been crucial. In many instances they have been used as a follow-up to discover owners, managers, addresses, and dates of a bath already found in a book or periodical article. Most frequently, information was found by a time-consuming search of directories found in every library visited. This provided enough basic information to use the resources of local history libraries and, latterly, the internet.

Unfortunately, much of the information found in local directories is selective—the poorer areas were not always included—and inaccurate, especially where dates and the spelling of names are concerned.

The dates used in this book

The date, or inclusive dates, in the title of a local directory give only the most approximate idea of how up-to-date its information is likely to be. Like today's periodicals, directories were often dated ahead to give them a longer life. Often not all the entries were revised for each edition. This means that, without confirmation from another source, most dates obtained from a directory are only approximate.

For an unaided author to undertake exact checks on every date within the book would probably result in its never being published so, following Voltaire's maxim, 'The best is the enemy of the good', I have had to compromise.

In general, therefore, when I have been able to give an exact date—to include year, month, and day—it is 95% likely to be accurate, while the inclusion of a year and month only means it is probably reasonably accurate. So, unless otherwise stated, when a date consists of a specific year only, it is most likely that this is when a bath was first sighted, or last heard of. Baths, like most businesses, are usually started with much publicity. Small businesses usually die quietly.

PART I

Background to the Victorian Turkish bath

1

Introduction: What is a Victorian Turkish bath?

Ask any small group of people sitting in a sauna or a steam room, 'What is a Turkish bath?' You will almost certainly get as many definitions as there are people. The phrase 'Turkish bath' conjures up very different images in the minds of those who come across it, so including it in the title of a book dictates that it needs to be defined very early on.

> **Turkish bath** ▸ noun **1** a type of bath in which the bather sweats freely in a room heated by hot dry air (or in a series of two or three such rooms maintained at progressively higher temperatures), usually followed by a cold plunge, a full body wash and massage, and a final period of relaxation in a cooling-room.
> **2** (sometimes pl.) an establishment offering Turkish baths.

Dictionaries do not offer any authoritative guidance. Most of their definitions are inaccurate in one way or another and serve only to confuse, because each definition is an attempt to define, as an entity, something which has never existed (Fig 1.1).

There is nothing specifically Turkish about the so-called 'Turkish bath', any more than there is anything English about an English bath, or American about an American bath.

But, for centuries, European travellers in the Turkish Ottoman Empire have been fascinated by the seemingly exotic public hot-air baths which they found there (Fig 1.2). It is their written accounts which have led to these baths becoming widely known as Turkish baths.

But they are not specifically Turkish; they are also widely found in the Maghreb (Fig 1.3), and wherever there is, or has been, a Moorish or Islamic influence.

These public hot-air baths—better and more accurately called Islamic ʿ*hammams*—are, as we shall see, quite different from the Victorian Turkish baths which are the subject of this book.

There is no mention of any steam or humidity in this definition; the hot air is dry. And, for reasons lightly touched on above, the words 'Turkey' or 'Turkish' do not occur within the definition.

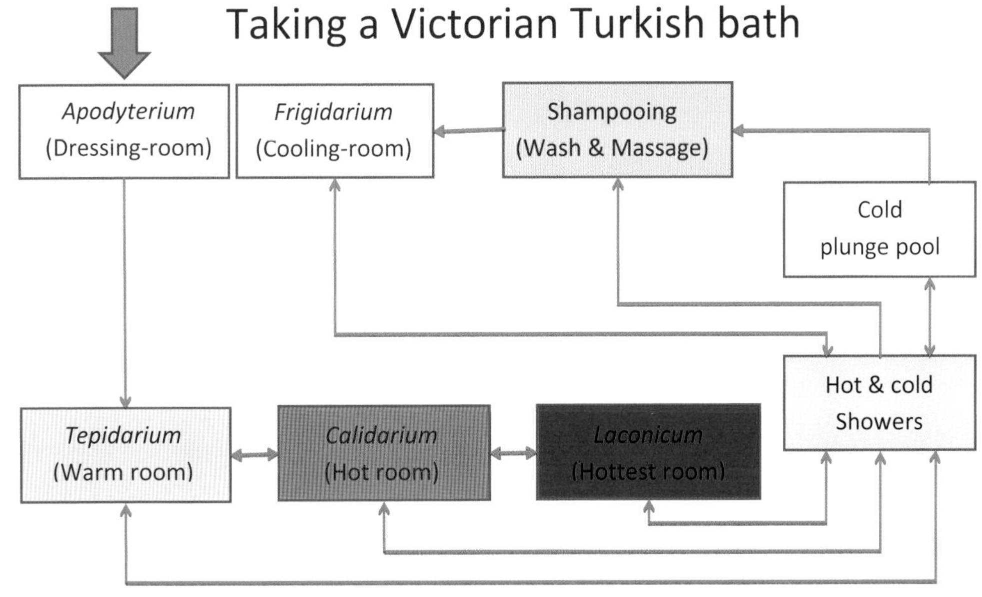

Fig 1.1
A typical route followed by a bather in a Victorian Turkish bath.
(© Malcolm Shifrin)

Fig 1.2
The outer cooling-room of the Psamatia Kapousi bath, Constantinople. Engraving by Thomas Abiel Prior (hand-coloured later) from an original illustration by Thomas Allom in his Constantinople and the Scenery of the Seven Churches of Asia Minor *(1838).*
(Author's collection)

Fig 1.3
A Moorish bath (hammam) at the turn of the 19th and 20th centuries. The photograph used on the postcard is variously credited to J Geiser of Algiers and Wilhelm Klee of Berlin.
(Author's collection)

For it is the dryness of the air which distinguishes the Victorian Turkish bath from other types of hot-air bath: from the humid steamy Islamic *hammam*; from the Russian Баня (*bania*, or *banya*) or steam bath; from its close relation, the Finnish *sauna* (in which cold water is periodically ladled on to a stove so as to dampen the otherwise dry atmosphere); and from the medicated vapour bath (usually found as a single-user cabinet in hydros, or as an added facility in early Turkish bath establishments).

Victorian bathers describing the bath would have used the word **shampoo* in place of 'full body wash and massage' because they were familiar with the two separate processes performed on them by a shampooer (sometimes called a rubber).

But *shampoo* is also absent from my definition because the word is now generally thought of in connection with washing one's hair or cleaning the car.

It would, of course, be unrealistic to suggest scrapping the phrase 'Turkish bath'. For reasons to be discussed later, either 'Roman bath' or 'Victorian hot-air bath' would be far more accurate. But long-established terminology is rarely replaced on grounds of logic or accuracy.

'Victorian Turkish bath', then, is an easily understood compromise term. But the word 'Turkish', as used here, is of no more significance than is 'Welsh' in 'Welsh rarebit', or 'Scotch' in 'Scotch egg'. Only the adjective 'Victorian' is wholly appropriate, for what it describes was truly a Victorian institution, and it flourished during Victoria's reign.

The impact of the hot-air bath on Victorian life

The first Victorian Turkish bath was built in 1856, and baths of this type continued to be built until 1981, when the last one opened within the Gateshead Leisure Centre.

Buildings of the 20th century may have benefited from more advanced heating and ventilation systems, but the Victorian layout and style, and the Victorian procedure for taking the bath, remain essentially unchanged even today.

Despite a burgeoning interest in the Victorian era—now separated from us by more than a century—the history of its 'Turkish' bath is virtually unknown.

You will not find it in works on British social history; it will rarely be included even in local histories, where some recognition of its past value to a community is surely worth mentioning. So it is difficult to understand why such a fascinating subject has been neglected when its study can give us fresh insights into so many aspects of Victorian life.

It has to be admitted that the Victorian Turkish bath—unlike that other popular Victorian development, 'the electricity'—never impacted on the lives of any but a small minority of the total population. Yet that is insufficient reason to ignore its contribution to the lives of those who *did* benefit from its use.

For the wealthy Victorian, in the context of health and wellbeing, the hot-air bath bridged the gap between the hydropathists' spartan *cold water cure (Fig 1.4), and the more relaxed approach which saw *hydropathy gradually morph into our modern hydrotherapy.

More generally, before the use of aspirin became widespread at the end of the 19th century, the bath was valued by many for its ability to help alleviate pain.

Sitz Bath & Wet sheet 6 o'clock, winters morn "This is delightful, very!!!"

Fig 1.4
One of a series of postcards based on 19th-century caricatures by Thomas Onwhyn, showing the various treatments available at a hydropathic establishment.
(Author's collection)

And in secure closed communities, such as the Victorian 'lunatic asylum', the bath was valued because it cheered the depressed and relaxed the tense.

The Victorian Turkish bath indirectly helped to improve everyone's quality of life, whether they used it or not. For its development contributed to advances in heating and ventilation; it helped to raise contemporary awareness of the benefits of personal hygiene and cleanliness; and it became part of the new Victorian leisure industry.

The years immediately preceding and following the beginning of Victoria's reign saw three devastating epidemics of cholera, starting in 1831, 1848, and 1853. In 1849, for example, there were 2,000 cholera victims in Bristol alone.[1] This triggered urgent calls for sanitary reform and the involvement of the state in matters of public health.

Special emphasis was placed, for the first time, on the value of preventative measures directed by the government. Despite some vigorous opposition, the Baths and Wash-houses Acts of 1846 and 1847 were enacted, and these allowed community baths to be erected at public expense. Unfortunately, the acts were not mandatory, and by 1865 only 20 towns in the whole of England and Wales had built municipal baths. Nevertheless, though the provision of public baths and swimming facilities started slowly, it gradually accelerated until it became the norm.

The second half of the 1850s was therefore a good time to open private bathing establishments which, in a small way, and for a short time, helped meet a previously unsatisfied need. At the same time, the growing popularity of Victorian Turkish baths gradually encouraged local authorities to provide them also—provision which, some argued, was not actually permitted under the acts.

Pioneering Turkish bath builders had no easy task, for the technology at their disposal was inadequate. Proprietors found it extremely difficult to raise air to the high temperatures required; contemporary heating devices often produced toxic fumes which had to be prevented from entering the bath; and it was difficult to remove stale sweat-laden air before the advent of an effective electric extractor fan.

Fig 1.5
Certificate No. 758 for one £10 share in the Brighton Turkish Bath Company Limited, dated 7 'Febry' 1870.
(Author's collection)

CERTIFICATE OF SHARE.

No. 758

THE Brighton Turkish Bath Company, LIMITED,
INCORPORATED PURSUANT TO ACT OF PARLIAMENT.

£10 Share

This is to certify that the Person whose name is on the Register of Members is the Proprietor of the SHARE Number 758 of the BRIGHTON TURKISH BATH COMPANY, LIMITED, subject to the rules and regulations of the said Company, and that up to this day there has been paid up in respect of such Share the full sum of Ten pounds.

Given under the Common Seal of the said Company, the 7th day of Febry in the year 1870.

DIRECTORS.

SECRETARY.

The Victorian Turkish bath led to the invention of new, more efficient stoves, which were then also used to satisfy other heating requirements. Experiments conducted to compare the efficiency of different types of heater exemplify an early use in the building industry of heat-loss calculations. These, and other problems, much exercised the Victorian mind and helped expand the boundaries of what was technically possible.

In the course of research for this book and its complementary website, I have so far identified more than 600 Victorian Turkish baths built in the British Isles since 1856. But there will certainly be others—in places too small to have their own classified trade directories, for example, or baths too small to advertise in the local paper.

An examination of the life histories and ownership trails of so many individual bath establishments tells us much about small 19th-century businesses, and why so many company-owned baths had shorter lives than those which were privately owned.

The rise of the Victorian Turkish bath was contemporaneous with the rise of the Joint Stock Company (Fig 1.5), made popular—fashionable even—by the liberalisation of regulatory procedures following the Limited Liabilities Act of 1855. In England and Wales alone, I have found over 110 such companies, 72 of which included the word 'Turkish' in their name. But many other companies, using alternative words such as 'swimming' or just 'baths', are more elusive.

Perhaps surprisingly, the first publicly financed body specifically set up to open a Turkish bath was not a joint stock company. In 1859—barely two years after the first bath opened in England—the Rochdale Pioneers formed the Rochdale Subscription Turkish Bath Society as a co-operative venture.

The majority of Victorian Turkish baths were started by entrepreneurs who ran a single establishment; very few owned more than one at a time.

Charles Bartholomew was one of the few, creating what was possibly one of the first multiples outside the field of banking. His seven establishments, each in a different city, with their standardised furniture, hand-painted glass screens, and decorated letter 'B' monograms, were instantly recognisable as Bartholomew establishments.

Later, other proprietors, such as William Cooper and the Neville family, came to own several branches in a single city. Most, however, remained in the ownership of a sole proprietor or a small company.

Discovering how the Victorian Turkish bath developed and spread round the British Isles enhances our understanding of a variety of Victorian attitudes: those of the gentry; of the emerging (but insecure) medical profession, and of the new industrialists; attitudes to the provision of Turkish baths for women, for the 'lower' classes, or for the poor; and attitudes to the mentally ill, to 'effeminacy', and to foreigners.

We also meet a remarkable group of workingmen who, while their fellows were engaged in campaigning for the vote, dedicated themselves instead to petitioning Members of Parliament on matters relating to their country's foreign policy.

These were the members of David Urquhart's Foreign Affairs Committees (FACs) who, in order to help support their families while they themselves engaged in political activities, opened more than 30 of the first Victorian Turkish baths in England.

The Victorian Turkish bath movement

The movement—for undoubtedly it was a movement—grew from a single seed planted in Urquhart's idiosyncratic travel book *The Pillars of Hercules.*[2] It was nurtured in the pages of a serious and somewhat humourless political newspaper, *The Sheffield Free Press,* and its successor, *The Free Press*, published in London.

Urquhart's flair for publicity enables us to trace the bath's rapid progress (Fig 1.6). Starting in 1856 with the first experiments in construction at Blarney, near Cork in the south of Ireland, it can then be followed across the Irish Sea to the industrial towns of the north of England, after which it travels—simultaneously—further north to the population centres and hydropathic establishments of Scotland, and south through the Midlands, until it finally arrives in London four years later in 1860.

About 75 per cent of the baths we know of were opened during Queen Victoria's reign. During the same period, similar baths were opened in many parts of the British Empire, while the first establishment in the United States—no less Victorian than any of its British predecessors—was opened in Brooklyn in 1863.

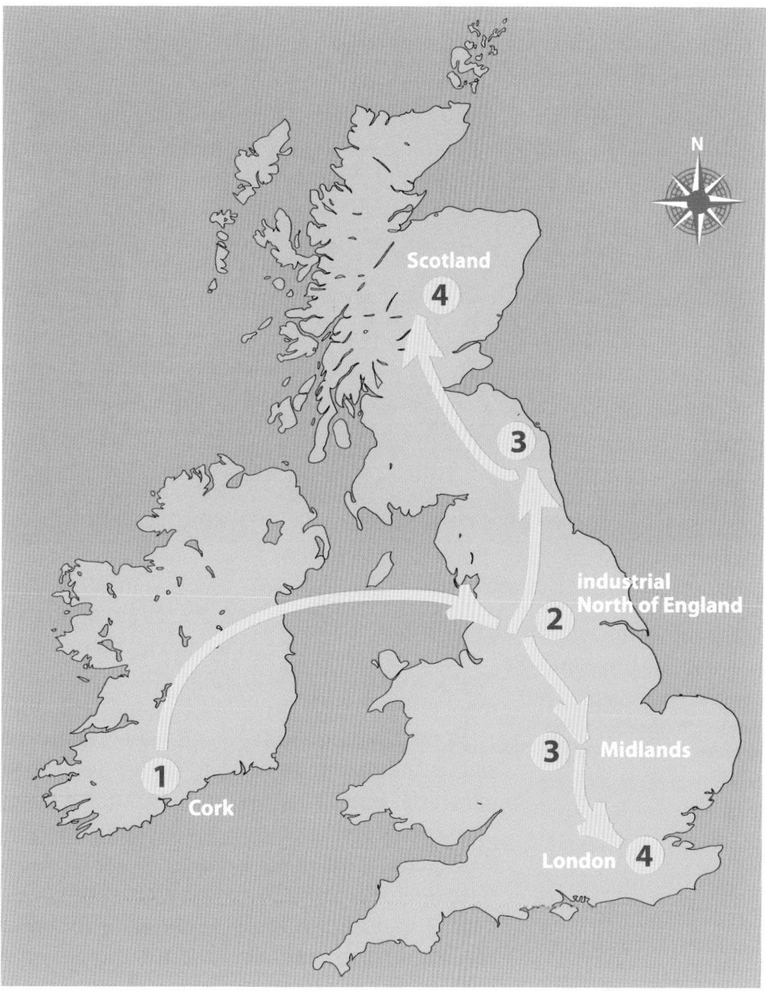

Fig 1.6
The Turkish bath crosses the Irish Sea to England and Scotland.
(© Tash Shifrin)

The decline of the Victorian Turkish bath

At the time of writing (April 2015), only twelve Victorian-style Turkish baths remain open in the British Isles, of which only five date from the Victorian era, and three, owned by private members' clubs, are not open to the general public.

During the past 20 years, many local authorities have closed their Turkish baths. Although some were in relatively modern buildings, four were Victorian, and two of these have since been demolished.

But while the Victorian Turkish bath seems to be in terminal decline, hot-air bathing in modern leisure centres and health clubs is growing in popularity; only the bathing medium and the type of bath have changed.

Free-standing Finnish wooden sauna cabins and prefabricated plastic steam rooms may not completely satisfy the Victorian Turkish bath

Fig 1.7
Bathtime in the home of a poor family in the 1890s. The same water would normally be used for all the children.
(Carol Adams, Ordinary lives, *Virago, 1982, p.16)*

enthusiast—because they *are* quite different. Nevertheless, they are increasingly enjoyed by a younger generation and, significantly, are much more economically provided and maintained.

Hot-air bathers today have expectations of sauna and steam room very similar to those which the Victorians had of their Turkish bath, though their priorities may have been different.

The ability of the sweating process to thoroughly cleanse the bather was increasingly valued as Victoria's reign progressed. For some, the hot-air bath compensated for the absence of even the most basic washing facilities in a home which was often shared and usually overcrowded (Fig 1.7).

Today, most people take for granted the running water, baths and showers in our homes. Yet the super-cleanliness provided by a hot-air bath is still much valued. Its effectiveness in contributing to skin care and a healthy looking complexion is widely recognised. Most of us enjoy the general sense of wellbeing which naturally follows, and appreciate the ease with which we can de-stress ourselves.

Some Victorians welcomed the hot-air bath for its therapeutic potential, especially those suffering from such conditions as rheumatism or gout (Fig 1.8). Contemporary medicine could provide no cure for these crippling complaints, but the heat of the Victorian Turkish bath frequently helped ease a patient's suffering.

Today, many hot-air bathers see the use of sauna and steam rooms as 'alternative therapies', and the power of heat to ease aches and pains is still known to be effective.

But while Victorian bathers purported to take hot-air baths for reasons of health or to cleanse themselves, the Victorian Turkish bath almost certainly *retained* its popularity because it was also extremely relaxing, because it was highly enjoyable, and because it was a social activity that could be shared with friends—an activity which was seen by many as being a positive alternative to the public house and the dangers of alcoholism.

Relaxation and enjoyment are acknowledged as being the primary motives for present-day visits to sauna or steam room. And in the quest for that sybaritic feeling of wellbeing which the hot-air bath satisfies, both today's bathers and Victorians alike are little different from the ancient Greeks and Romans who frequented, if not the first hot-air baths, then at least some of the very earliest ones.

Fig 1.8 (right)
The cover of Charles Shepard's booklet, Rheumatism, and its treatment by Turkish baths, *reproduced as a 20th-century poster published by The World of Massage Museum in the USA.*
(Author's collection)

2

Early communal hot-air baths

When people say they are going to take a bath, we tend to envisage them sitting or lying in a long container of hot water and washing themselves with soap, or cleansing gel.

But there are many other ways in which a person can take a bath. More generally, we can think of bathing as a process of immersing the body, or part of it, in a *medium* which enables it to be cleansed or medically treated.

Although water is the medium normally chosen, there are many others. According to Pliny the Elder, Nero's wife Poppæa Sabina favoured asses' milk.[1] More common alternatives, such as steam, hot dry air, or even mud (Fig 2.1), can all be used to medicate, beautify, or produce a cleansing sweat.

The wealthy have always been able, if they wished, to take hot baths in the privacy of their own homes. They had the servants needed to fetch the fuel, stoke the fires, heat and carry the water, and clean the bath afterwards.

But throughout the centuries, in many communities, the less well-off have availed themselves of communal baths, usually to cleanse themselves, but also for relaxation.

In Japan, for example, the first commercial communal bathhouse, or *sento* (literally, coin-bath), is thought to have opened at the end of the 16th century.[2]

Early steam baths

Public steam baths, however, were widely popular long before this. They are known to have been in use in the ancient city-state of Sparta, although public bathing, even in Europe, almost certainly predates this. Spartan bathers would remain in the steam until they were covered in sweat and then immediately plunge into an adjacent cold water pool to cool down again.

The use of steam baths spread, first throughout Greece, then later westwards to Rome. The practice seems to have travelled also in a northerly direction, originating from early Greek settlements in the south of Ukraine, and then becoming widespread in much of Russia (Fig 2.2), and the areas surrounding it or under its influence. As a result, steam and vapour baths are often still referred to as Russian baths (Fig 2.3).

Strictly speaking, the Finnish sauna is the name of the room rather than the bathing process

Fig 2.1 (above) Postcard showing the mud baths at Saki, Russia. (Author's collection)

Fig 2.2 (below) The South-Western Bathhouse, a modern Russian vapour bath, or banya, *in Mississauga, Ontario, Canada. (Courtesy of the South Western Bathhouse www.banya.ca)*

Fig 2.3
Rabbi Benjamin Schewzik's Russian vapour baths in the east end of London before they were destroyed by fire in 1940. 'Saracenic' features—the canopy and window frame overlays—were added to the original building to give an eastern effect.
(London Metropolitan Archives, City of London)

itself (Fig 2.4). It is often thought to have developed from the Russian bath, but most authorities believe it developed independently in Finland.[3]

Roman hot-air baths

However, it was the Romans who, by adopting the concept of the public bath and improving it to an extremely sophisticated level, were pre-eminent in the provision of bathing facilities to an extent which has not been surpassed to this day.[4] In Rome, the first public baths *(*balnea)* appear to have been built during the second century BCE, and in the following years public bathing found increasing favour.

It is difficult to determine when the Romans first began bathing in rooms heated by air which was not only hot, but dry. However, it seems unlikely that this would have been practical until after the development of the *hypocaust (Fig 2.5) as an effective hot-air central heating system.

Roman engineers were unable to measure *specific* temperatures, but they would have been only too conscious of the constraint that the temperature of their steam baths was limited to that of wet steam. The hypocaust made it relatively easy to maintain a sequence of rooms at increasingly high temperatures, depending on the size of each room and its proximity to the source of the circulating hot air.

It was this sequence of rooms heated by hot dry air which—as we shall see—became the model for the Victorian Turkish bath. As though to emphasise this link, it is significant that the Victorians often named the rooms of their baths by the Roman names rather than the Turkish (or Islamic) names.

So, the changing or undressing-room was often known as the **apodyterium*, the cooling-room as the **frigidarium*, the warm room as the **tepidarium*, the hot room as the **caldarium*, and the hottest room as the **laconicum*.

Such names may, to some, have seemed pretentious, but the Victorians were not only attempting to distinguish their baths from the steamy damp ones found elsewhere; they were, as we might now say, heritaging them by asserting that they were part of a long-lost tradition, thereby making them more generally acceptable and, of course, more likely to make a profit.

After the adoption of the hypocaust, Roman baths typically included—in addition to the rooms heated by dry air—a steam room, a cold plunge pool, and rest rooms. Roman bathers repeatedly moved between different types of bath, alternating between hot dry air and steam room, and between hot water and cold water baths.

During the centuries which followed, the range of facilities grew to such an extent that the great **thermae* of the emperors Caracalla and Diocletian were in effect palatial leisure centres set in beautiful gardens. They included

Fig 2.4
A modern sauna at the Panorama Therme Beuren in Germany. The attendant has temporarily shut the door to newcomers before adding water to the stove and spreading the ensuing hot air around the bathers by twirling a towel over their heads. Not for the novice bather!
(Panorama Therme Beuren, Germany www.beuren.de)

swimming pools, courts for ball games, and dedicated spaces for wrestling and exercising with weights, for relaxation, and for galleries and libraries.

As the area under Roman control expanded, so the number of Roman baths increased. Eventually they were to be found in almost every corner of their empire. In Britain, the most impressive baths were probably those in the City of Bath (the Roman *Aquae Sulis*) where their extensive remains can still be seen. In Britain there are currently more than 30 sites where partial remains of Roman baths are open to view.[5]

The Islamic *hammam*

In Rome, the building of baths as luxurious as those of Caracalla did not last. Increasingly frequent attacks on the western provinces led, in 476 CE, to the end of the western empire. Many public baths were among the buildings that were destroyed, or which later fell into disrepair and eventual ruin.

The Roman empire of the east, by contrast, was rich, well populated, and less subject to foreign attack. The Emperor Constantine's capital, the New Rome (later renamed Constantinople and, more recently, Istanbul) contributed to the economic wellbeing and survival of what later became known as the Byzantine Empire for almost another 1000 years.

Even after the fall of Constantinople in 1453, the Roman bath survived, being adapted, and then adopted, by the Muslim Ottoman conquerors. Cleanliness and ritual bathing, but not public nakedness, are intrinsic to Islam, and the Islamic bath (*hammam*) (Fig 2.6) is a felicitous combination of the religious bathing tradition of the Muslim, and the elaborate bathing procedures of the Romans.

A typical hammam includes a warm room, a hot room, and a steam room, with washing facilities, dressing rooms, space for shampooing (often on a raised, marble-covered platform in one of the hot rooms), and areas for relaxation and refreshment. The Roman cold plunge or swimming pool is normally omitted because many Muslims consider that still water (which

Fig 2.5 (below left)
Hot air tunnel leading to under-floor hypocaust in a Roman House, c 2 CE, at Trier (Trèves) in Germany. The pillars of the hypocaust are about 2ft (60 cm) high. An opening to another tunnel can just be seen in the centre of the wall on the right.
(© Malcolm Shifrin)
Fig 2.6 (below right)
Postcard showing a municipal hammam in Rhodes, Greece.
(Author's collection)

Fig 2.7
Eski Kaplıca: the oldest hammam (late 14th century) still in use in Bursa, the original capital of the Ottoman Empire. A postcard showing one of the few hammams with a pool. These are permitted under Islamic law when fed by continuously running water. (Author's collection)

is, by definition, stagnant water) is ritually unclean, just as Jews require running water for their ritual bath, the **mikveh*. Where *hammams* do have a pool as, for example, at Bursa (Fig 2.7), it is because they can be fed by a natural spring so that the water is constantly changing.[6]

While it is possible to indicate the areas and facilities within a typical Islamic *hammam*, it is more difficult to describe the appearance of one: for the individual bath styles differed from each other—usually according to the period and location of the bath—just as, for example, individual churches differ from each other.

If we conjure up an image of the 'typical' Islamic bath we probably envisage glazed star-pierced domes, minarets, *horseshoe arches, and highly decorative tiles. All of these are key elements of Islamic architecture, but not all are appropriate in a *hammam*. Indeed, as Nebahat Avcıoğlu has argued, such key elements as domes and minarets are not even essential in a mosque.[7]

So, while there would be many baths with some of these elements, practice varied widely. The arches around the Eski Kaplıca pool at Bursa, for example (Fig 2.7), are not horseshoe arches and are more Roman than Islamic, while those at Rhodes (Fig 2.6) are pointed.

Just as the Roman bath followed the Roman legions, so the Islamic *hammam* followed the Ottomans. The opulence of such pools, often lavishly enriched with mosaic designs and furnished with fountains and purely decorative pools, could be found as far afield as Aleppo (Fig 2.8) in Syria. More prosaic baths can still be found all over western Asia, Arabia, and the Maghreb, while the remains of disused baths can be seen, for example, among the Moorish buildings of Gerona (Fig 2.9) in Spain, and the 15th-century Islamic buildings of Baku (Fig 2.10) in Azerbaijan.

These early hot-air baths can be considered as ancestors of the Victorian Turkish bath. There are, of course, many other types of hot-air bath, perhaps the most important being the sweathouses (Fig 2.11) of Ireland and the sweat lodges (Fig 2.12) of the Americas. But they have been omitted here because they developed independently, and had no direct impact on the development of the Victorian hot-air bath.

The many bathhouses built in Britain during the Roman occupation fell into disuse or were destroyed when the Romans departed. It was to be many centuries before they were rediscovered.

Fig 2.8
The cooling-room at the 'men only' Hammam al-Nahasin, Aleppo, Syria. Urquhart would have seen this type of fretwork screen in several hammams, and he used it in the Jermyn Street Hammam (see Fig 27.7 p.292). (Richard Boggs, Hammaming in the Sham, *Garnet, 2010. Courtesy of Richard Boggs and Garnet Publishing (UK) Ltd)*

Fig 2.9 (top left)
A corner of the caldarium *in the 'Arab baths' in Gerona, Spain. These were built around 1195 on the site of earlier baths which had been demolished by the French. (© Malcolm Shifrin)*
Fig 2.10 (top right)
Ruins of the hammam in the 15th-century Shirvanshah Palace, Baku, Azerbaijan. (© Michael Shifrin)
Fig 2.11 (bottom left)
This beehive-shaped sweathouse in Tullynahaia, Co. Leitrim, is typical of many others still to be found in Ireland.
*(*Irish sweathouses and the great forgetting *www.irishmegaliths.org.uk/sweathouses.htm © Anthony Weir)*
Fig 2.12 (bottom right)
Postcard showing a Navaho Indian sweat lodge in the Southwestern United States. (Author's collection)

3

The British 'discovery' of the 'Turkish' bath

Before 1856, most of our information about the so-called Turkish bath came from books written by travellers returning from Turkey, the Maghreb, or other areas where Islamic culture was, or had been, predominant.

These included Lady Mary Wortley Montagu's much-quoted account of her visit to a women's *hammam* in the early 18th century,[1] Richard Robert Madden's travels in northern Sudan and the Mediterranean countries from Egypt to Turkey (1829),[2] Edward William Lane's book on Egypt (1836),[3] and the rather less serious *Notes on a journey from Cornhill to Grand Cairo* (1846) by William Makepeace Thackeray, who wrote:

> The Turkish bath is certainly a novel sensation to an Englishman, and may be set down as a most queer and surprising event of his life.'[4]

Thackeray's description of his first bath in Constantinople is designed to amuse, employing language typical of the time as, for example, 'I saw a great brown wretch extended before me.' But what Thackeray, amusingly or otherwise, is really saying is that although he, a habitué of Pall Mall, found it enjoyable, this is a very strange custom which *they* have *over there*.

And, in a letter dated 1 April 1717, Lady Mary Wortley Montagu, describing the nakedness within a women's *hammam* in Sophia, contrasts it with her insistence on leaving all her own clothing on, even within the hottest areas. Her letter, though not intended to be amusing in the manner of Thackeray, is nevertheless designed to entertain its recipient by comparing *their* customs with *ours*.

Even the two scholarly works by Madden and Lane fall into the category of works describing for us the customs of others, albeit to educate rather than entertain. Madden described the *hammams* of the Middle East, and Lane included a chapter on the Islamic bath complete with a plan and detailed description of the bathing procedure. But neither author suggested any practical lessons on personal hygiene which their readers might learn from these accounts.

In 1838, 12 years before Urquhart's book *The Pillars of Hercules* was published, he criticised the manner in which these earlier writers described what they had seen. The European traveller, having arrived,

> in the midst of habits and institutions so completely at variance with those of his country, and struck, of course, immediately with all those things which are worse and inferior to his own country, whether that inferiority exists in reality or in his previous opinion respecting excellence, his eyes naturally revert homewards, with a feeling of satisfaction and exultation; and, from the position on which he stands, where smaller objects are confounded or lost, he takes a more comprehensive view than, probably, he has done before, of the elements of his country's greatness...[5]

As Nebahat Avcıoğlu has perceptively argued,[6] Urquhart's criticism could almost have been written 140 years later by Edward Said in his ground-breaking work *Orientalism*.[7]

In it, Said maintained that all western study of the east, and particularly of the Middle East, was an exercise in diminishing its peoples and cultures in order to demonstrate the inherent superiority of the colonialist west. We need look no further than those paintings purporting to depict Islamic *hammams*—such as, for example, the much reproduced *Le Bain turc* (*The Turkish bath*) by Ingres (Fig 3.1) and *La grande piscine à Brusa* (*The great bath at Bursa*) by Gérôme—to see Said's analysis exemplified, almost literally, in the flesh.

Orientalism has had a seismic and largely positive effect on the manner in which non-European cultures are currently studied, though many scholars now suggest that a more nuanced view is needed. Said also, in effect, cautions those who, for whatever convenience, continue to use adjectives such as Saracenic, that they should tread most carefully.

Architectural historians argue, with considerable justification, that since a 'Saracenic style' never existed in the same way as, for example, the classical style does, the term is meaningless and should be avoided. It was, however, widely used in the 18th and 19th centuries by travel writers and others who used it to encompass a wide range of different styles from different locations and different periods.

In doing so, they encouraged the belief that there was but a single 'eastern' style—one which was clearly different from our own western one, and so 'exotic' and less 'normal' than their own.

But while buildings designed by Islamic architects often incorporated such key elements as, for example, horseshoe arches or minarets, many such buildings were without them, and these buildings were just as Islamic as those which had them.

So in considering—post-Said—early Victorian Turkish baths, we need to be aware that when we read contemporary accounts which use the term Saracenic, the writer was describing what, at that time, was considered to be an Islamic-style building.

And when, for convenience, 'Saracenic' is used here, it refers not to an Islamic style *per se*, but specifically to how Victorian architects and writers interpreted what they *thought* was an Islamic style. In practice, as we will find later (see Chapter 13), there were very few Victorian Turkish baths with an external appearance very much different from the buildings around them.

Strictures on the personal cleanliness of the English

Two works describing the bath were quite different in intent from all the others. The first was *Strictures on the personal cleanliness of the English, with a description of the hammams of the Turks, &c.*[8] The author, unknown and anonymous, self-published just 250 copies in 1828, the year before Madden's book appeared. It was distributed for the author by the radical publisher of *The Republican*, Richard Carlile of 62 Fleet Street, who described it as,

Fig 3.1
Possibly the painting most associated in people's minds with Turkish baths is the orientalist Le Bain turc painted in 1862 by Jean-Auguste-Dominique Ingres. It actually depicts a group of women in a harem and was inspired by the much quoted description in Lady Mary Montagu's Letters from the orient.

> a very useful book, and calculated to promote personal and general cleanliness, by showing us, that the Christians, in the aggregate, have been and are the filthiest people in their persons, of all the human beings that have existed on the face of the earth.[9]

As Carlile had realised, the author was—specifically—*not* comparing the British favourably with the Turks, as the orientalists were wont to do; on the contrary, he was positioning the Turks as a people to be emulated, by describing customs which his readers should adopt.

Although the author chose to address his strictures, in title and text, to the English, he clearly had a wider target in mind, as when he writes:

> Great Britain in fact is the only country where the people, from the day of their birth, go down to their graves with all their filth about them.[10]

To encourage the reader, the book includes a plan and full description of a Turkish bath found in a private house in Tripoli (Fig 3.2)—at that time in Ottoman Syria, but currently in Lebanon.[11]

The author wrote that he had wanted,

> to erect baths at the expense of government in different parts of London, after the manner of the Roman *thermæ*, publicly endowed like hospitals for the use of the people,[12]

and that in 1818 he had tried to interest George III in his project. In this, he had been unsuccessful.

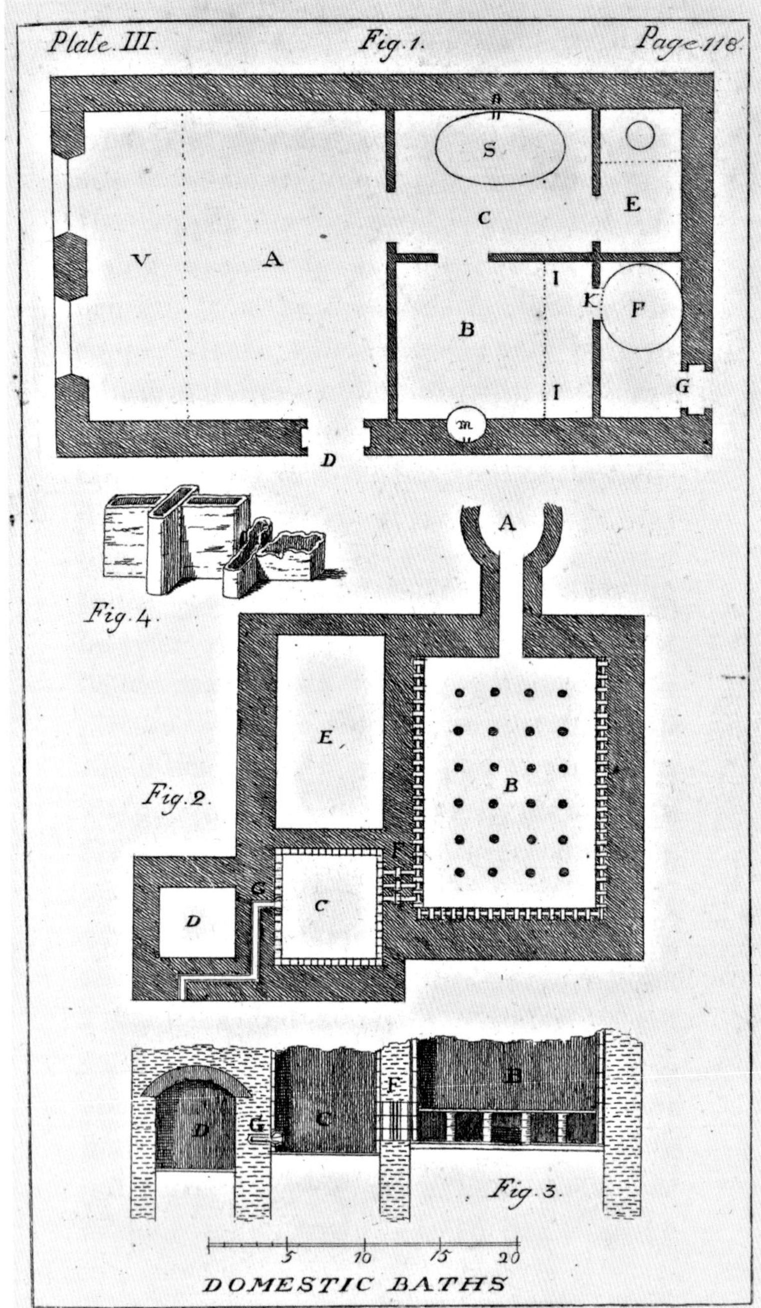

Fig 3.2
A plan of the Turkish bath found in a private house in Tripoli—at that time in Ottoman Syria, but currently in Lebanon. (Strictures on the personal cleanliness of the English, *1828. © The British Library Board, 7393.aa.5 [Pl III])*

The Pillars of Hercules

The second of these books, written by David Urquhart, a Scottish diplomat and sometime MP for Stafford, was *The Pillars of Hercules*, an account of his travels in Morocco and Spain in 1848 (Fig 3.3).

Urquhart was a lifelong sufferer from neuralgia who had found, in the heat of the hot-air bath, some relief from the severe pain to which he was frequently subjected. So, into this idiosyncratic travel book of variable quality, Urquhart—who was nothing if not a proselytiser—included a chapter on the Moorish bath, preceding it with one on 'the bath as it is used by the Turks, which, as more complete and detailed, is more intelligible.' [13]

This chapter on the bath of the Turks was to have a considerable impact, not only in the British Isles but also further afield. Urquhart was himself in no doubt of its importance, writing that it was,

> a chapter which, if the reader will peruse it with diligence and apply with care, may prolong his life, fortify his body, diminish his ailments, augment his enjoyments, and improve his temper: then having found something beneficial to himself, he may be prompted to do something to secure the like for his fellow-creatures.[14]

Later, following his own cue, he was quite down-to-earth when replying to correspondents who, having read *The Pillars of Hercules* or heard him speak, had then written for advice on how to build their own bath. His answers would be tailored to suit the financial implications of his advice for the enquirer, often suggesting bare-bones solutions which would cost but a few pounds.

However, in *The Pillars of Hercules* his writing was more flowery, describing the bathing procedure as though it were a theatrical performance:

> The operation consists of various parts: first, the seasoning of the body; second, the manipulation of the muscles; third, the peeling of the epidermis; fourth, the soaping, and the patient is then conducted to the bed of repose. These are the five acts of the drama.[15]

He continues by describing the set—the stage on which the performance takes place:

> There are three essential apartments in the building: a great hall or *mustaby*, open to the outer air; a middle chamber, where the heat is moderate; the inner hall, which is properly the *thermae*.

And then the programme details:

> The first scene is acted in the middle chamber; the next three in the inner chamber, and the last in the outer hall. The time occupied is from two to

four hours, and the operation is repeated once a week.

The performance starts:

> On raising the curtain which covers the entrance to the street, you find yourself in a hall circular, octagonal, or square, covered with a dome open in the centre ...

Urquhart actually begins the following section with the words:

> 2nd Act—You now take your turn for entering the inner chamber ...

and we find that the bather has now become part of the performance, and remains so while continuing through Acts Three, Four, and Five.

Strictures on the personal cleanliness of the English and *The Pillars of Hercules* were different from earlier books describing the bath because their agendas were different.

To their authors, the Turkish bath was not a curious custom, related by them merely to interest and entertain their readers. It was a model, to be admired and, most important, to be copied in order to raise British ideas of personal cleanliness to contemporary Turkish standards—a novel concept for a nation of empire builders, busily introducing Christianity and the benefits of British rule to the uncivilised foreigner.

At a time when the majority of Victorians had no indoor running water, let alone any experience of taking what we think of as an ordinary bath, these two writers argued that a network of public Turkish baths should be built at public expense.

Strictures is better argued and more readable than Urquhart's book. It is forthright and outspoken on the subject of personal cleanliness, with chapters on public, domestic, Turkish, and Roman baths, and yet it seems to have had no impact at all.

Urquhart, a natural publicist, largely succeeded in removing the Turkish bath from the exotic to the local high street.

And, in a caricature entitled *The Turkish bath*[16] (Fig 3.4), John Tenniel showed that by the 1870s everyone was familiar with what the inside of such baths looked like. Despite the Latin term *sudatorium* over the doorway, the bath had become an instantly recognisable avatar of Turkey and its culture; one which he used to good effect in commenting on the current scene.

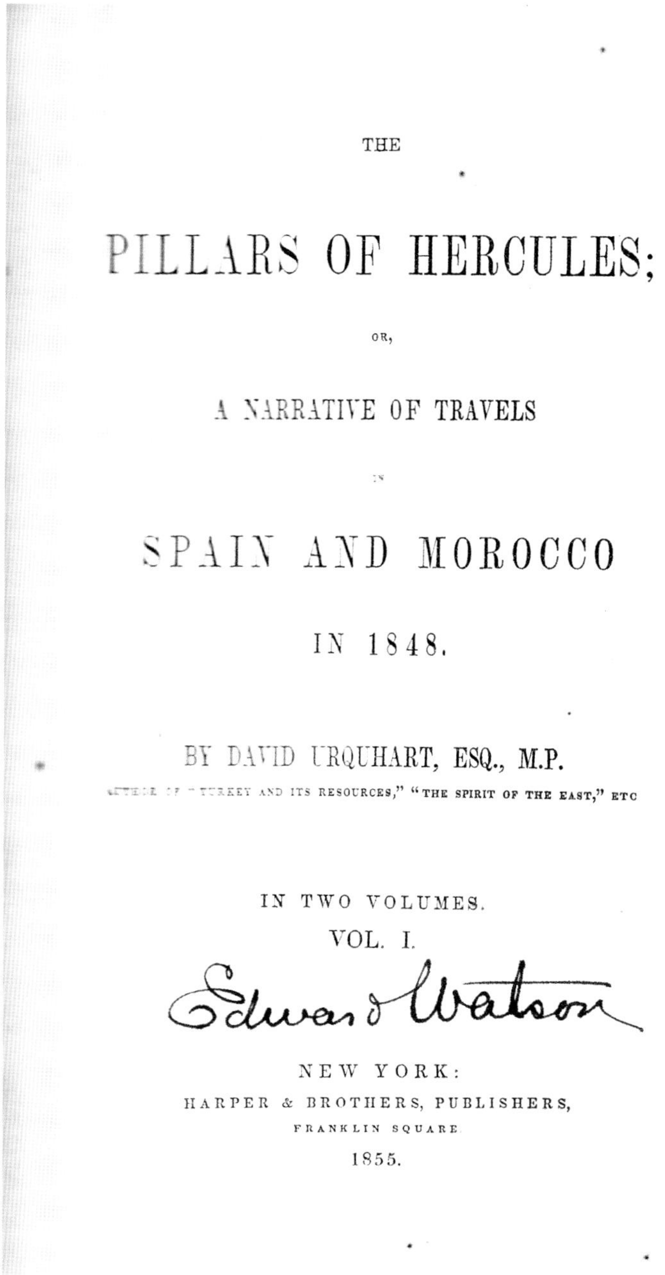

THE

PILLARS OF HERCULES;

OR,

A NARRATIVE OF TRAVELS

IN

SPAIN AND MOROCCO

IN 1848.

BY DAVID URQUHART, ESQ., M.P.

[illegible] TURKEY AND ITS RESOURCES," "THE SPIRIT OF THE EAST," ETC

IN TWO VOLUMES.

VOL. I.

NEW YORK:

HARPER & BROTHERS, PUBLISHERS,

FRANKLIN SQUARE

1855.

Fig 3.3
Title page of an American edition of David Urquhart's The Pillars of Hercules *which includes the two influential chapters on Moorish and Turkish baths.*

For around this time, the politically-minded were much concerned with what was widely known as the Eastern Question—how to stop Russia moving into the Balkans as the Ottoman Empire was seen to be disintegrating, and thereby posing a threat to British interests. Backing Turkey against the Russians had led Disraeli to turn a blind eye to the 1876 massacre at Batak of thousands of Bulgarians by Ottoman irregulars.

Tenniel depicts Disraeli (on the couch) conceding that Gladstone had made life difficult for

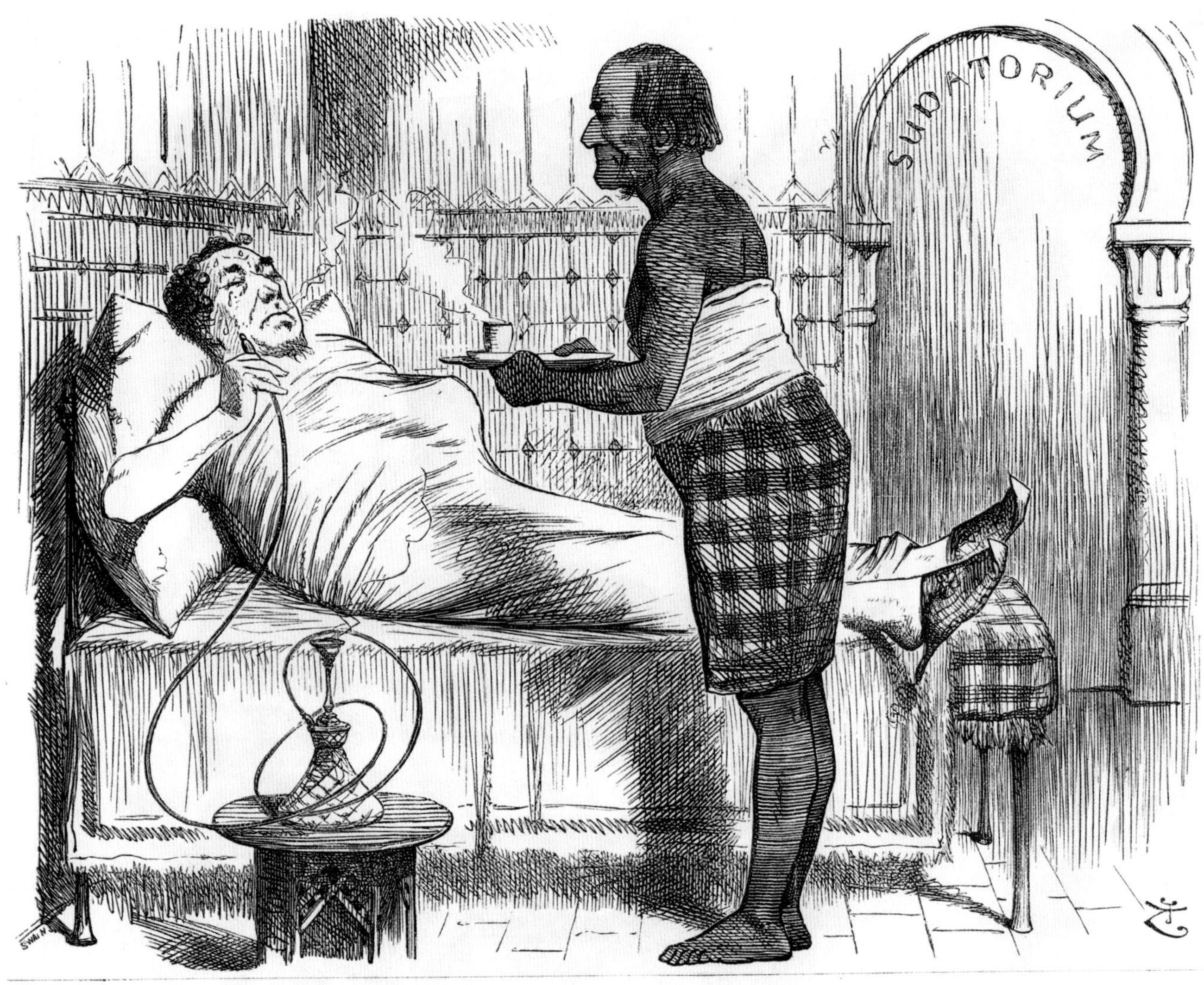

THE TURKISH BATH.

ATTENDANT. "*How do you feel after your bath, my lord?*"
LORD B. "*Pretty comfortable, thank you!*—(Aside. *Lost some weight, I fancy.*)—*You made it so confoundedly* HOT *for me!!!*"

Fig 3.4
John Tenniel's political cartoon relating to the Bulgarian victims of Turkish persecution.
*(*Punch*, 7 October 1876. Author's collection)*

him by appealing, on behalf of the Bulgarian victims, directly to the British public.

So far as actually opening Turkish baths was concerned, of these two authors—the anonymous writer of *Strictures* and David Urquhart—only the latter achieved even a modicum of success.

But, as we shall see, he did not do it alone and, as a later commentator was to write, the anonymous author of *Strictures* 'was not so fortunate as to find a Dr Barter to give practical effect to his suggestions.'[17]

PART II

EARLY HISTORY OF THE VICTORIAN TURKISH BATH

4

The birth of the Roman–Irish, or Victorian Turkish bath

Richard Barter (1802–70) (Fig 4.1) was one of the two people most associated with the introduction of the Victorian Turkish bath into the British Isles. He was born on the family estate, Cooldaniel, in the parish of Kilmichael in County Cork, Ireland. His father died while he was still a young child and, according to the anonymous writer of the memoir *Recollections of the late Dr Barter*, he was often left to his own devices by a mother who apparently preferred his elder brothers.[1]

Thus accustomed to looking after himself, Barter grew up with an independent mind and an ability to act decisively when undertaking projects in which he believed, even though he might be criticised for them or, on occasion, be subjected to ridicule.

After qualifying as a doctor in London at the College (later, the Royal College) of Physicians in 1828, he returned to Ireland. While working at the dispensary in the small village of Inniscarra, just to the west of Cork, he simultaneously built up a successful medical practice of his own. According to Richard Metcalfe, he was well liked, and one wealthy satisfied patient 'settled an annuity of fifty pounds a year on [him] during her life'.[2]

Soon after the 1832 cholera epidemic, he left Inniscarra for the market town of Mallow where he met and, in 1836, married Mary Newman. Barter now became interested in farming and was one of the founders of the Agricultural Society of the County of Cork.

Fig 4.1
Dr Richard Barter, builder of Victorian Turkish baths in Ireland, in whose honour many Europeans refer to the bath as the Irish-Roman Bath.
(Richard Metcalfe, The rise and progress of hydropathy, *Simpkin, Marshall, 1912, p.120)*

Barter, hydropathy, and St Ann's[3]

Dr Barter's interest in cold water as a therapeutic agent began in 1843 after hearing a lecture on *hydropathy given in Cork by Richard Tappin Claridge, who was by trade an asphalt contractor.

Captain Claridge, as he was generally known, was largely responsible for introducing hydropathy into the British Isles, travelling round the country giving lectures about what was popularly known as *the cold water cure.

Richard Metcalfe, describing Barter's conversion to hydropathy, suggests that he first became interested in the medical aspects of water during the cholera epidemic. He was, therefore, already amenable to Claridge's approach, reading his book *Hydropathy* (Fig 4.2), the first to be written in English,[4] in which the author describes the cure (Fig 4.3) as practised by its originator, Vincenz Priessnitz (Fig 4.4), at Gräfenberg, Silesia—now Lázně Jeseník, in the Czech Republic.

Travelling to England, Barter visited both Ben Rhydding (in Ilkley) and Malvern and,

> witnessed there the practical application of processes which hitherto he had only heard or read of, and thus conviction confirmed what reason had previously sanctioned and approved.[5]

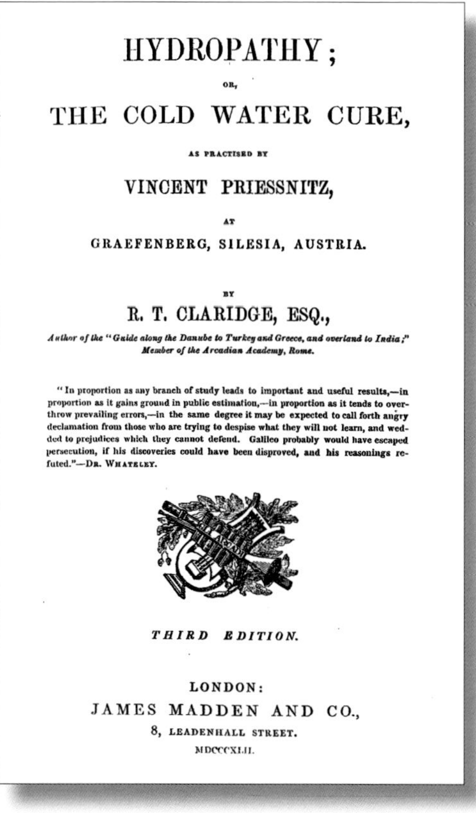

HYDROPATHY;

OR,

THE COLD WATER CURE,

AS PRACTISED BY

VINCENT PRIESSNITZ,

AT

GRAEFENBERG, SILESIA, AUSTRIA.

BY

R. T. CLARIDGE, ESQ.,

Author of the "Guide along the Danube to Turkey and Greece, and overland to India;" Member of the Arcadian Academy, Rome.

"In proportion as any branch of study leads to important and useful results,—in proportion as it gains ground in public estimation,—in proportion as it tends to overthrow prevailing errors,—in the same degree it may be expected to call forth angry declamation from those who are trying to despise what they will not learn, and wedded to prejudices which they cannot defend. Galileo probably would have escaped persecution, if his discoveries could have been disproved, and his reasonings refuted."—DR. WHATELEY.

THIRD EDITION.

LONDON:
JAMES MADDEN AND CO.,
8, LEADENHALL STREET.
MDCCCXLII.

Figs 4.2 and 4.3
Title page (left) of Captain Claridge's influential book on hydropathy, and frontispiece (right) showing four forms of treatment.
(R T Claridge, Hydropathy; or, the cold water cure, *3rd ed, Madden, 1842. Wellcome Library, London)*

Barter opened his Hydropathic Establishment at St Ann's Hill in 1843, paying scant attention to the 'most determined and paltry opposition from the Irish medical faculty'.[6] Its opening 'was greeted with every form of ridicule and contempt' yet an increasing number of patients came to consult 'the mad Doctor'.[7] The hydro was an almost immediate success, and it was soon treating many patients in residence there.

Barter's enquiring mind soon led him past the restricted path of the 'traditional' orthodox hydropathist for whom the cold water cure was a universal panacea. He quickly realised that cold water and *wet sheet packing were not suitable for every patient, or every malady.

Believing that heat might be more effective in some instances, he tried the use of a cabinet vapour bath with some of his patients. But he soon replaced this with a traditional Russian bath in which patients could sit or lie down, and so be totally immersed in the steam.

Barter's introduction of the vapour bath 'was regarded by the stricter followers of Priessnitz as an altogether unjustifiable substitute for the *blanket pack'. Many ridiculed him, contemptuously calling St Ann's 'a vapour establishment'.[8]

None of this prevented Barter's patients from attending St Ann's for any significant length of time, and the number in residence soon returned to its normal level of between 80 and 90. The establishment continued to grow and its premises had to be enlarged several times.

Fig 4.4
Vincent Priessnitz, father of hydropathy. All later practitioners paid homage to him and many visited his establishment at Gräfenberg, Silesia—now Lázně Jeseník, in the Czech Republic.
(Joseph Constantine, Hydropathy, health, and longevity, *Heywood, 1893)*

Inevitably, there were fewer patients during 1847–8 when famine swept over Ireland, decimating its population. But the check proved to be temporary[9] because, by now, St Ann's already had a justified reputation based on the successful alleviation of pain, and on the cure of many complaints for which traditional medical practice had no effective treatment.

Barter, Urquhart, and the beehive-shaped bath

Early in 1856, just over a decade after St Ann's opened, the Urquharts were travelling in Ireland and, needing medical assistance, visited Dr Barter. Afterwards, Barter read *The Pillars of Hercules* which was, by chance, in his library. He later wrote that, upon coming across the chapter on the Turkish bath, 'I was electrified; and resolved, if possible, to add that institution to my Establishment.'[10]

He immediately contacted Urquhart, offering him men, money and materials, 'besides a number of patients upon whom experiments might be made',[11] if he would visit St Ann's and help him build a Turkish bath. Urquhart accepted and arrived at the hydro early in 1856.

He was extremely impressed, both by the scale of St Ann's and also by Barter himself, who may have been an advocate of the water cure, but was certainly an advocate with a difference.

Urquhart wrote describing the place to his wife, Harriet, who forwarded it to the editor of the *Free Press* to publish:

> Certainly, this is the oddest place in the world. It reminds me of descriptions I have read of the settlement of a colony in a new country. Dr Barter has immense farms in his own hands, and this place seems to be the Head-Quarters of everything. There is a carpenter's shop, saddler, mattress maker, gas-works which supply the whole establishment with light, saw-mill, &c, &c, &c ... All the buildings are done by him and his men ... [12]

It was not just the maintenance of the hydro which was undertaken on the estate. A later visitor, Robert Wollaston, wrote:

> Every consumable article is produced on the estate; beef, mutton, pork, and poultry are supplied by the farm; the finest milk (untainted by London mysteries), butter, and eggs are also supplied from the same source: vegetables of every kind from the gardens, and fruits from the orchards, are abundantly supplied.[13]

Much less is known about the construction of their first experimental bath, or exactly how they heated it. The author of the anonymous memoir retained 'a grateful recollection of the little beehive-shaped thatched building in which the baths stood' and wrote that one of the workmen at the time related,

> that 'they used to add a bit of the circulating pipes every day to try how they would act, and perhaps pull their work to pieces in the morning' until the proper combination of heat and moisture was obtained.

The use of the beehive bath, the writer continued, 'enabled the bather to withstand 15° [Fahrenheit] more of heat than in the ordinary vapour bath.'[14]

Over 50 years later, Metcalfe wrote that Barter placed the heating flues under the floor of the bath as Urquhart had seen in Turkey, and that 'water ran in streams, cooling the floor and creating vapour.'[15]

It soon became clear that this bath was not able to heat the air sufficiently for therapeutic purposes, and that there was too much vapour in the air. But, as Durham Dunlop commented:

> It was scarcely to be expected that the first Bath ... should have been faultless. It was not constructed after the ancient Roman model of the period when the Bath flourished in its perfection, but rather after the slovenly and imperfect modern imitations with which Mr Urquhart was most familiar ...[16]

Dunlop was right. When Urquhart made his own personal discovery of the baths in Turkey, he was totally overcome with the effect of what he saw and experienced. He was not examining them with the eyes of one who would later try to construct such baths himself. Why should he? Nor did he realise that the baths he used—though a revelation to him—might in their practical details have fallen far short of the Roman ideal.

Urquhart was aware that the use of the bath helped to relieve the pain of his own neuralgia, but neither he, nor the habitués of the Roman or Turkish baths before him, realised that it could be used more generally as a therapeutic agent—provided the air was dry enough to enable the body to tolerate the high temperature needed. This realisation, this achievement, was Barter's alone.

But the beehive bath, its shape reminiscent of the traditional Irish sweathouse, had been disappointing, and Urquhart returned to

England and a short period of intense political activity.

Dr Barter, determined to improve his bath, sent a sculptor and architect living at St Ann's (coincidentally also named Richard Barter[17]) to Rome in order to study the construction of the baths of the ancient Romans. The plans he brought back, however, were very similar—so far as their method of heating was concerned—to Urquhart's description of the Constantinople baths. Nevertheless, Dr Barter now had enough confidence to set about building a bath which would, he hoped, hold many more patients in greater comfort.

The improved Turkish Bath at St Ann's

A celebration, attended by the Urquharts, was held at St Ann's on 5 June 1856 to mark the laying of the foundation stone of the new bath. About 300 guests, including some 80 patients, feasted and listened to speeches. Urquhart praised Barter and said that he had been waiting nearly 20 years before he had found someone who would try to re-create the Roman hot-air baths which, at that time, survived only in the Ottoman Empire. The doctor was presented with a dinner service by his friends and a bust of himself by his namesake. Finally, the evening closed with a ball.[18]

The Urquharts stayed on afterwards participating in the various experiments in heating. In August, the *Free Press* reprinted an article from the *Cork Herald* describing their reporter's visit to St Ann's. 'At some distance from the establishment, an elegant cottage is being built by Mr Urquhart, containing a hot air bath'. One of Dr Barter's patients, 'a delicate young lady' had benefited by enduring a temperature of 175°F (79°C) in it.

Nearby, the new Turkish baths building, with its semi-circular roof over the *tepidarium*, was linked to the original building used by patients for other hydropathic baths and treatments. The walls, like those of Urquhart's cottage, were 'built of turf, smoothly plastered'—here, because of its heat insulation properties rather than, as at the cottage, for reasons of economy.[19]

In mid-September, when the baths were at an 'advanced stage', Urquhart arranged a fête for 120 workmen and tradesmen who were involved in constructing them. The Mayor of Cork and the local MP were also present for a dinner at which there was a sheep roasted whole, and Turkish pilaff served with potatoes.[20]

Urquhart described the baths at a public meeting in Cork, so we know that the building—40ft × 20ft (12.2m × 6.1m) in size—was divided into three rooms, and that it was 'capable of bathing sixty persons at a time.' [21] (Figs 4.5a–c)

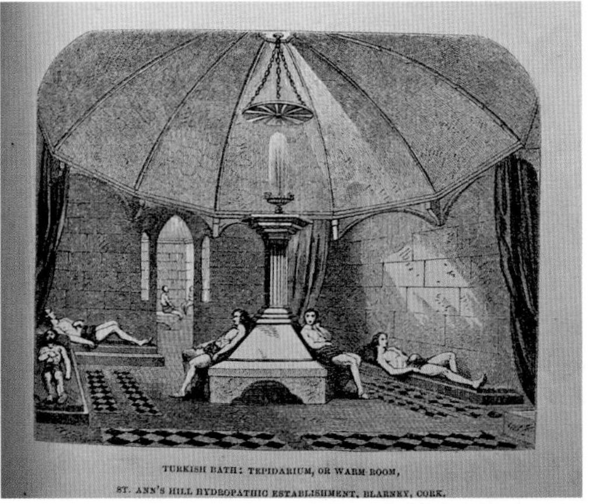

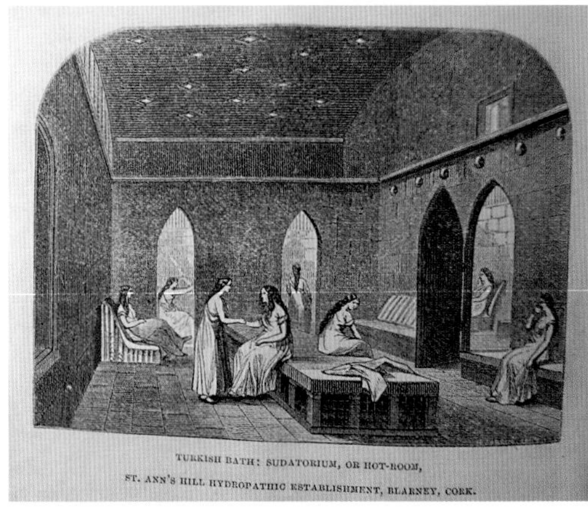

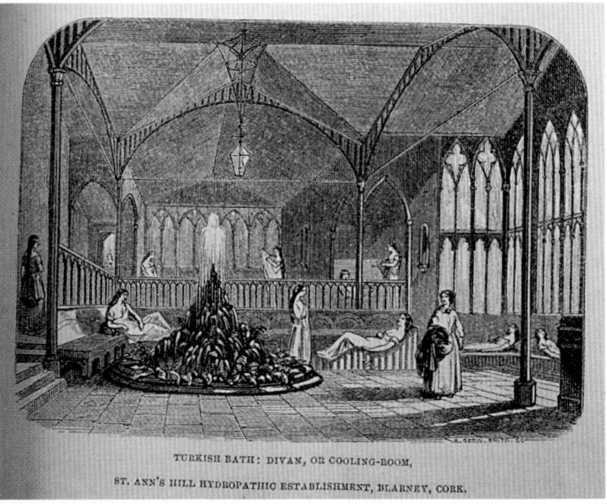

Fig 4.5a–c
The sudatorium, *or hot room (top),* tepidarium *(middle), or warm room, and* frigidarium *(bottom) in Barter's second, improved, Turkish bath at St Ann's Hydro, Blarney, near Cork. The captions to these images were wrongly printed in the original booklet, and the rooms are here named correctly.*
(Descriptive notice of the rise and progress of the Irish Graffenberg, *printed by Levey, Robinson and Franklyn, 1858, pp.21–3. Courtesy of Special Collections, UCC Library)*

When virtually complete, nearly a year later, the *Cork Examiner* described it as a 'pretty building, quite unique in style.' In addition to the **sudatorium*, or hot room, there was also a *frigidarium*, or cooling-room which had,

> large windows, an arched ceiling, supported by pillars, neatly carved, of polished oak; it is most profusely hung with drapery, of a rich character, and, with a capital eye to the position of colours, rich stained glass has been used.[22]

But even now, Barter continued to make changes to the heating and ventilation systems. He devised a method of arranging the flues 'in a particular way', so that, as he wrote to a friend, there was now a considerable saving in fuel cost.[23] This was later to become the subject of his patent application relating to improvements in heating and ventilating buildings.[24]

The baths (Fig 4.6) were not formally opened until 11 May 1858, when there was a celebratory lunch (Fig 4.7), and a 'presentation of plate to the Doctor', followed by dancing.[25]

Lecturing later in Bradford, Barter explained how the original bath, built 'under Mr Urquhart's instructions', had been unsatisfactory, becoming steamy because of the water introduced to cool the floors, and the bad positioning of the washing fountains. But,

> Under the influence of pure heated air, free from visible steam, and continuously renewed by a perfect system of ventilation, no one feels the distress which so frequently accompanies other heating appliances; for while perspiration is more fully obtained, the pulse is seldom found to rise much above its normal standard. This is the great feature of the Improved Turkish Bath, and one upon which its perfect safety and curative property will be found mainly to depend.[26]

Undertaking repeated experiments, and constructing new buildings involved considerable financial expenditure on Barter's part and, when the baths were fully operational, they were launched as an addition to the facilities of the hydro. An advertisement at the back of the published version of the Bradford lecture indicated that, whereas the existing baths were included in a patient's weekly charge, the new Turkish bath cost an additional three shillings per week.

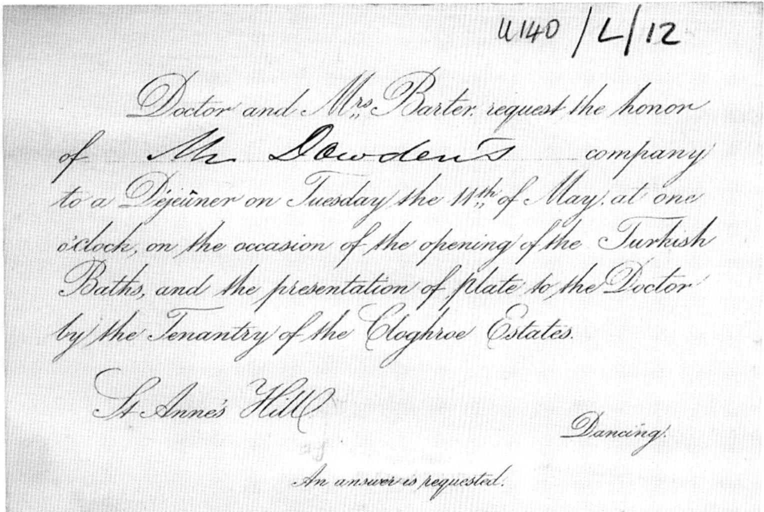

U140 / L / 12

Doctor and Mrs Barter request the honor of Mr Dowden's company to a Déjeûner on Tuesday the 11th of May, at one o'clock, on the occasion of the opening of the Turkish Baths, and the presentation of plate to the Doctor by the Tenantry of the Cloghroe Estates.

St Anne's Hill

Dancing.

An answer is requested.

Fig 4.6 (top)
The second Turkish bath at St Ann's.
(A glimpse of Saint Ann's, St Ann's: Sweeney, 1869, plate 8. Harvard College Library Widener Med 1878.69)

Fig 4.7 (bottom)
An invitation to the celebratory lunch on 11 May 1858 when the second Turkish bath at St Ann's was formally opened.
(Reproduced with the permission of Cork City and County Archives. Richard Dowden Papers, Ref. U140/L/012)

Even before the new building had been completed, Barter was busily promoting Turkish baths elsewhere in Ireland. A more cautious person might have waited until all the major problems had been solved; Barter preferred to open baths as soon as there was a possible demand, improving them as time went on.

This may have been a contributory factor leading to a bitter dispute, and an accusation that his baths were harmful and possibly dangerous—a dispute that was, unfortunately, not limited to medical journals, and to which we will return.

5

Urquhart, his committees, and their Turkish baths

Once the Victorian Turkish bath crossed the Irish Sea, it spread rapidly across the mainland. To understand how this happened we need to digress and examine in some detail the close relationship that existed, during the third quarter of the 1850s, between David Urquhart and his wife Harriet, his Foreign Affairs Committees (FACs), and the two *Free Press* newspapers.

Urquhart's entry in the *Oxford dictionary of national biography* concentrates on his diplomatic and political career, with only a single line mentioning the Turkish bath. Yet his political activity had virtually no influence on the government of the day and is largely forgotten, while more than a century later there are still 12 Victorian Turkish baths open in Britain. Furthermore, Urquhart's bath paved the way for the rapid mid-20th-century acceptance, and growing popularity, of the Russian steam bath and Finnish sauna which have taken its place.

'Therefore,' in the words of his contemporary (and friend), Karl Marx, 'a few remarks about a man whose name is on everyone's lips but whose actual significance hardly anyone can account for.'[1]

David Urquhart (1805–77)

Urquhart (Fig 5.1), the second son of David Urquhart (1748–1811) and his second wife, Margaret Hunter, was born in the Scottish Burgh of Cromarty at Braelangwell. After his father's death, he was educated by his mother, and then at St John's College, Oxford.

In 1827, he left for Greece, volunteering in the Greek War of Independence, later travelling to Constantinople (now Istanbul), then back through Albania and areas on the border between Greece and Turkey. While travelling, he sent back reports of what he had seen to two of his mother's friends, Jeremy Bentham and Sir Herbert Taylor (the former private secretary to George III and, later, to William IV).

These contacts, together with publicity resulting from his articles written for the *Morning Courier*, resulted in his accompanying Sir Stratford Canning as a diplomat to Constantinople in 1831. There, according to Miles Taylor, he 'went native, moving out of the embassy quarter and adopting Turkish dress.'[2]

Historians who have written about Urquhart have tended to focus on this period, and on his later creation of 'Foreign Affairs Committees'. These were formed, mainly in the mid-1850s, and particularly in the north of England and the Midlands, to promulgate his own political beliefs.[3]

Urquhart was a staunch Turcophile and an obsessional Russophobe (Fig 5.2)—an almost inevitable encapsulation of the political views he embraced while in Constantinople. Although most historians agree that neither Urquhart nor the FACs had any lasting impact on British foreign policy, all accept that he was 'one of the

Fig 5.1
David Urquhart, towards the end of his life. (Gertrude Robinson, David Urquhart, *Oxford: Blackwell, 1920, frontispiece)*

Fig 5.2
'Mr Urquhart appears to labour under the fearful fancy that [Tsar] Nicholas is about to invade this country mounted on the Great Bear, a constellation which our unfortunate dreamer was probably born under.' (Punch, *7 April 1849, 143)*

most remarkable publicists of his day',[4] and a knowledgeable, charismatic and eccentric person who, to the surprise of many, was often right.

In 1853, for example, Marx wrote to Engels, 'Strange though it may seem to you … I have come to the same conclusion as the monomaniac Urquhart—namely that for several decades Palmerston has been in the pay of Russia.'[5]

To his contemporaries, Urquhart's doctrines may well have been 'a specialised taste' but, as Anderson has noted, 'once acquired they became an addiction.'[6]

Joseph Constantine, the first important Turkish bath proprietor not to be connected with the FACs, characterised Urquhart as one who,

> founded the Free Trade and Foreign Affairs Association, and afterwards he tacked on to it the Turkish Baths, and the members loyally accepted it, and advocated it with vigour; he was their leader, and they were absolutely his followers … If Urquhart had added another tenet of faith of an opposite nature it would have been accepted. His followers had faith in him; he was their *law-giver*.[7]

Yet no one has satisfactorily explained *what* attracted so many workingmen to the committees, or why Russophobia (or any other aspect of *foreign* policy) bound them to Urquhart so loyally and for so long.

As for Urquhart's reintroduction of the Turkish bath to a Victorian society in which any form of bath was a luxury for the wealthy, historians seem to have thought such diversions not worthy of serious study. Neither have they sought to consider Urquhart the man, other than to notice, repeatedly, such obvious eccentricities as his refusal to shake hands with anyone—preferring, as he taught his children,[8] to kiss the hands of visitors.[9]

Several historians have studied the important unpublished collection of Urquhart correspondence at Balliol College, Oxford, but hardly any attention has been paid to those letters in the group labelled 'Turkish baths', nor to the significance of paragraphs on the subject to be found in some of the other letters, mainly political, dating from the 1850s and 1860s.

One of the few exceptions to this general neglect is an article by Asa Briggs on the FACs in the West Riding of Yorkshire. Briggs suggested that in their meetings can be found the prototype of the successful tutorial classes, founded in 1903 by the Workers' Educational Association (WEA), and still run by them today:

> However wild the personality and outlook of Urquhart himself—and he was the main inspiration of all this effort—the Foreign Affairs Committees mark an impressive stage in adult working-class education.[10]

Briggs noted also that 'another activity of the committees was the building of Turkish baths' and that 'Local letters were often headed "the Turkish Bath"'.[11] This article was written over 50 years ago, however, and no one seems yet to have followed up these acute observations.

The traditional view of Urquhart's positive side is of a well-read person, extremely knowledgeable on his own subjects, a clear thinker with reasoned answers to any question put to him, and,

> with a singular genius for impressing his opinions upon all sorts of men, from aristocratic dandies down to the grinders of Sheffield and the cobblers of Stafford.[12]

To this must be added some less attractive traits: that his unchecked enthusiasms 'often obscured his judgment;'[13] and that sometimes 'he put down with ostentatious insolence anyone who ventured to demur to anything he said.'[14]

Photographs seem to confirm a surly demeanour (Fig 5.3), but few subjects smiled in early 19th-century photographic portraits, possibly due to the need for a lengthy exposure time. Certainly such images seem to confirm the impression of humourlessness gained from reading his numerous speeches and pamphlets.

But Urquhart could be quite different. In 1920, the eldest of his children, David, sent a less than enthusiastic letter of polite thanks to Gertrude Robinson for her biography of his father.

> You have selected, and well selected those sections of his work which appeal to you and you have given a wonderful picture of the man he was, when working—He had a lighter side tho'—Brilliant conversationalist full of fun, jokes and quips—That does not show in his letters and with increasing bodily sickness and pain, there was little of that in his later years ... [15]

He was also aware that Robinson had been helped in her selection of Urquhart's correspondence by his younger sister, Harriet, her lifelong friend. But Harriet (known in the family as Hatty) was a timid girl of 15 when her father died. David related how, accompanied by Hatty and Maisie (the elder sister) he,

> used to go into [our parents'] bedroom in the mornings and have a real romp and fight in the big bed with him—I can well remember that little Hatty never really enjoyed these romps.

So it is, in part, a distorted picture which emerges from Robinson's biography, unduly coloured both by Hatty's view of her father and by the personality of an author who, immersed in political Catholicism, saw Urquhart (in the Kelmscottian subtitle of her biography) as 'a Victorian knight errant of justice and liberty'.

David's happier picture of his father is given credence by an amusing description by Lady Currie (the writer, Violet Fane) of a party at her parents' home around 1856 when she was just in her teens, and Urquhart (known to his friends as 'The Bey') was one of the guests:

> Upon one side of [my mother] was seated the Prince Frederick of Schleswig-Holstein ... From time to time, with a shrieking laugh which sounded almost hysterical, he bounded up and down in his chair, and slapped the table with his hands, by which one knew that the Bey, who sat upon his other side, had made some more than usually witty sally.[16]

Urquhart seemed to retain the friendship of those for whom he campaigned even when unsuccessful, for he was seen to be honest, caring, and had (unlike many of his contemporaries) genuine respect for those beyond the borders of Europe with whom he chose to work.

Fig 5.3
David Urquhart, shortly after his marriage to Harriet Angelina Fortescue in 1854. (Gertrude Robinson, David Urquhart, *Oxford: Blackwell, 1920, p.121)*

Ahmed Khan of Daghestan, for example, began a letter, 'Beloved Daoud Bey—Your Highness',[17] and if he had not fully grasped the specific British usage of the latter phrase, the intention is evident. While Hassan of Circassia began, 'Most noble Daoud Bey', extending his greeting to Urquhart's young son in his valediction, 'I salute thee and little Daoud Bey and all your friends.'[18]

Margaret Jenks has pointed out that Urquhart's personality particularly appealed to women. He welcomed their assistance, and 'almost all of the men who were most closely involved with him received the encouragement of their wives.'[19]

But he also worked well with women who were single. Harriett Ann Curtis was a longtime supporter of Urquhart's activities, although it is not known who she was, or how she first became involved. Already being sent political documents by him in 1849 when he was MP for Stafford, she wrote in the press under the name 'Fides' supporting his views.[20] While attending the committees' Christmas conference in 1858,[21] she was present at an organisers' meeting, and was important enough to be consulted by committee secretaries who needed advice and did not wish to trouble Urquhart.[22] She was staying at Rickmansworth on 7 April, the night of the 1861 census, entered as a visitor, and earlier that year had become the second largest shareholder in the London & Provincial Turkish Bath Co Ltd.[23]

But it was Harriet Angelina Fortescue who, after her marriage to Urquhart on 5 September 1854, became his chief support and collaborator in all things.

Harriet Urquhart (1824–89)

Harriet (Fig 5.4) was the sister of Chichester Fortescue MP, later Baron Carlingford. An independent-minded individual, and a believer in rational dress for women, she had earlier, with financial help from Ruskin, started a shirt factory for the unemployed of Ardee in Co. Louth.[24]

During the year before her marriage, she prepared an introduction to some of Urquhart's papers,[25] and the day after her wedding, the *Morning Advertiser* published *The words of Lord Palmerston* under her pseudonym 'Caritas'. [26]

In her memoir of Harriet, Maria Catherine Bishop wrote that she found it difficult to distinguish between Urquhart's writing and Harriet's. 'Half her articles in his paper, the *Free Press,* and her many other writings were by him, and half of his by her.' Bishop quotes a letter from their son David who wrote that, generally speaking, 'the argumentative work, the collating of extracts from despatches, treaties, &c., was done by her first, and then my father dictated the introduction and conclusion.'[27]

Historians do not seem to have given Harriet credit for the closeness of her collaboration with Urquhart, though it must be clear to all who study his papers. Their two temperaments complemented each other in exactly the manner needed to ensure that their work was most effectively undertaken. The retention of committee members' loyalty to Urquhart was in no small measure due to her calm, soothing rationality.

Her contribution was widely recognised by many of the FAC members themselves. Benjamin Morrell, for example, referring to her in a letter to her husband as 'your valuable partner Mrs Urquhart.'[28] They appreciated the trouble she took in her explanations of difficult points, David Scott writing to ask John Johnson to 'present my sincere and grateful thanks to Mrs Urquhart' for helping him overcome his habit of 'jumping to Conclusions without weighing evidence.'[29] And they responded to her personal interest in their lives, as when Thomas Dean, answering her query, wrote, 'My wife's name is Bridgett, but having lived in service where certain names are not liked, we have got the habit of calling her Ann …'[30]

Harriet could not, even had she wished, avoid involvement in Urquhart's campaign to reintroduce the Turkish bath; a bath was constructed as soon as they moved house. Harriet's memoirist wrote in 1897:

Fig 5.4
Harriet Angelina Fortescue, full partner in every aspect of Urquhart's work, and writer under the pseudonym 'Caritas'.
(Maria Catherine Bishop, Memoir of Mrs Urquhart, *Kegan Paul, 1897)*

> My first impression of the hot air room contrived in his Geneva villa was of a dimly lighted catacomb. Mrs Urquhart, in white bathing costume, slight and picturesque in the light of the lamp she carried, stood at the foot of the stairs in friendly welcome. She taught us as we lay panting on our shelves in a heat of 170°F [77°C] all the merits of what is truly a sanitary institution, but one that with its attendant shampooing was not then as freely recognised as now.[31]

Throughout his life Urquhart welcomed anyone wishing to try the Turkish bath, whether they were friends or neighbours, his servants, local doctors with their patients, FACs wanting information, or their members who were unwell.

The Turkish bath he built at Riverside, near Rickmansworth (see Chapter 22), was internationally renowned and considered 'a great boon to the neighbourhood.'[32] Harriet agreed that its use should be offered to those who sought to discover its worth, and kept many sciatic and invalid guests over for breakfast. 'Some days there were as many as twenty-five people using it', wrote John Johnson.[33]

If Urquhart received effusive letters from his acolytes, Harriet received them also—from those who realised the contribution she made to their common endeavours. John Harlow, writing from Small Heath, Birmingham, spoke for many when he wrote:

> To yourself Madam, I would only say—Who that has seen you, has heard you speak, and has known your acts as I have, can have other feelings towards you than those of humble reverend admiration.[34]

FAC members had 'an absolute conviction that they were right and an utter devotion to Urquhart and his cause', but Jenks, for one, found it difficult to explain how this was inspired.[35] Many factors were involved, but one of these must surely have been the feeling shared by committee members that within the movement there was a knowledgeable intercessor able to take the rough edges off any problems which might arise in their work.

The Foreign Affairs Committees

Asa Briggs memorably described the committees as 'not so much a cohesive movement as a series of bouts of agitation':

> Their interpretation of history was sometimes ... as confused and wild as their interpretation of foreign policy, but their claim to the right to study foreign policy for themselves and to exercise control over representatives was too serious in its implications to be dismissed lightly.[36]

Urquhart's first political campaign, following dismissal from the diplomatic service, was waged single-handedly in the late 1830s, with a barrage of pamphlets, and letters to newspaper editors, about British foreign policy towards Russia and Turkey.

In 1840 he began to gather round himself a group of middle-class supporters with whom he was to be involved in the formation of FACs.[37] For a while Newcastle-on-Tyne became a centre of Urquhartite activity, but this was short lived, and though he continued writing, ill-health, travel, and a short spell as MP for Stafford, all combined to put an end to Urquhart's first bout of committee-style activity until the early 1850s.

Starting again in Newcastle, he was encouraged to resuscitate some of the earlier committees by the growing hostility between Russia and Turkey, which was to lead to the Crimean War. Soon, committees were to be found in Preston and Manchester, and nearly 30 could be found in Yorkshire alone.[38]

They were at their most successful during the mid-1850s, and though often scorned by British politicians and newspapers, Karl Marx still retained a high opinion of them and their leader, writing in 1860 that,

> Urquhart is a power, of which Russia is afraid. He is the only official personage in England who has the courage and honesty to affront public opinion. He's the only one of them who is incorruptible (whether by money or ambition). Finally, and strange to say, I have so far encountered none but honest men among his followers ...[39]

There was a final spurt of activity at Keighley in 1874 when Urquhart briefly returned from his health-induced retirement abroad. But the committees had ceased to occupy the pages of the newspapers—or worry too many politicians—long before then.

Urquhart and Isaac Ironside

Sometime in the early 1850s, when he was starting to rebuild the FACs, Urquhart met the prominent Sheffield Borough councillor, Isaac Ironside (1808–70). The meeting was to have a considerable effect on the work of each of them during the next few years.

Ironside, three years younger than Urquhart, was a self-made man who was apprenticed at the age of 12 to an iron foundry.[40] He continued his studies at night school, being particularly gifted at mathematics, and later left the foundry to become an accountant like his father.

Inspired by Joshua Toulmin Smith's *Local self-government and centralization,* Ironside began calling local meetings, 'wardmotes', to discuss such matters as local libraries, or a new gas supply, hoping to encourage people to take such decisions out of the hands of central government.[41] He was also interested in foreign affairs and was staunchly anti-Russian, though it was probably local government and political methodology which brought the two men together as much as anti-Russian politics.

Ironside was using his wardmotes to 'authorise' his highway improvements; Urquhart, already a follower of Smith's doctrines, was using the same principle to campaign for his 'moral improvements', arguing that a country's foreign policy should be as moral as the everyday dealings between their own people.

The significant difference was that Ironside's followers could sometimes see a benefit which would directly affect their lives; Urquhart's committees selflessly engaged in a battle for the greater good and were, therefore, continually in need of encouragement and support.

The two men probably began their close involvement in each other's affairs early in 1854, after Ironside began calling for 'an honest war'[42] against Russia. By September, he had made Sheffield one of the centres of Urquhartite activity with himself as its leader,[43] and later, as Secretary of its FAC.

It has been suggested that Urquhart was drawn to work closely with Sheffield's ultra-radicals in 1854 because they had 'a newspaper in the shape of the *Free Press*, which was controlled both financially and editorially by Isaac Ironside.'[44]

§But when Urquhart started working with him in 1854, the *Free Press* did not yet exist, and although Ironside may at times have had some influence over the content of the *Sheffield Free Press,* he neither edited nor owned it at that time.[45]

When the editor of the Sheffield paper became ill, however, Urquhart recommended one of his protégés, the Secretary of the Longton FAC, William Cyples, as sub-editor, and shortly afterwards Cyples became editor.

The committeemen

Many of Urquhart's recruits were young and, unlike Cyples, often had only a basic education. It has frequently been remarked that in preparing them for the part they were to play in the political work of the committees—including the study of treaties, official documents, Vattel's *The law of nations*, and his own myriad pamphlets and articles—Urquhart was a hard taskmaster.

He would have considered such rigour necessary to ensure that the committeemen were able to stand on their own feet when corresponding with politicians and members of the government. And he knew that he was also providing a general education which would stand them in good stead for the future, while at the same time making their acceptance of government policy less automatic.

Urquhart taught them the use of Socratic dialogue as a means of converting an opponent to their point of view. They were required to compose practice dialogues—one of which was reprinted by Robinson—and then to submit them for approval.[46] This exercise made a considerable impact on committee members, perhaps because the more astute ones saw in it something which might also be useful in everyday life.

The secretary of the Stafford committee told John Johnson that when Urquhart visited them,

> He instructed us in the best method of dealing with our fellow-men and told us how to reply to all their objections to any proposition we advanced. Not to utter the contents of our own minds but to interrogate them as to the contents of theirs and to make them define correctly the meaning of the words they use.[47]

Another member seems only accidentally to have stumbled on an underlying reason for such study. 'I find from experience', he wrote, 'that the Socratic method is useless to me unless I know every side of the case on which I intend to question an opponent.'[48]

Of course, such an approach could not be expected to work for all members. Perhaps Thomas Woodruff was too humane, confessing to Urquhart, 'I don't think I have the ability or capacity of applying the result of a series of questions in order to expose my neighbour's ignorance.'[49]

As men showed ability, they moved to work with Urquhart, and this in itself must have been an education. Committees considered not up to the mark would receive an educational visit; the aim, however, was always to achieve improvement, not to belittle the efforts of fellow members.

The Crossroads committee had been visited by three committee 'supervisors' amongst whom was Urquhart's trouble-shooter Stewart Rolland, later to become a major shareholder in the London & Provincial Turkish Baths Company. Afterwards John Waddington wrote:

> We felt somewhat afraid of the visit of Major Rolland before he came, but on a nearer acquaintance we like him 'vastly well', he is so homely, and makes no parade of superior knowledge nor our ignorance.[50]

One of the reasons why some historians have been unable to understand how Urquhart held the loyalty of his committee members for so long is that, seeing only snapshots of particular moments, they often underestimated the men's innate abilities.

Richard Shannon, for example, commenting on Woodruff's confessed inability to use the Socratic method, refers to him as a factory operative of North Shields, implying that such intellectual rigours were therefore beyond him.[51] But Woodruff was only working 'twelve hours a day in a hot dusty factory'[52] because he had lost his previous employment.

One year later, he was running his own business, a Turkish bath in Stephenson Street.[53] Five years after that he was simultaneously running a second Turkish bath in Sunderland, an establishment which remained open after his death in 1885, and continued under his wife, and then his daughter, until it eventually closed in 1895.[54]

Likewise, Margaret Jenks also underestimated the high intelligence of many of the committeemen. Although she well understood that:

> One of the most important elements in Urquhart's appeal to these men was that he gave them a sense of importance and pride in themselves …'[55]

She also, looking at letters written by some of the committeemen, equated lack of specific skills with lack of intelligence:

> It is easy to say that the men had little education and were of a limited ability. That, indeed, was often the case. Bartholomew's spelling and grammatical constructions, for instance, left much to be desired.

This is a dismal assessment of Charles Bartholomew, the son of a Wiltshire farmhand, who was then in his early 20s. His inability to spell was soon rectified and had nothing to do with his exceptional intelligence and grasp of historical complexities, nor his ability to achieve success.

He opened his first Turkish bath in Bristol in1860, and when he died in 1889 he left a chain of Turkish baths (the largest in the kingdom) comprising one establishment in each of eight cities. Knowing where thanks were due, he named one of his sons Urquhart.[56]

Bartholomew was a naturally gifted publicist and, later, a writer of numerous pamphlets. One of these purported to report the evidence he gave on 11 and 12 June, 1866, 'before a group of medical men', on the prevention and cure of disease by the use of Turkish baths, refuting their accusation that the bath was dangerous. His account takes the form of a Socratic dialogue between himself and the doctors, and he had to reprint it several times.[57]

His highly embellished story of these meetings has become part of the mythology of the Turkish bath. Richard Metcalfe, for example, related in 1878 how Bartholomew 'was publicly examined in the Lecture Hall of the Bristol Athenaeum before a large audience of medical men and the general public.'[58]

One hundred years later, the story of his trial before the doctors was still being told, E S Turner concluding his account, 'It was Bartholomew's night and the doctors had to grin and bear it.'[59]

Anyone attending these meetings expecting a medieval disputation with a large crowd of doctors firing barbed questions at the hapless Bartholomew would have been disappointed. Although the first evening's proceedings achieved a quarter column in the following day's paper, it also noted that 'The attendance was not very large.' Bartholomew, it reported,

> read a kind of dialogue between a doctor and a believer in the Turkish Bath system, in which the objections of the former were answered … Mr Bartholomew displayed a very intimate acquaintance with his subject, and his observations were frequently applauded.[60]

In fact, the whole Socratic affair was stage-managed from beginning to end and would have done credit to a modern spin doctor. According to Leonard Park, whose father, William, worked for Bartholomew, some of those present were Bartholomew's own patients brought there by him, with complimentary tickets.[61] The following day the same paper reported that while Bartholomew 'continued his "examination" into the relative value of drugs and the Turkish bath … The attendance was very small.'[62]

Urquhart's gift was being able to recognise those who were, in today's parlance, underachieving through no fault of their own. He gave them a sense of purpose and of pride in themselves, inspiring them with a vision of what they *could* achieve and then, most importantly, gave them the skills to enable them to take advantage of their inherent ability so as to control their own lives.

The two *Free Press* newspapers

On 21 June 1856, two very different articles appeared in the *Sheffield Free Press*. One, the first of a series called 'Revelations of the diplomatic history of the eighteenth century', was by Karl Marx. The second, aimed at the same readership, was an article headed 'Introduction of the Turkish bath into Ireland' which suggested that,

> This transplantation of an institution from the East into the West is an event of which the historian should make a memorandum. Considered in the consequences that will result from it, I look on it as equal to a social revolution.[63]

To understand why the editor of a Sheffield political weekly should feel that each of these articles would interest his readers, we need to examine briefly the history of the paper.

The *Sheffield Free Press & Rotherham and Barnsley Advertiser* was founded in 1851 by a local printing firm. It was similar to many other provincial papers of its time, but its more radical political slant brought it to the attention of Isaac Ironside. In April 1855 he became one of its proprietors and, within a few months, a second cut-down version, omitting much of the local news and called the *Free Press,* was also being published.

This too was edited by William Cyples and, by mid-November, Ironside wholly owned both papers, though the new one was being subsidised by the Newcastle ironmaster George Crawshay (a longtime Urquhart supporter).

Nine months later, the *Free Press* moved to London, continuing publication without a break. It was now edited by Collet Dobson Collet, an Urquhartite convert, and published by Urquhart and Crawshay.

Collet, a person of infinite 'energy, resources and devices',[64] was also the active secretary of the Association for Promoting the Repeal of the Taxes on Knowledge—the newspaper stamp duty. Allan Merson points out that,

> from August 1856 onwards, the *Free Press* was the vehicle of two distinct campaigns: Urquhart's campaign against Palmerston and Collet's campaign against the remaining obstacles to a cheap popular press.[65]

But Merson fails to point out that the *Free Press,* for the next few years at least, was also the vehicle for Urquhart's Turkish Bath Movement.

Most of the occasionally acrimonious negotiations leading to the separation of the two papers was conducted by correspondence as Urquhart was at St Ann's for most of 1856, still working with Barter on the development of the bath.

When the discussion with Ironside became difficult, Urquhart asked Crawshay to visit him at St Ann's to see whether he could help. While there, he too was introduced to the latest version of the bath. Crawshay was impressed and, at the beginning of the following year, had a Turkish bath built at his home in Tyneside (see Chapter 22). Urquhart built his own first small bath a little later in the year at Lytham, and Stewart Rolland followed suit in 1859.[66]

Ironside also discovered the bath, shortly after Crawshay. For well over 18 months he had been suffering from a severe outbreak of boils which had failed to respond to any prescribed conventional medical treatment. Urquhart, whose relationship with him did not appear to be too disturbed by the removal of the *Free Press* to London, recommended that he visit St Ann's in order to try Barter's Turkish bath. However, in December, when Ironside arrived, the latest version was still incomplete, and he had to make do with the vapour bath instead.

Nevertheless, after three weeks of twice-daily bathing, the boils cleared up[67] and Ironside became the latest convert to the Turkish bath which, he was assured by Barter, would be even more effective because the body was able to withstand greater temperatures in dry air.

Neither Urquhart nor Crawshay had facilities for distributing the *Free Press* and this was taken on by Holyoake & Co—a connection which probably explains the regular coverage of Turkish bath matters in secularist George Jacob Holyoake's own paper, *The Reasoner.*

The Turkish bath had become, then, an integral part of the lives of those involved in the production of both *Free Press* newspapers.

Reporting the Turkish Bath Movement

We can now begin to get a clearer picture of how the Turkish Bath Movement started to develop, the role of the two political papers in the process, and the involvement of the various FACs and their members.

The *Sheffield Free Press* article, 'Introduction of the Turkish bath into Ireland', was an account of a dinner held at St Ann's in honour of Dr Barter, at which the foundation stone of his new Turkish bath was laid.[68]

The paper had already published a letter (describing the St Ann's estate) which Harriet had forwarded.[69] Then, barely a month after reporting the dinner, another article appeared entitled 'Introduction of the Turkish bath into our towns and cities'. Its author wrote:

> There appears promise of a 'movement' in favour of water and cleanliness; and it would not be astonishing if Turkish Baths became the rage, and succeeded the small bonnets and coloured shirts.[70]

If, as Gwyn Prins suggests, 'a movement' is 'a self-description which already has an evangelistic ring', then the *Sheffield Free Press* was the evangelist.[71] The issue dated 23 August 1856 included not only an article headed 'Mr Urquhart, the Apostle of the Oriental Baths'[72] (reporting a well-attended public meeting in Cork), but also a letter signed 'Balnea' suggesting that Urquhart be asked to give a public lecture on the Turkish bath when next in Sheffield.[73]

The account of his Cork lecture, mainly about the social implications of cleanliness, gave rise to a second article (this time in the *Free Press*) which triggered several more letters to the editor.[74] First, Charles Bartholomew, as secretary of the Bristol FAC, wrote saying how much he had enjoyed reading the lecture,[75] and the following week Charles Attwood wrote to say that, like the Turkish bath,

> Medicine chiefly acts by stimulating secretion … And how much poison does it—medicine—not also introduce and leave behind in order to excite this action?[76]

But, he suggested, unlike medicine, the Turkish bath was harmless.

The following month brought an account of the celebratory party given by Urquhart for the workers building the new Turkish bath at St Ann's,[77] and Bartholomew, clearly inspired by all this, wrote to Urquhart that he intended to build a Turkish bath in Bristol (Fig 5.5),

> Then Sir us Working Men Sum of us Masons, Carpenters Glazers & Smiths. We will set to work nights till it is completed. I shall if possible get the Committee to do it so after wards it may be its property. Thear are difficulties in this plan But nothing But what may be overcome and if the public see that we are introducing an Institution for their benefit we shall gain a larger influence upon other matters.[78]

This too was duly published in the paper—though with the spelling corrected.[79]

Although Bartholomew's approach was not taken up by the Bristol committee, Urquhart clearly liked his thinking and, when Benjamin Bishop of the Wakefield FAC wrote asking for advice on building a bath, he was sent a copy of Bartholomew's letter together with his own reply:

Fig 5.5
Part of an early letter from Charles Bartholomew to Urquhart, dated 26 September 1856, recounting his political work that week, and announcing his intention to build a Turkish bath in Bristol.
(Balliol College, Oxford. Urquhart Bequest. I: Letters G.4.7. Image supplied by the Master and Fellows of Balliol College, Oxford)

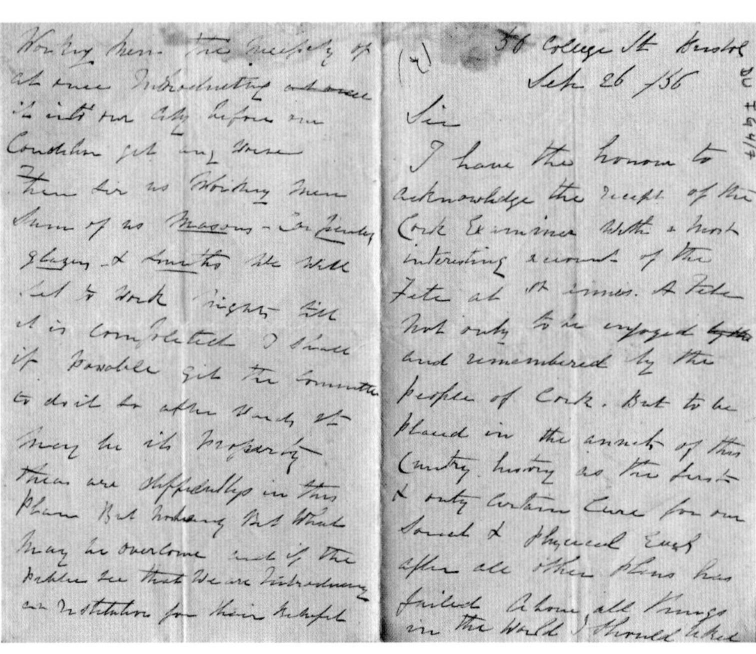

Working Men. The necessity of
... Introductory ...
... into our City before ...
Condition get any worse
Then Sir us Working Men
Sum of us Masons - Carpenters
Glazers & Smiths We Will
set to Work nights till
it is Completed I shall
if Possible git the Committee
to do it so after wards it
may be its Property
Thear are Difficulties in this
Plan But nothing But What
May be overcome and if the
Public see that We are Introducing
an Institution for their benefit

(2) 56 College St Bristol
Sep 26 /56
Sir
I have the honour to
acknowledge the receipt of the
Cork Examiner with a most
interesting account of the
Fete at St Annes. A Fete
Not only to be enjoyed
and remembered by the
people of Cork. But to be
placed in the annals of this
Country history as the first
& only Certain Cure for our
Social & Physical Evils
after all other Plans has
failed Above all things
in the World I should like

> It has long been an idea of mine, to associate with each committee a proprietary Bath; for the cleaning of the mind and body go hand in hand.[80]

Here were the beginnings of a second strand in the movement's development: a network of communication—by letter, person to person, and at meetings of the various committees.

After reading of Bartholomew's intention to build a bath, Ironside wrote to tell him how the vapour bath had cured his own painful affliction.

The two papers may have been yawningly serious politically, but even the smallest incident concerning the baths was reported. For instance, when Ironside decided to build a Turkish bath at home so that he could continue the treatment started at St Ann's, he consulted John Maxfield, a heating engineer who was a member of the Sheffield FAC.[81] After he told Maxfield about the letter he had written to Bartholomew, Maxfield wrote to the *Sheffield Free Press* saying that he had heard about Ironside's successful cure, and would the editor let readers know more about it.[82] The editor, of course, agreed and reproduced Ironside's letter to Bartholomew.[83]

Bartholomew, always a natural publicist, later quoted a shortened version of this letter in his pamphlets, though he always changed the phrase 'vapour chamber' into 'Turkish bath'.[84]

The committees and their baths

Without doubt, the major news item about the bath during 1857 was the announcement in both papers of the building in Manchester, with Urquhart's financial help, of the first Turkish bath in England to open to the public. This was managed, and later owned, by William Potter at his home in Broughton Lane. Potter had been secretary of the Birmingham committee, later moving to work with Ironside in Sheffield, before ending up in Manchester where, for a short time, he worked with the Manchester committee.

The bath seems to have opened some time around 12 July,[85] with Potter's wife, Elizabeth, supervising separate sessions for women,[86] for it was always taken for granted that Turkish baths were equally beneficial to both sexes.

The bath's success, passed along the grapevine and published in their papers, fuelled the committees' enthusiasm. Eighteen months later, at the end of 1859, there were nine Turkish baths in England so far identified as being owned by them, or by their members.

During the same period, seven establishments were set up in Ireland (mostly by, or under the guidance of, Dr Barter), and three in England which were independent of the committees, the most important of which was Joseph Constantine's first bath in Manchester's Oxford Street.

By 1860 *The Reasoner* was commenting that Turkish baths 'are now spreading like vaccination. It is becoming a sign of civilisation in a town to possess one.'[87]

The two political papers played an important part in keeping committee members in touch with progress around the country. In one issue alone, that of 26 May 1858, five out of the eight pages of the *Free Press* (Fig 5.6) were about the Turkish bath.

Eventually, there were at least 30 Turkish baths known to have been run by FACs members (Table 5.1).

Except in Ireland, where Barter's influence predominated, it was the committees, their members, and their baths which inspired other proprietors, perhaps more commercially minded, to start building and opening Turkish baths for the general public.

A self-help movement

Both David and Harriet Urquhart cared about the wellbeing of those less fortunate than themselves. They did so in a manner quite different from that so often associated with the picture—no doubt partly stereotyped—of the Victorian do-gooder. Urquhart believed as strongly as any Samuel Smiles that people had to help themselves. There was never any institutionalised charity in his work.

This did not preclude his contributing financially to help individuals from time to time, as when the Macclesfield FAC was raising funds to send one of its members, Henry Swain, to Dalton's Turkish baths in Manchester to try to cure his severe back problem.[88] This was successful and, when the committee opened its own Turkish bath in 1860, Swain was appointed bath attendant.

Initially, Urquhart saw the working men as a means of putting pressure on the government. However, he soon became aware of them as people: that they responded well to those who took an interest in them. He believed that everyone had a right to participate in public affairs by actively arguing for what they believed in, and continuing to do so whatever the result.

Table 5.1 Foreign Affairs Committee Turkish baths

Ashton-under-Lyne	Manchester (4)
Bath	Oldham
Birmingham (2)	Preston
Bradford	Rochdale
Honley	South Shields
Keighley	Stalybridge
Leeds (2)	Stockport
Liverpool	Sunderland
London (6)	Winchester
Macclesfield	Unknown area (1)

He realised too that the men needed the means to undertake the work he required of them, providing educational workshops to give them knowledge and skills which they were then also able to use in the course of their everyday lives. Not only did he do this without condescension, but he ensured that the helpers he chose were, like Rolland, colleagues who knew how to get the best out of people.

Fig 5.6
On 26 May 1858, The Free Press, *normally an extremely dry political paper, devoted five of its eight pages to matters relating to the Turkish bath.* (The Free Press, *26 May 1858, p.1)*

PUBLISHED ON THE FOURTH WEDNESDAY IN EVERY MONTH.] {REGISTERED AT THE GENERAL POST OFFICE FOR TRANSMISSION ABROAD.

THE FREE PRESS.

"I WISH THE PEOPLE OF ENGLAND WOULD TAKE THEIR AFFAIRS INTO THEIR OWN HANDS."—SIR R. PEEL.

VOL. VI.—No. 17.] WEDNESDAY, MAY 26, 1858. [PRICE ONE PENNY.

THE TURKISH BATH.

THERE are not many things more useful and there are few things more simple than a brick, when you have got it. Yet there was a time when bricks were unknown, and when they had to be invented. Their invention is connected with the first great epoch of the human race, for the tower of Babel was built of bricks, and thence have come the dispersion of races and the confusion of tongues among mankind.

But if methods are invented, inventions also are lost, and a far more remarkable history might be written on the loss of inventions, than ever has been compiled on their discovery. Brick-making flourished in England under the Romans, and yet for fourteen centuries no brick was made in the land. Surely it was easy to gather mud into moulds and burn it into stones; surely the remnants of Roman edifices showed that this was possible and how it was to be done, yet no brick-kiln flamed in England during these many ages.

Now, if during that course of time any man had said to his fellows, "Why don't you make bricks?" and discoursed to them upon the plastic nature of aluminous matter, and its induration by means of caloric, what would have been the unfortunate's fate? Would they not have said to him, "Now, go to; don't tell us that we are fools, for to say that we can make bricks and don't make them is to tell us so." This is the use made of conscience by mankind; to make themselves bitter against those who show them that they have been wrong, and especially when the wrong is committed upon themselves; then there is nothing for the innovator but hemlock and the stake.

The application of heat to the human body is no less a process than that of its application to a lump of clay. Being a process, it has to be invented, and an edifice is required, just as for burning coals; in fact, this is one of the uses to which in the earliest times bricks have been applied. This also is one of the first of inventions, and appears to be even of earlier date than the Tower of Babylon; traces of the peculiar ash which results from the method of combustion in the bath having been found in large quantities between the interstices of the blocks in the antediluvian structures of Baalbec.

This invention was also introduced into Great Britain by the Romans, and although it became a habit, and notwithstanding all its benefits and enjoyments, the practice went out. Doubtless the baths themselves stood disused for ages before they passed into the condition of ruins, and yet they conveyed no more the idea to the then mind of the Britons than did the splendid marble baths of the British hospital at Scutari to the civilised and medical mind of the English at Constantinople. And thus for fifteen or sixteen hundred years was this invention lost in these islands.

At the end of this period, namely, the present moment, one of the people says to his fellows, "Build Baths; it would be very good for you, and very profitable for you; see how it is done." But his fellows have a conscience, and they answer him, "Now, go to, you reviler; will you tell us that we are filthy and stupid? Are we, civilized Christians, to be taught by the Turks?"

After that talk had gone on for twenty years, one man gets up and says, "I will build a bath, and make money of it," and he builds a bath, and does make money of it. As in the case of bricks, when one brick was made, the invention was recovered, so does it happen also with baths; the profit having accrued, the bath passes from the domain of conscience, and enters into that of religion, for a people which worships gold venerates what is profitable.

We are required by some who have experienced the benefits of this invention to publish a number which shall contain an exposition of its nature, and instructions as to its use. This is easy to ask, but not so easy to perform. Let us take an analogous case. In a certain country the use of boats is unknown. You will not introduce navigation by publishing a number of the *Free Press*, containing elaborate disquisitions on the density of fluids and the buoyancy of timber, but you will do service, if you can make two announcements—first, that other countries have the means of going afloat, and secondly, that, in a certain village on your own coast, a boat has been built, or is in process of construction. We tell the English people that baths have been in existence from the earliest ages, throughout nearly the whole of the human race; that they did formerly exist in England; that the lost invention has now been recovered; that some score have already been constructed; that shortly no town, and prospectively no village in the land, will be without them; and that any one who is so minded may now see the thing with his own eyes, and experience it in his own person.

REVIEW.

The Turkish Bath with a View to its Introduction into the British Dominions. By D. Urquhart.
Bryce, Paternoster-row, 1856.

IN the history of this institution there is no point more remarkable than that the East should have been as mute in reference to the good it possessed as the West has been to the deficiency of which it was not conscious. The first spark of thought has been there elicited by what is doing in England. A series of articles has just appeared in the *Medical Gazette* of Constantinople, which commence with this explanation of their own appearance:—

"An English physician, Dr. HAUGHTON, has undertaken the journey to Constantinople to investigate upon the spot a subject so full of interest, and in consequence of an Eastern bath having been recently constructed in the neighbourhood of Cork from plans and directions furnished to the proprietor by the celebrated DAVID URQUHART. During the last two years Mr. URQUHART has devoted himself to the establishment of the Eastern bath in England, and he has gone through the country haranguing multitudes in the great cities upon the importance of sustituting the Oriental bath for the plan of immersion. From the success he has already obtained we may fairly anticipate that a hygienic reform will be effected by his great talent and indefatigable perseverance, and if this be the case amongst the practical people of England there can be little doubt that the example will be followed by the rest of Europe. This effort of Mr. URQUHART's is a reason the more why we who live in the East should hasten to do our part in bringing about this important change—this restoration of the golden age."

To have the bath it is not necessary for a people to be very civilised or very recondite or even very mechanical.

"The rudest people may have had the bath. The Red Indians are fully acquainted with it, and the means they employ are heated stones and a leather covering. They crawl in and throw water on the stones, and soak till the same effect is produced as the Balnea of Rome obtained."*

Nor are they very remote from our own country:—

"With respect to the sweating-houses, as they are called, I remember (says a recent writer) about forty years ago, seeing one in the island of Rathlin, and shall try to give you a description of it:—It was built of basalt stones, very much in the shape of a bee-hive, with a row of stones inside, for the persons to sit on when undergoing the operation. There was a hole at the top and one near the ground where the person crept in, and seated him or herself; the stones having been heated in the same way as an oven for baking bread is; the hole on the top being covered with a sod, while being heated; but, I suppose, removed to admit the person to breathe. Before entering, the patient was stripped quite naked, and on coming out, dressed again in the open air. The process was reckoned a sovereign cure for rheumatism and all sorts of pains and aches. They are fearful-looking things, as well as I remember."†

Yet the bath is not necessarily confined to the wild Irish, the Red Indian, the cruel Turk, or the enslaved Russian. The Phœnicians, the Greeks, the Romans, the Saracens, all possessed it. From the pamphlet under Review we select a few passages:—

"I cannot enter into a lengthened description to reason out the subject; I should require to be a profound physiologist and physician; but my deficiencies in this respect, and the appearance of presumption in speaking confidently on a medical subject, will not deter me from declaring that of which I have daily and hourly proof, that with full knowledge of the uses of water, and the means of employing it at different degrees of temperature, you have an entire command over those acute disorders which constitute nine-tenths of our maladies.

"Where the bath is the practice of the people, there are no diseases of the skin; all cases of inflammation, local and general, are subdued. Gout, rheumatism, sciatica, or stone, cannot exist when it is consecutively and sedulously employed as a curative means. I am inclined to say the same thing in reference to the plague. I am certain of it with reference to cholera. As to consumption, that scourge of England, that pallid spectre, which sits by every tenth domestic hearth among the higher or-

* Turkish Bath, p. 8. † Ibid. p. 64.

When he returned to England from St Ann's, he found that his workingmen were often practical people with manual and technical skills, and that they were interested in the progress of his bath-building. He saw how one after the other showed an interest in constructing and using them, in offering their use to fellow workers and, in groups, considering how best to share the fuel costs. Accordingly, he encouraged them to the adopt the idea of running Turkish baths as a means of financial support, thereby enabling them to concentrate more on their political activities, raise their standard of living, and become more independent.

In this he was satisfied and there are extant posters which advertise such meetings. But the rooms were also let out to other groups, providing additional income, and their use by Secularists is noted later (see Chapter 12).

One account, with a sketch of three stout men sitting in boxes with steam escaping into the air, celebrates the centenary of the Keighley Co-operative Society, relating that it was founded in the Market Place Turkish bath.[89] More prosaically, it was in the meetings room where 12 to 14 locals 'sat on both sides of a big, oblong table, with the Chairman at the far end.'[90] It was, however, several of the FAC members discussing matters in their baths who initiated the idea, and contacted their FAC colleagues at Rochdale, several of whom were involved in the Rochdale Turkish baths, for advice on forming a society.

More than half a century later, 27 women, 'much encouraged by their Rotarian husbands', held a meeting at Herriott's Turkish Baths in Manchester to form a women's club on Rotary lines to be called The Inner Wheel.[91]

This idea of supporting themselves financially was present almost from the beginning, and was seen as a means of giving his committee men, like Ironside's wardmote participants, an everyday motive for supporting his work.

The committees saw the value of utilising the bath premises as a meeting-place, providing an alcohol-free environment where the men, and on separate occasions their wives, could meet in the equivalent of the leisured man's club.

Urquhart's papers in the Balliol College Archives show letter after letter asking for advice on locations, temperatures, costs, and many other aspects of Turkish bath provision. The size of the proposed bath was irrelevant to Urquhart.

Some, like the one built in 1866 by the Secretary of the Winchester FAC, were very small indeed. Thomas Stopher notes, in his 1895 history of the city, that 155 High Street was for many years,

> occupied by Henry Butcher, a baker and very worthy man. He established here the first Turkish bath and indeed the only one there has been in the City. Many a good shampooing I have had at his hands. The arrangements were very primitive, the hot chamber being over the oven to economize heat. There was no plunge to cool you down, only warm water thrown over you, gradually colder, preceeded [sic] by the caution 'Cooler!' as he reduced the temperature of the water.[92]

Butcher wrote to thank Urquhart shortly after the bath had opened:

> Having opened this Bath for a fortnight free to anyone who we could induce to avail themselves of the opportunity, have much pleasure to inform you that about 40 persons have passed through highly pleased and delighted with the result.—the cost of this with the addition of the Dressing Room to our house, amounting to little over twenty pounds—We have great expectations of making it in a pecuniary point of view a profitable undertaking—for am glad to state we have already taken £1 2s 6d thus far—to realise the hope Mr Urquhart held out to us when at Winchester that it may be made a profitable investment, besides being a blessing to ourselves and neighbourhood.[93]

These baths remained open for just over 15 years, Mrs Butcher (Fig 5.7), who had looked after the women bathers, continuing to run them for a couple of years after her husband died.[94]

Requests from local committees for Urquhart to visit them to help decide whether to go ahead and build a bath were frequent, and if he was unable to go personally, he sent Rolland, Bartholomew, John Johnson, or A E Robinson. Each committee reported to the others on what the speaker said, and in which bath they went to relax after their meetings. After one hectic meeting John Johnson wrote to Urquhart:

> ... I spoke near one hour and half and went so hoarse next day that it was with difficulty that I could speak to be heard experiencing also a soreness in the throat and chest. I went to the Turkish Bath (to Mr Dalton) and getting a very good bath I felt very much relieved indeed.[95]

They also kept each other informed by letter. For example, when Joseph Foden wrote to John Johnson about the Turkish Treaty, his political comments were followed by a sketch plan (Fig 5.8) and description of a newly discovered Turkish bath in Stockport.[96]

Urquhart had helped them to provide for themselves not only a place where they could go to get clean, or ease their aches and pains, but also a point of social contact where they could relax or talk about the world with a feeling that they were doing something to make it a better place. After their few committee years, the men had skills of lasting value which few would otherwise have had.

It is undoubtedly true that Urquhart realised that those who enjoyed 'Turkish' customs would tend to be more favourably disposed towards the Turkish nation. But the many articles on the bath which were published in the *Free Press* papers reinforce the view that the Turkish bath campaign was actively planned, not a mere by-product of the political campaigns.

If we ignore these small Turkish baths set up by members of Urquhart's committees, we get a completely distorted view of the origins of the bath, because this important (mainly working-class) promotion of the bath as a cleanser and healer disappears from view. And that is to grossly distort the picture.

Fig 5.7
Mrs Butcher, the local baker's wife, ran his Winchester Turkish baths on women's days, and kept the establishment open for a short while after his death. (Hampshire Archives and Local Studies. Item 85M88W/16 fol.26, part)

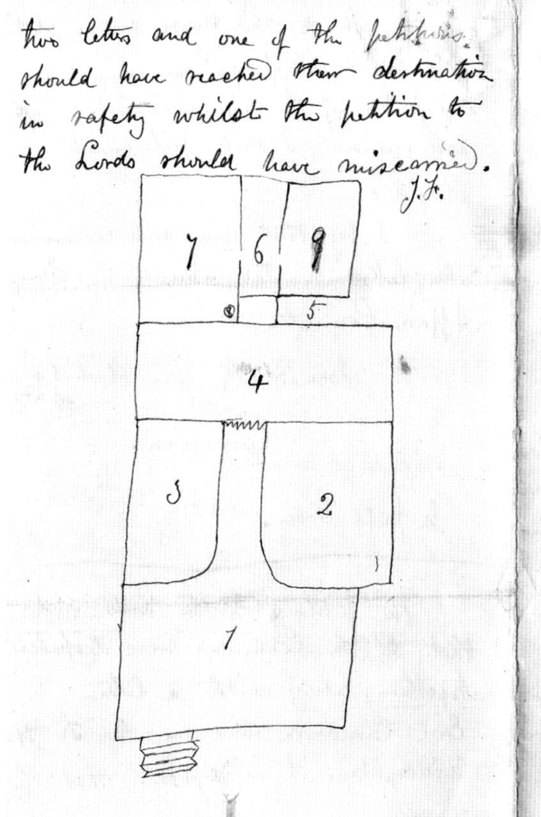
two letters and one of the petitions should have reached their destination in safety whilst the petition to the Lords should have miscarried.
J.F.

DU IG 14

Copy

3 Park St
Westminster
June 8. 1860.

Sir, I have to acknowledge your letter of the 2nd inst. — making enquiries as to a petition which it appears ought to have reached me about the middle of last month — which I should have replied to before this but that in consequence of its being directed to the Travellers' club it did not come to hand till late yesterday evening.

I received your first communication of the 17th of May stating that you would forward me a petition relative to the correspondence of Sir A. Burnes with the Govr Genl of India, but the petition itself never reached me either here or at the

Fig 5.8
The sketch plan of a newly discovered Turkish bath in Stockport. This was part of a letter about the Turkish Treaty, then occupying the minds of the Foreign Affairs Committees, sent by Joseph Foden to John Johnson on 9 June 1860.
(Balliol College, Oxford. Urquhart Bequest. I: Letters G.14 Pt.2. Image supplied by the Master and Fellows of Balliol College, Oxford)

6

Dr Richard Barter and the bath in Ireland

By the spring of 1859, less than three years after completing his first—and not completely successful—experiments at St Ann's, Dr Barter (Fig 6.1) had already partially opened a Turkish bath for public use in nearby Cork at 8 Grenville Place.[1] Furthermore, during the five year period 1859–63 he was actively involved in opening seven other Turkish baths in Ireland (Fig 6.2), and one in London.

The speed at which these baths were opened remains impressive (Table 6.1). Seven were in newly erected buildings. All were designed by Dr Barter's namesake, the sculptor and architect, Mr Richard Barter (c1824–96).

Table 6.1 Turkish baths, open to the public, associated with Dr Barter

Opened	*Town/city*	*Location*
1859	Cork	Grenville Place
1859	Killarney	[Near the station]
1859	Bray	Quinsborough Road
1860	Limerick	Military Road
1860	Dublin	Lincoln Place
1860	Waterford	Hardy's Road
1860	Belfast	Donegall Street
1861	Sligo	?
1862	London	Victoria Street
1863	Cork	Maylor Street
1869	Dublin	Upper Sackville Street

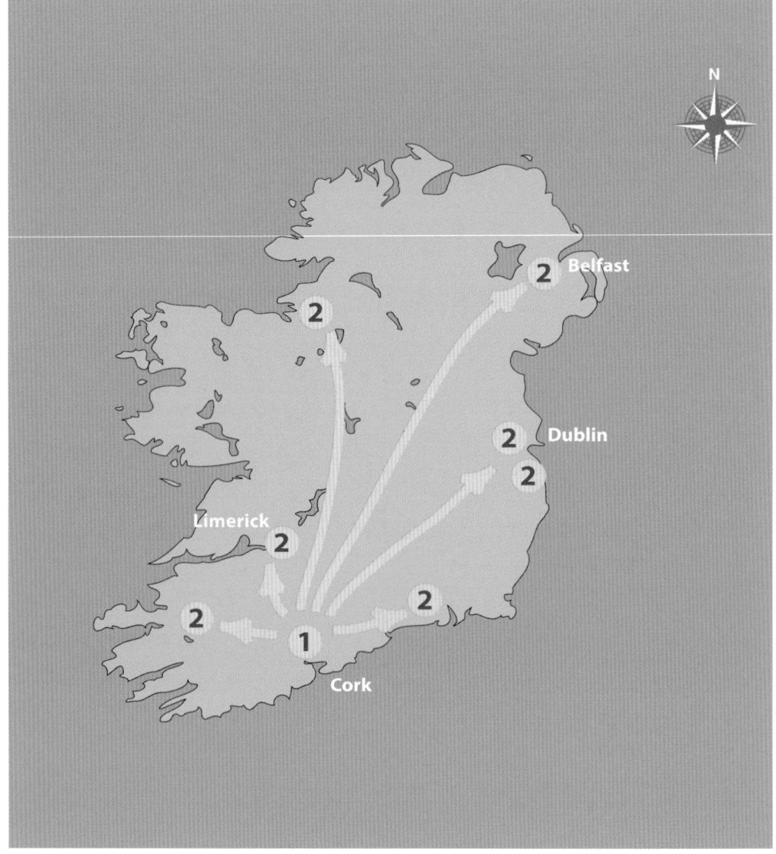

Fig 6.1 (below)
Dr Richard Barter, outside an entrance to his last Turkish bath at St Ann's, completed shortly before his death in 1870.
(A glimpse of Saint Ann's… *St Ann's: Sweeney, 1869 plate 1. Harvard College Library Widener Med 1878.69)*

Fig 6.2 (below right)
Barter's Irish–Roman bath spreads across Ireland.
(© Tash Shifrin)

Cork: Grenville Place

Dr Barter's Grenville Place baths (Fig 6.3), his first outside the grounds of St Ann's, were designed by Mr Richard Barter, constructed by local builder Denis Murray, and fully opened around May 1859.[2]

They had what was described as a 'Grecian' front with three windows and two doors, all arched and surmounted by circular lights of stained glass. Between the two entrances, one for men and the other for women, was a central ticket office. Both sets of baths were similar, being 80ft × 20ft (24.4m × 6m) in area.

From the outer hall, with its tessellated pavement, bathers entered the cooling-room lined with dressing cubicles and furnished with **duretas* for relaxation after the bath. A central passage led to the two hot rooms, each 16ft (4.9m) long and 18ft (5.5m) high, lit by star shaped coloured glass set into the ceiling. Round the walls were stone benches in the tepid room and marble slabs in the hot room.

The baths were open from eleven in the morning till five in the afternoon, and cost two shillings including 'the use of linen', with an additional sixpence for a shampoo. There was also a four-hour period after six o'clock when the price was reduced to half. On Sundays they were only open between ten and five. It was typical of Barter's approach that children under the age of 10 should also be admitted if they were with an adult. He encouraged this by offering them half-price tickets, though we do not know how successful this was.[3]

By the end of 1862, Barter was already dissatisfied with the baths and on 23 February the following year he opened 'new' ones. Probably only the actual bathing areas were new, though we cannot be sure because we do not know what facilities were provided after the rebuilding.

The baths seem to have closed in the late 1880s, and by 2006 the building appears, at first glance, to have been replaced by an apartment block (Fig 6.4). But closer examination shows that the ground floor façade is basically the same, while there are two additional floors above. The corners (Fig 6.5) of the front of the building remain rounded at the ground floor level although door and window openings have been interchanged, and an insurance company fire call plaque has been reaffixed at first floor level at the side.[4]

Fig 6.3
Barter's first Turkish bath for the general public opened in Grenville Place, Cork, in 1859.
(The Lawrence Photograph Collection Lab 6448. Image Courtesy of the National Library of Ireland)

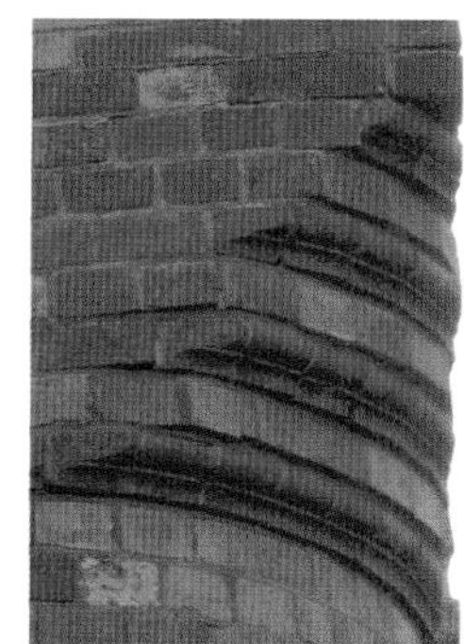

Figs 6.4 and 6.5
Part of the Grenville Place building incorporated into an apartment block, as seen in 2006; with a detail of the rounded corner brickwork supporting the upper floors added later.
(© Malcolm Shifrin)

Killarney and Bray

In April or May 1859, with the help of the Great Southern & Western Railway Company, Barter opened a Turkish bath near the station at Killarney.[5] There is no description of the inside of the building, but all were agreed that although small, it was 'handsome',[6] 'remarkably elegant' and with a structure which was 'entirely Turkish, with domes and minarets.'[7] These were the first of Dr Barter's four baths with a 'Saracenic' exterior, for which domes and small imitation minarets were thought to be a *sine qua non.*

But minarets, being towers from which the faithful are called to prayer, were meaningless in the context of a Turkish bath in Ireland. Architects who decided, or were commissioned, to follow the style of an Islamic *hammam*, did not seem to realise that the minaret belonged to the mosque of which the *hammam* was part, or to which it was adjacent. But accuracy was not essential. The domes and minarets created the *impression* of authenticity, which was all that was required.

When Queen Victoria and Prince Albert visited Killarney in 1861, Lord Castlerosse, at whose home they stayed, had wanted her to visit the Turkish baths. Unfortunately, 'pressure of time rendered it impossible' so we will never know what she thought of this intrinsically Victorian institution.[8]

The baths at Killarney, with a population of around 5,500, were not a great financial success. When an American visitor stayed 'with *very few guests*' at the Railway Hotel in 1867, he wrote:

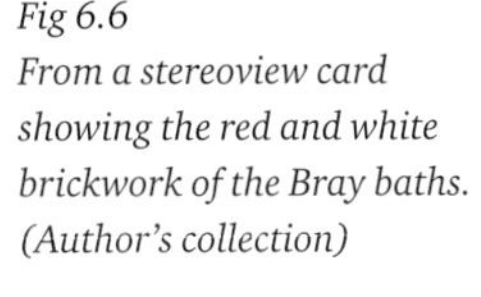
Fig 6.6
From a stereoview card showing the red and white brickwork of the Bray baths. (Author's collection)

> The Railway Company had built this house, and at the same time a large elegant building for a 'Turkish Bath.' Both this 'Bath' and the hotel are magnificent failures, financially. I was told that the Bath did not earn enough to pay for sweeping the dust out of it.[9]

The baths at Bray were even more magnificently 'Saracenic' and even more magnificently a financial failure. Yet long after the baths closed, the building was viewed with affection, especially by those too young to have used it.

William Dargan, a railway engineer and local benefactor who had been treated at St Ann's, commissioned the baths from Barter, who was to run them afterwards. They cost around £10,000, and were officially opened by Lord Meath on 15 October 1859.[10]

When finished, the building was the largest Turkish bath in the kingdom 'covering nearly half an acre', and providing separate men's and women's baths, each with their own entrance.[11] With domes and numerous decorative minarets, and a large 70ft (21m) high ornamented chimney, it was built of red and white bricks resting on a base of Dalkey granite (Fig 6.6).

Each set of baths included a cooling-room with a marble fountain surrounded by plants in the centre and, around the perimeter, a series of small dressing rooms, each with a couch. An *arabesque ceiling, windows of coloured glass, and a tessellated floor of Minton tiles completed a decorative scheme which more than adequately met Dargan's instruction that 'no expense should be spared'. The patterned floor continued through the two hot rooms, each furnished with marble seats, and with a dome pierced by coloured glass stars. Washing rooms, two small shower rooms and a shampooing room completed the picture.[12]

The opening hours, six in the morning till eleven at night, were unrealistically long, even on Sundays when shampooing was not available, and the baths closed for six hours in the middle of the day. Otherwise shampooing added sixpence to the two shilling admission charge. Also available, for an extra shilling, were private baths at the ends of the main building, each with its own entrance (Fig 6.7).[13]

The baths, commissioned by a Dargan completely over-enthused by the Turkish bath at St Ann's—and who had wanted to build one in Portrush also—were always going to be too large for a small town like Bray.[14]

The difference between the medical use of the bath by patients at a hydro and the leisure

Fig 6.7
There were entrances at each end of the building specifically for users of the private baths, who paid an extra shilling for the privilege.
(The Lawrence Photograph Collection SP.685. Image Courtesy of the National Library of Ireland)

activities of holidaymakers at a resort had not yet been understood. The baths struggled on for a few years only.

In March 1864, they were visited by Major Robert Poore, a director of the London & Provincial. A few days later he met Dargan who unsuccessfully offered to sell them to him for £4,000 or, at least, to lease them for £200 per year.[15]

They closed, either at the end of 1864 or early in January 1865.[16] Mary Davies, in her eminently readable history of Bray, has described how the building was then used for a variety of other purposes, even including, briefly, a small Turkish bath, until it was finally demolished in 1980.[17]

Limerick: Military Road

Barter's third 'Saracenic' baths (Fig 6.8), owned jointly with Samuel Wormleighton, were in Military Road (afterwards, O'Connell Avenue), Limerick.[18] They opened at the beginning of 1860 and were much smaller than those at Bray. Here, the men's and women's baths each comprised a *frigidarium*, two hot rooms, and two very small shower rooms.[19]

Soon after Barter died, Wormleighton refurbished the baths which were by then nearly 12 years old. The hypocaust was replaced by a heating system which 'confines the heating apparatus to a certain part of the room', possibly indicating the use of a radiator. Ornamental screens were added to increase privacy in the shampooing area, and a 15ft (4.6m) long plunge pool added to the men's area before the baths reopened at the beginning of September 1872.[20]

After Wormleighton's death in the late 1870s, the baths were run for his family by their superintendent, James Connolly, and from 1884 until they were auctioned in 1890, local directories named Mrs Connolly as proprietor. But she seems to have been unable or unwilling to continue running them for more than a few years, and business may have been affected by the new Turkish baths opened in 1887 by a Mr Taylor in Sarsfield Street. Although the baths were advertised as being 'in good working order, requiring very little, if any, outlay' they were not opened again as baths.[21] Most of the building seems to have been taken down some time in the 1950s, but small remaining parts were only finally demolished in 2006.

Fig 6.8
Barter's third 'Saracenic' Turkish baths. These were in Military Road (now O'Connell Avenue), Limerick. (Courtesy of Limerick Museum)

Dublin: Lincoln Place

By 1859, Barter had already invested a fair amount of money in Turkish baths and, while the Limerick baths were being built, he was also involved in setting up two limited liability companies to finance the establishment of baths in Dublin and Waterford.

There are no surviving national records for Irish companies of this period so it is not easy to discover the exact relationship between Barter and the Turkish Bath Company of Dublin. But we do know—according to Robert Wollaston, who had been told by the Deputy-Governor of the Bank of Ireland—that the shares had all been bought by a small group of men, and that 'not one share could be obtained'.[22]

We also know that one of Barter's friends, Richard Henry Bushe, the company's deputy chairman, would later become a founding director of the Oriental Bath Company of London, and that J E Hymes, of St Ann's Hill, would also become a director of both companies.[23] So it seems likely that there was some sort of informal connection between the two companies, although the hovering presence of Barter seems to be the only common link between all three.

The new Dublin baths, opened on 2 February 1860, were in Lincoln Place adjoining Trinity College.[24] The main frontage, about 186ft (56.7m) wide, comprised three sections, the central one slightly recessed and with an entrance porch. Adjoining this, opening off the obtuse angled pavement which connected Lincoln Place with Leinster Street, was a refreshment room, while at the rear in Leinster Street, was a Turkish bath for horses and other animals.[25]

§When first built, the new building was hard to miss, a local guidebook noting that its elevation,

> presents a quaint, but pleasing, appearance, with its many narrow pilasters, half-moon apertures, fretwork, ornamental minarets, etc, though, we believe, not quite orthodox as regards architectural principles.[26]

The sting in the tail was accurate; the baths, widely described as 'Saracenic', were built in a mishmash of styles. But writers in trade journals of the day approved, and were delighted that Irish builders were capable of executing so unusual a design which, with its *ogee dome and 85ft (26m) variegated chimney, formed 'a very novel and agreeable contrast to the "western" style of architecture prevailing here.'[27] Although the builders were universally praised, they were not named, though pride was taken in their being Corkonians. Only the plasterers, Hogan and Son, and the Clerk of Works, a Mr Dwyer, were mentioned.

This was the building called 'the mosque of the baths' by Leopold Bloom in the Lotus episode of James Joyce's *Ulysses*. But they could not have been 'one of Leopold Bloom's first ports of call on 16 June 1904', as claimed by several writers,[28] because they had already closed four years earlier. Bloom does indeed notice the *baths building* in passing, but actually only had time for an ordinary bath which he took at the Turkish and Warm Baths at 11 Leinster Street, on the opposite side of the road.

A visitor from England signing himself 'A Moist Man' described what he saw when taking his first Turkish bath. He is worth quoting at length because this is the first description we have of the interior of one of Barter's 'Saracenic' baths and, though we cannot be certain, his other baths may have been similar.

> I was conducted into a large room around which were arranged little curtained pavilions about the size and shape of a four-post bedstead. The room was decidedly Turkish in its aspect and appointments, the crescent form being as far as possible given to every thing, while *ottomans and other matters of oriental furniture were to be seen. The servants wore long scarlet flowing dressing gowns and Turkish slippers, and on stands were arranged trays with china coffee-cups, &c ...
>
> The *calidarium ... was still more ottomanic ... being in dim prismatic twilight, and without windows, unless the little star-shaped scraps of crimson, blue, and amethyst-stained glass, artistically inserted in the *vaulted roof, could be so-called.
>
> Inside the calidarium is another room, some five-and-twenty degrees hotter than that in which we were. Through the heavy curtains which guarded the door way between both, I could hear the wooden clogs moving about the inner apartment, and ever and anon the curtain was raised, and we were joined by a gentleman literally reeking from those still more torrid regions; for though it is requested that persons will not pass to the hottest place without permission or direction from the attendant, there seemed to be no objection to those who had passed the curtain emerging once more into the less ardent sphere. Every two or three minutes, a man entered with a tray full of glasses of cold water, which he politely handed round to us, and which we drank ...[29]

The word 'reeking' is used here in its older, Irish English sense of the body giving off vapour rather than an unpleasant smell.

There was also a shampooing room leading, through 'open oriental-shaped arches with piers and dressings of coloured bricks', to shower cubicles, each with water cisterns feeding hot and cold water sprays which could be directed over the body.[30] The floors over the hypocaust were covered with patterned Minton tiles.

When the baths opened, a first class ticket cost 2s 6d, while a shampoo cost an additional shilling. First class tickets were expensive in relation to typical wages of the day. Before the baths opened, the company advertised for a husband and wife team to become superintendent and matron of the baths. The major part of the salary offered comprised 'apartments, fire and light', to which was added £100 per annum.[31] So, in addition to their rooms, each of them was to receive just under 2s 9d per day, or just under 3d more than the cost of a single first class Turkish bath. In the event, both the superintendent and matron appointed were unmarried, so the matron would have received an even smaller wage.

Soon after the baths opened, the refreshment rooms were turned into a restaurant and run independently of the company. Between 1861 and 1870 it was known as the Café de Paris and run, in turn, by Burman & Muret, Olin & Muret, Pierre Olin, and then Mme Olin. Thomas Woycke ran it until 1875, after which Patrick Barrett, and finally Mrs Jane Barrett, continued until the baths closed. So the restaurant must have been profitable, though whether the company received a percentage of the profits, or only an annual rental, is unknown.

An advertisement which Muret & Olin placed in the *Irish Times* on 14 February 1861 also has a place in Irish restaurant history because, according to Máirtín Mac Con Iomaire, this is the first specific evidence of a French restaurant serving *haute cuisine* in Dublin. Mac Con Iomaire suggests its opening 'may have coincided with the introduction of the Refreshment Houses and Wine Licences' Act of 1860 which, by granting wine licences to restaurants, aimed to encourage sobriety.[32]

Changes in the management of the Lincoln Place baths were less frequent but of much greater significance. Some time around 1867, Dr Barter severed his connection with the Turkish Bath Company of Dublin (for whose directors he had built them). The company then leased them to Richard Bushe, their original deputy chairman, who had been a close friend of Barter.

One can only assume that there had been a major board room clash on matters of principle because in October 1867 an advertisement appeared in the *Irish Times* announcing that the new lessee,

> to meet the requirements of the Medical Profession and the Public has had the Baths newly decorated and fitted with CRYSTAL FOUNTAINS—Which create a genial moisture in the hot rooms ...[33]

Without any company records we will probably never know why such a dramatic volte-face was being proposed for one of Barter's showpiece establishments. Certainly, he would have been most upset by the introduction of moisture into the hot rooms, believing that this idea had been finally scotched after his baths emerged unscathed from a series of attacks made on them in January 1860.

The baths at 'B***' attacked

While Barter was involved in setting up the baths in Limerick, Dublin, Waterford and Belfast, he was accused of building baths which exposed bathers to poisonous fumes.

§The form of the attack was unusual. Dr Dominic John Corrigan, who was a well-known and respected medical man, wrote a letter to the editor of the *Dublin Hospital Gazette* asking him to publish an important article on the bath written by a medical colleague, Dr Richard Robert Madden.

Corrigan wrote that he was worried that many of the Turkish baths being built in Ireland had a 'deficiency of a sufficient supply of vapour'. Whether this defect arose by 'accident or ignorance it is a serious and dangerous mistake' which could produce in some bathers an effect 'not only dangerous but positively fatal'.

Madden had in fact published an account of his own travels in the Middle East[34] some 20 years before Urquhart, but his description of the *hammams* there had not been as widely noticed by medical practitioners as Urquhart's, nor as influential. In his *Gazette* article, Madden writes that in rheumatic diseases and those of the skin, he 'cannot sufficiently extol the advantages of the Turkish bath'. But, he complains,

> my own experience of the 'Turkish bath', as it exists in this country, taking the establishment at B*** as the type of all that have been established up to this time, leads me to the conclusion that the use of this bath must be attended with great aggravation of symptoms in several disorders, and with great danger in others ...[35]

Since everyone knew the baths in question could only have been at Bray it seems strange that he bothered to use asterisks. He referred to his own sciatica which had earlier shown signs of improvement but became more aggravated after each visit to the bath. He compared the eastern *hammam* with Barter's baths. The former,

> is a hot, humid air bath—a vapour bath, conjoined with a plentiful use of hot water and friction of a particular kind, which can only be employed with it advantageously. The other, or so-called 'Turkish bath' here in use, is a parched air bath, the dry heated air being generated from the combustion of coke in furnaces, which communicate by passages extending under the flooring of the bathrooms to them in various directions.

The loose wording of this last sentence could be interpreted as suggesting that the hot air and fumes from the burning coke were directly channelled by underfloor ducts into the hot rooms in order to heat them. This would be an extremely dangerous situation, and one without any foundation in fact, though the accusation would be made again, more directly, later in the article.

The *Dublin Hospital Gazette* refused to insert Barter's reply. The editor *had* been prepared to publish it; had 'gone over the letter line by line' and, together with Barter, had made a few alterations to it. But he was overruled by the governing committee; it appears that Dr Corrigan 'was an influential proprietor' of the journal.[36]

Barter was no stranger to ill-informed criticism. He had borne it stoically when he added vapour baths to St Ann's, and again when he built his first Turkish bath there. He had confidence enough to let it ride, firmly pursuing his medical objectives in the knowledge that he was right.

But he could not allow himself the luxury of such a response on this occasion. His reply showed that he was well aware that this time it was not merely his personal investment which was being threatened. The Turkish Bath Company of Dublin was a joint stock company; the investments of smaller shareholders were also at risk.

The day after the attack appeared in the *Dublin Hospital Gazette*, it was reprinted in the *Cork Daily Herald*. This was Barter's local paper and one which a much larger number of his potential patients would read. Barter sent his unpublished reply to the *Herald* whose editor was less constrained than that of the *Gazette*.

Barter was terse. He denied that the atmosphere of the bath was 'composed of dry parched air'; on the contrary it was pure and fresh, constantly renewed with an effective ventilation system and 'amply supplied with moisture'. The exclusion of 'visible vapour' had been explained on many occasions in his public lectures and in print, and 'ignorance on this point on the part of members of the profession' was inexcusable.

As for the serious accusation that the hot room was heated by a flue which channelled fume-laden hot air directly from the furnace, he said that he had 'a just claim' upon Dr Corrigan,

> to set this matter in a true light before the public, by correcting the errors or mis-statements in question, in as open a manner as he has now put them forward.[37]

Barter wisely chose to answer his critics briefly and with dignity.

The reprinting of the original letters in the *Herald* allowed others to participate in the fray, and there were several letters supporting Barter published within a week of the original attack. This must have helped to reassure potential bathers that they could continue to enjoy their Turkish baths in complete safety, for neither Corrigan nor Madden appears to have written any further letters to the press at this time.

In the more litigious world of the 21st century, a person so clearly libelled would have immediately consulted his solicitors. Barter does not appear to have done so. But apart from the correspondence in the Irish press, he did write directly to both Corrigan and Madden referring specifically to their incorrect statements on the flues, and the quality of the hot air, in his establishments.

In order that they might publicly correct these errors he offered them, or anyone they cared to nominate, every facility to visit and examine the construction of the baths, and the condition of its atmosphere. To further assist them, he enclosed copies of his patent specification, 'which ought to satisfy you that in constructing these baths, "accident or ignorance" were not the principles which guided me in carrying it out.'[38]

Neither accepted his offer, but the press controversy aroused much public interest, so that when Barter gave two lectures on the Turkish bath (on 8 and 9 February at the Rotunda in Dublin) there was 'a very numerous and fashionable assembly' there to hear him on each occasion. At the first of these, he made use of a plan of the baths to demonstrate 'the most ample provision, made for ventilation' and 'the most careful precautions taken to prevent the admission of impure air.'[39]

So while Barter was unsuccessful in obtaining public retractions or corrections, he did have the satisfaction of seeing an unwarranted attack speedily collapse at the first sign of opposition.

Waterford: Hardy's Road

The early history of the Waterford baths is more difficult to determine. As with the Lincoln Place baths in Dublin, the absence of any official records of Irish companies is a serious obstacle to accurate research.

In his lecture in Bray, on 13 October 1859, Barter was reported as saying that 'a company was now about being formed for the erection of [a bath] in Waterford.'[40] But by the middle of the following month, the baths had already been built, as were the Limerick baths, by Dr Barter and Samuel Wormleighton,[41] and according to Robert Wollaston's Cheltenham lecture, they were already open for business.[42]

We can deduce from the payment by the Waterford Turkish Baths Company of its 30th annual dividend on 1 October 1891, that the first dividend was probably paid in October 1861. The company was, therefore, likely to have been incorporated in 1860 and to have purchased the baths in Hardy's Road (later, South Parade) almost immediately (Fig 6.9).

The building was, externally at least, a far cry from anything 'Saracenic'—with its rounded windows and doors, and centrally positioned second floor tower, it is more reminiscent of a Spanish hacienda.

Little is known about the interior of the baths except that the symmetry of the building and its pair of doorways suggests that there were baths for men and women.

An early leaflet (Fig 6.10) describes the establishment as 'The improved Turkish or Irish bath, under Doctor Barter's patent' and, uniquely, the emphasis is on 'Irish Bath.' Even the first class baths were cheaper than Barter's earlier baths and, again, children under ten years of age were admitted at half-price.

We also know that there was no plunge pool. There was a proposal in 1907 to build one at a cost of between £100 and £150. A Special General Meeting was called at which the plans of the pool, 16ft 6in (5m) long and 6ft 6in (2m) wide were to be displayed. A letter to shareholders also stated that 'The Jewish community in Waterford offer £20 towards the cost, and would be constant patrons of the Plunge Bath', but it is not known whether the pool was ever built.

In 1888, the company leased the baths to Denis Dunlea who ran them until at least the first decade of the 20th century. They seem to have closed in the late 1920s, though the building was not demolished until the early 1940s.

Altogether, 1860 was a hectic year for Barter. Following on from the three baths at Limerick, Dublin and Waterford, the Working Class

Fig 6.9
The Waterford Turkish Baths in Hardy's Road, soon after they were built, showing the separate entrances for the men's and women's baths.
(Bernard Colclough, Waterford or thereabouts, *1993. By kind permission of Owen Colclough, son of the author)*

THE IMPROVED TURKISH

OR

IRISH BATH,

UNDER DOCTOR BARTER'S PATENT,

HARDY'S ROAD, WATERFORD,

Open on Week Days.

FIRST CLASS.

TICKETS ARE ISSUED FOR THE BATH

	s.	d.
From 6 to Half-past 8 a.m.	1	6
From Half-past 10 a.m. to 6 p.m.	2	0
From 6 to Half-past 8 p.m.	1	0

Children under 10 years of age, Half-price

Subscription Cards for 12 mid-day Baths, 16s.

Ditto for 12 morning do. 12s.

Ditto for 12 evening do. 8s.

Shampooing 6d. Extra.

SECOND CLASS.

TO MEET THE REQUIREMENTS OF THE MILLION

THE BATHS WILL BE OPEN

On SATURDAYS, from 6 to 8½ P.M.,

AND

ON SUNDAYS, FROM 6 TO 8 A.M.,

FOR SIXPENCE.

NO GRATUITIES ALLOWED.

T. S. Harvey, Quay, Waterford.

Fig 6.10
This early handbill for the Waterford Baths (issued when the baths opened around the end of 1859, or beginning of 1860) uniquely refers to them as Irish baths. (Waterford City Library)

Turkish Baths in Belfast (discussed in Chapter 16) opened on 1 October.

There is something of a mystery about a frequently mentioned bath in Sligo. At the beginning of November 1860, Miss Jane Lyons, eldest daughter of the mayor, laid the foundation stone of a Turkish bath there. But no further mention of this bath has been found and it is not known for certain whether it was actually opened, or even built.

Barter opened no further baths in Ireland during 1861 or 1862, being much involved in the setting up of the Oriental Bath Company of London Ltd, and the building there of the unsuccessful Oriental Baths in Victoria Street (Fig 6.11). He was probably unwise to venture away from his familiar home territory, though having been a student in London he must have known it reasonably well. But the site he chose, perhaps with bad advice, was not central enough to support such a large undertaking.

Barter now owned Turkish baths, or was associated with them, in most of the major cities in Ireland, and might by now have been sufficiently satisfied to stop. But in 1863, encouraged by his friend Mrs C G Donovan, he was persuaded to set up a second one in Cork, and so the Turkish Baths for the Destitute Poor, or the People's Turkish Bath (also discussed in Chapter 16) opened on 3 February at 15 Maylor Street.[43]

While all these developments were in progress, the Turkish bath at St Ann's Hydro, Barter's home and main business, was constantly being altered and improved. Apart from this, he probably thought that by now there would be no need to build any others.

But after the break with the proprietors of the Lincoln Place baths in 1867, things looked quite different.

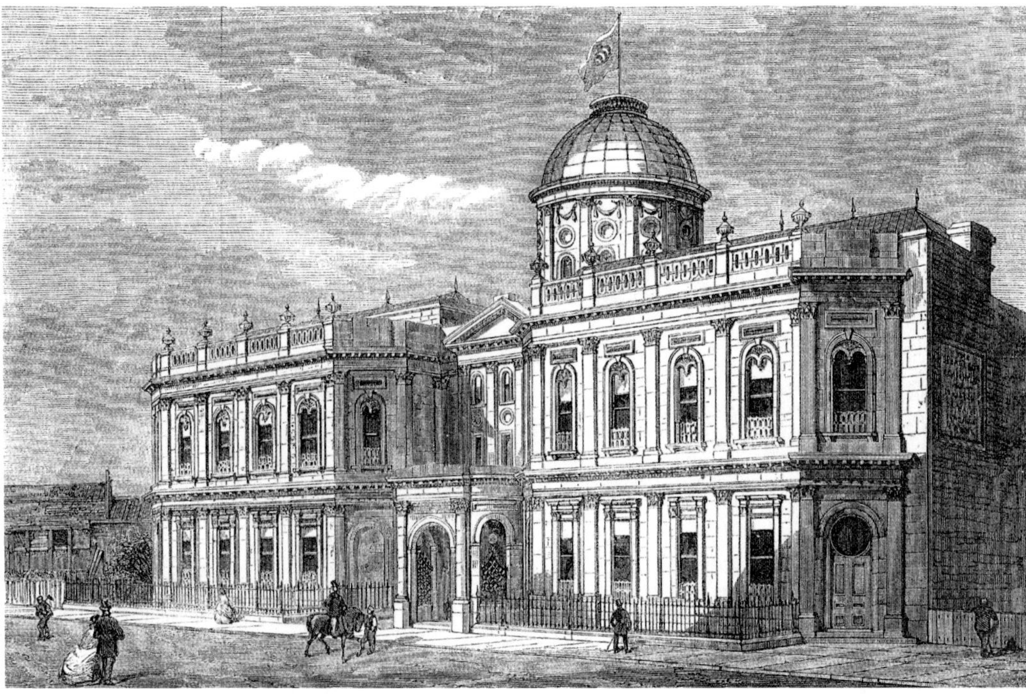

Fig 6.11
Barter's only venture in England, the Oriental Baths at 2, Victoria Street, London, opened early in 1862. Magnificently constructed by the Oriental Bath Company of London Ltd, it cost £28,000. They never lived up to expectations, and the company was fortunate that the site was bought by the Metropolitan Railway Company for its new Victoria Station. The baths were razed to the ground in 1865.
(Illustrated London News, 21 Jun 1862. Author's collection)

Second time around: The Hammam, Dublin

As father of the Turkish bath in Ireland, Barter would have found it inconceivable not to be associated with one in the Irish capital. And he would have seen it as important that the principles which had governed the design of all his earlier establishments should continue to be followed in Dublin.

He would have felt compelled to open another establishment there, and advertised for a suitable property, preferably to the north of the River Liffey.[44] He settled on a Georgian building known as Reynold's Hotel, situated at 11 and 12 Upper Sackville Street (now, O'Connell Street).[45]

The hotel's public rooms and its 30 bedrooms were refurbished, and in the garden at the rear—and also replacing the billiard room—he built a luxurious new Turkish bath. Reynold's Hotel became the Hammam Family Hotel and Turkish Baths (Fig 6.12) and opened on 17 March 1869.

Leading off the hotel entrance was a waiting room and—this not being St Ann's—a men's smoking room. The changing rooms were at the end of a corridor which was, the *Freeman's Journal* gushed,

> illuminated with lamps of every colour in the bow of Iris, and mottoes celebrating the glories of the plunge and the shower, the reclining and the Turkish are all writ out in letters of purple and gold ... When the whole building is lighted up it has more the appearance of a scene in one of Scheherazade's beautiful tales than of a solid, *bona fide* brick and mortar business in the centre of a great city.[46]

Beyond the dressing rooms were four separate suites of Turkish baths, two large ones for men, one for women, and a private suite which could be made available for men or women. There were also private rooms with hot, tepid, and cold water baths.

Bathers were able to experience temperatures ranging from 120–230°F (49–110°C) as they passed from one hot room to another. An underfloor hypocaust heated the rooms, and bathers were provided with cork-soled slippers to insulate their feet.

Adjoining the baths were separate coffee-rooms for men and women, with an ice-cream soda water apparatus which produced 'eight different kinds of delicious drinks, to cool and refresh the bather.'[47]

Barter ensured that in addition to hot rooms which were dry, and so provided an effective Turkish bath, the design and furnishing of the whole was especially attractive, with the ladies' section being 'even more sumptuously furnished and decorated than ... the gentlemen's.' After all, the Lincoln Place baths were still open and would be competing for business.

As with all Dr Barter's baths, apart from St Ann's, the day to day running of the establishment, with its 'numerous staff of efficient attendants', was entrusted to a manager, in this

Fig 6.12
Written on 26 April 1910, this postcard shows Barter's second Turkish bath in the Irish capital (the Dublin Hammam) at 11 and 12 Upper Sackville Street, later renamed Upper O'Connell Street.
(Author's collection)

case Mr James Walsh, who had previously run the baths at Bray.[48]

Dr Barter died on 3 October 1870 and The Hammam, as part of his estate, passed to his eldest son, Mr Richard Barter, who wisely retained Walsh as manager. Although Richard Barter's main interest was in agriculture and the farm at St Ann's—he was later knighted for services to Irish agriculture—he still kept a close watch on the Turkish bath establishments and was not slow to make improvements, even to The Hammam which was barely two years old.

At the beginning of 1871, an additional set of baths was opened adjoining the original ones which were now to be redecorated and reserved for the use of women.[49] The new baths were on such a scale that they may have been part of Dr Barter's original plan.

The 70ft × 34ft (21m × 10m) wide cooling-room was carpeted and amply supplied with seats and recliners, and its 25ft (7.6m) high ceiling allowed for 55 cubicles, each one upholstered and curtained, to be ranged around the room or on galleries above.

The main 60ft × 30ft (18m × 9m) hot room was kept between 120 and 150°F (49–65°C), and the smaller one between 180 and 200°F (82–93°C). Apart from a 17ft (5m) long cold plunge pool, there was a wide range of showers. This clearly met with bathers' approval; during the first three months after the new baths opened they were catering for around 200 bathers each day.[50]

Once the baths were firmly established, Richard Barter decided, as had his father before him, to end direct ownership of the baths. Instead, the premises and facilities would be leased to someone who would run the business independently. Walsh was succeeded on his retirement by a series of other managers until John North, previously manager of the County Galway Club, bought the hotel and baths in 1881.[51]

North continued the practice of regular refurbishment and renewal. In August 1890, for example, he added a fourth shampooing room, having earlier opened a separate set of second-class baths for men. These had their own entrance in Thomas's Lane at the rear of the building (where Mr Barter had run the Dublin People's Bath for a few years). They cost just sixpence, and were open from six in the morning till nine at night.

North died some time between 1901 and 1911, and The Hammam, together with the Belfast baths in Donegall Street which he had bought in 1892, passed to his son-in-law, Joseph Armstrong.[52]

The Hammam continued running smoothly and uneventfully during the next few years, but the Easter Rising of 1916, one of the defining moments in the struggle for Irish independence, interrupted its peaceful existence. The General Post Office (GPO), facing it, became the headquarters of the Irish Volunteers and was subjected to bombardment by the British. The GPO building was soon in flames, while others in the street were effectively under siege.

During this period, supplies of food for the 75 visitors and staff inside The Hammam began to run out and rations were severely reduced. There were too few bedrooms to house everyone and The Hammam cooling-rooms 'had to be used as bedrooms for a large number of people who were unable or afraid to occupy their rooms in the hotel during the revolution.'[53]

If The Hammam was under siege during the Easter Rising, six years later in 1922, it was right at the centre of the battle in O'Connell Street. Éamon de Valera—later prime minister, and afterwards president of what was to become the independent Republic of Ireland—was thought to be hiding there. On 3 July, when the end of the conflict had seemed near, a reporter wrote in the afternoon that,

> ... a large and expectant crowd is at this moment gathered along the quays in anticipation of seeing the white flag hoisted from the Gresham, Hammam's and other hotels in O'Connell-street amidst the bulging stout bins in which Mr de Valera and his adherents have ensconced themselves.[54]

But two days later the battle for O'Connell Street was still in progress, with shots being fired from both sides of the street. The Hammam was a major target, and was spectacularly and rapidly destroyed:

> There had been the usual early morning lull in hostilities, and the crowd of onlookers, which seems to beset every near approach to the actual fighting, took advantage of it to enter O'Connell Street at the lower end. They scattered on the approach of the eighteen-pounder gun, a single shot from which enlarged a breach in the ugly dull red front of the hotel. Incendiary bombs were then placed in the doorway, but these were ineffective. National soldiers entered the building, and afterwards emerged safely, having apparently encountered none of the opposing force. Immediately afterwards the flames broke out, and Hammam's was soon a roaring furnace.[55]

Nothing was left of Dr Barter's last public Turkish baths but a pile of bricks and masonry (Fig 6.13). Two years after the fire, Joseph Armstrong, as lessee of The Hammam, claimed £36,632 for the destruction of the hotel and Turkish baths attached, £9,982 for furniture and fittings, and £511 for his stock.

The Recorder of Dublin reduced the amount due for furniture to £7,000 but, under the post-war Damage to Property (Compensation) Bill, he was legally obliged to award the full cost of replacing the building as it had contributed economically to the area.[56]

Although the hotel and baths had now been in the family for 35 years, Armstrong decided to call it a day and the site was put up for public auction.[57] It may be that he did not have the will to start over again, or it may be that in such turbulent times he felt that his family, as Protestants, would have a better life concentrating on the Donegall Street establishment in Belfast.

The Hammam was never rebuilt. Offices and shops stand on the site today, their only connection with baths being their address—Hammam Buildings.

Fig 6.13
Armoured cars outside the Hammam during the 1922 Irish Civil War. Although pounded by rifles, grenades, and machine-guns from 2–5 July, those hiding inside escaped. A few hours after this photo was taken, the building was completely destroyed by shells and fire. (Courtesy of Dublin City Library and Archive)

Barter's last Turkish baths at St Ann's

The Turkish baths at St Ann's were, throughout Dr Barter's life, subject to a policy of continuous improvement. So much so that it is difficult to say what constituted a major improvement and what constituted a new bath. Even the buildings are difficult to keep track of.

In 1869, the *Hydropathic Record* commented that Barter was about to build two new sets of Turkish baths at the hydro, 'the largest this side of Constantinople' and the 10th to be erected there.[58] But the difficulty is compounded when some commentators count men's and women's adjacent baths as two sets. The new baths opened on 13 July 1870, just under three months before Dr Barter's death.

The building, again designed by Mr Richard Barter, was on a terrace at a lower level than the main building (Fig 6.14). It was a strange combination of styles, with its two wings of tall, slightly arched windows standing on either side of a *pedimented *portico, behind which was a tall windowed tower supporting a *cupola. Yet it seemed to work and was certainly impressive, the *Irish Builder* writing that 'for style of architecture and beauty [it] excels anything of the kind ever seen in this country.'[59]

The men's and women's baths together covered an area 180ft × 36ft (55m × 11m). Inside (Fig 6.15), there was a profusion of white Sicilian marble capping the top rails and red marble floors throughout. Between the hot room and the cooling-room in the men's baths, an arched opening, 12ft high by 6ft wide (3.7m × 1.8m), was filled with plate glass, and a marble fountain fed the large plunge pool. The lavish use of mirrors, stained glass and tapestry gave it 'internally quite an Oriental appearance', the *Irish Builder* suggested.

As was Barter's normal practice, a fête, attended on this occasion by the Lord Mayor of Dublin and the Mayor of Cork, celebrated the opening of the new baths on a date chosen to mark 'the fourteenth anniversary of the introduction of the Turkish bath into this country.' Barter's eldest daughter opened the baths, after which there was lunch, a ball and supper.[60]

Fig 6.14
From a stereoview card showing the exterior of Barter's last Turkish bath at St Ann's.
(Author's collection)

Fig 6.15
The cooling-room of the baths with a circular ottoman.
(The Lawrence Photograph Collection L_NS_01091. Image courtesy of the National Library of Ireland)

In 1859 Barter had provided a Turkish bath next door to the patients' bath for use by the poor of the area. After his death, his son Richard expanded on his father's work by building a home for those patients who lived further away and who needed a course of treatment. It accommodated 12 patients, young or old, of either sex and, being a hydropathic home, it was of course teetotal. The patients had to pay only for board and lodging (between five and ten shillings per week) but even this was cancelled for the very needy.[61]

Dr W Sack was the first of several doctors to look after the medical side of the hydro, first under Barter's son, and later under other family members until 1944 when the hydro was sold. By then it had already become more of a hotel than a hydro, and it soon began to suffer from neglect, finally closing in 1956.[62]

Barter's place in the history of the Victorian Turkish bath

Apart from Dr Barter's own baths, there were probably at least 30 others in Ireland opened by proprietors who, even if they constructed their baths differently, would have been inspired by the success of his baths.

He was, in Ireland, as much of a proselytiser as Urquhart was elsewhere, though he probably antagonised fewer people in the process. He did this without the advantage of Urquhart's locally based committees, though he too gave lectures on the bath right up to the year of his death.

His advocacy was largely responsible for the building of Turkish baths in Irish hospitals, asylums and, more successfully than Urquhart, in workhouses.

If there was, and perhaps still is, an Irish resentment that Urquhart is frequently given all the credit for the introduction of the Victorian Turkish bath, this is understandable, and was often remarked upon.

In a letter to *The Field*, for example, one of Barter's pseudonymous supporters argued, justifiably, that not only did Barter recognise the new idea, but he was prepared to set aside his earlier ideas in support of it. For a practitioner of the cold water cure to be able to recognise the value of hot-air treatments required not only a sharp mind, but preparedness to risk the considerable sum of money already invested in his hydro. It was only after his success at St Ann's,

> that the bath began to attract attention in England; and in all probability if Dr Barter had not taken up the matter as he did, and thrown himself body and soul into the work, Mr Urquhart might still be in search of a kindred co-operating spirit—the great apostle would have been, in short, without a convert.

And in a crisp postscript, he added,

> Dr Barter is well known as the founder of the Turkish baths in Ireland; and my object in writing the above is merely to set the matter in a true light before the English public.[63]

7

The Victorian Turkish bath travels overseas

In Chapter 1, the progress of the Victorian Turkish bath was depicted in terms of a journey, starting in 1856 from Blarney in the south of Ireland, along a path which crossed the Irish Sea to the industrial towns of the north of England. The path then split, one half turning north to the population centres and hydropathic establishments of Scotland, and the other turning south through the Midlands, until it finally arrived in London four years later in 1860.

But looking more closely (Fig 7.1), we unexpectedly find that on reaching the north of England the path actually split into three, the third branch becoming a superhighway leading overseas, with the result that a bath arrived at a destination 10,500 miles (16,900km) away before it reached London.

Australia

Dr John Le Gay Brereton opened his first Turkish bath in Sydney, Australia, several months before Roger Evans opened the first London bath in Bell Street.

Brereton, an English doctor who had qualified at St Andrews University, gained his knowledge of Victorian Turkish baths from the two people responsible for introducing them. First, he had seen Barter's bath at St Ann's. Then, for a short while in 1858, he was visiting physician at the Leeds Road Turkish Baths opened in Bradford by the local FAC 'under the advice and direction of Mr Urquhart'.[1]

According to George Jacob Holyoake,[2] Brereton had originally intended to open the first Turkish bath in London but was persuaded in 1859 to emigrate to Australia instead.[3] Almost immediately on arrival, he took the premises known as Captain Cook's Hotel at 15 Spring Street, Sydney, and converted it into a Turkish bath.

There was a changing room, a *frigidarium* at the same temperature as the air outside, a 120°F (49°C) *tepidarium*, and a 160°F (71°C) *caldarium*. Bathers were encouraged to spend 15 minutes in each of the hot rooms, before being shampooed and taken to relax and cool for half an hour.

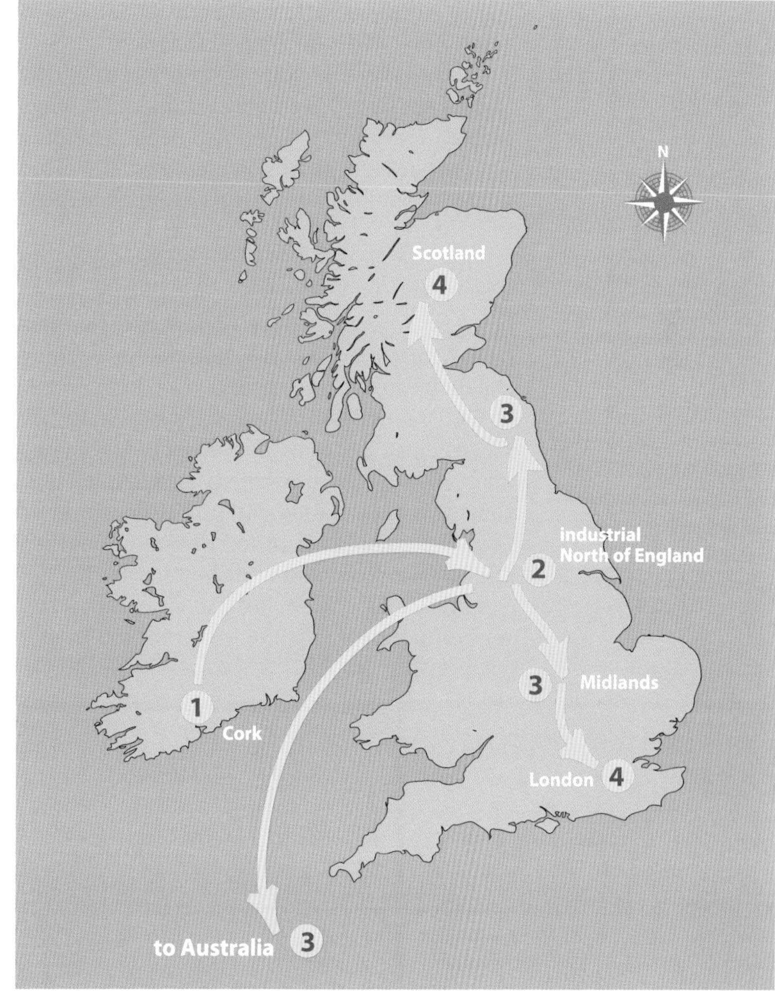

Fig 7.1
How the Victorian Turkish bath crosses to Britain, and beyond.
(© Tash Shifrin)

At the press preview, one reporter was particularly impressed by the hot and cold water shower. The bather, he explained, stood inside the circular *needle shower which, in addition to its central overhead spray, had, a little hand instrument like the 'rose' of a watering pot attached to a flexible hose, which can be used to direct a shower to any part of the body which may consider itself to have been neglected, or to stand in need of a little extra ablution.[4]

Drawing on his Bradford experience, Brereton set up a consulting room at the baths. Invalids were restricted to the mornings when a consultation, bath, shampoo and 'curative movements' cost 10s 6d. Otherwise, excepting Sundays, men used the baths from two till seven every day, and women on Tuesday and Friday mornings. A Turkish bath with shampoo cost 7s 6d, or four for a guinea (£1 1s).[5]

During the first nine months, over 4,000 baths were taken, averaging around 22 bathers per day. This was considered very encouraging, and within a few months Brereton was involved in plans to build a much larger establishment in Bligh Street.[6]

The Turkish Bath Company was set up to finance the building. Realising that it would be an exemplar for future Turkish baths in Australia, Brereton was concerned that everything should be absolutely correct.

On 10 July 1860, he wrote to Urquhart (Fig 7.2) enclosing a company prospectus showing 'the progress our movement is making here', though disassociating himself from some of the proposals. He had, for example, opposed the provision of additional *slipper baths, but 'having a majority against me could not carry my point, but [I] will take care that the Bath is honestly constructed'. In effect, seeking encouragement and support for his own proposals to the board, he concluded:

Will you inform me of the true order of colours in the Bath and also the epochs in its history which they indicate: also the Roman and Eastern names of each part of the Bath apparel—It is my endeavour, as far as I am able, to accompany the Bath with a true tho' necessarily imperfect history of the institution and of its modern restoration in which restorative Movement I regard you as our one true leader.[7]

Within a month of the prospectus being advertised, 300 of the 400 £10 shares had been taken[8] and building work began in August.[9]

The completed baths opened in Bligh Street on 15 March 1861. At an inaugural lunch the previous day, Thomas Holt, the company chairman, told the gathering—in a manner typical of the time—that while London was 'the metropolis of the greatest empire that ever existed',

here, in the metropolis of the Southern hemisphere—for no one would deny that such was Sydney (laughter)—we had a Turkish bath; and it was assured by Dr Brereton who knew what was passing elsewhere that this was the largest, most complete and noblest edifice of the kind in the world (cheers).[10]

Although narrow, the building, designed by local architects William Weaver and Edmund Kemp (*fl* 1856–64), had considerable depth. At the front were four *Doric columns supporting a pediment. We do not know anything about the appearance of its neighbours but while, according to the *Herald*, the new building looked strange standing next to them, it did acknowledge the Roman origins of the bath.

Immediately inside were a consulting room and a waiting room. Through a glass door and down a few steps was the *frigidarium*, paved with marble and lit by frosted blue glass windows (there being an open courtyard to the right of the building). At either end were changing cubicles and, around the walls, couches for relaxation after the bath.

A door led to the **lavatorium*, with its two needle showers and marble slabs for shampooing, and then on to the hot rooms: the *tepidarium*, heated to 120°F and the *caldarium* to around 170°F (77°C).

On the upper floor was a plunge pool, and a second *frigidarium,* where light refreshments were available and smoking was permitted.

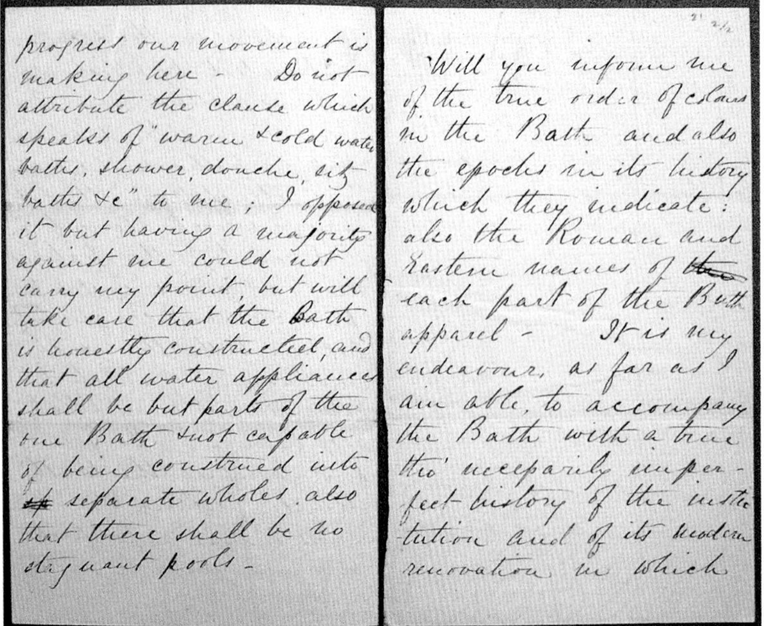

progress our movement is making here - Do not attribute the clause which speaks of "warm & cold water baths, shower, douche, sitz baths &c" to me; I opposed it but having a majority against me could not carry my point, but will take care that the Bath is honestly constructed, and that all water appliances shall be but parts of the one Bath & not capable of being construed into ~~a~~ separate wholes, also that there shall be no stagnant pools -

Will you inform me of the true order of colours in the Bath and also the epochs in its history which they indicate: also the Roman and Eastern names of ~~the~~ each part of the Bath apparel - It is my endeavour, as far as I am able, to accompany the Bath with a true tho' necessarily imperfect history of the institution and of its modern renovation in which

Fig 7.2
Part of a letter dated 10 July 1860 written by Dr Brereton asking David Urquhart for advice about the new baths to be built in Bligh Street. (Western Ms.6236. Correspondence on Turkish baths; 21. Wellcome Library, London)

There was also, in the basement, a variety of water baths—Brereton having lost the argument here—together with three bedrooms for the bath attendants, a kitchen, laundry, and the furnace.

Though the price of a bath at five shillings (or six for one pound) was cheaper than that at Spring Street, it was still twice as expensive as what had been proposed in the company prospectus.

The new baths seem to have been well patronised. But, as was so often to be the case elsewhere, takings which would allow a reasonable profit to a sole proprietor and his family were not sufficient to support a company, perhaps with loans to repay, certainly with wages regularly due, and yet still provide an acceptable return to its shareholders.

Slightly over 18 months after the grand opening, a special meeting was called for 2 December 1862, to consider dissolving the company and disposing of its property.[11] Two days later, the baths were 'CLOSED until further notice, in consequence of its undergoing repairs'.[12]

Confirming that the baths themselves were not in any sense a failure, they were bought for £2,750 by Brereton in partnership with a successful local businessman, Alfred Reynolds Huntley—after whom the Sydney suburb of Huntley's Point was named.[13]

In 1865 the two were increasing their investment, building a new set of women's baths at the rear (Fig 7.3). Unusually, the women's cooling-room and *lavatorium* were larger than the men's.[14]

After Huntley's death in 1868, his widow, Eleanor, inherited his share. She seems to have taken an active role in the business, appointing an immediate family member, Mr C A Sherwin, as manager. Minor improvements were made from time to time until 1884 when a completely new set of baths was built adjoining the original ones.[15]

The building, designed by French-born Gustavus Alphonse Morell (*fl* 1863–1888), had six floors (Fig 7.4), three of them below street level. The new facilities were more or less the same as the old, but larger, fitted out with rather more marble, and with tessellated floors. The major additions were a double-height galleried cooling-room with plunge pool (Fig 7.5) and, on the floor above, separate smoking and refreshment rooms. A top-floor flat was provided for

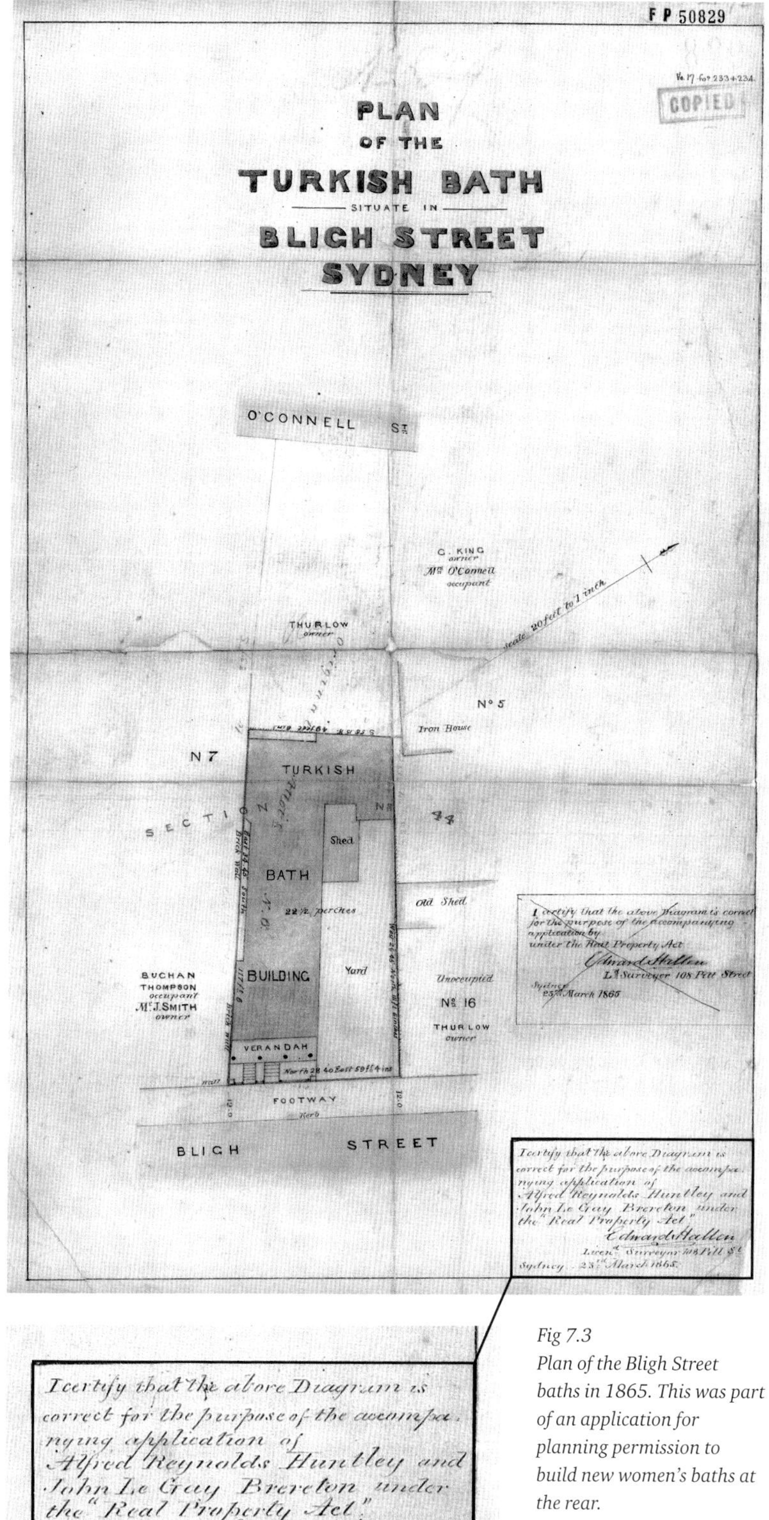

Fig 7.3
Plan of the Bligh Street baths in 1865. This was part of an application for planning permission to build new women's baths at the rear.
(Land & Property Management Authority 1 Prince Albert Road, Sydney NSW 2000 www.lpma.nsw.gov.au)

Fig 7.4
Façade of Gustavus Alphonse Morell's 1884 extension to the baths adjoining the original ones. (Author's collection)

Fig 7.5
The galleried cooling-room and plunge pool in Morell's new baths. (Author's collection)

the manager, and a more efficient heating system was installed in the basement. The original baths were now used in the morning by women bathers at 3s 6d, and in the afternoon and evening as second-class baths for men at 2s 0d.

Brereton died in 1886, and Eleanor Huntley, now sole proprietor, leased the baths to Sherwin. A year later, the buildings were altered for the last time.

The latest changes, by architects Coward and Bell, were partly cosmetic and partly designed to make better use of the original courtyard. The façade was changed to be more in keeping with the adjoining buildings, while inside, the consulting and waiting rooms, together with additional rooms on the upper floors, became lettable offices.

A new entrance to the basement opened off the street and an existing side passage was used for an unusual 'tramway' on which a trolley, loaded from 'a circular coal-shoot in the pavement' carried coke to the furnace at the rear.[16]

The changes may also have been about age. It was 20 years since there had been a major refurbishment and in 1883 new baths had been opened in Oxford Street by Charles E Wigzell who was now providing stiff competition (Fig 7.6).

Barely two years later, Mrs Huntley died and the Bligh Street baths were sold, with Sherwin's lease being terminated on 30 April 1890.[17] The baths, latterly known as Booth's Turkish Baths, 'the finest in Australia',[18] continued at least until 1917 and possibly into the early 1920s.

However, in November 1922, the site was sold for £18,000 and replaced by an eight-storey office block.[19] While the building was being demolished in August 1923 (Fig 7.7), an auction disposed of the fittings and building materials including the slates, wood and marble—'These slabs are only SCREWED TO WALL'.[20]

Brereton's baths were important for a number of reasons, but especially because he emigrated to Australia specifically to introduce the Turkish baths there. His expectation that they would be an exemplar was well-founded:

> The success... [which the Turkish Bath] presided over by Dr Brereton has met with in Sydney has been so marked that it cannot be a matter of surprise that some of our enterprising [Melbourne] citizens should be desirous of emulating his success, and a company, styled 'The Oriental Bathing Company' was accordingly formed some time back, having for its capital £10,000, in shares of £10 each.[21]

Within a year, the first Melbourne establishment opened (Fig 7.8), and soon there were others in Adelaide (Fig 7.9), Brisbane, Hobart (Fig 7.10), Launceston, Newcastle (Fig 7.11) and Perth. Later on, Turkish baths were also provided by several local authorities, either as separate buildings, or as additions to their existing swimming baths.

Fig 7.6 (above)
Charles E Wigzell's Turkish baths which opened in Oxford Street, Sydney, in 1883.
(Author's collection)

New Zealand

New Zealanders had to wait until December 1874 before their first Turkish bath was opened. This was set up by the Otago Turkish Bath Company in a converted biscuit factory in Moray Place, Dunedin (Fig 7.12).[22]

It consisted of two hot rooms, a shampooing room, a cooling-room, and a tepid water swimming pool, 36ft long by 24ft wide (11m × 7.3m). A Turkish bath cost three shillings, the swimming pool sixpence, and Wednesdays were reserved for women.

The company ensured that the baths were well run by appointing as manager William Scott Burton from the Russell Street Turkish baths in Melbourne.[23] Earlier, he had worked at London's Euston Road Turkish baths and may have been related to its proprietor, Joseph Burton.

Shortly afterwards, the company leased the baths to him.[24] They continued to be well patronised, remaining open under further lessees and owners until around 1908.[25]

Fig 7.7 (left)
The demolition of the Turkish Baths at 25, 27 & 29 Bligh St in 1923. Compare the portion of the baths to the left of the printer's sign with the original building (Fig 7.4, left).
(City of Sydney Archives NSCA CRS 51/1049)

TURKISH BATHS
MEDICAL BATHS

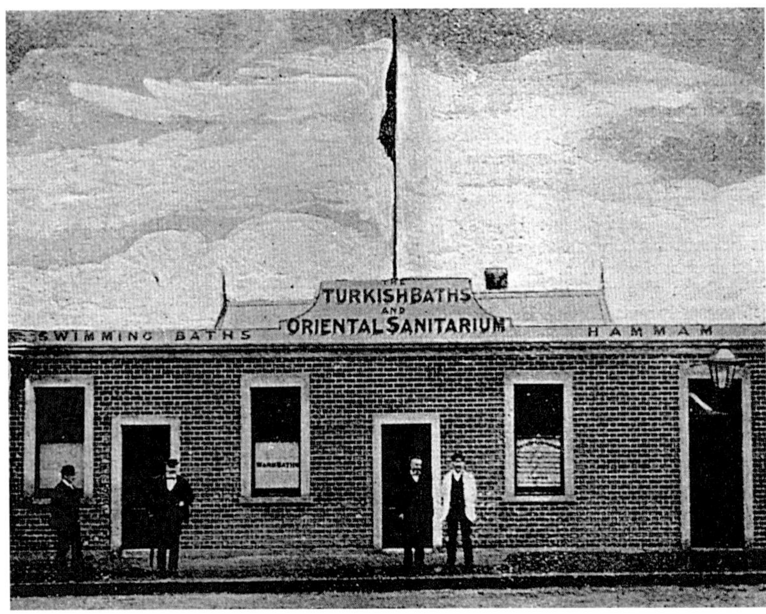
TURKISH BATHS
AND
ORIENTAL SANITARIUM
SWIMMING BATHS
HAMMAM

TURKISH BATHS
TURKISH BATHS
AUCKLAND
TURKISH BATH COMPANY
HOT & COLD PLUNGE BATHS
6 3 2 6

The Victorian Turkish bath in Australasia (opposite: left to right from top)
Fig 7.8
Women's day in the tepidarium *at the rebuilt Lonsdale Road baths in Melbourne in 1862. The original baths, opened two years earlier, had been destroyed by fire.*
('The Tepidarium' The Illustrated Melbourne Post, *18 October 1862)*
Fig 7.9
Adelaide's City Baths, in King William Road, opened in 1861; the Turkish baths were added six years later. Shown here is the cooling-room as it was around 1910.
(Image courtesy of Adelaide City Archives)
Fig 7.10
Although Tasmania's first Turkish baths opened in Launceston in 1861, we know more about those which opened in Hobart seven years later—the smaller building on the right. They cost £400, and remained open till 1928.
*(*Tasmanian scenery, *Melbourne: Fergusson & Mitchell, [188?] p.93. Tasmanian Archive and Heritage Office)*
Fig 7.11
The Turkish Baths at Denison Street, Hamilton, New South Wales, were built in 1879 by Francis W Reay, later to become the town's mayor. They survived well into the 20th century. The building was demolished in 1961.
(Courtesy of the Ellen G. White Estate, Inc)
Fig 7.12
The Turkish baths and Oriental Sanatorium, Moray Place, Dunedin, New Zealand, c1910.
(The New Zealand Electronic Text Collection License: Creative Commons Attribution-Share Alike 3.0 New Zealand Licence)
Fig 7.13
The first Turkish bath in Auckland was opened in Upper Queen Street by Mr King Daniel Sykes. It was soon purchased by the Auckland Turkish Baths Co Ltd for use while their new baths in Lorne Street, shown here at the beginning of the 20th century, were being built, and also, perhaps, to kill off the competition.
(The New Zealand Electronic Text Collection License: Creative Commons Attribution-Share Alike 3.0 New Zealand Licence)

The first Turkish baths in Auckland (Fig 7.13) opened just over eighteen months after those in Dunedin. In what seems to be a unique occurrence, the City of Auckland has placed a commemorative plaque on the location of these baths (Fig 7.14), which remained open till 1928. Later Turkish baths in New Zealand included establishments in Blenheim, Christchurch, Nelson and Wellington.

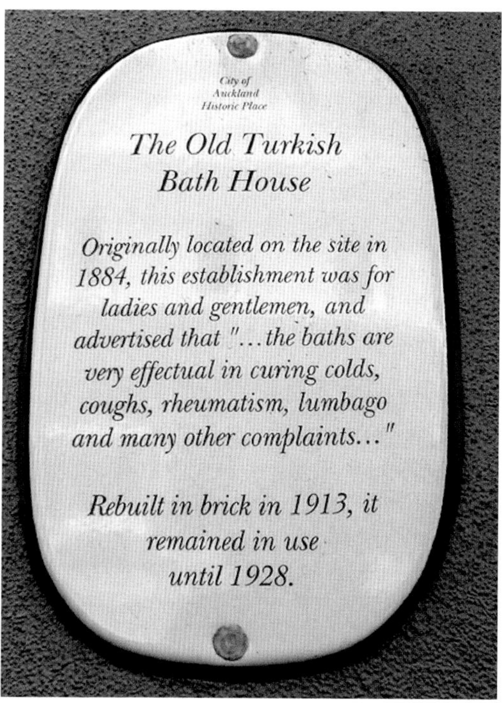

Fig 7.14
The Auckland Historic Place plaque commemorating the Lorne Street Turkish bath. Sadly, no organisation in Britain seems prepared to erect a plaque in London at 76 Jermyn Street, to similarly commemorate David Urquhart's iconic and internationally renowned London Hammam.
(© Sandy Austin)

Canada

In Canada, the first large Turkish baths opened in Montreal at 140 Monique Street in 1869 (Fig 7.15), but information about Canadian establishments has been difficult to find and there may have been an earlier bath in Joté Street. Other Turkish baths are known to have been opened in Dawson, Edmonton, Halifax, Toronto, Vancouver, Victoria, and one in Winnipeg with what was reputed to be the oldest neon sign in the town.

One of the grandest must surely have been the Turkish baths and pool complex added by Benjamin Trudel in 1897 to his Hotel Victoria at 44 Côte du Palais in the old quarter of Quebec (Fig 7.16).

The baths were on the site of the present-day hotel. The original hotel on the opposite side of the road was connected to the baths by a bridge 40ft (12m) long, built at first floor level to allow hotel guests to visit the Turkish baths without having to leave the building. Unfortunately, the bridge was constructed without planning permission and, in spite of a complicated legal battle, it had to be demolished.

The baths themselves did not survive much longer. When the original hotel was completely destroyed by fire in 1902, the new owner rebuilt it on the site of the old baths.[26]

Fig 7.15 (above)
Probably the first Turkish bath in Canada, opened in Montreal in 1869 by David B A MacBean at 140 St Monique Street. It was still open in 1911.
(Lovell's Montreal directory for 1891–92 *p.6. Bibliothèque et Archives nationales du Québec)*

Fig 7.16 (right)
The short-lived Turkish baths added by Benjamin Trudel to his Hotel Victoria in 1897. (Library and Archives Canada, Acc. No. 1970-188-1598 W.H. Coverdale Collection of Canadiana)

The United States of America

The spread of the Victorian Turkish bath was not limited to the British colonies. The United States was quick to follow Britain, and information is much more readily available about the first baths there.

Following a fortnight of cryptic advertisements in the local newspaper[27] consisting only of the words

> THE TURKISH BATH,
> ON BROOKLYN HEIGHTS

the first Victorian Turkish bath in the USA (Fig 7.17) was opened by the hydropathist Dr Charles H Shepard at 63 Columbia Street, Brooklyn, NY, round about 3 October 1863. Shepard added the Turkish baths to his 'Sanitorium', a water cure establishment he had opened two years earlier.

Later, a more detailed advertisement appeared, emphasising the bath's remedial benefits, its use as a preventative, and its success in Great Britain.[28] The ad fulfilled its purpose. The building's original hydropathic use was soon overshadowed by the almost immediate success of the newly installed Turkish baths.

'As long as men delight in health and cleanliness, the names of Urquhart, Barter, and Shepard will be held in grateful remembrance', wrote R E Van Giesen nine years later,[29] typically omitting any mention of women, for whom the baths opened every morning.[30]

Shepard first became interested in Turkish baths in 1859 after reading about their success in the British Isles. His bath was not purpose-built, but accommodated in an ordinary three-storey house on the corner of Columbia Street and Cranberry Street.

Even before the baths had been open for three months, they were reported in the *Brooklyn Standard Union* to be 'doing a prosperous business'[31] helped, no doubt, by the six-page pamphlet written by Shepard to publicise them.[32]

He took pains to ensure that his innovative facility had the backing of important people in the locality. At the top of the second page is a statement about 'the benefits of the TURKISH BATHS, as given in the well-ordered establishment of Dr Shepard.' The thirteen signatories included four ministers of religion, two professors, three doctors and Miss Catharine E Beecher (co-author with her younger sister Harriet Beecher Stowe of *The new housekeeper's manual*).

Fig 7.17
The first Victorian Turkish baths in America, opened in 1863 at the home of Dr Charles H Shepard (sometimes spelled Shepherd) at 63 Columbia Street (later renamed and renumbered 81 and 83 Columbia Heights), Brooklyn. When the baths opened, Brooklyn was still a separate town and not incorporated into New York City until 1898.
Charles M Robinson and Charles H Shepherd Philosophy of health and beauty *(Author's collection)*

The baths comprised a suite of four rooms: the *frigidarium* with curtained recesses ('dressing rooms') leading off; a *tepidarium* maintained at around 100°F (38°C); a *caldarium* at around 180°F (82°C) with 'marble couches'; and a *lavatorium*, where the bather was 'completely lathered with perfumed soap, and rubbed with a brush or sponge' before a final wash down.

Soon after the baths opened they were visited by a reporter from the *Eagle* who fulsomely described how, draped in a large sheet, he took his first Turkish bath. The separate shampooing process was completed before the bather entered the *lavatorium* and, after 20 minutes or so in the *caldarium*, an attendant 'manipulated our person in a manner that promptly developed the locality of all the sore spots on our body'. He concluded, 'Already does the Doctor find himself overwhelmed with visitors, and ere long we have no doubt he will have to enlarge his bath.'[33]

A shrewd comment—barely 10 months after opening, the baths were closed for alterations and extensions. A letter to the editor of the *Eagle* from 'D.H.J' after they reopened shows that these were quite significant.[34]

The main change was that couches had been added to the *tepidarium,* as well as to the *frigidarium* where the curtained changing recesses had been enlarged to take them. And in a change to the procedure, the bather returned to the *frigidarium* clad not only in a dry sheet, as previously, but also in a turban.

The baths closed again at the end of 1866, this time for a major expansion. A new set of baths for men, including plunge and swimming pools, was opened next door at number 65, while the original baths were converted for use by women.[35]

Shepard had earlier made a grand tour of Turkish baths in England, Ireland, and as far afield as Constantinople. This may be why, during his speech at the opening ceremony on 3 April 1867, he referred to the new baths as his Hammam.[36] But with one or two exceptions, advertisements in the local paper continued to refer only to Shepard's Turkish baths.

Towards the end of 1879, the baths were 16 years old. The day they opened, they were patronised by one solitary bather; five years later they were averaging over 40 per day over a 12-month period.[37]

Since 1865, at least seven Turkish baths had opened in other boroughs of New York, and at least two in Brooklyn—though Shepard had no real rival there, his only inconvenience being a changed address when Columbia Street was renamed Columbia Heights.

Yet he may gradually have lost some business to those who worked in Manhattan and bathed there with friends before returning home. In

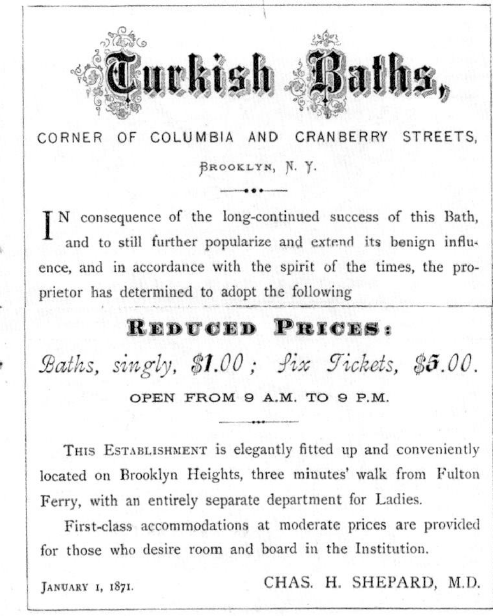
Turkish Baths,

CORNER OF COLUMBIA AND CRANBERRY STREETS,

BROOKLYN, N. Y.

IN consequence of the long-continued success of this Bath, and to still further popularize and extend its benign influence, and in accordance with the spirit of the times, the proprietor has determined to adopt the following

REDUCED PRICES:

Baths, singly, $1.00; Six Tickets, $5.00.

OPEN FROM 9 A.M. TO 9 P.M.

THIS ESTABLISHMENT is elegantly fitted up and conveniently located on Brooklyn Heights, three minutes' walk from Fulton Ferry, with an entirely separate department for Ladies.

First-class accommodations at moderate prices are provided for those who desire room and board in the Institution.

JANUARY 1, 1871. CHAS. H. SHEPARD, M.D.

Fig 7.18
A charges card advertising a general reduction in prices at Shepard's baths, possibly in reply to competition from the newer Manhattan baths, which might have been catching clients straight from work before returning to their Brooklyn homes. (Author's collection)

any event, for whatever reason, at the beginning of 1871, a new leaflet showed a reduced rate of $1 per bath (or $5 for six) (Fig 7.18).

Shepard did not seem to have any real competition until 17 April 1880 when the Brooklyn Turkish Bath Company opened a large new Turkish bath at 32 Clinton Street.[38] Its president was Dr A L Wood who, with Dr Eli P Miller, had opened Manhattan's first Turkish bath in Laight Street in 1865 (Fig 7.19).[39]

Shepard responded by further enhancing his own establishment, adding a reading room, several dressing rooms and, for the women, a new swimming pool.[40]

Shepard was the author of at least two pamphlets: *Rheumatism and its treatment by Turkish baths* (see Fig 1.8, p 8), published in 1892,[41] and *Hydrophobia*, a paper read before the American Medical Association at Philadelphia, in June 1897, and published by them later that year.[42]

He was indeed a pioneer and dedicated promoter of Turkish baths in the States, and his reputation was such that, when Brooklyn decided to build five public baths, he felt confident enough to campaign for one of them to be a publicly funded Turkish bath.[43]

Although he died on 29 October 1910, it has been suggested that his Turkish baths remained open till 1913, though this has yet to be confirmed.[44] Shepard had a tremendous influence on the history of the bath in the United States. There is hardly a city of any size where his example was not followed, and at least one bath opened.

France and Germany

When describing Turkish baths in mainland Europe, especially those which no longer exist, it is difficult to determine which were Islamic *hammams*, and which were Victorian Turkish baths.

In Paris, Le Hammam on the Rue Auber (Figs 7.20 and 7.21) was the first, opening to the public in March 1876. Despite its name, it

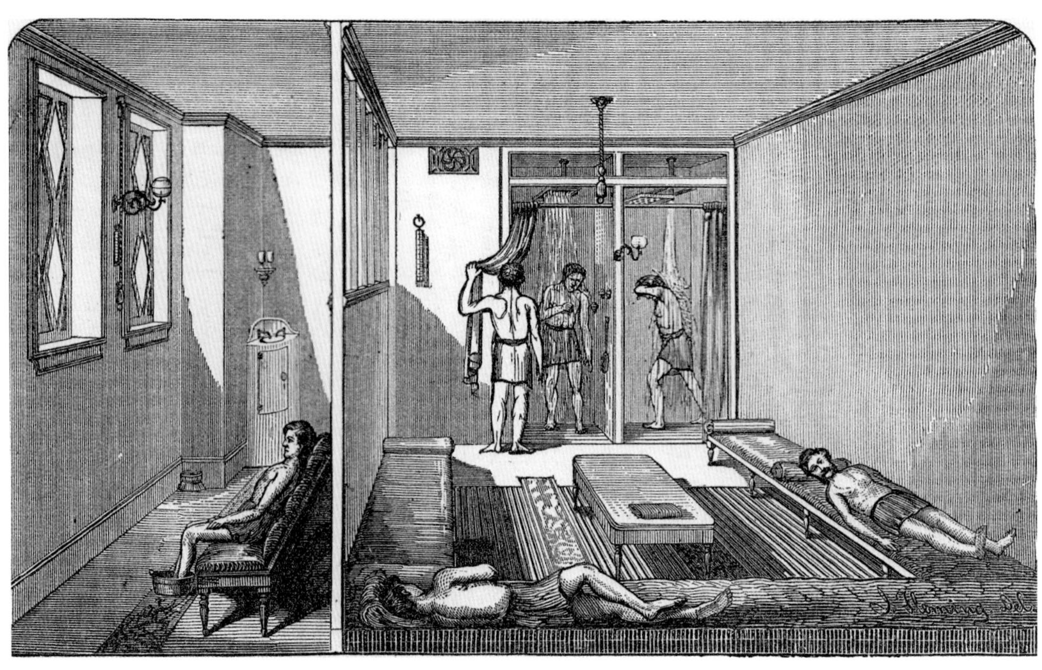

Fig 7.19
The sudatorium *and* tepidarium *in Dr Miller's Turkish baths at 13 Laight Street, Manhattan, New York, in 1867. (Erasmus Wilson* The eastern, or, Turkish bath, *New York, Miller, 1867, p.8)*

Fig 7.20
Today, only the façade remains of Le Hammam *in Paris, the interior having been rebuilt as modern offices.*
(© Nabahat Avcıoğlu)

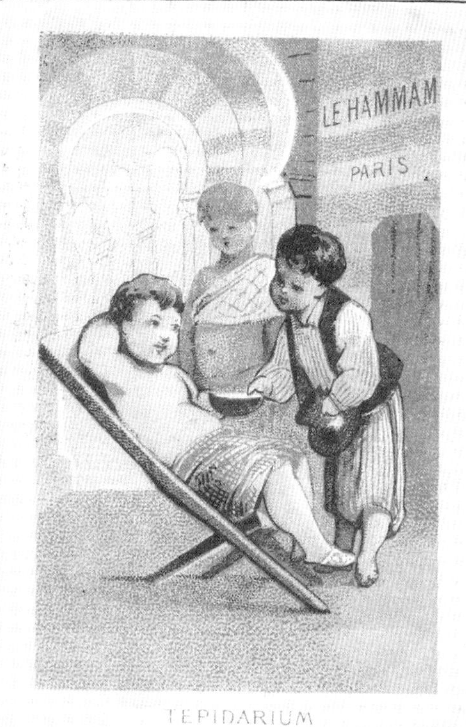

Fig 7.21
This trade card, (or possibly the first sides of a folder) indisputably claiming that Le Hammam *is a* bains turco-romains, *probably dates from around 1876 when it opened.*
(Author's collection)

Fig 7.22
Though the 'Saracenic' appearance of Les Bains Dunkerqouis *make them an ideal subject for a postcard, they comprised only swimming pools and vapour baths, and were not Victorian-style Turkish baths. (Author's collection)*

was definitely a Victorian Turkish bath, and not a *hammam*. Nebahat Avcıoğlu, in her illustrated account, *From* The *Hammam to* Le *Hammam*, convincingly shows how much the building was influenced by Turkish baths in Britain, and especially by Urquhart's Jermyn Street Hammam, opened 14 years earlier.[45]

Whereas the 1920s baths which are still open next to the Paris mosque in rue Geoffrey St-Hilaire are just as definitely Islamic. Like many Turkish *hammams* built during the Ottoman period, these were part of a large charity complex known as a *külliye*. In addition to the mosque and baths there could also be schools, shops, a clinic, museum, library and kitchens.

However, the long-closed bath at Dunkirk (Fig 7.22), the 'Saracenic' exterior of which has recently been beautifully restored (Fig 7.23), is more problematic because it is not possible, by merely looking at a ruined exterior, to determine whether it was really a *hammam*. In fact, its hot-air bath was actually *un bain à vapeur*.[46]

There can be no doubt, however, about Das Friedrichsbad at Baden-Baden in Germany (Fig 7.24) which is unashamedly called a Römisch–Irisches Bad—a Roman–Irish bath.

Magnificent both inside and out, the baths were opened on 15 December 1877 after taking eight years to build at a cost of one-and-a-half million Deutschmarks. They were designed by Karl Dernfeld (1831–79) to meet the Grand Duke Friedrich of Baden's wish that, in their 'utilisation of the hot waters, [the baths] should surpass those known hitherto, and be in accordance with all the requirements of modern balneo-therapeutics.'[47]

These famous baths are still open and exemplify the best Turkish bath practice available

Fig 7.23
The exterior of the baths after the 2010 restoration of the exterior shell. (© Pascal Delénin)

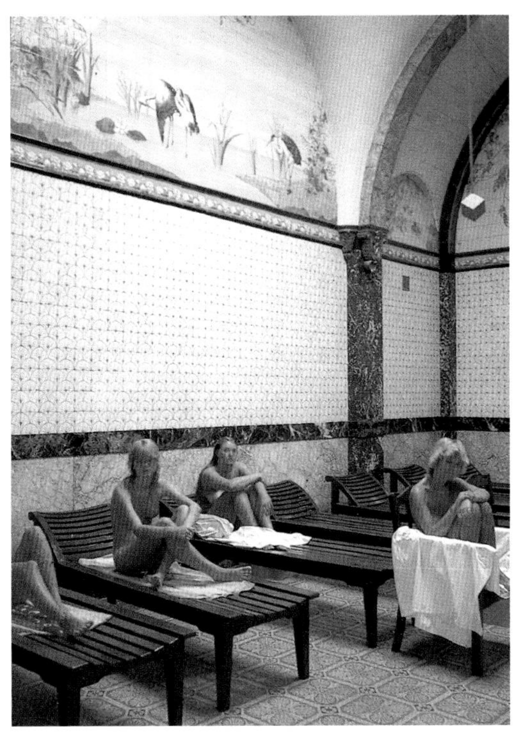

though the notice does not warn how icy the second shower is.

Then, after the Turkish bath, on to various steam baths, the round domed pool filled with warm thermal water at 82°F (28°C), the whirlpool, a cold water bath, and a final silent rest in the cooling-room.

It is claimed, though without any supporting evidence, that Mark Twain wrote to a friend, 'Here at the Friedrichsbad you lose track of time within 10 minutes, and track of the world within 20 ...' Apocryphal or not, the remark itself remains true, and today the baths are a heritage-protected historic monument.

Other Victorian Turkish baths can be found, for example, at Weisbaden and Munich in Germany, at Budapest in Hungary, and elsewhere in Europe. But the point has been well enough made that the Victorian Turkish bath travelled far beyond Victoria's realm.

Fig 7.24
The magnificent Friedrichsbad *at Baden-Baden in Germany, seen here in the 1990s, was opened in 1877 as a Roman–Irish bath.*
Courtesy of Carasana Bäderbetriebe GmbH www.carasana.de/en/friedrichsbad/home/

anywhere today. The unseen mechanics of the baths, and the more visible automatic locker systems may have been updated, but the baths themselves appear essentially unchanged since they opened (Fig 7.25).

On display is a 16-point timed plan for 'optimal' use of the baths but, within a three hour visit, bathers are actually free to follow their own preferences. The first suggested steps are:

1. Shower
2. Warm dry air room: 15 minutes at 55°C [130°F]
3. Hot dry air room: 5 minutes at 68°C [155°F]
4. Shower
5. Shampoo
6. Shower

Fig 7.25
That the tiles at the Baden-Baden Friedrichsbad *are in such good condition after more than 135 years, demonstrates how successful they are as a decorative wall cladding able to resist the continuous heat of the hot rooms.*
Courtesy of Carasana Bäderbetriebe GmbH www.carasana.de/en/friedrichsbad/home/

8

Building the Jermyn Street Hammam

After the 1857 opening in Manchester of the first commercial Turkish bath in England, three years were to elapse before Roger Evans opened the first in London. This was at his home in Bell Street, near Marble Arch, and by May he had already opened another in Palace Street, Pimlico.

Although Urquhart had advised Evans on Bell Street, he felt that the Pimlico establishment did not do justice to his own concept of the Turkish bath and was concerned that poor standards of hygiene would militate against the bath's wider adoption.

The Pimlico opening was noticed in *The Field* and, although praised, clearly not everything was perfect.

> Mr Evans, the proprietor, is aware of the defects under which his establishment labours, and is now engaged in remedying them. But imperfect as they are, they have already conferred great and, we believe, lasting benefits on the sick and ailing, as numerous grateful letters which we have received ... amply prove.[1]

A second article, the following week, rejected a suggestion that the baths were opened in haste and would improve. It argued that there was no hurry, and the opening should have been delayed till everything was in order 'rather than run the risk of sending people away with a false impression of the bath.' The writer continued:

> So far as we know, there is not yet any establishment in this country which realises the public Turkish bath, and we question very much whether there ever will be until some one who really understands the subject, and who has sufficient influence to command obedience, consents to take the matter up. The only person likely to do any good in this way is Mr Urquhart, and we earnestly hope that it will not be long before he makes up his mind to carry out this great public good.[2]

This seems like the beginning of a typical FAC-style newspaper campaign prior to the opening of one of their baths, and it may have been written by *The Field*'s angling correspondent, Francis Francis who, as a future shareholder in the shortly-to-be-formed company linked to Urquhart's name, would not have been totally disinterested.

Setting up the company

Urquhart, who had always made his own Turkish baths available to others, also met regularly with friends in London's first private bath. This was in Prince's Terrace at the home of George Witt, a physician, Fellow of the Royal Society, and noted collector of phallic antiquities. He and Urquhart had been friends for 20 years or so and it was at his baths that they, together with Stewart Erskine Rolland, decided to set up a large Turkish bath on 'genuinely' eastern lines. The venture was to be financed by setting up a joint stock company.[3]

Unfortunately, during the days immediately before the meeting called to form the company, Urquhart and Witt fell out. No record has been found specifically indicating the cause of the rupture, but some of the letters passing between the two men, and then between Witt and Harriet Urquhart, leave little doubt but that Witt was in the process of publishing a book on the Turkish bath without having fully consulted Urquhart beforehand.[4]

Nevertheless, on Monday 19 November 1860, a number of 'Gentlemen favorable to the use of the Turkish Baths' met at the Law Institution in Chancery Lane with George Crawshay in the Chair.

Urquhart, significantly not himself a subscriber though recorded as being one 'who was present', argued the need for a bath which would be a paradigm. Erasmus Wilson, the noted dermatologist and future author of a book on the eastern bath,[5] emphasised its value 'for the benefit of the health of the people'.

In due course it was agreed that a company be registered with the rather grand name of The London and Provincial Turkish Bath Company Limited (Fig 8.1) with a capital of £100,000 divided into 20,000 shares of £5 each, the latter aspiration showing an optimism soon to be proved quite unrealistic. The stated objects of the company were:

> For the establishment and construction of Turkish Baths on correct principles as same existed in ancient times, and as is still practised in the East, [to be opened] in London, Westminster and elsewhere within the United Kingdom.[6]

It was typical of Urquhart to insist, even in such a prosaic document as Form C of the Joint Companies Act, that phrases emphasising both the correctness and historical pedigree of the baths should be included.

The minutes of the meeting give no hint of the true nature of a meeting which was, by all less formal accounts, little short of disastrous.[7]

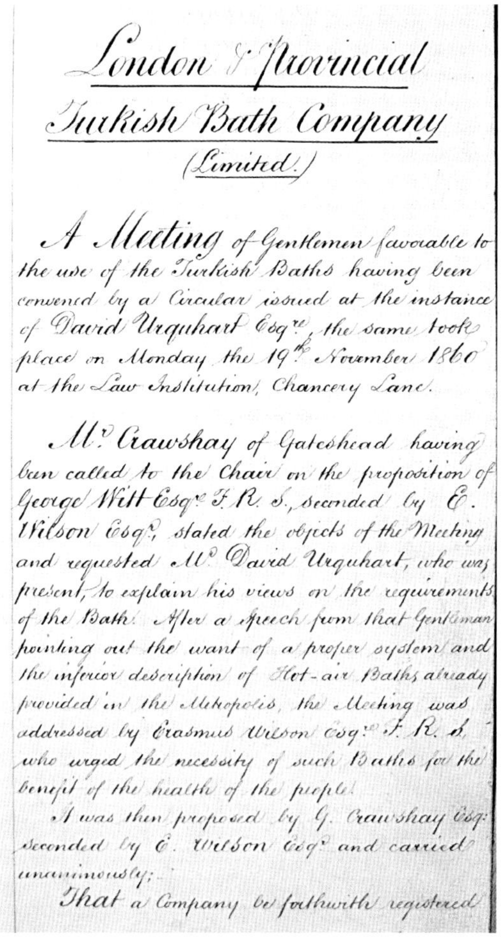

London & Provincial Turkish Bath Company (Limited.)

A Meeting of Gentlemen favorable to the use of the Turkish Baths having been convened by a Circular issued at the instance of David Urquhart Esqre the same took place on Monday the 19th November 1860 at the Law Institution, Chancery Lane.

Mr Crawshay of Gateshead having been called to the Chair on the proposition of George Witt Esqre F.R.S., seconded by E. Wilson Esqre, stated the objects of the Meeting and requested Mr David Urquhart, who was present, to explain his views on the requirements of the Bath. After a speech from that Gentleman pointing out the want of a proper system and the inferior description of Hot-air Baths already provided in the Metropolis, the Meeting was addressed by Erasmus Wilson Esqre F.R.S. who urged the necessity of such Baths for the benefit of the health of the people.

It was then proposed by G. Crawshay Esqre seconded by E. Wilson Esqre and carried unanimously;—

That a Company be forthwith registered

Differences of principle were quick to emerge and two of the main participants, Urquhart and Witt, were now no longer on speaking terms.

Neither of them was among the five persons present at the adjourned meeting of subscribers held the following day at 15 Bedford Row to agree the company's Articles of Association. Rolland was elected chairman of the company, Philip Augustus Hanrott was asked to be the company solicitor, and Septimus Beardmore—who, the following year, was to be the main instigator of the unsuccessful Roman Baths in Cambridge—was asked to act temporarily as honorary secretary.[8]

The company's articles enshrined Urquhart's position as an honorary director for as long as he wished; he was to be exempt from the normal requirement that a company's directors retire by rotation, yet he was also to have the full rights of an elected director. Another article determined that the 'mode of construction and general arrangement of the Baths' should be carried out under his 'advice and supervision' in return for which he could be allotted shares. Both these provisions resulted in later difficulties.[9]

Preliminary decisions and early skirmishes

Urquhart saw himself not only as an expert on the use of Turkish baths, but also on their construction. Having already built or supervised the building of a number of baths of varying sizes, he did have perfectly valid ideas about the practicalities of constructing one, the types of materials to be used for different purposes, and the positioning of its different areas. But none of these baths, even that at Riverside, was designed in anything approaching a Turkish style.

Even Urquhart did not quite believe he had the professional knowledge required to produce working plans and specifications for such an important bath, or to give appropriate instructions to the builders. Had he done so, he would undoubtedly have dispensed with an architect's services altogether.

We do not know why the directors considered George Somers Leigh Clarke (1825–82) to be a suitable architect to work together with someone as wary of another's expertise, or lack of it, as Urquhart. Somers Clarke had no previous experience of building a public Turkish bath—unlike, for example, Henry Francis

Fig 8.1
The minutes of the first meeting called to form the London and Provincial Turkish Bath Company Limited on 19 November 1860.
(Wiltshire and Swindon Archives WSA 1915/217)

Lockwood (1811–78) who, in partnership with the Mawson brothers, William (1828–89) and Richard (1834–1904), had already designed the Turkish bath building at Ben Rhydding Hydro (see page 210).

Somers Clarke had been a pupil of Sir Charles Barry. This led to his being invited to submit designs for major buildings such as the National Gallery, and though his design for the Midland Hotel at St Pancras was unsuccessful, he did win a premium for it. It is, of course, possible that he might have been chosen because he had previously worked for one of the company directors.

Urquhart reported to the board that, after a preliminary discussion, Somers Clarke had agreed 'to superintend as architect the erection of the Baths and that he would do so under Mr Urquhart's supervision.'[10]

While Urquhart had been typically forceful, it seems surprising that Somers Clarke, who was no tyro undertaking a first commission, should agree to conditions which might be considered by most professionals to be somewhat demeaning, yet they were duly incorporated in his contract.

Although, in the event, Barter's Oriental Baths in Victoria Street opened two months before the new company's own establishment, it had initially seemed as though the Jermyn Street baths might be the first major Turkish baths to be built in London. So the unusual nature of the project might have made it seem worthwhile for Somers Clarke to bite his tongue in order to participate. Also, he appeared to work well with Urquhart; only after the building was finished did the relationship end in recriminations and angry letters.

The earlier quarrel between Urquhart and George Witt continued to affect the company and, at the beginning of December 1860, Witt wrote a long letter attempting to explain why he had distanced himself from the project. Urquhart responded with an unusually pacific letter clearly intended to heal the breach, to which Witt briefly replied, giving the impression that he too wished to put the quarrel behind him.[11] But the two never reverted to their previous relationship and Witt had no further connection with the company.

Almost immediately, Urquhart became involved in another drama, this time to do with his own relationship with the company and how, or even whether, he should be remunerated. There had already been much discussion and correspondence about this, some with Harriet Urquhart who played, as not infrequently, the role of intercessor, just as she did with members of the FACs.

At the beginning of the month, Urquhart had contented himself with stating that, while he appreciated the directors' proposal to pay for his services, he was determined 'not to accept any remuneration', though he 'would not decline an indemnification of his actual expenditure.'[12] Yet within a fortnight he wrote informing Rolland that he had sent Hanrott, the company secretary, a letter asking for his name to be removed from the company share prospectus (Fig 8.2)—just weeks after it had been published in a wide selection of papers including *The Times*, *Morning Post*, the *Field*, and the *Builder* and, additionally, noticed in the *Lancet*.[13]

As often happens, people with different aims and objectives are not always able to work together. This can be exacerbated when one of the parties—in this case, Urquhart—himself had two irreconcilable objectives: first, to build a bath which exemplified the best practice for others to follow; second, to ensure that the working classes could afford to use it. Even with such Urquhartites as Rolland and Crawshay, and such medical advocates as dermatologist Erasmus Wilson, surgeon Sir John Fife and the father of neurochemistry, Dr John Louis William Thudichum, the company also needed shareholders who invested their money in order to make a reasonable profit.

Urquhart knew he could not afford to build an exemplar without the money that a company could provide; the company knew it would not easily survive without him and could not afford, and probably did not wish, to offend him. Yet his 'idiosyncratic' ideas about, for example, class or finance, frequently meant that decisions relating to his position within the company's organisational structure needed continual amendment.

Paramount was his disapproval of the capitalist system. His instinct was to have nothing to do with a joint stock company; he did not intend to invest in one; he foresaw numerous arguments about entrance charges. 'The Company will be looking to its profits. I shall be looking to charges lowered for the Working Classes', he wrote to Rolland.

On the other hand he did not wish the project to fail. He therefore withdrew his refusal of remuneration so that it would be possible to use it, to that object w^h I have had from the beginning in mind namely the establishment of Baths for the Working Classes free from any charge beyond that requisite for work.[14]

By now, Rolland had several years' experience in sorting out difficulties arising from Urquhart's principles. Having already seen the instigators of the company riven by dissent, and the resultant far-from-satisfactory initial meeting of subscribers, he acted quickly to resolve this latest problem. After conferring with Hanrott, he smartly put the matter on hold, and immediately diverted Urquhart's thoughts towards the exciting potentialities presented by the finding of suitable premises.

This had not been easy. After considering a number of possibilities, Somers Clarke had been to see an 'eligible site in Jermyn Street', with a main frontage of about 70ft (21m), leased by the Crown to a Mr Holmes.[15] Number 76, in the heart of London's clubland, had previously been the St James's Hotel where the fatally ill Sir Walter Scott had stayed for three weeks awaiting his last journey home to Abbotsford.[16]

Although it was a condition of the lease that the appearance of the front of the building could not be changed, there were stables and outbuildings at the rear which could be demolished. There was also an area behind the hotel which could be acquired later to provide a second entrance to the baths from Ryder Yard, together with room for expansion. But even without this, the site was large enough for a building which, internally at least, could be as Turkish in style as Urquhart wanted.

After the toing and froing which seems an inescapable part of acquiring a property, Holmes agreed to rent the building for £500 per annum, supplemented by two deposits, each of £1,000.[17] The company's initial offer for the stables was refused, but at least they were able to gain access to the main building by the end of December.

The public share offer had not gone well and Rolland, reporting to Urquhart on their board meeting, wrote that they had £4,500 in hand, of which £3,400 was already committed, leaving just over £1,000 with which to start building.[18]

There were only two large shareholders at this time, Rolland with 400 shares, and Crawshay with 200. Urquhart, still refusing to buy shares or accept remuneration, wanted to lend the company any money they thought was due to him. Harriet, however, had agreed with Rolland that an allotment was the best solution[19]

THE

LONDON AND PROVINCIAL TURKISH BATH COMPANY,

LIMITED.

REGISTERED OFFICES: 76, JERMYN STREET.

CAPITAL £100,000, IN 20,000 SHARES OF £5 EACH. DEPOSIT 10s. PER SHARE ON APPLICATION.

TO THE DIRECTORS OF THE ABOVE-NAMED COMPANY.

GENTLEMEN,

Having paid to the Bankers of the Company the Sum of £ ________ being the amount of the Deposit of Ten Shillings per Share, I hereby request you to allot me ________ Shares in the above Company, or any less number, subject to the Regulations of the Company.

Dated this ________ day of ________ 18 ____

Name ________

Address ________

Occupation (if any) or Description ________

*** This form, with the blanks filled up, and stamps affixed to the receipt, is to be presented entire to the Bankers, the Applicant retaining the Receipt, which will be exchanged for the Share Certificate after the usual Notice.

DEPOSIT RECEIPT.

(To be retained by Applicant, and delivered up in exchange for the Share Certificate.)

THE

LONDON AND PROVINCIAL TURKISH BATH COMPANY,

LIMITED.

RECEIVED from Mr. ________

to the credit of the above Company, the sum of £ ________, *being the Deposit of Ten Shillings per Share on* ________ *Shares in the Company.*

£ : : ________ *Bankers' Signature.*

*** The corresponding deposit on Shares not allotted will be returned at the above-named Bankers, after the expiration of seven days from the day of Allotment, on presentation of this Receipt, marked for the sum to be repa'd, for which purpose it must be previously produced at the Company's Registered Office.

Fig 8.2
Application form from an early prospectus offering shares in the company. (Wiltshire and Swindon Archives WSA 1915/220)

and, late in January 1861, 200 shares were put in Urquhart's name.[20] They remained untouched till after his death even though, after 1864, the Urquharts lived abroad.

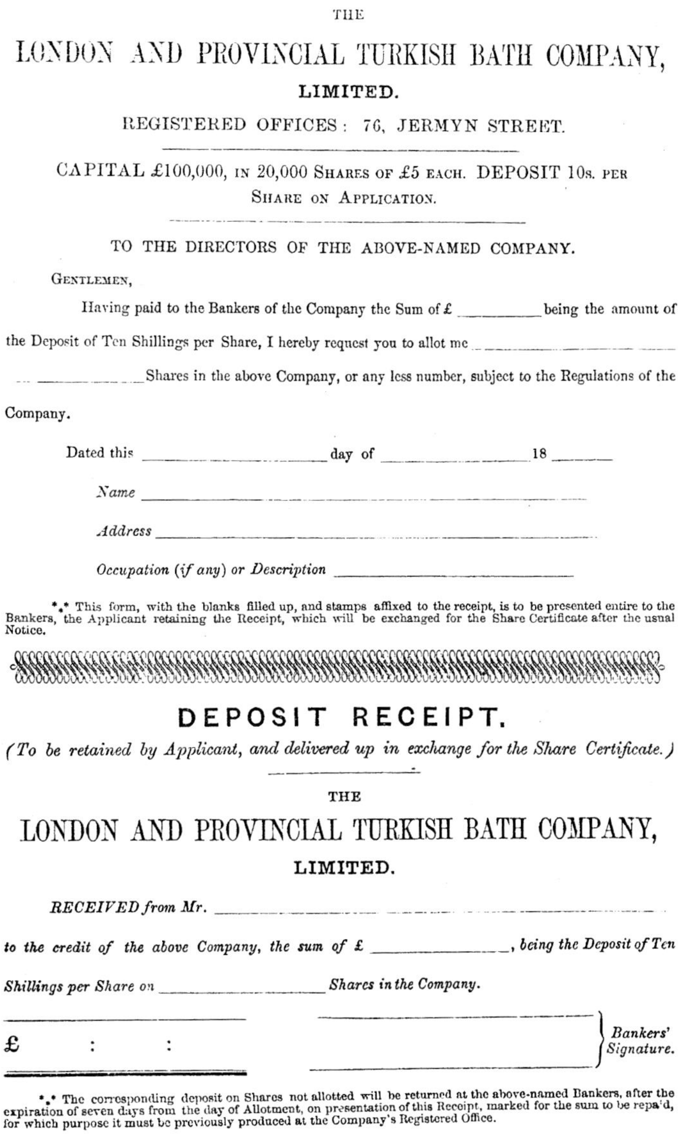

Designing the bath

Given that Somers Clarke had not previously designed an Islamic-style building, and that it was nearly 25 years since Urquhart was last in Turkey, the company approached Dr Julius Michael Millingen for help.

Millingen was one of the two doctors who unsuccessfully 'treated' Byron on his deathbed. While Turkish correspondent for *The Times*, he became politically involved with Urquhart during the latter's diplomatic posting in

Constantinople. A much sought after doctor, he was court physician to five successive sultans.

In 1858, Millingen had written a series of articles in the *Gazette Médicale d'Orient* about the Turkish bath, and Crawshay had written asking for a copy of one of them—an earlier one having already been translated and reprinted in *The Free Press*.[21] Millingen sent 'the article' and 'the two plates', one of which was an image 'copied after nature' and the other, a 'plan of a public and also of a private bath', so that it would be 'an easy matter for an intelligent architect to build baths of any dimensions.' He added that he would 'not only be happy, but consider it a duty' to help with any further information Crawshay might require.

By the beginning of February 1861, alterations to the inside of the main building had started although they were, reported John Johnson, 'going on very slowly.'[24] Totally trusted by Urquhart, Johnson had been involved in FAC work since the 1850s. Becoming ill, he had been invited to stay at Riverside so he could use the bath there, and appears there on the 1861 census as a clerk, though he would later become Baths Superintendent at The Hammam.

On 19 February, Urquhart wrote a long letter outlining his vision of how he saw the new bath. The catalogue of the Wellcome Library, in whose collection it is,[25] suggests that it may have been written to Dr Thudichum. But this seems most unlikely. Thudichum was a director of the company, and would already have been familiar with its content.

Moreover, the letter begins 'Sir' whereas Urquhart's normal salutation to friends and, indeed, to Thudichum 12 days earlier, was 'My dear Sir.' Finally, the letter ends:

> 'I have the honour to remain
> & & &
> D Urquhart'

and Urquhart's letters, or copies, do not normally include ampersands in this context.

One strong possibility is that the letter was a draft for a letter to be sent to several of those who knew about the bath, in an attempt to persuade them to take up shares, or even additional shares, in the company. Support for this theory can be found in Urquhart's caveat, two thirds of the way through the letter, where he follows the pattern of a share prospectus, writing:

> As I am giving you this summary to enable you to judge of its remunerating faculties, I must refer to the probability of competition.

Such a letter would have been a matter of some urgency because it was written on the same day as a draft agreement was initialled for the purchase of the Jermyn Street lease.[26] Although half of the agreed £6,000 had already been paid, this still left another £3,000 to find, with the company having just over £1,000 in its account. Of the initial shareholders in the company, only Rolland and possibly Crawshay had increased their holding during 1861. Yet the remaining £3,000 was paid in full on 9 April.[27]

In spite of the 'Sir' salutation in the draft, it seems inconceivable that one of the recipients would not have been Urquhart's long-time political supporter, Harriett Ann Curtis. One week after the letter was posted, 400 £5 shares were allotted to Miss Curtis.[28]

It is highly significant that, with the exception of Erasmus Wilson, all the large shareholders, including Miss Curtis, came to be involved with the company through their work with the FACs—the committees which had also been the core of the 'popular' Turkish Bath Movement. Without the initial support of these shareholders there would have been no Hammam.

Almost immediately, the company had to pay the Crown a further £5,000 for the stables and ground behind the hotel.[29] Rolland took a further 100 shares and another director, John Henry Nathaniel Da Costa, helped out with a loan of £1,500 for which he charged the company interest at 5%.[30] Finally, in order to gain permission to demolish the stables, Rolland had to undertake to rebuild them at a later date if called upon to do so.[31]

In his letter, Urquhart wrote that he had originally rejected the site because of the constraints imposed on modifying the exterior, but the difficulty of finding another one located so centrally changed his mind and,

> after long and painful labour on the part of Mr Somers Clarke and myself, we have fixed upon a plan partly of construction, and partly of adaptations, which altho' not according to the proper form of an Eastern Bath, still in all essentials, and in a very great degree even in appearance, will represent the Bath of the East.[32]

Describing their plan, already approved by the Crown Surveyor (subject to a 'slight modification'), he wrote that there were to be three galleries around a central hall, linked to the cold rooms on the floors of the main building. There would also be a pool. Then, he continued,

> at the further extremity there will be a descent to the basement story affording entrance for the

cheaper class of bathers and for more extensive facilities of washing without raising vapours.

It has been suggested that since the entrance for 'the cheaper class of bathers' and the 'more extensive facilities of washing' are mentioned in the same sentence, Urquhart was indicating that the working-class bathers would have to wash before being allowed into the bath.[33] Distinguishing between classes in this manner would have been anathema to Urquhart. He was merely describing what would be in the basement, and emphasising the importance of ensuring that the air in the hot rooms would remain dry and not, as in an Islamic *hammam*, humid and vaporous.

Urquhart described how the space would be used and how the company would make a profit. It is worth quoting this part of the letter at some length as it shows how naive Urquhart was in financial matters, and how unrealistic were his expectations and, therefore, his calculations:

> There requires for the taking of a Bath five distinct allotments of space (independently of the Tank [ie, the plunge pool]) … A quarter of an hour being allowed for each operation, the time on an average will be an hour and a quarter. In these operations, the space required for each person varies from ten to 20 square feet, passages not included. The general result is that 300 persons can be accommodated simultaneously for bathing, on the Men's side, and 70, for bathing on the Women's. The scale of prices will vary, at least according to my present lights on the subject, from 9 o['clock] to 5/o['clock] and taking an average of 1/6 you will see that the Bath may hold at one time for a single bathing, £25; and taking 12 or 13 working hours, these numbers might be repeated 10 times. Of course the throng will be only at two periods—in the afternoon at the higher prices, and in the evening at the lower. Say that the Bath is filled but twice during the day, the gross returns would be £15,000 a year; and if the practice took, of course it would be 5 or 6 times that amount. The expenses on the other hand, would be £2,400 fixed.

He did accept, when looking at possible competition, that London would be unlikely to support the 4,000 baths suggested by his comparison of its population with that of Constantinople. But, having asked Evans for a copy of his accounts (Fig 8.3) for the first 16 weeks (11 September to 29 December 1860) of his third establishment in Golden Square,[34] he then noted that two small London establishments which had been open for about a year were making returns of 150 per cent and 300 per cent.

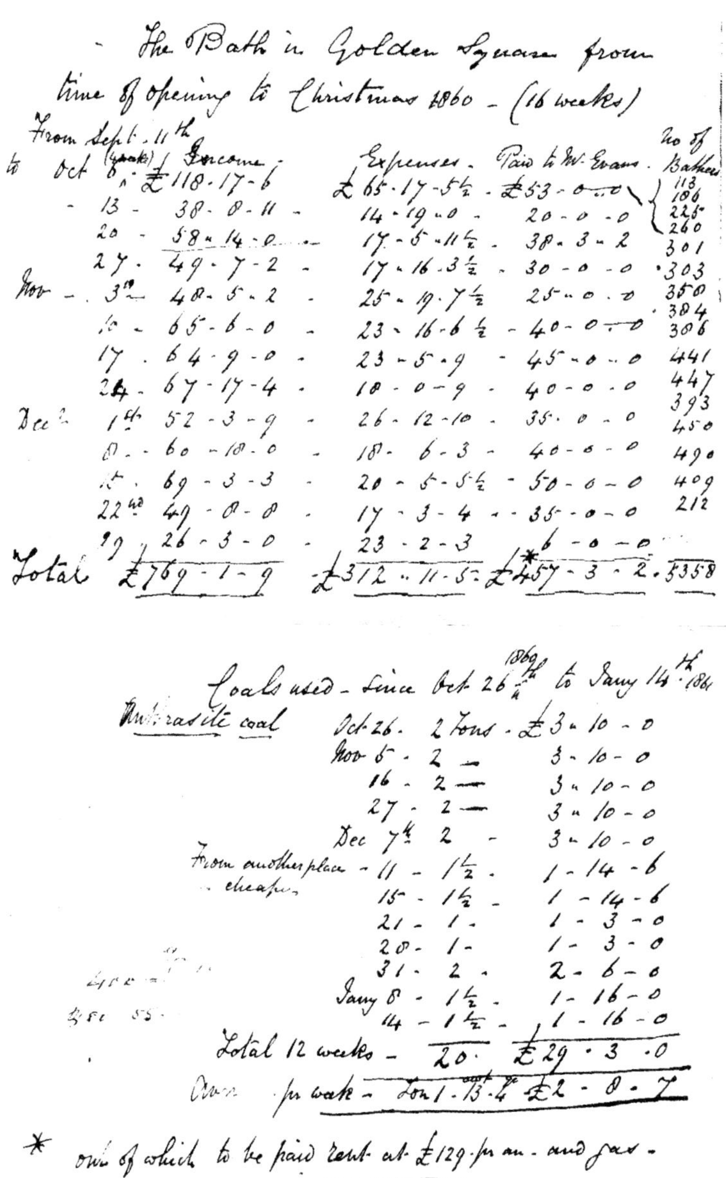

The Bath in Golden Square from time of Opening to Christmas 1860 – (16 weeks)

From Sept. 11th		Income	Expenses	Paid to Mr Evans	No of Bathers
to Oct	6 (4 weeks)	£118-17-6	£65-17-5½	£53-0-0	113 / 186 / 225 / 260
	13	38-8-11	14-19-0	20-0-0	301
	20	58-14-0	17-5-11½	38-3-2	303
	27	49-7-2	17-16-3½	30-0-0	350
Nov	3rd	48-5-2	25-19-7½	25-0-0	384
	10	65-6-0	23-16-6½	40-0-0	306
	17	64-9-0	23-5-9	45-0-0	441
	24	67-17-4	10-0-9	40-0-0	447
Decr	1st	52-3-9	26-12-10	35-0-0	393
	8	60-10-0	18-6-3	40-0-0	450
	15	69-3-3	20-5-5½	50-0-0	490
	22nd	49-8-8	17-3-4	35-0-0	409
	29	26-3-0	23-2-3	6-0-0	212
Total		£769-1-9	£312-11-5	£457-3-2*	5358

Coals used – since Oct 26th 1860 to Jany 14th 1861

Anthrasite coal

	Oct 26	2 Tons	£3-10-0
	Nov 5	2	3-10-0
	16	2	3-10-0
	27	2	3-10-0
	Dec 7th	2	3-10-0
From another place cheaper	11	1½	1-14-6
	15	1½	1-14-6
	21	1	1-3-0
	28	1	1-3-0
	31	2	2-6-0
	Jany 8	1½	1-16-0
	14	1½	1-16-0
Total 12 weeks		20	£29-3-0
Aver. per week		Ton 1-13-4	£2-8-7

* out of which to be paid rent at £129 per an. and gas.

This was an exaggeration. When the letter was written, no Turkish bath in London had been open for more than seven months, and he did not mention that these baths were owned by individuals and not by companies.

In the event, it was fortunate that the original design was 'found to exceed the means of the company'[35] and it had to be redone on a smaller scale. The new baths would have two floors instead of four and be connected to the main building at entrance level only.

By mid-July, the directors had approved the revised plans which Urquhart and Somers Clarke had worked on together, and the firm of Kirk & Parry of Little Queen Street had been appointed builders.

Fig 8.3
Accounts for the first 16 weeks of Roger Evans's Turkish baths in Golden Square, his third establishment.
(Wellcome Library, London Western MSS.6237 Notes on Turkish baths; 3)

One of those who used Urquhart's Riverside bath was his friend Dr Arthur Leared, a physician at the Brompton Consumptive Hospital. His visit to Jermyn Street while construction was in progress led to Urquhart's asking the board to build a small Turkish bath in the main building for use by invalids, and later for women bathers. Initially, it would be used by a number of Leared's patients suffering from phthisis (tuberculosis) to determine whether the bath was therapeutically beneficial in such cases.

Spurred on, no doubt, by Urquhart's sense of social responsibility, not to mention the possibility of some favourable publicity in the medical journals, permission was granted, provided the cost did not exceed £100.[36]

The suggestion was a good one and in December its use was extended to the members of the board. The company was still far short of the capital it needed. Being able to use the small bath enabled directors to encourage their friends to try it, become interested in the company, and then become shareholders.[37]

Urquhart probably also had in mind that experience gained from its use would be helpful in avoiding mistakes in the main baths. It seems to have been a valuable source of feedback because it was soon closed for alterations—though unfortunately there is no record of what changes were made, or why.[38]

Preparing to open

By the middle of May 1862 the company began to prepare seriously for the opening of the baths. The need to appoint staff and to fix opening hours and charges was becoming urgent. Robert Boxer Punnett, the Company Secretary, and an office boy had both been in post, at salaries of £10 and 10s per week respectively, since the first prospectus was issued in December 1860.[39]

But now a housekeeper, Mrs Doggett, was appointed to look after the chambers in the main building at £75 per year all found; Youssouf Hieronymus, an Armenian, was retained as head shampooer—today, chief shampooer would be a more appropriate title—at two guineas per week, and 10 shampooers were to be engaged at £1 5s per week, though it is seems unlikely that the full complement was ever appointed.

John Buxton, who had been secretary of the Manchester FAC, was appointed as baths manager at an annual salary of £200. This may well have been at Buxton's request since, due to the cotton famine in Lancashire that year, not much was happening with the Manchester committee. He would have had little experience yet of running a bath and the appointment was for a trial period of six months.[40]

Finally, John Johnson was appointed as money taker. Even after Buxton's appointment, Johnson was the person more likely to keep the Urquharts up to date. Often it was gossip as well as news. He wrote to Harriet, for example, that one of the directors,

> Mr Lowe brought five gentlemen to the Bath last night whom he was anxious to interest in the Bath. Several calls have been made during the week & enquiries also as the probable time of opening the Bath. Every one seems disgusted with Dr Barter's establishment.[41]

It is difficult to know whether the last remark about the newly opened Victoria Street baths was in any way true, or merely what people thought Urquhart would want to hear. That it seems likely to have been true is supported by a comment in *The Standard*, 11 months later, that the building's 'hitherto incomplete state has prevented their as yet coming into anything like full operation.'[42] And, in England at least, a bath run by Urquhart would in any event make a greater impression on prospective bathers.

On 17 June the subject of opening hours and charges 'was discussed at great length'. The basic rate was 3s 6d for men and 5s for women, presumably on the basis that fewer women were expected. We can only assume that the concept of the vicious circle was unknown to members of the board. Men's baths were 2s after seven in the evening and as low as 1s (but without a shampoo) on Saturday evening. Rates for monthly, six-monthly and annual subscriptions were at a discount, and the small bath could be hired for private use for one guinea. The baths were open till midnight and closed on Sundays, and could be used by women on Tuesday and Thursday mornings from eight till noon.[43]

To put these charges into perspective, even to take one of the cheaper 2s evening baths with a shampoo cost the equivalent of one fifth of their own office boy's weekly salary. These prices would have displeased Urquhart and justified his earlier worries.

John Johnson, though now paid by the baths company, was still involved in the day-to-day running of the FACs. In July, when Urquhart was ill, he wrote asking Miss Curtis for advice on how to deal with a major dispute about the separate Turkish baths owned by each of two committee secretaries in Leeds. He also thanked her for a cheque for £12 0s 8d. This may have been related to their committee work, but it may instead have implied that Miss Curtis was looking after the day-to-day disbursements on behalf of the company. Johnson told her he was still living at Riverside, and would be travelling to the baths every Tuesday.[44]

The Hammam was now almost ready to open and the directors and their friends were invited to use it for the first time on Wednesday 16 July. By this time, a description of 'the one perfect Turkish Bath in London'—the first part of which could almost have been written by Urquhart himself—had already appeared in *Building News*.[45]

The Jermyn Street Hammam

The entrance lobby and ground floor of the old hotel continued in use, modified to suit the baths. Additions included a ticket office and a cloakroom where bathers were able to deposit their valuables.[46] A door led to an inner hall where, at the bottom of a short wide flight of stairs, bathers left their shoes before entering the main baths area.

The full 50ft (15m) width of the new building was divided into two main areas (Fig 8.4): first a 70ft (21m) long *frigidarium*; and second, a square space encompassing the *tepidarium*, hot rooms and, at a lower level, washing facilities.

The *frigidarium* (Fig 8.5) was an impressive 35ft (10.7m) high, the main structural components and its wooden roof being left open to view, finely complementing the varnished fretwork partitions and decorative balcony balustrade. On either side of a broad central avenue were eight spacious alcoves (or *leewans*) slightly raised off the main floor. These were separated from each other, and from the main aisle, by 'low level perforated balustrades ... so that, while having an uninterrupted view of all around, perfect privacy is still provided.' Each alcove was carpeted and furnished with two couches, except for one near the entrance. This was equipped for making Turkish coffee to accompany the sherbet, **narghile* or **chibouk* available to bathers after their bath. The temperature ranged from 70 to 80°F (21 to 27°C).

In the centre of the room was a fountain, its marble basin feeding the 30ft (9m) long white tiled cold plunge pool. Through a 15ft (4.6m) high Moorish arch, its opening completely covered by a sheet of plate glass, could be seen the *tepidarium* and the far end of the plunge pool. Bathers swam under the protected glass

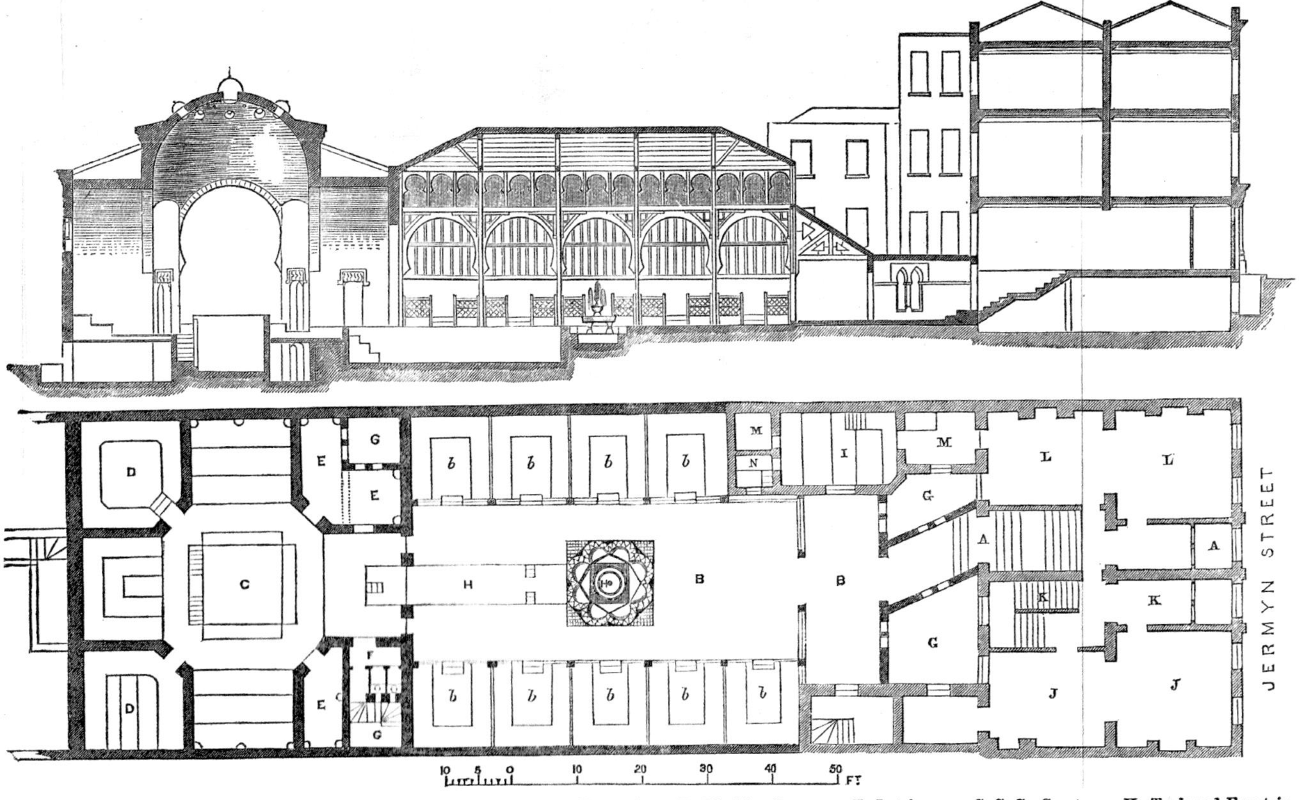

Fig 8.4
Section and plan of the London Hammam (left and centre) built behind the existing Jermyn Street hotel. (David Urquhart 'On the art of constructing Turkish baths...' J Soc Arts, *28 Feb 1862. Author's collection)*

between *frigidarium* and *tepidarium*, though on either side of the pool a doorway, covered with a sandwich of insulating felt between two red curtains, also allowed bathers to move from one room to the other.

The *tepidarium* was maintained at 120°F (49°C), and in the centre was a raised 11ft (3.4m) square platform 2ft 6in (0.8m) high (Fig 8.6). Three of its sides had a half height seat on which bathers could sit or have a massage, and

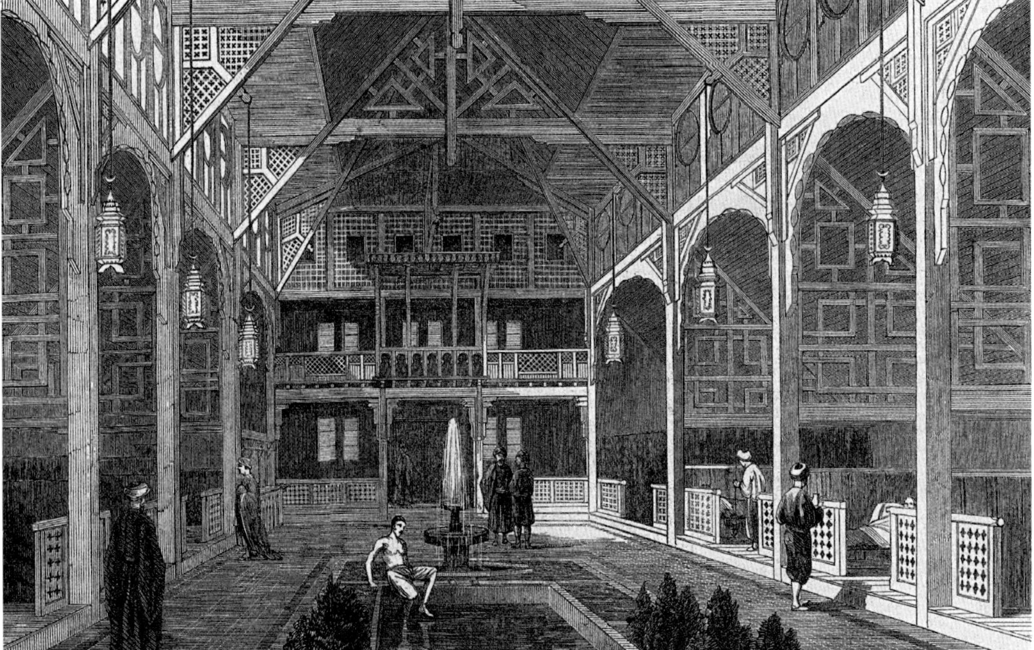

Fig 8.5
Artist's impression of The Hammam's frigidarium, *engraved and printed before the baths opened.*
*(*Illustrated London News, *26 Jul 1862. Author's collection)*

Fig 8.6
Artist's impression of the platform in The Hammam's tepidarium, *engraved and printed before the baths opened.*
(Author's collection)

on the fourth side, steps led down to a *douche room below the platform. This was fitted with a needle shower and a single 2½ inch (64mm) wide douche.

Above the platform was a large central dome of red brick pierced with star-shaped openings covered with coloured glass. The platform, floors, and dado were all of marble, and the two hot rooms had similar but smaller domes. Air, heated by the furnaces, flowed between the pillars supporting the floors.

In each of the four areas between the arms of the Greek cross was a square room, its entrance placed in a wall which diagonally cut across one of its corners (Fig 8.7).

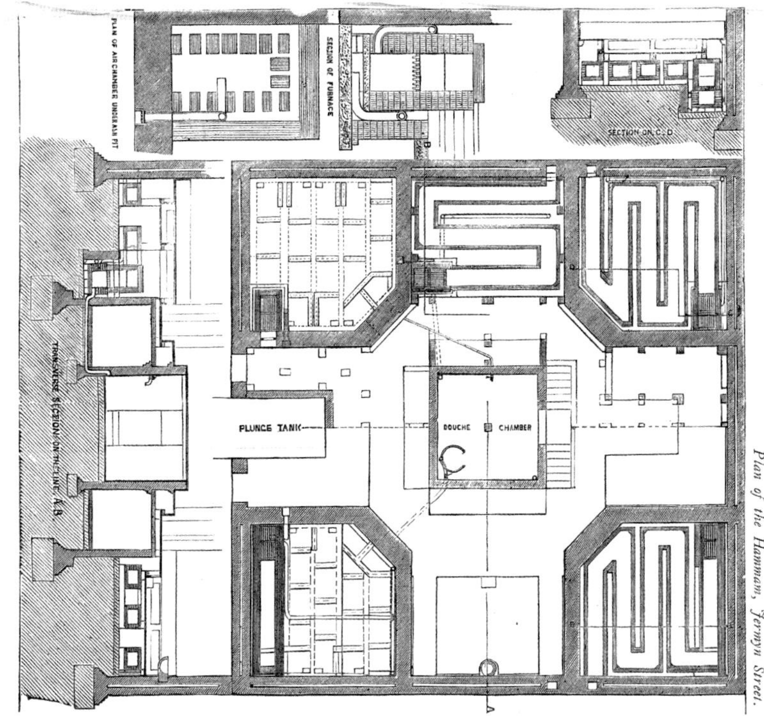

Entering the 120°F (49°C) *tepidarium*, the rooms immediately on either side were subdivided, the one on the right into washing and shampooing areas, and that on the left into toilets and another washing room. Facing the entrance were the two hot rooms, each with its own furnace below. It is not known exactly what the temperatures of these rooms were when the baths first opened, but they ranged 'upwards from 170 or 180 degrees [77 or 82°C].' The room on the right had a supplementary experimental curved iron radiator and stepped seating so the temperature would vary according to how high the bather sat (Fig 8.8).

At night, the *tepidarium* was lit by coloured glass Turkish lanterns suspended from the roof, and by what *Building News* called *sunburners. But these were more likely to have been ventilating sunburners fixed outside the stained glass apertures in the hot room domes.[47]

The baths were officially opened to the public, after a couple of postponements to complete the work, at 10 am on the morning of 28 July 1862.[48]

Fig 8.7
Plan of the tepidarium *at The Hammam.*
Fig 8.8
Plan showing the plunge pool passing under the glass screen between the frigidarium *and the* tepidarium. *Also shown is the stepped seating in one of the hot rooms, unusual in a Victorian Turkish bath. (John Fife,* Manual of the Turkish bath, *Churchill, 1865)*

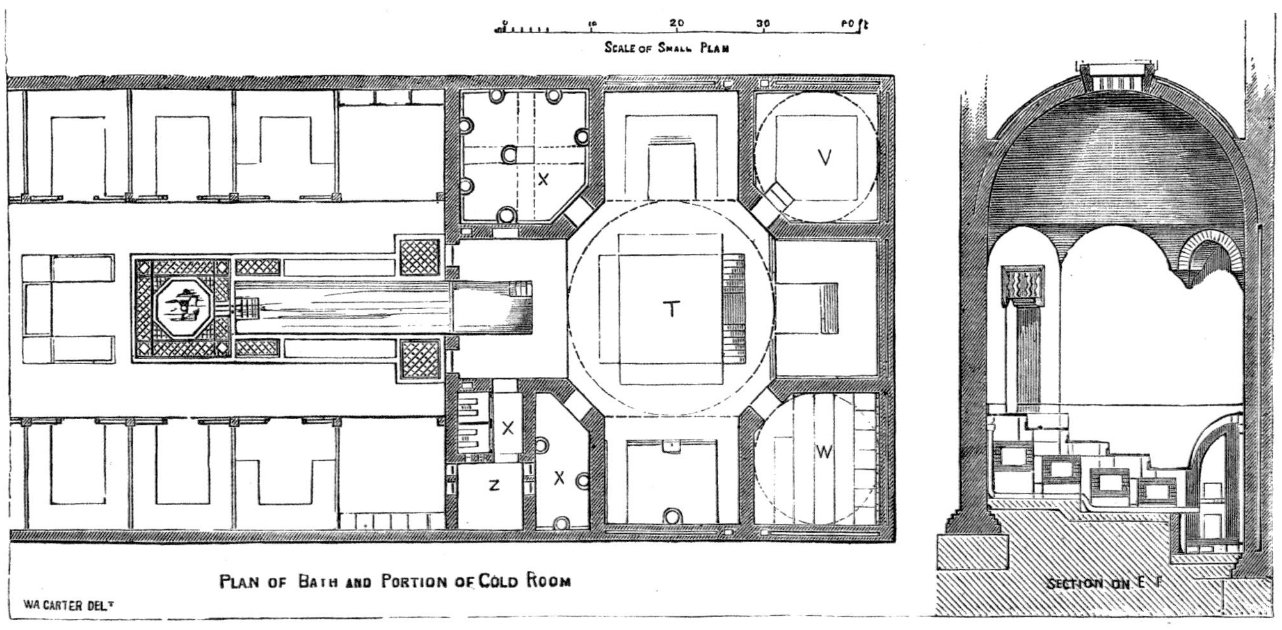

9

The Jermyn Street Hammam, 1862–1941

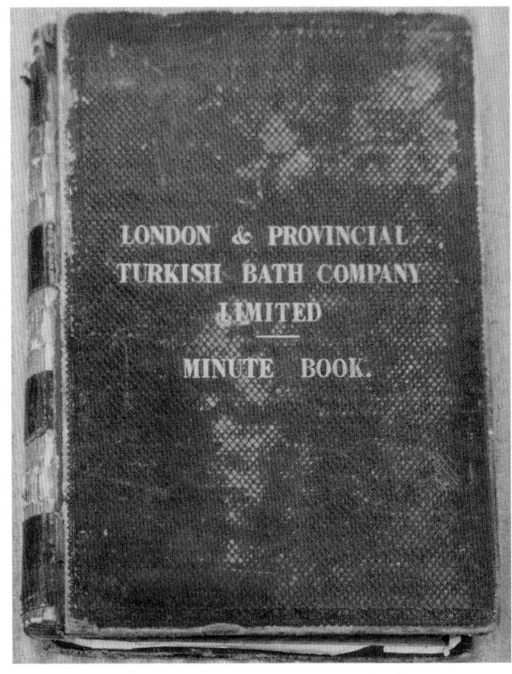

Fig 9.1
The Minute Book of the London and Provincial Turkish Bath Company Limited.
(Wiltshire and Swindon Archives WSA 1915/217)

Although there were Turkish baths that survived longer, such as those at Swindon and Harrogate, the connection between Urquhart and The Hammam makes it by far the most important historically. We are fortunate that there is so much detailed information about its origins (from the collections of letters at Balliol College, Oxford, and the Wellcome Library, London) and its running (from the minute book (Fig 9.1) and other documents at the Wiltshire & Swindon History Centre). These documents still await a more detailed study.

Even so, there is only space here for a broad outline of how the baths were run. Many interesting facets are barely touched on and will in due course be added to the more detailed accounts which are possible on the *Victorian Turkish Baths* website.

The early years

There were, inevitably, a number of problems arising during the first months. Just two weeks after the opening, Urquhart 'explained to the Board that he had suspended the Manager, Mr Buxton, for delinquency.'[1]

It is not clear what Buxton had or had not done, and there was some sympathy for him from Dr Thudichum when the chairman proposed confirmation of Urquhart's action. Thudichum moved an amendment that before any decision was taken they should determine exactly what powers had been delegated to Urquhart.

Although this was defeated, it took a second meeting, and a reading by Hanrott of the appropriate Articles of Association, to confirm that he did indeed have such powers. Buxton's solicitor, meanwhile, had issued a writ for the amount of salary due to his client.

The incident gave rise to a further dispute. Thudichum, presumably to gain support for Buxton, had written about the case to Miss Curtis who, though a major shareholder, was not on the board. This was understandably considered improper by the others and, although Thudichum retained his five shares for another 20 years, he resigned his directorship and offered to apologise to Miss Curtis. Later, the board sent her a vote of thanks 'for her kind assistance during the trying period of the opening of the Bath.'[2]

John Johnson was appointed superintendent in Buxton's place, though he continued to assist Urquhart in his political work by co-ordinating the work of the committees. After one heavy four-hour Saturday meeting which he had arranged in order to formulate a letter to Lord Russell, he wrote to Urquhart at Riverside (Fig 9.2), 'I have just come in. There is not another scrap of paper but this in the room. So I must write small and clear …' Writing on the back of one of the leaflets advertising the breakfast menu, Johnson first recounts the meeting, and then reports on The Hammam, 'The numbers not so good this week. The fog frightened them …'[3]

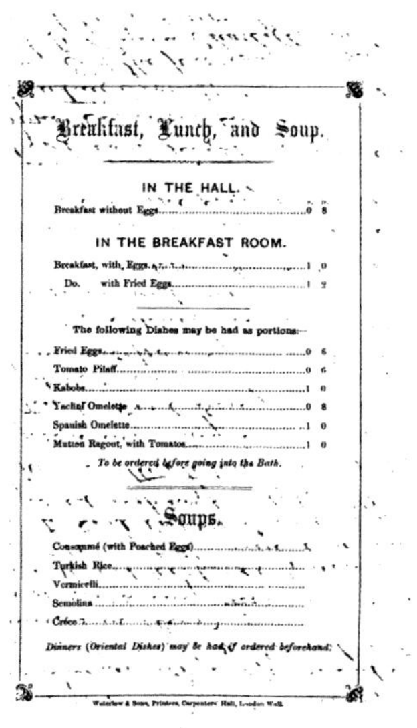

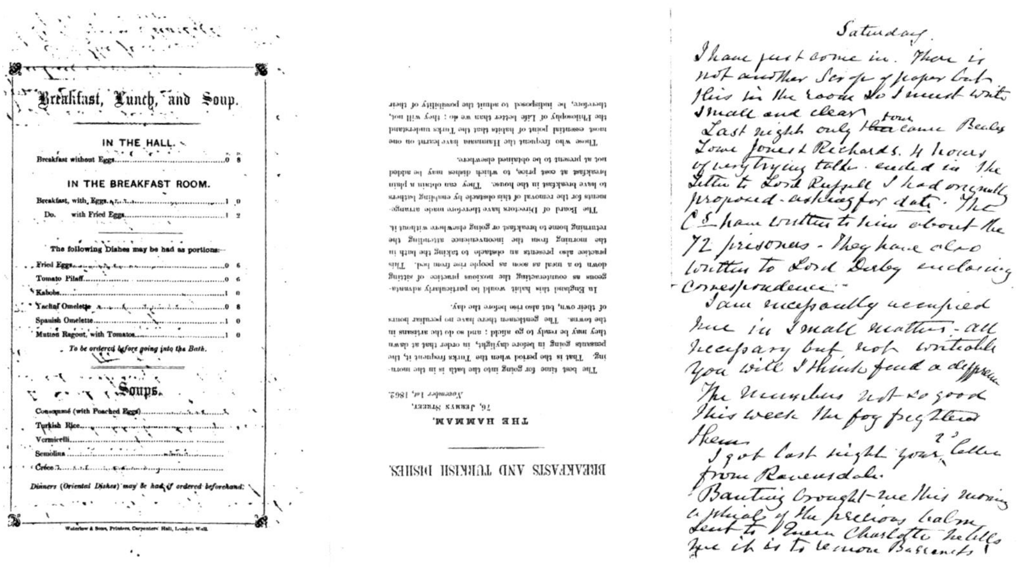

Breakfast, Lunch, and Soup.

IN THE HALL.

	s.	d.
Breakfast without Eggs	0	8

IN THE BREAKFAST ROOM.

Breakfast, with Eggs	1	0
Do. with Fried Eggs	1	2

The following Dishes may be had as portions:—

Fried Eggs	0	6
Tomato Pilaff	0	6
Kabobs	1	0
Yachaf Omelette	0	8
Spanish Omelette	1	0
Mutton Ragout, with Tomatos	1	0

To be ordered before going into the Bath.

Soups.

Consommé (with Poached Eggs)
Turkish Rice
Vermicelli
Semolina
Crécy

Dinners (Oriental Dishes) may be had if ordered beforehand.

Waterlow & Sons, Printers, Carpenters' Hall, London Wall.

Fig 9.2
On the only available paper, John Johnson writes to Urquhart on the back of a breakfast menu. He describes the political meeting he had arranged and just returned from, and notes the drop in the weekly number of bathers due to the fog. The price of breakfast at The Hammam was kept low to encourage early morning bathers.
(Balliol College, Oxford. Urquhart Bequest. Image supplied by the Master and Fellows of Balliol College, Oxford)

Not surprisingly, the number of bathers turned out to be far fewer than Urquhart had forecast by comparing the populations of London and Constantinople. Someone who knew Turkey as well as he did should have taken more account of the importance of ritual bathing in the Islamic lifestyle. And perhaps, even more important, he should have considered the differing climates in the two cities, and that a bad winter could prove financially embarrassing for the company.

If the weather reduced the number of bathers at the Hammam, in the north the main cause was the economic situation. Abel Andrew, who had been running the Stalybridge FAC and, since shortly after its 1859 opening, the Turkish bath also, wrote to John Johnson—10 months after soup kitchens were opened in the town—to say that the business employing him and his son was closing the following week.

> I wish to ask you if there is a vacancy at the great Turkish Bath for a shampooer. My son, Alexander has been acting as Shampooer on a Saturday for a long time and I think by a little instruction he will be an adept if he should be so fortunate as to obtain a situation in the Bath in Jermyn St.
>
> I have also a Daughter 19 years of age stout made she has been accustomed to wait on the ladies in the Bath & is much beloved by them.

Then in the next paragraph, seamlessly as usual, on to the political issues occupying the FACs at the time:

> Our limited means has prevented us from inviting the noble Circassian Chiefs to address a meeting at Stalybridge. The Bath is doing no more than defraying expenses which is as much as we can expect at present.
>
> The American War still continues to be the Chief topic of Conversation.[4]

Only months after the Buxton affair, the company secretary Robert Punnett was suspended and later dismissed. Urquhart could be unforgiving of those who had, in his eyes, erred. And there can be little doubt that his natural pedantry must, on occasion, have made him a difficult person to work for.

However, he had also shown, with his committee members, a gift for inspiring a total dedication which enabled them to undertake work which was often intellectually difficult, and which offered no immediate reward.

So when he found someone akin to the resident housekeeper, Mrs Doggett, who was hard-working and totally trustworthy, he was quick to offer unstinting support, arguing to the board that her £75 salary was quite inadequate. When she was appointed, before The Hammam opened, Urquhart had no practical experience enabling him to predict the duties she would perform. Less than a month after the opening, these had already multiplied and when Urquhart asked for her salary to be increased to £100, the board agreed.[5]

But when, barely four months later, Urquhart asked for a further increase, the board began to have serious doubts and set up a small committee to look into the matter.[6] She was asked to attend, and prepare for them an account of what she did.

§Her account provides a detailed picture of the work required of someone in her position, and of how little time she had left for her own interests. It also describes much of what went on behind the scenes to ensure that the bathers were able to enjoy their relaxation unconcerned by the actuality of life downstairs.

Urquhart was asked to comment. His explanation of her totally unforeseen impact on the company's catering profits proved to be the clinching argument, for it had originally been arranged that the refreshment bar in the cooling-room should be let to an outside caterer. Urquhart said that under the housekeeper's management,

> 'the profits for seven weeks have been £26.19.2 that is to say an average of £3.17.0 a week. During the same period (from 1st Dec[r] 1862 till the 17th January 1863) the profits on the sale of refreshments in the House and on the letting of the Chambers have amounted to £29.10.2 making a total of £56.9.4 so that the Company is now deriving from the exertions of the House keeper a weekly income of £8.1.4 or nearly £420 a year.'

He also mentioned that the profit would have been even larger had they not decided to serve breakfast at cost, to encourage more bathers in the morning.

Noting that Urquhart thought highly of Mrs Doggett, that she was working an average of more than 14 hours a day (even though, since mid-January, women no longer used the large baths) and that the company was making an annual profit of more than £400 from her department, the committee recommended that her salary be raised to £150 per year.[7]

Urquhart was familiar with the hardship suffered in the struggle for survival by several of his leading supporters within the FACs. His influence on the board when considering salaries and working conditions probably made the company, at least by the standards of the day, one of the more enlightened of employers. One of his last acts was to write to the board supporting the setting up of a 'Superannuation or Sick Fund' for their employees.[8]

But even earlier, when John Johnson died in 1867, a sum of money was invested for the benefit of his children.[9] Cash gifts were sometimes given for exceptional service, as when Rogers, the fireman, was rewarded 'for the care he has taken in reducing the consumption of fuel',[10] and pensions were provided for those who retired through illness.[11] Later, the company decided that the shampooers should receive 12 days holiday with pay each year and, if sick, full pay for four weeks with half pay for a further four.[12]

On Friday 12 September 1862, The Hammam was visited for the first time by Major Robert Poore (Fig 9.3) who was living in nearby Bury Street. He visited again on 16 October and, according to his diary, on each of the following five days, sometimes even indicating how long he spent there.[13]

On Poore's third visit, Urquhart introduced himself, so beginning a lasting friendship between the two men, and later their families. Urquhart would have seen in him a man of principle who 'left the military service to which [he] was particularly attached on the ground ... that there was a certainty of a soldier's being illegally employed.'[14] Thirty-three years after Urquhart's death, Poore, himself now aged 76, still revered him, telling his daughter that one of his sayings, 'It is the business of a man's life to be right', was an 'invaluable gift to hand to my children.'[15]

Within a few weeks of meeting Poore, Urquhart introduced him to Rolland and eight days later, Poore agreed to take up shares in the company.[16]

Newly enamoured of the bath, he continued to record all his Turkish bath visits, at home and abroad, for two more years. The entry for 19 February 1863, 10 days after he became a director of the company,[17] notes that 'Nina Corry took her first Turkish bath.' It was something she presumably enjoyed; six days later Poore proposed to her and was accepted.[18]

By 1866 he was the largest shareholder with 600 shares[19] and he and his sons were to play an important part in the running of The Hammam

Fig 9.3
Major Robert Poore, who was to become the largest shareholder in the London & Provincial, and a lifelong friend of the Urquharts, seen here seen in 1911 at the age of 77.
(Wiltshire and Swindon Archives WSA 1915/168)

until it closed. He also became involved in the work of the FACs and, later, in promoting Urquhart's other political endeavours.

After the baths had been open a few months, it was clear that there would always be far fewer bathers than Urquhart had projected. In fact, the number was probably quite acceptable for a new venture where the charges were not particularly low. Nevertheless, the directors had every sensible reason to seek additional ways of augmenting their income.

Letting chambers in the main building was one obvious approach. The Jermyn Street building was renamed The St James' Private Hotel, and the necessary licences obtained in the name of Mrs Doggett.[20] The company had already let accommodation to Robert Douglas of Bond Street for a hairdressing salon with access from the baths and the street. This generated additional rent and augmented the facilities available to bathers.[21]

Altogether, cashflow was very healthy allowing the company to pay a first dividend of 6%, though it 'could have given eight, but preferred being careful.'[22]

By the time the baths had been open for a year, things were running smoothly, and staff relations were much better, unlike 'the very different spirit that at one time prevailed', wrote Harriet Urquhart to Frances Waldegrave, her brother Chichester's wife.

However, there had been 'an accident to the great sheet of glass' between the *frigidarium* and the *tepidarium*.

> I daresay Chichester has laughed at David's printed notices that 'fifty pounds penalty would be required from the person, or his executors, who by violent proceedings in the tank should break it.' Well it is broken at last, but by a shampooer.[23]

After another incident, the company was taken to court by Edward Adams who slipped on some steps and burnt his leg on a heated flue. He claimed negligence on the basis that at the time of the accident there was no handrail next to the steps, and was awarded £100 damages.[24]

The company also received complaints from their neighbours. A Mrs Roberts, in particular, claimed to have suffered financially and wrote, not for the first time, that the heat from the baths had made it impossible to let her cottage which adjoined them.

Although the board asked Hanrott to negotiate a sum as compensation for Mrs Roberts, no attempt seems to have been made to rectify the problem itself. Today it seems obvious that if escaping heat could be retained then less coal would be consumed, but very few Victorians were environmentally aware, and any practical science of insulation was non-existent.[25]

Somers Clarke, although previously congratulated by the board for his work on the design and conversion of the baths, showed himself less helpful in dealing with problems which arose after the settlement of his account with the company.

In the first place he had not handed over a copy of the plans, as is normal at the end of a contract. More serious was the dilatory manner in which he dealt with the architect's section of a report into a series of three accidents on the premises. In each of these, marble flooring slabs had collapsed beneath bathers.

After the last occurrence, Urquhart, who had three years experience of the effect of heat on marble floors at Riverside, sent a lengthy report for consideration by the board.

The slabs were laid on open brickwork and he had agreed with Somers Clarke that the distance between the supporting piers would nowhere be greater than nine inches (229mm). But the slabs had in fact only been supported by walls 2ft 6in (0.8m) apart in one direction, and not at all in the other.

Urquhart added other complaints, such as the placing of a courtyard which reduced the size of the washing areas, finally claiming that the alterations and repairs had cost the company hundreds of pounds.[26]

The board backed Urquhart, requesting Somers Clarke's response, and again asking for their plans to be forwarded.[27] But Somers Clarke's only response was to send a letter cutting all links with them.[28] The following week the board decided, probably without too much hope, to try to enforce their rightful claim to the plans, but there is no indication that they succeeded.[29]

The Hammam, it soon became apparent, was increasingly unlikely to become available to the working class; it was, on the contrary, becoming a very fashionable place in which to be seen.

An early visit by 'Prince Napoleon and suite' was duly noted in the press,[30] and after a royal visit in October 1865, Edinburgh's *Caledonian Mercury* ran a long column describing the bathing process headed 'The Prince of Wales in the bath.'[31] A shorter account in the *Huddersfield Chronicle* reported that the baths were reserved exclusively for the prince and Major Teesdale, and the visit had lasted under two hours.

Fig 9.4
The new façade of the converted hotel area, designed by Arthur Cates. (American Architect and Building News, *3 Nov 1871)*

> The Prince was waited upon by the manager of the bath and some of the principal shampooers. He conformed very readily to all the regulations of the establishment. Before quitting the Hammam, the Prince ordered a very handsome *baksheesh* to be distributed among the attendants, and expressed himself greatly pleased with his experience.[32]

Prince Napoleon later had a bath built for himself at the Palais Pompéien in Paris; the Prince of Wales preferred to visit the baths of others.

It was not long before there was informal talk of rebuilding the interior of the hotel, though the directors were still uncertain as to what facilities it should contain.

In the meantime, the small bath was converted into a private bath intended 'for the use of Ladies and Invalids.'[33] A further hot room was added to the main baths also. This was capable of providing 'a temperature varying between 200 degrees and 230 degrees',[34] and was heated by a 'new Radiating Apparatus recently patented by Mr Urquhart.'

Another 18 months passed before the board decided to turn the hotel into unfurnished men's chambers of the type popular around clubland. It was to be initially funded by a £5,000 loan from Major Poore in response to a letter, written by Crawshay on behalf of the board, which started:

> My dear Poore, I think I cannot recommend anything better for you to do with your £5000 than to lend it to this Company on Debenture at 5 per cent.[35]

This sum was later supplemented by a £13,000 bank loan.

Although the Crown had ensured that the façade of 76 Jermyn Street could not appear in any way 'Saracenic', there was evidently no objection to a new building as such, so long as it fitted in with its neighbours.

The company directors, though by now extremely dissatisfied with their architect, Somers Clarke, had been very pleased with Kirk & Parry, their builders, and appointed them to undertake the new work. This time, the architect was Arthur Cates (1829–1901) who had been a pupil of Sydney Smirke, designer of the great circular reading room at the British Museum. Cates contributed greatly to many organisations related to architecture, becoming vice-president of the Royal Institute of British Architects and completing the production of *The Dictionary of Architecture*, the nine-volume work published by the Architectural Publication Society. Unlike Somers Clarke, Cates had shares in the baths company and later became a director.

Although the chambers were not finished and advertised for letting until the beginning of 1871, The Hammam itself was only closed for two months towards the end of August 1868.

Entrance to the baths was now through the ground floor of the new red brick-faced building (Fig 9.4). Above were four floors of apartments, each of which comprised a reception room with curtained alcove for a bed, together with 'necessary conveniences attached.' A basement and a top floor accommodated staff and offices. The only design concession to indicate the function of The Hammam was a circular plaque decorated with a star and crescent placed over the central fourth-floor window.[36]

These symbols were to be widely found as part of the decorative schemes of Victorian Turkish baths. But their external use in this manner sometimes became a code to indicate the existence of a bath when it was not possible, or not desirable, to use a more obviously Turkish design as, for example, on the façade of the 1920s municipal baths at Plumstead (see page 169).

Shortly after the apartments were completed, it was finally decided to discontinue the women's baths. The Urquharts had moved abroad for health reasons late in 1864. Nevertheless David wrote to the board objecting strongly to the closure although, as usual in such cases, without success.[37]

In 1873, now resident (according to season) in Montreux, Nice, or St Gervais, Urquhart wrote again. This time it was to protest—perhaps with tongue in cheek, 'as a shareholder'—against a proposed increase in charges—the only time he ever acknowledged his share ownership.[38]

Reality—the inescapable drive for companies to make bigger profits—had finally defeated Urquhart's idealistic wish that The Hammam would be inexpensively open to all.

At the end of 1873, the agreement with Robert Douglas to run the hairdressing salon was ended, though it is not known at whose request.[39] The new contract, to take effect the following May, was with one of Douglas's staff, William Henry Penhaligon, an arrangement which was to be highly beneficial to both parties.[40] It was to last until the early 1890s when the enlarged Penhaligon & Jeavons moved up the road to 66 Jermyn Street to gain a second entrance round the corner in St James's Street.[41]

In addition to hairdressing, Penhaligon sold *eau de toilette* and perfume, and began to manufacture his own range. The most widely known was The Hammam Bouquet, probably created slightly later than the 1872 claimed by today's Penhaligon's—otherwise it would have belonged to William's employer Robert Douglas.

Urquhart died on 16 May 1877 in Naples on the way home from a trip to Egypt. It is an unsolved mystery why, in the minute book of a company which recorded illnesses and deaths of so many of its employees, there is no mention of Urquhart's death. Neither was there any indication as to whether a letter of condolence was sent to Harriet on behalf of the company which owed him so much.

Though the work of the FACs had long ceased, the reaction of his committee members was quite different. A memorial meeting was held in Manchester on 17 June organised by the Lancashire and Cheshire committees, and 25 of their surviving local members signed a letter to Harriet, respectfully venturing to 'intrude upon you in your great sorrow to express our heartfelt grief.'[42]

With this, and other letters of condolence in the Urquhart Papers at Balliol College, Oxford, is a printed leaflet containing a poem of remembrance by James Hindle, a committee member and owner of a Turkish bath in Ashton-under-Lyne. The poem, 'Daoud Bey', starts,

> As if made of steel,
> Seeing truth he spoke it,
> Falsehood finding, broke it
> On his hardest wheel.

Accompanying the leaflet is a letter to his brother John, secretary of the Stockport committee and, earlier, owner of a Turkish bath at Tiviot Dale. James apologised for his absence from the memorial meeting and concluded, 'It is a great work of good for Mr Urquhart to have done, had Turkish bathing been all he had attempted.'

The Hammam after Urquhart

Twenty years after the Jermyn Street site was acquired, the company finally leased the adjoining land in Ryder Yard, giving it space for expansion and access from Ryder Street. Both *The Lancet* and the *British Medical Journal* announced the company's intention to build additional hot rooms and, at the same time, noted that physicians could now use the baths at the reduced price of two shillings.[43]

The extension (Fig 9.5), completed shortly afterwards, led off the existing *frigidarium*, adding around 30ft (9m) to the length of the

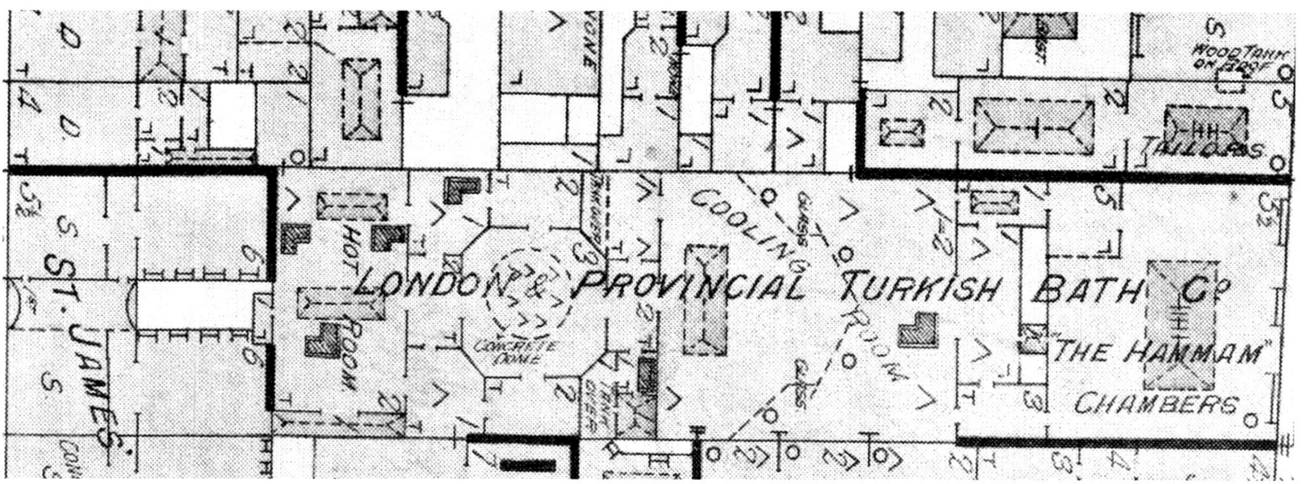

Fig 9.5
Detail from a Goad fire insurance map showing the extension of The Hammam with its additional entrance (left) in Ryder Street, and the Hammam Chambers entered from Jermyn Street (right).
(London Metropolitan Archives. City of London, LCC/VA/GOAD/A/1889)

building. In the centre was a smoking room, with extra toilets beyond, and an additional hot room on each side. On the floor above, a new laundry and drying room was built over the smoking room.[44] Also around this time, Mr Gregory, a chiropodist from Bond Street, rented one of the downstairs divans bringing in another £75 per annum and adding to the facilities available to bathers.[45]

But new facilities alone did not guarantee a well-run establishment. With the deaths of Urquhart and (four years later) Rolland, standards at The Hammam declined. One regular bather who became dissatisfied was Thomas Gibson Bowles (Fig 9.6), founder of *Vanity Fair* and *The Lady*, and grandfather of the Mitford sisters.

He bought himself a single share in 1882, had himself elected to the board, and took it upon himself to become a one-man ginger group, an activity not always combined with tact and modesty. By the old guard, Bowles was regarded, if not as a threat, then certainly by implication as a critic of their own unwillingness to put things right.

George Crawshay had been elected chairman of the company after Rolland's death, but there were fewer board meetings because it was difficult to achieve a quorum. Crawshay lived in Newcastle and soon had to be replaced as chairman by General Keane who, together with Major Poore, Dr Lockhart Robertson and Francis Francis, became the most frequent attenders. But the last-named director had recently had a severe stroke and, of the others, only General Keane lived in London.

The son of Francis Francis, also named Francis, was another holder of a single share, though not yet himself a member of the board. He wrote to a friend,

> I was in at the Turkish bath the other day. They tell me that the new Director, 'Vanity Fair' Bowles had rather upset the formerly placid order of things there. He swaggers about in the bath advertising himself as a Director, & 'means to have things done properly,' etc, bullies the servants & so forth ...[46]

Bowles wrote a long letter to his fellow directors. The two main issues related to the decline in the standard of shampooing, and the bad choice of materials used in refurbishing one of the washing rooms.

> It is not that the Shampooers of the Hammam have any want of energy or any want of industry. It is that they lack knowledge of the very difficult art of Shampooing. They do the best they know, no doubt, but they do not know the best for they lack the traditions that are behind the Eastern Shampooer ...[47]

Fig 9.6
*Caricature by 'Spy' of Thomas Gibson Bowles ('Tommy'), the one-man ginger group aiming to return The Hammam to its previous high standards. (*Vanity Fair*, 13 July 1869, Author's collection)*

Such standards would have appalled Urquhart, but the matter of the refurbishment of the washing room was even more important. Bowles had been informed that the alterations had been carried out 'in accordance with the usual system pursued in the management of affairs', and he argued that, except in an emergency, such work should not be carried out in future without authorisation.

Bowles had pinpointed a total lack of financial control in the daily running of The Hammam, and the absence of any line of control between the board and the company's management. A subdued board gave him the authority to rectify matters.

Two indicators tell us a little more about the type of bathers using the baths in the mid-1880s. First, a notice, warning bathers to be careful how they walked on the wet marble floors, was written not only in English, but also in French and German, suggesting that The Hammam was well used by visitors from abroad.[48]

Second, a list of periodicals selected for the cooling-room in 1887,

Blackwood's
Cornhill Magazine
Fortnightly Review
Longman's Magazine
Macmillan's Magazine, and
United Service Gazette

enables a comparison to be made with a similar list from the City of Gloucester Baths Committee just over a decade later,

Answers
Graphic
Pearson's Royal
Strand
Tit-Bits

all of which, they decided, should be sent to Gloucester hospitals after use.[49]

Perhaps the most gifted person to be employed at The Hammam was Sutherland Macdonald (Fig 9.7) who was appointed steward at the end of 1888. He was already knowledgeable about Turkish baths, having grown up in those which his father Robert opened in Guildford around 1874, and ran for 20 years.[50] As a young man, Sutherland spent some years in the army where, as an accomplished artist, he learned to tattoo, rapidly becoming an expert (Fig 9.8). On leaving the army he ran a small Turkish bath and tattooing service in Aldershot.[51]

Once installed at The Hammam, the 28-year-old Macdonald set up a tattooing salon in 'a large airy room on the basement'.[52] He achieved great fame there, tattooing numerous famous clients of both sexes, including several crowned heads. He bought 30 shares in the baths company in 1897, only disposing of them, and 30 others subsequently purchased, in 1937.[53]

With the baths now also able to offer a variety of additional facilities, its reputation abroad continued to attract eminent visitors. One such was the Shah of Persia (now Iran) who evidently much enjoyed his bath, and purchased 'a dozen scent-sprinklers' from Penhaligon's before leaving.[54]

Around this period, relationships between the various directors were not as smooth as

Fig 9.7
Gambier Bolton's rare photograph of Sutherland Macdonald, Steward of The Hammam, shareholder, and tattooist extraordinaire. *(Source unknown)*

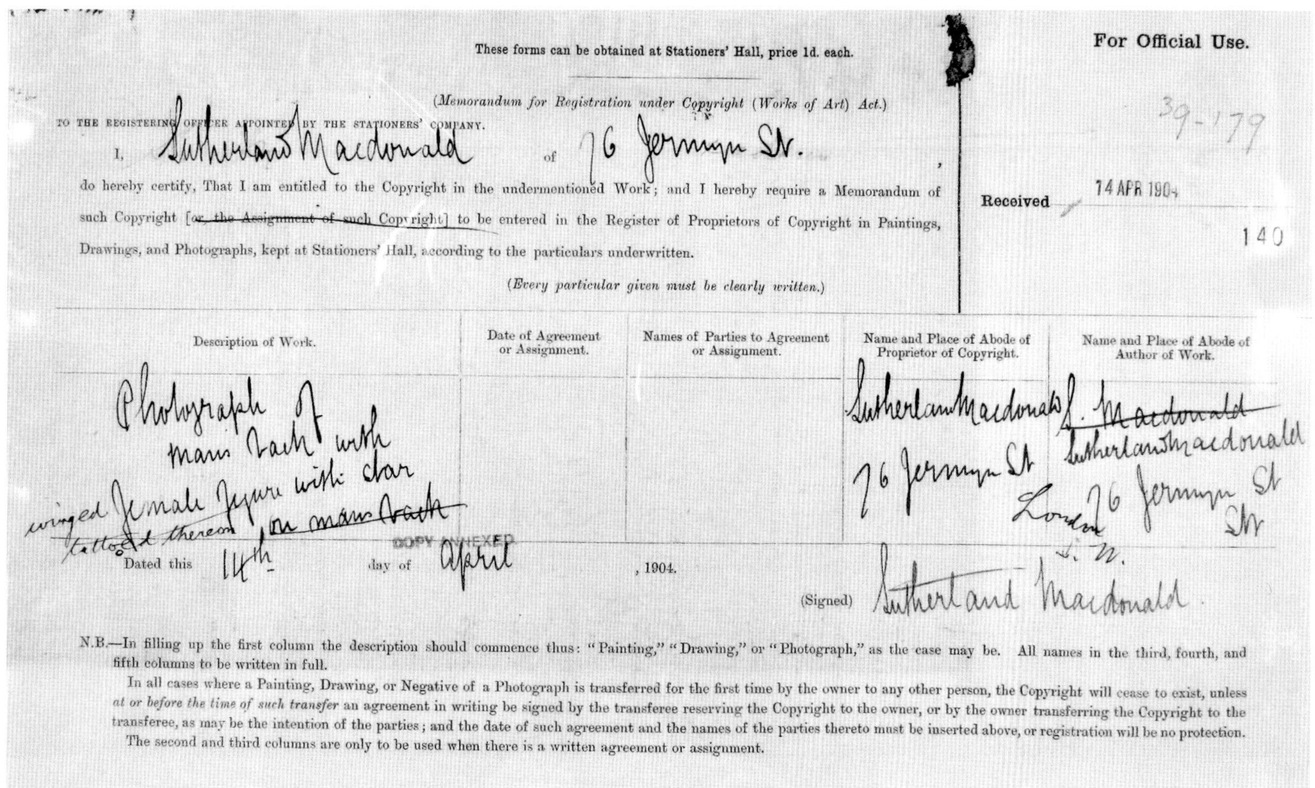

These forms can be obtained at Stationers' Hall, price 1d. each.

(*Memorandum for Registration under Copyright (Works of Art) Act.*)

For Official Use.

39-179

Received 14 APR 1904

140

TO THE REGISTERING OFFICER APPOINTED BY THE STATIONERS' COMPANY.

I, Sutherland Macdonald of 76 Jermyn St.,

do hereby certify, That I am entitled to the Copyright in the undermentioned Work; and I hereby require a Memorandum of such Copyright [~~or the Assignment of such Copyright~~] to be entered in the Register of Proprietors of Copyright in Paintings, Drawings, and Photographs, kept at Stationers' Hall, according to the particulars underwritten.

(*Every particular given must be clearly written.*)

Description of Work.	Date of Agreement or Assignment.	Names of Parties to Agreement or Assignment.	Name and Place of Abode of Proprietor of Copyright.	Name and Place of Abode of Author of Work.
Photograph of man's back with winged female figure with star tattooed thereon ~~on man's back~~			Sutherland Macdonald 76 Jermyn St	~~S. Macdonald~~ Sutherland Macdonald 76 Jermyn St London S.W.

COPY ANNEXED

Dated this 14th day of April, 1904.

(Signed) Sutherland Macdonald.

N.B.—In filling up the first column the description should commence thus: "Painting," "Drawing," or "Photograph," as the case may be. All names in the third, fourth, and fifth columns to be written in full.

In all cases where a Painting, Drawing, or Negative of a Photograph is transferred for the first time by the owner to any other person, the Copyright will cease to exist, unless *at or before the time of such transfer* an agreement in writing be signed by the transferee reserving the Copyright to the owner, or by the owner transferring the Copyright to the transferee, as may be the intention of the parties; and the date of such agreement and the names of the parties thereto must be inserted above, or registration will be no protection.

The second and third columns are only to be used when there is a written agreement or assignment.

Fig 9.8
Sutherland Macdonald's signed application (sent from 76 Jermyn Street on 14 April 1904) for copyright on a photograph of one of his tattoos on a man's back. (The National Archives. Copyright Office, Stationers' Company COPY 1/472/140. Author's photograph)

once they had been. Several crises occurred, one to do with travel expenses drawn by Major Poore. Another appeared to be a thwarted coup by several members of the board. Fortunately, none of this seemed directly to affect the running of the baths.

The last years of The Hammam

Towards the end of the 1890s, and well into the first decade of the 20th century, there were a number of significant alterations to the building and its facilities but, unlike earlier changes, it has not been possible to determine exactly when each occurred.

The first company minute book was filled by the early 1890s and only survived because it was taken home by Major Poore and kept with his other papers, now to be found at the Wiltshire & Swindon History Centre. The second minute book was lost during World War II.

Electricity was installed some time between February 1891 and May 1892, when advertisements in *The Times*—which offered shop or office space 'on the ground-floor entrance to the Hammam'—first included the phrase 'with electric light fittings'.[55]

In March 1890 there had been a discussion about whether Urquhart's Islamic-*hammam*-style platform in the centre of the *frigidarium* should be removed—an idea which would have infuriated him. Nevertheless, a photograph published in 1902 shows men still being massaged on it (Fig 9.9),[56] although by the 1930s, a Hammam brochure—published (or reprinted) soon after Frank Fells became manager in 1928—shows an attractive new shampooing room replacing one of the old washing rooms (Fig 9.10).[57] Another photograph shows a gallery with additional divans above those on the ground floor, and exactly matching them (Fig 9.11).

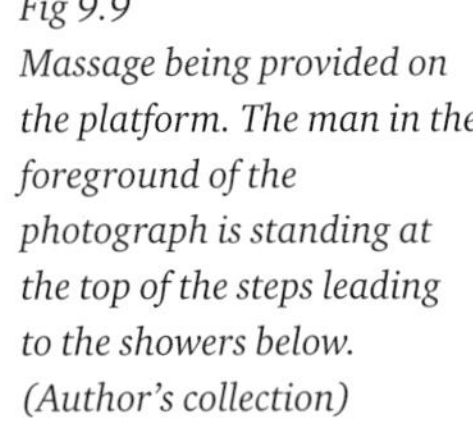

Fig 9.9
Massage being provided on the platform. The man in the foreground of the photograph is standing at the top of the steps leading to the showers below. (Author's collection)

These additions were part of a major extension designed in 1907 by London architect Ernest Fletch (1866–1929), and in use by 1908.[58] It included the gallery, and a much larger basement area. Here, for the first time, and well away from the dry heat areas, a Russian steam bath was installed, and proudly advertised.[59]

The directors' innate conservatism seems to have disappeared almost overnight with the addition of every conceivable passing fad—including 'Pine and Electric Light Baths, *Vichy and Aix Douches, Galvanic and Sinnsoidal [sic] Treatments, Electric Vibrators and Liver Packs'—all in order to challenge a new establishment opening round the corner in (Duke of) York Street (Fig 9.12). This perceived threat of competition also spurred The Hammam Board to register their logo which had already been in use for some time (9.13). Within a couple of years, the new establishment was to expand and gain an entrance further down Jermyn Street at No.92, when it would be renamed The Savoy Turkish Baths.[60]

In truth, although writers about Turkish baths seem constantly to confuse the two establishments, their clients never did. They belonged to different classes, expecting to pay different prices. While The Hammam was charging 6s in the morning and 4s after noon, the Savoy was charging 3s all day long. The Hammam closed at nine o'clock in the evening, and a sleeping cubicle cost 5s 6d per night; the Savoy baths were open all night and charged 5s including a bed.

The number of bathers at The Hammam, and therefore its profits, only started to decline in 1933; and in 1940, seriously affected by the war and the bombing which began in September, it made a loss for the first time.[61]

A NEW TURKISH BATH HOUSE.

York House Hydro,

12, YORK STREET, JERMYN STREET, ST. JAMES', S.W.

(AT BACK OF ST. JAMES' CHURCH, PICCADILLY).

OPEN DAY AND NIGHT. . . . . . NEVER CLOSED.

PORTION OF SHAMPOOING ROOM.

Hydropathic Treatment as at Matlock, Buxton, Harrogate, Bath, &c.

FIXED MODERATE TARIFF:

TURKISH BATH, Including Vapour Bath and Shampoo ... 3/-
ELECTRIC LIGHT BATH 4/-
VIBRATORY MASSAGE 3/-
ELECTRICAL Do. 3/-
HAND Do. 3/-

AIX DOUCHE 3/6
VICHY DOUCHE 4/-
ELECTRIC WATER BATH 5/-
ALCOHOL RUBBING 1/6
LIVER PACKS 3/-

NAUHEIM BATHS, HIGH FREQUENCY TREATMENT and other MEDICAL APPLICATIONS GIVEN UNDER PRESCRIPTION ONLY.

SUITES—BACHELOR CHAMBERS IN CONNECTION WITH THE BATHS

TO LET AT MODERATE RENTALS.

Figs 9.10 and 9.11 (top). Two images from the brochure published in the 1930s show recently added facilities. A shampooing room (left) has replaced one of the original washing rooms, and the interior of the frigidarium *(right) shows the newly constructed upper floor, and the use of sofas downstairs. (Wiltshire and Swindon Archives WSA 1915/220)*

*Fig 9.12 (above) Possible competition from new baths round the corner. These were actually aimed at a different clientele, and prices were accordingly much lower. (*Winning Post Summer Annual, 1908*)*

Fig 9.13 (right)
The company logo, now registered at Stationers' Hall under the Copyright Acts in force from 1842 to 1912.
(The National Archives Copyright Office, Stationers' Company COPY1/270, 214)

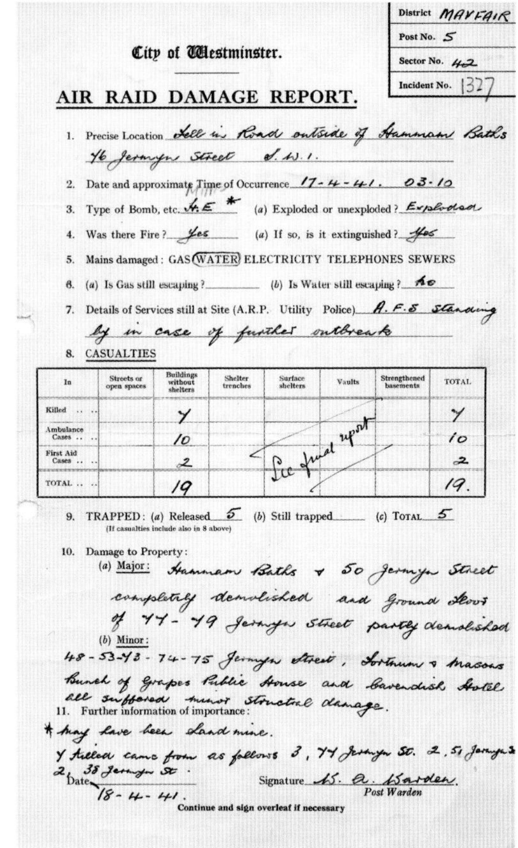

District MAYFAIR
Post No. 5
Sector No. 42
Incident No. 1327

City of Westminster.

AIR RAID DAMAGE REPORT.

1. Precise Location Fell in Road outside of Hammam Baths 76 Jermyn Street S.W.1.
2. Date and approximate Time of Occurrence 17-4-41. 03-10
3. Type of Bomb, etc. H.E * (a) Exploded or unexploded? Exploded
4. Was there Fire? Yes (a) If so, is it extinguished? Yes
5. Mains damaged: GAS (WATER) ELECTRICITY TELEPHONES SEWERS
6. (a) Is Gas still escaping? (b) Is Water still escaping? No
7. Details of Services still at Site (A.R.P. Utility Police) A.F.S standing by in case of further outbreak
8. CASUALTIES

In	Streets or open spaces	Buildings without shelters	Shelter trenches	Surface shelters	Vaults	Strengthened basements	TOTAL
Killed		7					7
Ambulance Cases		10					10
First Aid Cases		2					2
TOTAL		19					19.

See final report

9. TRAPPED: (a) Released 5 (b) Still trapped (c) Total 5
(If casualties include also in 8 above)
10. Damage to Property:
(a) Major: Hammam Baths + 50 Jermyn Street completely demolished and Ground floor of 77-79 Jermyn Street partly demolished
(b) Minor: 48-53-73-74-75 Jermyn Street, Fortnum + Masons Bunch of Grapes Public House and Cavendish Hotel all suffered minor structural damage.
11. Further information of importance:
* may have been Land mine.
7 killed came from as follows 3, 77 Jermyn St. 2, 51 Jermyn St 2, 38 Jermyn St.

Date 18-4-41. Signature [illegible] Warden.
Post Warden

Continue and sign overleaf if necessary

Fig 9.14 (far right)
Cyclostyled air raid damage report on the destruction of The Hammam, 17 April 1941.
(City of Westminster Archives Centre)

On 13 December the company announced that they were closing the baths and winding up the company. All debts would be paid and it was expected that shareholders would eventually be fully repaid.[62] The closure was just in time.

Fig 9.15 (below)
The aftermath of the destruction of The Hammam.
(City of Westminster Archives Centre)

At ten past three on the morning of 17 April 1941, a high explosive bomb (Fig 9.14) or land mine fell in Jermyn Street outside the baths which were completely destroyed (Fig 9.15). Seven people were killed and twelve people injured, though fortunately the baths and chambers were empty at the time.[63]

Finally, on 1 May 1944, Helena Francis, who had inherited five shares from Francis Francis, received a first payment of £22 10s for them, with a further 5s 8d on 22 January 1948.[64]

In the company's original lease, the Crown Surveyor had stipulated, as a condition of being allowed to build behind the hotel, that in the event of the baths closing, the site had to be returned to its appearance at the time of the lease being granted. So the site of the baths has not been built on since, and by 2012 had become an office car park, the 21st-century equivalent of the original stables and courtyard.

PART III

PROBLEMS AND ATTITUDES

10

Early problems and controversies

From our 21st-century perspective it might seem surprising that the first Victorian Turkish baths should have presented so many practical problems, or caused so much controversy.

After all, vapour bath establishments had been around for a considerable time, some of them also providing a range of medicated vapours. In the first half of the 19th century alone, there were, for example, Sake Deen Mahomed's vapour baths in Brighton (Fig 10.1),[1] and Mathias Roth's Russian baths in London (Fig 10.2).[2]

At first glance, the only immediately noticeable technical difference between the established vapour, steam, or Russian bath on the one hand, and the Victorian Turkish bath on the other, is that in a Russian bath, sweat is produced by bathing in a room full of hot vapour, while in a Victorian Turkish bath, sweat is produced by bathing in a room, or rooms, heated by hot dry air.

Why then was there so much controversy, and so many issues to be resolved? It seems as though there was almost no aspect of the bath which was not controversial.

Here we examine a few of the technical problems which the 19th-century innovators had to conquer, and in the next chapter we look at some of the (frequently prejudiced) attitudes which had to be overcome.

However, this division into technical and attitudinal considerations is an artificial one. It should not be assumed that the solution to every

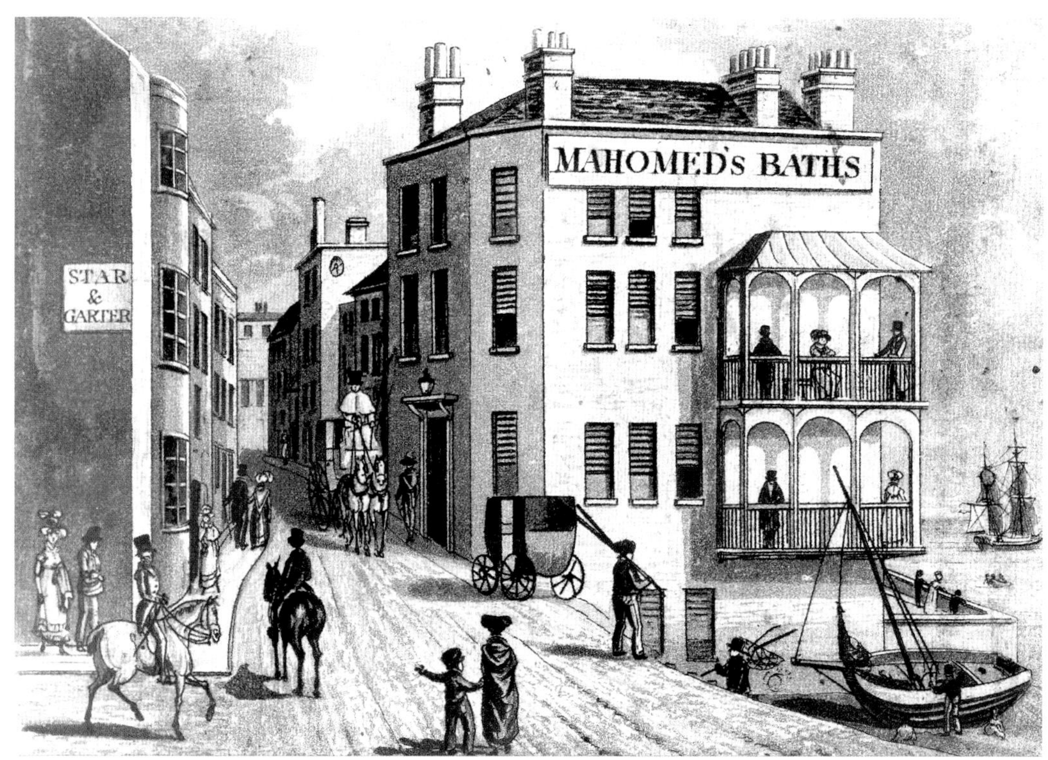

Fig 10.1
Mahomed's Medicated Baths, Brighton.
(Royal Pavilion and Museums, Brighton & Hove)

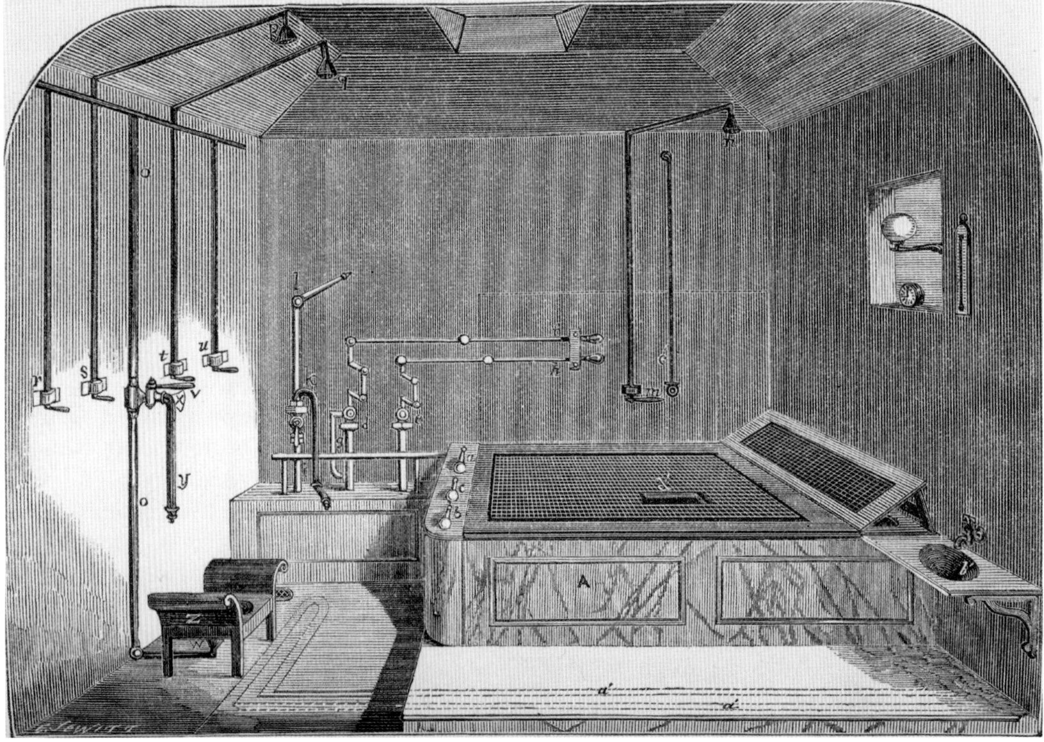

Fig 10.2
Roth's Russian Bath in London, 1855.
(Mathias Roth, The Russian bath, *Groombridge, 1855.*
© The British Library Board, 7470.d.58 [frontispiece])

technical problem was completely unaffected by the attitudes of those discussing them.

Heating the air

The problems faced by the Turkish bath builders were, first, how to raise the temperature of the air in the hot rooms to the high levels needed, and second, how to maintain it there for long periods without destroying the stove in the process.

But when considering, for example, the effort expended in developing the technology needed to heat air to around 200–240°F (93–116°C), it should not be assumed that everyone agreed that such high temperatures were necessary, or desirable, even in the *laconicum*, or hottest room.

The first Victorian Turkish baths were heated using the traditional Roman hypocaust, continuing the approach followed in eastern baths built during the period of the Ottoman Empire.

The Romans may not have been able to measure a specific temperature, but they knew that it was hot enough to ensure that bathers wore wooden *pattens to avoid burning their feet. Victorian bath builders soon realised that the hot floors could be dangerous if a patten slipped off, or if someone fell and was unable to get up quickly enough.

As the Romans had done, the Victorians also began to conduct the heated air in ducts behind the walls. These were separated from the seating by a gap, so the bathers were not at risk of burning their backs.

Then, early in 1861, Dr John Adams Bolton (Fig 10.3) devised and patented 'An Improved Apparatus for Heating Turkish Baths, Public and Private Buildings, Vineries, Hothouses, and Cooking Ovens'.[3] This was described by one journalist as ensuring that 'the pure, fresh air of heaven, already heated to any degree, is directly admitted into the bath chamber, from the external atmosphere'.[4]

Bolton's own Turkish bath, which he opened on 8 April at 9 New Street in Leicester, became the first in which heated air was circulated through the rooms.[5] By the following year, it had already been installed to replace an earlier unsuccessful system at the Newcastle-on-Tyne Infirmary, where Dr Bolton's younger brother Andrew was house surgeon.[6]

In the Leicester establishment, fresh cold air was guided over heated metal plates covering the furnace so that the hot air was completely separated from the combustion fumes and smoke. The clean hot air then flowed in a continuous current through the hot rooms until it escaped outside the building through a grating.

Fig 10.3
John Adams Bolton, whose bath was the first to have hot air circulating through the rooms. His younger brother, Dr Andrew Bolton, was house surgeon at the Newcastle-upon-Tyne Infirmary, the first hospital to install a Turkish bath. (Courtesy of Dr A R Bolton, great-great-grandson of Dr Andrew Bolton—of the Edinburgh Infirmary—who was Dr John Adams Bolton's younger brother)

Quite separately from this, the hot smoke from the furnace, on its way out through the chimney, was first diverted through floor-level ducts around the rooms and back again, so that *its* heat could also be used. The ducts were partially hidden, being covered by cushioned benches which bathers could then sit or lie on.

Bolton's bath had been designed by local architect Francis E Drake (*fl* 1868). He was so buoyed by its success that he placed advertisements in *The Times*, and a variety of local newspapers around the country, stating that he would,

> be happy to PREPARE PLANS OF TURKISH BATHS, treated on entirely New Principles, as recently erected in Leicester, and which have been Patented, and completely remove all objections against the Turkish Baths as hitherto employed.[7]

Though Bolton's heated metal plates were never universally adopted, circulating the heated fresh air through the hot rooms was an important development. It was an improvement on earlier methods of heating the bath, and it impacted on the inextricably linked problem of ventilating it.

Previously, a way had to be found of disposing of the stale, sweat-laden air because effective electric fans were not available until the development of Nikola Tesla's alternating current motors in the 1880s.[8]

But when fresh cold air was drawn into the furnace room from outside, heated, and then passed through the hot rooms until it escaped outside through a ventilator, the heating and ventilation of the bath was carried out simultaneously (Fig 10.4).

The Leicester bath was generally considered to be an improvement on existing ones. Drake later wrote that while he was there he had seen 'as many as thirty bathers present at one time' without 'the slightest disagreeable odour.'[9]

But it was not quite that simple. Dr Edward Haughton (Fig 10.5), manager of the Oriental Baths at 113 Mulberry Street, Liverpool, had visited two establishments heated on Bolton's principles. In one of them, he wrote in a letter to the *Medical Times*, the furnace door was red hot 'showing a pretty rapid combustion of fuel', and 'the "pure, fresh air" was, in both cases, obtained from the dusty precincts of the stoke-hole.'[10]

Haughton had a valid point. Bolton's system used his own patent air heater. Elsewhere, the air circulation principle itself did not always produce the expected continuous flow of fresh hot air because of the nature of the then commonly used cockle furnace. This was originally designed to heat the large areas typically

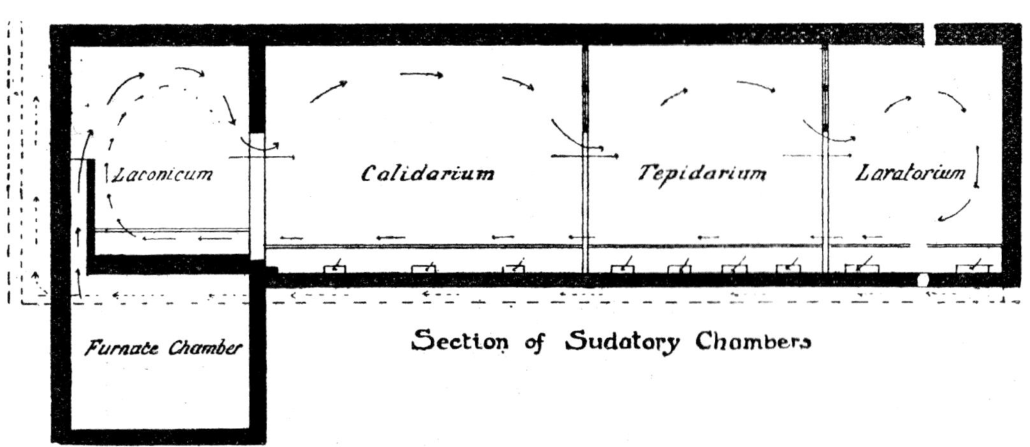

Fig 10.4
The flow of hot air through the rooms of a Turkish bath. (Robert Owen Allsop, The Turkish bath, *Spon, 1890 p.84)*

Fig 10.5
Edward Haughton: hydropathist, author, and baths manager.
(Richard Metcalfe, The rise and progress of hydropathy, *Simkin Marshall, 1912, p.142)*

required in manufacturing processes such as drying sugar in a refining-house or for large buildings such as the innovative Derby Infirmary designed by William Strutt in 1810.

It was popular in such locations because, although the area to be heated was much larger than that to be found in any room in the average house (where wood or coal were usually burned in a fireplace), the air temperature required was little different from that in a house.

The cockle stove maximised the heat obtained by placing a large metal dome directly above an open furnace, the air being heated as it passed over the dome.[11]

Unfortunately, the harshness of the heat gradually destroyed the dome, and minute particles of metal were carried along with the airflow to be inhaled by the bathers. Another hazard was the danger of fire if the air flow was insufficient and the dome overheated.

The invention of the Convoluted Stove (Fig 10.6) in 1866 by two Turkish bath proprietors, Joseph Constantine (Oxford Street, Manchester) and Thomas Whitaker (Bridge Street, Bolton),[12] was a major improvement. It avoided overheating, completely separated the required hot air from the poisonous furnace fumes, and saved fuel while protecting the stove by ensuring a slow and uniform rate of combustion.[13] The stove, which was also manufactured by William Crumblehulme & Sons, gradually became an industry standard, as well as being used to heat such large buildings as Manchester's first Free Trade Hall and numerous smaller halls and churches around the country.

Not all managements necessarily adopted a stove which was only later recognised as being superior. Kidderminster was not the first council to have its heating and flue systems fail, but few local papers took such glee in their difficulties as *The Kidderminster Shuttle*.[14]

> THE TURKISH BATH.—Malignant are the stars which preside over the inception of this institution. The difficulties which retard its realisation form an epos of no mean interest. On Tuesday, after months of delay, it was opened to the public, and on Wednesday it incontinently closed. Eight gentlemen were properly stewed in their own gravy, shampooed, bathed, and dismissed rejoicing in the feeling of a renewed physical nature on the Tuesday. But on Wednesday morning the heating apparatus broke down, and hot smoke, instead of pure hot air, [poured] into the sweating rooms. Numerous would-be bathers called during the day, but had to be disappointed. The Baths Committee meet to-day.

Providing air at the right temperature for Turkish baths moved the boundaries of heating science forward. On 30 April 1879, John Leck Bruce (1850–1921) read a paper before the Glasgow Philosophical Society describing a comparative study of the heating and ventilation of the Turkish baths at two of the city's baths clubs, the Victoria and the Arlington. This appears to be the first time that heat loss calculations had been used in this context and, possibly, in any other building context.

The Arlington (see page 229) opened in 1871. Its Turkish baths were heated by two Constantine Convoluted Stoves. The Victoria (see page 231) opened in 1877, and its Turkish baths were heated by one of Pennycook's Patent Caloric Multitubular Stoves.

Bruce's detailed study considered all aspects of the problem, including the different stoves, temperatures, air flow and the design of the baths themselves. He concluded that heating power should be 'slightly in excess of the theoretical requirements', 'that the air as it leaves the stoves should be kept at the lowest temperature which will supply the requisite heat', and that increasing 'the quantity of air passed through the stoves … will secure at once better ventilation in the rooms and better value from the stoves.'[15]

Even for the non-technical interloper, Bruce's paper makes fascinating reading, especially its account of the difficulties experienced in making the measurements. It was favourably received in the *Builder*,[16] and Joseph Constantine, in congratulating Bruce on his paper, said that it would be,

> of the greatest possible help in the scientific consideration of the subject of heating generally, which, with the kindred subject of ventilation, is at present sadly in want of a definite basis of facts. Not only are the conclusions valuable, but the method pursued will be a good guide to future experimenters.[17]

However, in spite of the gradual improvement in stoves, boilers, and heating systems, and the replacement of coal, coke, and anthracite by oil, it appears that at least one cockle furnace survived to heat the air at Bartholomew's Baths, in the City of Bath, until well into the late 1940s.

The 'correct' temperatures and humidity

There were almost as many opinions as to the correct temperature and humidity required in each part of the Victorian Turkish bath as there were individual establishments and individual (self-proclaimed) experts.

Discussion about temperatures started with the building of the first bath and continued long afterwards. Many early proponents of the bath were avid pamphleteers and letter writers, sometimes making quite personal attacks on each other. There was no shortage of letters or comment in *The Lancet* and the *British Medical Journal*[18] because there were no precedents for supposedly correct temperatures or humidity.

Some writers, like Dr Edward Haughton, suggested that the baths in Constantinople *did* provide a precedent. He had measured the temperatures in several baths there, finding that the rooms were typically around 77°F, 95°F [25°C, 35°C], and (as an absolute maximum in the hottest room) 104°F [40°C].[19]

There was disagreement even on this. Dr Robert Wollaston had also taken his thermometer to the baths in Constantinople where he 'invariably found the hot room verging about 150°F or 160°F [66°C or 71°C].'[20]

One of the reasons for such discrepancies is that only rarely does a writer indicate the height at which the thermometer was placed in the bath. That this makes a significant difference is immediately apparent when rising from a sitting to a standing position in any Turkish bath or modern sauna.

But none of these temperatures was really relevant because the air in the Victorian Turkish bath was dry, whereas in the *hammams* of Constantinople it was usually extremely humid, not to say steamy. And, as George Wyld and several other doctors pointed out,

> In the treatment of certain forms of disease, the hot-air bath … can be borne at a temperature of 250°F [121°C], while the thick-steam bath can scarcely be endured at 115°F [46°C], or the hot-water bath at 100°F [38°C].[21]

ALL CHURCHES, CHAPELS, SCHOOLS, AND PUBLIC BUILDINGS

CAN BE THOROUGHLY WARMED AND VENTILATED WITH LITTLE FUEL BY THE PATENT

CONVOLUTED STOVE.

Efficiency in all cases Guaranteed.

THE CONVOLUTED STOVE supplies a want which has long been felt. The largest building can now be warmed with ease. This is proved by the complete success of the apparatus at the ROYAL EXCHANGE and the FREE TRADE HALL, Manchester (two of the largest rooms in the world).

Two large Convoluted Stoves fixed in the basement warm the immense area of the ROYAL EXCHANGE most effectually, and with less labour and fuel than are required for small churches under the old system. The coke consumed from the 1st of November, 1875, to the 30th of April, 1876, was 21 tons 12 cwt. 2 qrs. (costing £8. 0s. 0d.), being less than 2½ cwt. for every 24 hours the building was warmed. The consumption of coke at the FREE TRADE HALL for the four winters commencing 1872 has been 17 tons 16 cwt. 2 qrs., being an average of 4 tons 9 cwt. 14 lbs, costing about £2. 10s. for the whole winter. The Exchange is warmed daily, but the Free Trade Hall only in very cold weather for the evening, a comfortable temperature being produced with four hours' firing.

In both the above cases references are kindly permitted.

Estimates and Plans of Warming arrangements for Churches, Chapels, and Schools, Town Halls, Hotels, Mansions, Halls, Workhouses, Turkish Baths, Disinfecting Rooms, Warehouses, Drying Rooms, Shops, Offices, &c., on receipt of tracing showing area to be warmed, and situation of apparatus chamber.

For Illustrated Circular, with Testimonials, address

J. CONSTANTINE,

CONVOLUTED STOVE WORKS, Chorlton Mills, Hulme Street; or 23, Oxford Street, Manchester.

[See Testimonials over.]

Fig 10.6
Leaflet advertising Constantine's Convoluted Stove.
(Author's collection)

It was not just that dry air could be *tolerated* at higher temperatures. The whole rationale behind Barter's use of dry air was that an air bath was most effective therapeutically when the temperature *was* higher. He found that '... visible vapour was a great imperfection' and after much study substituted pure air for vapour. This was also safer, as well as being more agreeable for the bathers.[22]

Barter patented his dry-air bath, calling it 'The Improved Turkish Bath'.[23] Some, including Urquhart, ridiculed this name, implying arrogance, and assuming that the improvement related to the dryness of the air.

But Barter's patent was about economising fuel by reheating already used (and still warm) air—a bad idea which was to cause him trouble in the near future. But the sobriquet 'Improved' may have come about because, in British law, the subject of a valid patent application must be either a new invention or an improvement on one; Barter's was for an 'improved' air circuit to save fuel.

But Urquhart had earlier been honest enough to admit that the dryness of the air *was* important. When, in 1856, Barter had reprinted the chapters from *The Pillars of Hercules* which dealt with the bath, Urquhart wrote,

> Postscript: the foregoing [book] was written ten years ago; the part on the Turkish bath still ten years earlier ... I cannot suffer this reprint without stating, that I had then but most imperfectly apprehended the value of HOT AIR, to which, as distinguished from vapour, the Turkish bath owes its peculiar excellence. D.U.[24]

It was Dr Thudichum who put it most forcibly, in a lecture on the bath to the Royal Society of Medicine.

> The discovery that was lost and has been found again, is this, in the fewest possible words: The application of hot air to the human body. It is not wet air, nor moist air, nor vapoury air; it is not vapour in any shape or form whatever. It is an immersion of the whole body in hot common air.[25]

In practice the air was never *completely* dry. However carefully the spaces required for sweating, plunging, shampooing, and relaxing were positioned to maintain a separation between dry and wet areas (Fig 10.7), it was not possible. Every time a wet bather entered the dry rooms, every time a door opened, air which was slightly damp penetrated the dry areas. But compared with a *hammam*, the hot rooms of a Victorian Turkish bath were dry.

Needless to say, there were also some doctors who maintained that a *reasonable* amount of humidity was not only desirable, but absolutely essential. The twin problems of humidity and temperature much exercised their minds.

In 1861 *The Lancet* reported the registration of a new company set up to re-establish the Roman bath in Cambridge. It noted that, in order to reassure medical people, the company would consult doctors about what would be the most appropriate temperatures for the hot rooms in their projected new baths in Jesus Lane.[26] During the following weeks, several doctors wrote to express their views but without any consensus becoming apparent.

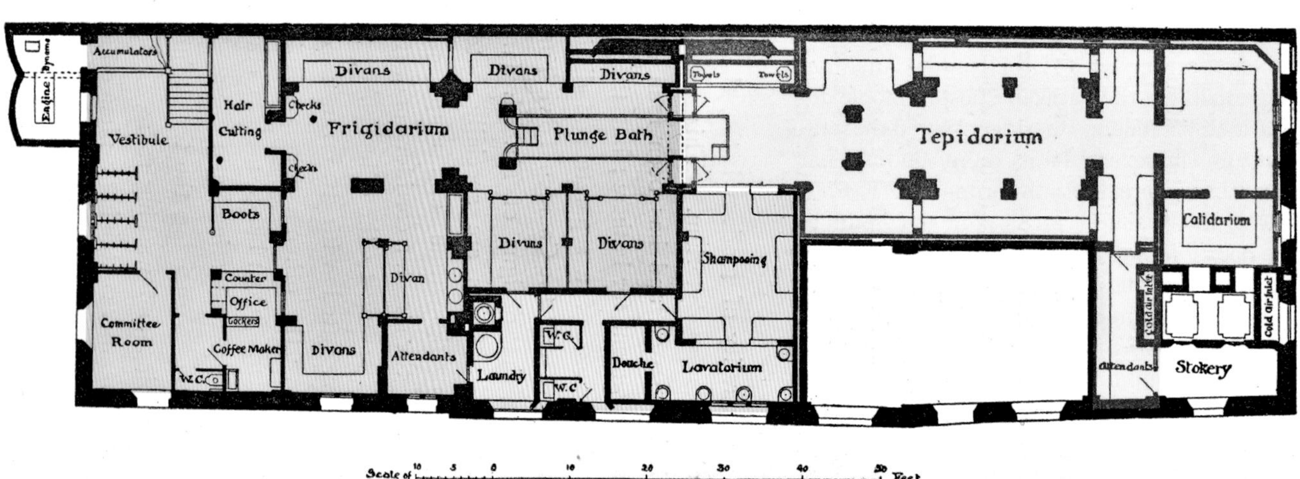

Fig 10.7
The separation of wet and dry areas in a Victorian Turkish bath.
(Robert Owen Allsop, The Turkish bath, *Spon, 1890, p.21)*

By all accounts it seems that, until the mid-1860s, the maximum temperature in Turkish baths in Ireland—almost all built by Dr Barter, or under his guidance—was 160°F (71°C).

In the remainder of the British Isles, where Urquhart was the greater influence, top temperatures were sometimes slightly higher. Exceptionally, by 1866, the Jermyn Street Hammam had a *laconicum* which, by means of a radiator, was able to reach a temperature of 220°F (104°C).

After the invention of the Convoluted Stove in 1866, though not necessarily as a *direct* result, temperatures generally rose. From then until the end of the 19th century, the average *tepidarium* would be maintained somewhere between 125°F (52°C) and 140°F (60°C), the *caldarium* between 170°F (77°C) and 180°F (82°C), and the *laconicum* between 230°F (110°C) and 240°F (116°C).

Setting standards

These later temperatures were probably considerably influenced by the recommendations of Robert Owen Allsop who had written a series of articles on the design of Turkish baths. Almost nothing is known about Allsop except that he was an engineer rather than an architect. He wrote three books on baths of various types, followed by *Engineering work in public buildings*, a travel book, and an article on Norwich for a popular magazine.

Allsop's articles on the Turkish bath appeared in *Building News* between 1888 and 1889, and were published as a book the following year, soon becoming the standard work on the subject. Allsop recommended that hot rooms should be provided at 120°F (49°C), 140°F (60°C), 180°F (82°C) and 250°F (121°C).[27]

Another influence was the architect Alfred Hessell Tiltman (1854–1910). Though his architectural practice was not particularly successful, he was adept at winning competitions for hospitals and public baths, including the Windsor Baths in Bradford (see page 155). He went on to adjudicate several competitions for the design of local authority public baths. In a paper given in 1899 at the Royal Institute of British Architects,[28] Tiltman generally followed Allsop's recommendations, except that he preferred to specify for only three hot rooms.

The architect Alfred William Stephens Cross (1858–1932) was another important designer of public baths; his *Public baths and wash-houses* of 1906 became the standard work on the subject.[29] Although Cross does not appear to have designed any Turkish baths—that at Ironmonger Row is in the extension built after his death, and designed by his son and partner Kenneth—Alfred's book does include a chapter on them. This recommends temperatures similar to Tiltman's except for the *laconicum* which is 20 degrees cooler at 230°F (110°C).

Finally, two professional bodies made their recommendations, the Institution of Municipal and County Engineers (IMCE—now part of the Institution of Civil Engineers) in 1935, and the Institute of Baths and Recreation Management (IBRM—now part of the Institute for the Management of Sport and Physical Activity) in 1967.

Both organisations brought the highest temperature down to 220°F (104°C), and suggested a range between 160°F (71°C) and 180°F (82°C) for the *caldarium*. But for the *tepidarium*, the IMCE specified a temperature between 140°F (60°C) and 160°F (71°C) and, 32 years later, the IBRM settled on a lower range, starting at 120°F (49°C).

So, from the information available, it does seem possible to detect certain trends. As the bath became more established, temperatures started to rise, while in the latest phase of the bath's life, we find that they have fallen slightly. But this may be more a result of contemporary fuel prices allied to less crowded baths than anything related to the efficacy of the bath.

At present, all known temperatures come from what is, in effect, a random sample of baths, taken over a period of more than 150 years. So these trends are extremely tentative, and far more research is needed to make any sort of accurate assessment.

11

19th-century attitudes to the Victorian Turkish bath

The main technical problems arising from the reintroduction of the Turkish bath were all solved sooner or later—as usually happens in any developing technology. The negative attitudes towards the bath took much longer to overcome and some still remain.

In truth, the advent of the Turkish bath was not universally welcomed. Many doctors saw the bath proprietors, especially those who were not medically qualified, as competitors for their patients' fees. They found it particularly galling when they were unable to provide cures for their regular patients who suffered from complaints such as rheumatism or gout and who found that the Turkish bath provided relief from their pain.

Others who thought the bath especially threatening were the hydropathists who had sometimes invested considerable sums in the building of large residential establishments where the water cure had been promulgated as the universal medical panacea. They could not have enjoyed seeing the ease with which a relatively small Georgian town house could so inexpensively be converted into a busy Turkish bath.

Admittedly, some of the earliest establishments, particularly those in London, would not have competed with any of even the least expensive hydros; their clients were, as we should say today, from a different sector of the market. Nevertheless, they were perceived as being an early warning of what *might* happen.

Doctors' attitudes

It is conceivable that if the Turkish bath had been introduced solely as an improvement on the vapour bath as a cleansing agent, it would have met with little opposition. What set the cat among the 19th-century pigeons was that, from the beginning, it was also promoted as a therapeutic agent.

In the hands of someone like Dr Barter, this should have been perfectly acceptable. However, physician he may have been, but his primary approach was through hydropathy—the cold water cure—thought by many doctors to be just another form of quackery.

Medical practitioners were by no means fully professionalised in the mid-1850s and many ordinary doctors, if not most, were against the bath from the start. It might seem, at first glance, that they had a good case.

Probably the first display advertisement for Turkish baths in England claimed that,

> It fortifies the body against colds, influenza, consumption, gout, rheumatism, nervousness, neuralgia, *tic-doloureux*, tooth ache, all skin diseases, and disorders arising from the liver.[1]

The next paragraph blithely asserted that 'the right use of it will *cure* any of the above diseases' (my emphasis).

This was, of course, unwise. But it was not completely outrageous at a time when bloodletting was still a major treatment for almost anything, and when there were very few diseases which the doctors themselves were able to cure.

It is easy to understand why James Laurie—himself a hydropathic doctor and proprietor of the Sciennes Hill Turkish Baths in Edinburgh—felt it appropriate, in his book on the bath, to quote Voltaire's view that 'Medicine is the art of amusing the patient, while nature cures the disease.'[2]

Durham Dunlop had much to say about doctors' attitudes. In his book *The philosophy of the bath*, dedicated to Richard Barter, he went even further, quoting Sir Astley Cooper's contention that, 'The science of medicine is founded on conjecture, and improved by murder.'[3]

Although Turkish baths gained acceptance in a number of hospitals, some doctors forbade their patients to use them. Others grudgingly allowed their use, but only if under the supervision of a doctor.

From the opening of the first baths until the middle of the 20th century, proprietors had to fight back with a stream of advertisements, publicity brochures, and even books.

Five objections to the bath, clearly reflecting the warnings given by doctors to their patients, were regularly—almost automatically—refuted in publication after publication. These were:

1 that the Turkish bath was injurious to the blood;

2 that bathers were likely to catch a cold when leaving its heat;

3 that it should be avoided by those with a weak heart;

4 that it was weakening and enervating;

5 that it should not be taken by the elderly.

Proprietors knew that well-conducted baths would be unlikely to do any such harm, but they did not wish to antagonise doctors who might otherwise send their patients to them. A number, like Robert Parry of Liverpool, made postal overtures to their local doctors with the aim of gaining their approval (Fig 11.1).

Some, like the Turkish baths companies in Cardiff and Bolton, offered them free passes to try the baths for themselves, while others, like Charles Bartholomew, advertised that,

> Medical men are invited to send their own prescriptions for medicated baths with instructions which will be strictly carried out.[4]

When an establishment was owned by doctors, there was another type of problem. One London doctor, signing himself 'Dubious' in a letter to *The Lancet*, was worried about the Turkish baths in Alfred Place owned by two physician brothers, Charles and Edward Pollard. Accepting that they were 'practitioners of some standing' he asked,

> Do they undertake to give advice or opinions to patients sent to them by medical men, and, by superseding us, virtually withdraw such patients from our care? It would be as well if the Messrs Pollard would let it be clearly understood if their establishment is solely for the administration of the Turkish and medicated baths, that there is no attempt to interfere with the patients confided to them, and that the instructions given by the medical attendant are strictly carried out—in fact, that we may be assured that we still retain the charge of the patient.[5]

CENTRAL TURKISH BATH,
128, DUKE STREET, LIVERPOOL.

Messrs. PARRY & LINGARD

Beg to thank their numerous Patrons and Friends for their warm appreciation of the efforts made so to Ventilate *their* TURKISH BATH, *as to render it a* Curative, Hygienic, *and* Luxurious *Agent. Encouraged by this success they now beg to announce the addition of* Vapour, Russian, *and* Medicated Baths *of every description, including* Sulphur, Mercurial, *and* Sea Weed ; *the latter combining the Effects of a Vapour and Warm Salt Water Bath.*

The LADIES' BATHS *are fitted up with every accommodation requisite for Invalids, also to afford an agreeable and soothing relaxation to the robust.*

☞ As the LADIES' BATHS can only be used during the Day, the Tickets are Reduced to the Evening charges, viz., 2/- for a Single Ticket, or a Book of 6 for 9/-

Fig 11.1
Robert Parry, among others, mailed postcards to local doctors seeking a recommendation to their patients. (Rodney Street is Liverpool's Harley Street.) (Author's collection)

To which the editor added a reassuring note that, 'Messrs Pollard scrupulously avoid interfering in any way with the patients entrusted to them by their medical brethren.'

Even when a doctor simply offered advice or consultations at a Turkish bath, he could find himself in trouble with his colleagues through no fault of his own.

William Haigh, owner of the Chapel Street baths in Southport, had stated in newspaper advertisements that a doctor (who was not named) could be consulted at his baths. This had occasioned a complaint that the consultant, Dr John Balbirnie, had himself broken the prohibition on doctors advertising their services.

Haigh wrote a well-reasoned letter of apology to the editor of the *Medical Times and Gazette*.[6] He pointed out that the offending advertisement bore his own signature, and that if the phraseology had 'compromised or placed the gentleman in a false position with his Medical brethren', then he regretted the circumstances for which he alone was responsible.

He explained that because many poor invalids sought his advice on the use of the bath, it seemed far safer for the patient, and himself, if the advice was given by 'a gentleman who had an established reputation in the Profession, on the one hand, and whose knowledge and experience of the operation of the Turkish Bath on the other' would best qualify him to give such advice. To this, no logical retort from a doctor was possible.

Thirty-five years later, there seems to have been a more pragmatic approach to a doctor's involvement in rather more blatant commercial activities. The *British Medical Journal* was asked by a correspondent whether it would be unprofessional for his name to be included, as a shareholder and director, in the prospectus of a company being set up to provide 'Turkish baths, with shops and offices in front'. The journal replied that,

> there can be no objection to the simple insertion of our correspondent's name ... the well understood medico-ethical rules by which the dignity and status of the profession are maintained have no reference to legitimate commercial enterprise.[7]

But the question was quite unnecessary; doctors had been identified in prospectuses since the first Turkish bath companies were set up a year earlier. Such a company was hardly considered respectable without one. The prospectus of the London & Provincial Turkish Bath Company Ltd named Dr Thudichum in 1860,[8] and the following year, that of the Roman Bath Company included two doctors and a surgeon.[9]

Attitudes to cleanliness

In Ireland, the early emphasis on the therapeutic value of the Turkish bath was because it was first used in a hydropathic establishment. But Barter's city baths, and Urquhart's baths in England, placed an equal emphasis on cleanliness, for the overwhelming majority of the population were at that time unaccustomed to regular bathing. There were no easily available facilities.

Urquhart reportedly upset the inhabitants of Cork when he told them that they needed Turkish baths because they were a dirty people.[10]

When the hydropathist and Edinburgh-qualified physician Dr Edward Wickstead Lane opened the City Turkish Baths in London's South Street in 1861—barely a year after he bought James Ellis's Hydropathic Sanatorium at Sudbrook Park in Surrey—a long article about it was reprinted in an American magazine.[11]

Towards the end, a table analysed the reasons given by 221 bathers for taking a Turkish bath there. Since the article was originally published soon after the establishment opened, there is reason to believe that the figures relate to the first 221 bathers to use the baths, though we cannot be certain about this.

The bathers were first divided into groups according to the frequency of their visits. Then bathers in each group were asked why they had visited the baths (Table 11.1).

This is a very small number of bathers for a survey so we must be wary of drawing any other than tentative conclusions from the results. But what is especially interesting is that no one had given bathing to cleanse oneself as a reason for the visit.

This may be because the city businessmen who frequented this particular establishment would have considered themselves already clean as they would probably have had bathing facilities, however rudimentary, at home. But it may be because the proprietor felt that it would not be politic to ask whether this was the reason for the visit.

What is clear, however, is that already, within five years of the introduction of the Turkish bath into the British Isles (and only one year after the first one opened in London), it was already perfectly acceptable to admit that one went to the Turkish bath for enjoyment—and this despite all the advertising which concentrated on the bath as the ultimate cleanser, or as the cure for an astonishing range of illnesses.

Dr Samuel Jeaffreson, a strong supporter of the bath, told the British Medical Association a few years later:

> It is somewhat repugnant to the English notion to be told that we are a dirty set of fellows; that our [hot water] baths, our sponges, our soap, and flannels, only increase our filth by rubbing the

Table 11.1 Why bathers said they went to the City Turkish baths

BATHERS	*Pleasure*	*Colds*	*Rheumatism and gout*	*Other ailments*
Frequent	54	3	8	4
Occasional	53	4	14	9
First bath	47	4	9	12
	154	**11**	**31**	**25**

dirt in; and that cleanliness can only be obtained, not 'by the sweat of our brows' only, but that we must be washed from within outwards by myriads of rippling streams of perspiration.[12]

To those unused to bathing, the Turkish bath introduced a whole range of strange new experiences. In 1860, for example, the manager of the co-operative Turkish bath in Rochdale wrote a short pamphlet for prospective bathers in which he indicated that he understood that many were,

> afraid of the Turkish Bath, simply because of the cold shower after being in the hot room. We cannot blame such, because a short time ago we should have thought of nothing but instant death if such a change had been proposed to us.

He then explains how to take a shower (Fig 11.2):

> The proper plan, and one which makes the matter quite easy, is to stand firmly with the feet exactly under the centre of the rose. Make an effort to brace up the nerves, and assume a defiant attitude as though about to encounter an enemy. Let the first shock of cold fall on the face and chest, then move the upper part of the body gently to and fro, so that the water may fall on the back and front alternately; then on the sides in turns, holding up the arms alternately, that the armpits and sides may have their due share of the bracing stream.

And after dealing with other parts of the body, he continues:

> When there is time and opportunity, the pleasure may be increased by the bather putting his hands on the floor, and moving about, or laying down, so as to receive the shower on different parts of the body. By laying on the back the feet may be held up, which is very agreeable. In short, the shower should be a source of fun to all who take the Turkish Bath ...[13]

We may find this amusing today, but in the middle of the 19th century, no less a person than George Jacob Holyoake wrote that Mr Jagger's pamphlet was 'a very sensible and practical tract'.[14]

Fig 11.2
A French postcard illustrating a needle shower at Vichy.
(Author's collection)

Class attitudes to the use of the bath

David Urquhart, who had seen people of all classes mixing freely in the baths of Constantinople, believed that the Turkish bath could bring classes closer to each in other in Britain.

> No barrier of ceremony, of pride, or of habit, is so great as that of filth which, in these times, especially in large towns, separates the poor from the rich, as if they were not members of the same state, but, as Disraeli has phrased it, 'the two nations.'[15]

Fig 11.3
A modern American postcard shows that John Abel's attitude to drunkenness among the 'higher orders' persists to this day.
(Author's collection)

The Times, in its account of a lecture to the Society of Arts under the chairmanship of the Duke of Wellington, reported that Urquhart, speaking of the advantages of perfect cleanliness among all classes,

> pointed out that our intercourse with the lower orders was broken off by there being no settled occasions on which we are in contact with them, and by the want of cleanliness in their persons. In the bath, both classes were constantly brought into the presence of each other. Contempt and distaste were removed on one side, degradation and irritation on the other.[16]

Urquhart seemed to be a person totally unaware of class, and this influenced all those with whom he worked. A few months after the opening of the committee-owned Leeds Road establishment in Bradford, the local paper published a letter from 'A Lover of the Turkish Bath' who complained that because the prices were cheaper in the evenings and weekends, those who had to work during the day, and who would willingly pay the higher price, found there was no provision made for them. He admitted that they,

> might mix in the crowd that generally is present in the evening, but I apprehend that, as society is at present, this respectable and influential portion would not be among the patrons of the bath. There is an undisguised reluctance to mix at random with any of the working classes who might chance to be present. Whether this arises from an expected discourtesy of demeanour, or the offensiveness of some of their callings, or an uncertainty of their cleanliness, I will not say.[17]

The working men of the Bradford FAC who ran the bath mischievously responded that if the correspondent would care to attend their next committee meeting, which for all their convenience was held in the evening straight from work, they would be happy to discuss the matter.

Class attitudes to drunkenness, seen as a loser of productivity in the new 19th-century factories, led to temperance and abstinence movements aimed at the working class, but some Victorians believed there was a need to treat the non-labouring classes with more understanding. The Quaker, John Abel, saw a session at the Turkish bath as the solution (Fig 11.3).

> Notwithstanding the numbers that have been rescued by Total Abstinence Societies, there is a large class unreached by them amongst the higher orders, who are addicted to intemperance. The remedy proposed offers to them a means of escape which does not hurt their self-esteem—a boon which those who have tried it, speak of it in terms of affectionate remembrance.[18]

Many medical officers of health and local politicians were just as prejudiced against the provision of inexpensive Turkish baths for the working classes as the doctors who feared for their livelihood.

In response to a questionnaire from the hydropathist Richard Metcalfe, Sir William Gull, Queen Victoria's physician, replied, 'Turkish baths are probably more adapted to the indolent and luxurious, than to those who toil for their livelihood.'[19] And Thomas Stevenson, Medical Officer of Health for the London borough of St Pancras, wrote, 'The Turkish bath is of great value as a sanitary and cleansing agent. The great difficulty in introducing them for the use of the lower orders is the expense.'

Metcalfe, who was a member of the Paddington Vestry, wanted Turkish baths provided under the Baths and Wash-houses Acts, but the vestry incorrectly believed that this was not allowed because the acts, which predated the Victorian Turkish bath, did not specifically mention them.

However, a few daring authorities, such as those in Bury and Bradford, went ahead anyway without incurring any dire consequences. Southampton Corporation provided them by the simple ruse of wickedly calling them vapour baths,[20] and Birmingham did the same by initially calling them 'hot-air lavatories'.[21]

Because the acts were not mandatory, the majority of early Turkish baths were commercial establishments which needed to make a reasonable profit. As a result, they were rarely built in the poorer areas where they were most needed. This can clearly be seen in London if we superimpose establishments on Booth's 1889 Poverty Map (Fig 11.4).[22] Preferred

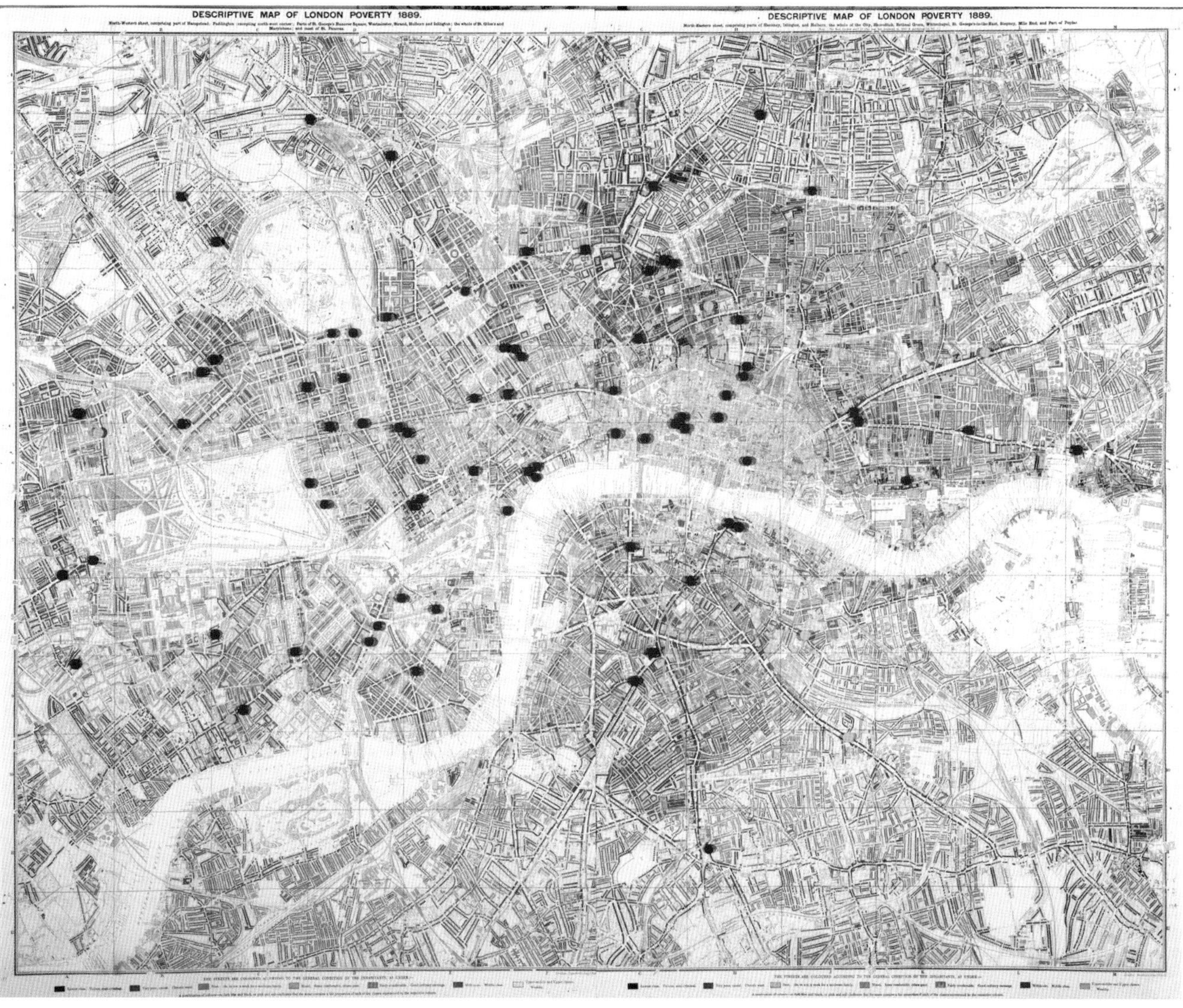

Fig 11.4
The spread of the Turkish bath in London overlaid on Booth's Poverty Map. (Image enhancement: © Malcolm Shifrin. Photo: © Historic England DP166127, from map in Author's collection)

locations were more often adjacent to railway stations used by commuters travelling home to the suburbs.

Working-class bathers faced another barrier. When, in 1864, Bury Improvement Commissioners unanimously decided to open their Turkish baths for a few hours on Sunday mornings, there was an outcry. Letters to the local papers, on both sides of the argument, continued for several weeks.

'J.W.A.' wrote to the *Bury Times* that 'it was a disgrace to the town' and asked bathers to boycott the baths on Sundays.[23] William Cooper, who came from outside Bury (and who did not indicate that he was a Secularist and one of the Rochdale Pioneers), wrote supporting the council:

> We have a Turkish Bath in Rochdale which is open on a Sunday, and the Christians here—who are I suppose as good as the Bury Christians—make no objection. And why should they? They are not compelled to go.[24]

Eventually the correspondence was closed, and the baths remained open. Yet, over 20 years later, pressure from church and chapel prevented William Bishop's Putney Baths from opening on Sunday—the only day, he argued, the working classes had sufficient time to use them.[25]

Perhaps the strangest manifestation of class prejudice occurred even later. When London's borough of Camberwell opened its Old Kent Road baths in 1905, according to the programme of the opening ceremony,

> A Russian Vapour Bath, which will accommodate nine persons at one time, is provided for the second class bathers. For the first class bathers there is a Turkish Bath to accommodate fourteen persons at one time, with plunge bath attached.[26]

The council seems to have considered this message to have been an important one to proclaim. Perhaps Camberwell was just less hypocritical than those councils which allowed their price lists to perform the same function?

Other prejudices

Members of the leisured class saw further reasons to deny the benefits of the Turkish bath to those whose work supported them in the manner to which they were accustomed.

The bath led, they claimed, to indolence and would destroy the manliness which created the British Empire, as it had destroyed the Roman Empire, and as it was then destroying the Ottoman Empire.[27]

Such attitudes inevitably led to xenophobia and what we should now call racism. On 28 January 1861, Dr Thudichum read a paper on the bath to the Medical Society of London[28] which, on several other issues also, triggered a lengthy correspondence in the medical journals.

Dr Thomas Garlike wrote to *The Lancet*, 'Can the active, fox-hunting, cricketing, boating Englishman bear the same kind of treatment that benefits and gratifies the indolent, languid, luxurious Turk?'[29]

While an editorial in the same week's *British Medical Journal* stated that,

> The [Turkish bath] may be adapted to the mental and physical constitution of those lazy Eastern voluptuaries, who have cost us so much trouble and so many lives, and the well-fed and fatted contents of their harems. The slothful pasha may work off his superfluous hydrocarbons and nitrogenous materials through the sudoriferous ducts and the pulmonary mucous membrane; but healthy men of business and of sense in this country will, we venture to prophesy, never consent to the dissipation of time and matter involved in the idea of a periodical Turkish bath.[30]

Such editorial arrogance led seamlessly into the accusation, made sometimes even by those who were strong advocates of the bath (if not, always, of shampooing), that the regular use of the Turkish bath led to effeminacy and loss of manliness. Dr Lockhart Robertson, for example, wrote that much of the prejudice against the bath,

> and the contrasts drawn between its health giving use and that of a good day's hunting or shooting, result from the popular and just notions of the effeminacy of the modern Eastern bath, with its abominable practice of shampooing and its luxurious ease and enervating cooling process.[31]

These views fitted the general prejudices of the time. In 1906, a popular dictionary of medicine in the home remarked that the bath was then 'chiefly patronised by the disciples of Mahomed', adding, 'How much of the effeminacy and sensuality of that race may be attributed to its use or abuse, it is not easy to say.'[32]

Loss of manliness and effeminacy were frequently ascribed to the regular bather, though this might have been due to a fear of homosexuality, for which no word existed at the time (see Chapter 27). Such arguments were contradicted (but ever so warily) by Dr Henry W Kiallmark:

> Except in the case of those who take the bath for a specific purpose, I think its use should not be regarded as an affair of daily recurrence. It must never interfere with, or take the place of, the Englishman's daily 'tub'; and, with this proviso, the alarm expressed by some, that it will lead to effeminacy and degeneracy of race, as it is said to have done with the ancient Romans and the modern Turks, may be looked upon as fallacious.[33]

Dr Edward Haughton, another baths advocate (and himself a bath manager), also disapproved of shampooing—but left himself a typical escape route.

> One thing more is required before the bath can be brought within the reach of the public, viz, the costly, tedious, and effeminate custom of shampooing must be totally got rid of, except when prescribed as a therapeutic agent.[34]

But shampooing remained an important component of the Turkish bath (Fig 11.5). Not until the very end of the century was any suggestion made, and then in the most discreet manner, that in a few establishments, not necessarily Turkish baths, massage may have had unseemly and unacceptable connotations.[35]

Other advocates of the bath had a different prejudice. Erasmus Wilson, in his book *The eastern, or Turkish Bath*, saw nudity as a moral issue. But this, again, might have been a fear of encouraging homosexual activity in the bath. '... a costume', he wrote, in the year when the death penalty for sodomy was abolished,

> is indispensable. Without a costume in the presence of others, the bath is not the bath—it is an evil, and as an evil it should be suppressed with the utmost severity.[36]

But the previous year, Mr Jagger, who advised us earlier on the use of the shower, expressed a rather more representative view.

> Some object to the Bath, because of the time they are liable to be seen in a state of comparative nakedness. This seems to spring from the too common notion of no sin if the world does not see it. We think it a piece of over-fastidiousness to shrink from being seen by the same sex, when there is no special reason for so doing. The vicious

LOW
RUBBER (before starting) "HAVE YOU GOT ANY ACHES, SPRAINS OR STIFFNESS, SIR?"
TERRY: "N-NOT YET."

Fig 11.5
One of David Low's caricatures commissioned by Nevill's Turkish Baths.
(A Visit to the Turkish bath by Low and Terry, Nevill's Turkish Baths)

Fig 11.6
Erasmus Wilson, dermatologist, and philanthropist.
(Photographs of eminent medical men, *ed Wm. Tindal Robertson, J Churchill, 1867. Wellcome Library, London)*

> and the unfortunate may be pardoned if they try to hide the evidence of past folly, or of natural deformity; but the healthy, well-formed man, need not be ashamed to be seen by his neighbour.[37]

Usually, at most of the early Turkish baths in the British Isles, bathers were partially covered by towels, though in the plunge pool the majority swam in the nude, as they generally did in the sea at that time.

A towel is a perfectly adequate covering for even the most modest Turkish bather. Erasmus Wilson (Fig 11.6) was the most respected dermatologist of his day, and his several books on the diseases and care of the skin went into multiple editions over a period of over 35 years. He must surely have known that any benefit to be gained by exposure of the skin to hot air would be negated by covering up the skin so the hot air could not reach it.

But then logic was not always the motivating factor at the forefront of a doctor's mind when discussing the bath. Speaking from the floor after Dr Thudichum's lecture, one doctor appears merely to have resented the possibility that those from a class lower than his own were enjoying themselves.

> From the use of the heated air bath as a therapeutical agent to its use as a social enjoyment or luxury, is a wide step, and a step which I, for one, hold back from taking. It seems to be the misfortune of this remedy, that its administration is for a time attended by a sensation of great pleasure and satisfaction ...[38]

Yet it was just such enjoyment which was found to be so beneficial in the use of Turkish baths in the Victorian asylum, as we shall see in Chapter 18.

PART IV

VICTORIAN TURKISH BATHS FOR ALL

12

Ownership

Proprietors of Victorian Turkish baths intended for use by the general public were of three types. The first was the individual entrepreneur, sometimes with one or more partners; the second was the joint stock company on behalf of its shareholders; and the third, though not a proprietor in quite the same way, was the local authority. But both the type of proprietor and the actual proprietor could change throughout the life of the bath, sometimes several times.

Over the past 20 years I have identified over §600 Victorian Turkish baths in the British Isles alone. How I found them, and how representative they may be, are described in 'Dating the baths' (see page xviii). In discussing ownership in this chapter, however, I have excluded baths provided for special users, such as hospital patients or club members, and any which were part of a hydropathic establishment or hotel. I found that, although these baths had the same three types of proprietor, it was easier to discover accurate information about stand-alone baths which were open to everyone.

I looked at a group of 488 baths, of which 404 were in England, 34 in Ireland, 40 in Scotland and 10 in Wales (Fig 12.1), and found that 343 were set up by individual entrepreneurs or partnerships, 57 by companies, and 88 by local authorities (Table 12.1).

I also identified just over §100 companies which were formed to open or run Turkish baths. Only about half of these are included in the table because some bought existing baths, and a dozen or so progressed no further than registration, neither trading nor even allotting shares.

Table 12.1 Who opened Victorian Turkish baths?

Individuals and partnerships	343	70.29%
Limited liability companies	57	11.68%
Local authorities	88	18.03%
	488	100%

Fig 12.1
Opening page of a delightful illustrated manuscript telling the story of a visit to the Llandudno Turkish baths.
(Richard Greene, Llandudno: its attractions and amusement *[Sketch book], title page. Supplied by Llyfrgell Genedlaethol Cymru, The National Library of Wales, WlAbNLO 04441110)*

Entrepreneurs and partnerships

Most establishments passed through several phases during their lifetime. In common with many other small businesses, they frequently changed hands, the unsuccessful ones closing when their owners could no longer pay their way.

These baths might then be sold as a going concern, or the premises used for a different type of business. In the 1880s, according to Michael J. Winstanley, a change of proprietor usually involved a change of business use.[1] But, in the case of Turkish baths, there would be an incentive to retain facilities which had been costly to build, and even a tendency to improve them (unless it was the business rather than the management which had been poor).

Occasionally, creditors might take possession of a Turkish bath in lieu of long overdue rent, or because the owner had defaulted on interest which was due on a loan or mortgage. They might then attempt to run the baths on their own account. But this too could fail, as in the case of the High Street Turkish Baths in Birmingham, which led to the former creditor's own bankruptcy.[2]

Often, baths which failed would have been profitable were it not for loan repayments. In 1904, for example, Albert Barnes-Moss bought the Central Turkish Baths, already established for nearly twenty-five years in London's Newington Causeway, and ran it successfully for another five. Then, with his masseur and shampooer among the subscribers, he formed a new company to purchase and run the baths, with himself as managing director.

The following year, in order to finance necessary improvements, the company made a public share offer of 1,400 £1 shares. This was not a success; instead, it had to raise the £800 it needed by issuing two debentures secured on the business. Then, when no interest was forthcoming, the senior debenture holder, Edgar Brandon, took the baths over, ran them for a couple of years, and then sold them on.[3] Ironically, they later became one of the more successful establishments of William Cooper's Savoy Turkish Baths Ltd, and only closed when the premises were destroyed during the 1941 Blitz.

In time, even successful establishments changed hands: partners disagreed and one or other would leave the business; baths would be sold when proprietors decided to move on, or retire; executors might be compelled to sell an establishment on the death of a proprietor, or the business might be inherited by a spouse, or by a son or daughter. And if such a daughter were to marry (or a widow to remarry), further change lay ahead because, until the Married Women's Property Act of 1882, ownership of the baths would have had to pass to the new husband, unless an equitable settlement had previously been made.

Inevitably, the first Turkish baths were started or purchased by proprietors with little or no experience. They recognised an opportunity and decided—or hoped—there was a living to be made. Often, as we have seen, they came to the bath through their involvement with one of the Foreign Affairs Committees (FACs), or else they themselves were frequenters of Turkish baths.

Those who had previously worked in one (and gained experience of how they were run) could be expected to stand a better chance of success, and several bath attendants became successful managers.

John Nicol, for example, was a bath attendant for at least four years at Duke's Baths in Sauchiehall Street, Glasgow. He became manager there in 1870 and remained in that position, apparently without feeling any need to start on his own, until a new proprietor took over in 1883, or possibly even later.[4]

But it was difficult for bath attendants, shampooers, or even managers—many of whom had families to support—to save or raise enough capital to start on their own. One of those who did was Benjamin Bell who, in 1879, managed to buy the §Grosvenor Baths in Buckingham Palace Road from the liquidator of the company who owned it previously.

Bell was a lively personality who used caricatures in the booklet advertising his baths (see page 313), and was later to show his receptivity to original ideas.

In the mid-1880s, when British farming was depressed, an attempt was made to see whether tobacco could be added to the country's crops and give employment 'to great numbers of women and children'. With special Inland Revenue permission, small quantities were successfully grown in a number of areas and attempts then had to be made to dry and cure the crop. According to a report published in December 1886:

> Some fine leaves have been cured in the pure, hot-air chambers of the [Grosvenor] Turkish baths near the Grosvenor Hotel, having been put there by the honorary secretary of the Ensilage Society.[5]

Sometimes, a manager's experience of how difficult it was to make a good living from a small establishment acted as a deterrent. Nevertheless, some did succeed, traversing a variety of routes.

In 1888, William Park , who had first worked at Ben Rhydding Hydropathic Establishment, was employed by Charles Bartholomew as bath attendant at his Turkish baths in the City of Bath (Fig 12.2). Park was almost certainly the manager in all but name, but Bartholomew probably calculated that if he allowed him to use the designation 'manager' he would ask for more money. As attendant, Park started at just '25/- per week and perquisites', or perks.[6]

After Bartholomew's death in 1889, Park stayed on for another year managing the baths for Charles's niece, Kate Bartholomew. But by then he wanted to run his own establishment. Moving to Worcester, he bought the §Sansome Walk baths (Fig 12.3) from Bartholomew's executors.

Ambition alone, however, does not purchase a thriving Turkish bath when one is earning little more than 25s a week. A normal bank loan would have been difficult or impossible, but sometimes a capable manager might have been able to obtain a loan from a wealthy sponsor, probably a regular bather who knew the potential profitability of the bath and the manager's ability and reliability.

Park's son Leonard, interviewed at the age of 92, told me of two such loans. His father, a staunch Methodist, was helped by a loan from a co-religionist, the philanthropist Sir William Hartley, after whom Hartley Victoria College in Manchester is named.[7] Bartholomew himself received an initial loan from Sir Isaac Pitman who was already a regular bather.[8]

Park appears to have decided early in his time as bath attendant that he would work towards becoming a proprietor. But sometimes a transfer of ownership happened almost by chance.

Mr A Samwell (or Samuels), manager of the New Street Turkish Baths in Leicester, for example, soon realised that the baths were not being marketed in the most effective way. But he was unable to persuade the owner to experiment, perhaps by trying different opening hours or lower prices. In 1873 he wrote to Richard Metcalfe relating how he had been there for eight years,

> during the first four of which it was difficult to pay expenses; but, since taking them on my own account, the prices have been 2s. 6d., 1s. 6d., and 1s., the working classes availing themselves of the opportunity immediately, and now the establishment pays 12 per cent. I have also been well supported in opening from 5am to 8am for 6d., without shampooing.[9]

Four years later, he completed a questionnaire for Birmingham's Baths and Parks Committee which was considering whether to approve the provision of their first Turkish baths at Kent Street. His receipts for the previous year, he wrote, were £800, though he omitted to say whether he was still achieving his 12 per cent.[10]

Not everyone was so successful in assessing their potential market. A somewhat rueful Mr T Roberts, for example, also wrote to Metcalfe in 1873, reporting that after seven difficult years, '… I gave up my Turkish bath, as I could not get sufficiently supported. Perhaps the population of Skipton was too small.'[11] But in staying open for as long as he did, Roberts outperformed many other entrepreneurs and also, as we shall see, almost one third of the companies running baths.

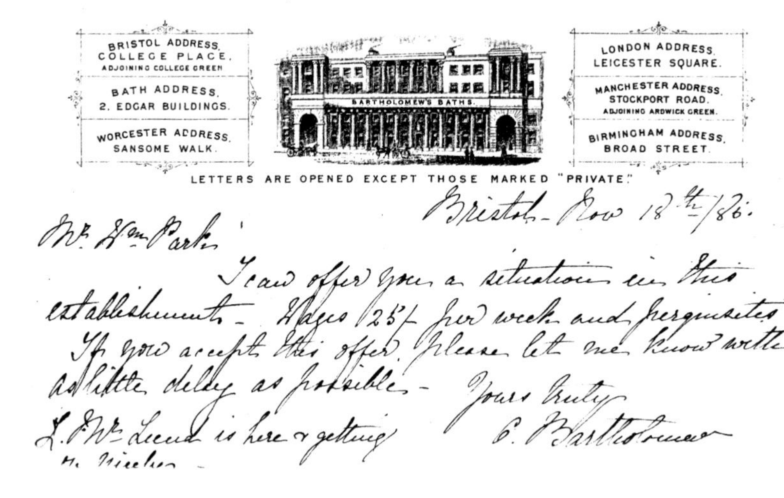

BRISTOL ADDRESS. COLLEGE PLACE. ADJOINING COLLEGE GREEN
BATH ADDRESS. 2. EDGAR BUILDINGS.
WORCESTER ADDRESS. SANSOME WALK.
BARTHOLOMEW'S BATHS.
LONDON ADDRESS. LEICESTER SQUARE.
MANCHESTER ADDRESS. STOCKPORT ROAD. ADJOINING ARDWICK GREEN.
BIRMINGHAM ADDRESS. BROAD STREET.
LETTERS ARE OPENED EXCEPT THOSE MARKED "PRIVATE."

Bristol – Nov 18th/86.

Mr Wm Park

I can offer you a situation in this establishment – Wages 25/- per week and perquisites. If you accept this offer please let me know with as little delay as possible – Yours truly

C. Bartholomew

Fig 12.2 (top)
'I can offer you a situation in this establishment.' Charles Bartholomew to William Park, 18 November 1886. (Courtesy of the late Leonard Park, William's son)

Fig 12.3 (bottom)
The cooling-room in the Sansome Walk Turkish Baths, c 1910. (Courtesy of the late Leonard Park, William's son)

Running a family establishment. A case study: the Hunts

Even small establishments required several people to run them efficiently. If the baths were open to both sexes, female staff—usually part-time—would also be needed. So the most cost-effective approach for a sole proprietor would be to involve his whole family in the venture.

After William Park left Bath around 1890, Henry (Edward) Hunt, the son of a local millwright, became manager. By 1907, he had purchased the establishment from its then owner, Robert M Herriott, and made it a family business (Fig 12.4), keeping costs to a minimum by employing outsiders only when absolutely necessary.

Henry's wife Alice looked after the women's days, and three of his four children would take on an increasing share of the workload as they grew up.[12]

His son, Edward Arthur Hunt, known as Ted, was given his first Turkish bath at the age of eighteen months, shortly after Henry started working at the baths.[13] In 1910, when Ted was nineteen, he started work as bath attendant, followed later by his younger sisters, Winifred and Ellen, and in 1941 when his father died, he inherited the business.

Fig 12.4
The Hunt Family, owners of Bartholomew's Turkish Baths in Bath, 1907–1961. Back row (left to right): Edward Arthur Hunt (Ted), Henry, Leonard; Front row: Ellen (Nell), Alice, Winifred (Win), with Ted's daughter Muriel on Alice's knee. (Norman Ashfield)

Neither Henry nor Ted made any significant changes to the baths or the way they were run, apart from the addition of some slipper baths in the basement. Ted's grandson, Norman Ashfield, used to visit his grandfather in the late 1950s and he told me how the family operated, and how hard they worked. In these baths, the first half of the 20th century was very little different from the last quarter of the 19th.

The working day was a long one, starting early in the morning, with the cleaning of the bathhouse, and checking the boilers and coke supply (Fig 12.5). This was delivered to the boiler room through two large doors opening onto Edgar Mews at the rear of the building. Inside, stone steps (Fig 12.6), led to the laundry above.

The sisters would be dealing with the washing long after the baths closed, often as late as two o'clock in the morning. Referring to his two great-aunts, known as Win and Nell, Ashfield recalls:

> Sometimes, while my hard-working aunts were washing at gone midnight, a constable's voice would call up from the delivery doors 'Is everything alright up there?' And they would call down in the inky blackness (working by gaslight, of course) 'Yes thank you—water baths staff here'.

All the towels and lounger sheets had to be washed in a very basic laundry (Fig 12.7) which, although clean, was very dark, lit only by a single gasolier (gas mantle). The table was worn and pitted with scrubbing down over the years.

> I remember there were two huge china sinks; one had taps, and there was a piece of wooden channelling to carry water across to the second tub. The towels were scrubbed hard and after they were wrung out by hand, there was a mighty mangle through which the towels were rolled and they came out squeezed flat, not needing much ironing ... There was a black flat metal iron in the downstairs kitchen which was heated on the range and with a woollen protective cloth for the hands round the rather conductive handle. [Anything that required it] was ironed down there.

The items which did not need ironing were hung out to dry on a line on the roof.

The receptionist, using a speaking-tube which led to the kitchen in the basement (Fig 12.8), passed on any orders for refreshments to be served in the cooling-room. When ready, the food was sent up to reception by means of a *dumbwaiter, and one of the shampooers came out to collect it, since propriety would not allow

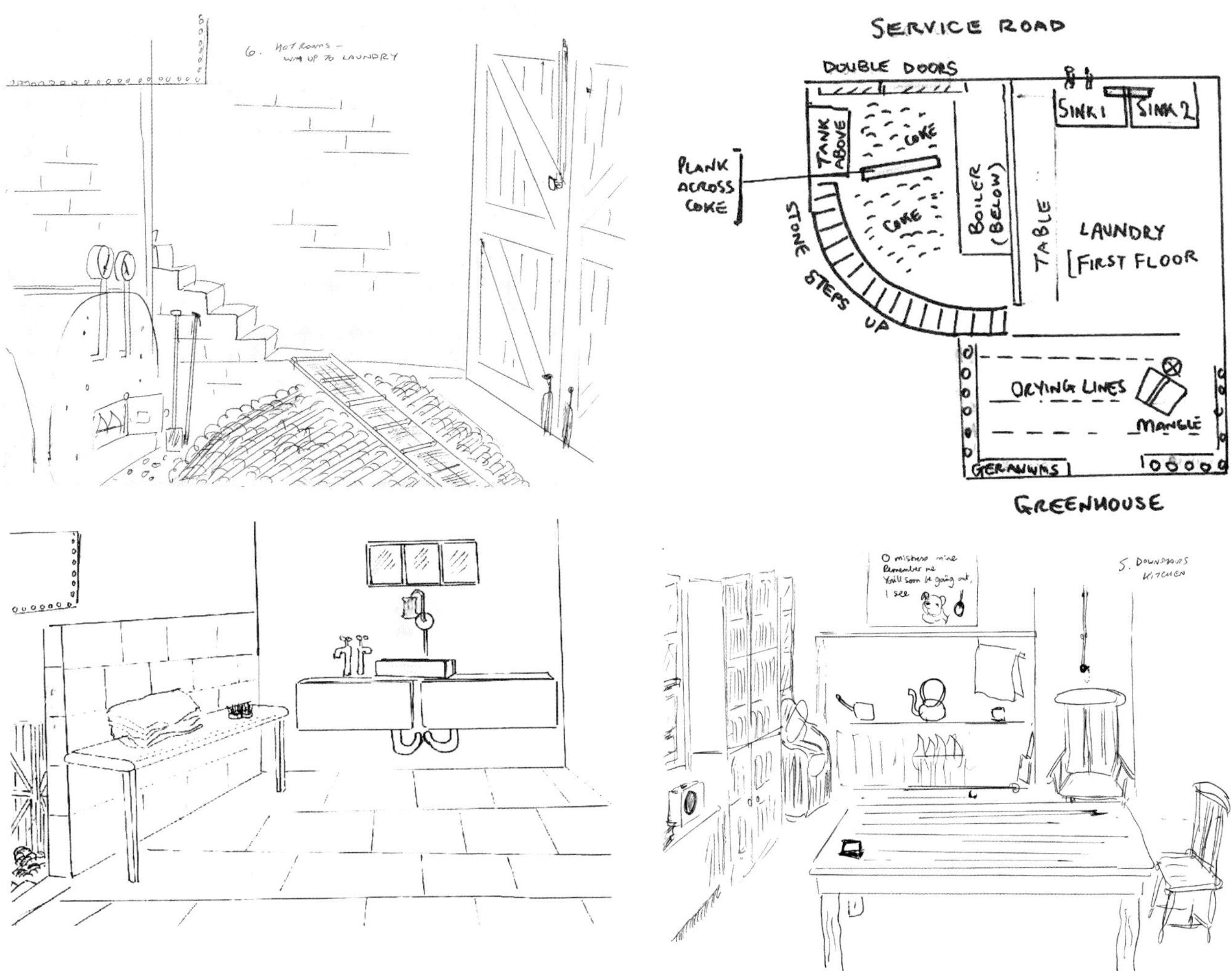

Figs 12.5–12.8
Norman Ashfield remembers the baths in the late 1950s: (L–R from top)
1 the boiler room, coke store and rear entrance.
2 sketch plan of coke store and first floor laundry.
3 sketch of the laundry.
4 the kitchen.
(Author's collection)

the female tea-makers to enter the cooling-room on a men's day. On women's days, Win and Nell did the shampooing, and extra help had to be employed to look after the reception area.

Amazingly, there was no electricity in the building until after the baths finally closed on 11 June 1961, slightly less than 80 years after Bartholomew opened them. All the illumination was by gaslight, and this was seen to suit the ambience of the baths because, as Ashfield remembers,

> The cooling-room was particularly romantic on a cold winter Saturday afternoon with the yellow, warm lights hissing gently, the red couches at the ends without bed linen on them looking smart, and the others set up with white linen and bathers reclining on them, reading a paper or supping their tea from ornate metal stands next to them. Small white cups, a miniature pot of milk and pot of tea to accompany that, plus digestive biscuits. It was a warm, venerable, lived-in smell, not new and fluorescent as our accommodation is nowadays.

Henry Hunt and William Park, both taught by Bartholomew—a disciple of Urquhart—clearly knew what they were about. But, too frequently, proprietors would get carried away by an overenthusiastic assessment of the potential number of bathers in a town. Or they would underestimate the number of regular bathers needed to ensure that takings were sufficient to allow them to maintain the baths in good condition and yet still make a profit.

Anyone considering whether to invest in a company which intended to build new baths, or to purchase an establishment which had only been profitable as a family-run enterprise, could make very similar mistakes.

Change of ownership—a revolving door?

In 1891, the *Darlington & Stockton Times* reported that,

> the people of Barnard Castle want Turkish baths! 'Barney' with an eighth of the population of Darlington! It certainly is awkward for the inhabitants of Barnard Castle to travel many miles in order to get a bath, and it wouldn't be surprising if business-like steps were taken to make the provision at home. Some of the people of the town seem to think the speculation would pay. If so, why shouldn't it pay in Darlington?[14]

The warning was well justified. Two Turkish baths in Darlington, both owned by James Wright, a local hairdresser who also manufactured and repaired umbrellas,[15] had closed the previous year because they could not be made to pay, and Darlington's population at that time was about 40,000.

Wright had opened his first Turkish bath in Valley Street in 1876.[16] The following year, he built Granville House, a new Turkish Baths and Hydro, at the corner of Woodland Road and Portland Place. His hairdressing and umbrella businesses were also carried on at the new baths—an odd combination perhaps, but such disparity was not unusual. Many Turkish baths proprietors combined a range of activities which had little in common, their baths becoming a personal micro-version of the clumsy corporate conglomerates which were to become, for a while, so fashionable a century later.

Granville House had yet more to offer. A year after opening, an advertisement stated that 'James Wright will take 1st class residents for £2.10.0 per week', and warned that third-class bathers at £1.5.0 'must use the back entrance in Portland Place.' Both these charges included medical attention from Dr Howison, physician to the establishment. Non-residents' tickets for the Turkish bath cost 2s 6d (or 12 for £1) and included the use of a cold swimming pool in the basement.

Wright, a public-spirited man, also offered to provide a course of 12 swimming lessons for boys in the workhouse at 2s per boy. This was rejected, however, because there appeared to be no available public funding.[17] In December 1882, Wright, who was apparently also carrying on business at the Northern Iron Foundry under the name of Wright & Co, Ironfounders and Moulders, filed for bankruptcy.[18]

The following June, The Darlington Turkish & Swimming Baths Company Limited was set up to lease the premises and take over the running of the Turkish baths, together with the hairdressing and umbrella businesses.[19]

By 1885, 18 months later, the baths had been sold to a Mr John Lye and the company had ceased trading. By 3 October 1890, the baths had closed and the building taken over by the YMCA.

How could the new company have got it so wrong, with three solicitors and an accountant as subscribers, supposedly able, and presumably expected, to consider its prospects in a highly professional manner? Also among its first shareholders were a baronet, three Justices of the Peace, two wine merchants, and a Member of Parliament. The MP was Arthur Pease who, with 20 £1 shares, was undoubtedly influenced by his use of the Turkish bath at Hutton Hall, the country house designed for his father by Alfred Waterhouse (1830–1905).[20]

Perhaps the subscribers thought that Wright's problems were caused by losses at the foundry. Even so, did the directors really believe that any small profit which might satisfy a sole proprietor could finance the regular payment of dividends to their shareholders?

The starry-eyed prospective bathers of Barnard Castle were fortunate to have received such sensible advice from their local paper, and to have taken note of it.

Ownership by joint stock companies

The records of the Registrar of Companies held at The National Archives, Kew (TNA), bear witness to the many investors who subscribed to new companies before undertaking any real research into their prospects.

Peter Beirne, in one of the very few recent journal articles about an individual Turkish bath, relates the history of Ennis Turkish Baths Company (Limited) (Fig 12.9). Apart from the sad fate of the proprietor, it is in many ways typical. The company was formed in 1870 in County Clare, Ireland. At that time, Ennis had a population of around 6,500—not much more than Barnard Castle in the late 1880s.

> Initial high running costs for energy, followed by continuing poor attendance figures ... ensured the baths' demise. The patience, philanthropy and deep pockets of the investors were exhausted ... The failure of the baths also took a human toll. Writing from Ennis in 1880, English journalist Bernard Becker noted that 'the ruined proprietor is now in the lunatic asylum on the road to Ballyalla'.[21]

THE IMPROVED
TURKISH BATHS,
MILL ROAD, ENNIS,
ARE NOW OPEN DAILY.

HOURS OF ADMISSION :—

	CHARGE.
From 6 to Half-past 8 a.m.	1s 0d
From 10.30 a.m. to 12.30 p.m. (for Ladies)	1s 6d
From 2 p.m. to 4 p.m.	2s 0d
From 6 to Half-past 8 p.m.	1s 0d
Reclining Bath	1s 0d
Shower Bath	0s 6d
Plunge Bath	0s 3d

Children under 10 years of age Half Price.

Subscription Card for 12 Morning Baths	10s 0d
" 12 Mid-day "	18s 0d
" 12 Evening "	10s 0d
" 6 Morning "	5s 0d
" 6 Mid-day "	10s 0d
" 6 Evening "	5s 0d
" 3 Months Plunge "	10s 0d
" 3 Months Shower "	10s 0d

On FRIDAYS, from 10.30 a.m. to 12.30. p.m., the Price for Ladies will be ONE SHILLING.

SHAMPOONING 6D. *EXTRA IN ALL CASES.*

On SATURDAY EVENING the Baths will be open from 6 p.m. at Half Price.

Fig 12.9
An 1870 advertisement for the Ennis Turkish Baths in Co. Clare, Ireland.
*(*The Clare Journal, *19 September 1870. Courtesy of Clare County Library, Ennis, Ireland)*

Other investors—though they may not have realised it at the time—may have been more fortunate when their newly incorporated companies, formed to purchase a specific establishment, had to abandon their plans because they were unable to conclude the deal, or raise enough money to proceed.

I found it difficult to come to any but the most general of conclusions about company ownership of Turkish baths. English companies are the only ones for which a significant number of records is available. Those of ten companies, six of which owned establishments of great importance in the history of the bath, were destroyed while in the care of Companies House as part of an apparently arbitrary weeding policy.

Information from the records of 68 English companies which owned Turkish baths (Table 12.2) clearly shows how short a life most of them had. Fewer than half survived for longer than 10 years. But whether a company acquired a Turkish bath or started one, over half the baths survived, in different ways, after their company folded.

The two longest surviving companies were the London & Provincial Turkish Baths (80 years) and Nevill's Turkish Baths (67 years).

The former's Jermyn Street Hammam rarely failed to make at least some profit. But income from the baths was being supplemented by rent from the 'gentlemen's chambers' in that part of the main building which had earlier housed the St James's Hotel. Like many others, the company was initially under-capitalised, although this was mitigated by the existence of several long-term shareholders. And, from 1863 till the baths closed, there was the continuing influence on the board of Robert Poore and, later, of one of his family.

Under-capitalisation was usually because initial share offers generally met with a poor response, although there were some exceptions. The 500 £10 shares of the Leicester Turkish Bath Co Ltd were fully taken up by just 53 shareholders. Thirty years later, when the company sold its baths, there were only 24 shareholders remaining, but all 500 shares were still being held between them.[22]

Another success was the Leamington Royal Pump Room Co Ltd, which was registered in 1861. From the start, all but 53 of its 1,700 £5 shares were held by 127 shareholders, each of whom received a small distributed surplus when the business was sold in 1869 to the local Board of Health for the District of Leamington.[23]

Unlike those in Leamington, most publicly funded Turkish baths were built by the local authorities themselves. They provided them, usually in conjunction with a swimming pool, for people living in their area. But 13 authorities

Table 12.2 Survival of Turkish baths companies in England

Life of the company	*Number of companies*	*Percentage of sample*
Up to 5 years	13	19.12%
6 to 10 years	22	32.35%
11 to 15 years	9	13.24%
16 to 20 years	6	8.82%
21 to 25 years	8	11.76%
26 to 30 years	4	5.88%
31 to 40 years	3	4.41%
41 to 50 years	0	—
51 to 60 years	1	1.47%
61 to 70 years	1	1.47%
For 80 years	1	1.47%

Fig 12.10
The Lewes Turkish Baths in the 2014, over 130 years after they closed.
(© Malcolm Shifrin)

took over what were, in the main, well-patronised establishments. Their proprietors, almost always companies, were unable to keep them open because of problems with cash flow, loan repayments, or maintenance costs.

Some baths, for example those taken over by Manchester Corporation, had a long life afterwards. And when William Park retired from his Worcester baths, the city council compulsorily purchased them, employing his son Leonard as superintendent until his retirement 13 years later.

The companies in Lewes and Folkestone, however, failed to persuade their local councils to save them. The Lewes (Fig 12.10) baths closed; Folkestone (Fig 12.11) was more fortunate, finding an entrepreneurial saviour who kept the baths open for another 20 years.

Not all the companies were failures, and the baths of some of the more successful ones are described in later chapters. Almost all of them are interesting for one reason or another. For example, the 35 shareholders in the Hartlepool's Bath Company, including Henry Withy, one of the founders of Furness Withy, were all connected with shipping, either as shipbuilders or ship owners; all four directors of the Cardiff Electro Bath Company, which owned the Charles Street baths, were magistrates; and all the original directors, the secretary, and the architect of the Brighton Turkish Baths Company Ltd were Freemasons.[24]

Four Turkish baths, although stand-alone establishments, were owned by companies not normally associated with baths: these were the ones provided for the management, casts, and stage crew at the Wimbledon Theatre, and for workers and their families at the company towns of Crewe, Saltaire, and Swindon (see Chapter 16).

Running a successful Turkish bath, keeping it clean and accident-free, and maintaining its equipment in good condition, was not an activity to be undertaken lightly. Yet there were some proprietors who owned more than one establishment, and even a few who owned several.

Owners of several Turkish baths. 1: Dr Richard Barter

Chronologically speaking, the first name which springs to mind in this context is Dr Richard Barter. Two or three of the baths associated with him were not open to the general public: that at St Ann's Hydro, the Cork Turkish Baths for the Destitute Poor, and possibly Dr Curtin's hydro at nearby Glenbrook (with which he may have had an undisclosed link).

Local directories recorded his connection with at least 10 other establishments in their

Fig 12.11
The Folkestone Turkish & General Baths, now converted into private residences.
(Author's collection)

Table 12.3 Turkish baths, open to the public, associated with Dr Barter

Opened	Town	Location	Relationship	Associate
1859	Cork	Grenville Place	Proprietor	—
1859	Killarney	[Near the station]	Partner	Gt S & W Railway Co
1859	Bray	Quinsborough Road	Partner	William Dargan
1860	Limerick	Military Road	Partner	Samuel Wormleighton
1860	Dublin	Lincoln Place	Director	Dublin company
1860	Waterford	Hardy's Road	Director	Waterford company
1860	Belfast	Donegall Street	Partner	Thomas Cockson
1861	Sligo	?	?	?
1862	London	Victoria Street	Director	London company
1869	Dublin	Upper Sackville Street	Proprietor	—

early years, either as a director, or as proprietor (Table 12.3).

But apart from St Ann's and Upper Sackville Street, all is not quite what it seems. Once Barter had established his first stand-alone baths in Cork—the town nearest to St Ann's—he decided to spread the financial risk involved in building those which followed. This enabled him to quickly open seven other baths in Ireland, as well as the one in London. It also ensured that they were built to his satisfaction, and usually with the involvement of his architect namesake, Mr Richard Barter.

Dr Barter was, as Ronan Foley has perceptively suggested, franchising his brand, the so-called 'improved' Turkish bath.[25] The franchisee of each bath was either the partner who would eventually become its sole owner, or a locally based company of which he was a director.

In 1867, Barter disassociated himself from the Dublin Turkish Bath Company following its decision to introduce humid air into the hot rooms of its Lincoln Place baths. Only then did he again retain sole ownership of a new bath, his last, opened in Upper Sackville Street to re-establish his presence in the Irish capital (see Chapter 6, page 47).

Owners of several Turkish baths. 2: Charles Bartholomew

Charles Bartholomew, the most ambitious of the early Turkish bath proprietors, was inspired, while secretary of the Bristol FAC, by Urquhart's charisma. Although he failed to persuade the Bristol FAC to build the bath mentioned in his letter to Urquhart (see Fig 5.5, page 34),[26] he waited until he was financially able to move ahead on his own, and then opened a small bath in the south Bristol district of Bedminster.

He launched the bath as though he was organising another of his Bristol FAC activities, starting with a public meeting, followed by an event, and concluding with letters to the press.

On 17 December 1860, an advertisement appeared in the *Western Daily Press*:

> WANTED, 500 PERSONS to attend THIS EVENING at the BEDMINSTER HALL, at Eight o'clock when Mr BARTHOLOMEW will show by some important Experiments and Illustrations how the Turkish Bath abstracts from the Human System the following Diseases, viz., Consumption, Gout, Rheumatism, Boils, Stone, Cholera, Fevers, and every kind of Skin Disease.—For particulars see Bills.[27]

The following Saturday, advertisements appeared in a number of papers announcing that a Turkish Bath was now open at Mr Bartholomew's [Chemical] Works, Mill Lane, Bedminster. 'And to bring this blessing within the reach of all', the ad stated, the prices would be 1s from 9 am till 4 pm, and 6d from 4 pm till 8 pm.[28]

Finally, a week later, a letter to the editor of the *Mercury* from Robert Killip, John Harris, and John Bond Charles (a Wesleyan Minister), described in great detail how they took a Turkish bath at Bartholomew's. 'We found the premises were certainly not very imposing in external aspect, but everything was very clean, and arranged as well as the limited means and the experimental nature of the project would allow.'[29]

There was a 'changing and lounging room' and two hot rooms at 100°F (38°C) and 150°F (66°C). The bathers were then showered using a watering can, first with lukewarm water and then with cold, before being shampooed by Bartholomew 'all over the person with the open hands.' These were low temperatures even for an experimental bath, but they were probably the maximum that could be achieved in those premises without the expense of installing a new stove.

But Bartholomew's main chance came when the lease of the Royal Western Hotel became available at a low rental. The hotel, in College Green, was designed by local architect, Richard Shackleton Pope (*c* 1793–1884), and opened in 1839. It was conceived by Isambard Kingdom Brunel as an overnight stop on what was to be an integrated Brunel journey from London to New York. Passengers would start from his Paddington Station, travel on Great Western Railway (GWR) trains to his Great Western Hotel, and then cross the Atlantic on his Great Western steamships. But the hotel closed in 1855, for it was already clear that Cunard's choice of Liverpool for embarkation had made it passengers' preferred port for transatlantic crossings.

Bartholomew, stretching his resources to the full, and with at least one large loan, seized his chance and took a lease on the hotel. The Turkish baths (Figs 12.12 and 12.13), when opened on 2 January 1861, occupied the best part of two floors, and also included a range of other bathing facilities.[30] Initially, Bartholomew's wife Emma supervised the establishment on Wednesdays and Fridays when the baths were set aside for women, but within a few months, due to lack of custom, Friday became an additional men's day.[31]

In less than a year Bartholomew had—either knowingly or unknowingly—over-extended himself financially. On 26 November 1861 he was 'adjudicated bankrupt on his own petition', according to the *Bristol Mercury*, which went on to suggest that many of its readers would be pleased to hear that, 'arrangements have been made for keeping the Turkish Baths open to the public.'[32]

Bankruptcy did not hold Bartholomew back for long. By 1865, a full-page illustrated advertisement for his Turkish Baths Establishments informed the reader that there was now,

> a separate establishment for Ladies' and that … The Bristol Great Western Hotel, under the same roof with the Turkish Baths, Warm and Cold Water Baths, Tepid Swimming Baths, and Gymnasium, has been reopened on an improved Temperance Principle for the convenience of Commercial and other Gentlemen, Bathers and Patients, who will now find the largest Commercial Room in the City, an excellent Reading Room with all the London and Provincial Newspapers, 40 well-appointed Bed Rooms with well-aired Beds and clean Linen.[33]

Placed at the bottom of the page, were the addresses of two other establishments which he briefly ran, one at Church Place, Neath, and the other at Dock Street, Newport, both in nearby south Wales. Neither was a success. Bartholomew had over-reached himself again, this time by trying to branch out too quickly.

The Neath baths were owned by the Neath Bath Co Ltd from whom Bartholomew had taken a lease before the baths were completed.[34] The opening, on 14 April 1864, was marked by a public meeting in the town hall, chaired by the mayor, and attended by Dr Balbirnie, author of *The sweating cure*.[35] Ominously, the *Cambrian* reported that 'there was not a large attendance, although we noticed several ladies present.' On the design of the baths it noted with gentle cynicism:

> The first floor of the house is artistically decorated with half moons and other emblematical designs, which we suppose are intended to convey (certainly somewhat remote) the idea that the baths are a *fac simile* of those in use in Turkey and the Continent generally.

But it also remarked that everything was 'scrupulously clean and in proper order for use.'[36]

Fig 12.12 (left)
One of a range of postcards illustrating Charles Bartholomew's first major Turkish bath establishment, at College Green, Bristol. (Author's collection)
Fig 12.13 (right)
The cooling-room in Bartholomew's Turkish Baths at College Green, Bristol, shown on an early 20th-century postcard. (Bristol Record Office: BRO 43207/32/2/13)

The failure at Neath was not entirely Bartholomew's fault, partly due to problems with the town gas supply which was universally acknowledged to have been 'bad in illuminating power, and deficient in pressure.'[37]

In addition, although by now accustomed to running a large establishment in a populous and prosperous city, Bartholomew had underestimated the problems of running a small bath in a town where the reliability of public utilities could not be taken for granted. He may also have been misled, for example, as to the likely number of bathers who could be expected to patronise the baths.

We do not know how long he continued to run the baths, but he did leave Neath, and his bills unpaid, in a somewhat unsatisfactory manner. §The baths, however, under a succession of managers, survived until at least 1885.[38]

The Newport baths which Bartholomew also leased were not a success either, and by 1866 they had been sold by his creditors to the newly formed Newport (Mon) Turkish & Warm Baths Company Ltd which ran them until the early 1870s.[39]

For Bartholomew, Neath and Newport seem to have been his only failures. He was to wait almost 10 years before opening another Turkish bath, by which time he was a far more experienced businessman, and he never again leased an establishment.

The mid-1870s were a time when individual retail shops were beginning to be replaced by multiples (known in the US as chain stores). These were extremely successful, according to Dorothy Davis,

> in footwear, men's clothes, chemists' goods and sewing-machines, all of them trades where the manufacturers were making great strides in mass-production and found that it paid to control their own shops, to ensure a steady outlet for their enormous, planned production. At the same time other chains of shops were appearing whose owners were concerned only with distribution in newspapers, for instance, and hardware and tobacco ...[40]

Bartholomew (Fig 12.14), aware of these changes, realised that this was a development not only applicable to the distribution and sale of goods, but equally effective in providing services. He began by buying an existing Turkish bath in Manchester (1875). This was followed by baths in Birmingham and Worcester (1878), Bath (1881), and London (1882) (Fig 12.15). Finally, in 1887, he designed a new Turkish bath, and the following year began operating it, for the Grand Hotel in Eastbourne.

Fig 12.14
Bartholomew, in mid-life, from a self-published pamphlet.
(Charles Bartholomew, A lecture on Turkish baths, *Marshall, 1886, [frontispiece] Author's collection)*

Though we now take such things for granted, Bartholomew's genius lay in creating a house style for his baths. Many competitors' baths displayed the star and crescent; Bartholomew's baths also had their own logo, the decorated initial B which first aroused my own interest in Victorian Turkish baths. And so far as the shape of the building allowed, all his baths had a similar appearance (Fig 12.16), with similar screens of painted glass (Fig 12.17), and similarly designed furniture (Fig 12.18) and fittings.

BARTHOLOMEW'S
London Turkish Baths.

SECOND-CLASS TICKET, 1/6.

This Ticket entitles the holder to one Bath, such holder being bound by the Rules and Regulations of the Establishment, which are exhibited in the Hall at the principal entrance, the Office, and the Bath Rooms; and Visitors are requested to make themselves acquainted with such Rules and Regulations.

No. 953

Fig 12.15
A second-class ticket for Bartholomew's London Turkish Baths in Leicester Square.
(Author's collection)

Mr Bartholomew and the cripple

'Will you walk into my Turkish Baths?', said sly Bartholomew;
'Tis such a pretty little Bath, and just the thing for you;
You've only got to pop your head just inside the door,
To be cured of every pain you have, or haven't, which is more.
So will you, will you, will you, will you, walk in and be cured?
Will you, will you, will you, walk in and be cured?'

'My Baths are always open', said sly Bartholomew,
'I'm always glad to cure the bad, and set them up anew.'
'Yes, I've heard of you before, my boy, 'tis said that men are stew'd
In their own gravy at your Baths, so do not think me rude
If I will not, if I will not, walk in and be cured,
If I will not, if I will not, walk in and be cured.'

But none could ever get the best of sly Bartholomew,
And so this Cripple, 'twas from gout, inside he somehow drew;
I cannot tell the frightful sounds that people outside heard,
'Twas said that he was smoked and CURED like ham, but that's absurd;
But whether he was really cured, or whether he preferred
To keep his gout till he got out, will presently be heard.

But that Cripple ne'er was seen again to pass out of the door,
Though, in an hour, a spruce young man, in what the Cripple wore,
And VERY like him in the face, went forth upon his way
I offer here no comment, so judge of it as you may,
But won't you, won't you, won't you, won't you walk in and be cured?
But won't you, won't you, won't you, won't you walk in and be cured?

He also, as suggested earlier, had a flair for publicity. In 1868, a verse parody of 'The Spider and the Fly' *(left)* appeared in a local paper purporting to be written by a patient of his.[41] But was it?

According to Michael J Winstanley, whereas the aim of a franchiser is to share responsibility within a standard framework of practice, the multiples,

> were the brainchilds of single entrepreneurs who often controlled their empires dictatorially from a central office or, later, through the board of a limited liability company.[42]

Bartholomew certainly supervised his establishments, visiting them regularly, and advertising that he was available for consultation on specific days of the week at each of them. When, in 1886, just before he started on the design of the Eastbourne bath, he indicated that he was open to sell or lease his baths, he wrote that,

> After 30 years hard work with 700 miles a week on the Railway, he finds that he cannot give to each and all the personal attention they need.[43]

Bartholomew and exaggeration were not strangers. Noting his advertised consultation

Fig 12.16
Edgar buildings, Bath: the hottest room, showing Bartholomew's trademark painted glass panels. (Author's collection)

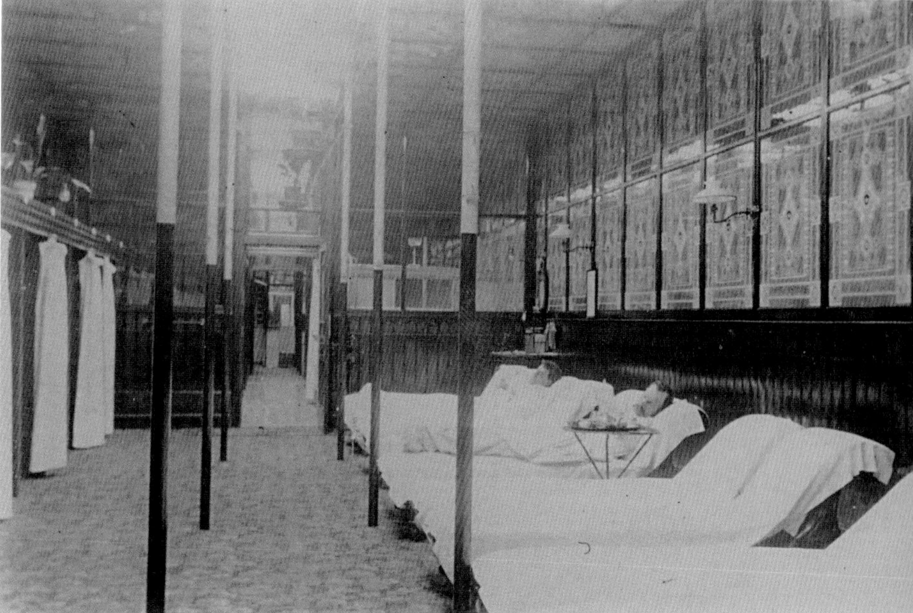

Fig 12.17 (left)
One of the smaller decorative glass panels from Edgar Buildings, Bath. (Author's collection)
Fig 12.18 (above)
The cooling-room at Edgar Buildings, Bath. (Author's collection)

days and using the August 1887 edition of *Bradshaw's Railway Guide*, we can roughly estimate his most economical weekly route during the 11 years from 1875 to 1886. He would probably be spending about 16 hours per week on trains and covering a total of around 600 miles.

Even so, by 1886 this was a hefty weekly itinerary to follow for someone approaching his 60th birthday. It is not difficult to see why he should wish to sell some of his establishments, given that none of his children was able (or possibly, willing) to take over the business. Nevertheless he continued running them till he died in 1889, and most of his baths outlived him by many years.

Later Turkish baths multiples

Bartholomew was the only owner of a multiple where each establishment was in a different town, although John North simultaneously owned a bath in Belfast and a second in Dublin, and a Mr J James briefly had one in Cardiff and another in Nottingham.

Other proprietors owned two or three baths in the same city. Thomas Andrew, for example, owned two in London, while Robert Parry and Benjamin Bell owned three each in Liverpool and London respectively.

But apart from Bartholomew's, the big Turkish bath multiples were all in London. Between 1879 and 1896, Jonathan Hurn Faulkner (Fig 12.19) appears to have built his chain of six Turkish baths—including one in Fenchurch Street Station—by converting, or adding to, existing businesses, mainly hairdressers. His base was the City Central Hotel in Newgate Street and a contemporary trade card calls him a general provider and contractor (Fig 12.20). Exceptionally, and for only a short while, he was lessee of the White Rock Turkish baths in Hastings.

Alfred Hooper Neville—he dropped the final 'e' when naming the baths—was 50 years old in 1871 when he opened the London Bridge Turkish baths at 35 and 36 Station Approach (later renamed and renumbered 7 and 8 Railway Approach).

In 1875 he opened the first of his adjacent pairs of separate baths for men and women in Whitechapel, possibly spurred on by the opening that year of a second establishment in Railway Approach. This was Samuel Thomson's Terminus Baths, at numbers 19 and 20, which aimed, like his own baths, to attract the London Bridge commuters.

On Alfred Neville's death in 1883, the baths passed to two of his sons, James Forder Neville and his younger brother Henry. By the end of the century they owned seven establishments, including their prestige headquarters in Northumberland Avenue (Fig 12.21), designed by architect Robert Walker (1837–1896) for their father. By 1900, the eighth bath had been added, and Henry was practising as a barrister, with James Forder listed as sole proprietor.

In 1908, Nevill's Turkish Baths Ltd was formed to take over the baths, their leases (ranging from 25 to 60 years), and the two freehold properties in Northumberland Avenue and Commercial Road East. Both brothers were directors, as was Herbert Edwin Sentence, a civil servant.

As the 20th century progressed, the lessening demand for Turkish baths was matched by a diminishing number of establishments. In 1957, with its last surviving bath, Nevill's was sold to the Jermyn Street Turkish Bath Company Ltd, which had been set up 11 years earlier to purchase the last of William Cooper's Savoy Turkish Baths.

Fig 12.19 (above)
J H Faulkner, at one time owner of six Turkish baths. From Margaret Molyneux's photograph of a contemporary painting by an unknown artist. (Courtesy of Margaret Molyneux and Jill Melia, Faulkner's great granddaughters)

Fig 12.20 (below)
Front and back pages of a folded trade card listing some of Faulkner's businesses. (Author's collection)

Between 1910 and 1912, William Cooper, owner of a large eponymous garden buildings and bicycle factory on the Old Kent Road, bought eight establishments to form the Savoy Turkish Baths Ltd. Two of them, for women only, backed on to adjacent men's baths. Curiously, at some stage, the name of the garden buildings company was changed to T Bath and Co, short for 'Turkish baths'.[44]

Nevill's also owned eight London baths including, like their Savoy rivals, two baths for women, backing on to adjacent men's baths.

Fig 12.21
Headquarters of Nevill's Turkish Baths in Northumberland Avenue until 1948.
(© Malcolm Shifrin)

The intertwining of these three companies, and the story of what happened to their baths, some of which are discussed in later chapters, is fascinating but lengthy. Like many such stories it includes a directorial squabble which ended in court. This one set a legal precedent which is still studied by law students.[45]

The Rochdale Pioneers' co-operative Turkish bath

Uniquely, one Turkish bath was opened neither by a joint stock company, nor by an individual entrepreneur, but by a co-operative society.

David Urquhart, who battled with his board of directors at The Hammam about their high entrance price, was especially gratified when he learned that a people's bath was being opened in Rochdale. He retained a newspaper cutting reporting that the baths initially cost £200 raised by working men in 1s shares, and that they reputedly realised 12½ per cent on their capital in their first year.[46]

Unfortunately there is little information to help us understand exactly how this was achieved; how many subscribers there were; whether the shares had to be paid for on application or over a period of time; and what proportion of the £200 'cost' was actually paid for by the share capital—for the whole amount would have involved 4,000 shares being taken up.

Urquhart firmly believed that small baths did not need to be expensive. Indeed, in 1862 he built one for £37 'in the rudest fashion and at the lowest possible cost' at his new home in Worthing (see Chapter 22).[47] And if, as seems to be the case, there were, amongst the working-men, craftsmen with the necessary skills to construct the baths themselves, then the reported outcome seems much more achievable.

Urquhart had every reason to be pleased. In March 1857, the Rochdale FAC appointed James Smithies as its chairman.[48] Smithies was crucial to the success of this particular baths project, for he was one of the original members of the Rochdale Society of Equitable Pioneers, known as the Rochdale Pioneers, and credited with the formulation of the Rochdale Principles and the foundation of the British Co-operative Movement.

Through the FAC network, Smithies asked John Johnson for some information about the bath.[49] Then, as acting secretary, he called a meeting of those wishing to subscribe to a new society which proposed to build a Turkish bath with attached news and refreshment rooms.[50] At the beginning of July, Smithies had been elected secretary of the Rochdale Subscription Turkish Bath Society.[51] By the end of the month, the subscribers had taken a two-year lease on Church Cottage at the corner of School Lane, and were intending to begin 'fitting up the premises for baths on the Oriental principle' the following month.[52] On 14 November, the baths opened for members of the society.[53]

The first manager was Joseph Jagger, leader of the West Riding Secular Union, whose pamphlet has already been quoted, and who greeted visitors 'in his Turkish bath dress.'[54]

Jagger's appointment brought the proselytising FACs and their Turkish Bath Movement closer to another group of proselytisers, the secularists, whose leader George Jacob Holyoake, editor and publisher of *The Reasoner,* regularly published news of the bath to a wider public, and whose firm Holyoake & Co was by now distributing Urquhart's *Free Press*.

Edward Royle has noted the number of secularists, especially in the north, who, in addition to Jagger, were also FAC bath owners and managers: men such as Abel Andrew (Stalybridge), Roger Evans (London), John Hindle (Stockport), John Maxfield (Huddersfield and London), John Shaw and Frederick S Rawnsley (Leeds), Hezekiah Thornton (Bradford), and Thomas Wilcock (Bradford and Liverpool). These were all staunch supporters of Urquhart, strong-believing Christian though he was. Royle saw 'the continuing appeal of Urquhart through the Turkish bath movement' as 'a constant threat to secularism, even though the baths often gave secularism a home.'[55] Rather, it shows much mutual tolerance. Conversation in the Rochdale bath would have been lively with such a mix of fervent Urquhartites, co-operators, and secularists.

Early advertisements for the new Turkish baths included a surprising range of prices. Until five years earlier, co-operative society members were limited to a maximum shareholding of £4 so that no individual could have a controlling vote, and everyone had a more or less equal say in how the society was run. Yet they established three classes of bath, ranging in price from 2s down to 6d. Even on Thursdays, 'reserved for ladies when a Female will be in attendance', there was still a three-class structure.[56]

In 1881, the Rochdale Subscription Turkish Bath Society needed to restructure itself so as to take advantage of changes in the law which now offered co-operators the protection of limited liability. The baths were also in need of refurbishment and the society had made a loss of £9 during the previous six months. A special meeting of subscribers on 2 March elected a committee to consider how best to proceed.[57]

On 28 April the first general meeting of the newly registered Rochdale Turkish Baths Co Ltd was held with Abraham Greenwood, another Rochdale Pioneer, in the chair. He, with six others, would form the first board of directors, and the new company would buy the society's assets and goodwill for around £80, having already obtained a seven-year lease on their building at an annual rent of £21. This would be financed by a public share offer of 250 £1 shares in the new company, with a 3s payment on application and a similar one on allotment (though this was changed to two payments of 5s when the offer was made).[58]

By 23 June, barely 12 weeks later, there were 60 shareholders. Most of them were members of the working-class or small traders, all but nine of whom had but a single share. Five years later, the number had risen to 244.

There were still three classes of bather in the refurbished baths, all priced as before. Shareholders, however, could buy a second-class ticket for 6d instead of 1s. And bathers could now get a vapour or sulphur bath for 1s and a slipper bath or a shower douche for 6d.[59]

The baths closed in 1891, a few months after Rochdale Corporation opened its own refurbished Smith Street baths, now with its own Turkish baths suite.

13

Housing the Victorian Turkish bath

Since 1857, more than 600 Victorian Turkish baths have been opened, with lifespans varying between nearly a century and barely a year. Just under 500, some of which are discussed more fully in later chapters, were open to members of the general public.

Here we look at some of the similarities and differences between baths loosely divided into three convenient categories: stand-alone baths, Turkish baths which are part of a larger baths and wash-house complex, and those which are converted houses or shops.

The baths and wash-house complex is straightforward enough. It includes wash-houses (where local people can wash their clothes and linen), slipper baths, swimming pools, and hot-air baths—Turkish, Russian, or both, sometimes with their own dedicated plunge pool.

Such complexes were usually provided by a local authority, although 10 were originally built by commercial companies. These were taken over by local councils when their proprietors either sold them (as in the case of the Leamington baths) or, more usually, could not make them pay and went into voluntary liquidation.

But stand-alone baths are more difficult to categorise because I have not excluded a few which, like the Cookridge Street Oriental Baths in Leeds, or the much smaller Bridge Street Turkish Baths in Bolton, have added a swimming pool or a Russian bath at a later date. In this type of building, the pool was complementary to the Turkish baths whereas, in the complex, the Turkish baths were just one of a wide range of facilities.

Also considered as stand-alone are those Turkish baths which were part of a shop and office development, such as those built for the Doncaster Oriental Chambers & Turkish Baths Co Ltd. These were designed by Thomas George Edwards, surveyor to a local sanitary authority, and opened on 25 January 1897.

At the third general meeting of the company, it was suggested that if the baths did not make a profit, the other buildings erected on the site would do so.[1] This was a sound judgement; in fact, the Turkish baths remained open for over 30 years, after which the company changed its name to Oriental Chambers Ltd and continued in business until 1965.[2]

Bradford Corporation, at Lister Terrace in Great Horton Road, was the only local authority to provide stand-alone Turkish baths by converting a house. Whether this was an economy considered appropriate because the baths were specifically for women is not known.

Stand-alone Turkish baths

Very few of these were what might be called 'set piece' Turkish baths; but 14 were 'Saracenic' in appearance, and three were neoclassical.

In Chapter 6 we looked at the 'Saracenic' buildings designed by Dr Barter's namesake, Mr Richard Barter, in Lincoln Place, Dublin and Military Road, Limerick, and also those in Bray which he designed with Sir John Benson (1812–74) for William Dargan.

In England there were, most notably, the Oriental Baths at Cookridge Street, Leeds, designed by Cuthbert Brodrick (1821–1905), and discussed in the next chapter.

Brighton's residents had been familiar with an eastern style of architecture since its iconic Royal Pavilion was built between 1787 and 1823. Nevertheless, though on a very much smaller scale, the §Brighton Hammam in West Street (Fig 13.1), designed by Horatio Nelson Goulty (1830–1869) of Goulty & Gibbins,

> rising like some Moorish Temple, resplendent with crimson and gilt, *encaustic and *terracotta in total contrast to the very English-looking 'gables and bow-windows' surrounding it,[3]

Fig 13.1
The Brighton Hammam, converted around 1910 into the Academy Cinema, and seen here in the 1930s. (Royal Pavilion and Museums, Brighton & Hove)

This is to certify that Mr. Henry Parker acted as Clerk of the Works under us during the erection of The Turkish Bath, Brighton to our entire satisfaction.

Cost of building, £9,000.

Contractors: Messrs. G. Cheesman & Co.

Goulty & Gibbins.

November, 1868. Architects. London & Brighton

Fig 13.2
Illuminated testimonial from Goulty & Gibbins, architects of the Brighton Hammam, to Henry Parker, their 'Clerk of the Works', November 1868.
(Henry's great-great-grandson, Alan Parker, and his great-great-great-granddaughter, Barbara Reader [cousins])

retained a certain 'Saracenic' elegance even after the baths had closed and the building was being used for other purposes.

It has been suggested, with much justification, that builders generally get neglected by historians in favour of architects. Here we can safely assume that the Brighton Turkish Bath Company was well pleased with their builders, for Goulty & Gibbins passed on their own satisfaction at the contribution made by their Clerk of (the) Works, Henry Parker, in the form of a most imposing testimonial (Fig 13.2).

The baths closed around 1910, and the building was converted into the 400-seat Academy cinema. This, with several name changes and refurbishments, remained open till 1973 and was demolished the following year.[4]

There were two important examples of 'Saracenic' exteriors in London. The first, in §Ashwin Street, was built in 1882 (Fig 13.3). In the days before every large city had at least one mosque, this extrovert building designed by John Hatchard-Smith (1853–1939), standing right opposite Dalston railway station, must have surprised travellers seeing it for the first time and, perhaps, tempted them to try a Turkish bath on the way home from work. But it survived barely eight years before being destroyed by fire on 7 May 1890.

The other was Nevill's New Broad Street baths (Fig 13.4), in the heart of the City of London. Designed by architect Harold Elphick (*fl* 1890), this is the only British baths building with an eastern style exterior still standing. It does so proudly, having survived the 1940s Blitz—a 'Saracenic' extravaganza in what is now Churchyard Passage, happily diverting our attention from the monotonous modernity which almost totally surrounds it.

There had been baths on this site since 1817, but the present building was erected in 1895, shortly after they were bought by Henry and James Forder Neville. The new building was very attractive, though much smaller than their flagship baths in Northumberland Avenue, and it did not cater for women.

Before many of the streets in the area were renamed, the main entrance was in Alderman's Walk (now Bishopsgate Churchyard). The baths themselves were partly underneath the original New Broad Street House (now demolished), and partly underneath Alderman's Walk. The entrance forms part of a kiosk in the upper portion of which were water tanks, masked by a Moorish-style wall, and surmounted by a similarly styled ogee cupola, decorated with a star and crescent.[5]

Fig 13.3
The Dalston Junction Turkish Baths, Ashwin Street, London.
(Historic England Library DP172002, The Builder, *14 Jan 1882)*

Fig 13.4
Nevill's New Broad Street Turkish Baths in the City of London, ten years after it closed.
(From London overlooked *by Geoffrey Fletcher. Artwork © Geoffrey Fletcher. Reproduced by permission of The Random House Group Ltd)*

Architectural journals of the day described the baths in glowing terms, praising both the overall decorative scheme, the quality of its fittings, and also the imaginative manner in which a very small ground-level area was utilised.[6]

Entering the kiosk, the bather went down a winding oak staircase, lined with *faïence, to the entrance vestibule, where he bought his ticket. After paying, he continued on to a cooling-room decorated in the style of the Alhambra in Granada. A fountain of cold filtered water, with a Doulton basin, reinforced the Moorish ambience.

The room was divided into a series of divans, or cubicles (Fig 13.5), each of which was provided with couches, an elaborate mirror, and an occasional table. The ceiling was clad in cream tinted panels with coloured borders, and the floors were covered with soft, richly patterned carpets.

Leading off the cooling-room were three hot rooms, each with marble mosaic floors, and tiled walls and ceilings. Marble seats, stained-glass windows, and wall alcoves in faïence, gave the rooms a comfortable and luxuriant air. The *caldarium* could be raised to a temperature of 270°F (132°C), the *tepidarium* to 180°F (82°C) and the *frigidarium* to 140°F (60°C). All were lit by electricity.

As in other Nevill's establishments, fresh hot air came through a grated opening below the ceiling, while the stale air was extracted through ventilators in the seats near the floor level, or gratings in the floor itself.

An additional feature was a Russian vapour bath of marble, with hot water pipes (under the seat) throwing out fine jets of steam, producing instant perspiration for those bathers who were unable to sweat in the dry heat of the Turkish bath. The adjacent shampooing-room was also fitted with marble slabs, and the walls were tiled throughout.

The bather then had a choice of showers, after which there was a 30ft (9m) cold plunge pool, 5ft (1.5m) wide, lined with marble, mosaic and tiles, complete with a decorative frieze (no pun intended).

The ceilings of the hot rooms and the shampooing room were of enamelled iron fixed to a solid roof of cement, and the windows were treble glazed to prevent rapid transmission of heat. The design and colour of the various apartments differed, and a richly modelled *stalactite cornice surrounded all the main rooms.

At the top of the staircase leading to the baths below, and throughout the relaxation areas, were walnut screens with panels of coloured leaded glass in peacock blue and gold, while the walls, beams, and columns were encased with faïence and tile-work. Even the joints were part of the design, the tiles being purpose-made in various interlocking shapes, in the Moorish manner (Fig 13.6). These were manufactured at Jackfield in the Ironbridge Gorge by Craven Dunnill[7] to the designs of the

Fig 13.5
Inside Nevill's rebuilt New Broad Street Turkish Baths when they opened in 1895. (Copyright and Courtesy of the Ironbridge Gorge Museum Trust Library, IGMT Ref. 2011.590)

Fig 13.6
Interlocking tiles specially designed by architect G Harold Elphick for use inside his New Broad Street Baths.
(© Malcolm Shifrin)

architect, who had the shape of his interlocking tiles registered.[8]

Elphick was fortunate that he was allowed to build his 'Saracenic' kiosk above ground but, as we saw earlier, the London Hammam had to be built in the area behind the main Jermyn Street building in order to conform with specific planning requirements. Elsewhere, in similar circumstances, if no additional land was available, an architect wishing to create a 'Saracenic' appearance was limited to the interior of the baths.

Several architects chose this approach, most notably the London firm of Baggallay and Bristowe (*fl* 1890s) who beat 25 other competitors to build the §Royal Baths, Harrogate (Fig 13.7). Winning the competition did not seem to overly affect Mr Baggallay who, describing the baths a few months after they opened, told the 1897 Leeds Sanitary Conference with masterly understatement that,

> I do not know that there is much I could say to interest you, unless I were to describe the oriental appointments and decoration [Fig 13.8], which are rather more luxurious than is quite usual.[9]

The gazetteer published by the Tiles & Architectural Ceramics Society (TACS) is more forthcoming, Lynn Pearson describing the interior as a 'glazed brick nirvana with Moorish-style arches, columns (Fig 13.9) and screens, *terrazzo floors (Fig 13.10) and walls of colourful brickwork.'[10] These baths were completely refurbished in the early 2000s and, happily, remain open for bathing.

Those living in Leamington Spa are not so fortunate. The 'Saracenic' Turkish baths, which opened in 1863 behind the Doric colonnade fronting (Fig 13.11) the 50-year-old §Royal Pump Rooms, closed in the 1970s.

Recently, however, the structure of the baths, including the domed octagonal room (Fig 13.12) with its slightly pointed horseshoe arches, stained glass, rose windows, and tiled floors, has been well restored as part of the town's new library and museum. This section, now a permanent exhibition about the history of the baths, is definitely worth a visit.

The façade of the Guildford Road Turkish baths, Northampton, designed by local architect Charles Dorman (*c* 1837–1901) was not 'Saracenic'; neither did the interior structure incorporate any horseshoe arches. Yet the decorative scheme adopted in the cooling-room (Fig 13.13) seems to suggest a vaguely 'Saracenic' appearance. This was achieved by the use of wooden fretwork ogee arches over the doors and scalloped arches across the curtained relaxation areas, together with a liberal provision of potted palm fronds around the 30ft (9m) long plunge pool.

There is not even the slightest suggestion of a 'Saracenic' interior behind the impressive portico of §the Roman Baths at Jesus Lane in Cambridge (Fig 13.14). Designed by the Wyatt brothers, Thomas Henry (1807–80) and Matthew Digby (1820–77), neoclassicism prevails. Long occupied by the Pitt Club, much of the

Fig 13.7
The cooling-room, looking towards the changing cubicles, at the Royal Turkish Baths, Harrogate, shortly after they opened.
(Harrogate for health, Royal Baths, c 1950. Author's collection)

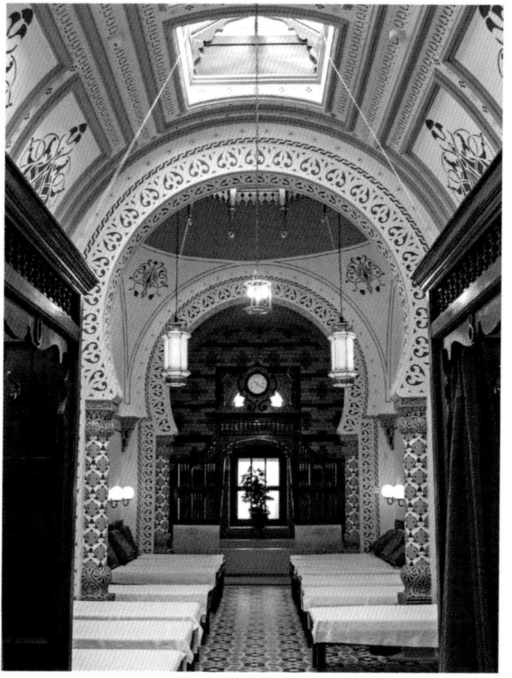

Fig 13.8
The cooling-room, looking towards the plunge pool, at the Royal Turkish Baths, Harrogate, shortly after refurbishment.
(© Jean F Smith)

Fig 13.9
Part of one of the pillars after the refurbishment.
(© Jean F Smith)

Fig 13.10
Part of the Italian mosaic floor.
(© Lenora Genovese)

Fig 13.11 (below)
Pre-1920s postcard of the façade of the Royal Pump Rooms, Leamington.
(Author's collection)

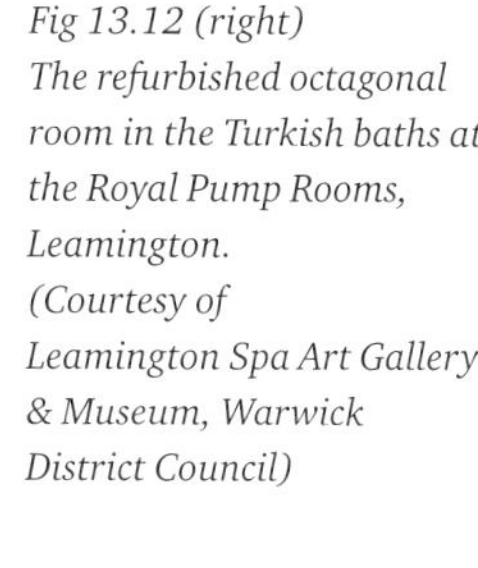

Fig 13.12 (right)
The refurbished octagonal room in the Turkish baths at the Royal Pump Rooms, Leamington.
(Courtesy of Leamington Spa Art Gallery & Museum, Warwick District Council)

Fig 13.13
The cooling-room at the Guildford Road Turkish Baths in Northampton, shortly after opening. (Author's collection)

Fig 13.14
The classical façade of the Roman Baths in Jesus Lane, Cambridge, in the 1930s, when it was home to The University Pitt Club. (Walter Morley Fletcher, The University Pitt Club, 1835–1935, *The Club, 1935)*

Fig 13.15
The façade of the Working Class Turkish Baths in Belfast prior to their demolition in 1946. (© Belfast Telegraph. *Collection Ulster Folk & Transport Museum HOYFM.BT.775)*

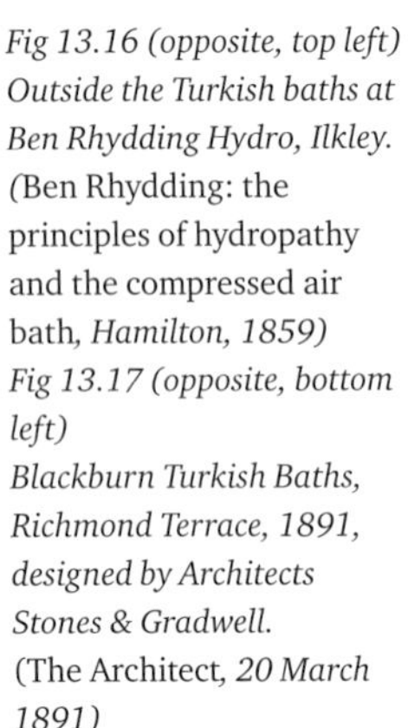

Fig 13.16 (opposite, top left)
*Outside the Turkish baths at Ben Rhydding Hydro, Ilkley. (*Ben Rhydding: the principles of hydropathy and the compressed air bath, *Hamilton, 1859)*
Fig 13.17 (opposite, bottom left)
*Blackburn Turkish Baths, Richmond Terrace, 1891, designed by Architects Stones & Gradwell. (*The Architect, *20 March 1891)*

ground floor interior, now a restaurant, can still be seen.

There were two other neoclassical baths buildings, both associated with Dr Barter. The first, in London, was the grand, but short-lived, Oriental Baths in Victoria Street, again designed by Barter's namesake and opened in 1862. But, 'inconveniently placed' in the wrong part of London, the baths were a failure, closing after less than three years.[11] The financial loss suffered by the shareholders of the Oriental Bath Company of London was only partially reduced by the District Metropolitan Railway's purchase of the building to make room for a section of its new Victoria station.

The other building, much smaller, was in §Donegall Street, Belfast (Fig 13.15). Originally opened by Dr Barter in 1860, the Belfast Working Class Turkish Baths initially remained open for around 30 years. At the beginning of the 1890s, shortly after they closed for the first time, they were bought by John North who, for the previous 10 years, had owned the Dublin Hammam in Upper Sackville Street.

North felt that a complete rebuild was necessary and appointed Dublin architect James Franklin Fuller (1835–1924) to undertake the work. The baths reopened as the Belfast Hammam in 1892, but it is not known whether its neoclassical façade was also Fuller's work, or whether it was part of the original building.

Apart from these Roman-style and 'Saracenic' buildings there were few design surprises. The separate Turkish baths building at Ben Rhydding Hydro in Ilkley (Fig 13.16), designed by Lockwood and Mawson (1849–74), was strangely Scottish Baronial in appearance. The §Richmond Terrace baths in Blackburn (Fig 13.17) and those at Great Moor Street in Bolton (Fig 13.18) are considered to be in the Queen Anne style. Of these three, only the Bolton building survives, with its strong stonework indication of purpose outside, and a few remaining vestiges of 'Saracenic' design inside. It has since been used for a variety of purposes, including a police station.

Sometimes the existence of a Turkish bath was almost completely hidden. In Coventry, at the end of 1890, Francis James fitted out his Priory Street Turkish baths in a building which was originally intended as a Wesleyan Chapel, though never used for that purpose. And William Edward Wiley's Frederick Street Hammam in Birmingham (Fig 13.19) seemed completely invisible, its exterior, on the right,

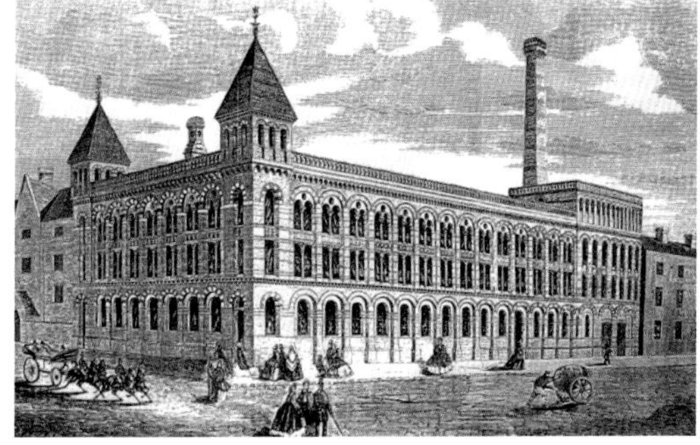

Fig 13.18 (top right) Bolton Turkish Baths, Great Moor Street, 1891.
(The Architect, *20 March 1891)*
Fig 13.19 (bottom right) The men's and women's entrances to W E Wiley's Hammam and Turkish Baths can be seen on the right at the end of his pencil factory in Frederick Street, Birmingham.
(Building News, *21 August 1863)*

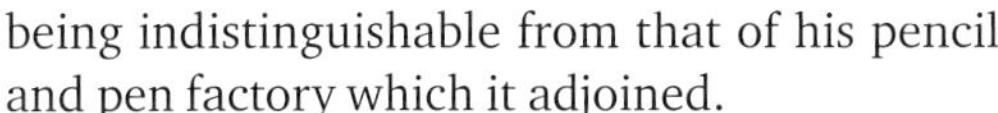

being indistinguishable from that of his pencil and pen factory which it adjoined.

Most of the remaining stand-alone baths were in the vernacular, fitting in more or less appropriately with their neighbours. In the main, they were built by individual proprietors, small under-capitalised companies and, in the case of the Biggin Street Turkish Baths, by the corporation of the relatively small town of Dover. For all of these, the cost of an unusual design would have been a major disincentive.

Turkish baths within the public baths complex

Because Turkish baths were not mentioned in the Baths and Wash-houses Acts, local authorities in London were slow to provide them. Further away from the seat of government, provincial authorities showed more willingness to treat Turkish baths as just another type of hot-air bath which, in the form of vapour baths, *were* specifically permitted.

For local authority architects, many of whom were actually borough surveyors rather than professional architects, the main choice was between designing and furnishing the Turkish bath to match the other facilities in the complex, or having to defend the extra cost of a more eastern approach.

The inevitable result was that anything out of the ordinary was as rare inside the baths as outside. Many councillors and several newspapers were quick to point out that councils were spending, or squandering—according to the political views of the writer—ratepayers' money.

Such attitudes persisted into the 20th century. Even for straightforward, simply designed baths such as those designed by Robert John Angel (*fl* 1892–1926) for London's Bermondsey Council in 1927, the *Daily Mirror* was critical.

Under the front page headline:

BERMONDSEY'S NEW £150,000 PALACE OF BATHS

were two photographs. The first, of the cooling-room (Fig 13.20), was captioned 'The luxurious Turkish baths, where the charge will be 3s. 6d.' The second, an exterior view, was captioned,

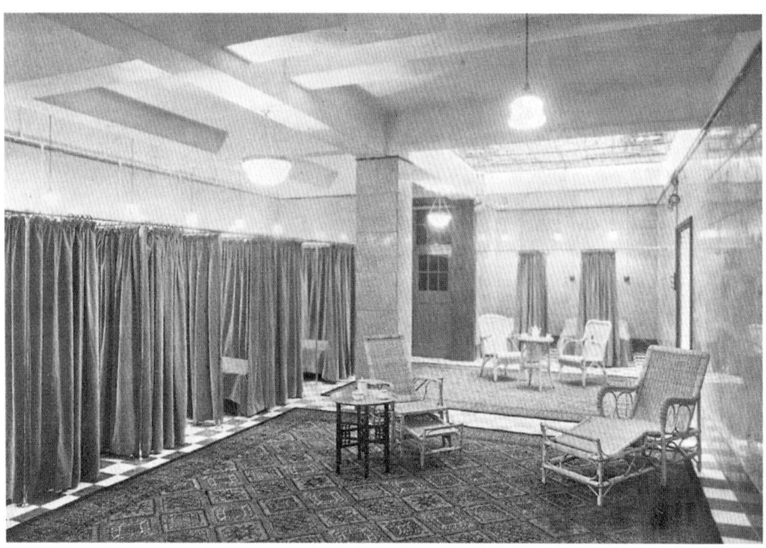

Fig 13.20
The cooling-room in Bermondsey Council's 'new £150,000 palace of baths'.
(Souvenir of the opening of New Central Baths, *Metropolitan Borough of Bermondsey, 1927. From the collections of the Southwark Local History Library & Archive)*

> Bermondsey's palatial new baths, built by the Socialist-controlled Council at a cost of over £150,000, and described by the mayor, Mr G Catchpole, at the opening ceremony on Saturday, as 'better than the best.' The building comprises marble halls, first and second-class swimming pools with stained-glass windows, private, Turkish and Russian baths, a recreation-room and baths for babies.[12]

There were many local councils where proposals to provide Turkish baths were discussed, often over an extended period, and finally rejected. But some went ahead and built baths with interiors that were designed to a very high standard.

Those at Carlisle were built by William Johnstone, a local builder, for around £2,300.[13] They were designed by Henry C Marks, the city engineer and surveyor, and his assistant, Percy Dalton (*c* 1884–1957), who later succeeded him in the post.[14] The Turkish baths opened in 1909 and, though altered, are still in use.

The interior, with its cooling-room, changing cubicles (Fig 13.21), and plunge pool all faced with green and white tiling by Minton Hollins of Stoke-on-Trent, and its 'Moorish-style keyhole arch and curious capitals' (Figs 13.22 and 13.23), has justly been called a 'remarkable survivor.'[15]

Other notable tilework can still be seen in Scotland at the Carnegie Baths in Dunfermline, although the Turkish baths, having just passed their centenary, closed in 2008.

The outside of the building, in Classical Revival style, is faced in grey stone. Inside, the mainly blue and green polychrome glazed wall tiles, mosaic floors, and 'the use of horseshoe arches at openings and niches, as well as a proliferation of traditional curvilinear patterns', emphasise the Moorish theme.[16] Untiled walls were plastered and painted in restful pastel shades. In contrast, the cooling-room (Fig 13.24), furnished with curtains and carpets, seemed at the time,

> a veritable Turkish apartment with its carved and decorated wood screens, and wall surfaces all elaborately treated in positive colours of rich reds, blues, and gilding all forming a pleasing and attractive eye scheme adding to the perfect comfort of the bath.[17]

In the 1970s, the baths were renovated 'with no great sensitivity',[18] and when they closed were replaced by a health suite with a single *tepidarium* kept at around 120°F (49°C). The Turkish

Fig 13.21 (left)
Changing cubicles at Carlisle.
(© Malcolm Shifrin)

Fig 13.22 (centre)
A keyhole arch at Carlisle.
(© Malcolm Shifrin)

Fig 13.23 (right)
Curious capitals at Carlisle.
(© Malcolm Shifrin)

baths, with their original tiling, have been converted into a couple of meeting rooms.[19]

The Turkish baths at Harrogate (1897), Dunfermline and Carlisle, straddling the end of the 19th century and the beginning of the 20th, seem to be the only local authority baths to adopt a mainly 'Saracenic' interior. But, in doing so, they helped—as did the baths at Glossop Road, Sheffield (1877), and Hathersage Road, Manchester (1906)—to bring about 'the full flowering of tiled decoration which came with the development of Russian or vapour baths and Turkish baths.'[20]

Even the subtle use of just a few Islamic features could suggest an eastern bath without the expense of, for example, using tiles with moulded surfaces.

The Reginald Street baths in Derby, for example, which opened in 1904, had a plunge pool reached through an 'inward curving screen of

Fig 13.24
Postcard of the cooling-room at the second Carnegie Baths, Dunfermline, when they opened in 1905.
(Author's collection)

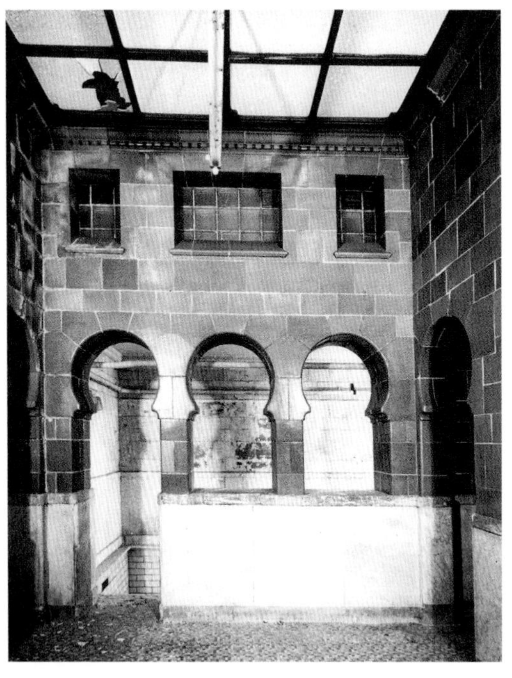

Fig 13.25
'Three Islamic arches' at Reginald Street, Derby. (Historic England Archive FF98/00342)

three Islamic arches'[21] (Fig 13.25), with similarly styled windows and doors in the cooling-room. Although the building was designed by the English architect, Alexander MacPherson (1847–1935), the plans were signed by the city surveyor, John Ward, with whom he often worked. Although some parts of the building are still in use, the baths closed in 1982.

Other architects, before and after 1900, tended to use plain tiles in the hot rooms, with perhaps the addition of a coloured stripe or two. In Scotland, William Mackison (1833–1906) the architect newly appointed as Burgh Engineer of Dundee, was probably responsible for the Turkish baths added to the swimming pool at West Protection Wall in the early 1870s, though the actual design may have been by his depute, James Thomson. Although plain tiles predominated, some walls did have elaborately tiled patterns.

Fig 13.26
Mainly plain walls and encaustic tiled floors at West Protection Wall, Dundee, Scotland. Here, early in the 20th century, David Edwards McGarry, Turkish Baths Attendant, sits in a weighing chair next to the plunge pool. (Photograph courtesy of McGarry's great-grandson, Graeme Ewen McGarry)

Cooling-rooms were frequently quite plain (Fig 13.26), with simple curtains on a rod or rail facilitating changing-cubicle privacy—perfectly adequate, if somewhat unexciting. Some cooling-rooms had elaborate couches (Fig 13.27), but most had easy chairs, or ordinary café-style chairs and tables (Fig 13.28).

Even the plainest baths often had some features to set them apart. Sometimes there were arched openings between the various rooms which, if not ogee or keyhole, were often, as at Bury (1864) (Fig 13.29), still quite attractive. Manchester's Whitworth baths (1890) had an ornate series of repeated pattern mosaic dados (Fig 13.30), while others had a simple tessellated floor, as at Stow Hill in Newport, Wales (1890).

In 1933, Birmingham's Baths Department replaced the city's first Turkish baths in Kent Street where, in 1879, they had superseded a disused wash-house. The new baths were designed by Archibald Hurley Robinson (1883–1953) and built behind a long neoclassical façade (Fig 13.31).

If including Turkish baths in a different style from the rest of the building seems strange, we need look no further than Kent Street for proof that it really did have a positive effect on bathers. With its adoption of the keyhole arch (Fig 13.32), the Turkish Bath suite was 'truly sumptuous with an Eastern style' of its own. Even as late at 1954, according to one bather,

> walking through that door into the Turkish Baths transformed everybody. They began to act as if they were living in that period … The Attendant called everybody 'Sir'. And when you came out it was a rude awakening.

At Kent Street the classes mixed, as Urquhart had hoped they would in all Turkish baths. A non-professional man who bathed,

> alongside the bankers, solicitors, schoolmasters and dealers from the jewellery quarter recalls that 'While you were in there—for your shilling—you were made to feel really important.'[22]

Though severely damaged during World War II, the baths later reopened, remaining in use till 1977. In 2009 the building was demolished to make room for a car park.

Fig 13.27 (top left)
Chunky chairs and solid couches in the cooling-room at Plumstead Baths in Woolwich, London. (Greenwich Heritatge Centre)

Fig 13.28 (centre left)
The cooling-room at Gilkes Street, Middlesbrough. (Courtesy of Teesside Archives)

Fig 13.29 (bottom left)
An arched entrance at Bury. (Bury Central Library GB126.Bury RIS)

Fig 13.30 (below)
Mosaic dados at Manchester's Whitworth Baths. (© T Ford www.whateversleft.co.uk)

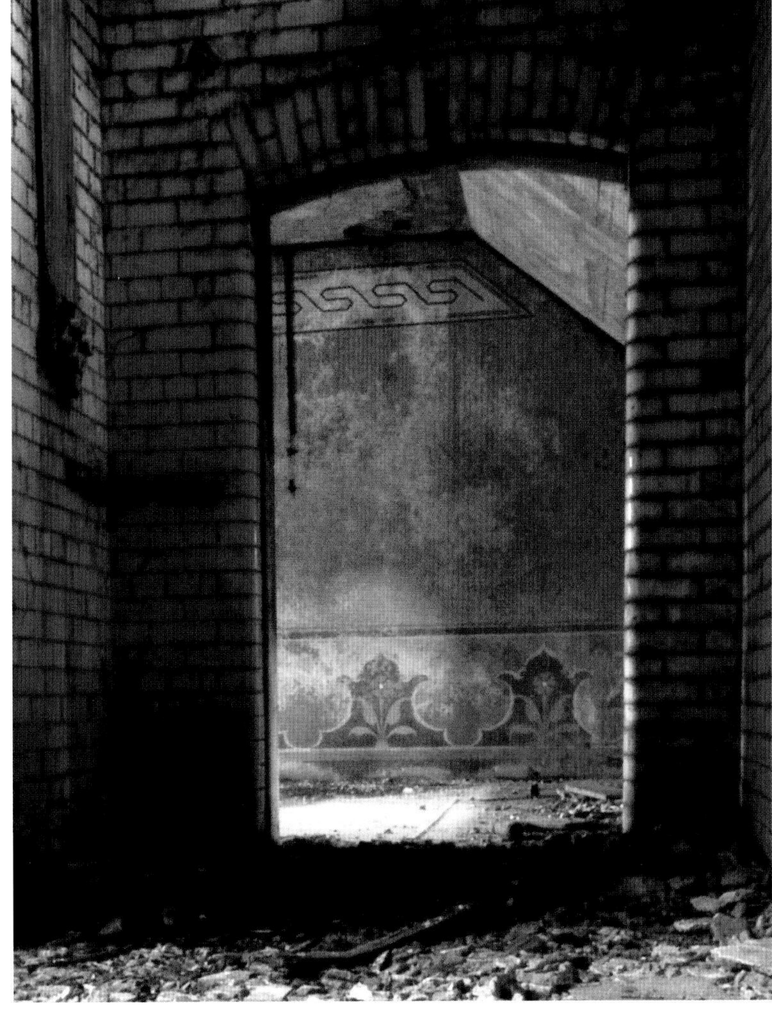

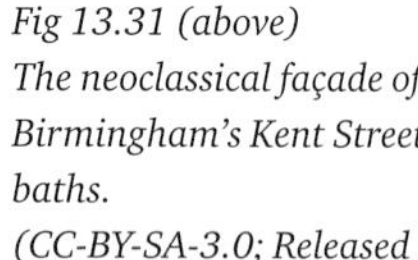

Fig 13.31 (above)
The neoclassical façade of Birmingham's Kent Street baths.
(CC-BY-SA-3.0; Released under the GNU Free Documentation License)

Fig 13.32 (above right)
The style of the Kent Street Turkish baths is in complete contrast to the outside of the building.
(Rachel Wilkins, Turrets, towels and taps, *Birmingham Museums, 1984, p.13. Reproduced with the permission of the Library of Birmingham)*

The Gilkes Street Turkish bath in Middlesbrough, designed by S E Burgess, the borough engineer, was also built in 1933. Its cooling-room may have been unexceptional, but in the hot rooms, as in the Kent Street baths, there was a 1930s take on the keyhole arch. The baths closed some time in the late 1980s.

Fortunately there are still some 19th-century baths buildings with well-designed interiors and beautiful tiling which, though their Turkish baths are no longer open, can still be visited.

One of the largest is at Glossop Road in Sheffield, opened in 1877 in a building externally similar to many other Victorian buildings of its period. The Turkish baths were built on a triangular site behind an existing swimming pool, and the resulting floor plan must surely have been the strangest layout of a Turkish bath to be found anywhere (Fig 13.33).

Yet the rooms, octagonal, pentagonal, triangular as well as rectangular, all fitted well into the scheme of things. The cooling-room, with its curtained changing cubicles, easy chairs and felt-clad marble benches, occupied two floors of one of the octagons. The upper floor, a wide balcony overlooking the main area, was reserved for smokers. The hot rooms were

Fig 13.33
The Turkish baths at Glossop Road in Sheffield were built behind an existing building on a triangular site, yet the arrangement of the differently shaped rooms seemed to work.
(Author's collection)

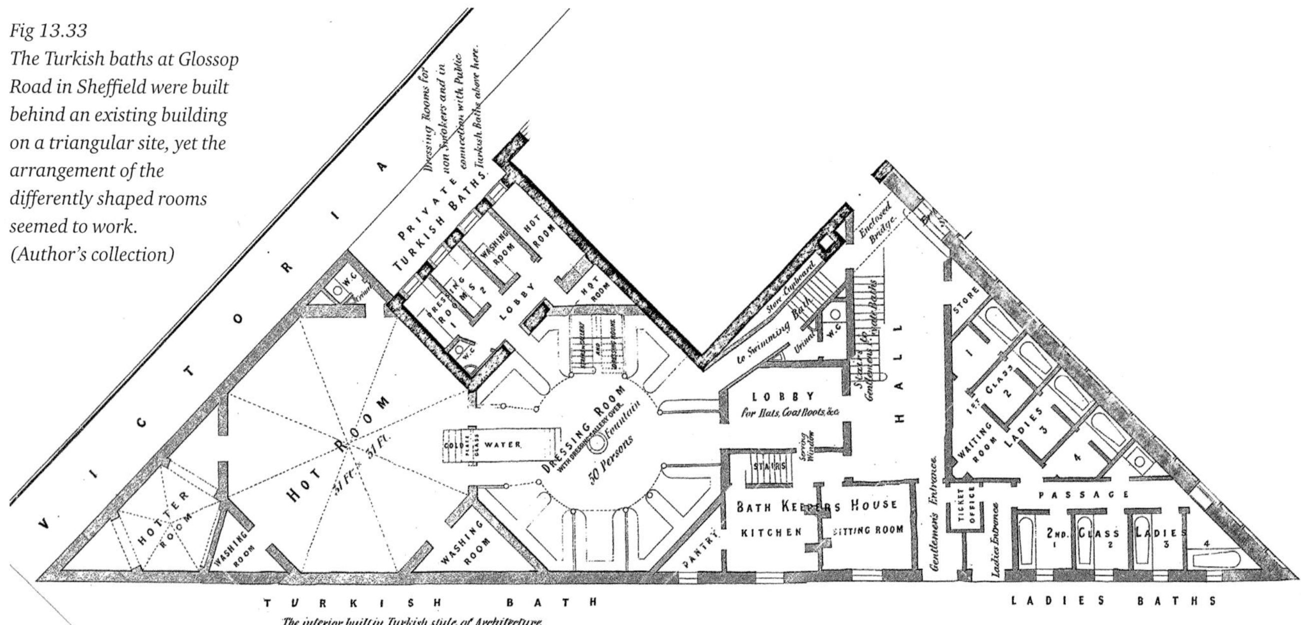

'luxuriously fitted out with tessellated pavements (Fig 13.34), white and coloured glazed brick walls, [and] arched ceilings' built to a high standard.[23]

The baths were designed by Sheffield architect Edward Mitchel Gibbs (1847–1935) for the Sheffield Bath Co Ltd, and its heating system designed and supplied by Thomas Edward Vickers, one of the company's directors.

Like many similar companies, this one was under-capitalised. By 1886, the baths complex, originally costing £33,000 to build, had been sold to the first of two successive sole proprietors, before being bought for £4,000 by Sheffield Corporation in 1895.

The baths closed in 1990, remaining empty until the whole corner was privately redeveloped to include a public house and 23 luxury apartments. Finally, the Turkish baths were sympathetically refurbished to reopen as a luxury day spa. But although the Turkish baths largely retain their original appearance, they are now used for steam baths and various spa treatments.

The other splendid Turkish baths suite was at §Manchester's Victoria Baths in Hathersage Road. This was designed by city architect, Henry Price (1867–1944), and opened on 7 September 1906. If its tessellated floors are not as decorative as those in Sheffield, there are compensations, including several walls covered with green tiles designed by Frederick C Howells and probably manufactured by Pilkingtons (Fig 13.35). The polished woodwork of the doors (Fig 13.36), internal windows, and bannisters, is of a very high quality. Perhaps most impressive of all are the many stained-glass windows and door panels made by local glass stainer, William Pointer. Especially fine is the large panel known as the Angel of Purity in the cooling-room (Fig 13.37).[24] These baths were closed on 13 March 1993 despite a protest

Fig 13.34
A mosaic tiled floor in a hot room at Glossop Road.
(© Malcolm Shifrin)

Figs 13.35 and 13.36
At Manchester's Victoria baths, the rooms are extensively tiled (left), while the doorways (right) are of polished woodwork with stained glass panels.
(© Malcolm Shifrin)

Fig 13.37
The Angel of Purity stained-glass window by local craftsman, William Pointer. (Jon Parker Lee, Victoria Baths Trust)

Fig 13.38
The local community marches in protest before closure on 13 March 1993. (Courtesy of Victoria Baths Trust)

march (Fig 13.38) and a two day sit-in by an estimated 200 demonstrators.

There could hardly be a greater contrast than that between the Edwardian splendour of these baths and Edward Harding Payne's design for London's first local authority baths, opened in 1905 in the Old Kent Road, Camberwell. Yet they opened within a year of each other. It is not that the latter skimped on materials; plenty of Sicilian marble was used for Camberwell's benches, shampooing slabs, and a fountain. The hot rooms had walls of glazed brickwork, and the floors were of mosaic and terrazzo.

But while the appearance of the Manchester baths exemplifies the pinnacle of Victorian Turkish baths design, the Camberwell baths, destroyed in the Blitz, were a harbinger of how the clean lines and simplicity of 20th-century baths would develop.

After Camberwell, few highly decorated baths were built, apart from those already mentioned. There were, in any event, fewer Turkish baths built after World War I, and barely a handful after World War II.

Three baths from the interwar period deserve mention. In London, the Porchester Hall baths built by Paddington Borough Council are still open (see Chapter 15, page 166).

The baths in Cliftonville Avenue, Margate were originally opened in 1927 as an adjunct to the Hydro Hotel and were bought at auction four years later by the Borough of Margate. The building, in a modernist style (Fig 13.39) with, perhaps, touches of art deco (Fig 13.40), was of white glazed terracotta pierced by metal-framed multi-pane windows (Fig 13.41), some decorated with the star and crescent. The interior was also modern, with walls and floors of Italian marble, yet it also had a Victorian needle shower, pseudo Grecian motifs decorating the walls (Fig 13.42), and the star and crescent on the floor.

The Turkish baths at the Newcastle-on-Tyne City Pool, a Grade II Listed Building designed by John Edward Dixon-Spain (1878–1955) and Charles Nicholas (*fl* 1892–1926), were opened on the site of earlier baths in 1928.

While the shampooing and hot rooms had no special design features, the cooling-room was particularly attractive with its simple inlaid floor decoration, circular glazed dome, and mahogany panelled changing rooms and doors (Fig 13.43).

The council's main boast in its celebratory opening booklet was the ventilation system which passed clean air through a water spray chamber before being heated. The hot air was then directed separately to each of the hot rooms, instead of passing through each in turn.[25] The booklet suggested that this was the only such system in the country, but there were also separate airflows to the hot rooms in the baths at the Royal Automobile Club (see Chapter 21).

Fig 13.39 (left)
The hydro in Cliftonville Avenue, Margate, in 1927. (Reproduced by kind permission of Dixon Wilson)
Fig 13.40 (centre left)
Exterior detail showing touches of art deco. (© Malcolm Shifrin)
Fig 13.41 (centre right)
Star and crescent window at the side of the hydro. (© Malcolm Shifrin)
Fig 13.42 (bottom left)
Hot rooms with a Grecian motif on the floor. (Reproduced by kind permission of Dixon Wilson)
Fig 13.43 (bottom right)
*The cooling-room at Newcastle-on-Tyne when the baths opened in 1928. (*Souvenir to commemorate the opening of the City Hall and Northumberland Baths, *The Council, 7 November 1928, p.18. Author's collection)*

The Newcastle baths were still open when this chapter was started, but are now closed as a result of savage government cuts to local authority funding. The stupidity of such an irreversible response to a temporary difficulty stands out by comparison with an earlier, wiser approach; Middlesbrough's Gilkes Street baths were built as a result of the county borough council's successful application in 1930 for a grant after the government 'pressed Local Authorities to submit schemes for the relief of unemployment.'[26]

In 1975, one of the last Turkish baths to be built was part of Nottingham's Victoria Leisure Centre. Totally modern in style, this was a mid-20th-century realisation of the clean lines of the Camberwell baths, exemplifying all that was best in the Victorian Turkish bath before its demise.

The walls of the shampoo and hot rooms were faced with Italian glass mosaics in pale bronze and gold, the plunge in dark blue flashed with gold (Fig 13.44). The massage slabs were of white Sicilian marble, with the floors finished in brown vitrified ceramic mosaic, while the carpeted cooling-room had a cedar-lined ceiling. There was also a steam room and an *Aeratone bath.[27]

When opened, there were separate Turkish bath and sauna suites so that 'If a man visits the Turkish section his wife can have a sauna. They can then meet in the solarium, situated between the two suites.'[28] The baths closed in 2010 and the building is currently due for demolition.

Turkish baths within shops and houses

Around 70% of the nearly 500 Turkish baths built for the general public were not purpose-built and were located in part, or the whole, of an existing building.

Some of them occupied a shop, such as Joseph Constantine's establishment in Oxford Street, Manchester, catering for business people and those in town for the day. Constantine's was among the minority which had the advantage of shop windows (Fig 13.45) and was able to show, if not the actual baths, then at least its accompanying hairdressing salon.

Others, such as the working-class baths opened by the Leeds FAC at St Peter's Square (Fig 13.46), were behind or below a shop, sharing its entrance and hoping to attract those who lived and worked in the locality. Domestic basements were also converted into baths, such as James W Bryning's Surrey Turkish Baths in Blackfriars Road, just south of the Thames.

Unlike Constantine's, these baths had to rely on small signs or posters to attract custom, though this did not always apply when baths were in a converted house.

In Wales, at the Merthyr Tydfil Turkish Baths, opened around 1868, Thomas Atkins, the original proprietor, discreetly painted the words 'Turkish Baths' on the longer, road-facing wall of his house. A later proprietor, William Pool, was not so shy, applying much bolder lettering on several walls, with a large star and crescent

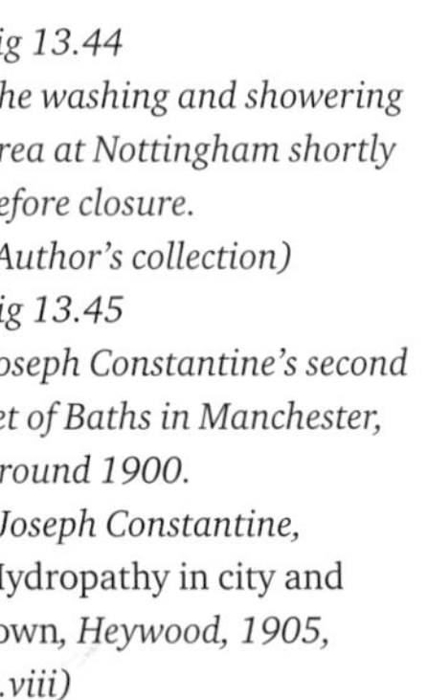

Fig 13.44
The washing and showering area at Nottingham shortly before closure.
(Author's collection)
Fig 13.45
Joseph Constantine's second set of Baths in Manchester, around 1900.
(Joseph Constantine, Hydropathy in city and town, *Heywood, 1905, p.viii)*

Fig 13.46
Turkish baths opened in 1858 by the Leeds Foreign Affairs Committee, photographed at an unknown later date.
(By kind permission of Leeds Library and Information Services. Leodis ID: 20031017_79638309)

on the main façade (Fig 13.47). His advertisements showed that he also had a sense of humour (Fig 13.48).

When Mr D Taylor opened his Turkish baths at 15 Sarsfield Street in Limerick, he originally just painted TURKISH BATHS 1887 on part of the wall over the front door. This gave no indication that inside there was a 40ft × 28ft (12m × 8.5m) cooling-room with 26 upholstered dressing boxes, a 15ft × 9ft (4.6m × 2.7m) plunge pool, a fountain, hot rooms, shampooing room, needle showers, a laundry with drying rooms and, in the basement, a caretaker's flat. By the time of the 1916 Easter Rising, when British tanks blockaded Sarsfield Bridge (Fig 13.49) and troops had been billeted in the baths, Michael J O'Brien, the new owner, had added a small supplementary hanging sign over the front door.[29]

Fig 13.47 (below)
The building as an advertising hoarding—the Merthyr Tydfil Turkish baths.
(Carolyn Jacob, The County Borough of Merthyr Tydfil, *Alan Sutton, 1994. Merthyr Tydfil Public Library Service)*

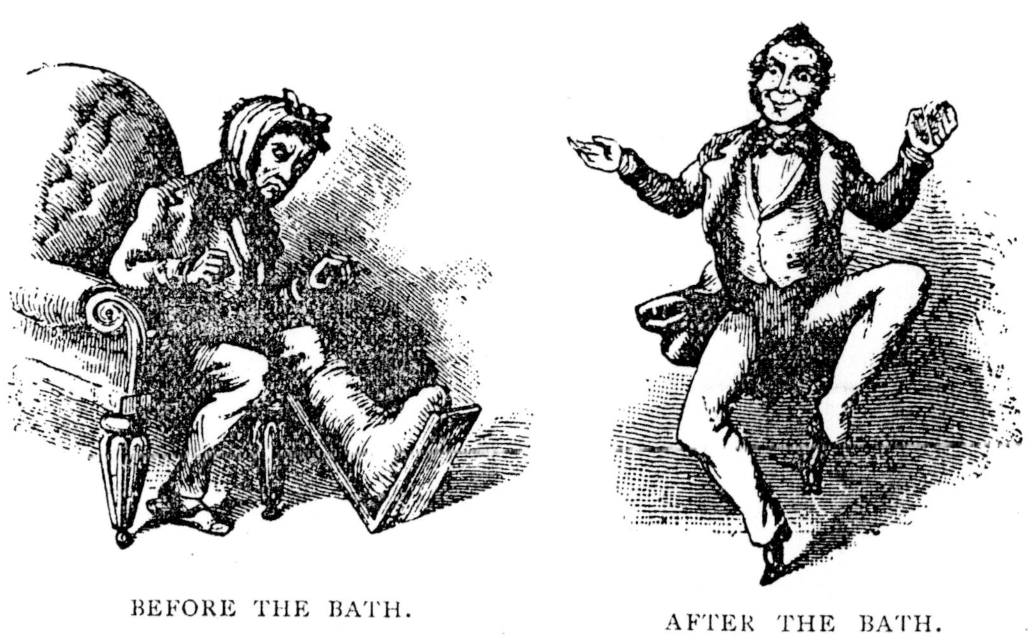

Fig 13.48
One of several 'Before and after' type advertisements. (Express almanac and year book for Merthyr Tydfil, *1897, p.48. Merthyr Tydfil Public Library Service)*

Fig 13.49
British tanks blockading Sarsfield Bridge in Limerick during the 1916 Rising. (Courtesy of Limerick Museum)

Another approach was adopted by Henry Collis. He made his Southsea baths in Portsmouth (*c* 1872) more prominent by painting ogee shaped outlines around the existing windows of his corner house in King's Terrace (Fig 13.50). During the 1880s the baths were patronised by the Duke of Edinburgh, enabling Collis to advertise his establishment as the Royal Turkish Baths, though it seems unlikely that it was the windows which persuaded royalty to bathe there.[30]

There were also a few establishments where, as at Burton's Turkish or Roman Baths for Ladies and Gentlemen (in London's Euston Road), the baths were on several floors of two adjoining houses. This allowed separate entrances for male and female bathers, and, according to Holyoake, 'the Turkish crescent now graces the front of the garden leading to it.'[31]

Many of the baths housed in existing buildings had to make do with access through a door or passageway between two shops, or down

Fig 13.50 (left)
Orientalising the windows at Southsea Baths in Portsmouth.
(Author's collection)

Fig 13.51 (above)
Inside the Savoy Hill Turkish baths—the first in London to be lit by electricity.
(Author's collection)

steps to a basement entrance. So there was, in practice, no exterior to design. This could also be the case for quite large establishments such as the Cork Turkish Baths in South Mall, and at the Savoy Turkish baths at 92 Jermyn Street. The owners of these baths, like those of baths in buildings with a frontage constrained by planning restrictions, had to limit their designers' ambitions to the interior.

It seems that none of the baths in converted shops or houses adopted a Roman or neoclassical style for their interiors, although some, such as the Savoy Hill Turkish Baths in London (Fig 13.51), did try to incorporate a few 'Saracenic' features—a fountain, horseshoe arches, decorative tiles, divans, and an occasional octagonal Turkish-looking table.

The first baths in England to have a 'Saracenic' interior opened in 1859. This was William Potter's second establishment, in Clifford Street, Manchester, which even had a dome (Fig 13.52). The remains of these baths (Fig 13.53), including parts of the columns (Fig 13.54), were discovered in 2013 while preparing foundations for the new National Graphene Institute at Manchester University.[32]

In most of these conversions, however, the internal decoration was about as authentically Turkish as Ingres's painting *Le Bain turc* authentically represents an Islamic *hammam* (see page 15).

It is very difficult, for example, to know what to make of this artist's impression of the men's baths at Earls Court Gardens in West London (Fig 13.55), or to discover whether it bore any

Fig 13.52
William Potter's second Turkish bath, Clifford Street, Manchester.
(Author's collection)

Figs 13.53 and 13.54 William Potter's second Turkish baths unearthed in 2013 (left), and part of a 'hypocaust' uncovered at the site of the bath (right). (Courtesy of Oxford Archaeology)
Fig 13.55 (below left) Orientalising the image—the men's cooling-room at Earls Court Gardens, London, 1930s. (Author's collection)
Fig 13.56 (below right) The women's cooling-room at the same establishment, and at the same time. (A R James, Why go for a cure?*, James's Hydro, c 1925)*

resemblance to actuality. Even the image of the women's cooling-room (Fig 13.56) is of little help because women's facilities so often differed from the men's. But as the baths closed in 1941, it is impossible to tell.

Many of the small baths in working-class districts were very short lived and questions about a decorative style probably never arose. Their proprietors were too concerned with getting their bath to function in the limited amount of space at their disposal to worry about design.

It is, perhaps, understandable that it is the set piece establishments which are written about, and about which theories of design and orientalism are woven—it is, of course, easier to find out about them.

'Saracenic' or Roman?

When proprietors decided that they wanted their baths to be 'Saracenic' or neoclassically Roman in appearance, it was not just because they thought this would result in attractive buildings. They were also making a statement about what they thought their baths should be.

The Victorians discussed, in a variety of journals,[33] whether the bath should be called Roman or Turkish. Nebahat Avcıoğlu has suggested that in preferring the term Roman bath, the west was reclaiming its ancestry from the east. Or, in other words, that Roman (read European) baths would be more acceptable to a British public than Turkish (read oriental) baths.[34]

But to Dr Barter, 'Roman' simply meant dry air, in contrast with 'Turkish', which implied

vapour. And Urquhart's use of 'Turkish' was a deliberate choice consequent on his seeing the bath as an effective means of introducing Turkish culture to the British people. Most importantly, this was not as a curiosity to amuse them, but as something worthy of emulation.

So the way in which many proprietors saw the history of the bath and its terminology, inevitably impinged on discussions about which architectural style they should adopt. This was especially so around 1861, by which time over three dozen establishments had already opened. Architects asked whether the baths actually had to *look* Turkish or Roman.

Early that year, a cynical William Hardie Hay (1813–1901), responsible the previous year for the design of the 'Saracenic' Turkish bath at §Lochhead Hydropathic Establishment in Aberdeen (Fig 13.57), gave a lecture at the Liverpool Architectural Society. He admitted that he had not been happy about the style adopted. His brief, he said, was 'to produce a certain accommodation at the very smallest outlay' and his original plan was 'based upon the baths of ancient Rome', but,

> I have adopted the Turkish or oriental style of architecture with a touch of Eastern grandeur, so that the Turkish Baths might not be altogether a misnomer to the uninitiated; nevertheless, there is a very large demand made upon the practical skill and experience of an architect in the erection of works of this kind. But I was employed to design Turkish baths, and Turkish baths they must be; to arrange the interior as I pleased; but the bulbous domes and gilded minarets must appear in all the cheapest and most showy style, so that the Oriental character might be realised as freshly as from a perusal of [Thomas Moore's popular book-length poem] *Lalla Rookh*.
>
> I should be inclined, however, to recommend a thoroughly English style of architecture as decidedly preferable to this.[35]

The Roman emphasis of the baths at Jesus Lane, Cambridge, was deliberate and intended to emphasise that *their* bath was to be no steamy *hammam*. With perhaps typical academic insouciance, it was advertised in the local paper as 'public and private *thermae*', it being assumed that anyone living in Cambridge would know what *thermae* were without any further explanation.[36]

The Roman design was also intended to give a historical background to what was a novel experience by linking it to an established tradition. The problem was that in Cambridge the proprietors chose the wrong tradition. With the not inconsiderable amount of publicity and discussion of the bath in contemporary newspapers and magazines—all referring to *Turkish* baths—it is hardly surprising that the Roman baths were not a success and survived less than a year.

LOCH-HEAD TURKISH BATH, near ABERDEEN.
Bath, 87 Feet long.
Hot Rooms, 18 to 25 Ft. high.

Fig 13.57
Trade card for the Turkish Baths at Lochhead Hydro, Aberdeen.
(Image courtesy of Aberdeen City Libraries)

Proprietors who chose a 'Saracenic' appearance (Table 13.1) were linking to a tradition just as much as the Roman Bath Company in Cambridge, but to a tradition which at that time was actually in the public eye, and so their baths' unusual appearance became a marketing asset.

Significantly, 11 of these baths were built between 1856 and 1866—while the bath was still establishing itself. Thereafter, apart from Dr Barter's last building at St Ann's (1870) and the London ones at Ashwin Street (1882) and New Broad Street (1895), no further baths were built in this style—it was no longer necessary. The Victorian Turkish bath had already gained acceptance.

Table 13.1 Turkish baths with 'Saracenic' exteriors

Year	Place	Address
1859	Blarney	St Ann's Hydro (2nd baths)
1859	Bray	Quinsborough Road
1859	Dublin	Lincoln Place
1859	Limerick	Military Road
1860	Killarney	
1861	Aberdeen	Lochhead Hydro
1862	Bridge of Allen	
1863	Glenbrook	Victoria Baths & Family Hotel
1863	Scarborough	Bland's Cliff
1864	St Leonards-on-Sea	West Hill
1866	Leeds	Cookridge Street
1870	Blarney	St Ann's Hydro (3rd baths)
1882	London	Ashwin Street
1895	London	New Broad Street

14

Commercial Turkish baths

In this chapter, I aim to give a general impression of what commercial Turkish baths were like. The last of them closed almost 40 years ago; from first to last, barely 120 years passed (Fig 14.1).

There is no easy way to select, from nearly 400 such establishments, those to be discussed here. Inevitably, instead of a detailed and logically presented history, there can only be a loosely connected sequence of partial accounts and points of interest which exemplify some of the unique features, similarities, and differences between the baths.

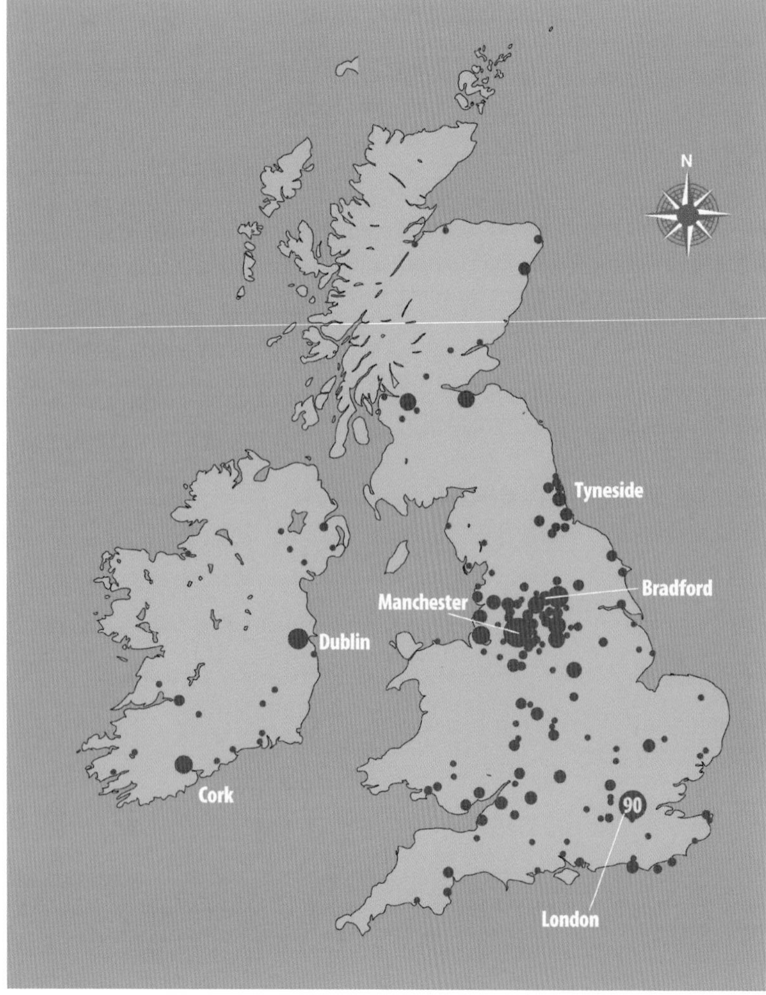

Fig 14.1
Commercial Turkish baths opened outside London from 1857 onwards. Some of them lasted a very short time. None remains open. Apart from London, the size of the dots indicates the number of baths opened in each place, eg, 10 in Dublin; 1 slightly south, in Bray.
(© Tash Shifrin)

Choice is also affected by the amount of information which can be found. This in turn probably leads to an initial emphasis on establishments which have either survived longest, or else been spectacular failures; on those which have appeared frequently in newspaper reports; and on those which have advertised and produced publicity materials which have survived (Fig 14.2).

This approach may be no bad thing. Unless you are a specialist, there is, after all, a limit to the number of descriptions—of more or less similar baths—that can significantly add anything to the general picture. But if you do wish to know as much as possible about a specific establishment or, as a local historian, to learn about all the baths within a specific area, then the book's complementary website may help fill in more of the details.[1]

London's first Victorian Turkish baths

Roger Evans, like Urquhart a sufferer from neuralgia, discovered the bath while at Riverside on FAC business. He determined to build one at his house in Bell Street, just off the Edgware Road, and at the beginning of July 1860, he opened it for use by fellow mechanics at a charge of 1s a time—the first Victorian Turkish bath in London.

The hot room was heated by a brick flue, about 3ft (0.9m) high and 9in (229mm) wide, running along three sides of the room, and raising its temperature to 160°F (71°C).[2] The bath was so successful that by 11 September Evans had already built and opened a larger establishment at Golden Square.

This one, with two hot rooms, was managed by John Johnson, who had served on both the Stafford and Manchester FACs. During its first

MASSAGE GIVEN IN THE HOME CITZ. PHONE 5888

U. E. WHITEIS

Turkish and Electric Baths

MASSAGE CHIROPODY

Men Exclusively

112 East Broad Street

Columbus, Ohio

LADIES' BATHS
150 EAST BROAD STREET

CLOSED FROM SUNSET FRIDAY TO SUNSET SATURDAY

Fig 14.2
Blotter card from Columbus, Ohio.
(Author's collection)

five months, 6,000 Turkish baths were taken there, and income and expenditure accounts were copied and sent to Urquhart for his information.[3]

Some early baths in the north

The Leeds Road Turkish Bath in Bradford was important for a number of reasons: it was started, as was William Potter's first bath in Manchester, by the local FAC under the direct guidance of David Urquhart; it continued Potter's practice of making the baths available to women; it arranged to have a physician available for consultation at set times; and it inspired Dr John Le Gay Brereton to set up the first Turkish baths in Australia.

When George Jacob Holyoake (Fig 14.3) visited the Leeds Road bath in 1858, the year after it opened, he was unable to resist poking gentle fun at the seriousness of the committee members who ran it.

> [After the bath] there remained with me a distinct sense of additional warmth, from early morning this day, until late the next day. Of course my bath being made by our foreign affairs bretheren, was heated with blue books, and towards the end, an autograph letter of Mr Urquhart's was thrown into the furnace. I imbibed a considerable suspicion of Russia, while undergoing the operation, and at the end had visions of Tower Hill with Mr Collet bringing up Lord Palmerston, Mr Urquhart reading his sentence, and Major Rolland feeling the edge of the axe. Beyond this slight mental disturbance, I found the effects of the bath good.[4]

At the beginning of May 1858, one of the regular letters to Urquhart from FAC member A E Robinson mentioned some handbills he had seen. These were about a Turkish bath which some unnamed proprietor intended opening at Boddy's Buildings in Northgate, Halifax.[5] A local advertisement indicated that there would be a single 'heated chamber of dry air, from 140 to 160 degrees [60–71°C]', a tepid shower, and shampooing. Not until mid-July did the proprietor reveal himself to be a Mr Joshua Waddington.[6]

In the mornings, his baths were reserved for private use by individuals at a cost of 1s; in the evenings, first-class baths cost 6d and second class 3d, with Wednesday evenings reserved for women.

To get a feel for these prices, it is interesting to compare them with those in a contemporary advertisement in a local paper. This stated that for a two-hour reading by Charles Dickens from

Fig 14.3
Portrait of George Jacob Holyoake, by Rowland Holyoake, 1902
(Rationalist Press Association with thanks to Conway Hall Library & Archives.)

Fig 14.4
Joseph Constantine: wool comber, bathman, hydropathist, inventor. (Joseph Constantine, Hydropathy, health, and longevity, *Manchester: Heywood, 1895, frontispiece)*

A Christmas Carol, reserved and numbered seats cost 5s, tickets in the area 2s 6d, and those in the gallery 1s.[7]

The baths seem to have closed before the end of the year and there were no further advertisements after August. Just before Christmas, William Potter thought it might be worthwhile trying to fill the gap by advertising his Manchester baths in Halifax, but we do not know if he was at all successful.[8] Waddington's establishment was probably one of several similarly short-lived ventures which have not yet come to light—a hopeful entrepreneur spurred on by the publicity surrounding the baths in Manchester and Bradford.

In one such instance, the only reference found has been a short paragraph in the *Bradford Observer*. This described how the proprietors of the (otherwise unknown) West End Turkish Baths in Lamb Lane, 'admitted, free, a large number of the children of the Ragged School to their recently opened bath-rooms—a treat which is not likely soon to be forgotten' by 'these comparative strangers to ablutionary blessings.'[9]

Thomas Lowe, a medical botanist, seems to have been the first non-FAC member to open stand-alone Turkish baths which survived for any length of time. Little is known about them except that they opened on 28 February 1858 at Union Street in Barnsley,[10] and that they were still open, owned by Morris Poppleton, in 1901.[11]

Fig 14.5 (opposite top)
Plan of the Mulberry Street Turkish Baths, Liverpool. ('Short description of The Oriental Baths', Proc Lpool Archit & Archaeol Soc, *1861. Liverpool Record Office, Liverpool Libraries)*

The immediacy of the first Manchester bath's success in 1857 was not lost on hydropathist Joseph Constantine (Fig 14.4). Since 1850, he had been running vapour baths close to the centre of town at 3 Oxford Street. Within months of Potter's opening, Constantine had added Turkish baths to his own establishment and, unlike Potter, also offered a vapour bath, wet sheet packing, and other hydropathic treatments.

By 1859 he had opened a second establishment 50 yards away, in St James Street. And the following year, an advertisement at the back of his *Handy book on hydropathy*, one of several works by him on the subject, announced that both baths would be replaced shortly by a larger and more up-to-date one, a little further up Oxford Street at Number 23.[12]

By 6 June 1861 the new baths were open, fitted out to Constantine's own specification.[13] In August, a long, densely printed advertisement was published in the *Manchester Times* listing and briefly describing the five suites of Turkish baths, in addition to his Russian, slipper, sulphur, alkaline, electro-chemical and galvanic baths. There were also sections on *General Rules for Taking Baths*, and *A Few Hints on Ordinary Affections* about the use of the bath in treating a variety of complaints.[14]

In 1866, after he and Thomas Whitaker had invented the Convoluted Stove, Constantine went on to design Turkish baths for others, advise local authorities and, of course, become a supplier of stoves across the country. In the process, he became—with that other self-taught bathman Charles Bartholomew—one of the two most important non-architect consultants on the heating of Turkish baths.

One of the first limited liability companies set up to run Turkish baths throughout the English provinces was the Oriental Bath Company of Liverpool Ltd. Registered on 2 February 1861 with a capital of £10,000 divided into £10 shares,[15] its first bath, and in the event its only one, was opened on 3 August later that year.[16]

Its prime mover was Dr Edward Haughton who had been staying at St Ann's when Urquhart and Barter were experimenting with their first bath. Haughton became the first manager of the Oriental Baths, though he handed over to his deputy, Thomas Gardiner, within the year.

The building, at 113 Mulberry Street, had originally been a Welsh Methodist Chapel. It was converted into three separate sets of Turkish baths (Fig 14.5) by the architect Cornelius Sherlock (*c* 1824–88),[17] who went on to design Liverpool's famous Picton Reading Room beneath the main William Brown Library.

The men's, women's, and private baths each had a *frigidarium*, *tepidarium*, and *caldarium*, and the men's bath additionally had

ORIENTAL BATHS.

BUILT UNDER THE SUPERINTENDENCE OF DOCTOR HAUGHTON.

GROUND PLAN.

GENTLEMEN'S

A FRIGIDARIUM.
B TEPIDARIUM.
C CALDARIUM.
D LACONICUM.
E LAVATORIUM.

LADIES'

F LAVATORIUM.
G CALDARIUM.
H TEPIDARIUM.
I FRIGIDARIUM.

PRIVATE.

J CALDARIUM.
K TEPIDARIUM.
L FRIGIDARIUM.
M ENTRANCE.

N STOKING-ROOM.
O YARD.
XX W. C.
VV VESTIBULE.
Z PRINCIPAL ENTRANCE.
R HOUSE.
S DO.
2 TICKET-OFFICE.

C. SHERLOCK, *Archt.*

The Circles marked I represent fountains, intended to prevent too great aridity in the air; the effect of which will be to render the process more rapid, so that a bath may occupy less time.

The room D, or Laconicum, will be kept comparatively dry, and of a higher temperature than the other rooms, so as to be more suitable for medical use.

W. CALLIHAN, *Del.*

MULBERRY STREET.

a *laconicum*. There were separate entrances for men and women and, inside both baths, 'ample bath dresses' were worn by bathers and attendants.'[18]

Sherlock had not previously designed a Turkish bath, and would have needed guidance on heating systems from Haughton, who had briefly run a small hydro adjacent to Dr Barter's baths in Bray. But the floors were hot and the ventilation poor, and the following year Gardiner had to install a new system, lowering the already relatively cool temperature of the hottest room from 150°F (66°C) to 110°F (43°C).[19]

The company went into voluntary liquidation in 1883, when the baths were purchased by William George Sloane who ran them until they closed, around 1906.

In a factory and on the beach

One of the strangest locations for a purpose-built Turkish bath must surely be at the end of William Edward Wiley's Birmingham pencil and pen factory in Frederick Street. Wiley had started making pens and pencil cases in 1850, and in 1862 commissioned a new three-storey L-shaped factory from local architect John George Bland (*c* 1828–98). Most of this survives as the Argent Centre, a Grade II* Listed Building in the Jewellery Quarter currently occupied by small businesses (Fig 14.6) and a unique pen museum.

Built mainly of red brick, it is exuberantly decorated with polychrome brick chequered arches and panels, and black and white banding. According to the National Heritage List for England, 'The building's arcaded elevations take their inspiration from Florentine-Lombard early Renaissance palazzi with corner towers…'[20] although these were originally topped with pyramids and the parapet is a later addition.

Fig 14.6
W E Wiley's Turkish baths (far right) at his pencil factory, Birmingham. Compare with the original towers and parapets (Fig 13.19, page 127).
(Historic England Archive AA000617)

Fig 14.7
William Edward Wiley. (Courtesy of David Gardiner-Hill, great-great-grandson of William Edward Wiley)

At the northern end is a four-storey section, behind which is a tall tapered square chimney next to what was originally the boiler house. It is here that Wiley (Fig 14.7) decided to build his baths. The beauty of this location, from his point of view, was that fresh air could be inexpensively heated by being passed over the flues and steam pipes connecting the boiler house to the factory, and then ducted into the hot rooms.[21]

There were three complete suites of Turkish baths: for working men on the first floor, gentlemen on the second and (opened slightly later) for ladies on the third. There were, of course, separate male and female entrances, one of which has since been bricked up. Each suite was the same, comprising a cooling-room 110ft (33.5m) long, three hot rooms, and a shampooing room.

After being greeted by a bare-footed boy in full Turkish costume, male bathers would remove their shoes and be taken up to the cooling-room. Its walls were decorated with arabesque scrolls, its windows with stained glass, and its floor covered with matting. Around the walls were red curtained cubicles for changing and couches for reclining. Relaxation after the bath was encouraged by the provision of *chibouks*, papers, chess, draughts and billiards.

The hot rooms at 130°–160°F (55°–71°C) and higher had Sicilian marble seating round the walls and, in the first, a wooden bench in the centre. In the shampooing room, a long hose with a shower rose at the end was within reach of the slab.[22]

The baths were opened to the public experimentally after Boxing Day 1862, and more formally on 13 February the following year. In fixing the charges at 3s 6d, 2s 6d, 1s 6d, and 1s, Wiley exactly matched those of his only competitor, James Melling, who had opened baths at The Crescent, Cambridge Street, the previous September.[23] But additionally, Wiley offered free admission to the working classes 'on the recommendation of any Medical Gentleman.'[24]

Although Wiley calculated that the baths could accommodate 200 bathers per day, he more realistically suggested an average of fifty when he put the refreshment department out to tender.[25]

The baths appear to have closed around 1870 when Wiley's merged with three other closely related companies to form Perry & Co Ltd, and no further advertisements appeared. But whether the baths closed because they were unsuccessful, or because the new larger company needed the space, is not known.

Not all baths which opened in the late 1850s or early 1860s were as large as those of Wiley and Bartholomew. Even some company-owned baths were much smaller, and the Bland's Cliff baths in Scarborough were quite different from either of these two.

They were built by the Scarborough Public Bath Co Ltd to a design by J F Fairbank, a local surveyor. The company was incorporated in 1858 under the chairmanship of a local physician, Dr Richard Cross. Judging by its name, it may originally have been set up solely to provide sea water swimming baths[26] which it had originally wanted to lease to an independent manager.[27]

The baths were built on the beach itself—before the construction of Foreshore Road—and when they opened around the middle of 1859, the 100,000-gallon pool of fresh sea water was heated to 65°F (18°C).[28] This compares favourably with present-day outdoor lidos which maintain their water within the range 65–75°F (18°–24°C).[29]

We do not know for certain when the Turkish baths opened, but it was most likely to have been in 1863 when the building was enlarged.[30] The earliest available image dates from around 1875 (Fig 14.8),[31] and this suggests that the Turkish baths were either there from the beginning, or that it was always intended to provide them. Otherwise it is difficult to understand why the horseshoe windows and ogee cupola were placed on the left-hand side of the building, when the Turkish baths were located on the right.

Compared with a price of 6d for a swim, 2s 6d seems expensive in 1863 for a Turkish bath,[32]

Fig 14.8 (left)
The Bland's Cliff baths in Scarborough. When built, before the construction of Foreshore Road, they were still adjacent to the beach . (Author's collection)

Fig 14.9 (right)
All that remained of the Bland's Cliff Baths in the 1990s. (© Malcolm Shifrin)

and by the following year, there were three evenings when tickets were reduced to 1s.[33]

The baths company survived till 1904 when the premises were sold for £4,250. The pool remained open till around 1931, though the Turkish baths may have closed earlier.[34] Parts of the building still survive as an amusement arcade (Fig 14.9).

The Oriental Baths in Leeds

To the left of the Bland's Cliff Baths in Scarborough stands the imposing Grand Hotel, designed by Cuthbert Brodrick (1821–1905). James Stevens Curl's apt description of its being 'indubitably, staggeringly, hugely, above all, Victorian' [35] could also, with the addition of the word 'Saracenic', aptly be applied to the Turkish baths in Leeds, which Brodrick designed a couple of years later, in 1864, for the Oriental and General Baths Company of Leeds Ltd.

The company was incorporated in 1862 with a capital of one thousand £10 shares. Brodrick himself was the largest of the first shareholders, though his ten shares may have been allotted to him in lieu of an initial fee.

In common with most architects at that time, Brodrick had no previous experience of designing Turkish baths but, as the foremost Leeds architect of the day who had just completed the city's prestigious town hall, he would have been the obvious choice for an ambitious new company.

He would certainly have studied the well-known illustrations of Constantinople by architect and artist Thomas Allom (1804–1872). Allom had been an early partner of Henry Francis Lockwood who, with the Mawson brothers, had already designed Turkish baths at Ben Rhydding Hydro (opened 1859) and Saltaire (opened 1863). Brodrick, who was articled to Lockwood in the 1830s, may well have benefitted from discussing his plans with all of them.

During the four years it took to build the baths and the 99 years they remained open, everything about them changed—their planning, their external and internal design, even their ownership—sometimes several times. And while we know, in general, what facilities were available at different periods, we cannot be absolutely certain what the outside of the building looked like before 1928, when some surviving photographs were taken.

Brodrick's first design is the most integrated (Fig 14.10), each section of the building fitting perfectly with the other—though Cookridge Road never looked this idyllic, even in 1862.[36]

His drawing shows a single-storey building, with a central section flanked by two wings, each with a small pointed dome at the end, its façade decorated with horizontal polychrome brick stripes and surmounted by a decorative

Fig 14.10
Cuthbert Brodrick's original watercolour design (unrealised) for the Cookridge Road Oriental Baths in Leeds.
(RIBA Library Photographs Collection, RIBA 12126)

parapet. The central section has a wide arched recess which frames the doorways for male and female bathers. Above this is a pointed dome; behind it two pointed saucer domes; and behind that, a much large saucer dome with a low cone-topped *lantern. At the rear—not, as has been suggested by Derek Linstrum, rising out of the central saucer dome—is a tall minaret-styled structure.[37]

This is the most frequently reproduced image of the Oriental Baths, and most writers imply that this is the design which was adopted. Lindstrum, here on safer ground, doubts that this was so, suggesting that 'some of the richer details on the perspective were probably modified'.

But the building actually constructed had more than its 'richer details' modified. Apart from the striped façade, decorative parapet, and some domes, the building was considerably changed, as can be seen from a second watercolour which was reproduced on an early poster advertising the baths (Fig 14.11).

Here there is no longer a 'minaret' or a large central saucer dome, and the remaining three central domes are differently shaped and sized. The central archway is now purely decorative and there are two separate entrances, for gentlemen (on the left) and ladies (on the right). The building is smaller, with five instead of six windows in each wing, and these are of a simpler, less expensive design. Finally, the absence of any boiler house flue in a building with Turkish baths, suggests that even this view is not an accurate representation of what was built.

For this we need to examine the more prosaic drawing on the letterhead used by the company at the time (Fig 14.12). In general the features are as in the poster image, but here a plain business-like flue is clearly shown behind the central, square-based pitched roof which has replaced the saucer dome.

Even so it must have looked stunning to those who saw it at the time.

The baths, which cost £13,000, were opened in stages: the swimming bath on 28 July 1866, and the Turkish and other baths later in the year. The swimming pool, with its water maintained at 74°F (23°C), was opened at different times for first- and second-class bathers, all of whom were required to wear drawers. There were also vapour baths and showers, and two classes of Turkish baths and slipper baths, all of which were reserved for women on Wednesdays.

Though Brodrick was still a shareholder, he did not wish, or perhaps was not asked, to design the new baths, and the virtually new building was designed by Leeds architect, William Bakewell (1839–1925).

While the provision of bathing facilities was an undoubted improvement, the same could not be said for the exterior (Fig 14.13). Even before they were opened, the *Mercury* was frankly critical:

> The additions to the Oriental Baths, Cookridge-street, will attract considerable attention, both on account of the public interest attaching to the building, and architecturally because of the attempt to transform into a nondescript modern Gothic front the well-designed Saracenic elevation of Mr Broderick [sic]. The result, as far as we can judge at present, can scarcely be considered a gain from an art point of view, and the change from the old familiar dome to the turret over the central block is, I think, by no means an improvement, and it is to be regretted that the architect was not allowed to design an entirely new front.[38]

Fig 14.11
A poster advertising the Oriental Baths in 1858, showing the baths as originally built.
(By kind permission of Leeds Library and Information Services)

In 1880, the company directors discussed with shareholders the financial loss and inconvenience of only having a single set of facilities for both classes of user. There was also a pressing need to increase their income and it was decided to rebuild the baths, and at the same time add a second storey to provide lettable office accommodation. As this would necessitate the removal of all the domes, it was felt appropriate to reface the façade so as to fit in better with its surrounding buildings.

When the baths reopened on 29 April 1882, however, the facilities were impressive, with interior surfaces faced with an abundance of black, white, and red marble. The first-class Turkish baths had a cooling-room with fourteen divans, a fountain 'with a figure representing one of the naiades holding a water-lily from which a jet of water is thrown', a plunge pool, and a gallery for smokers made possible by the addition of the second floor. There were three hot rooms at 125°F (52°C), 170°F (77°C), and

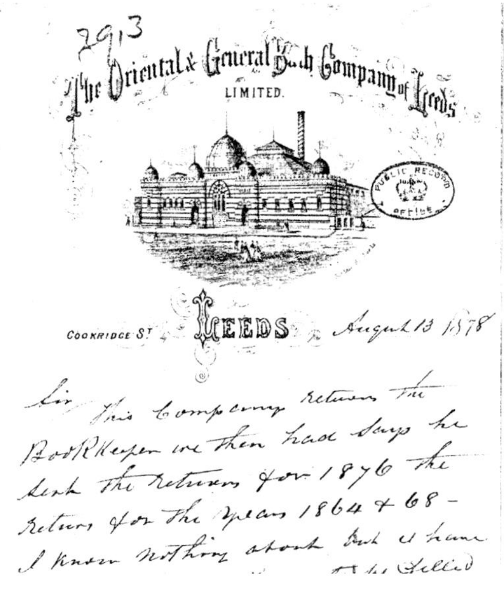

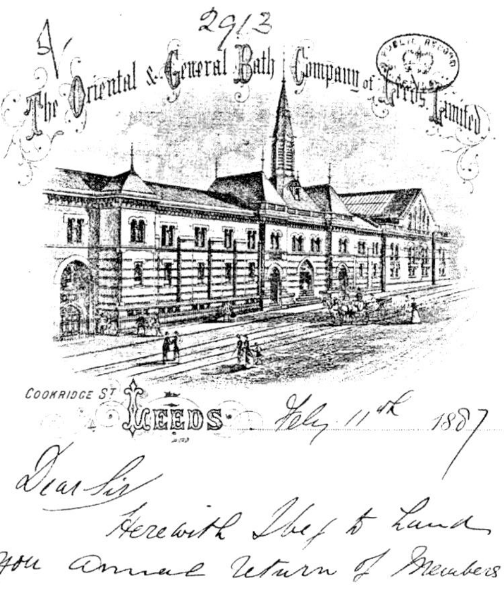

Fig 14.12
Two letterheads showing the Oriental Baths in 1878, and after rebuilding, in 1886.
(The National Archives. Contains public sector information licensed under the Open Government Licence v3.0.)

Fig 14.13
The Oriental Baths prior to closure in 1969.
(By kind permission of Leeds Library and Information Services. Leodis ID: 2002815_47864932)

230°F (110°C) heated by Whitaker's Convoluted Stoves,[39] an ante-room to the shampooing room with its four slabs, and a washing room with a variety of showers. The second-class baths were similar, but without a third hot room.

Yet there were still no separate facilities for women. These had to wait another five years, finally opening on 2 February 1887. Also designed by William Bakewell, they were similar to the men's second-class baths in having only two hot rooms.

Unlike Dr Barter's baths, the Oriental Baths did not advertise cheaper rates for children, but at least a few did accompany a parent, and enjoyed it. In 1888, a letter appeared in the *Leeds Mercury* Children's Column from Frank B, Leeds (aged 10) in which he gave a lively account of a visit with his father.

> ...and then I went into the hot room to get the dirt off if you have any on (it appears that I had, but it was soon off), and after being in the hot room a time I went and got a good shower-bath, which is very nice, and then I went into the hot room for a bit...[40]

Frank goes on to describe his shampoo, and his tea, and ends, 'If any of the readers of this column would like to go, I'm sure the lady [at the ticket box] will be very pleased.'

With the facilities now available it was expected that the company would make increased profits and be able to pay reasonable dividends, but by the mid-1890s the situation was becoming difficult.

An initial agreement with the corporation had ensured a particularly favourable water rate, on the understanding that this would rise when the company was making a profit and paying a 'reasonable dividend.' In the 35 years since the company was formed it had paid ten dividends, which over its life gave an average rate of just under one per cent. It still had a mortgage of £8,000, and around 1880 the water rate was doubled from an initial 3d per 1,000 gallons to 6d. So to change the water in the two pools twice each week (totalling 140,000 gallons) would cost £7.[41]

The corporation had also recently opened its own swimming baths and was offering free admission to schoolchildren if accompanied by a teacher, a facility which had earned the company £40 per year. Against this, the company was sitting on a central city site of about 2,000 square yards (1,672 square metres) which, if sold at the same rate as the adjoining site had just achieved, would bring in £25,000, or £4,500 more than had so far been spent on the building.[42]

The company had first offered to sell the baths to the corporation in 1897 for £20,000. But a year later it was only being offered £18,000, the same as the higher of two private bids received. The company preferred to sell the baths to the corporation rather than to a private individual who would close them, and the sale was finally agreed.[43]

The corporation spruced the baths up at the beginning of 1901, adding a Russian bath,[44] and continued running them until 1965. By this time it would have been difficult to recognise Brodrick's original design, though underneath the grime, the photograph still shows traces of horizontal stripes. The building was demolished in 1969.

The others

In selecting just a few of the commercial Victorian Turkish baths to represent them all, I have not been able to say that any single establishment is wholly representative. But almost all of them are interesting in some way, and I have tried to offer a small taste of the whole in the hope that a first bite encourages you to discover some of the others on the *Victorian Turkish Baths* website.

15

Municipal Turkish baths

The Public Baths and Wash-houses Acts of 1846 and 1847 enabled local authorities to build sanitary facilities at public expense (Fig 15.1).

These included wash-houses where people could launder their clothes, slipper baths (Fig 15.2), vapour baths, and open-air swimming pools—indoor pools not being permitted until later.

The acts were permissive and stipulated that if an authority decided to adopt them, and chose to provide baths, then there had to be twice as many of the cheaper ('Second Class') baths as there were of the more expensive ('First Class') baths. They also laid down the maximum charges for each class of bather.

The acts did not apply in Scotland, where specifically Scottish legislation was enacted, baths usually being built under the provisions of a local police act. Glasgow's baths, for example, followed the Glasgow Police Act of 1866, enabling the city to provide one class of baths for all to use together.

But the Scottish legislators and planners were ahead of their time. Instead of their intended outcome, the provision of only a single class of baths led, as we shall see in Chapter 21, to the creation of relatively exclusive private baths clubs, of which there were five in Glasgow alone.

Nor did the acts apply in Ireland where, in 1873, Kilkenny Corporation became the only one to open a public baths complex with Turkish, shower, plunge and reclining (*ie*, slipper) baths.[1]

In England and Wales, over 90 authorities are known to have provided Turkish baths between 1864 and 1981, almost always as part of a larger baths complex (Fig 15.3).

Of all the major cities, Liverpool and Bristol were the only ones without municipal Turkish baths.

After a slow start, the number of Turkish baths opened by local authorities started to rise. Between 1870 and 1939 an average of around 12 baths were opened every 10 years, apart from the decade which included World War I. But local authority provision never really recovered after World War II, and the years of austerity and severe building controls which followed it. Turkish baths were unsuccessful not only in competing with other claims on public expenditure, but also with newer, more economical means of providing hot-air baths.

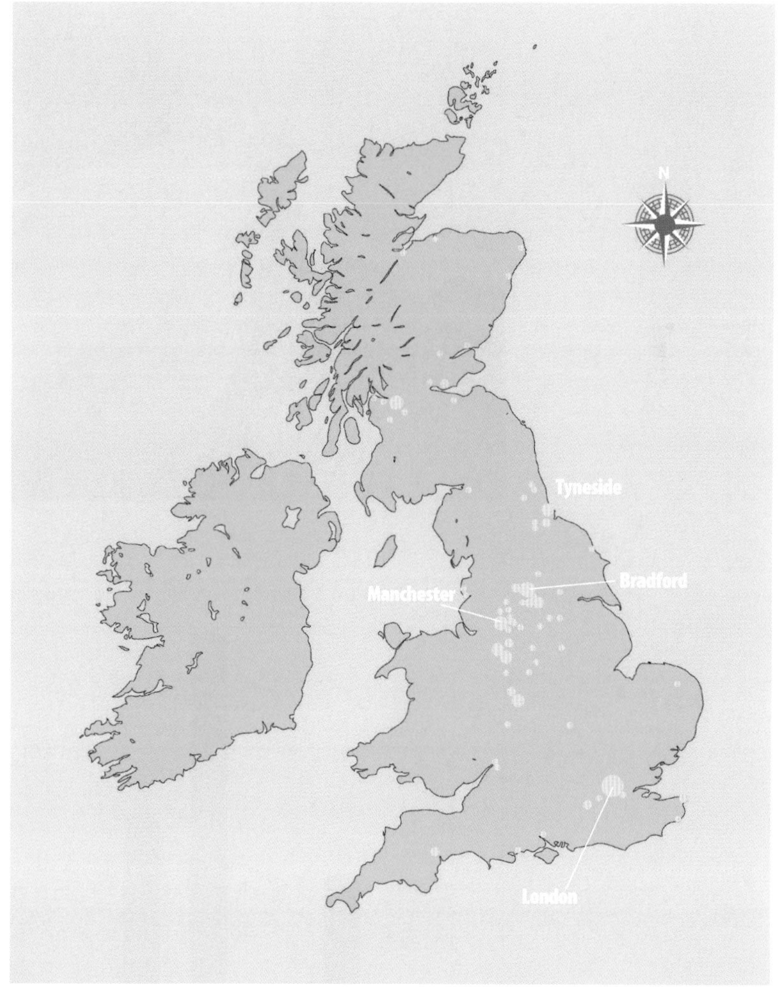

Fig 15.1
Municipal Turkish baths opened between1865 and 1965. Some of them lasted a very short time. Twelve were still open at the time of writing (January 2015). The size of the dots indicates the number of baths opened in each place, eg, 11 in London; 1 in Southampton. (© Tash Shifrin)

Fig 15.2
These slipper baths in Birmingham were typical of those provided by many local authorities.
(Agnes Campbell, Report on Public baths..., *Edinburgh University, 1918)*

The first local authority Turkish baths

The first local authority to *initiate* the provision of publicly funded Turkish baths was Bradford Corporation, but such baths were already in use in two other locations owned by local authorities.

In 1850, Nottingham Corporation opened public open-air swimming pools at Gedling Street, but it was corporation policy to lease them annually to a tenant who 'kept all fees and was responsible for all payments.'[2]

In 1859, they were let to the local Chief Inspector of Nuisances, William Richards, 'Mr Richards to pay for the Towels and Furniture.'[3] The following year, the committee responsible for the pool did consider providing Turkish baths, but decided to consult local doctors first.[4]

In January 1861, a petition with 105 signatures was presented to the corporation asking for a Turkish bath.[5] There had clearly been some effective campaigning, possibly by Richards himself, possibly by members of the Nottingham FAC, or most likely by both.

In September, Richards attended a meeting of the Public Offices Committee and offered to provide a bath at his own expense.[6] His offer was accepted and the minutes of the following

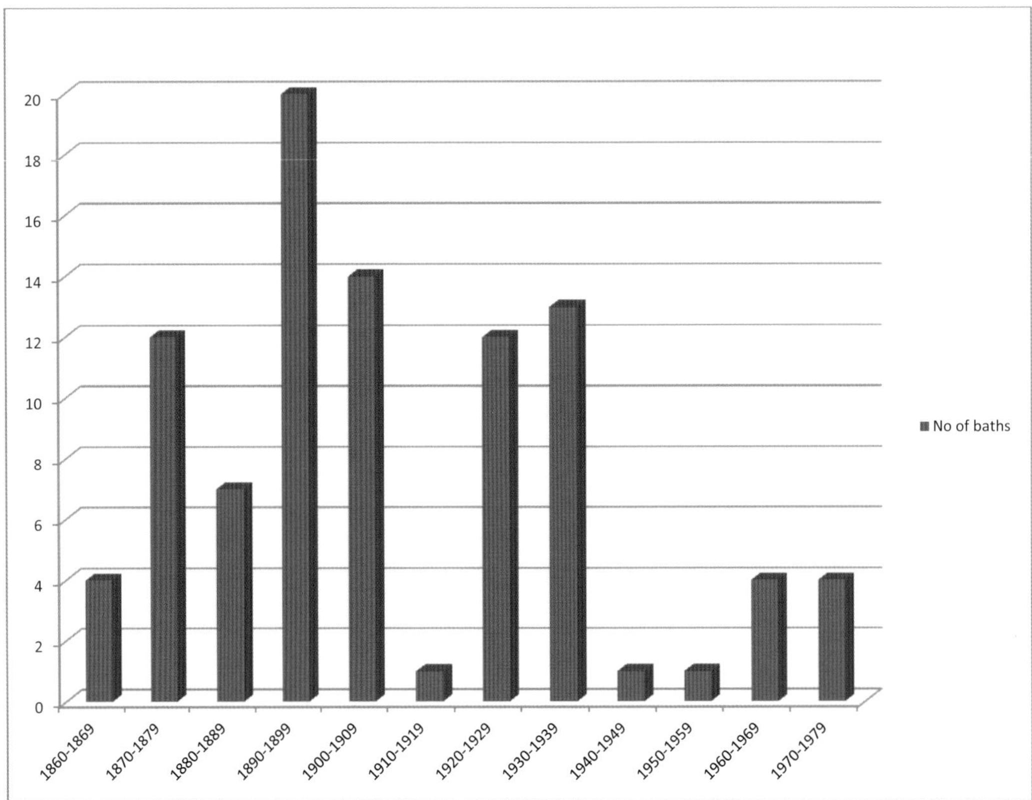

Fig 15.3
Graph showing the number of municipal Turkish baths opened per decade.
(© Malcolm Shifrin)

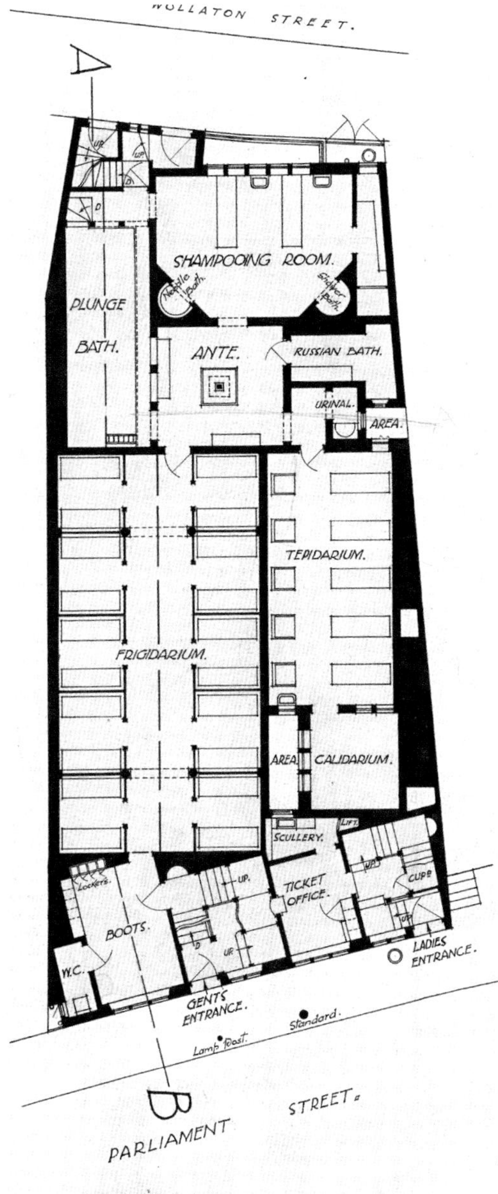

Fig 15.4
Ground floor plan of the Turkish baths in Upper Parliament Street, Nottingham. (Nottinghamshire Archives CA/EN/20/181)

committee meeting recorded, rather condescendingly, that the committee 'are unanimously of the opinion that they see no objection to Mr Richards erecting a Turkish Bath on the premises now occupied by him…'[7]

By the following June, Richards had completed the bath, paid for additional repairs and improvements, and was then generously allowed to renew his lease 'at £100 a year instead of £80 as formerly.'[8] As to maintenance costs, it is unlikely that the Baths and Washhouses Committee did anything 'other than [exercise] a benevolent supervision.'[9]

Tickets cost 2s first class and 1s second class. The baths, which were reserved for women on Thursdays, opened from eight in the morning till eight in the evening, and remained operational for just over 30 years.[10]

In 1894, the Turkish baths, now managed by the council on its own account, were demolished to make room for new baths. When the new building opened two years later, however, there were no Turkish baths. As though in accordance with some hidden agreement, 1896 also saw the birth of the Nottingham Turkish Baths Co Ltd, one of whose shareholders was Jesse Boot, founder in Nottingham of the chain of chemists which still bears his name.[11]

The new company built Turkish baths in Upper Parliament Street (Fig 15.4) designed by local architects Arthur William Brewill (1861–1923) and Basil Edgar Baily (1869–1942). Externally, the fenestration, asymmetrically positioned doors, and off-centre drainpipe all combined to give the building a slightly unsettling appearance (Fig 15.5). Internally, the decidedly 'Saracenic' hot rooms, shampooing rooms (Fig 15.6) and marble-lined plunge pool contrasted strangely with the reception rooms and pew-like mahogany changing cubicles in the *frigidarium*. Women's baths, with their own entrance to the right of the building, were provided on the first floor, with a laundry above.

The baths were built with the help of a substantial loan from a corporation whose elected members may well have felt relieved that they no longer had to provide them. But if there *was* relief, it was short-lived.

Opening in May 1898, the baths started well, and in 1902 the company bought out its main competitor, the 25-year-old James' Turkish Baths in Lower Talbot Street, in order to close

Fig 15.5
Main façade of the Upper Parliament Street Turkish baths.
(Baths and bathing, *Nottingham: The Hammam, 1898. Courtesy Nottingham Local Studies Library)*

Fig 15.6
The 'Saracenic' shampooing room at Upper Parliament Street.
(Baths and bathing, *Nottingham: The Hammam, 1898. Courtesy Nottingham Local Studies Library)*

it down.[12] But the onset of World War I affected business badly. The Corporation refused the company's request for a further loan, though it did agree to purchase the baths. It took negotiations lasting more than a year before a price of £5,400 was agreed, and in 1917 the Corporation once again found itself running Turkish baths.[13]

The outbreak of World War II had a greater effect, and the baths were closed 'for the Duration', the staff transferred to ARP (Air Raid Precautions) duties,[14] unused prepaid tickets were refunded, and one gross tablets of 'toilet soap which was not suitable for use in other establishments' were disposed of at cost.[15] Like so many other businesses closed for 'the duration', they never reopened. The building was demolished in 1962.

The second of these early local authority Turkish baths was opened on 2 May 1864 at St Mary's Place in Bury. Building work had started the previous year on behalf of a company set up specifically for that purpose. After construction started, however, the company found itself unable to raise more than one third of the money required. Fortunately, the project was taken over by the town's Commissioners of Baths and Wash-houses and this allowed its completion to be paid for from the rates.[16]

Unlike many other authorities, Bury's Commissioners did not seem concerned about whether the Baths and Wash-houses Acts allowed them to provide Turkish baths instead of vapour baths. But they did consider it important that there should be separate Turkish baths for first- and second-class bathers, whereas most other authorities provided a single set of baths to be used by each class at specific times.

Thirty-four years later, in a brochure produced to mark the opening in 1898 of a rather more luxurious single suite of replacement baths, the council was happy to admit that in the original baths, 'The rooms were small and dingy, and the whole appearance gloomy and foreboding, and, in addition, the ventilation and heating were very unsatisfactory.'[17]

The new baths, designed under the direction of Joshua Cartwright, the Borough Engineer, had a *frigidarium* with mahogany partitioned changing cubicles (Fig 15.7), two hot rooms heated by a Crumblehulme Convoluted Stove able to provide a temperature up to 240°F (116°C), and a shampooing room with marble slabs, basins, and needle showers (Fig 15.8).

Local authority provision in Bradford

When the Bradford FAC opened its Leeds Road establishment in December 1857, Bradford became the second city in England to have a Victorian Turkish bath. During the following six years, four other commercial baths opened there, though only the one in George Street remained open for any length of time. So Turk-

Figs 15.7 and 15.8
The frigidarium *(left) in Bury's second set of Turkish baths opened in 1898.*
The shampooing room (right) at Bury.
(Opening of the Turkish bath, *Bury: The Council, 21 February 1898)*

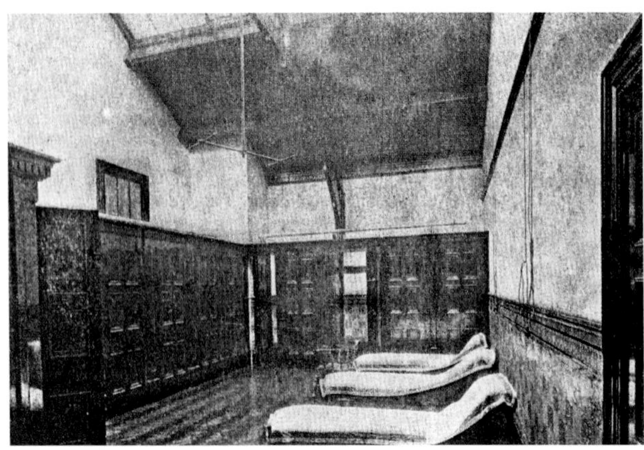

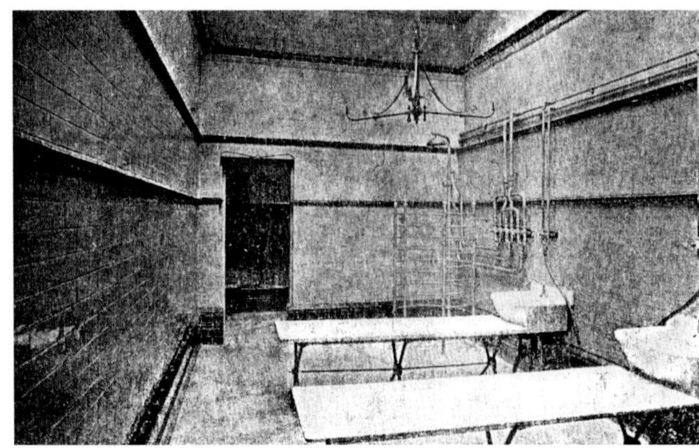

ish baths were already well established in the city when the corporation opened its Central Baths at 111 Thornton Road in 1865.

The suggestion that Turkish baths should be added was probably made by John Howarth who had just been appointed Bradford's first Baths Superintendent. The building had originally been the offices of the local waterworks and were converted into baths and washhouses at a cost of £7,500 by local architects Eli Milnes (1830–1899) and Charles France (1833–1902).[18]

When the Turkish baths opened in 1867, the cold air was heated by steam pipes. The cooling-room was furnished with eight cubicles formed by panelled partitions, each with a damask curtain over the entrance and a couch inside. The floors were fireproof and laid with mosaic tiles.[19] It is not known how many hot rooms there were, or what other facilities were available apart from the shampooing room, but the following year a vapour bath was added.

The men's baths were well used. 8,152 tickets were issued in 1882, for example, and for the 15 years 1882–96, there was an average of 11,836 tickets annually, or 227 each week.

But the women's baths, supervised by Mrs Howarth, were not as popular. In 1882, only 2,413 tickets were sold—just over one quarter of the total. Nevertheless, the corporation, possibly wishing to enlarge the men's baths, opened separate Turkish baths for women at Lister Terrace. At the same time, tickets were reduced from 1s 6d to 1s 0d and the number of women rose to just under 40 per cent of the men. But over the same 15-year period (1882–96), the average annual number of women's tickets sold was only 3,629, or under 70 baths per week.[20]

Towards the end of 1896, a disappointed Sanitary, Baths and Cemetery Committee regretfully decided to close the women's baths, and clearly felt that if they set aside any time at all for women to use the men's baths, they would be losing money.[21]

It is not known whether any of the corporation's other baths had Turkish baths for women at this time. When the West Bowling Baths were built in 1887, vapour baths were provided, and Turkish baths were only added at an unknown later date—though certainly before 1935.

A completely new Central Baths, later renamed the Windsor Baths, was designed by Alfred Hessell Tiltman (1854–1910), and opened in Great Horton Road on 13 September 1905. Its large Turkish baths suite covered nearly half the area of the lower ground floor (Fig 15.9), and a separate entrance enabled women to use them on Mondays.

Three hot rooms, the largest being 36ft × 18ft 6in (11m × 5.6m), were arranged in the form of a letter 'L' and heated by a Constantine's Convoluted Stove. Their walls, as in most local authority baths, were of glazed brick, with adjacent marble seats. The two large cooling-rooms were fitted with couches for a total of 34 bathers, and their walls and ceilings were lined with decorative glazed tiles. A 30ft (9m) long plunge pool, a Russian steam bath, and a shampooing room with three fixed slabs, needle douche and *sitz bath, completed the setup. Interestingly, although the Turkish baths suite

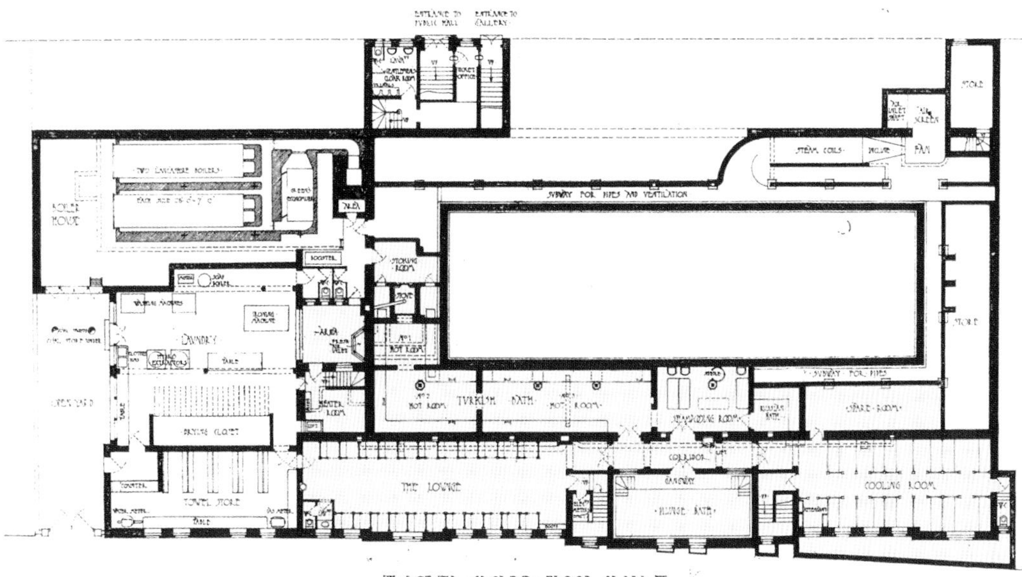

Fig 15.9
Enhanced plan shows Alfred Hessell Tiltman's Turkish baths suite at the Windsor Baths, Bradford. (Photo credit: Bradford Council)

was lit by electricity, gas lamps were preferred for the main swimming pool.[22]

The baths closed in 1983 but, according to William Park, proprietor of the Sansome Walk baths in Worcester, they were the best municipal baths in the country when they first opened.[23]

Bradford is important in the history of Victorian Turkish baths. Not only was it the first municipality to initiate their provision, but it continued to provide them for nearly 120 years and, although Nottingham's baths spanned a longer period, they were not provided continuously.

Some other municipal Turkish baths

Between 1867 and 1875, eight other local authorities, including Paisley—the first in Scotland—and Kilkenny in Ireland, opened Turkish baths. But not all were what they seemed.

The Rochdale public baths in Smith Street were opened in 1868 at a cost of £9,500. Local architect, E N Macdougall, had not been asked to include Turkish baths, presumably because the nine-year-old co-operative baths in Church Lane were still popular. But some time around 1872, the corporation added three 'excellent and peculiar' first-class Turkish bath cabinets—two for men and one for women—specially designed by their Superintendent, Mr J Milligan.[24] They do not seem to have been very popular, however, and when the baths were refurbished in 1881 they were replaced by a more conventional Turkish bath.

In Scotland, there had been commercial Turkish baths in Glasgow and Edinburgh since 1861, supplemented later by those in the private swimming clubs. But in 1896, when Edinburgh was amalgamated with the small seaside town of Portobello three miles away, the resort was promised improved facilities, including a new town hall and its first public baths.

The inclusion of Turkish baths had been suggested as early as 1897 but not all members of the Plans and Works Committee had agreed. After an amendment to exclude them was proposed, local pride was invoked when a Mr Grieve pointed out that the baths were for Edinburgh people as well as those from Portobello. 'It was most undesirable', he said, 'that Edinburgh should be behind Aberdeen and Dundee, which had already erected Turkish baths.'[25] Such a possibility was clearly unthinkable, and the amendment was defeated.

The Portobello Baths (Fig 15.10) were designed by Edinburgh's City Architect, Robert

Fig 15.10
Hot rooms on the grand scale (with steps to plunge pool) at Edinburgh's Portobello Baths.
(Author's collection)

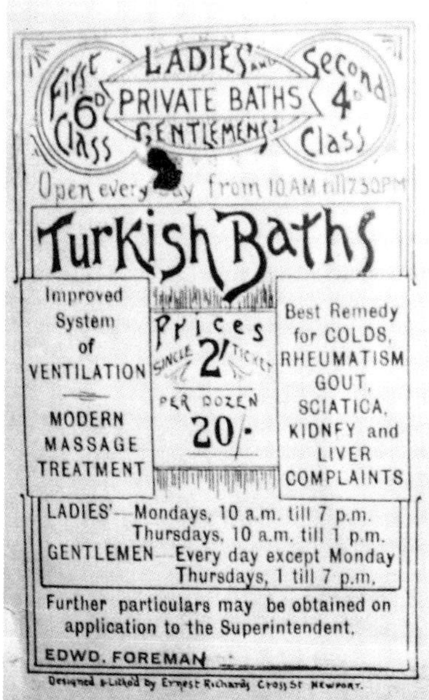

Fig 15.11 (top left) Recently refurbished changing cubicles above the Portobello frigidarium. *(© Crown Copyright: RCAHMS. Licensor, SC_1242932, www.rcahms.gov.uk)*

Fig 15.12 (bottom left) Refurbished plunge pool with 'curtain' through to the tepidarium. *(© Crown Copyright: RCAHMS. Licensor, DP_037119, www.rcahms.gov.uk)*

Fig 15.13 (top right) The outside of a folded card advertising the Stow Hill baths in Newport, Wales. (Kent History & Library Centre, Maidstone, DO/CA11/14/12)

Morham (1839–1912). Opened in 1901 and refurbished in the late 1990s, they remain in use as Scotland's only Turkish bath still open to all. There are changing cubicles in the *frigidarium* (Fig 15.11), and the cold plunge pool continues under a screen into the next hot room (Fig 15.12).

Newport, third city of Wales, had the only municipally built Turkish baths in the country until the 1950s. They were part of the public baths, opened on 19 June 1890 in the converted offices of the Stow Hill Waterworks which the corporation had recently purchased (Fig 15.13).

Designed by the borough engineer, Conyers Kirby, the Turkish baths suite comprised three hot rooms, a shampooing room (Fig 15.14), plunge pool, and a large cooling-room (Fig 15.15). According to *The Builder*, the hot rooms ranged from 180°F (82°C) to 300°F (149°C),[26] but the top temperature must surely have been a misprint, and a booklet published in the 1930s suggested a more realistic 150°F (66°C) to 210°F (99°C).[27]

Prior to their opening, the Baths Sub-committee, having consulted other towns about staffing, advertised for a Baths Superintendent in the *Daily Telegraph* and the *Daily News*. They offered 35s per week with residence, coal and gas, for a married couple, the wife to supervise the women's baths.[28] There were 33 applicants, of whom 4 were short-listed.[29] Other staff appointed later included an 'Engineer, boilerman and stoker' at 30s per week, a male attendant at 21s, a female attendant at 15s, and a boy attendant at 6s. It is dispiriting to compare these wages with ticket prices when a first-class bath cost 2s and a second-class bath (on Saturdays only) cost 1s.[30]

The baths were regularly upgraded, adding, at various times, a *mikveh* for the Jewish community, a vapour bath, *Zotofoam baths, a Vichy douche, and *sun-ray lamps.[31] The baths survived for 95 years, closing in May 1985.

The Cardiff Baths in Guildford Crescent, were built in 1862 by the Cardiff Baths Co Ltd and designed by the Cardiff Borough Architect, Thomas Waring (1825–91), who was also the Company Secretary.

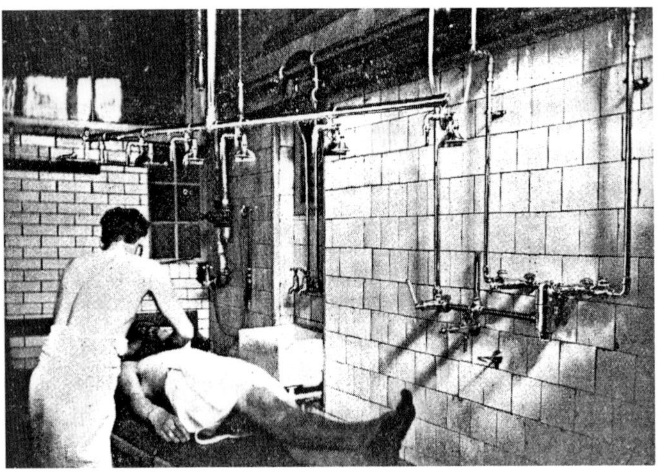

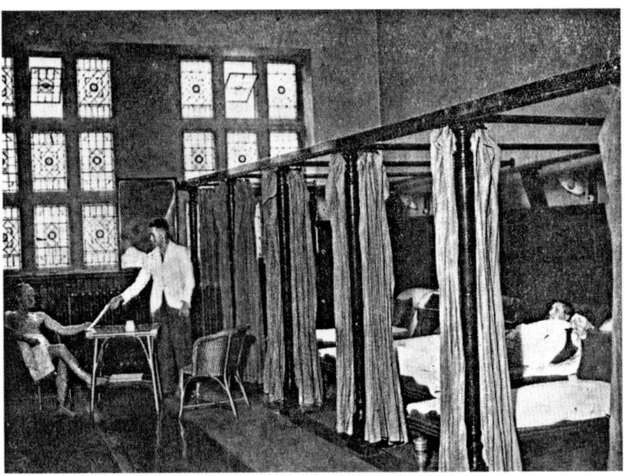

Figs 15.14 and 15.15
The shampooing room (left) and the cooling-room (right) at Stow Hill Turkish Baths. (Opening of the Maindee Baths; Newport: the baths, 1938. Newport Community Learning and Libraries)

As befitted the attractions of a major port welcoming foreign sailors, the company also advertised its facilities in French (Fig 15.16), and to encourage their use by local residents the company gave free passes to doctors.

When the baths first opened, there was a gymnasium and,

> two large swimming baths, each holding upwards of a million gallons of water supplied by the Bute Docks feeder, hot water baths, and a Turkish Baths; the whole costing £3,700.[32]

The cooling-room, which was divided into changing cubicles, was followed by two hot rooms. The first, at 130°F (55°C) had covered couches, and a grating in the centre of the decoratively tiled floor allowed the hot air to enter. The second hot room reached 160°F (71°C), and there was also a washroom with hot and cold showers.[33]

When the company went into voluntary liquidation around 1873, the baths were taken over by the corporation and renamed the Cardiff Corporation Baths. They then remained in use until replaced in 1958 by the international Wales Empire Pool, built for the 1958 British Empire and Commonwealth Games.

Although an international pool, the Empire Pool was paid for by the city and, after the games, became municipal by default. The Turkish bath, usually credited to the City Architect, John Dryburgh (1919–88), is one of the few Victorian Turkish baths recorded on film.[34] With a commentary typical of the early 1960s, a ten-minute sequence shows two women using the bath's facilities, carefully ministered to by Mrs Miller, the Baths Attendant on women's days.

After changing and showering, they pass through the two hot rooms (130°F/55°C) and 160°F/71°C) the needle shower, plunge pool, shampooing room, Aeratone bath, and cooling-room, before dressing again and returning to their car, conveniently parked all this time in the street right outside the baths.[35]

The pool was demolished in 1998 and, in due course, replaced by a new Wales National Pool in Swansea and the International Pool in Cardiff, neither of which had Turkish baths.

Fig 15.16
Advertisement aimed at French-speaking visitors to the port, 1863. (Duncan & Ward's Cardiff directory, 1863, p.158. Courtesy of Cardiff Council Library Service)

LES BAINS PUBLICS
DE CARDIFF,
SITUÉS PRÈS DE GUILDFORD-STREET.

Sont ouverts chaque jour à toutes heures, et les dimanches de 7 à 9 heures du matin.

	1ère Classe.	2e Classe.
BAINS CHAUDS	1 Scheling.	6 Pence.
Pour les personnes âgées de moins de 20 ans	8 Pence.	4 Pence.
BAINS ORIENTAUX	2 Schelings.	1 Scheling.
Massage (dit Shampoo) 6 Pence extra.		
BAINS DE NATATION	6 Pence.	3 Pence.

LES EMPLOYES N'ONT DROIT A AUCUNE GRATIFICATION.

Philanthropy

A recent estimate suggests that 'ten per cent of public baths built between 1870 and 1901 benefitted wholly or in part from philanthropic gifts.'[36] Only a few of these, however, included Turkish baths.

In 1870, for example, the then Manchester partnership of Henry John Paull (d.1888) and George Thomas Robinson (*c* 1827–97)[37] designed baths near Manchester for two mill owners. Those in Church Street, Stalybridge, cost £6,000, opened on 7 May, and were

Fig 15.17 (left)
The long-closed Turkish and swimming baths at Ashton-under-Lyne.
(Historic England Archive bb81_06477)

presented to the town by Mr and Mrs Robert Platt. Those in Henry Square, Ashton-under-Lyne, were much larger, cost £16,000—most of which was paid for by Hugh Mason—and opened on 5 September.

Though different in size, there were some similarities. Both were of red brick and each had a chimney stack (Fig 15.17) 'constructed with a hollow chamber round the smoke flue for ventilation.'[38] Both had Turkish baths designed by Charles Bartholomew.

The Stalybridge baths were demolished in the 1970s but the shell of the Ashton baths still stands, awaiting a new use in the Petersfield regeneration scheme. The eleven circular first-floor windows of the cooling-room—three more than in the original Paull & Robinson design (Fig 15.18) which was reproduced in *The Builder* when the baths opened—can still be seen to the left of the main 120ft (37m) high chimney stack. The original plan shows three hot rooms, but the shampooing room is not specifically indicated, and there are only a few small changing cubicles.[39] It seems that at some stage the Turkish baths area was extended up to the limit of the ground floor area. This might explain why the heating system was found to be inadequate in 1879, and part of the reason why Bartholomew was asked to install a larger one, costing £100 (Fig 15.19).

One of the problems often associated with a generous gift of this nature is that the recipient usually has to finance the cost of running and maintaining it. So Turkish baths, often thought by some councillors to be a luxury, had to pay their way in order to survive. There were moves to close the ones at Ashton during the early 1930s but, as in Edinburgh, civic pride and local rivalries were invoked. One alderman argued that they had to be saved: 'Otherwise we shall have to go to Stalybridge and we do not want to go to Stalybridge for owt.'[40]

In the event, the Turkish baths remained in operation until 1937 when, 'owing mainly to the extraordinary high price of fuel', the 'hot room' was discontinued and replaced by three *Zotofoam baths.[41] The main swimming baths remained open till 1975.

Nowadays such philanthropic activity—by a town's largest employers on behalf of those who were, in effect, mainly their employees—is considered somewhat patronising, but this does not seem to have been openly expressed at the time.

Not all donors were similarly motivated. Andrew Carnegie, for example, made his

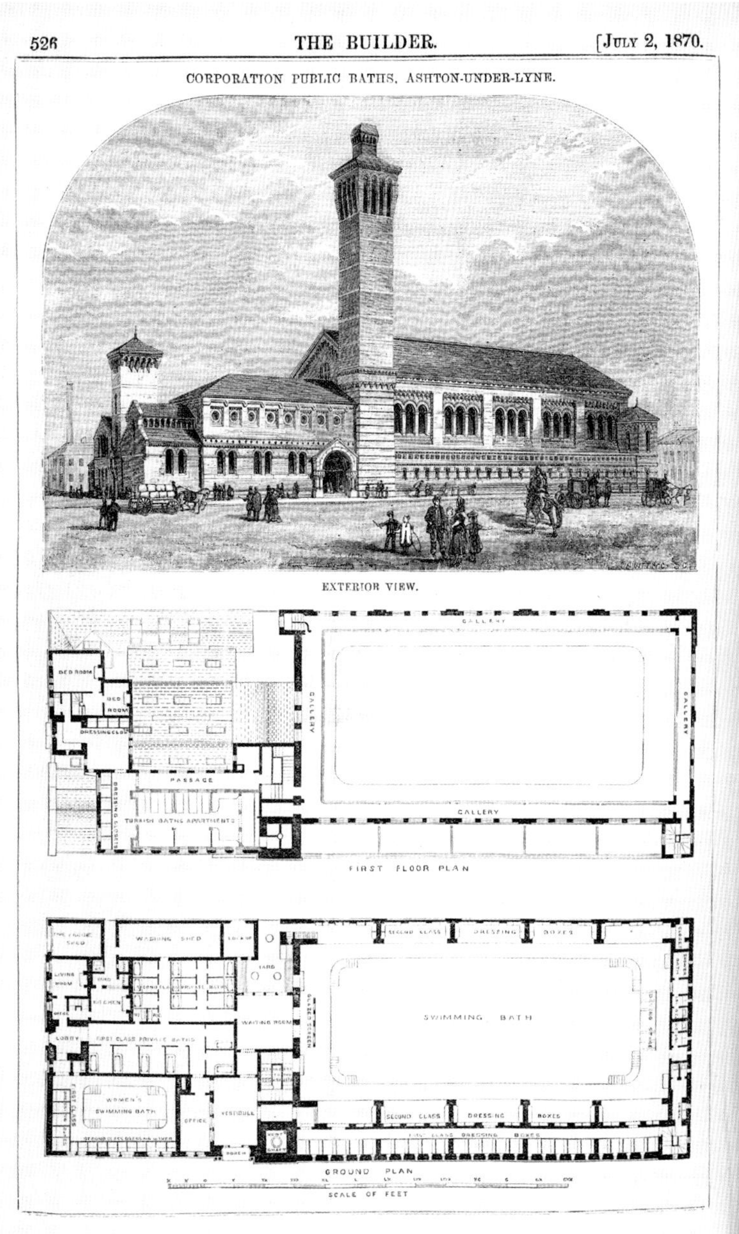

526 THE BUILDER. [July 2, 1870.

CORPORATION PUBLIC BATHS, ASHTON-UNDER-LYNE.

EXTERIOR VIEW.

Fig 15.18 (below)
Elevation and plans of the Ashton-under-Lyne baths.
(Historic England Archive DP172001, The Builder *2 July 1870)*

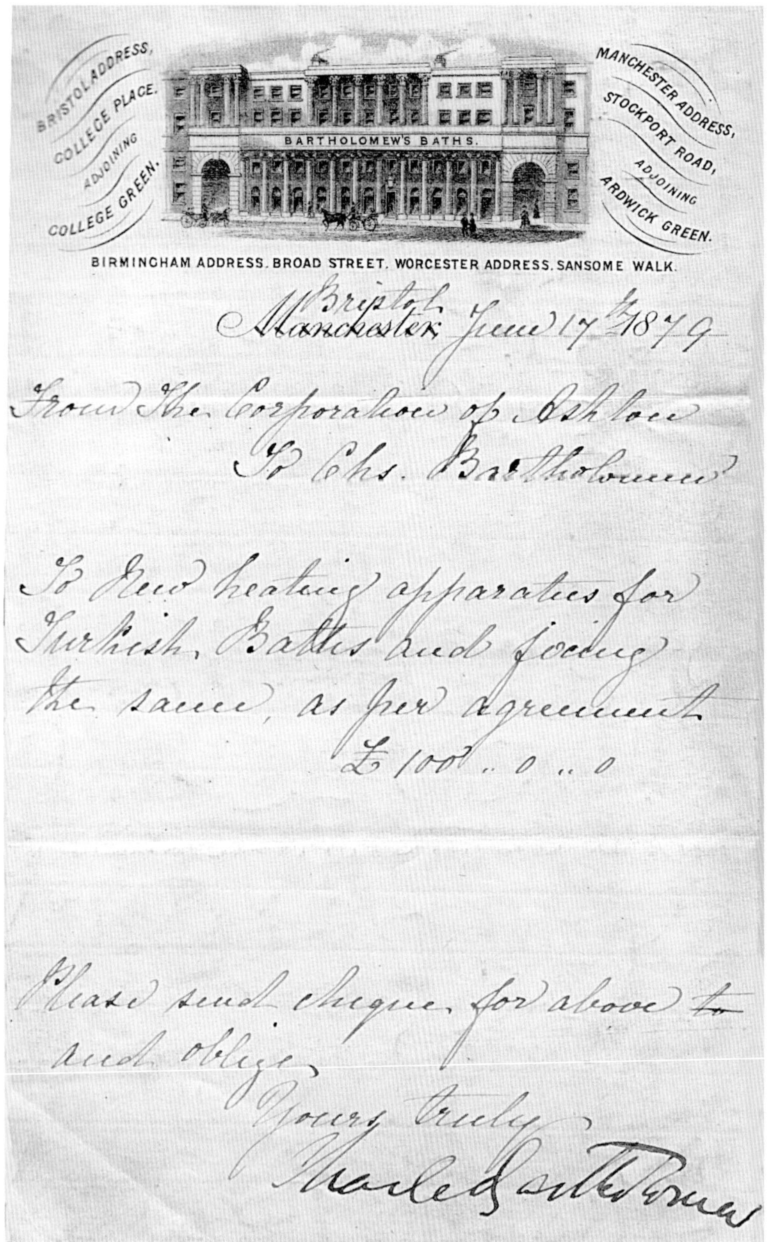

BRISTOL ADDRESS, COLLEGE PLACE, ADJOINING COLLEGE GREEN.
BARTHOLOMEW'S BATHS.
MANCHESTER ADDRESS, STOCKPORT ROAD, ADJOINING ARDWICK GREEN.
BIRMINGHAM ADDRESS. BROAD STREET. WORCESTER ADDRESS. SANSOME WALK.

Bristol
Manchester June 17th 1879

From The Corporation of Ashton
To Chs. Bartholomew

To New heating apparatus for Turkish Baths and fixing the same, as per agreement
£100 . 0 . 0

Please send cheque for above & and oblige,
Yours truly
Charles Bartholomew

Fig 15.19 (above) Charles Bartholomew's invoice for heating apparatus, slipped into the Corporation of Ashton Minute Book. (Tameside Local Studies and Archives)

Fig 15.20 (above right) One of the central radiators used to heat the hot rooms at Alloa. (© Crown Copyright: RCAHMS. Licensor, SC_681727 www.rcahms.gov.uk)

fortune in the United States. His several gifts to Dunfermline were expressions of thanks to his hometown with no hidden expectation of personal gain.

Carnegie gave the corporation £5,000 to build its first public baths. The building, on a corporation-owned site in Schoolend Street, was designed by local architect Andrew Scobie (*c* 1847–1924), and was officially opened on 12 July 1877.[42] Later, when it was clear that they had become so popular that they were too small, Carnegie gave a further £45,000 for a second set of baths and a gymnasium—a Christmas present to the town. These baths, in nearby Pilmuir Street, were designed by French-born Edinburgh architect Hippolyte Jean Blanc (1844–1917) and opened on 31 March 1905. Both buildings included Turkish baths.

Shortly after the start of World War I, they were made available for soldiers to use at half-price, so they were able to have a Turkish bath for 4½d or 6d. A hot water bath cost 1d or 2d and 'matters [were] so managed that no military man may be in the city for more than a week without a bath.'[43]

Another mill owner, John Thomson Paton, donated public baths in 'Scottish Renaissance' style to Alloa. Built at a cost of £40,000, the building also housed a billiards room, club room, and gymnasium. Designed by Glasgow architects John Burnet & Son (1882–1918), it was opened by Mr John Blair Balfour on 29 April 1898.[44]

The Turkish Baths, internally 'Saracenic' in appearance, comprised a cooling-room and two hot rooms. These were heated to 140°F (60°C), and 180°F (82°C), by a main central radiator (Fig 15.20) with three smaller supplementary ones.

A passage between the cooling-room and *tepidarium* led to the shampooing room and a Russian bath. The latter was unusual in being heated by steam introduced through perforated pipes at the discretion of the bathers themselves. There was also a large plunge pool.

By the 1960s the baths were in dire need of refurbishment and a major modernisation plan was drawn up. But in 1965, cuts were deemed necessary and the new scheme slashed. Some improvements to the Turkish bath were approved, and the work started, but in the midst of refurbishment, fire broke out and the Turkish baths were destroyed, although the swimming baths survived till 1986.[45]

Yet another northern mill owner, (Sir) John Henry Maden, included Turkish baths in his 1893 gift to the town of Bacup. And the Turkish baths at Openshaw in Manchester (1890), with their highly decorative mosaic-tiled walls, were a gift to the city from the legatees of the engineer Sir Joseph Whitworth, who established the eponymous British standard screw thread gauge.

Notwithstanding such philanthropy, the overwhelming majority of municipal Turkish baths were built by local authorities themselves, not always without lengthy deliberations, many of which led to a decision not to provide them.

Sanitas sanitatum et omnia sanitas

During the 1870s, the hydropathist Richard Metcalfe (Fig 15.21) served on the Paddington Vestry in London, originating several environmental schemes such as the laying out and planting of Paddington Green. In particular, he strongly advocated the adoption by the vestry of the Baths and Wash-houses Acts.

The arguments used by Metcalfe, and much of the information he collected, were later included in his book *Sanitas sanitatum et omnia sanitas* (*Health of health, all is health*). Like Disraeli—who had adopted this parody of 'Vanity of vanities, all is vanity' from Ecclesiastes as a political slogan—Metcalfe strongly believed in the need for sanitary legislation to improve public health.[46]

Although originally intended as the first of several volumes, it remains the only one published. Even so, the book is a remarkable document which, in spite of some exaggeration and over-simplification, was written by a knowledgeable enthusiast who himself had nothing to gain financially should his proposals be accepted.

In the chapter 'Hot-air *versus* warm water baths' Metcalfe compares the health and cleansing capabilities of each, convincingly demonstrating, to me at least, the advantages of hot air.

Discussing the economics of the hot-air bath, he admits that in Britain, the Turkish

Fig 15.21
Richard Metcalfe: hydropathist and committed propagandist.
(Richard Metcalfe, hydropathist: the man and his work, *Bemrose, 1894. Wellcome Library, London)*

bath had always been considered costly and time-consuming. Opponents had argued that no parochial authority could provide Turkish baths on the rates because the Baths and Wash-houses Acts limit them to a maximum charge of sixpence—a price, it was thought, which could never recoup the original cost of providing them.

Metcalfe then explains how such a problem might be solved, suggesting that publicly funded provision should comprise two complementary facilities,

> first, to give an ordinary Turkish Bath for sixpence—a sum quite within the reach of the working classes; and, secondly, to provide the facility for a perfectly cleansing ablution in a *lavatory, heated from 100°F to 115°F, for twopence.[47]

Furthermore, he designed and included a plan of his 'improved bath for the working classes', together with an estimate—from a local builder, Charles French of Lisson Grove, Marylebone—of the cost of constructing two possible versions of the building.

Metcalfe argued that although additional capital would be required in order to add a Turkish bath to existing facilities, there were other important factors which needed to be taken into consideration.

First, he showed that for a given capital expenditure the Turkish bath was more efficient because the downtime of the facility (as we would now say) was less than that for warm water baths. He estimated that the Turkish bath 'would be capable of bathing from 1500 to 2000 per week with ease', whereas warm water baths could only cope with a quarter of that number of bathers because each time a bath was used it needed emptying, cleaning, and refilling before it could be used again.

Second, while admitting that (in 1877) there were no municipal baths 'that have cleared off the first cost of erection from their profits', their use had been responsible for other, indirect, savings. Thinking especially of those who suffered from complaints like rheumatism, he maintained that the use of the Turkish bath would 'result in such an increase of health as to considerably lighten the rates, by keeping the poor from falling sick and so becoming dependent upon the parish.' There were also more quantifiable indirect savings such as, for example, passing the surplus heat through ducts around a drying room to dry all the linen and towels.

Third, he pointed out that slipper baths and wash-houses were used less frequently during the winter months, whereas the opposite was true in the case of Turkish baths, as had been shown at the People's Bath in Cork (discussed in the next chapter). So, he argued, adding a Turkish bath to an existing facility would help to stop the loss during the winter of the operating profit previously made during the summer.

Before writing his book, Metcalfe campaigned hard to persuade the Paddington Vestry to accept his proposals. At some time around the end of 1873, he wrote letters to well-known statesmen, noblemen, literary men of eminence, all Medical Officers of Health, and the superintendents, proprietors, and managers of all Turkish baths of whose existence he was aware.

He explained that the Commissioners of Baths for the Parish of Paddington were about to erect baths and wash-houses for the working classes. He, and a number of other Commissioners were, 'anxious to add the Turkish Bath and heated Lavatories (in which to wash and bathe)' to the usual facilities. Seeking assistance from all who might be able to add weight to his arguments, he wrote:

> Would it be too much at ask for your view on the Bath as a sanitary and cleansing agent, and the desirability of affording the Working Classes the facilities named? [We] do not ask your opinion of the Bath as a remedial agent, that being beyond the scope of [our] proposal.[48]

Amongst those he wrote to were all the current ministers of state, although only two replied: A S Ayrton from the Office of Works, who felt that 'for the purpose of cleanliness, it is better to provide the very cheapest means of washing, and not the most costly'; and Lord Carlingford (Harriet Urquhart's brother) from the Board of Works who wrote that he would 'be very glad to see its use extended to the working classes.'

Metcalfe must have been pleased with the results of his survey. We do not know how many did not reply but, to his credit, *Sanitas* included excerpts from every one of the 153 replies he did receive, even when he disagreed with the writer's views.

It is possible—but, given Metcalfe's character, unlikely—that he may have omitted to write to those he knew did not favour the Turkish bath. But we should not be too surprised to find that all but two respondents agreed with his first proposition—that the bath was an effective 'sanitary and cleansing agent' since anyone with opposing views would probably not have bothered to reply.

Only one person, a Dr Thomas Ballard, replied that he did not regard it as more convenient 'for cleansing purposes than a hot water bath.' While the other dissenter was the celebrated artist and caricaturist George Cruikshank, who wrote that he washed in cold water all year, and had never even seen a Turkish bath.

As to whether the Turkish bath should be made available to the working classes of Paddington, Metcalfe was able to show that 115 respondents (75.16%) thought that it should, and only 25 respondents (16.34%) thought otherwise. Cruikshank, again, did not know, and 12 respondents (7.84%) did not reply to this question.

As was to be expected, all the Turkish bath proprietors and managers answered both questions in the affirmative and remarkably, like Shepard in New York, none appeared to see a publicly funded bath taking custom away from his own establishment.

Of nine clergymen, all but one—the famous Baptist preacher Charles Haddon Spurgeon—strongly approved of providing such facilities for the working classes. His objection, expressed by others also, was that 'the great length of time required for the proper taking of a Turkish Bath will prevent the working classes using it very extensively.'

Spurgeon had visited the London Hammam over a decade earlier, and had, perhaps, overestimated the importance of its ritual, not realising that much simpler Turkish baths could be no less effective as a cleansing agent or source of pleasure.

Metcalfe understood that in spite of all this data, his fellow-members of the vestry might believe that he was merely suffering from a troublesome *idée fixe*. He felt, therefore, that they needed to read arguments which had been published prior to, and therefore independently of, his respondents' views. He related how, 'like a drowning man catching at a straw', he decided, at considerable cost, to give each of over seventy vestry members a copy of Durham Dunlop's *The philosophy of the bath*. But he sadly became aware that it was a wasted effort, writing,

> As a proof of their indifference to the subject I found, a few weeks afterwards, copies of the book I had presented, and bearing the mark of the Vestry, exposed for sale in the immediate neighbourhood.'

When his proposals were turned down, Metcalfe, who had a decade earlier run a Turkish bath at the short-lived Ragged Castle and Workman's Hall in Notting Hill (see page 175), and believed that he understood the needs of the poor, was understandably disappointed and withdrew from the commission.

In his view, when the vestry decided to build warm baths of the traditional type, they did not obtain the best value for the public money they were spending. He also believed that they had neglected their proper responsibilities in another important matter by building the baths on a site surrounded by the residences of the well-to-do and wealthy, instead of being in the vicinity of the poor, for whose benefit the Acts were intended.

The Dover Corporation survey

Several local authorities investigated how successful others had been before deciding whether to build Turkish baths, though this did not always result in their subsequently making the right decision for their own area.

In August 1901, Dover's town clerk sent a questionnaire to a selection of other English and Welsh town clerks, asking whether they had municipal Turkish baths, and if so whether they could provide some information about them. He received forty-three replies.[49]

Thirty-two stated that they did not have them, including five who mentioned that their town already had 'Turkish baths owned by private companies', and one from Maidstone which emphasised that they had 'no intention of having one.' Carlisle wrote that they had 'ordered' one, and the remaining ten towns had baths and completed the questionnaire. These ranged from Bacup with a population of 22,505, to Southampton with a population of 105,000.

Respondents were asked about the cost of building the baths, but it was difficult to make comparisons because, in many cases, the cost of the Turkish bath was not separated from that of the other baths or facilities in the building. In Dewsbury (Fig 15.22), for example, the cost was also combined with that of the library. For similar reasons, it was not possible to compare annual income or expenditure, or staff wages.

There were too many variables: some towns employed married couples; some were provided with accommodation; and many attendants were required to do different additional duties. All but the three largest towns (Newport, Stockport and Southampton), managed

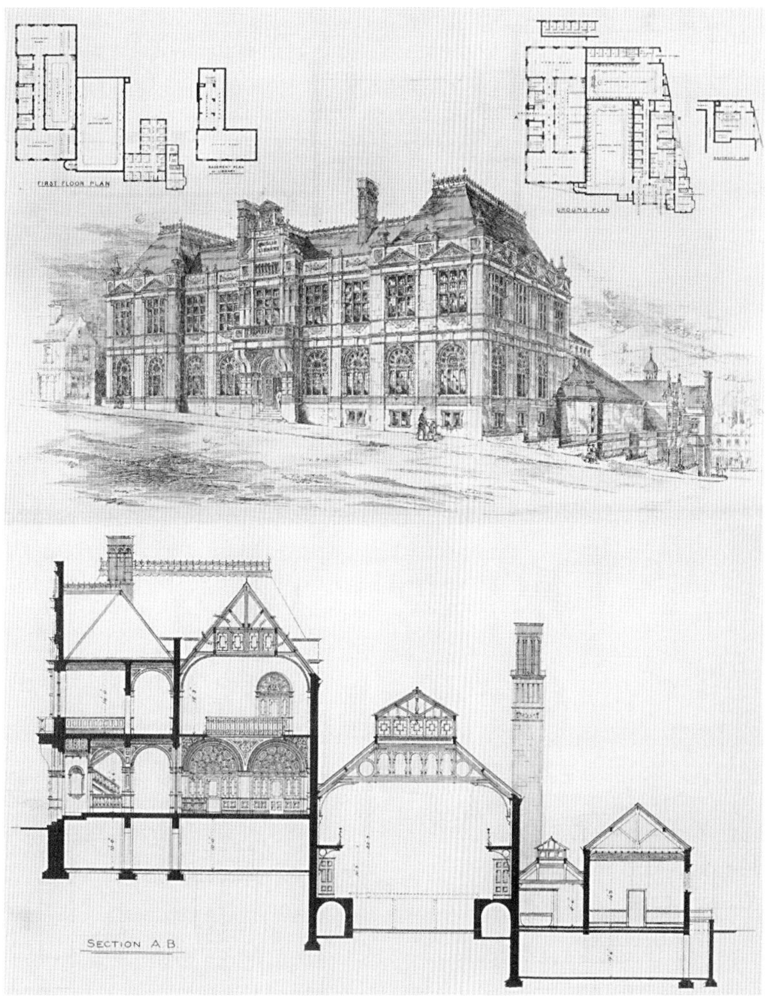

Fig 15.22
The first of three designs for the Dewsbury Baths—rejected because of cost.
*(*American Architect and Building News*, 26 September 1891. Author's collection)*

with one full-time attendant, together with a part-time female attendant for women's days.

The most expensive first-class baths, at 2s, were those at Lancaster and Newport (Mon), followed by Bacup, Southampton and Stockport at 1s 6d, and the remainder at 1s. Most second-class baths cost 1s, though Stalybridge charged 9d, and Batley, Burslem, Dewsbury and Longton charged only 6d.

Asked 'What are the sizes of the rooms?', all but Batley specified the names of each room, but the comparison tables presented by the clerk to his members unhelpfully gave only the sizes.

Neither Bacup nor Burslem mentioned having a shampooing room, and Batley did not mention a cooling-room. It may be, therefore, that some respondents interpreted the question as applying to hot rooms only, because some Russian baths and plunge pools known to have existed were not mentioned either.

Whether Dover's policy makers understood the limitations of the survey is unknown, but the only useful information to be had from the room size question is that, of the ten baths responding, seven provided three hot rooms and the remainder only two.

Respondents were also asked what their population was, 'what number of persons can be accommodated at one time in the various rooms', and 'What number of people use the Baths annually'. Table 15.1 is an attempt to show what percentage of a town's population it was thought necessary to provide simultaneous provision for.

While it would be tempting to indicate the percentage of the town's population which used the baths, this is not possible because, despite the questionnaire referring to *people* using the baths annually, this is universally translated into the number of *baths taken* per year. But I have used the data to calculate the ratio of baths taken to a town's population. So we can see, for example, that in one year in Longton, one Turkish bath was taken for every six people who lived there. Of course, the 5,300 baths were taken by far fewer than the stated 'number of bathers', most of whom would have taken several baths in the year. But the calculation does enable a very crude comparison to be made of a town's success in encouraging its population to use the Turkish baths provided. It is important not to make too many inferences from this type of table, because the towns surveyed were randomly chosen, during an accidentally chosen year, using questions which were not ideal.

Nevertheless, it does seem as though Longton, which notionally provided one bath for every six inhabitants, did better in promoting its baths than Burslem, which made the largest provision, but only managed one bath for every eleven inhabitants.

To obtain a more accurate picture, many additional factors would need to be considered, in a much more scientific survey. For example, in the larger towns, a person's distance from home to baths is just one factor which immediately comes to mind; it can probably be seen here affecting the figures for Southampton.

Dover went ahead with its proposal. May 1903 saw the opening of Turkish baths built within an existing building to the design of the Borough Engineer, Henry E Stilgoe. They included a cooling-room with ten cubicles, three hot rooms, a plunge pool, vapour bath, medicated and *electric baths (Fig 15.23), two shampooing rooms and a caretaker's flat.[50] They remained open till 1935 when, perhaps to take account of more urgent bodily needs, they were converted into public conveniences.

Although the Dover survey only begins to show this—the questions were too restricted—many small town Turkish baths had features in

Table 15.1 Results of Dover Corporation's Turkish baths survey, 1901

Town	*Population*	*Places*	*Places to population*	*Baths per yr*	*Approx ratio baths to population*
Bacup	22,505	8	0.035%	813	1:27
Batley	30,321	16	0.053%	2,869	1:10
Burslem	38,766	30	**0.077%**	3,362	1:11
Dewsbury	28,050	8	0.029%	4,000	1:7
Longton	35,371	15	0.042%	5,300	**1:6**
Newport (Mon)	67,292	11	0.016%	4,367	1:15
Southampton	**105,000**	42	0.040%	3,200	1:32
Stalybridge	27,674	20	0.072%	1,850	1:14
Stockport	78,871	20	0.025%	3,273	1:24

Lancaster has been excluded from the table as not all questions were answered.

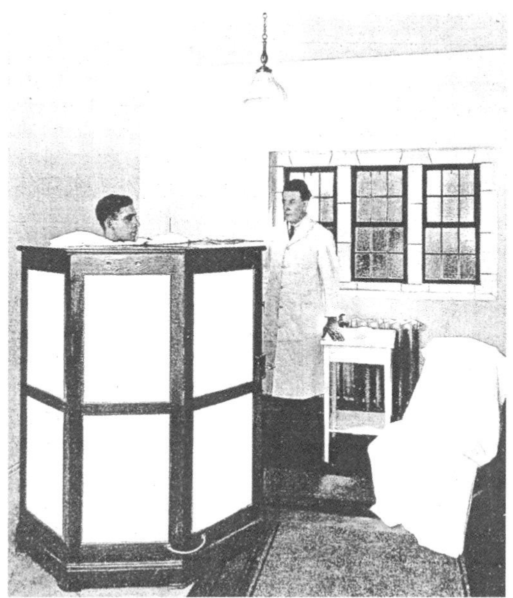

Fig 15.23
Electric bath cabinet at the Turkish baths in Margate, similar to that at Dover. (Reproduced by kind permission of Dixon Wilson)

common, differing only in the number of hot rooms provided, whether the cooling-room had changing cubicles or an adjoining dressing room, whether there was a plunge pool, or whether shampooing was provided.

Similarly, the interior decoration may or may not have been 'Saracenic', but the surface finishes were usually of glazed bricks or tiles, the floors were laid with plain tiles or decorative encaustic ones, and sometimes their floors or walls were partially faced with decorative mosaics.

London's municipal Turkish baths

Four years elapsed between the building of the first Victorian Turkish bath at St Ann's and the first one in London; nearly 40 years elapsed between the first municipal Turkish bath in Bradford and the first in London. Why it took so long is difficult to fathom.

By 1900 there were already over 40 municipal baths in the provinces. No authority had been prosecuted for providing Turkish baths. The Paddington authorities were not the only ones to consider the possibility and then reject it. Chelsea Council (Fig 15.24) ran an architectural design competition, awarding the prize to architects Wills & Anderson, but when the baths opened in 1907 the Turkish baths had been omitted.

Eleven of the twenty-nine pre-1965 London boroughs built Turkish baths as part of a new complex (Fig 15.25). The first was Camberwell in 1905. Then came a 20-year gap, only partly accounted for by World War I. Nine more followed between 1927 and 1938, with Lewisham, the sole straggler, in 1965.

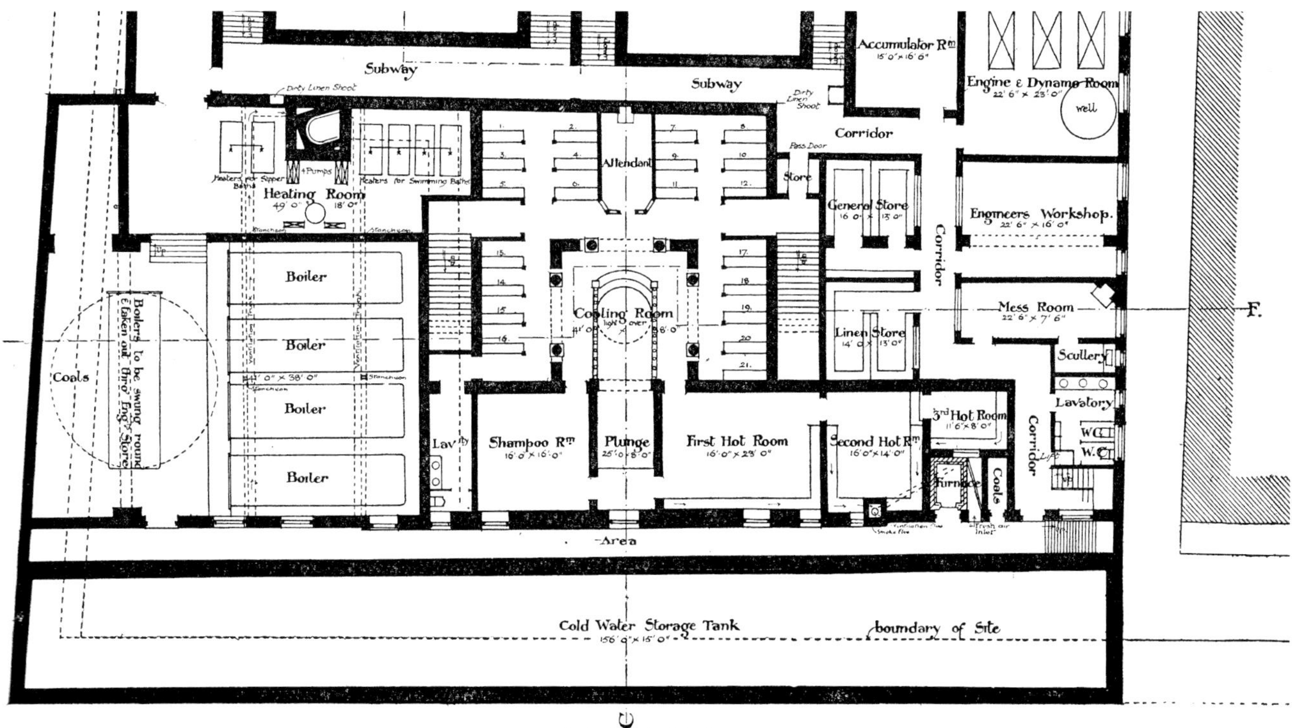

Fig 15.24
This competition-winning Turkish bath, for London's Borough of Chelsea, was never built. There were other baths, similarly proposed around the country, which never reached fruition, usually for financial reasons.
(Alfred W S Cross, Public baths and washhouses, *Batsford, 1906)*

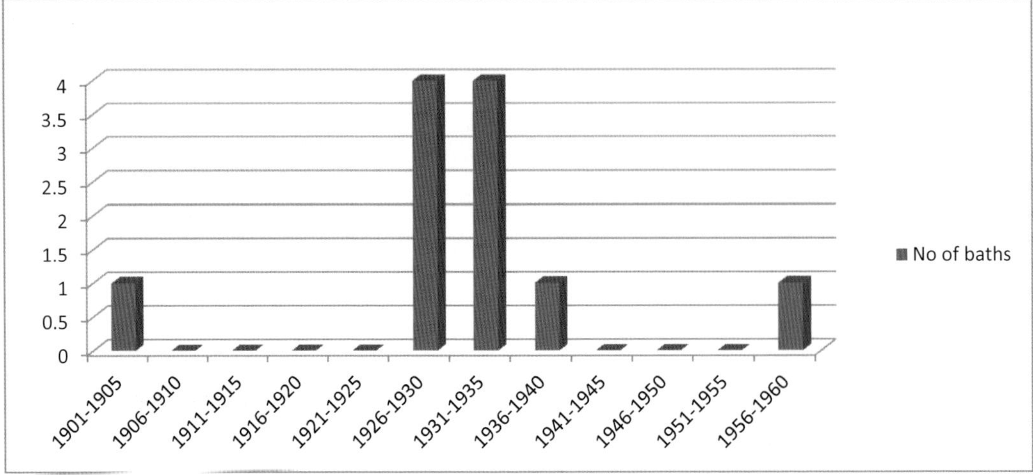

Fig 15.25
Graph showing the number of municipal Turkish baths opened in London per half-decade.
(© Malcolm Shifrin)

The Turkish baths at Camberwell were in the basement of a new building in Old Kent Road. They were designed by architect Edward Harding Payne (1866–1951), opened on 19 October 1905, and were destroyed in the Blitz during the last months of World War II.

They were built and fitted to a high standard, a green-banded white marble staircase leading down to the cooling-room (Fig 15.26) with its black and white marble floor and multi-coloured fountain. Fourteen curtained cubicles, each with a couch, provided the privacy which women bathers were said to prefer on the days set aside for them.[51]

The temperatures of the three hot rooms could be raised to around 120°F (49°C), 180°F (82°C), and 280°F (138°C) by a Crumblehulme Convoluted Stove. Their walls were of glazed brick with coloured bands, their ceilings of enamelled iron panels, and their floors of mosaic and terrazzo, with marble benches. A shampooing room, with two marble slabs and basins, a 24ft (7.3m) long plunge pool, an array of needle and other showers, and a Russian vapour bath completed the facilities.

Even the staff were thoughtfully provided for, with a chute down to the laundry for dirty towels, and dumbwaiters supplying clean ones to the ticket office.

Few of the later London baths matched Camberwell in the quality of their fittings or the clean modern design of the whole, though the unique art deco plunge pool at Paddington Baths (Fig 15.27), designed by local architect Herbert Shepherd (1873–1944), was an exception. These baths, now in the London Borough of Westminster and known as Porchester Spa, are still open. Indeed, a poster, probably dating from the bath's opening in 1929, shows that the pool and the spacious ground floor cooling-room have hardly changed at all during the past 85 years (Fig 15.28).

Most of London's post-Camberwell municipal baths had the same basic provision of three

Fig 15.26 (below left)
The cooling-room at the Camberwell baths in Old Kent Road.
*(*Souvenir of the opening of the public baths...*, 19 October 1905) p.17. From the collections of the Southwark Local History Library & Archive)*
Fig 15.27 (below right)
The art deco plunge pool at the Paddington baths.
(Unknown photographer)

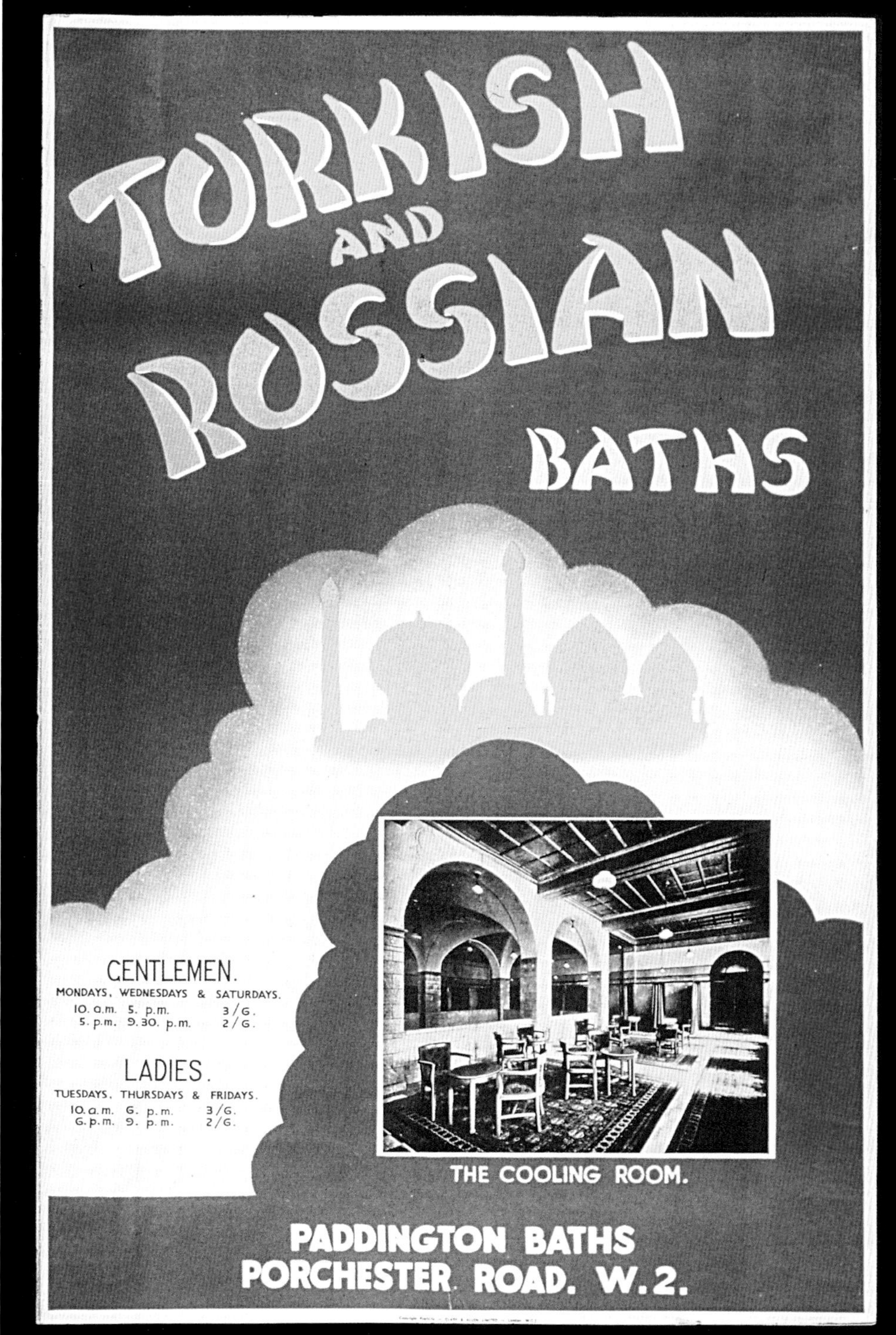

Fig 15.28
A poster advertising the Paddington baths shortly after their opening. (Author's collection)

hot rooms, a cooling-room with changing cubicles, a shampooing room, plunge pool, and Russian bath.

There were a few differences. Bermondsey's baths in the basement at Grange Road, in addition to a cooling-room, had separate dressing rooms for males and females even though they used the baths on different days. There was also a separate second Russian bath and cooling-room for those bathers who did not want a Turkish bath.

Even better was the provision at the Stepney Baths, designed by Stepney's Borough Engineer and Surveyor, Harley Heckford (1867–1937).

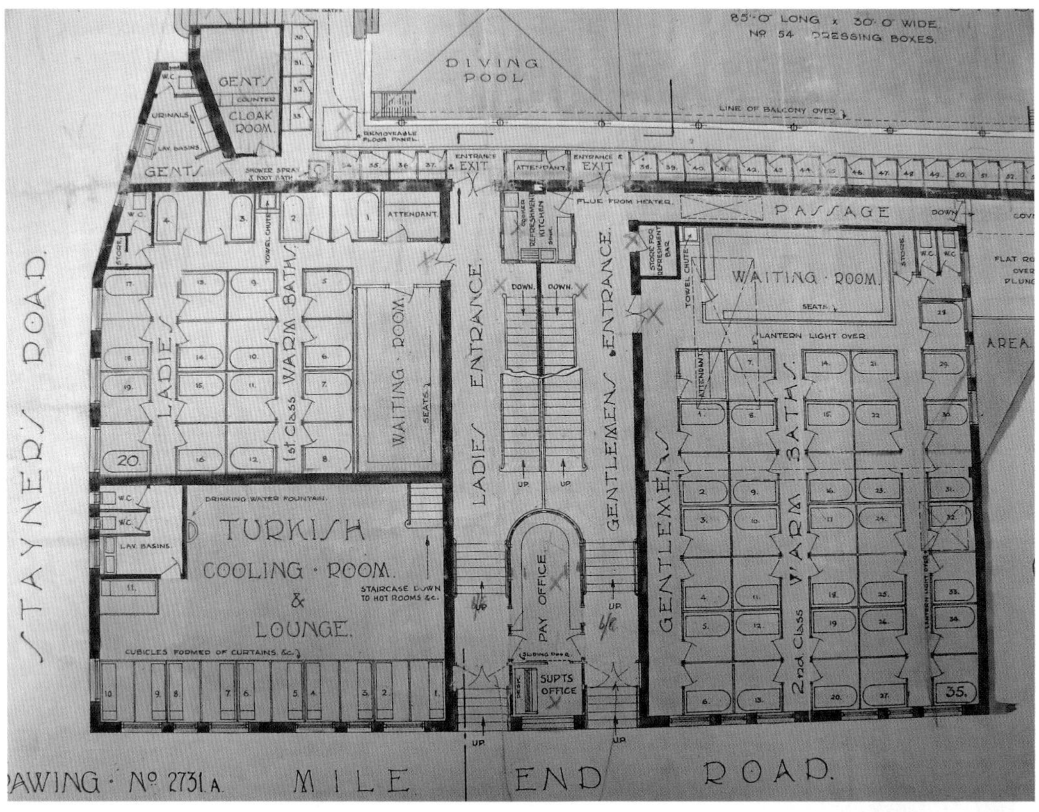

Fig 15.29
Stepney's Mile End baths: part of the ground floor plan.
(London Metropolitan Archives. City of London)

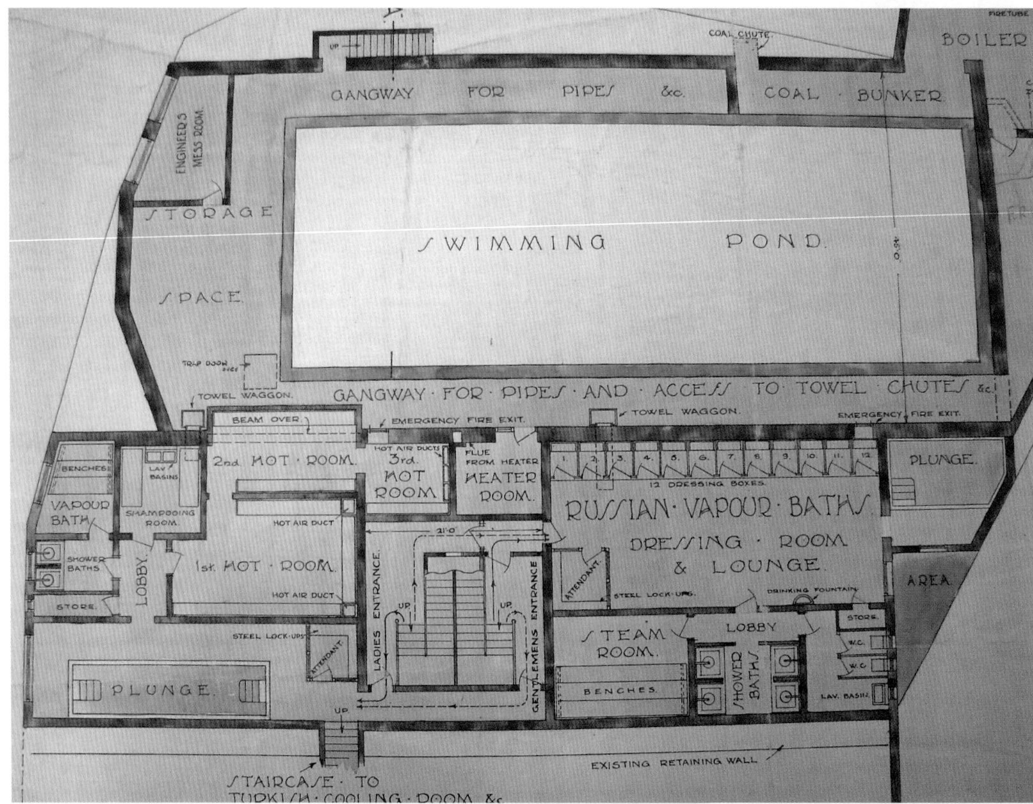

Fig 15.30
The Mile End baths: part of the first floor plan.
(London Metropolitan Archives. City of London)

Fig 15.31 (opposite top)
Notices in the Mile End in 1940 were in Yiddish and English, and probably had been since the baths opened.
(Unknown photographer)

Here the entrance and cooling-room were on the ground floor (Fig 15.29), while the Turkish baths themselves (with an additional small vapour bath) were on the floor above (Fig 15.30). Also on this floor was a separate Russian baths suite, with its own lounge, changing cubicles, and plunge pool for those preferring not to use the Turkish baths. Again, men and women bathed on different days, but separate entrances allowed the simultaneous use of their own slipper baths elsewhere in the building.

At the end of the 1930s, most of the important signs within these baths included a Yiddish translation (Fig 15.31) because so many of the bathers were Jewish—refugees from the Russian pogroms or, later, from Hitler's Germany.

Unusually, when Woolwich baths were opened in 1913, the typical installation sequence (hot-air baths followed by vapour baths) was reversed, Woolwich initially providing only Russian baths. These soon proved quite inadequate for the needs of the local popula-

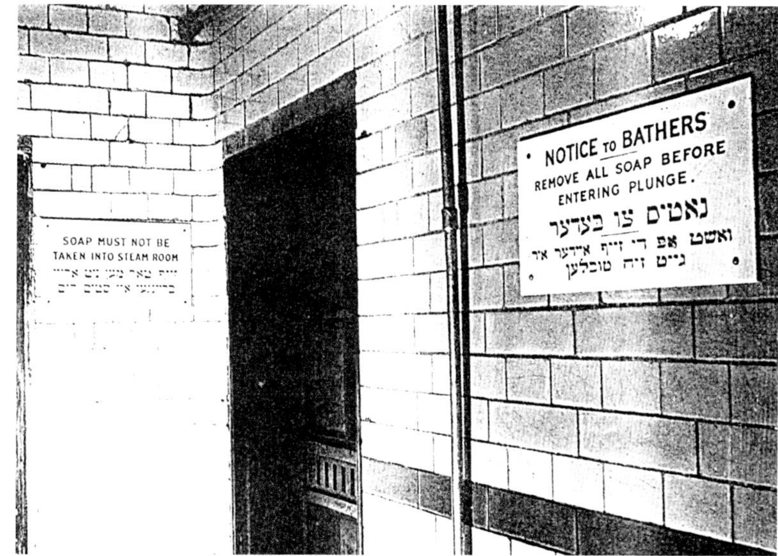

tion and a suite of Turkish baths was included in the new Plumstead High Street baths.

This was designed by the borough engineer's department under F H Clinch and opened in 1927. Apart from its Turkish baths sign and, above it, a star and crescent roundel (Fig 15.32), there was nothing of particular note externally.

Inside, the hot rooms, plunge pool, and showers were similar to most others, but its cooling-room—though perhaps overcrowded—was designed with comfort in mind and lavishly furnished with fully upholstered couches and easy chairs (see Fig 13.27, page 131).

Finsbury's cooling-room at its Ironmonger Row baths (now within Islington) was probably no less comfortable, but the possibility of slightly more privacy would have made for easier relaxation (Fig 15.33).

Fig 15.32 (above) Exterior of the Plumstead Turkish Baths, with men's and women's entrances, and a star and crescent roundel above. (Turkish and Russian vapour baths, *Borough of Woolwich, 1928. Greenwich Heritage Centre)*

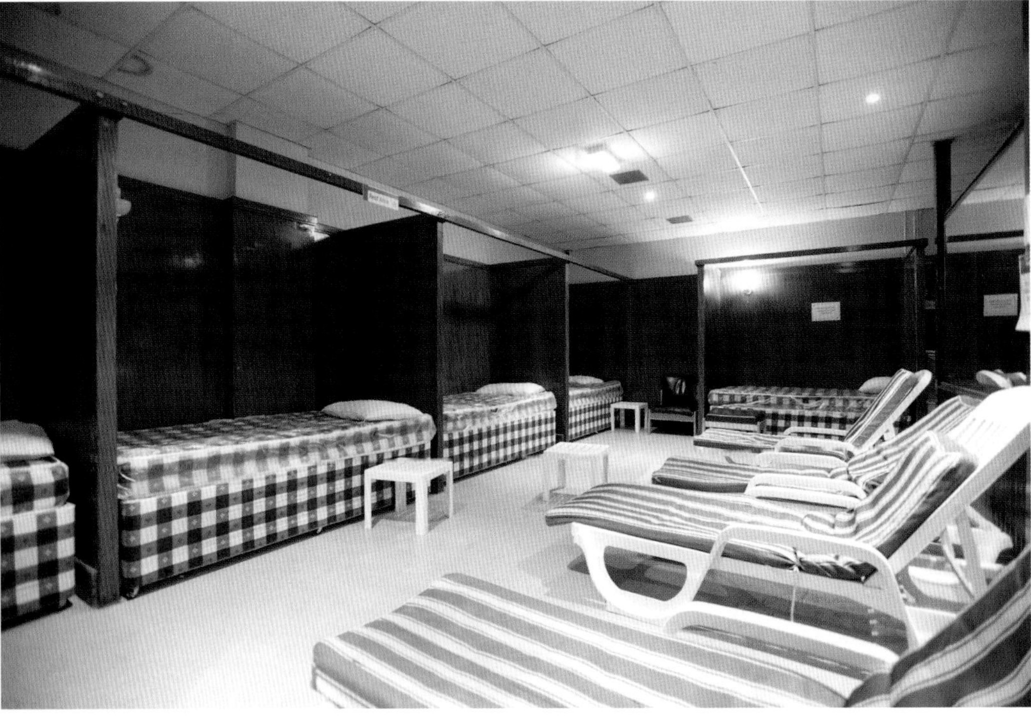

Fig 15.33
Finsbury's Ironmonger Row cooling-room.
(© Grant Smith)

Comparing London's municipal Turkish baths

So if London's municipal baths were all built in the 20th century and all had more or less the same number of rooms, fulfilling the same functions, were they all the same in appearance?

For anyone other than a specialist it would probably be tedious to do a room by room comparison for all of them. But to get a general impression of the differences, it is probably sufficient to compare shampooing rooms because this allows us to consider usability as well as appearance.

What is particularly interesting is the similarity between the rooms at Camberwell built in 1905 (Fig 15.34), Woolwich built more than 20 years later in 1927 (Fig 15.35), and Greenwich more than 50 years later still, in 1959 (Fig 15.36). From a bather's point of view, the only difference between the first and last rooms is that curtains could be used to separate the slabs for greater privacy—only the rails are shown in the photograph, which was taken just before the baths opened. Apart from that, there were

Fig 15.34 (below left)
Shampooing room at Camberwell's Old Kent Road baths.
*(*Souvenir of the opening of the public baths…, *19 October 1905, p.17. From the collections of the Southwark Local History Library & Archive)*

Fig 15.35 (below right)
Shampooing room at Woolwich baths in Plumstead High Street.
*(*Turkish and Russian vapour baths, *Borough of Woolwich, 1928. Greenwich Heritage Centre)*

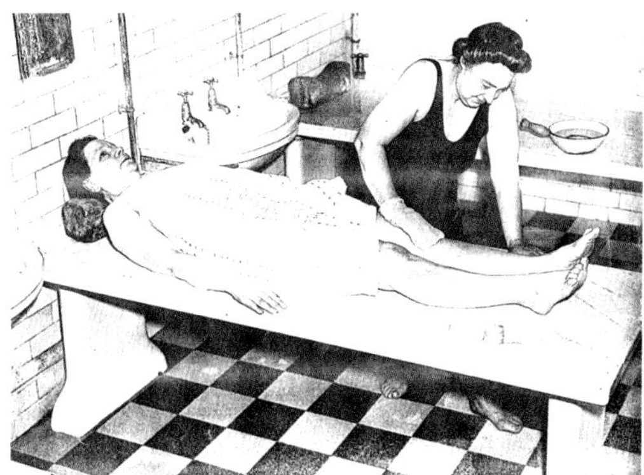

Fig 15.36 (left) Shampooing room at Greenwich baths in Trafalgar Road. (Opening of the Turkish and Russian vapour baths, *Borough of Woolwich, 1959. Greenwich Heritage Centre)*
Fig 15.37 (right) Shampooing room at Bethnal Green's baths at York Hall in the 1920s. (Unknown photographer)

a few unhidden pipes at Woolwich, making the room slightly more difficult to keep clean.

Opened barely two years after Woolwich, the shampooing room at York Hall in Bethnal Green (1929) seems, with its open pipework, to take a step backward. More important, the lack of space between the slabs made it almost impossible for two shampooers to use both slabs simultaneously (Fig 15.37).

But least satisfactory was the shampooing room at Ironmonger Row (1938). Here the shampooer could only stand on one side of the bather (Fig 15.38). Not only did this affect the massage, but could lead to severe back problems for the shampooer.

Surprisingly, this room was designed by Kenneth Mervyn Baskerville Cross, a public baths specialist.[52] Yet the shampooing room designed by Cross for the Pier Approach baths in Bournemouth (which opened the previous year) was altogether more spacious (Fig 15.39). We must assume that Bournemouth had more money to spend.

Most of these baths were built during the inter-war years, 1927–1938, in the poorer areas of London. Other boroughs were not so fortunate. Both Hackney and Stoke Newington were in the midst of planning Turkish baths in the late 1930s, but the war intervened and eventually the plans were abandoned.[53]

Fig 15.38 (below left) Cramped shampooing room at Finsbury's Ironmonger Row Baths. (Islington Local History Centre)
Fig 15.39 (below right) Spacious shampooing room and plunge bath at the Pier Approach baths, Bournemouth. (Bournemouth Pier Approach Baths, *The Corporation, 1937. Reproduced by permission of Bournemouth Libraries)*

16

Turkish baths for the working classes

The Baths and Wash-houses Acts, with their requirement to provide separate classes of bath, did not apply to commercial baths, though most of them provided more than one class by choice. This may have been so that the working classes did not come into contact with those 'above' them, but it was also because, in order to make a profit, it was necessary to broaden a bath's potential customer base as much as possible.

Even in Ireland and Scotland, where the acts did not apply, commercial baths often made separate provision. At §Lochhead Hydropathic Establishment near Aberdeen, for example, the baths were also open to members of the public for two hours in the afternoon at a cost of 2s 6d. In the evening they cost 1s for 'the Working Classes (who require to provide themselves with a Sheet and Towel)', with two days being reserved for women in each class. Similarly there were differing charges for shampooing.[1]

So even before the first local authority Turkish baths opened, the typical commercial establishment catered in this way for the better paid working-class bather.

Here we are interested in two other types of establishment: those which, when opened, were specifically intended to provide for the poorest of the working class; and those provided by individual companies for their employees.

Yet again, in Ireland, Dr Barter set the pattern by providing a bath at St Ann's where,

> 'At the end of the week the numerous workmen and labourers, and after them their wives and children, have the privilege of being refreshed and cleansed by the Bath.'[2]

A red flag was displayed outside the bath when it was occupied by men, and a white one when occupied by women. When there was no flag showing, the bath could be seen by any interested visitors.

Barter's first commercial baths, however, were expensive, and in 1860 Dr Edward Haughton, in his *Facts and fallacies of the Turkish bath*, wrote that in Ireland,

> up to the present date, the baths called 'Turkish' have been, from the prices charged, necessarily beyond the reach of the poor, except as a favor; and, therefore, their use has been chiefly confined to the rich. This is to be regretted, as there is nothing in the real Turkish Bath to exclude the poorest of the poor.[3]

And there were others who were also aware of the problem.

Turkish baths for the poor in Belfast

Two public meetings were held on 22 March 1860 at the Belfast Music Hall. Both were well-attended by 'the most respectable portion of the inhabitants of the town'.[4]

Their objective was to seek support for a new company, the Belfast Turkish Baths Company Ltd, which would build and operate working class Turkish Baths in Donegall Street. But when it was clear that there was insufficient financial support, Barter decided to build them at his own expense, and the company was later dissolved.[5]

The baths opened 'for the use of the Working Classes' on Monday 1 October, with bathers entering at the rear of the baths from number 43 Little Donegall Street, a smaller road running parallel to the main one. But the price of the least expensive Turkish bath, at an establishment supposedly designed for the working classes, was still too high (Fig 16.1).

Even in what were called the second-class baths there were two price levels. At each end of the day, between six and eight o'clock, a bath cost 6d, while in the intervening period between ten in the morning and four in the afternoon, the charge was 50% higher. Shampooing 'with

ADVERTISEMENTS. 183

TURKISH BATHS,

112, DONEGALL STREET,

BELFAST.

THESE improved TURKISH BATHS are in constant operation, Sundays excepted.

These Baths were built by Dr. Barter, on his patent principle, and are managed by proved attendants from Blarney, under his directions, the same as at Dublin, Cork, Limerick, Waterford, Sligo, Bray, Killarney.

TERMS.

FIRST CLASS.

	S.	D.
From 6 to 8 a.m.,	1	6
From 6 to 8 p.m.,	1	6
Shampooing,	0	6
Subscription Ticket for 12 Baths at the above-named hours,	15	0
From 10 a.m. to 4 p.m.,	2	6
Subscription Ticket for 12 Baths,	24	0
Shampooing,	0	6
Subscription Shampooing Ticket for 12 Baths,	4	0

SECOND CLASS.

	S.	D.
From 6 to 8 a.m.,	0	6
From 6 to 8 p.m.,	0	6
From 10 a.m. to 4 p.m.,	0	9
Shampooing, with the use of Sheet,	0	3

Children under four years, Free to the Baths.
Children under ten years, Half-price.

Come, and take "THE BATH."

ENTRANCE TO FIRST CLASS, 112, DONEGALL STREET.
ENTRANCE TO SECOND CLASS, 43, LITTLE DONEGALL STREET.
M

Fig 16.1
Advertisement for the Belfast Turkish baths 'for the use of the Working Classes', 1861. (M'Comb's guide to Belfast, 1861. *Author's collection)*

the use of a sheet' cost 3d. However—a typical Barter touch—children under ten years old were allowed in at half price and for those under four the baths were free.[6]

Later, when the first-class baths opened (entrance this time through the front door) there was a similar two class structure based on the time of day, the cost of a bath being 1s 6d or 2s 6d, with a shampoo costing 6d. There were also reduced prices for those buying 12 tickets at a time.[7]

The baths were, therefore, very slow to catch on. Articles about them appeared in the local press, some singing their praise, others patronising and preaching.

> If working men would visit the second-class baths on Saturday evenings, instead of the public-house, which too many of them frequent, they would find their health benefited by it, and their strength invigorated for the labours of the ensuing week.[8]

When Dr Barter died on 3 October 1870, the baths, as part of his estate, passed to his eldest son, Mr Richard Barter. The working class Turkish Baths continued as such for at least another two years, although they do not appear to have been very successful in this guise. Thomas Coakley, the baths manager in 1872, wrote to Richard Metcalfe saying that,

> ...though ... in operation here about twelve years, yet, so very few avail themselves of them, that, in fact, they are not worth keeping open, inasmuch as they are not paying expenses.[9]

In an attempt to reduce these, an appeal was made to the Belfast Water Board for a reduction in their water rate. Mr Barter's representative, Mr Ruddell, said that in March 1871 he was paying £14 15s 3d per year, but now, only a year later, he was being asked £22 11s 6d because the premises had been enlarged.

To encourage the working classes to use the baths more, Barter offered to reduce their entrance charge by a quarter if the commissioners were prepared to supply his water at a fixed charge of £20, thereby conferring 'a boon upon the inhabitants of the town.'[10]

Although several commissioners looked favourably on the proposal, the chairman ruled that a written application should be made and an agreement drawn up indicating what each side undertook to do—and there the matter ended.

The baths were offered for sale in July 1881, although it is not known with what immediate result.[11] In November the following year, however, they were acquired by John North.

When they reopened on 26 June 1893 [12] (with four sets of baths, male and female, first and second class) North had renamed them 'Hammam Turkish Baths' to emphasise their link with his Dublin Hammam Hotel and Baths. They no longer catered specifically for working-class bathers, but under North, his son-in-law Joseph Armstrong, and Joseph's son Oliver, the new baths remained open till early in 1936.

The People's Turkish Bath in Cork

In the south of the island, the Turkish Baths for the Destitute Poor, popularly known as The People's Turkish Bath, opened in Cork at 15 Maylor Street on 23 February 1863. The bath was formally under the proprietorship of Dr Barter, its supervisor was Miss Lizzie Barter, and 'a number of Ladies ... consented to act as a Managing Committee.'[13]

Women had been the main campaigners for the bath, under the leadership of Mrs C G Donovan, a close friend of Dr Barter, and probable author of the memoir written after his death.[14] She had long campaigned for the wider use of the bath. In August 1858, when

Charles Dickens gave a reading in Cork,[15] she wrote asking him to 'make the bath a "household word,"'—making a play on the title of his magazine, *Household Words*, which was published weekly between March 1850 and May 1859. But it seems she had no reply, Dickens 'not having the prevision for which I gave him credit'.[16]

Mrs Donovan's committee, over a period of two years, raised the £500 needed. This included a grant from the trustees of the Barter Bath Charity Fund, £50 from J F Maguire, the local MP and proprietor of the *Cork Examiner*, and £100 from the Corporation of Cork.[17]

Announcing the opening of the bath, and clearly displaying the prejudices of the time, the *Cork Examiner* wrote,

> The bath, while comfortable in every department, is devoid of the unnecessary refinements which prevail in those for another class of the population, but which would be useless and out of place in an establishment designed especially for 'the people.'[18]

A one-penny bath ticket was purchased just inside the main entrance. On the left was the cooling-room with eight changing cubicles. A short passageway led to the two hot rooms and, opening off the second one, a bathroom. Access to the boiler room, strangely, was also through the cooling-room.

While this may seem a very basic provision, there were plenty of commercial baths with the same or less (having, for example, one hot room instead of two or three).

After a slow start—there were only 1,865 bathers (ie, baths taken) during the first year—the bath became more popular. The price rose in two stages to threepence, yet in 1869 there were more than 20,000 bathers.[19]

Still involved with the promotion of the bath in 1875, Mrs Donovan wrote, in a style similar to that of a comic-strip dialogue, an anonymous pamphlet on hydropathy and the use of the Turkish bath called *Chat upon health: Pat Dennehy visits Mrs Magrath*. The booklet concludes,

> N.B.—At the People's Bath, 26 Maylor Street, Cork, a Turkish Bath may be had gratis, or for a nominal charge. Advice given, and cold-water bandages and various hydropathic appliances may be purchased.[20]

The baths closed some time between 1894 and 1896, by which time the premises were occupied by Haden & Company's mineral water factory.[21]

A people's Turkish bath for Dublin?

In October 1871, Mr Barter offered to found 'a cheap Turkish bath for the working-classes of Dublin.'[22] Throughout the following six months, letters in support were periodically published in the *Irish Times*. These included a lengthy one from Mrs Donovan, signed 'An Irishwoman'[23], and another from one of her supporters, 'Irene.'[24] Then, on 10 April 1872, a meeting was held at Barter's Upper Sackville Street Hammam.[25]

As in Belfast, no financial support appears to have resulted from the meeting. Nor were there any actual contributions arising from an earlier letter in the *Irish Times* from William Ledger Erson who indicated that contributions of £50 'from a medical friend' and £20 'from a mercantile gentleman' had already been offered.[26]

When the baths opened just over seven weeks later in Thomas's Lane, more or less at the back of The Hammam, they had been entirely paid for by Mr Barter.

The cost of a Turkish bath between six in the morning and eight in the evening was sixpence, and the *Freeman's Journal* wrote that the new bath would be seen,

> as a great boon to thousands of the hard worked sons of toil, who, after a long day's labour, can for a few pence, take a refreshing bath that will thoroughly cleanse the skin, relieve their weary limbs, promote their health and self-respect, and fit them, if necessary, to go in without sleep for another 12 hours' labour. It will be entirely the fault of the working classes if they do not avail themselves of a great comfort and luxury which will be placed within their reach, but we are sure it will be generally availed of by thousands.[27]

They do not appear in any major directory, no advertisements have been found, nor have I found any advertisements for them. At the same price as the Belfast baths, success seems to have been unlikely.

The timing of Mr Barter's offer does not seem propitious. He must have known that the number of baths taken in Belfast was far lower than expected, and he must surely, by then, already have been considering whether to keep them open. It is also significant that while Mrs Donovan and 'Irene' both mentioned the success of the Cork baths, neither they, nor anyone else, mentioned Belfast.

It may be that Barter's offer, coming so soon after his father's death, was intended to show that he was no less generous. Or, perhaps more likely, that he was carrying out one of his father's last intentions.

On the mainland, no baths similar to these Irish ones have been identified, but other different ways of putting Turkish baths within the reach of the poorest people were tried.

The Turkish baths at the Workmen's Hall, Notting Hill

The hydropathist Richard Metcalfe had, 'at considerable inconvenience, opened a Turkish Baths at The Ragged Castle and Workmen's Hall, Notting Hill in connection with an Hydropathic Dispensary.'[28]

There is some confusion about the year the bath opened. Metcalfe, whose dates are not always reliable, gives two different ones in his written accounts, neither of which tallies with that in a contemporary newspaper. But he was correct in stating that the bath remained open only for 18 months.

In 1859, Mrs Mary Bayley and supporters from the Rescue Society (later renamed the Temperance Society) had converted two houses in Portland Terrace (now Portland Road) to meet their needs.[29] The hall aimed to provide working men with an attractive alternative to the public house, where light refreshments, reading material, popular board games, and bathing facilities were available.

The Workmen's Hall and Reading Rooms, the first of its kind, was opened on 12 March 1861 in the presence of Archibald Campbell Tait, Bishop of London and future Archbishop of Canterbury.

When the hall opened, Metcalfe, with Mrs Bayley's support, set up his dispensary in two basement rooms, 'one of which, a small three-cornered room, and heated by a brick flue running round it, was used as a Turkish Bath'.[30] Charges were nominal, and frequently waived.

Reasons for its early closure varied. According to Metcalfe, the trustees 'refused to allow the fire necessary to heat the Turkish bath, thinking it endangered the safety of the building', and so it was 'brought to an abrupt termination.'

Safety was probably just an excuse. According to Henry Solly, contemporary historian of the working men's social clubs, a new manager, appointed to improve the usage of the hall, claimed that,

> the first great drawback to success was that the reading-room was always so oppressively hot, the chimney of some Turkish baths running up at one end of it.[31]

But, just over 18 months after the hall opened, a *Daily News* article, probably much closer to the truth, reported that the baths, 'were not much patronised, and are now abandoned.' The article was generally critical of the hall, and its total lack of success was attributed to the fact that it was 'specially devoted to the diffusion of teetotal principles, and the dissemination of religious tracts for the conversion of the infidel.'[32]

In Wales, support was provided more acceptably by adopting a different approach.

The Ladies' Sanitary Association: free tickets at Cardiff Baths

The Cardiff Baths in Guildford Street were opened by the Cardiff Baths Company Ltd on 1 May 1862.

Admission to the Turkish baths cost 2s, or 1s between seven o'clock and ten in the morning. During the six months ending 1 November 1863, there were 1,425 bathers (excluding season ticket holders) and a letter from 'Aqua Pura' in the *Cambrian* noted that 'The shilling admission to the Turkish Baths appears to be largely appreciated by the working classes.'[33]

But 1s was a hefty sum, especially for women bathers, most of whom would not have had an income of their own. Starting in 1866, their needs were met, for a while at least, by the Ladies' Sanitary Association.

The Ladies' National Association for the Diffusion of Sanitary Knowledge (to give its original name) was founded in the autumn of 1857, under Royal patronage, for 'the diffusion of sanitary knowledge and the promotion of physical education among the female sex'. From the outset it dedicated itself to the task of health education, preaching that disease and early death were not inevitable.

It published a series of tracts with titles as varied as *The worth of fresh air*, *The value of wholesome food*, *The power of soap and water*, and *Hints to working people about personal cleanliness*.[34] However, their work was not limited to publishing. In Aberdeen, for example, they distributed soap, disinfecting powder, and even brushes.

Their members, some of whom would themselves have used Turkish baths, frequently visited working-class homes as part of their educational work. They would have seen for themselves how impossibly expensive even the cheapest bath was for those who might possibly have benefited most from its use.

Those working in Cardiff tried to remedy this situation by reaching an agreement with the baths company. This allowed the association to provide reduced price tickets for the women's sessions to 'deserving cases' at 'nominal prices'.[35]

But less than a decade after the baths opened, the company was in financial difficulties. The baths closed for a short while, and when they reopened as the Cardiff Corporation Baths the concessionary tickets were no longer available.

Company baths. 1: Swindon

During the second half of the 19th century there were two Swindons. On a site separated by fields from the original old town, the Great Western Railway Company (GWR) built a village adjoining its huge railway works for those who were employed there. New Swindon was a railway town and, more specifically, a company town.

From 1840, when Isambard Kingdom Brunel designed the first row of cottages, until 1906, when the medical centre and baths building on Faringdon Road was more or less completed, the GWR built a range of facilities for their workers and their families. Apart from housing, a hospital, schools, a library, a covered market, and a park, there was a Mechanics' Institution and a Medical Fund Society which, by 1947, was considered to be a model worth following by the new National Health Service.[36]

Those employed in the GWR works became members of the fund, originally compulsorily, though later voluntarily. A weekly subscription, ranging from ½d to 10d, was deducted from members' pay. In return, they were able to get free first aid and treatment after an accident, together with any necessary hospital treatment. In addition, they and their families could call on a doctor, and obtain medicines, dental treatment, physiotherapy, and a variety of baths.[37]

Some time, early in February 1858, David Urquhart was invited to the Mechanics' Institution to give a lecture on Turkish baths. But due to the sudden tragic death of his baby son William, the lecture was given by Stewart Erskine Rolland in his place.

When questioned afterwards about the cost of building such a bath, Rolland undertook, at a cost of £100,

> 'to build a bath at New Swindon capable of accommodating one hundred persons per day, and costing only from fourpence to sixpence per day for fuel.'[38]

Rolland's offer was not accepted. After all, the first Turkish bath in England had opened only seven months earlier. But, at some time during the following two years, the GWR directors were asked whether Turkish baths could be built at the back of the institution building which, on the first floor, already had eight slipper baths.[39]

It seems that, while the directors gave their permission for the baths to be built, the cost would have to be borne by the fund. Its response was to instruct its secretary to write for more information about the Turkish baths to the newly formed London & Provincial Turkish Baths Company, and to 'all other sources they possibly could'.[40]

Not until July the following year, after several failed attempts, was the Turkish bath proposal discussed again. With William Gooch in the chair, Mr Burton proposed, and Mr West seconded, that the meeting was,

> of an opinion that the erection of a Turkish Bath in New Swindon would confir [sic] great benefits to the inhabitants both in a Medical and Sanitary point of view and that the Sum of 250£ be appropriated for that purpose.[41]

This was a large sum for the fund to find, and an amendment 'that it is inexpedient to have a Turkish Bath in New Swindon' was carried 'by a large majority'. This was a great disappointment to the proposers, and William West would, in due course, return to the fray in a most effective, if surprising, manner.

It was soon recognised that the provision of only eight slipper baths, with no showers or changing facilities, was totally inadequate for a growing village population. In February 1863, it was decided to build a new bathhouse in the yard of the nearby Barracks.[42] This was not, as might be expected, a military establishment, but a rather severe-looking men's lodging house in the high street—today's Emlyn Square, where the building still stands.

But the baths, now overseen by an elected committee, and managed for the fund by Mr West, had to move again in 1868 when the barracks was converted into a Methodist chapel. A new bathhouse was to be erected on a narrow triangle of land between Taunton Street and Faringdon Road.

In the meantime, William West had taken matters into his own hands and, by 1867 (possibly even earlier), he was also running (on his own account) a small Turkish bath at his home in Cromwell Street.[43] This must have been successful because when the Baths Committee of Management met in September, it minuted that it would be 'advantageous to members' if Turkish baths were included in the new building being constructed in Taunton Street.[44]

West had played his hand well, and in November was invited to a meeting of the committee 'to make arrangements about the bath'.[45] By September 1868, the building was almost complete and West met the committee again, this time to hand in his resignation as manager of the slipper baths.[46]

Two weeks later, the committee accepted his tender of £30 to run the combined slipper and Turkish baths for a period of 15 months, though he had to agree to provide all the sheets and accessories needed as part of the deal.[47] The Turkish baths were to be open from 6 am to 9 pm on weekdays, and from 2 pm till 9 pm on Saturdays, while on Wednesdays, the baths were to be reserved for women from 2 pm till 5 pm. There were to be two prices for fund members—though no mention is made of whether this should also apply to non-members.

The new building opened on 1 October 1868, West having closed his own establishment and, by 1869, moved house to Taunton Street.[48]

Proud of its new facility, the 1869 edition of the fund's rules for members boasted 'a Bathing Establishment for the Company's Servants' with 'Washing, Turkish, Swimming and Shower Baths'.[49] The indoor swimming pool, however, was actually within the works site itself,[50] an unsatisfactory location from a safety point of view.

The bathhouse was divided into two (Fig 16.2), with an entrance to the slipper baths from Faringdon Road, and to the Turkish baths from Taunton Street. There were two hot rooms, a shampooing room, and a cooling-room with nine changing cubicles.

The Turkish baths, though moving across the road to new premises in 1905, and coming under successive new managements after the NHS began, are still in operation. They are, therefore, the longest surviving Turkish baths establishment in the British Isles, though not the oldest surviving baths building.

In 1878, ten years after the new baths opened, the fund's practice of leasing them to be run by others came to an end. They had just been let to Charles F Ponter at £20 per year, plus half the rates of the building;[51] but, almost immediately, Ponter had difficulty making them earn their keep and was unable to pay the rent. His ability to manage the baths efficiently was not in doubt and the society wisely

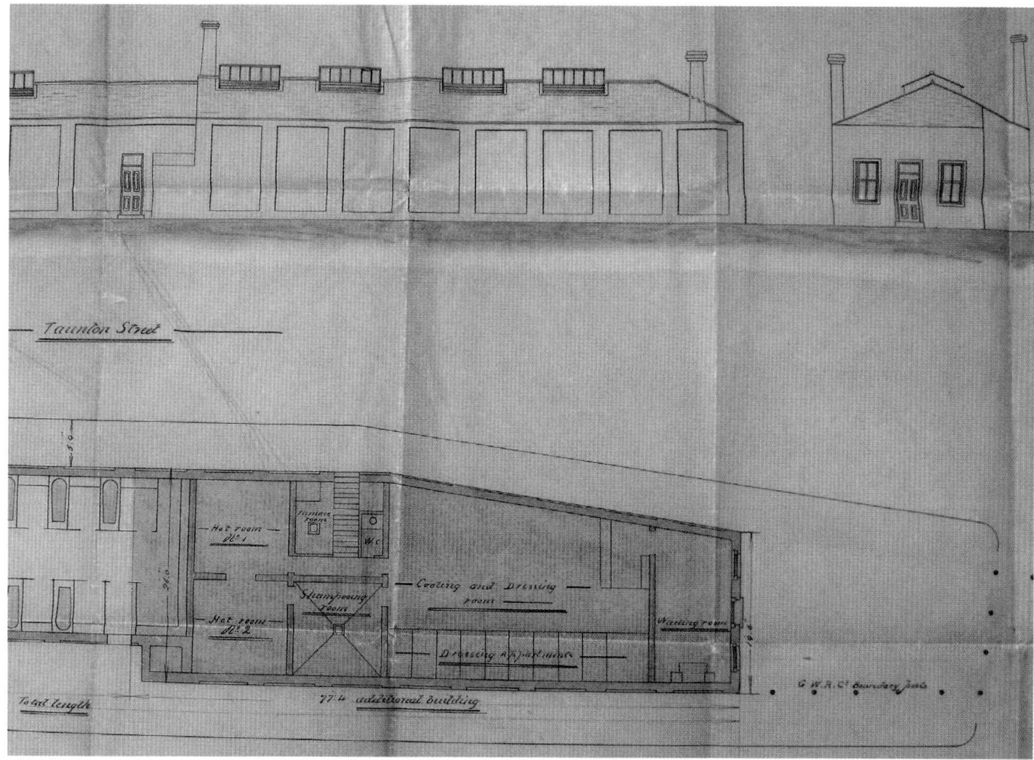

Fig 16.2
The Swindon Turkish baths, opened in 1868, lay between Farringdon Road and Taunton Street.
(Wiltshire and Swindon Archives, WSA G24/760/410 [Detail])

cancelled the lease and appointed him their paid manager.[52]

By this time, the Turkish baths opening hours were much shorter—daily from 1 pm till 8 pm—and they were open for women only by prior arrangement. But they were now free for the society's members and for their wives and families, a small charge being made for 'tea, coffee, and other refreshments.'[53]

By the standards of the time, the society treated its staff fairly. When the baths were closed for maintenance, for example, Mr Ponter was paid 3s 10d per week for the loss of wages.[54] And when, in 1888, Mr T Rice, a member of the Washing and Turkish Baths Subcommittee, designed and installed 'a new heating device' for the Turkish bath, he was paid an honorarium of £3.[55]

In 1891, the company built a large new red-brick building opposite the baths, on the corner of Faringdon Road and Milton Road. Designed in a simple 'Queen Anne' style by local architect, John James Smith (d 1915), it housed the fund's new dispensary, treatment rooms, various offices, and separate swimming pools for men and women, all reached from the main entrance in Faringdon Road.

It made sense to bring the two sets of baths together and, in 1904, new Turkish and slipper baths were built with their own 'Washing & Turkish Baths' entrance in Milton Road (Fig 16.3).

Fig 16.3
Milton Road entrance to the Turkish baths suite added in 1904 to the recently built Farringdon Road Swimming baths.
(© Malcolm Shifrin)

The men's Turkish baths suite on the ground floor was well laid out (Fig 16.4), and although, over the years, many alterations were made within the building, the structure and appearance of the three original hot rooms is virtually unchanged (Fig 16.5).

The adjoining shampooing room had two marble slabs and a circular needle shower.

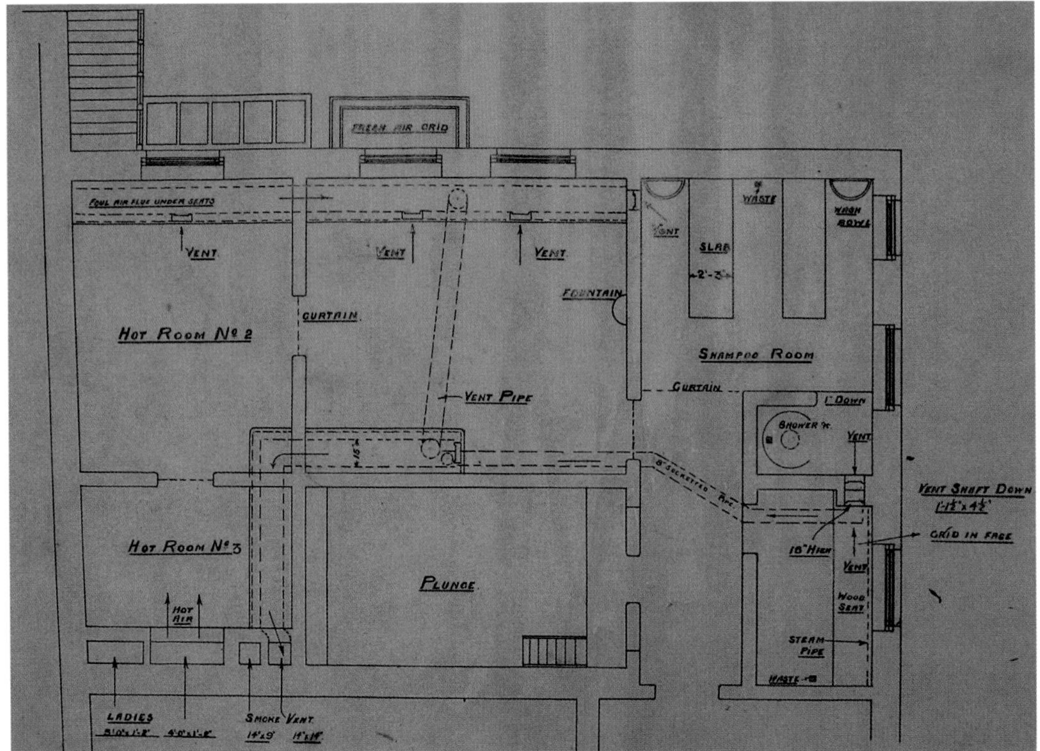

Fig 16.4
Plan of the Great Western Railway Medical Fund Society's Turkish baths suite.
(Wiltshire and Swindon Archives, WSA 2515/404/1288ms [Detail])

Fig 16.5
Swindon Turkish baths: inside one of the GWR hot rooms in 2013.
(© Malcolm Shifrin)

Shampooing is no longer offered at the baths, though it continued well into the 1990s. In its place are three additional modern showers—and one of the original slabs is on display in the entrance lobby.

The position of the large top-lit cooling-room is also unchanged (Fig 16.6), though its fireplace, the large clock mounted over it, and the glass-panelled screen on the opposite wall have long since gone.

The men's baths also include a Russian steam bath and a cold plunge pool. When it was built, the pool, at 9ft (2.7m) wide, was twice the width of most of those later provided by local authorities. When the baths were refurbished, probably at the end of the 1980s, it was split in two lengthwise, and one half is now aerated like a whirlpool. On the downside, the original tiling (Fig 16.7) has been replaced by rather plainer examples of the craft.

There is some doubt as to where the Russian bath was positioned when the baths opened. The original plans show it leading directly off the first hot room.[56] This would have been totally unsuitable as wet and dry areas need to be as far apart as possible. But a 1930 plan shows it positioned directly opposite the plunge pool, where it remains.[57] What is not known is whether the change was made before the building work started, or later, some time after the baths opened. There were also 12 changing cubicles. These are currently arranged in separated areas for men and women.

The original women's Turkish baths on the first floor (Fig 16.8) have been closed since at least the mid-1950s, though the door leading into them remains, complete with its coloured glass panel designed, like the heating device in the Taunton Street baths, by the company's Mr Rice. This beautiful door now leads, rather incongruously, into offices.

The women's baths were smaller than the men's, with only two hot rooms. These led off the shampooing room, with its slab, needle shower, wash basin, and drinking fountain. A cooling-room, toilet, and six dressing cubicles completed the suite.[58] The women's hot rooms—which each had a window overlooking the men's single-storey cooling-room—were directly above those of the men. This enabled the heated air to be ducted vertically up from the furnace in the basement to the hot rooms above.

Fig 16.6
The Swindon cooling-room in the 1940s.
(Bernard Darwin, A Century of medical service, *Swindon: GWRMFS, 1947. Author's collection)*

Fig 16.7
Original tiling round the still undivided plunge pool. (© Malcolm Shifrin)

Fig 16.8
Door leading to women's Turkish baths, long since closed.
(© Malcolm Shifrin)

After 5 July 1948, when the fund's medical services were replaced by the NHS, responsibility for the swimming and Turkish baths passed to Swindon Borough Council.

Bathers employed by the GWR became a smaller percentage of the total, many now coming from the old town. Some also came from nearby cities like Bath (where Bartholomew's Turkish bath had closed) and towns such as Cirencester (where there had never been one). In 1958, a Turkish bath in Swindon cost 6s, including shampoo.[59]

As long as the baths were under the aegis of the GWR's Medical Fund Society, the bathing procedure and behaviour of the bathers would have been appropriately formal. Gradually, the general ambience became more informal. Ray Parry, masseur and attendant between 1955 and 1970, was solely in charge and had a very free hand. When he first arrived, the baths appear to have been much underused, though it has been suggested that the actual number of bathers was higher than shown in the books. Similarly, massages would be provided as required, and these might have been considered perks.

During his time, alterations were made to the cooling-room. Larger cubicles, in which bathers could relax, were added and then, years later, removed again. The original cubicles were really no more than cupboards for depositing bathers' clothes, but even so,

> every fixture was Great Western. Every cubicle had a GW mirror and GW hooks … Heavy carriage locks on the doors. It was all GWR.[60]

The clients were varied, mostly business people, jockeys, bookies—with whom bets could be placed, although off-course betting was not yet legal—farmers, surgeons, parsons, dancers, even 'titled people'. Parry described the baths during his years there.

> … certain days, my first job was to look at the racing calendar—to see if the jockeys were likely to come. Look up the day, to see what races were on today or tomorrow, so if they was near, the jockeys would be in to sweat for the next day … I could knock off about 10lb.
>
> … My main job was—in the Turkish bath—you had to look after people—fix things—introduce people—deter people—bring them together. There was all different groups. They liked to keep separate … Lot of business done there. All the time. All day long. The cubicles had their own beds—They'd spend all day—I used to arrange food from outside—In those days things worked like that. It doesn't happen now.

Today, the Turkish bath is part of the Health Hydro run by Thamesdown Council.

Company baths. 2: Crewe

Like New Swindon, Crewe was a railway town. In 1865 its population was somewhere between 12,000 and 13,000, most of whom were railway workers or dependent in some way on the London & North Western Railway Company (L&NWR).[61] Almost all the facilities of the town were provided by the company, from houses to cooking facilities for the unmarried, from churches and chapels to schools and public baths.[62]

The first bathing facilities, slipper baths for men and women, were opened in 1845. They were managed by a subcommittee of the Council of the Mechanics Institute. By 1862, the company had expanded so rapidly that the baths were now right in the middle of the railway works, and access was difficult for workers' wives and for the general public.[63]

So new public baths were built by the company at the northern end of Mill Lane (later Mill Street) and opened in 1866. These consisted of hot, tepid, and cold baths, showers, and an open-air swimming pool.[64] The pool was fairly basic, as was common at that time. Water was changed once per week, and 'the price of admission was reduced as the water became progressively murkier'.[65]

It is not known exactly when the Turkish baths were added, but it must have been sometime before 1874 when they were first included in the local directory. Although the swimming pool was open from six till nine on Sunday mornings, and till nine o'clock in the evening during the rest of the week, the Turkish baths were open less often. They were closed on Sundays, but otherwise there were two separate sessions each day: from ten to twelve in the morning, and from two till seven in the evening.[66]

The entrance tickets (Fig 16.9) were produced using the same type of machine which printed the company's standard travel tickets. But otherwise, we know far less about these baths than about those of the GWR.

In 1923, the L&NWR became part of the London, Midland, and Scottish Railway (LMS). The new company continued to operate the town's baths for another 13 years, although its open-air swimming pool was already quite inadequate for a town of the size and importance of Crewe. Elsewhere, bathing facilities were provided by the local authority, and the company understandably saw no reason to expend the large amount of money required to build a modern facility.

Fig 16.9
The London and North Western Railway Company's Crewe Turkish bath tickets were similar to their train tickets.
(Image from a postcard by Dalkeith Publishing)

In the mid-1930s, Crewe Corporation finally agreed to provide a new bathing establishment. The LMS offered to sell the existing baths to the town for £500 but the corporation, feeling the site was too small, turned down the offer.[67]

The Mill Street baths closed on 31 March 1936 after serving the town for 70 years. The new baths were built on another site, but without Turkish baths.

Company baths. 3: Saltaire

Unlike the two railway towns, Swindon and Crewe, Saltaire was more a village.[68] And while the towns were built by companies each responsible to a board of directors, Saltaire, on the banks of the River Aire, was the creation of a single entrepreneur, Titus (later, Sir Titus) Salt.

After working for a number of years in the family wool-stapling business, Salt set up on his own in the centre of Bradford, spinning and weaving alpaca wool. Long concerned about the squalid conditions in which his workforce lived, in 1853 he relocated to a purpose-built mill near Shipley, constructing a village next to it to house his workers.

In addition to housing them, Salt provided for their education (schools, a library and reading rooms), for their souls (a congregational church), for their leisure (a billiards room and gym), for their health (a cottage hospital), and for their cleanliness (a clothes wash-house, slipper baths, and a Turkish bath). There were no public houses.

The Saltaire Baths and Wash-house opened in Caroline Street on 6 July 1863. Like the rest of the buildings in the village, the baths were designed by architects Lockwood & Mawson who had previously designed the Turkish baths at Ben Rhydding Hydro in 1859, and went on to design those in Albert Street, Keighley, some years later. The Saltaire baths and wash-house together cost Salt £7,000.[69] The wash-house was well equipped with six washing machines, together with drying and ironing facilities, so it would not be easy to discover the cost of the Turkish baths alone.

We do not know precisely what facilities were provided in the baths or how they were arranged. But although a complete set of drawings no longer exists, the local archive does have a plan of the 'basement'—we would now consider this a cellar—and a cross-section through the centre of the building.[70]

On either side of a central ticket office, there were separate ground floor entrances for women (on the left) and men (on the right). Also on each side was a plunge bath (possibly slightly warmed). On the men's side there were enclosed steps leading down to the Turkish bath furnace and coal store.

On the first floor there were 12 slipper baths on each side, and sandwiched between them was the Turkish bath. This was used by men and women on different days, probably reached through the appropriate slipper baths entrance.

As far as we can tell, the baths themselves (Fig 16.10) comprised one, or probably two hot rooms, perhaps with an internal dome, and a much larger cooling-room. The hot room(s) were at a higher level than the cooling-room, entered through an airlock entrance, possibly doors, but more likely heavy curtains, at the top of three steps. The difference in height allowed hot air to travel beneath the hot room floor(s), probably through ducts, so that bathers would need to have worn pattens.

Initially, the baths were open every day except Sunday between 8 am and 8 pm.[71] But in 1870, only seven years after they opened, it was reported that 'the luxury of an excellent Turkish bath' seemed, at a cost of sixpence, 'to be hardly appreciated by the workmen'.[72] However, when Charles Dickens Jnr wrote about the village the following year in *All the year round* he reported that the bath 'as I was told, is extensively patronised by the operatives', which sounds like a gross exaggeration, or a plug—no pun intended.[73]

In 1878, when Seth Bentley was manager, they were only opening two days in each month.[74] We do not know when they finally closed, but they were still open, with the same manager, as late as 1887.[75] The mill and most of the village still stand as a UNESCO World Heritage Site, though the baths building was demolished many years ago.

Turkish baths were well used in nearby Bradford, where many of the mill workers originally came from. So why were these baths so much less popular than those provided for workers in the railway towns? Perhaps the rules 'available from the manager' put bathers off.[76] Or perhaps the whole approach was too paternalistic, a failing which people can better tolerate from an anonymous company than from a man whose presence was all around them. Without further evidence it is difficult to tell.

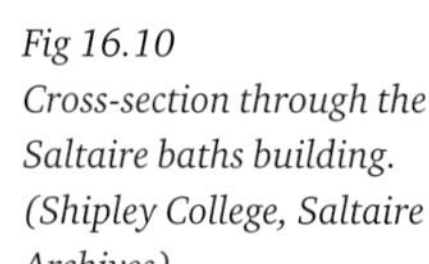

Fig 16.10
Cross-section through the Saltaire baths building. (Shipley College, Saltaire Archives)

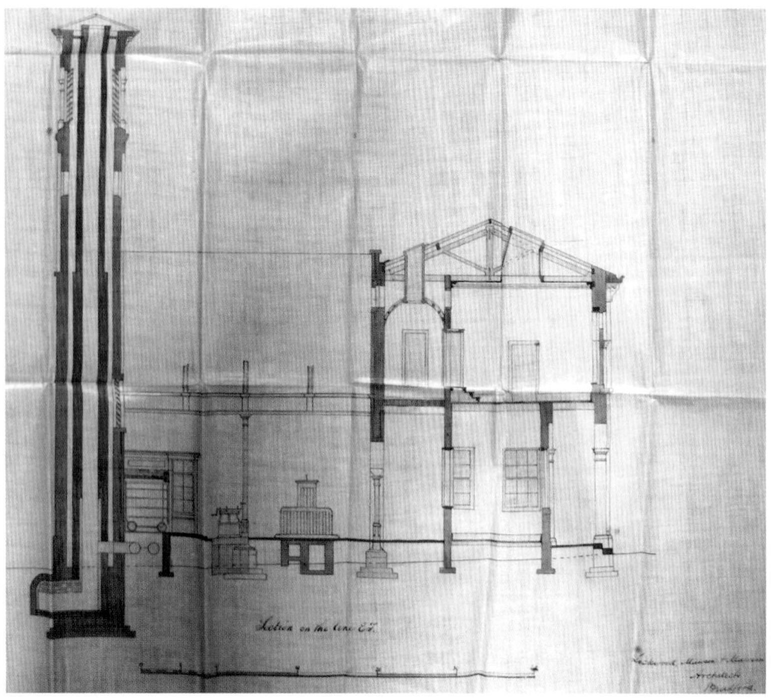

Company baths. 4: Wimbledon

Unlike the users of the three earlier company baths, the staff and actors of the Wimbledon Theatre (just south of London) would not, at the beginning of the 20th century, have thought of themselves as working class. But the Turkish baths within the theatre were provided by the proprietor for use by (at least some of) his employees and must, therefore, be considered company baths.

Although a number of cinemas opened in former Turkish baths—the Academy in Brighton and the Central Kinema in Edinburgh, for example—the Wimbledon Theatre seems to have been the only one which had its own Turkish bath in the basement.

It was designed by the theatre and cinema architect Cecil Aubrey Masey (1880–1960) and Roy Young, possibly based on an earlier design by Frank J Jones. Owned and managed by J B Mulholland, the theatre opened on 26

December 1910 with a pantomime, *Jack and Jill*. In addition to the theatre and Turkish baths, the building also included shops, an assembly hall, and two floors of offices.

However, as the only entrance to the baths was through one of several doorways leading off a lobby *within* the theatre, it seems safe to assume that they were intended mainly for the benefit of the actors and theatre staff, perhaps to relax the former and de-stress the latter. Furthermore, the absence of a women's toilet suggests that it was intended for use only by the male actors and theatre employees.

Although the lobby did have an entrance from the street, it is unlikely that the Turkish baths were ever open to members of the public. They were not included in contemporary local directories, and neither dedicated advertisements, nor mentions in advertisements for the theatre itself, have so far been found.

One local paper, describing the building prior to its opening, did note the existence of the Turkish bath but made no mention of who it was for. What *did* interest them was the use of the Turkish bath to augment the heating of the theatre.

> There are Turkish baths on part of the site occupied by the theatre and a series of ducts from the hot rooms have been arranged connecting with gratings in the floors and walls of the theatre, so that in the event of the climate playing one of their sudden pranks with which it afflicts us, the temperature can be raised from 40 to 60 degrees in 15 minutes.[77]

We must presume that the Turkish bath was empty of sweating bathers while the theatre temperature was being raised in this novel manner.

The theatre closed in 1938, and the Turkish bath remained closed when the theatre reopened after the war.

The baths then disappeared from view for over 60 years—part closed off and part, like the plunge pool, boarded over. But, in 2001, Steve Sotiriou took over an existing wine bar at street level and, with the help of a conservation grant and an extremely sympathetic architect, restored most of what remained of the original Turkish baths, turning them into an attractive bar and music venue.

The whole of the theatre building is Grade II Listed and the architects, Tijen and Brian O'Reilly, incorporated many features from the original rooms. Working on this unique conversion must have been an exciting project leading, as it sometimes did, to unexpected discoveries. 'We just drilled a hole in the wooden floor, and saw the plunge pool underneath', explained Tijen.[78]

Like the original baths, the transformed area has a complicated floor plan. In effect, it is set out on four floor levels (Fig 16.11). Three steps up from the street take you into the lounge.

This has been created from the space occupied by two separate shops. Originally each shop had a toilet in the cellar, though there is no longer any indication of how they were reached.

Apart from two stylised wall graphics of a woman bathing—created by backlighting drilled sheets of aluminium—there are no clues to the bar's origin when first entered. Only after mounting the six steps leading to the bar itself, in what was originally the Turkish bath cooling-room, can you look backwards to the left and see a restored staircase leading down to the rest of the baths (Fig 16.12).

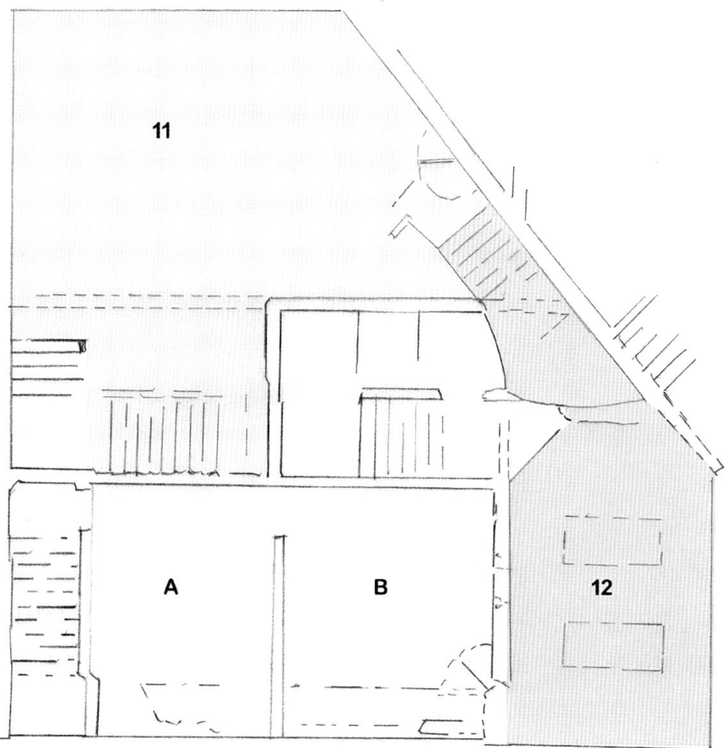

Fig 16.11
Plan of the upper floors at Wimbledon Theatre Turkish baths.
(Author's realisation)

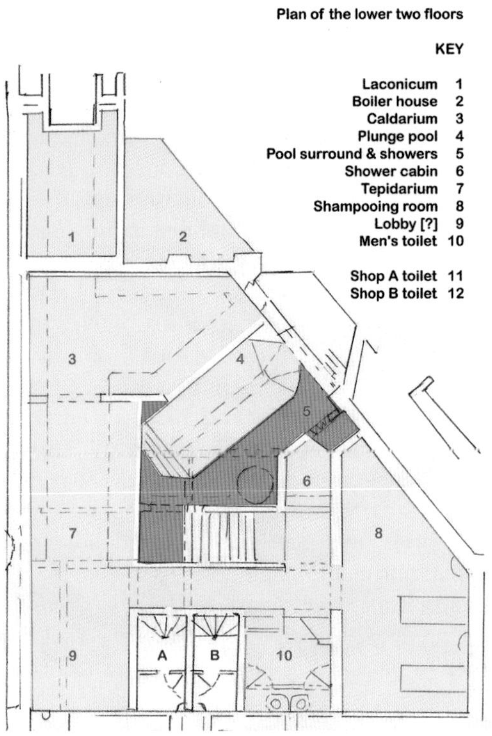

Fig 16.12
Plan of the lower floors at the theatre baths.
(Author's realisation)

Plan of the lower two floors

KEY

Laconicum 1
Boiler house 2
Caldarium 3
Plunge pool 4
Pool surround & showers 5
Shower cabin 6
Tepidarium 7
Shampooing room 8
Lobby [?] 9
Men's toilet 10

Shop A toilet 11
Shop B toilet 12

Half way down, a landing originally led directly into the plunge pool mezzanine, complete with its own showers. This ensured easy access both for bathers coming up from the hot rooms, and also for those going down from the cooling-room.

There was also a showering 'cabin', a shampooing room with marble slabs for two bathers, and three hot rooms arranged so that the air temperature increased as the bather progressed towards the boiler house end of the baths.

No changing area has so far been specifically identified, and bathers probably undressed in the cooling-room, which may have been fitted with clothes lockers. But it is impossible to say for certain how it was furnished as no traces of the Turkish bath remain in this part of the building.

The shampooing room is no longer open to view. Its marble slabs were removed years ago by a previous leaseholder, and the room is currently used as a store, with a lift shaft serving the theatre. Neither is it possible to see the hottest of the hot rooms or the boiler room, both of which have been blocked off. The two toilets serving the original shops have now been transformed into a modern washroom to serve the bar's women customers. Even so, what remains of the original Turkish baths is quite remarkable.

All the rooms have terrazzo floors, and their walls and the staircase are faced with white glazed bricks, with a green glazed brick double dado at about hand height. The floor, seating supports, and plunge pool walls are also faced with white glazed brickwork.

In the hot rooms (Fig 16.13), the benches were originally marble, though the seats themselves—like the shampooing slabs—had earlier been removed. Tables and extra seating have been provided, and the benches given cushioned tops (Fig 16.14). The rectangular hot room was converted into a bar with a disc jockey booth.

Perhaps the most radical alteration has been in the plunge pool (Fig 16.15) where tables and chairs have been installed (Fig 16.16). Some might disapprove, but this seems far better than boarding it over and hiding it again.

If the idea of having a drink in the middle of a plunge pool seems strange, it is hardly new. In 1892, a civic dinner to mark the opening of new public baths in Southampton was held with the guests seated at tables on the floor of the women's swimming pool.[79]

Fig 16.13 (below)
One of the hot rooms before renewal.
(Tijen & Brian O'Reilly at Brian O'Reilly Architects)

Fig 16.14 (below right)
Part of two hot rooms after renewal.
(Tijen & Brian O'Reilly at Brian O'Reilly Architects)

Turkish bath enthusiasts will surely appreciate that new fixtures (like, for example, the handrails) have not been made to look as if they are of the same period as the original baths, but stand out immediately as modern functional necessities.

On the other hand, when items have necessarily been removed from an area, it is not immediately obvious that what was originally a shower (Fig 16.17) has been transformed into a cosy alcove (Fig 16.18).

For more than six decades, no one has thought to restore the old baths as part of their business plan—or if they did, they must have been dissuaded by the cost. We must be grateful that so much of this unique Turkish bath can still be seen.

Figs 16.15–16.18
(Top left) The plunge pool before…
(Top right) …and after renewal.
(Bottom left) The shower before…
(Bottom right) …and after.
(Tijen & Brian O'Reilly at Brian O'Reilly Architects)

17

The Turkish bath in the workhouse

That there could have been any workhouse with a Turkish bath for its inmates may seem surprising. Many of the gentry thought the bath unsuitable even for the labouring classes, let alone the publicly supported poor. But there were several workhouse unions where the board of guardians decided it might be beneficial—almost all in the south of Ireland, Dr Barter's main sphere of influence. Information is sparse, however, and anything other than the barest details is difficult to find.

The Cork Union Workhouse

As early as June 1859, Barter had approached the guardians of the Cork Union Workhouse with a novel proposition. He offered to build, operate, and maintain a Turkish bath in the workhouse at his own expense. When it was ready, it would be used for a controlled experiment to see whether it was beneficial to the inmates.

Addressing the board, he noted that they classified their inmates into those on the threshold of the workhouse infirmary, those who were hospital cases, and those who were convalescing.

> Now what I propose to do is get 50 of them together, and let one of your body and myself select one alternately until we divide the 50 into two divisions, and 25 are to be treated in the ordinary way, but the other twenty-five are to be left to me, using the Turkish bath, but having the same food and the same treatment as the others.[1]

He went on to explain that after the end of an agreed period, independent assessors would 'report on the relative sanitary condition of the different groups.' If the report was favourable, he would consider his work accomplished. He would then either remove the bath at his own expense, or give the board an option to purchase it.

Understanding the realities of the workhouse and the difficulties faced by its occupants, Barter also undertook to train some of the junior inmates as bath attendants and skilled shampooers. They would then be able to support themselves.

The idea was looked on favourably by the medical officers and those on the board, and Barter was asked to put the proposal in writing as it would have to be approved by the Poor Law Commissioners.

But the proposal was never put into practice; two years later Barter wrote that the commissioners had refused to sanction it.[2]

The Lismore Union Workhouse, Co. Waterford

So far as is known, the Turkish bath at Lismore Union Workhouse in County Waterford—in use early in 1863, and possibly a little earlier—seems to have been the first installation of its kind.

It is significant that it was built only six or seven years after the first Turkish bath opened at St Ann's in 1856. And, remarkably, it was paid for out of public funds, sanctioned by the Poor Law Commissioners who, only a few years earlier, had refused Barter's offer to build a free bath in the workhouse at Cork.

At the end of February 1863, the Lismore Turkish bath was visited by the master and the medical officer of the workhouse in Fermoy, County Cork, when they were considering whether to install a bath at their own institution.

In his report of 2 March,[3] the Fermoy medical officer described the Lismore bath as having two rooms instead of the more usual three. The hot room was heated to around 120°F (49°C) and this, he reported, 'appears to work satisfactorily'. The second room was just a few degrees above the temperature of the outside air, gaining its heat only from being positioned next to the hot room. By comparison with a commercial establishment of the time, this provision would be the equivalent of a *tepidarium* and *frigidarium*, and would normally be supplemented by two much hotter rooms.

But he clearly considered the bath to be a success as, 'all the inmates, with the exception of the extremely old and infirm, take it weekly with benefit, and in no instance has its use been attended with injurious consequences.' The overall cost, he concluded, was less than £50.

He must have succeeded in convincing his board of guardians because just over three and a half months later, in June 1863, the Fermoy workhouse had its own Turkish bath, already installed and in use.

The Lismore bath continued in use well into the 1890s, almost 30 years after it had been built. An item in the local paper noted that, in March 1892, the workhouse porter, Mr Stokes, had finished 'putting them in order',[4] and a further item, published four months later, reported that he was to be paid 18s per quarter for maintaining them.[5]

The Fermoy Union Workhouse, Co. Cork

Nothing definite is known about the layout of the Fermoy bath, but it seems most likely to have been more or less a copy of the one that had been built at Lismore.

The Fermoy medical officer's report, minuted at the board's meeting on 1 July 1863, records that the bath had already been in operation almost daily during the past fortnight and,

> I am happy to state that its use has been attended with marked benefit in several cases of chronic rheumatism and skin diseases; a great many of the able-bodied of both sexes have also availed themselves of it.

Three weeks later, the minutes of the meeting held on 22 July show that progress was being maintained. Like the bath at Lismore, the Fermoy facility was used both as a cleansing facility and as a therapeutic agent for a wide variety of complaints, the medical officer reporting that, 'the beneficial results attending its use have in several instances exceeded my most sanguine expectations.'

His note about its success with rheumatism and skin problems tallies with the type of results experienced in most places where the Turkish bath was used to alleviate health problems at this time.

He thought that a more extensive trial would confirm its usefulness in other diseases, and was confident,

> that its introduction will be found economical as well as useful, from the circumstance that its employment has in numerous instances greatly shortened the duration of disease requiring hospital treatment.

As at Lismore, all but 'the very old and infirm' took a weekly bath which was conducive to an improvement in their general health.

This use of Turkish baths in the British workhouse was also of interest further afield. In 1867, for example, the New Zealand *Otago Witness* published an excerpt from one of the Fermoy medical officer's reports to his board.

> The Turkish bath, after a trial of four years in the Fermoy workhouse, has been found a useful remedial agent in a large class of cases—for example, in congestive and inflammatory states of the internal organs and viscera, the lungs, liver and kidneys in particular, renal dropsy, Bright's disease, &c. In virtue of its eliminating process it has been successfully employed in the treatment of rheumatism, sciatica, and gout. On the whole, I regard the Turkish bath as a valuable aid to medicine in the treatment of disease, and of very extended, though not universal, applicability.[6]

The Midleton Union Workhouse, Co. Cork

Three years earlier, in 1864, a Turkish bath had been installed at the Midleton Union Workhouse. In the absence of further information, we must assume that this, too, bore a family resemblance to those installed a few months earlier in nearby Lismore and Fermoy. But we do know, from Benjamin Johnston, Midleton's medical officer, that it was well used.

His report to the workhouse board of guardians in April 1870 was reprinted later that year as part of a House of Commons reply to a question from John Whitwell, the Member for Kendal.[7] Whitwell had asked to what extent Turkish baths were used in workhouses and asylums. In order to provide an answer, letters had been sent in March to the Inspectors of Lunatic Asylums and the Poor Law Commissioners who had forwarded them to those institutions which had baths.

Johnston's report was written after the Turkish bath had been in use at Midleton for six years, 'a period sufficiently long to form a somewhat correct estimate of its merits.'

He was very positive, writing that although Middleton was 'particularly well provided' with washing facilities, the Turkish bath was a useful addition which was in almost daily use; that with no other form of bathing could 'the same absolute cleanliness be insured', and that the bath's existence made possible savings in a quite different area of the institution's daily work because,

> its value as a means of drying the clothes (and thus affording all times an ample supply of thoroughly aired clothing at an expense not exceeding that hitherto expended on fuel for a similar purpose, which answered the purpose comparatively very inefficiently) can scarcely be over-estimated…

The bath had occasionally been used by the workhouse schoolchildren, and both the schoolmaster and schoolmistress reported the beneficial effect of 'the occasional judicious use of this invigorating luxury.'

Johnston continued by indicating how the Turkish bath had helped those with medical problems, and ended by summarising the value of the bath while, in effect, praising the guardians for providing a facility which few other workhouses could equal and without which 'any other public institution can be properly mindful of the health of its inmates'.

In addition to Benjamin Johnston's report on the Midleton bath, the commissioners included excerpts from the reports of the medical officer at Fermoy. So although, strangely, there was nothing about the Lismore bath, we at least know that the Fermoy and Midleton baths were still in use in 1870, if not for how much longer.

Not all workhouse baths in Ireland were successful. In 1895, one of a series of reports on Irish workhouses and infirmaries, conducted by the *British Medical Journal*, found that a Turkish bath in the workhouse at Clones, County Monaghan, was long disused and had been turned into a laundry drying room with no ventilation.[8]

In London in 1873, three years after John Whitwell's Parliamentary question, the Bethnal Green board of guardians declined an offer from the Marchioness of Salisbury to provide a Turkish bath for the inmates of their workhouse; in some places, attitudes to the poor had not changed since Barter's offer to the Cork guardians was refused 14 years earlier.[9]

The King's Lynn Union Workhouse, Norfolk

There was at least one successful workhouse Turkish bath in England, that in Norfolk at King's Lynn. This was certainly open in 1864 as it was mentioned in an article in the *Medical Times and Gazette*. The author, Dr B W Richardson, senior physician to the Royal Infirmary for Diseases of the Chest, wrote that the bath 'proves of great service both to the sick and the healthy' and recommends it for consideration by all workhouse managers.[10]

He goes on to praise Mr Kendall, the medical officer to the King's Lynn Workhouse who, he claims, was responsible for introducing the first hot-air bath 'for the benefit of the poor in the manner described'.

If this is correct, then the Turkish bath must have been installed early in 1863—or even before—because Fermoy and Lismore both had their baths by then.

But it is possible that Dr Richardson was unaware of the baths in Ireland, and really meant that the King's Lynn bath was the first to be installed in an English workhouse.

Nothing is known about the design of the bath or how it was used, when it was actually opened or when it closed. The workhouse itself survived, latterly as St James' Hospital, until 1985.

It seems unlikely that this could have been the only English workhouse to install a Turkish bath. But while it would be interesting to know of others, examining their practice might not significantly increase our understanding of such provision. As we have seen, existing contemporary reports tended only to repeat the same type of basic information.

18

The Turkish bath in asylums

One might imagine that private asylums, built for those able to pay, would lead the way in innovation. But in the provision of Turkish baths, they were many years behind the publicly funded local authority institutions.

In this chapter, I have retained terms such as 'lunatic asylum' and 'inmates' which reflect contemporary usage but, like the Imperial foot and inch, which I have also retained, they are, of course, no longer in use.

Dr Power and the first Turkish bath in an asylum

The close proximity of the Cork District Lunatic Asylum to St Ann's Hydro was a major factor influencing the building there of the first Turkish bath designed for the inmates of an asylum. Dr Thomas Power, the resident physician, had been impressed by the therapeutic results achieved by the use of the bath at St Ann's and had been in contact with Dr Barter.

In 1860, with Barter's help, Power persuaded the asylum's board of governors, 'after much discussion and opposition',[1] to install a Turkish bath there—a decision which was then, necessarily, sanctioned by the Privy Council.[2]

The bath, which was constructed under Dr Barter's supervision, would have been very simple. We know that in 1889 it had two hot rooms, one for men and the other for women,[3] but it seems likely that initially there was only a single room, with separate times being allocated for each sex.

Though not completed until February 1861, the bath was already in use the previous December. After being prepared for two or three days beforehand under the supervision of Dr Barter and Inspector-General Hatchell of the Dublin Office of Lunatic Asylums, 16 patients volunteered to use the bath. All enjoyed it and wanted to use it again.

At the beginning of May, Dr Power reported to the governors that, since January, 124 patients had used the bath. Of these, 10 had been discharged cured and another 52 had 'improved or were improving'.[4]

Of course this was no controlled scientific experiment, as both *The Lancet* and the *British Medical Journal* were quick to point out. The former noted that Power's experience would 'need to be corrected and tested by that of other physicians'; that it was not clear if other treatments had also been used; and that such a discharge rate was not all that unusual in a well-conducted asylum without a Turkish bath.[5]

The *British Medical Journal* contented itself with the snide remark that 'If this Turkish bath goes on spreading throughout the country, it is quite clear that the practice of physic will soon come to an end!'[6]

But Power was not writing a scientific paper, merely reporting progress to his governors and, buoyed up by these initial results, he made a plea for the introduction of Turkish baths in all the asylums, workhouses and prisons in the kingdom.[7]

In his second report, Power wrote that, while patients were, at first, limited to one bath per week, this had been increased, and that between 50 and 80 patients a day were now using the bath.[8] While some used it for remedial purposes, a larger number used it for personal cleansing, although this too had resulted in much healthier patients.

His results were still informally presented, but this time he was rather more careful with his use of figures for the numbers of cured and improved patients. Instead, he emphasised that because the percentage of cures obtained was higher than it had previously been, the Turkish bath must have played at least some part in the improvement; that the patients themselves believed that it helped them; and that relapsed patients returning to the asylum asked to be taken to the bath at once 'as they considered that nothing else would cure them.'[9]

The Lancet commented more supportively this time, suggesting that Power's experience 'may well be recommended to the consideration of the managers of other public and private asylums.'[10]

The baths were still in use in the early 1890s.[11] The introduction of the Turkish bath into an asylum was not only of interest to the medical profession, or even to readers of the British press, but as far away as Australasia.

Power's report was covered in the Australian papers and, a month later, it was raised in Parliament when Mr Sadleir asked if the Government intended to introduce the Turkish bath into Australian asylums. Mr Cowper, the Colonial Secretary, replied that he would refer the suggestion to the medical superintendent and that he, personally, thought it might be established with advantage in other establishments also, in the Parliament, for example—a suggestion evidently greeted with much laughter.[12]

The Sussex County Lunatic Asylum at Hayward's Heath

As with the initial introduction of the Turkish bath into the British Isles, Irish innovation was soon followed in England. The new asylum at Hayward's Heath had been opened in 1859 and its medical superintendent, Dr Charles Lockhart Robertson (Fig 18.1), was a firm believer in reform, totally opposed to the use on patients of any form of physical restraint, and well disposed towards hydropathy.

Fig 18.1
Dr Charles Lockhart Robertson, medical superintendent at Hayward's Heath Asylum. (Photograph by G. Jerrard, 1881. Wellcome Library, London)

He was one of a number of medical practitioners who been introduced to the Turkish bath in George Witt's private bath at his home in London's Knightsbridge. Like Power, Robertson was a member of the Medico-Psychological Association which, in 1971 would finally become the Royal College of Psychiatrists. He would have known about the Cork bath at a very early stage, and decided to install one at Hayward's Heath.

We know more about this bath than the one at Cork because, soon after it was built, Robertson included a full description, together with a plan (Fig 18.2), in his 1861 review of Erasmus Wilson's *The Eastern or Turkish bath* in *The Journal of Mental Science*.[13]

He was proud of the fact that it had cost less than £50, even including piping in water for the showers, and that it was probably 'the cheapest bath which has yet been built'. This was achieved, in part, by constructing it as a lean-to against a new wash house, so that an existing chimney-flue and stoke-hole could be used, and only two exterior walls had to be built.

The main part of the bath was 10ft × 30ft (3m × 9m), divided into three rooms, each with its own window. The hot room (*caldarium*), with a tiled floor, was 12ft (3.7m) wide, while the washing-room (*lavatorium*) and the dressing-room (*frigidarium*)—through which bathers entered the bath from the wash-house yard—were both 9ft (2.7m) wide.

The rooms were 12ft (3.7m) high at the wash-house end, sloping down to 9ft (2.7m) where they met the exterior wall. This was hollow and, like the space over the ceiling, filled with sawdust as insulation.

The much smaller furnace room—part of the new wash-house—was divided into two, with a door leading from the area housing the shared furnace into the hot room. A curtain, placed across the upper part of the room and over the furnace, effectively provided a *laconicum*, as David Urquhart had done in his Riverside bath.

A Sherringham ventilator allowed fresh air into the hot room (Fig 18.3), and the hot air passed from the furnace, travelling round the room through a flue which, with a board on top, acted as a seat. The room could, if required, be heated to 200°F (93°C) in four hours.

Although the washroom, sensibly built a step lower than the other two rooms, had several

on the Roman Bath. 219

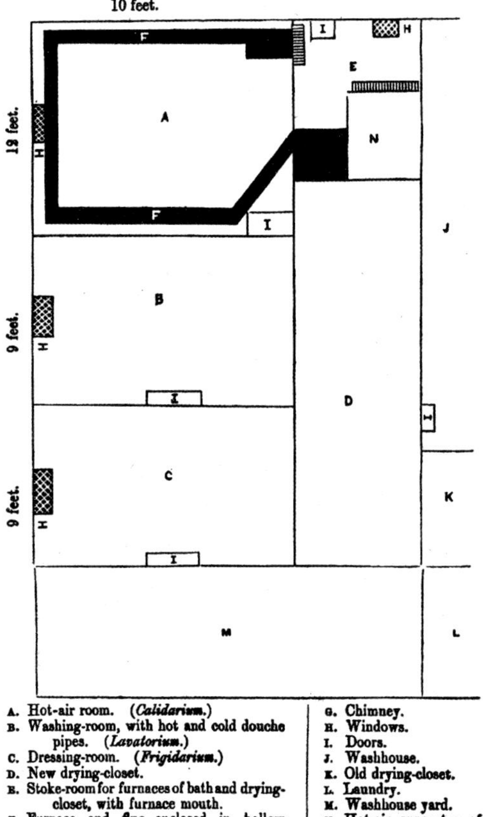
GROUND PLAN OF THE ROMAN BATH ERECTED AT THE SUSSEX LUNATIC ASYLUM, HAYWARDS' HEATH. *June*, 1861.

A. Hot-air room. (*Calidarium.*)
B. Washing-room, with hot and cold douche pipes. (*Lavatorium.*)
C. Dressing-room. (*Frigidarium.*)
D. New drying-closet.
E. Stoke-room for furnaces of bath and drying-closet, with furnace mouth.
F. Furnace and flue enclosed in hollow channel.
G. Chimney.
H. Windows.
I. Doors.
J. Washhouse.
K. Old drying-closet.
L. Laundry.
M. Washhouse yard.
N. Hot-air apparatus of drying-closet.

Fig 18.2
Plan of the Turkish bath at Hayward's Heath Asylum. (C L Robertson 'Review of Erasmus Wilson's The eastern or Turkish bath' *J Ment Sc, July 1861. Wellcome Library, London)*

types of shower, 'a pail of water', wrote Robertson, 'when an attendant is at hand, is more convenient, and to many insane patients less alarming, than the douche-pipe.'

The bath was not yet in regular use so Robertson was unable to give any significant clinical information. Although he quoted from an advance copy of Power's first report, his own rather more cautious belief was that the use of the bath in an asylum would have a general therapeutic value rather than result in specific cures.

In February 1863, Robertson received a letter from Urquhart asking for some information about the use of the asylum bath. Robertson's reply shows that in the intervening period there had been some constructional changes to the bath, and also to the manner in which it was used.

First, he had replaced the flues underneath the seating by heat-radiating iron pipes from the furnace. Second, he had increased the temperature in the hot room from around 145–150°F (63–66°C) to 170° (77°C) and, third, he had increased the once or twice weekly time spent in the bath from 20 minutes to an hour. 'I fully realize', he modestly wrote, 'how much I have to learn yet of the therapeutic uses of the bath; how little I know of its operations.'[14]

Robertson found the results of these changes encouraging. After such a short period, he wisely refrained from assigning cures for specific conditions, although the following year, with rather more experience, he wrote an article for the *British Medical Journal* about the specific case of a man with suicidal tendencies being successfully treated by the bath.[15]

For now, he contented himself with telling Urquhart that the bath had been helpful in cases of melancholia, with patients who had been refusing food and, with young women, in restoring regular menstruation.

Not least important was the general improvement in health gained from the cleansing effects of the bath, which was 'a remedial agent grateful to the feelings of the insane, and which they do not, like other means of washing, associate with the idea of punishment.'[16]

Although Robertson does not need to spell this out to Urquhart, a patient's mental association of washing with punishment was not, in the mid-19th century, a form of persecution complex.

It is true that asylums at that time could not be compared with those of a century earlier, when patients were chained to the wall in order to restrain them.

Yet, even in the early 1850s, the treatment books of the York Retreat (established in 1796 by the Quaker reformer William Tuke for 'the humane care of the mentally ill') showed that the prolonged use of 'showers' was frequently

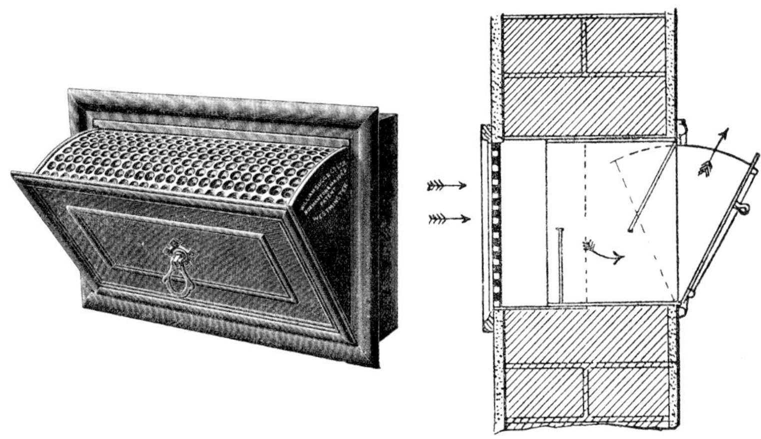

Fig 18.3
The Sherringham ventilator, with cross-section diagram showing it set into a brick wall.
(Principles and practice of modern house-construction, *ed G Lister Sutcliffe, Blackie, 1899. Historic England Archive, DP172006)*

Fig 18.4
The hosepipe shower, or, la grande douche *(used voluntarily in hydros, as shown on this French postcard from Vichy) were inappropriately used in asylums, where they were often seen by patients as a punishment, and where the procedure was open to abuse.*
(Author's collection)

resorted to as a means of quieting patients prior to the later, and widespread, prescription of bromides as sedatives.

Such 'showers' were usually hosepipe douches (Fig 18.4), the temperature and water pressure being determined by whichever attendant was administering it.[17]

When Urquhart went to visit the bath that November he had been expecting to find, he wrote to Sir John Fife, a 'low temperature, repulsive filth, and unventilated cellars. I found these chambers light and airy, and a temperature of 180°[F] [82°C]!'[18]

He remarked that Robertson, as physician and manager, had been typically cautious with his initial temperatures and his use of brick flues. But, having changed to radiating pipes, the cost of fuel was halved and he found the higher temperature obtained to be 'more bearable and more agreeable to the patients and to himself'. He even seemed prepared to try Urquhart's suggested temperatures of 200° (93°C) or 220° (104°C).

As with so many Turkish baths that opened to the accompaniment of much publicity, it is difficult to determine how long this one remained in use. But it appears to have still been in operation in 1899, when plans were drawn up to build a new one.

Limerick District Lunatic Asylum

Plans for a Turkish bath at the Limerick asylum designed by the local architect, William Fogerty (*c* 1833–1878), were already out to tender at the end of 1861, and the bath was operational the following year.

Nothing further is so far known about its design, but given that Barter was likely to have been consulted, and the bath at Cork asylum visited, it seems fair to assume that they were more or less similar. It was standard practice to examine existing baths before building a new one, and Limerick itself was visited in 1871, prior to the construction of the one at Denbigh asylum in Wales.

Not everyone was convinced of the value of Turkish baths in an asylum. After the Limerick bath had been open just a few months, 'Ratepayer' wrote to the *Freeman's Journal* asking what the benefits had been.[19]

Robert Fitzgerald, the resident medical supervisor, replied that it was a little premature for any detailed findings, but his impression was of 'unmistakable beneficial results' and, echoing Charles Lockhart Robertson, continued that it was particularly helpful in cases of melancholia and that 'As to its detergent and ablutionary powers ... [it] has no parallel'.[20]

It is not known how long the bath was in use, but there is no mention of it in the asylum's annual report for 1889.

The Second Middlesex County Asylum, Colney Hatch

The foundation stone of England's largest lunatic asylum, Colney Hatch, was laid on 8 May 1849. By 1852, when it had been open for a year, it was costing 8s 2d per week to keep each of its patients, of whom there were, by 1856, nearly 1,500. Even as late as 1914, when the establishment was run by the London County Council, the cost was still only 10s per week per patient.

Dr Edgar Sheppard became medical superintendent of the Male Department in 1862. He had long been a hydropathist and an advocate of the Turkish bath since the first one was built.

Sheppard visited Dr Power's Turkish bath at the Cork Asylum in 1863, and this strengthened his resolve to have one installed at Colney Hatch.

There is also a strong possibility, though as yet unconfirmed, that some time between Sheppard's appointment and the building of a bath at Colney Hatch, some patients were allowed to visit Richard Metcalfe's Graffenberg House Hydropathic Establishment, two railway stations down the line, at New Barnet. Writing in 1906, Metcalfe claims that he,

> had a licence to receive cases of mental alienation, and the Lunacy Commissioners did me the honour to approve of my methods of treatment; that is by hydrotherapeutics, but especially by the Turkish or hot-air bath.[21]

On 16 May 1864, Sheppard invited David Urquhart and Robert Poore to visit the asylum and 'discuss the possibility of building a Turkish bath for the inmates'.[22]

While there, Urquhart thought that a suitable Turkish bath could be constructed for around £300, but when he wrote to Sheppard the following Monday, he suggested a much grander affair, estimated to cost a further £200.

The plan, later submitted to the asylum's board of governors on 24 May, was for a building of 1,500 square feet (457m) which, Urquhart wrote, 'will become the model for the asylums, hospitals, unions, and barracks of the three kingdoms...'[23]

Urquhart realised that the board would be concerned that money spent on what was at that time still a relatively new type of facility should benefit as many patients as possible. He continued,

> As you dispose of the patients' time, and can arrange relays from six in the morning till eight at night (and herein lies your facility), you can pass 700 patients through the operation of the bath daily.

He estimated that fuel would cost less than 1s 6d per day, while the cost of soap and towels would be no more than at present.

In mid-October, Sheppard and Mr Wood, the asylum's clerk of works, were taken round the Jermyn Street Hammam by John Johnson who showed them the new room, experimentally heated to 205°F (96°C) solely by radiation.

Thanking Urquhart for the visit, Sheppard wrote that 180°F (82°C) would seem most appropriate for the proposed bath at Colney Hatch, and that their contractors already had the plans and specification and were preparing an estimate. After that, he hoped they would start construction without delay.[24]

In this, Sheppard proved to be somewhat overoptimistic.

Perhaps the most innovative aspect of Urquhart's original idea was the proposal that:

> The whole will be arranged panoptically, so that a superintendent, himself unseen, can, with the exception of one apartment, watch every patient.[25]

Urquhart was following a plan proposed by his family friend Jeremy Bentham who, in 1791, had designed the Panopticon (Fig 18.5) as the basis for a new type of prison which allowed the maximum supervision of prisoners by the minimum number of warders.

Like Bentham's prison, however, this Turkish bath was never built. The asylum board rejected the plan on account of its cost, and Sheppard noted in his report for 1865 that Mr Wood was 'now engaged upon plans of a less elaborate description' for submission to the next meeting of the visiting Justices of the Peace, who were responsible for ensuring that practice within the asylum satisfied the relevant statutory requirements.[26]

The bath approved by the board later that year was, at approximately 700 sq ft (213 sq m), less than half the size of that originally proposed, and of a much simpler construction (Fig 18.6). The rooms were heated by radiation, and even though the doorway was only covered with a blanket, the temperature reached a steady 190°F (88°C).

The building work cost £180; equipping, fitting, and furnishing it, a further £120. The total cost, £300, was the equivalent of half Dr

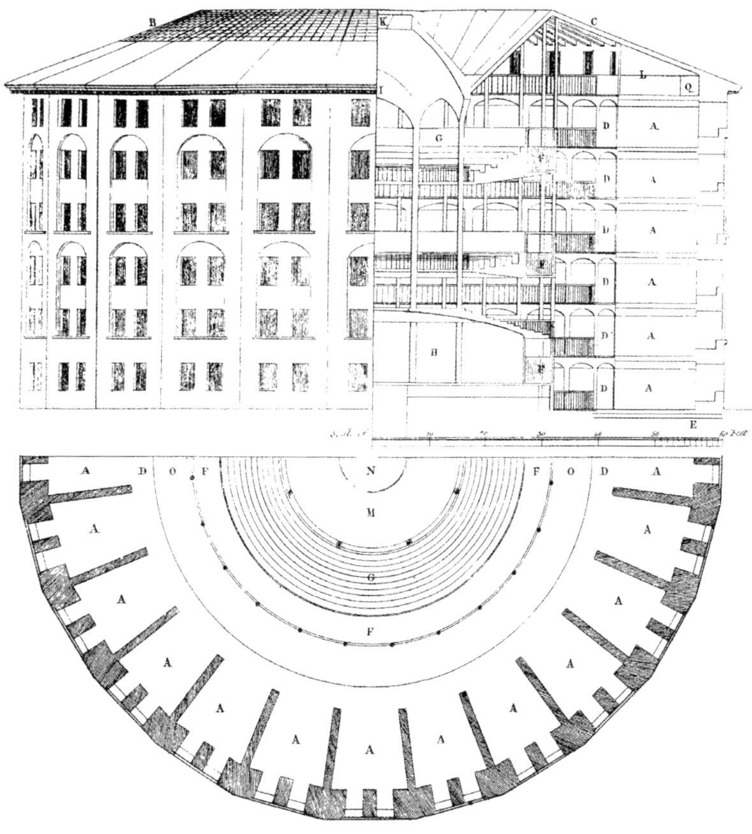

Fig 18.5
Elevation, section and plan of Jeremy Bentham's Panopticon penitentiary, drawn by Willey Reveley, 1791.
(Wikimedia Commons)

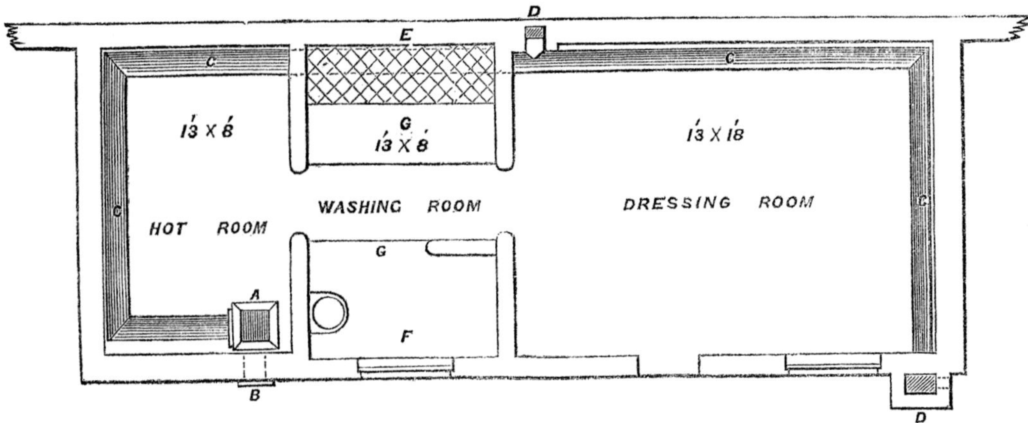

Fig 18.6
Plan of the Turkish bath at Colney Hatch Asylum. ('Opening of the Roman bath at Colney Hatch', JMenSc, 1865–6. Wellcome Library, London)

Scale ⅛ *in.* = 1 *foot.*

A.—Stoves.
B.—Doors for Stoves and Ashes.
C.—Iron Flue.
D.—Chimneys.
E.—Shampooing Slab, raised.
F.—Wash-Basin and Douch.
G.—Sunk Floor.

Sheppard's annual salary, or of feeding just over 600 patients for one week.

The Turkish bath was opened on 26 July 1865, and in the asylum's annual report for the following year it was mentioned several times and its success acknowledged.

The secretary to the board noted that 'several of the Patients themselves, when coming before the Committee for their discharge, have attributed their cure in some measure to its influence'.[27]

But although there were always more female than male patients at Colney Hatch, he also noted that women had been unable to use the bath because their nurses were not trained in its use, and this was about to be rectified.

Sheppard then dwelt on his pet project at some length pointing out that visiting justices and the medical superintendents of several other asylums came to Colney Hatch to see it for themselves.

It is no wonder that Sheppard should have achieved good results with the Turkish bath and gained the approval of his patients. At that time even the provision of toilets was inadequate, and the normal bathing facilities were considered unacceptable by the Commissioners in Lunacy.

At this time, according to the commissioners' reports, 'about 3 Men and from 3 to 6 Women are bathed in the same water', and it was 'not until 1883 that every patient was bathed in fresh water.'[28]

Sheppard was no less upbeat the following year. He reported that,

> The success of the Turkish bath, established in 1865, is abundantly confirmed by the experience of 1866. Upwards of 80 male patients, besides attendants and servants, can testify as to its usefulness.[29]

The bath was now being used by female patients, with equal success. Mr W G Marshall, the male superintendent of the Female Department—the first woman doctor was not appointed at Colney Hatch until after World War II—referred in his report to a patient with 'dementia after puerperal mania' (post-natal depression) who attributed her recovery to the bath.

> Previous to her having the baths she suffered from small abscesses of a furuncular character [*ie*, boils], which she prevented from healing by constantly picking, and she would sit listlessly about the ward, not taking any interest in objects around her. After the third bath her habits became much improved, her health re-established, and she began to employ herself in needlework and general household work, and was a most useful Patient during the remainder of the time when she resided in the Asylum.[30]

In 1868, the bath was used 600 times by 104 patients.[31] This was, of course, a very small percentage of the total number of patients, a point noted by the commissioners themselves, who wrote confirming, in effect, Urquhart's initial preference for a much larger building:

> The Turkish bath is in active and beneficial operation. We witnessed its application, and from the reports made to us upon the subject, it is we think to be regretted that from its small extent, its use is necessarily much limited and infrequent.[32]

Although Sheppard asked for the bath to be extended, this does not appear to have happened. By now, however, the success of the Turkish bath in helping some of the patients to a speedier recovery was taken for granted, warranting no more than passing mentions in future reports.

It is not known how long the bath survived, but it was still in use between 1882 and 1888 when Robert Jones, later Sir Robert Armstrong-Jones, was superintendent. He was so impressed that he took the idea with him to his next post at Claybury Asylum in Woodford,[33] setting up a Turkish bath there in 1893.

North Wales Counties Lunatic Asylum, Denbigh

At the end of the 1860s and beginning of the 1870s, the North Wales Counties Lunatic Asylum, Denbigh, cared for just under 400 patients, more or less evenly divided by gender.

As his fellow members of the Medico-Psychological Association had done before him, Dr George Turner Jones recommended, in his medical superintendent's report for 1869, the building of a Turkish bath at Denbigh.[34] He admitted that it had not yet been extensively used in the treatment of mental disease, but that many patients had benefited from its use for a number of physical complaints, and that he, personally, could speak 'as to its efficacy in rheumatic attacks'. His Committee of Visitors asked him to investigate further.

During the following year, together with the asylum's clerk and steward, John Robinson, he visited Limerick and then Cork. There they had been shown around by Dr Power, who considered the bath beneficial in almost all cases of insanity, especially when combined with melancholia, scrofula (tuberculosis of the lymphatic glands), and rheumatism. He also thought that, in the early stages of consumption (tuberculosis of the lungs), it could not only stop the disease, but cure it. Today, this seems extremely unlikely, but it was a view held by other doctors at that time. They also visited St Ann's Hydropathic Establishment at Blarney, where they discussed the use of the bath with several of the patients there.

Turner Jones wrote that 'when the prejudice against it subsides, the Turkish bath will come to be found in all large institutions'. Furthermore, he reported that 'as a means of cleansing it is found to be the cheapest mode adopted'.[35]

This last point carried the day. The visiting Justices approved the construction of a Turkish bath costing £400—approval which, perhaps predictably, aroused the scorn of *The Lancet* for the manner in which the decision was taken.

> In the desultory discussion which preceded the adoption of this resolution, some extraordinary statements were made respecting the wonderful percentage of cures alleged to have been effected by the bath; but we miss in the arguments used, as well as in the medical superintendent's report which was the occasion of the discussion, any exact statement of the real scientific value of the Turkish bath in the treatment of insanity. Some of the Visitors appear to have desired such a statement before sanctioning the required outlay, but to have obtained only, in place of it, an assurance that the bath is found to be the cheapest mode that can be adopted as a means of cleansing …

The visitors were then invited to provide the journal's readers with a 'precise report' on the results of using the bath after it had received a reasonable trial.[36]

Jones was successful in ensuring that the bath cost less than the approved estimate, the actual amount being £397 6s 6d. In his annual report for 1871, he subdivided the total into its constituent parts indicating the relative costs of such work at that time.

The bath had still only been open for three months, so Jones can be excused for not yet having attempted to satisfy *The Lancet*'s request for precision. Nevertheless, he felt confident that the bath would produce good results, and that it had been valuable in several cases of 'acute mania'. He was also 'fully persuaded' of its superiority over warm water for cleansing. He continued,

> This bath is much more liked by the patients. Many had a great aversion to the ordinary one, so much so that persuasion and in some instances gentle force was required to induce them to enter the bath. This has now almost entirely disappeared, and the pleasures of the baths are eagerly sought for. There is also great economy in labour and water.[37]

It is not clear whether Jones realised that removing the threat so often felt by patients being persuaded by 'gentle force' to cleanse themselves, had in itself a curative value.

The asylum (later hospital) closed in 1995 but, again, it is not known how long the Turkish bath survived.

The Retreat, York

The iconic asylum known as the York Retreat was founded by the Quaker philanthropist, William Tuke, in 1792. When it opened for patients four years later, its approach was considered a radical departure from contemporary asylum practice, especially in its minimal use of restraint, and its rejection of physical punishments.

Innovative it may initially have been, but more than 15 years elapsed between the installation of the first Turkish bath in an asylum, and the one at The Retreat.

In 1874, John Kitching, on his retirement after 25 years as superintendent, wrote a paper for his committee of management suggesting, as one of 18 proposed improvements, that a Turkish bath would be 'exceedingly useful' in treating their patients.[38]

Why did Kitching wait so long? As a member of the Medico-Psychological Association it is inconceivable that he was unaware of the bath's success in other asylums. It is true that Power's early report of successful 'cures' was greeted with cynicism by the medical press. And many doctors, already wary of quacks and suspicious of hydropathy, sensibly queried the claims of some doctors who implied that the bath was a therapeutic panacea.

But it seems more likely that his tardiness merely supports Anne Digby's view that 'After the mid-19th century The Retreat became rather a symbol of historical achievement than a current model in the world of asylumdom.'[39]

Kitching argued that the proposed Turkish bath would help reduce the 'monotony and ennui' of a patient's life to a minimum, becoming as much a part 'of the treatment of the insane, as the taking of medicine.'[40]

A sub-committee was set up to consider Kitching's suggestions, and Dr Robert Baker (Fig 18.7), his successor, was already in post when its report was presented on 15 December 1874. It recommended that the first improvement should be a new single-storey gentlemen's lodge with 17 bedrooms and sitting rooms, that the best place 'for the erection of a Turkish bath, and rooms in which other hydropathic treatment may be administered', was in the court at the end of the bedrooms, and that, following the usual practice, Dr Baker should visit other institutions 'to thoroughly inform himself respecting Turkish baths, Hydropathic and other improved modes of treatment'.[41]

Fig 18.7
Dr Robert Baker, superintendent at The Retreat, York 1874–92. (Borthwick Institute for Archives: Retreat archive)

To all of this, the committee of management agreed, and at its meeting on 16 February 1875, The Retreat architect, Edward Taylor (*c* 1829–1908), was instructed to work with Baker in drawing up plans for the Turkish bath at a cost not to exceed £1,400, including equipment and furnishing.

Taylor's plan, already completed and with the committee by 27 May, benefited both from Baker's visits, and from experience gained generally in running Turkish baths during the previous two decades.

Within its red brick and stone-faced building,[42] the facilities were far superior to those at Hayward's Heath or Colney Hatch, neither of which had provision for any form of hydropathic treatment, nor even a complementary vapour bath. Indeed, the Turkish baths suite at The Retreat was superior to that in several commercial establishments.

Taylor's plan (Fig 18.8) included two hot rooms,[43] a *tepidarium* at 120–130°F (49–55°C), and a *caldarium* at 130–180° (55–82°C).[44] Possibly due to expense, but more likely for safety reasons, there was no *laconicum*.

The air was heated in a boiler room situated in a cellar beneath the shampooing room. This had a direct fresh-air intake from outside the building, while the hot-air duct led straight into the *caldarium*, cooling as it passed into the *tepidarium*.[45]

The suite also included a vapour bath, which would have been a cabinet model constructed so the bather's head remained cool in the outside air.

In 1889, Baker gave a paper on 10 years' use of the Turkish bath at The Retreat, the published version of which included a plan (Fig 18.9) with only one significant change from Taylor's original.[46] The dressing room (Fig 18.10) was now much larger, and divided into cubicles, with couches enabling bathers to relax after their bath.

Although the alteration might have been made after the bath had been used for a while, it seems more likely to have been built that way initially. For Baker's investigative tour of other baths would surely have impressed upon him the need to provide a cooling-room if the bath was to be totally effective.

More surprising is that the later plan retains the bath and wet sheet packing room in which hydropathic treatments were to be provided. Although wet sheet packing was popular in hydropathic establishments for several years, it is not mentioned in Baker's paper, and this would be due to the fact that the Commissioners in Lunacy felt it necessary to include it among their deprecated forms of mechanical restraint.[47]

It appears that originally it was intended to open the baths to men only but, with its external entrance from the courtyard, there was no logical reason to exclude women.

Running costs were relatively small. Baker put the heating cost at between 9s and 11s per week,[48] and part of this was met by opening the baths to the public,[49] a practice already well established at the Newcastle-upon-Tyne Infirmary.

It is difficult to discover how many non-patients there were, as records were only partially kept. One of the first members of the public

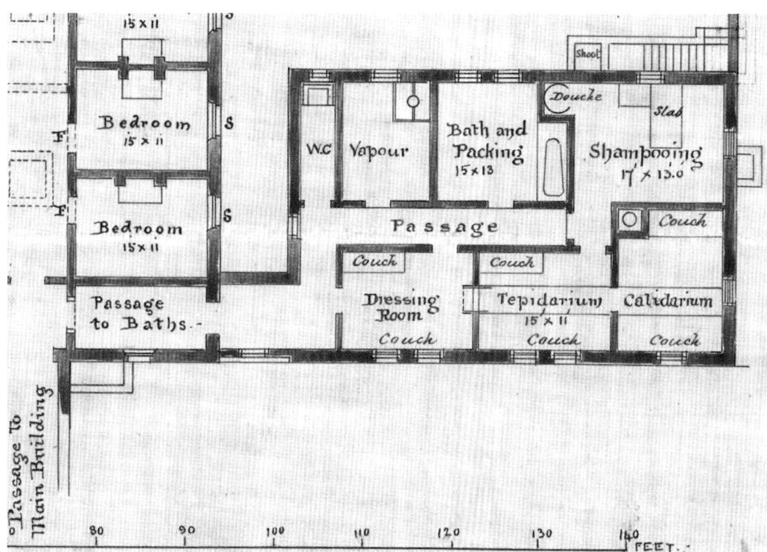

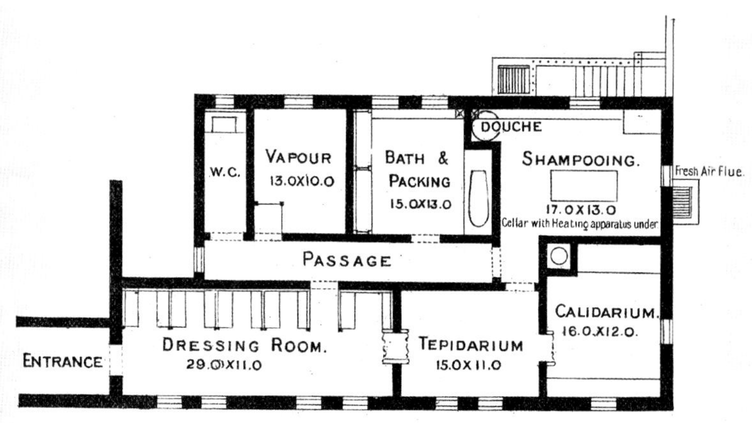

Fig 18.8 (above top) Edward Taylor's original plan for the Turkish bath at The Retreat. (Borthwick Institute for Archives: Retreat archive)

Fig 18.9 (above bottom) Plan of the Turkish bath at The Retreat after ten years' use. (Robert Baker, 'Notes of ten years experience…' JMenSc, *July 1889)*

Fig 18.10 (left) Section of the altered dressing room at The Retreat. (Robert Baker, 'Notes of ten years experience…' JMenSc, *July 1889)*

to use the Turkish baths was so impressed that he wrote to the *York Herald* praising them and asking the corporation, unsuccessfully it seems, to include them in their own proposed baths.[50]

Baker's 1889 paper is a thoughtful, carefully considered document. Bearing in mind the limits of contemporary medical knowledge, his claims on behalf of the bath are understated.[51]

He separates usage into two categories: the bath as a curative agent, and the bath as a palliative agent.

In the first category, he includes the bath's use with alcoholics, writing:

> I do not wish to undervalue the use of drugs in the treatment of the various forms of alcoholic insanity, but I have been so pleased with the power of charming away the condition of irritability and suspicion, so generally seen in these cases, by the frequent use of the Turkish bath that I would wish very decidedly to commend it to your notice.

He suggests that this was also applicable to those who abused morphia, chloral and other narcotics. And he also includes successes in middle-aged sufferers from gout, and from melancholia accompanied by a 'dry skin' and by a 'disordered and congested condition of the liver'.

Baker, feet firmly on the ground, continues:

> Far be it from me to imply that the use of the Turkish bath will invariably cure these cases. All I wish to say is that in some cases I have thought it to be a useful adjunct to the use of other remedies.

And in the case of 'puerperal insanity' he maintains only that the bath will tend to speed the cure of those who would, in any event, recover.

As a palliative, Baker first approves its effect with epileptics, reporting 'the chorus of unanimous indignant complaint' received if, on occasion, the bath was out of use.

Second, for what Baker refers to as cases of general paralysis of the insane—the now rare syndrome at that time occurring in tertiary syphilis—he notes 'the soothing and calming influence of the careful use of the Turkish bath', remarking how such patients,

> enjoy the luxurious sense of ease that a bath affords, and they are gratified at being for a couple of hours the sole recipients of the close personal attention of their bath attendant.

Third, in the treatment of the chronic insane, the bath was something to look forward to in a world of monotony, besides being the most efficient means of effecting patients' personal cleanliness.

Baker also draws attention to the situation in asylums where members of staff, who have lived with the anxieties and pressures of working with the mentally ill for many years, have themselves then shown signs of mental stress. He writes:

> I have seen several instances during the past seventeen years, but since our attendants and nurses have been allowed the free use of the Turkish bath only one such case has come under my notice.

The baths continued in use until at least 1908.

Holloway Sanatorium, Virginia Water, Surrey

While The Retreat set a new standard of comfort in its Turkish bath, this might well have been expected a decade later by those entering the Holloway Sanatorium, a 'hospital for the insane' designed for middle-class paying patients of both sexes.

The sanatorium (converted in the late 1990s into up-market housing units) and nearby Holloway College (now Royal Holloway, University of London) are two magnificent Victorian Gothic buildings, built as a gift to the nation by Thomas Holloway from the profits of his eponymous pills.

The buildings were designed by architect William Henry Crossland (1835–1908) who, with John Philpot Jones and Edward Salomons, won the competition held on the advice of the Commissioners in Lunacy. Among the judges who were knowledgeable about the technical aspects of the building was Dr Charles Lockhart Robertson, who had installed the baths at Hayward's Heath.[52]

In August 1872, the plans were placed on exhibition in the Regent Street Gallery. There were to be baths for men and women and 'There is provided in the basement, central on both sides, a series of rooms for a Turkish bath, hot-air and vapour bath.'[53]

When the sanatorium opened in 1885, however, the vapour baths had been omitted. But the Turkish baths (Fig 18.11), in common with

Fig 18.11
The Turkish bath at the Holloway Sanatorium, Virginia Water, Surrey. (Illustrated London News, *20 June 1885, p.622. Author's collection)*

the lavish style of the whole edifice, were built to a high standard with the marble seats and wall linings, while the shampooing room had a marble basin and pedestal.[54]

The sanatorium continued in use, latterly within the National Health Service, until 1981, but the use of the Turkish bath almost certainly ended many years before then.

West Riding Pauper Lunatic Asylum, Wakefield

In 1871, James (later Sir James) Crichton-Browne installed a Turkish bath at Wakefield Asylum. He was specially concerned about asylum hygiene and drainage, and so the Turkish bath had a wide range of showers, baths, and steam cabinets.

The building work was undertaken by a group of patients who were skilled artisans and who carried it out to an extremely high standard. On occasion some of the patients were unable to attend and this necessarily slowed completion of the building. But the delay was considered worthwhile, because of the competence of the builders and the elegance of the building and its fittings, which could not otherwise have been obtained.[55]

The six-room Turkish baths (Fig 18.12) had doorways ornamented with stone arches in the Moorish style, frosted glass windows, and encaustic tiles. The entrance, at the end of the building, led into a passageway with two doors on the right and a toilet at the end.

The first door opened into the Turkish baths 'dressing room', furnished with four relaxation couches. Next was the 'mild room' kept at 110°F (43°C), and then the 'hot room' which could be maintained at any temperature up to 190°F (88°C).

Unusually, the hot room could also, if required, be filled with steam and converted into a Russian bath. When this was done, bathers would also be able to use a needle shower, and a 'fountain bath' from which a 'stream of water' could be 'applied to the rectum or anus'. Both of these were on the far side of the room, close to the shampooing area in the next room. The hot and cold taps supplying them with water were under the control of the shampooer, within the shampooing room itself. Apart from safety considerations, this would also ensure that they could not be turned on when the hot room was being used with dry air.

The shampooing table had its own basin and flexible water spray, while on the other side of the room there was a 'wave bath from which a broad sheet of cold water can be made to sweep over the body.'

The fifth room was a bathroom with slipper, sitz, and hip baths, together with a weighing machine. The last room, which was also accessible from the entrance corridor, housed three cabinet baths which could be used for steam or a variety of medicated vapour baths.

The baths were reported as being particularly useful in relieving melancholia and in treating skin diseases and rheumatism. Crichton-Browne's claim that 'there are no baths in this country … which are more complete or more pleasing in their general effect

Fig 18.12
Plan of the Turkish bath at the West Riding Pauper Lunatic Asylum, Wakefield. ('Architect's plan' Annual Report, *1871. West Yorkshire Archive Service: Wakefield Ref. C85/1/12/3)*

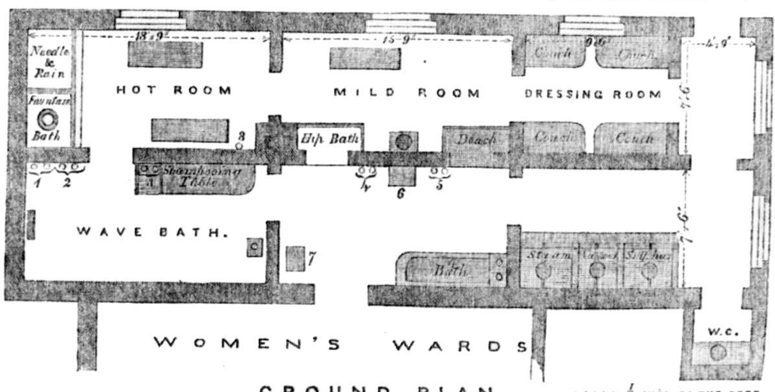

than those of the West Riding Asylum' seems to have been well justified.

Other Turkish baths in asylums

The bath set up in 1893 by Dr Robert Armstrong-Jones after he moved from Colney Hatch to Claybury, the London County Council's first asylum, located at Woodford in Essex, has already been noted. This was discontinued during the two world wars, and was not reopened after the second.[56]

One of the last, possibly *the* last, of the asylum Turkish baths to be installed was that at the new Reception Hospital of the St Andrew's Hospital for Mental Diseases at Northampton, in 1927. As 'asylum' had changed to 'hospital for mental diseases', so had the vaguely disreputable sounding 'hydropathy' morphed into 'hydrotherapy'.

At St Andrew's, each block had its own hydrotherapy department with a comprehensive array of baths, showers, and treatments located next to the dormitories. The department was completed by 'a Turkish bath installation in a separate building close to the hospital, where all forms of hot air and vapour treatments are provided.'[57]

There were other asylums which had Turkish baths, but it is doubtful whether they adopted any significant new approaches or treatments.

The plea of the satisfied bather who had used the Turkish bath at The Retreat and asked York Corporation to build one for public use, was not the only unsuccessful one. In 1863, W E Wiley, proprietor of the Turkish bath within his Birmingham pencil and pen factory, offered to put it at the disposal of the medical superintendent of the Birmingham Asylum between seven and ten each morning 'until he is satisfied of the beneficial effects of the Turkish baths upon lunatics.'[58]

The use of Turkish baths in asylums was not without occasional management failures. In 1889, for example, there was a serious accident at the Cork asylum where the bath was divided into male and female rooms. Twenty-five men and forty-five women were in the baths when fumes escaped from a duct, and nine men 'fell down insensible' and eleven women 'were prostrate and senseless.' Two of the women were unconscious for a short time, but fortunately all recovered in due course.[59]

Even more serious was the death of a woman at Denbigh Asylum from burns caused when she had an epileptic fit in the bath.[60] And there were, of course, other accidents and failures, just as there were in all types of hot-air baths used by all types of bather.

How beneficial were Turkish baths in the asylums?

Did the Turkish baths installed in these asylums deliver on the promise repeatedly made for them?

The level of medical knowledge in the second half of the 19th century suggests that in the many cases where a disease was not yet understood, or in the many more where there was no medical cure, the bath must have been beneficial. Many confirmed that it could often help alleviate chronic pain. We know that, in common with other types of hot-air bath, the Turkish bath can certainly help reduce stress, and thereby improve a patient's general sense of wellbeing.

The conclusion of Robert Baker's paper on the use of the bath at The Retreat, addressed to his medical colleagues, is apposite:

> ... first, I believe that the Turkish bath will probably assist you in promoting the recovery of some of your patients; and, second, that I know, and am sure, that by its judicious use you may infuse additional happiness, solace, and brightness into the lives of some of those whom we know to be amongst the most sorely-tried of the members of the family of 'suffering, sad humanity'.[61]

And with that, whatever modern medicine may teach us, it is difficult to disagree.

19

The Turkish bath in hospitals

Both Urquhart and Barter argued for the provision of a Turkish bath in every hospital, asylum and workhouse. In 1860, the year after Barter's unsuccessful offer to pay for a Turkish bath in the Cork Workhouse, Dr Edward Haughton wrote in his *Facts and fallacies of the Turkish bath*:

> There should be no hospital or poorhouse without its Hammam; for it is in these places that it is most wanted, and in which its beneficial effects will be soonest apparent.[1]

The 19th-century link between hospital patients, inmates of the lunatic asylum, and inmates of the workhouse, was that the institutions housing them were all built for the poor. The workhouse was publicly funded by a local authority; hospitals and asylums were paid for, and run by, privately funded charities.

Individual donors (or 'subscribers') to these charities often determined who would be accepted as patients. At the Newcastle Infirmary in 1860, for example, those who subscribed one guinea per year were entitled to recommend one out-patient for treatment. For two guineas the entitlement was two out-patients or one in-patient, and so on *pro rata*.[2]

The wealthy who were ill were normally treated at home; only the 'deserving poor' were to be found in hospitals, while the rest, the 'undeserving poor', were relegated to the workhouse.

Neither hospital patients nor inmates, similarly confined within their institutions for greater or lesser periods of time, were able to use Turkish baths open to the general public. Often the institutional confinement was not voluntary. In some respects this must have felt little different from the deprivation experienced by those in prison.

Although some advocates maintained that even prisoners should have access to a Turkish bath,[3] this was very much a minority view. I have not been able to find any prisons which had one, however beneficial this might have been to the prisoners.

The relatively few Turkish baths which were provided in the three other types of institution usually had in common the need to keep costs to a minimum, although there were exceptions such as, for example, the baths suite at the York Retreat.

The Turkish baths at the Newcastle-upon-Tyne Infirmary

The first use of a Turkish bath within an English hospital was, like so many milestones in the bath's history, due to the involvement of those connected with Urquhart's Foreign Affairs Committees—in this case George Crawshay (Fig 19.1) and his father-in-law, Sir John Fife (Fig 19.2), who had been invited to try the private bath which Crawshay had built on his return from Ireland in 1857.

Fife, an ex-Chartist and, according to Urquhart's wife Harriet, one of Urquhart's oldest political associates,[4] was surgeon at the Newcastle-upon-Tyne Infirmary and one of the founders of its medical school.

Just as Crawshay had been impressed at St Ann's, so was Fife impressed, not only by the bath itself, but also by its many therapeutic possibilities. He wrote to Charles Attwood, another Urquhart supporter:

> I have been restored to youth by being boiled, or rather roasted, alive in the bath of the Romans. It is one good thing done by Mr Urquhart, to bring this agent to us; and I am about to introduce it to the Infirmary.[5]

In November 1857, Fife reported on his bath experience in a talk to the Newcastle and Gateshead Pathological Society.[6] Soon after, on the joint recommendation of Fife and Crawshay, the House Committee of the Newcastle-upon-Tyne

Fig 19.1 (above)
George Crawshay (1821–1896) by an unknown photographer, c 1850. Crawshay was a longtime supporter of David Urquhart.
(Supplied by Llyfrgell Genedlaethol Cymru, The National Library of Wales, LlGC/NLW -PE4213)

Fig 19.2 (above right)
Sir John Fife, surgeon at the Newcastle-upon-Tyne Infirmary.
(By permission of the librarian, Robinson Library, Newcastle University)

Infirmary approved the construction of a bath there.

It was designed by the eminent local architect, John Dobson (1787–1865), whose earlier buildings included the city's Northumberland Baths (1839) and its imposing Central railway station (1850). He had also been responsible for a new wing, which opened at the Infirmary in 1855, and was named the Dobson Wing after him.[7] The hospital bath, which cost £60 to build and equip,[8] was completed and in use by July 1858.

When Dobson set to work, there was almost no professional expertise on which he could draw. He therefore followed Barter's practice of heating the bath by means of a Roman-style hypocaust. Yet the plan of Dobson's bath shows it to have been different from Barter's in several respects (Fig 19.3).

First, the hypocaust appears to have run only under the *sudatorium* (its hottest room), so that the *tepidarium* relied on ambient heat and the *frigidarium* was not heated at all. Perhaps as a result of this (or possibly by design), the room temperatures were lower than those usually found in a commercial establishment, with the *sudatorium* ranging from 130–160° F (54–71°C), and the *tepidarium* being maintained at 100°F (38°C).

Second, Barter believed that for optimal therapeutic effect the hot air in a Turkish bath should be as dry as possible; Dobson's inclusion of a shower in the hot room goes against a fundamental principle, already generally accepted by designers of Victorian Turkish baths, that wet and dry areas should be separated.

Nevertheless, the medical staff were pleased with their bath, and Dr Andrew Bolton, in his house surgeon's report for 1859, seemed to be writing as much for house surgeons elsewhere as for his own house committee.

During the opening year to July 1859, 11,891 baths were given and, based on the experience gained, Bolton chose to pre-empt one of the standard contemporary objections to the bath—that it should not be taken by those with any sort of heart problem. He had found that the extreme heat of the Turkish bath exerted less influence on the heart and circulation than an ordinary warm bath, remarking that,

> in some cases in which the pulse and stethoscope give unmistakeable evidence of heart disease, such patients have undergone the [Turkish bath] process without attendant mischief, and with almost unlooked-for benefit.[9]

The bath, he wrote, had also helped patients with liver and kidney disease, and had been

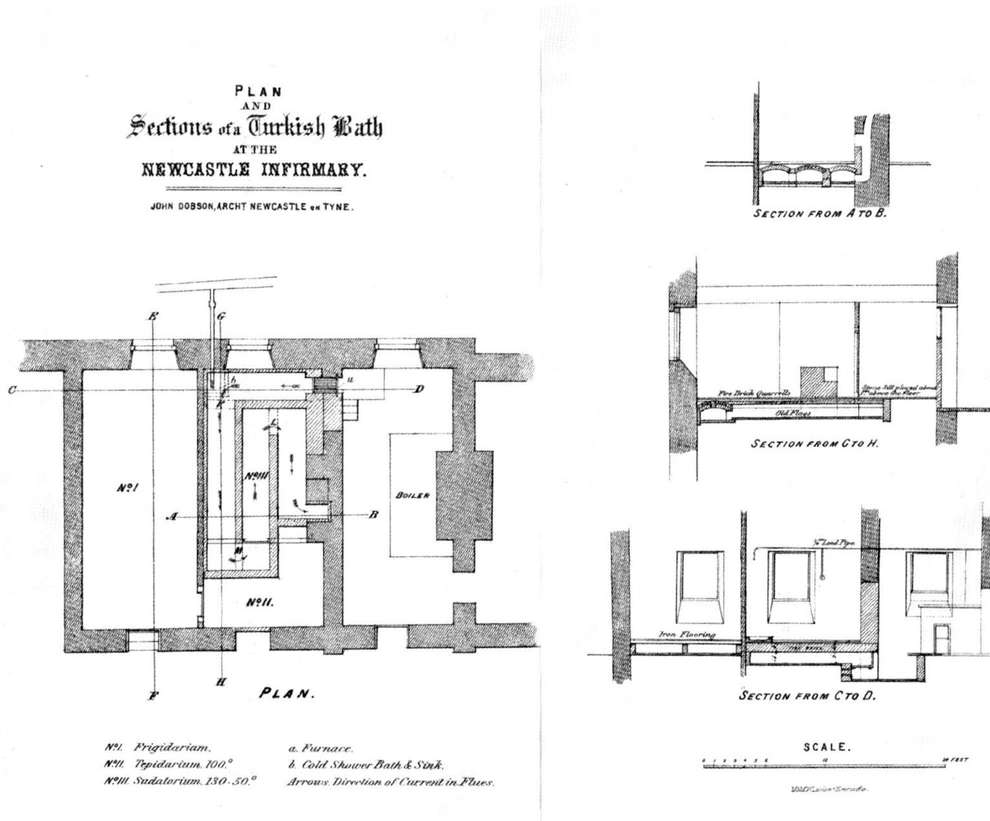

Fig 19.3
John Dobson's plan of the Turkish bath at Newcastle-upon-Tyne Infirmary, the first to be installed in a hospital.
(109th annual report of the Newcastle Infirmary, *Newcastle: the Infirmary, 1860. Author's collection)*

especially beneficial to those who suffered from rheumatism.

During the year, from 1 January to 31 December 1861, 11,946 baths were given.[10] The bath seemed to be working well, appeared to satisfy all the hospital's medical expectations, and was widely visited by others wishing to follow suit. Neither were all the enquiries from other hospitals.

When the Roman Bath Company was planning the Turkish bath which it intended to build in Cambridge, Mr E F King, the company secretary, wrote to Bolton to ask for an account of its use at the infirmary.

Bolton replied, with an enthusiasm rather more glowing than might be expected in a sober medical assessment, that the first cases they had treated were,

> of a rheumatic character, both acute and chronic, lumbago, neuralgia, sciatica, and gout; and with such beneficial results, that in the course of a few weeks the bath had become most popular, and rheumatic cripples were being brought from all quarters; some with their joints much swollen and suffering a martyrdom, were conveyed helplessly down to a bath, into a species of Elysium, where ache and pain vanished as by magic.[11]

Bolton's reply suggests that 12,987 persons used the bath during the year ending 31 March 1861—a slightly different period from that in his annual report. And rather than giving King the actual total, he chose to provide the number of bathers grouped according as to whether the baths were given to in-patients (1,720), out-patients (1,778), or to the overwhelming majority which he called 'casuals' (9,489). He does not explain what is meant by 'casuals', but it seems highly likely that in addition to members of the public (who would have paid for a bath), some of the hospital staff were also included.

While confirming the benefits of using the bath, he also warns King about what to avoid in Cambridge. For the infirmary had already abandoned the hypocaust as a means of heating the bath when a number of bathers were burnt, usually after their pattens came off. The change became essential after a particularly serious accident. A bather had fallen onto the hot floor and was unable to get up quickly enough to avoid being seriously burned and 'life for a time was endangered.'

After this, the hot air was circulated in ducts around the walls of the bath, underneath the seating. But this too was quickly abandoned as the heated air became sweat-laden and there was no adequate ventilation.

Fortunately for the infirmary, Dr Bolton's brother, Dr John Adams Bolton, previously an assistant surgeon at Newcastle, had opened his Turkish bath in Leicester the previous year where he had installed his own newly patented heating and ventilation system (see page 88). This was soon installed at the infirmary to replace the existing unsatisfactory one.

In the infirmary's *Annual Report for 1864*, which included a plan of the new baths (Fig 19.4), Dr Andrew Bolton commented that the Turkish bath had been favourably received by the medical profession. He added, rather over-optimistically, that its adoption by hospitals, asylums, and workhouses generally, seemed highly probable.

More realistically, he was convinced that, after a three-year trial, the principle of circulating a continuous current of fresh heated air into the hot rooms had shown itself to be 'superior in every respect' to the methods adopted in the earlier baths.[12]

The Turkish bath was now open for patients three days in the week but, since the number of baths taken was no longer stated, it is not clear whether they were closed for the remainder of the week, or whether this was a period reserved for non-patients and staff.

The report also gave some information about costs, and procedures. Coke for the furnace, for example, cost £9 7s 0d for the whole of the year 1863–4. This was a great saving on the cost of the hypocaust because the rooms did not need to be kept hot at night. Firing the furnace at six in the morning ensured that the *sudatorium* would reach the desired 160°F (71°C) by 11 o'clock. The furnace was then closed down and the heat was found to be sufficient for their bathing requirements for the rest of the day.

At some time between 1874 and 1883—we do not know exactly when because both local collections of the house surgeon's annual reports have gaps in their holdings—the infirmary stopped running the Turkish baths themselves and leased them to the Newcastle-upon-Tyne Turkish Bath Company Ltd.

This was the company which, together with its financially restructured successor, the Newcastle-upon-Tyne Turkish Baths Co (1894) Ltd, owned and ran the Pilgrim Street Turkish Baths in the city centre. Significantly, one of its directors was Dr Charles John Gibb, the infirmary's house surgeon from 1849 to 1855, and then an honorary surgeon till 1870.[13]

Each of the infirmary's annual reports for the years between 1884 and 1897 includes, in its statement of income and expenditure, the receipt of £300 'To One Year's Rent to 30 November ... from Turkish Bath Co'. From this sum, income tax had to be deducted, ranging from £7 0s 2d (in 1884) to £10 0s 0d (from 1895–7).[14]

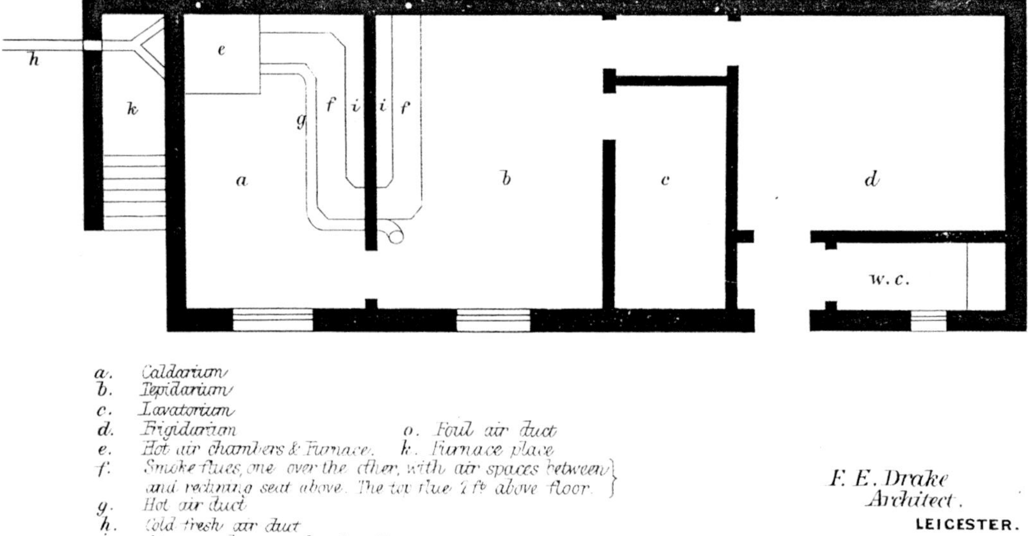

Fig 19.4
Plan of the third Turkish bath at Newcastle-upon-Tyne Infirmary.
(Annual report for 1864, *Newcastle: the Infirmary, 1865. Author's collection)*

This convenient leasing arrangement came to a halt at the end of 1897, when the Turkish bath company sold its Pilgrim Street Baths to William Priestley.[15] It seems unlikely that the infirmary reverted to running the baths themselves, and they probably closed when Priestley took over. But even if this was not so, the infirmary moved into new buildings in 1906, and there is no mention of any Turkish baths on the new site.

The medical press calls on hospitals to undertake research

By 1861, the bath had already been established in Ireland for five years and in the north of England for nearly four years. Yet professional journals in the capital only became 'medically' aware of them after the first London baths opened half way through 1860. And at the beginning of 1861, the Royal Shrewsbury Infirmary seems to have been the only other hospital to follow Newcastle's example.

In London, St Mary's Hospital in Paddington adopted a different approach, possibly as a very cost-effective experiment. For 1s each, they sent a number of their patients in the evening to a Turkish bath in nearby Conduit Place, 'with very great benefit', according to Dr Goolden of St Thomas's Hospital. But it is not known how long this continued, and there is nothing else known about these baths except that they were small and very plainly decorated.[16]

Not all doctors agreed with their Newcastle colleagues about the value of the Turkish bath as a therapeutic agent. The house surgeon's annual reports gave figures for the number of baths taken each year, as we have seen, and also named specific medical conditions for which the bath was stated to have been beneficial. But this was not significantly different from the sort of information included in the advertisements of commercial Turkish baths.

Very little serious research *had* been undertaken, and this was pointedly noted in medical journals during the year. An editorial in *The Lancet* commented:

> It is not important to know how agreeably or how luxuriously two hours may be spent in the bath, for few of us, who have the work of life before us, have time to spare; but we really wish to know how the air bath operates on the human organism. If any, what is the nature of the danger to be apprehended, when a healthy body is the subject? What is the kind of relief produced in disease? What are the constitutional or pathological peculiarities that are injuriously influenced?[17]

The journal offered its columns to those who had real research results to contribute, and continued:

> Our hospitals should afford us the information we are now seeking, especially such as have large schools and ample funds, since in them only can a sufficiently-organized investigation be instituted, checked by public observation. No private institution can be free from the imputation of interested representations, and we must zealously guard against enthusiasm as well as charlatanry.

Yet again it was Urquhart who provided the necessary support, by inviting Dr Arthur Leared, a physician at the Brompton Royal Infirmary for Diseases of the Chest, to bring some of his hospital patients to the London Hammam which was then being built in Jermyn Street. The directors agreed to build a small experimental bath for invalids and Leared was encouraged to document the effects of the bath on those with consumption.

The experiment was later continued in the main bath. For a number of reasons, only two patients carried on using the bath for any length of time, but their health improved, and Leared's results were very detailed. They were published in *The Lancet* at the end of 1863 under the title *On the treatment of phthisis by the hot-air bath*.[18]

Although several articles with single-line references to the Turkish bath appeared in the *British Medical Journal* and *The Lancet* during the 1860s, there were very few which dealt with the use of the bath in the treatment of a single specific disease.

Other hospitals which are known to have installed Turkish baths during this period include the Royal Victoria Military Hospital at Netley, near Southampton, in 1864, and the Denbighshire Infirmary, Denbigh, towards the end of 1869.

The Denbigh baths cost 'about' £311[19] and, like Newcastle's baths, were also open to the general public, making, according to its annual report for 1871, a useful profit of £12 12s 6d.[20]

In 1879, the Brompton Royal Infirmary expanded into part of a new 'south block'. The building was designed by Thomas Henry Wyatt (1807–80), and the basement housed two specialised baths which were considered beneficial to sufferers from consumption, a compressed air bath and a Turkish bath. After 16 years, Leared's experiment had finally borne fruit.[21]

When *The Lancet* called for hospitals to undertake research back in 1861, they wrote,

> It is gratifying to hear that the governors of St Thomas's Hospital are contemplating building a Turkish bath in their establishment, and that the medical officers, as a body, are prepared to examine its value as an addition to the ordinary means of treating diseases.[22]

But although one or two doctors prescribed the bath, and published their research results, there was very little evidence that 'the medical officers, as a body' became involved.

The strange case of the bath at St Thomas's Hospital, London

The story seems to have started at the beginning of 1860, or possibly slightly earlier, when Dr R H Goolden and a small group of doctors asked for a Turkish bath to be built at St Thomas's for therapeutic purposes.

A staff committee was set up to consider whether to recommend approval of the proposal. According to Goolden, in a letter published in *The Lancet* on 26 January 1861, no one had objected when the committee had originally considered the matter. But afterwards, three of its members had written privately arguing against the proposal. Accordingly, the hospital treasurer—as senior resident member of staff responsible for the running of St Thomas's and for reporting to the hospital governors—wrote to each committee member asking for his views.

We know that Goolden's reply was very long because a copy was attached to his letter to the editor of *The Lancet*.[23] This was at Goolden's request as he felt that its content might be useful to other hospitals considering the addition of a Turkish bath. It is difficult to imagine an editor today finding two-and-a-half pages of small print for such a rambling communication, but it is only through his letters that we know of these discussions, or of Goolden's description of other baths and his ideas as to what a hospital bath should provide.

He began by expressing surprise that three physicians should have such influence when 15 other physicians and surgeons had requested the bath. They had presented no arguments against it during the committee meeting and he could see no reason to counter the original decision, especially since no one was forced to prescribe the bath until convinced of its value.

He dismissed the suggestion that the bath was expensive to construct, use and maintain. He then listed all the people he had consulted about the value of the bath, and noted that he had personally visited every London bath open to the public, as well as several private ones. In particular, he described in some detail his visit to the first London bath—that run by Roger Evans in Bell Street.

> I went into the bath at such times as that I could observe its effects upon the lower classes, who resorted there in great numbers, not as a luxury, but as a remedy, as they supposed, for disease ... There were often ten people in the hot room at one time, all invalids, and I found them quite willing to tell me all their complaints, and to let me examine them. They were principally artizans, small shop-keepers, policemen, admitted at a small fee.

After naming a score of the bathers' complaints and illnesses, he continued:

> To expect a cure, or even benefit, in all these cases, would be unreasonable; but I found relief produced to a far greater extent than I was prepared for. The most marked relief was found in cases of gout, rheumatism, periosteal nodes, and sciatica ...

He then described the type of bath which he thought would satisfy the hospital's needs:

> The hospital bath should consist of several chambers: a hot room (150°[F] [65.5°C]), a tepid room (100° [F] [37.7°C]), and an ante-room with a supply of hot and cold water, so arranged that the bather can have a shower-bath or douche at any temperature. There should also be a tap of cold water supplied to each room. The rooms should be warmed by a flue, not necessarily under the floor. In attending to this matter much saving can be effected without lessening the efficiency. The floor should be of brick, and the walls may be of cement, brick, or Dutch tiles; and the rooms must be so constructed as to admit of perfect ventilation. The estimated cost of fuel is about 1s 6d a day.

St Thomas's Hospital was at this time located in Borough High Street in Southwark, but for some time there had been a possibility—soon to be realised—that it was going to have to vacate its premises in order to make room for the enlargement of London Bridge Railway Station.

In the meantime, the hospital's architect, Henry Currey (1820–1900), soon to design the new hospital in Lambeth opposite the Houses of Parliament, was asked to draw up plans for a Turkish bath. Only two drawings survive, preserved in the hospital's papers at the London Metropolitan Archives.[24]

The first, labelled 'Hot Air Baths' at 'St Thomas's Hospital', is dated 22 May 1860 and shows the ducting underneath the floors of the various rooms of the bath, together with the position of the furnace. The ducts carrying clean air to the hot rooms are coloured olive green, and those for removing the stale air are coloured black.

The second plan (Fig 19.5) dates from September 1860 and shows each of the rooms with its size, purpose, and layout. On the left of the baths, sharing both furnace and water supplies, are two private slipper baths, and on the right, a wash-house and drying closet.

A small lobby leads into the cooling-room (*frigidarium*) which has its own toilet. Leading directly off this is the 'intermediate room' (*tepidarium*) with its toilet and shower, and an opening to the 'Hot Chamber' (*sudatorium*), also with toilet and shower. Unfortunately the plan gives neither any indication of the building materials to be used, nor the internal finish of the walls or seating. Excluding the wash-house, furnace room and slipper baths, the Turkish bath is approximately 48ft × 25ft (14.6m × 7.6m), which seems very generous.

By January 1861, it was known that the hospital would definitely have to move the following year and, since it would need to be in temporary premises for quite a while, the building of the Turkish bath was put on indefinite hold.

The interval between the altercation described in Goolden's letter to *The Lancet* and the date on the first of Currey's plans would seem to indicate that the differences between the two groups were resolved fairly quickly. However, nine years were to pass in temporary accommodation between the hospital's departure from Southwark in 1862 and moving into its new premises in Lambeth.

In 1863 Dr Goolden published a paper in the *British Medical Journal* on his use of the bath in the treatment of diabetes.[25] However, it is not clear whether there was a Turkish bath in the hospital's temporary premises or whether he

Fig 19.5
Henry Currey's plan of the Turkish bath at St Thomas's Hospital, London.
(Guy's and St Thomas' Charity London and Metropolitan Archives. City of London)

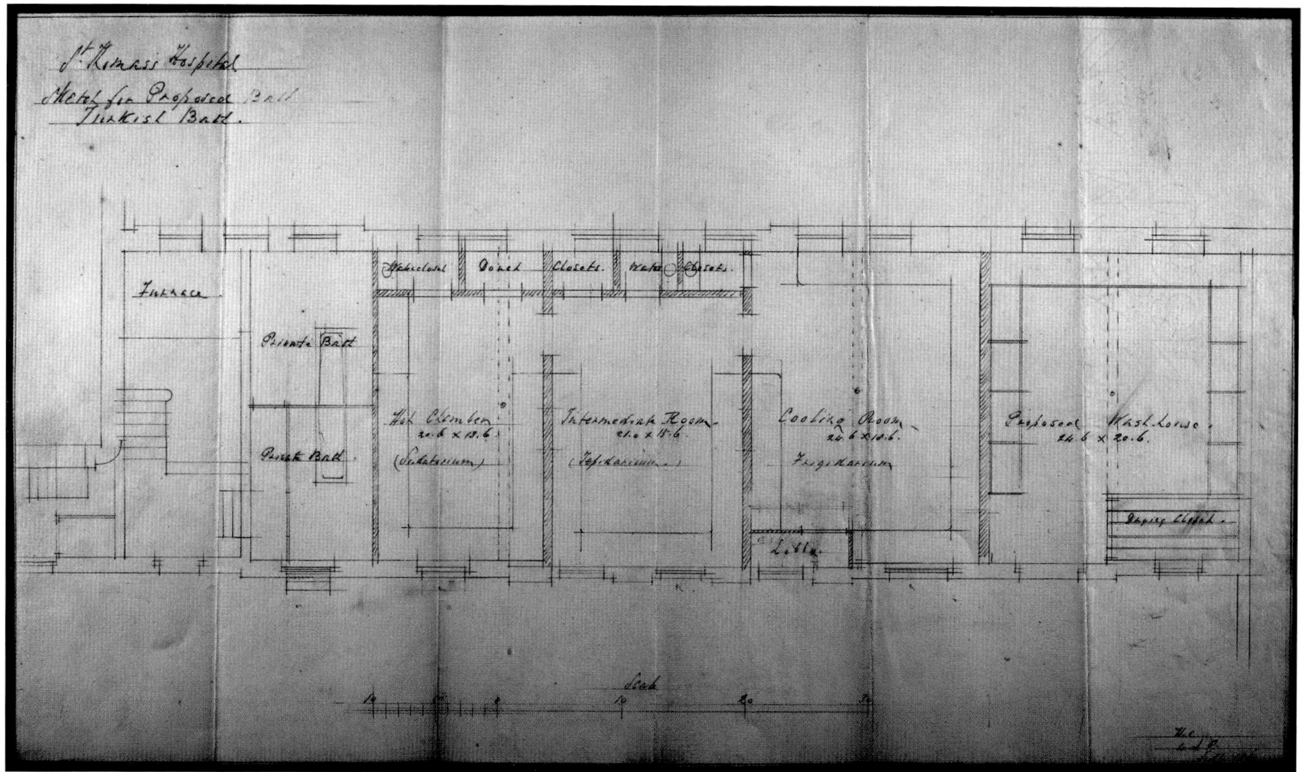

supervised the patient's use of one in a commercial establishment nearby.

After Currey's two plans, nothing further is heard about a Turkish bath in the hospital for 17 years until the publication in 1877 of Metcalfe's *Sanitas sanitatum et omnia sanitas* with its excerpts from the replies to his questionnaire.

One of these was from James Bryning, whose reply was intriguing. Bryning was proprietor for seven years of the Turkish baths at 191 Blackfriars Road, just a short walk away from the new hospital. He was a strong believer in the value of the bath, but emphasised that it would need to be 'ever so cheap' if those living in Paddington were to use it. For the poor, he wrote,

> like the rich, have their prejudices, and being uneducated, you cannot persuade them that it is either necessary or beneficial, therefore, it makes it a work of time.
>
> When you find prejudice in educated medical men, you cannot wonder that the masses should be so.
>
> There is a Turkish bath in new St Thomas's Hospital, and they will not avail themselves of its curative powers; therefore it is not used, although Dr Erasmus Wilson, and Dr Goulden [sic] are both so favourable to its use.[26]

Did the bath that was built differ from Currey's original plans? And was it really never used? At present, these questions do not seem to be answerable, either in the hospital archives or elsewhere.

By contrast, if St Thomas's Hospital had a bath which was never used, the Southport Convalescent Hospital prescribed the Turkish bath even though it did not itself possess one. During the year 1887, for example, 3,761 patients stayed at the hospital for its normally recommended period of three weeks (though there were a few extended visits). Considering the bath to be a valuable contribution to an effective recovery, the hospital arranged for 517 of these patients to take Turkish baths at a local establishment—probably the one on The Promenade—with the cost paid for by the hospital.[27]

Turkish baths at Huddersfield and Edinburgh Infirmaries

It is difficult in practice to discover which of the many hospitals in the British Isles installed Turkish baths, as the bath is such a small part of a large hospital. Nor would anything new necessarily be discovered in attempting to track them down, since all of them attempted to treat a variety of complaints in more or less the same way.

Huddersfield Royal Infirmary may have been the last of the large hospitals in England to install a Turkish bath. Although, like Newcastle and Shrewsbury, its baths were open to the public, Huddersfield offered more facilities, and there are surviving price lists.

The Turkish bath was not new to 1890s Huddersfield. The commercial Turkish bath in Albion Street was one of the first in the country, being opened in 1857 by John Maxfield (the Elder). In 1884 and 1885 its then proprietor, William Tuley, placed advertisements in the local paper suggesting to the reader that,

> If you want Health and Beauty, visit the Albion Street Turkish Baths. Rheumatism, Gout, Lumbago, Indigestion, Colds, &c, cured by a delightfully pleasant operation. Open Daily, 10 to 10. Admission till 9. [28]

Even so, the need for a medical bath establishment at the Royal Infirmary was well enough argued, a decade later, to encourage Mr George Brook of Springwood Hall to donate a sum sufficient to enable one to be built and opened in 1897.

The establishment included Turkish, Russian, and 'other remedial baths, which were available to patients under the direction of their medical advisers'. It had its own entrance, proved to be well used both by patients and the general public, and was,

> much resorted to by many persons, on payment of the rate charged, who would not ordinarily receive treatment at the Infirmary.[29]

Interestingly, although the Infirmary emphasised the medical supervision which was provided, the governors poached John Shoesmith from Albion Street to be their first baths superintendent. This was a wise appointment, since Shoesmith had well over 25 years' experience managing Turkish baths, latterly in Huddersfield and, before that, in Bolton.

In 1912, (Fig 19.6) the baths were open three-and-a-half days in the week for men and a full day and two halves for women. But the cheaper second-class baths (available after 7 pm) could only be used by women once each week as both their half day openings were in the morning.[30]

World War II had its effect on the baths, as on all other aspects of daily life. More women were working in factories to support the war effort. This, together with the blackout, undoubtedly contributed to a decrease in the number of women bathers, with the result that by 1940 the baths were only open to them for one-and-a-half days each week. About this time also, possibly due to shortage of staff, the medicated baths and the individual slipper, sitz and shower baths were all discontinued, leaving only the Turkish and Russian baths in operation.

After the end of the war, with an increasing proportion of families having their own bathrooms, and with the number of bathers availing themselves of the Infirmary baths constantly diminishing, it was decided to close them in 1949.

Tuley's baths, which had moved to Ramsden Street in 1906, had already closed in 1927, so the Turkish baths at the Infirmary were the only ones remaining in Huddersfield. As in so many similar cases, there was an active—but unsuccessful—campaign to keep them open, but they finally closed in 1951.[31]

If the Turkish suite at Huddersfield Infirmary was superior to those provided in other English hospitals, then the most luxurious facility must surely have been that provided at the Royal Infirmary of Edinburgh, probably the last British hospital to install a Turkish bath.

Its bathing department was designed by architects Sydney Mitchell & Wilson (*c* 1887–*c* 1908).[32] Located in the basement of a new red stone medical pavilion, built in a 'modified Scottish baronial style of architecture',[33] it was intended to commemorate Queen Victoria's Diamond Jubilee. The Pavilion was formally opened on 26 October 1900 by Princess Henry of Battenberg.

The new bathing establishment contained a Turkish bath with three hot rooms, vapour, electric, sulphur and other medicated baths, a douche room and a needle shower. The large cooling-room was 10ft wide × 70ft long (3m × 21m), and the suite had its own dressing-rooms, toilets, and accommodation for the bath attendants.

So as to avoid overheating or steaming the ward above, the basement was separated from the first floor by a double-concrete fireproof floor, with an intermediate ventilated air space. Within the suite, the walls and floors were covered 'with tiles of various patterns and colours', and presented 'a pleasing appearance'.

The concept of the hospital Turkish bath went out in style.

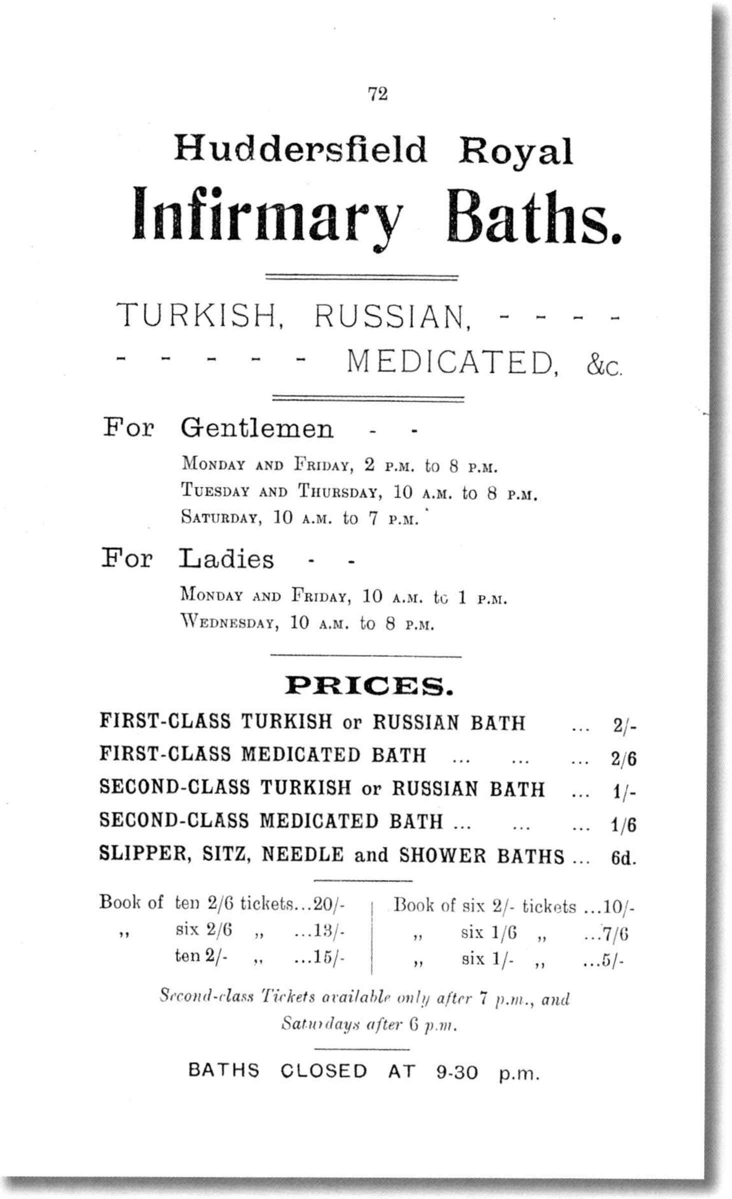

72

Huddersfield Royal

Infirmary Baths.

TURKISH, RUSSIAN, - - - -
- - - - - MEDICATED, &c.

For Gentlemen - -

Monday and Friday, 2 p.m. to 8 p.m.
Tuesday and Thursday, 10 a.m. to 8 p.m.
Saturday, 10 a.m. to 7 p.m.

For Ladies - -

Monday and Friday, 10 a.m. to 1 p.m.
Wednesday, 10 a.m. to 8 p.m.

PRICES.

FIRST-CLASS TURKISH or RUSSIAN BATH ...	2/-
FIRST-CLASS MEDICATED BATH	2/6
SECOND-CLASS TURKISH or RUSSIAN BATH ...	1/-
SECOND-CLASS MEDICATED BATH	1/6
SLIPPER, SITZ, NEEDLE and SHOWER BATHS ...	6d.

Book of ten 2/6 tickets...20/-	Book of six 2/- tickets ...10/-
,, six 2/6 ,, ...13/-	,, six 1/6 ,, ...7/6
ten 2/- ,, ...15/-	,, six 1/- ,, ...5/-

Second-class Tickets available only after 7 p.m., and Saturdays after 6 p.m.

BATHS CLOSED AT 9-30 p.m.

Fig 19.6
Opening hours and charges for the general public at Huddersfield Royal Infirmary Turkish baths. (Royal Infirmary annual report, Huddersfield: the infirmary, 1912, p.72. Huddersfield Library Local Studies)

20

The Turkish bath in hydros and hotels

Fig 20.1
William Macleod was the first to add a Turkish bath to an already existing English hydro.
(Richard Metcalfe, Rise and progress of hydropathy…, *Simpkin, 1912)*

Although the first Victorian Turkish bath was built at St Ann's Hydropathic Establishment, this was not the first British hydro, nor even the first in Ireland. Dr James R Wherland opened a much smaller one in Cork at 22 Warrens Place a few months before Barter's.

Alastair Durie, in the introductory chapter of his essential book on hydros and health tourism in Scotland, summarises the rapid spread of hydropathic establishments.[1] Starting in the 1820s in Europe, especially in Germany and Austria, hydros soon appeared in London, Malvern and other places in the south-east of England. Further north, they severally developed so that villages such as Ilkley and Matlock, already famed for their pure water, became important hydropathic centres.

After Claridge's visit to Cork, Wherland and Barter independently visited some of these hydros and then set up their own establishments in Ireland. Finally, Claridge's visit to Glasgow, also in 1843, provided the impetus for hydropathy to take off in Scotland, so that eventually it had more hydros than anywhere else in the kingdom—though not always the most successful.

In 1857, Barter built the third of his Turkish baths at St Ann's—the first wholly successful one, and it was not long before other hydros followed suit. Though many hydropathists initially derided any form of therapy not practised by Vincent Priessnitz, the father of hydropathy, they had to take note of the fact that patients found sweating in hot dry air more comfortable than spending long periods wrapped in cold wet sheets.

The Turkish bath at Ben Rhydding

In 1859, less than two years later, William Macleod (Fig 20.1) had a Turkish bath built at §Ben Rhydding in Ilkley. Macleod's bath, like Barter's, occupied its own separate building and was designed by architects Lockwood and Mawson, making them the first major architectural practice to build a Turkish bath in England.[2] It cost £2,000 and was called—rather more accurately—a Roman bath.

As soon as bathers entered, their clothes were exchanged for a bathing dress (for women) or a sheet (for men), together with a pair of wooden pattens.[3]

The first of its three main rooms was the *frigidarium*, over 1,000 sq ft (305 sq m) in area, maintained at about 100°F (37.8°C) (Fig 20.2). Around the walls were dressing rooms, with couches so that bathers could relax after their bath, soothed by the gentle sound of a decorative fountain in the middle. Above, curved ribs

Figs 20.2–20.4 (clockwise, from far left)
The frigidarium, tepidarium *and* caldarium *at Ben Rhydding.*
*(*Ben Rhydding: the principles of hydropathy and the compressed air bath*, Hamilton, 1859)*

supported the coved and vaulted 30ft (9m) high ceiling, in the centre of which a stained-glass lantern filtered the daylight.

The *tepidarium* (Fig 20.3), at a temperature of around 125°F (52°C),[4] was smaller than the *frigidarium* and octagonal in shape. On one side was the doorway, and on each of the other seven sides was a curtained recess, also furnished with a couch.

The *caldarium* (Fig 20.4), though square, had a domed ceiling 'of rich *groined work, ornamented with *bosses' supported by carved *corbels of cream-coloured limestone from Caen. This room, too, was lit by a central stained-glass lantern. Drinking fountains were provided on either side of the entrance, with long seating units against the walls. Other doors led to cold water baths, a *wave douche, and spray showers. The floor, as in all the rooms, was laid with patterned encaustic tiles.

When the baths opened, the air temperature in the *caldarium* was 150°F (66°C), but this was later reduced to 135°F (57°C). In fact, all the temperatures adopted by Macleod were relatively low by comparison with those of Barter. Macleod also decided against the rough Turkish style of shampooing considered so important by Urquhart as a cleansing agent. Instead he adopted Ling's System of Movements which is, perhaps, better known as Swedish massage.

It may be that Macleod's gentler approach was the result of his already having decided to relax the regime which Ben Rhydding founder Hamer Stansfield copied from Gräfenberg. Before Macleod's arrival, discipline was very strict and the *Directory of Ben Rhydding* noted that, 'The Scriptures are read in the drawing-room every morning after breakfast.'[5]

Such practices were the norm in other hydros too, and patients and their guests were required to obey numerous rules and regulations. At Smedley's Matlock Bank Hydro, for example, patients were warned of a 2s 6d fine for 'Any person who shall come to meals after a blessing has been asked.' There was also one of 10s 6d for 'Any gentleman entering the ladies' sitting-room', a fine which, curiously, was the same as that for 'Any gentleman entering the ladies' bath-room',[6] possibly bringing to mind a fleeting image of sheep and lambs.

Some patients were accompanied by their wives and children, for whom the hydro was little different from a hotel. It may have been this which encouraged Macleod to make Ben Rhydding more attractive to a wider clientele by becoming what was essentially a hydropathic hotel.

Later, he abandoned one of the main tenets of traditional hydropathy by obtaining a licence to serve alcoholic drinks with meals. According to Richard Metcalfe, the immediate result of this radical approach was that 'a group of some fifty quakers, who were in the house when this change was effected, at once left'.[7]

The change from hydropathic establishment to hydropathic hotel, and finally to hotel, was to become increasingly common as hydropathy became less popular towards the end of the 19th century.

However, long before this, patients' families began to accompany them to hydros, finding that recreational facilities were available, and that normal meals were served to non-patients. It was only natural that nearby hotels should respond by adding Turkish baths and pools to their own facilities to help retain what they saw as *their* clientele.

Rivalry at Glenbrook, Co Cork

At Glenbrook, a small riverside resort near Cork, for example, there was considerable rivalry between §Dr Curtin's Hydropathic Establishment and §The Royal Victoria Hotel and Baths.

The Royal Victoria Monkstown and Passage Baths opened in August 1838 on the western bank of the River Lee and were the first public baths in the area.[8] When built, they comprised slipper baths, showers, and a cold plunge pool, all of which were luxuriously fitted out.[9] It was not long before these facilities were supplemented by the provision of food, accommodation, gardens, and outdoor activities designed to attract those living in the nearby villages.

The Royal Victoria Baths did not remain the only bathing facility at Glenbrook for long. Early in 1852, according to local historian Colman O'Mahony, Dr Timothy Curtin, a well-respected hydropathist and homeopathic doctor, purchased or leased the nearby Carrigmahon House, together with '13 acres of wooded and landscaped gardens' with the intention of opening a hydropathic establishment in Glenbrook. Already, by the middle of the year, 'guests, including some from England, had arrived at Carrigmahon and were paying two guineas per week.'[10]

That such guests were already staying at the hydro in the absence of any advertising, seems to suggest that good fortune alone was not responsible. It is possible that Dr Barter had advised Curtin on setting up his establishment and was sending him those patients for whom the fees at St Ann's were too high. And after his death, the lease of the land on which Dr Curtin's hydro was built was found to be in the name of Barter's son.

The hydro prospered. Additional land was acquired soon after it opened, and in 1856, the year in which Barter was experimenting with his first Turkish baths at St Ann's, Curtin decided to expand so that additional guests could be housed.

By now the original Royal Victoria Monkstown & Passage Baths were owned by a Mr Robert Watkin Jones, who purchased them some time around 1856. He changed their name to The Glenbrook Victoria Hotel and Baths, thereby also changing the relative importance of the different services provided.[11]

At the time, a campaign was being mounted to get a pier built at Glenbrook so that visitors would be encouraged to travel by steamer from nearby Cork. This was successful and the pier was scheduled to open in 1858.

Jones knew that the pier would help his business and, at the end of January 1858, the *Cork Examiner* reported that additional bedrooms, private rooms, breakfast rooms, and a large dining room were to be built. The report went on to say that before the start of the bathing season, 'Mr Jones is about adding to his establishment that imported luxury of which so much is spoken now-a-days, the Turkish Bath'.[12]

The opening of these new facilities some time in the middle of May was marked by a celebratory dinner on 9 June, at which the Mayor of Cork asked Barter, who was also present, to say a few words.

Barter was less than wholeheartedly enthusiastic about Jones's bath. 'It needed but the carrying out of a few alterations such as he could suggest', he said, 'to enable it to give much greater accommodation, and become much more profitable to the owner.'[13]

But with its 'stained dome lights, crimson hangings, a central fountain, richly tessellated floors and handsome couches', less knowledgeable critics merely noted that its decorative features maintained the high standard set by the marble fitments of the existing baths.[14]

According to an early advertisement, hotel guests were charged two guineas per week—the same as at the hydro. This included the use of the hot, vapour, plunge and shower baths, though the Turkish bath cost an additional 2s 6d per week. For day visitors, a Turkish bath cost 2s or, with a return ticket for rail and boat travel from Cork, 3s.[15]

Meanwhile, Dr Curtin somewhat belatedly recognised his missed opportunity to be first with a Turkish bath. Galvanised by the thought of the coming publicity about Jones's celebratory dinner, he determined on damage limitation. A second article duly appeared in the *Cork Examiner*, on the same page as the article describing Jones's opening, and only marginally shorter. This described the new Turkish bath being built at the hydro, which was 'very far advanced, and will in all probability be completed, and in working order, in about three weeks from this'.[16]

Such a completion date could never have been a real possibility, but the article was intended as what we should now call a spoiler, designed to diminish the impact of Jones's publicity.

In fact the hydro baths were built in stages, each area being opened as it was completed.[17] It was not until 11 months later, in May 1859, that the *Examiner* carried an advertisement indicating that Dr Curtin's hydropathic baths included 'an elegantly constructed Turkish Bath, now in constant use'.[18]

Curtin's baths, less flamboyant than the hotel's, comprised two hot rooms and two cooling-rooms, the larger of which was partitioned into areas suitable for 'cosy knots of three or four to ... chat without the presence of a crowd.' The smaller second one had none of the usual furniture or fitments, and was designed for 'temporary cooling ... either as a matter of pleasure, or through inability to bear the continuous heat.'

Each of the hot rooms was roughly 14ft (4.3m) square, surmounted by an octagonal dome about 9ft (2.7m) high. The heating apparatus, normally close to the hottest room in a Turkish bath, was here placed midway between the two rooms, a set of dampers being used to regulate the temperatures.

A fountain, surrounded by seating in the shape of an octagon, occupied the centre of the *tepidarium*, while around the walls were couches for those who preferred to recline. An adjoining douche room was fitted with showers at a variety of temperatures and pressures. Shampooing was undertaken on a slab in the centre of the *caldarium*.

The Turkish bath at the hydro was seen as one of a series of available therapies, whereas at the hotel it was more a luxury designed not only for resident guests, but also to attract Glenbrook's day visitors.

On 11 July 1859, a fire destroyed the hotel's north wing and Turkish bath, and Curtin had the field to himself.[19] This was a considerable setback for Jones because Glenbrook was then at the height of its popularity. It was a short-lived peak, lowered when nearby Crosshaven also built a steamer pier, and virtually flattened after 1862 when a new railway took trippers further afield.

It took Jones two years to rebuild the burnt part of the hotel, and the new Turkish baths were quite different from those at the hydro, and from those they replaced.

In 1861, local historian Charles Bernard Gibson wrote that, 'Viewed from the river, they remind the traveller of a Turkish temple on the Bosphorus.'[20] Hardly—though orientalism was still awaiting Edward Said for its modern interpretation. And if the Irish painter John E Bosanquet was no Ingres, he too seems guilty of a certain romanticism in his painting of the hotel (Figs 20.5 and 20.6).

But it was the bath itself which was completely different from the original one, its successor being built at the time of the controversy in the Irish press about whether the hot air in a Turkish bath should be dry or humid.

Though Barter's baths had been unaffected by the attack on them by Drs Madden and Corrigan, the lack of an easily understood outcome (see Chapter 6) would have been confusing to an entrepreneur such as Jones, who was without any medical training.

Being persuaded by the arguments of Barter's adversaries, and determined to have what he thought of as *genuine* Turkish bath, he introduced steam artificially into his hot room. By arranging a complicated series of dampers, taps, and flues running between an upper and a lower floor (for which he submitted a patent application[21]), he was able to deliver adjustable quantities of hot air at appropriate temperatures through one flue, and steam-heated vapour through the second.

So when the new bath opened in July 1861, it was advertised as 'THE ORIENTAL HAMAAM, OR REAL TURKISH BATH' which was, it claimed,

Fig 20.5 (top)
Glenbrook *by the Irish painter John E Bosanquet (fl.1854–71)*
Fig 20.6 (bottom)
Detail of Bosanquet's Glenbrook*, showing the artist's impression of the* Victoria Hotel and Baths. *(Crawford Art Gallery, Cork)*

'infinitely superior' to the 'Improved Turkish Bath'.[22]

In some ways the introduction of a steam flue was a precursor of the ubiquitous prefabricated steam room found in modern health clubs, but it was definitely not a Victorian Turkish bath and seems to have had a fairly short life.

Jones announced his retirement just over a year after the new bath opened, and put the hotel up for sale despite his investment in the new bath and the effort involved in his patent application.[23] Perhaps he foresaw the coming decline in the popularity of Glenbrook.

In November 1868, Barter wrote to the *Irish Times* rebutting an anonymous suggestion that Jones built the first Turkish bath in Ireland. Referring to the wet and dry air controversy Barter noted:

> Mr Jones's bath is long since closed, as are all the baths erected after his model, while the baths on my principles are extending rapidly over Western Europe and America.[24]

The Turkish bath at Dr Curtin's Hydropathic Establishment continued in typical low key manner and was well respected, according to Charles Bernard Gibson who noted that, 'Here we have the Turkish baths in perfection, and the hydropathic system, conducted with ability and professional skill, by the proprietor, T Curtin, Esq, MD' [25]

Curtin died in 1876 and, three years later, the *Irish Builder* reported that it was 'intended to erect sixteen blocks of first-class houses at Carrigmahon'.[26]

The design of Turkish baths in hydros

In his definitive work *The Turkish bath: its design and construction,*[27] Robert Owen Allsop included a plan of the baths at the Mont Dore Hotel, Bournemouth (Fig 20.7), suggesting that it might be a useful model for hydropathic establishments, and adding a few general principles to be followed in their design.

At Mont Dore, more space was allocated to specialised medical baths than Turkish baths, but the latter had been designed by Charles Bartholomew. They comprised the standard three hot rooms, a cooling-room, shampooing room and plunge bath all laid out logically and compactly, and Allsop thought well of them.

The following year saw the publication of his second book, *The Hydropathic establishment and its baths*. Although there is no separate chapter specifically dealing with Turkish baths, the author wisely preferring not to repeat the content of his earlier work, there is much information about the layout of bath departments and what facilities they should provide.

Plans show Turkish baths built in, or added to, six hydros between 1874 and 1889, including Smedley's (Fig 20.8) (1874), Dunblane (Fig 20.9) (1878), and Craiglockhart (Fig 20.10) (1880). They give us a good idea of what was considered essential by proprietors of commercial hydros needing to hold their own in the competition for clients, and to ensure that, having won them, they were well provided for.

Also included is Allsop's own plan of a model bath-house with separate sets of Turkish baths for men and women (Fig 20.11). In both books he argues strongly for separate baths, each with its own approach corridor and entrance, but initially all six hydros built a single set for use

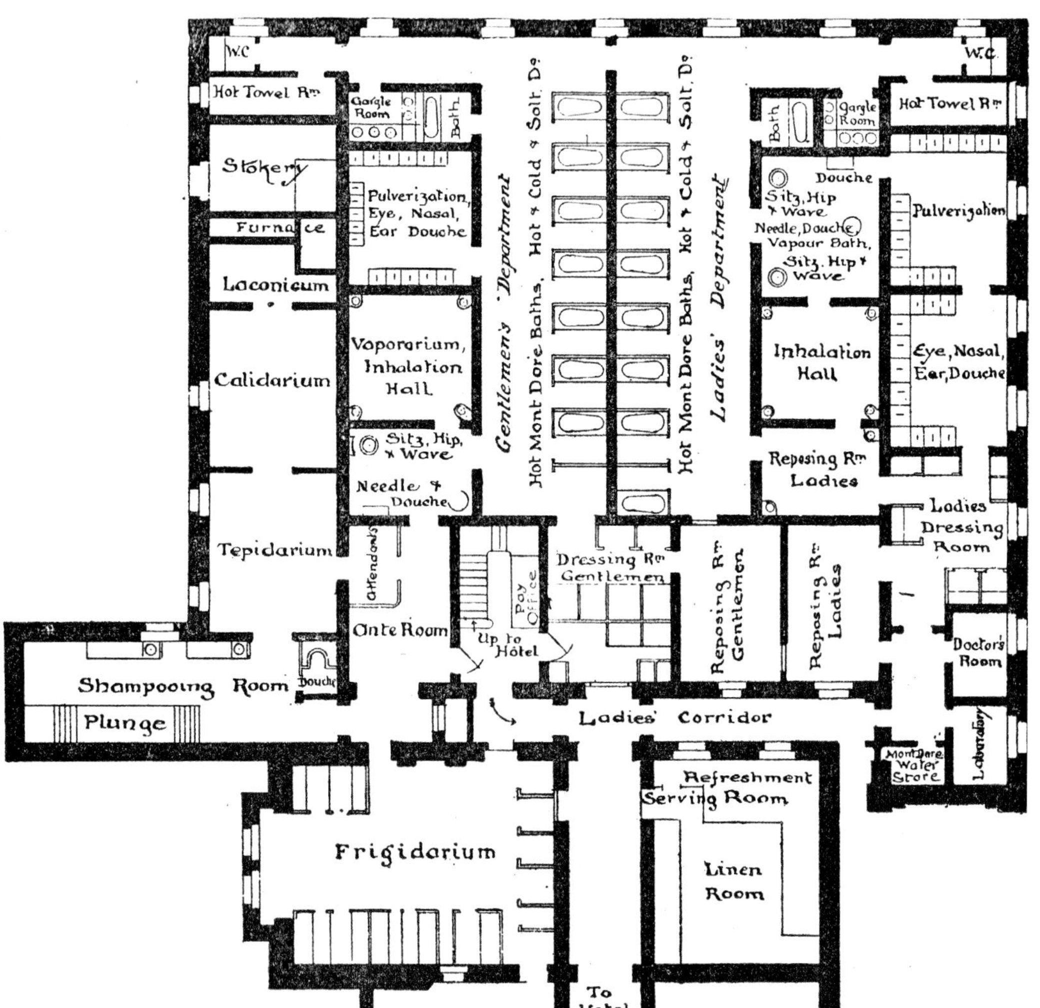

Fig 20.7
Plan of the baths at the Mont Dore Hotel, Bournemouth.
(Robert Owen Allsop, The Turkish bath, *Spon, 1890, p.135)*

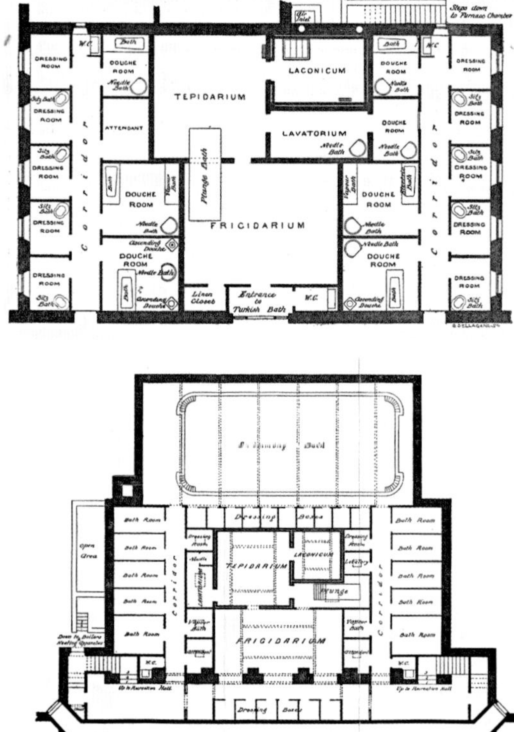

Figs 20.8–20.10 (clockwise) Plans of the baths at Smedley's Hydro, Matlock; Dunblane Hydro, Scotland; and Craiglockhart Hydro, Scotland.
(Robert Owen Allsop, The hydropathic establishment and its baths, *Spon, 1891, pp.32, 68, 54)*

by both sexes at different times. Only 21 years after it was originally built did Smedley's, able to accommodate 300 patients, build separate baths for women.

Allsop maintained that hotels differed from hydros because, for hotel visitors, taking a Turkish bath was one of several activities only available at specific times. But hydro patients often needed to use the baths more than once a day and were following a timetabled routine prescribed by their doctors. For this reason he argued that women were disadvantaged by not being able to use their baths whenever necessary.

Of course Allsop was advising on optimal provision, whereas the hydro proprietors were the ones who had to pay for expensively heating Turkish baths which may have had less frequent use. They also knew that although patients taking the various medicated baths, showers, massages, and treatments often required attendants on a one-to-one basis—and therefore by appointment—several patients could use the Turkish baths simultaneously and so timing was not critical.

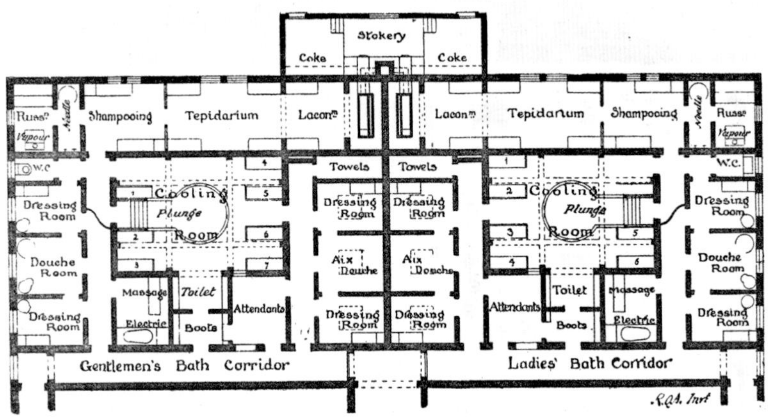

Fig 20.11 Plan of Turkish baths for men and women designed by Allsop.
(Author's collection)

Allsop countered this by noting that the rooms in their Turkish baths were often too large, and that two smaller sets would be more useful and no more expensive. Strangely, he never suggested insulation as a means of cutting costs, even though the architect-designed Turkish baths at Lochhead Hydro utilised cavity walls as early as 1861.

He was critical of the majority of British hydro facilities:

> Frequently one may hear expressions of disapproval from visitors, more particularly from ladies, who are not disposed to put up with the rough-and-ready accommodation that suffices for men. The bath-rooms are commonly dull and dismal, and the dressing-rooms, or *boxes*—for rarely do we meet with decent *rooms*—are cramped and uncomfortable.[28]

Their facilities even compared unfavourably with those in some public baths, and 'cramping and cutting-down of bathing accommodation', he continued, 'is false economy in the hydropathic establishment.'

All six of the establishments discussed by Allsop had three hot rooms and a cooling-room. In addition, four had plunge pools, three had a shampooing room, four had needle showers, and three had Russian steam baths, though at

Craiglockhart these were not directly accessible from the Turkish baths.

Craiglockhart incidentally, though long closed, remains of interest because of its association with the poets Wilfred Owen and Siegfried Sassoon who stayed there when it was used as a military hospital between 1916 and 1919.[29]

Scattered around the British Isles were many smaller hydropathic establishments with Turkish baths. However, there is little new to be learned about the Victorian Turkish bath from them, even though some, like the long-forgotten Harrogate Hydropathic, achieved a modicum of fame after a film, *Agatha,* reclaimed it as the hydro at which Agatha Christie stayed when she left her husband and disappeared for 10 days.

Less well remembered is the hydro at Blackpool, which on 21 May 1881 unexpectedly welcomed a group of visitors not foreseen by those who planned it. Some time in the afternoon, a small boat, the *Margaret Jane*, with a four-man crew and a load of paving stones, on its way from Ireland to Liverpool, capsized within 90ft (27m) of the beach at North Shore:

> A number of those who had been watching the progress of the little craft immediately went into the water with ropes round their waists in order to secure the bodies of the men as they were thrown up by the terribly rough sea which was then raging. Two of the number were brought out insensible, and their lives for a long time hung in the balance. They were immediately taken up to the Imperial Hydropathic Establishment, where they were placed in the Turkish baths and, happily, by the untiring exertions of Dr Wartenberg, the physician to the establishment, and other local doctors, respiration was restored, and the men brought well on their way to recovery.[30]

Turkish baths in hotels

As in Glenbrook, many small hotels—like the §Charlemont Arms in Armagh, Philp's Cockburn Hotel in Glasgow, and the Granville in Ramsgate—added Turkish baths to attract customers away from nearby competitors.

But those at the Granville are worthy of note for being designed, like the hotel itself, by Edward Welby Pugin (1834–75), architect son of the more famous Augustus Pugin. At 5s a time they were expensive, but they were elaborate—their floors and walls were faced with Minton's encaustic tiles—and they were efficiently run.[31] Edward Pugin was a bather himself and later designed the Grosvenor Turkish Baths in Buckingham Palace Road.

Turkish baths were also a feature of some of the larger city hotels. Charles Trubshaw (1841–1917) included them in the Midland Hotel, Manchester (1903), and Robert Frank Atkinson (1869–1923) in the Adelphi Hotel, Liverpool (1912), both built for the Midland Railway Company, and both now Grade II Listed, although their baths were long ago replaced by health spas.

The eminent Victorian architect Alfred Waterhouse (1830–1905) designed Turkish baths as part of the Metropole Hotel (1890) in Brighton (Fig 20.12). There was already a large establishment, the Brighton Hammam, in West Street, but this was now nearly 30 years old and though still 'comfortable and commodious', according to a local guide,[32] by 1895 it was 'perhaps not so luxurious or so well patronized as the Turkish Bath in connection with the Hotel Metropole.' The Hammam staggered on till 1910, whereas the Metropole baths continued until at least the 1960s.

But the most impressive hotel Turkish baths were undoubtedly those at London's Imperial Hotel in Russell Square.

Fig 20.12
Vignette of the cooling-room at the Hotel Metropole, Brighton.
(Illustrated London News, *26 July 1890, p.116. Author's collection)*

The Imperial Turkish baths (1913–1966)

The long demolished Imperial Hotel was once described as 'a fantastic dream, unbelievable to those who never saw its green copper pinnacles over the rooftops of Georgian Bloomsbury, its gargoyles sneering at modern progress.'[33] It was designed by Charles Fitzroy Doll (1851–1929) and built in two stages, the first being completed in 1907.

Its proprietor, Harold Walduck, also owned two other Bloomsbury hotels, The Bedford and The Premier. In April 1911, The Imperial London Hotels Ltd was set up to purchase all three, and to finance the building of a large extension to the Imperial (Fig 20.13). Apart from Walduck and the three other directors, many key members of staff were shareholders, some holding as many as 500 £1 shares.[34]

Fig 20.13
The postcard shows the exterior of the Imperial Hotel, London, before the extension was built. (Author's collection)

The following month the company set about raising £200,000 with an issue of five per cent debenture stock. The first £100,000 raised was to be spent on the extension which, in addition to a number of public rooms and 384 new bedrooms, would include—and here the abridged prospectus launched into capital letters, 'A PALATIAL TURKISH BATH, WHICH IT IS INTENDED SHALL BE THE LARGEST AND MOST LUXURIOUS IN LONDON'.[35]

There is a certain irony here, in that Walduck saw the personal cleanliness of his guests (and convenient access to their washing facilities) as being less important than providing Turkish baths as an optional desirable luxury. For the original building had only one bathroom for every 7 of its 300 bedrooms, although the Savoy Hotel (built nearly 20 years earlier) already had a ratio of 1:1. Yet the proportion of baths to beds in the extension remained frugally the same as in the original building.

The Turkish baths were located in the basement and sub-basement beneath the hotel dining room. Doll's 1911 plans[36] show that the baths (Fig 20.14) could be reached directly from the street through a small lobby, or from the hotel through the bar and down the stairs. Shoes and any outdoor clothing were deposited in a cloakroom just outside the main entrance. A passage immediately ahead led to a hairdresser and five private bathrooms, while on the left was the inner hall at the side of, and leading into, the main open area of the baths.

This was a long 'great hall' (Fig 20.15) best described as 'a nave of nine bays formed by octagonal piers.'[37] Towards the top of these were terracotta figures in elaborate niches, a few of which have been placed in the courtyard of the current hotel (Fig 20.16).

On either long side of the 'nave' were aisles—and above them galleries (Fig 20.17)—mostly divided into rest areas furnished with beds surrounded by red curtains. At either end of the hall was a 'mean staircase' starting as a single flight, and dividing into two, each at right angles to the first, and leading up to one of the galleries. Painted coats of arms decorated the Jacobean style ceiling (Fig 20.18), from which were suspended rotating fans, and the hall was lit by 'spiky' lights from the Connaught Rooms whose then proprietor, (Sir) George Harvey, was now a director of the Imperial.

Halfway between the two aisles was a decorative fountain and, two-thirds of the way along

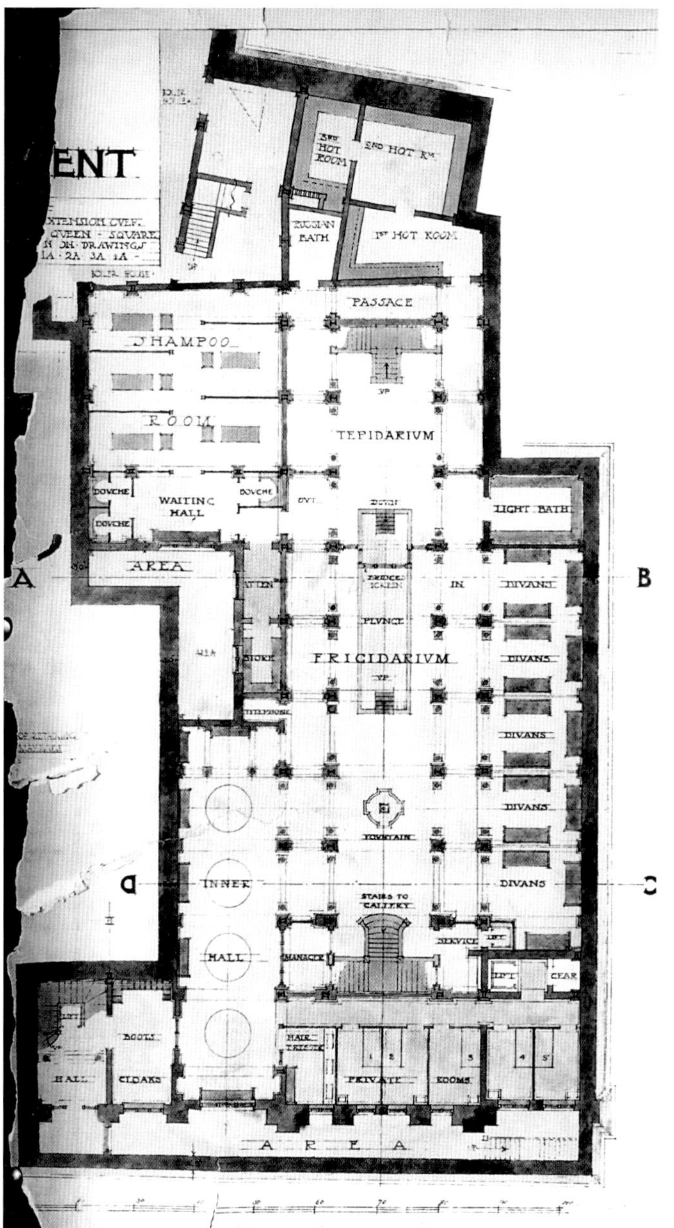

Fig 20.14 (left)
Fitzroy Doll's 1911 plan of the main floor of the Imperial Turkish Baths, located mainly in the hotel's sub-basement.
(RIBA Library Drawings & Archives Collections, PA67/1 23)

Fig 20.15 (above)
The Long Hall (frigidarium) *of the Imperial Turkish Baths.*
(Author's collection)

the hall, 'like a Black Mass chancel screen, a wall of wandering stained glass reptiles lit up from within'[38] divided the first part of the room, the *frigidarium,* from the *tepidarium* beyond. In the centre of the room, continuing under the screen, was a plunge pool allowing swimmers to pass beneath it from one area to the other, while in the aisles non-swimmers made do with rather more prosaic doors. The sofas on the dry side gave way to deck chairs of canvas and wood on the wet side.

To the right of the *tepidarium* was an electric light bath, and to the left, through the waiting room with its three needle showers, the shampooing room with five marble slabs and basins,

Fig 20.16
One of the terracotta figures from the baths, currently mounted outside the modern hotel.
(© Malcolm Shifrin)

and five masseurs pummelling and soaping their docile clients.

• THE REST ROOMS RUSSELL SQ TURKISH BATH •
©Mike Young 2000

Finally, at the far end of the hall, behind the staircase, was a small Russian bath and three hot rooms. Their walls were faced with tiles of elaborate Moorish design, their mosaic floors almost completely covered with thick red Turkish carpets, and their white marble seats furnished with white canvas slab cushions and canvas hanging backs, to protect bathers from being burned.[39]

An early 1913 poster (Fig 20.19) indicates that the baths were open to women as well as men, though since there are no separate women's baths shown on the original plans it must be assumed that these baths were reserved for women at set times.

However, it must soon have become apparent that the number of women bathers was not great enough to outweigh the financial loss arising from their being closed to a greater number of men. Less than a year after the baths opened it was decided to build a separate set of women's baths at 20 Queen Square, a property adjoining the back of the hotel and already owned by it. This would give women the opportunity to enter directly through their own entrance, while still being able to gain access from the hotel if preferred.

It is not possible to describe the layout of the women's baths in any detail, because the two surviving plans show only their position and general outline.[40] But the main entrance,

Fig 20.17 (above)
Part of the Long Hall in the 1960s, remembered by Mike Young nearly 40 years later. (Illustration © Mike Young, 2000, reproduced by kind permission of the artist)

Fig 20.18
The ceiling and lights. (Historic England Archive bb66_03074)

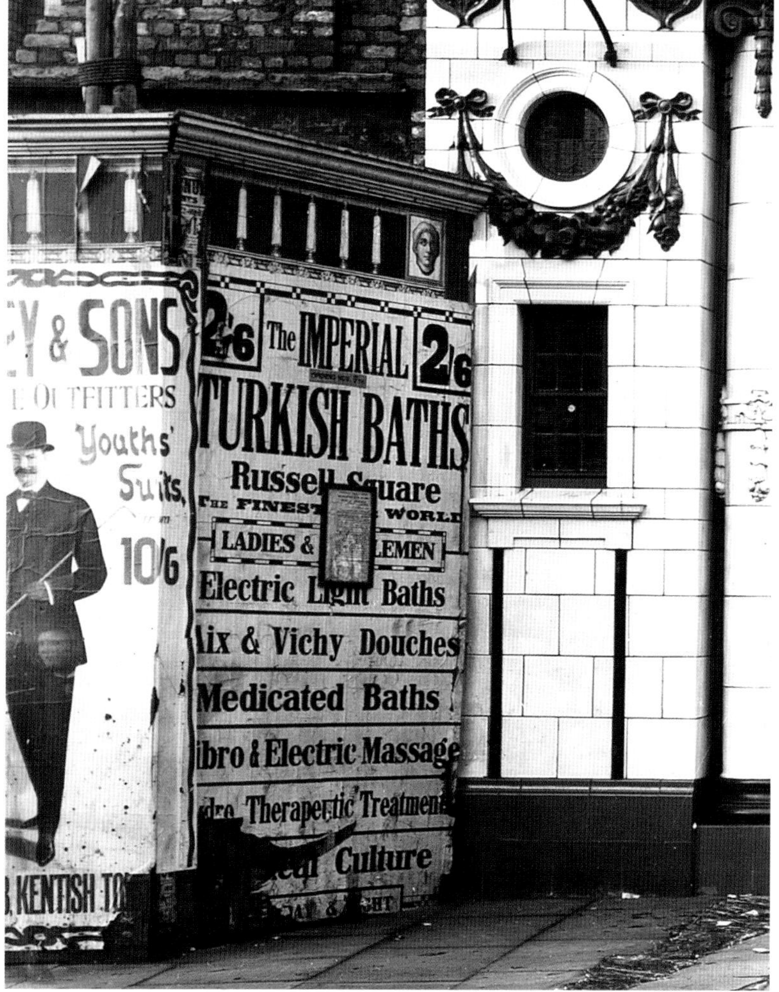

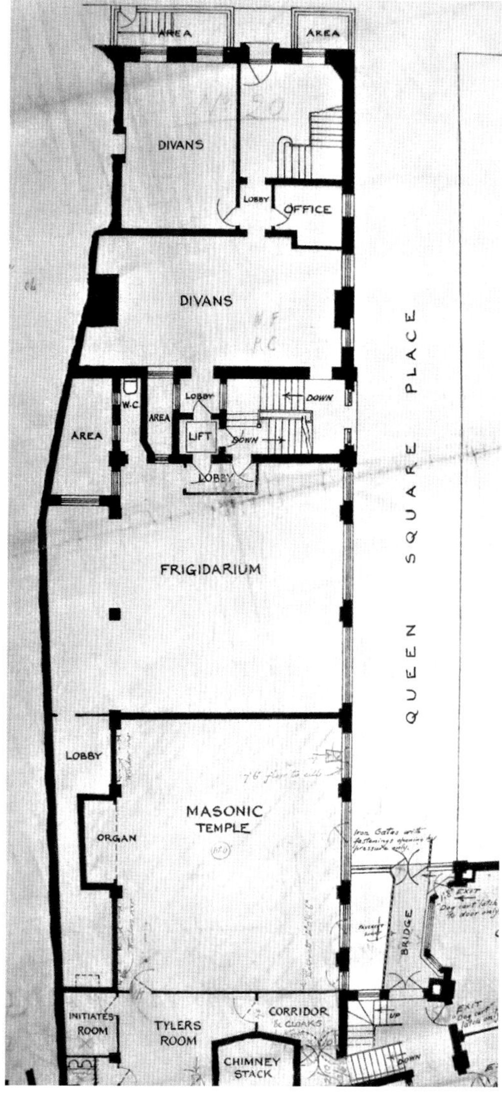

changing area, and *frigidarium* (Fig 20.20) are known to have been on the ground floor, with the remaining rooms located in the basement.

Price lists (Fig 20.21) from the 1920s and 1950s show that a full range of facilities and treatments was available to women, even though their baths were much smaller. And it is possible to fill in some details from Wendy Stacey's description of visits made in the late 1950s and early 1960s. There are so few accounts by women describing their use of Turkish baths that it is worth quoting her joyful account at length:

> As I remember it, to get into the Turkish Baths, we entered the Imperial Hotel by its main entrance on Russell Square. I remember my friend and I climbing the red-carpeted stone steps to the massive front door and being amazed by the mahogany and brass splendour inside. It was like stepping back several generations, even in the 1950s.
>
> I think we travelled down to the basement by lift to reach the Bath but first we were weighed and given red and white checked cotton rectangles in which to wrap ourselves after undressing. Once in the vast chamber we were invited to take as much time as we wished steaming and cooking before presenting ourselves to the masseuses for a scrub and a splash in the plunge pool. There were two dry-heat rooms, one hotter than the other, and a steam room with stepped platforms to sit on—a great place for a gossip. Looking back I seem to see a stone pool and fountain ... The scrub was wonderful and the cold plunge a shock to the system.
>
> Afterwards we were weighed again and tucked up in bed in adjoining curtained cubicles—I remember crisp white sheets and a soft blanket—and served with tea and biscuits on a tray. We were told we should rest and recover strength before setting out again into the November night

Fig 20.19 (above left)
Poster advertising the baths, targeting a cinema audience in Kentish Town.
(Historic England Archive BL22454)

Fig 20.20 (above)
General outline plan of the women's Turkish baths at the Imperial Hotel.
(Photograph of a detail from a plan of Doll's Imperial Hotel at the London Metropolitan Archives. City of London. Photograph © Malcolm Shifrin)

Ladies Turkish Bath Prices.

	£	s.	d.
Turkish and Russian, including shampoo-massage, shower and plunge		8	6
Special Treatments			
Belt Massage		5	0
Hand Massage (20 mins.)		7	6
Foam and Zotofoam Baths		12	6
Sulphur and Brine Baths		12	6
Pine Needle or Seaweed Baths		12	6
Radiant Heat Bath including Massage		15	6
Colonic Lavage	1	1	0
~~Vichy Douche~~	~~1~~	~~1~~	~~0~~
Electrical Treatments			
Short Wave Therapy		12	6
Ultra Violet Ray		7	6
Ultra Violet Ray (face only)		5	0
Infra Red		5	0
Infra Red, with Massage		15	0
Wax Baths		15	0

CHIROPODY 9.30 a.m. to 6. p.m
(by appointment)

Refreshments may be obtained from attendants in Red Room.

Hairdressing and Beauty Culture.

	£.	s.	d
Cut to Style		7	6
Trim .... from		2	6
Cream Shampoo and Set		8	6
Henna or Cammomile Shampoo & Set		8	0
Egg Shampoo and Set		10	0
Set Only		5	6
Frictions by Coty		2	6
Special Rinses, from		1	6
Bleach Retouch Shampoo and Set		15	6
Bleach first time Shampoo and Set	1	12	6
Henna application Shampoo and Set from	1	1	0
Tinting Retouch " " "	1	5	0
Tinting, first time " " "	2	2	0
Jamal Permanent Waving, whole head	3	3	0
Jamal Permanent Waving, ends only	2	12	6
Wax Depilatory Treatment from		5	6
Facial with Make up		12	6
Manicure with Revlon		5	0
Eyebrow Shaping		2	6

Fig 20.21
Price list for services available at the women's Turkish baths. (Author's collection)

but we certainly didn't feel fragile and spent our rest time chatting.

I've been trying to recall how much it all cost but can't be sure. A price of ten shillings comes into my head but surely it must have been more than that! [41]

The price of a Turkish bath at the hotel in the late 1940s and early 1950s was 8s 6d and it may be that the tea and biscuits topped it up to 10s. The women's baths remained open until around 1962.[42]

The other major alteration to the baths came with the early realisation that the Russian bath—which was smaller than the hottest of the hot rooms—was totally inadequate. A plan dated 15 February 1915 (Fig 20.22) shows that a completely new Russian bath was built directly over the existing hot rooms

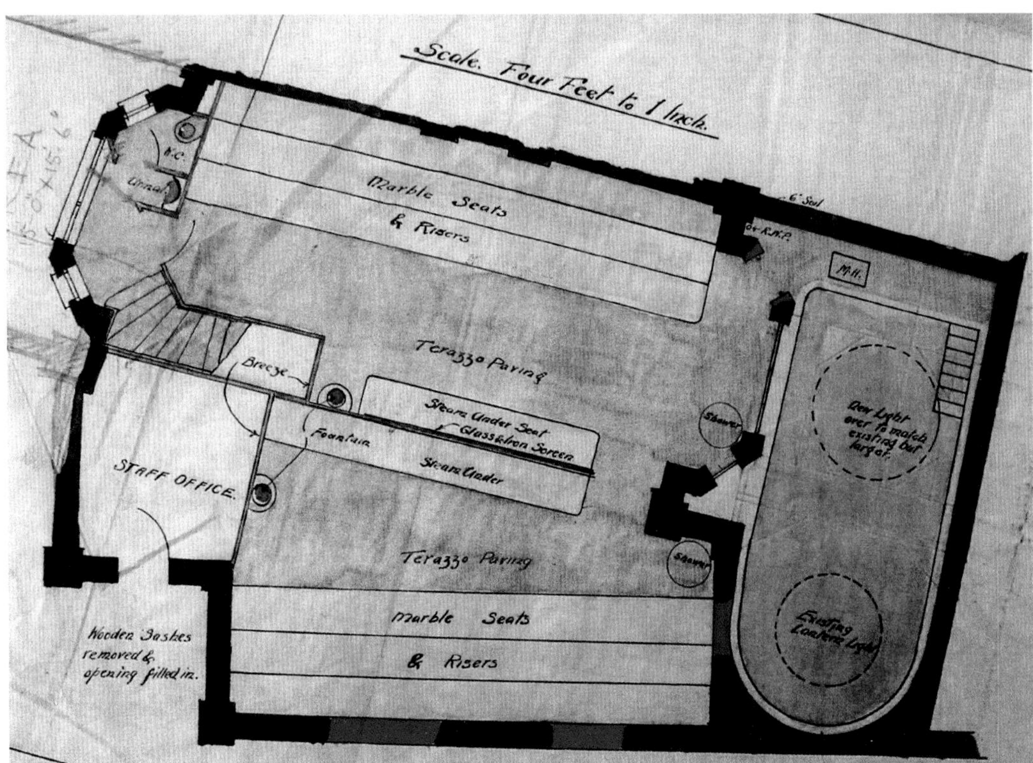

Fig 20.22
Plan of the Russian bath and its possible future extension. (Photograph of a detail from a plan of Doll's Imperial Hotel at the London Metropolitan Archives. City of London. Photograph © Malcolm Shifrin)

but occupying a larger area.[43] The door to the original bath became an arched opening into a passageway which led to 'a dimly lit staircase, which curved upwards to a steam room.'

The room was nearly 30ft (9m) long with three wide marble steps running down the left-hand side, each step wide enough to lie on. At the far end, to the left of a shower, a canvas-covered archway led to a cold plunge pool (Fig 20.23), 'the dimly lit water' stretching 20ft (6m) down to a 'dark domed circular chamber.'[44]

The architect's plan shows that provision had been made for almost doubling the capacity of the steam room, by placing a second tier of seats along the angular wall at the other end of the pool, but this was never done.

To some people these baths were almost a second home (Fig 20.24). Here, for less than the cost of bed and breakfast, one could stay the night. Chaim Bermant, normally a bather at Glasgow's Govanhill baths, stayed overnight at the Imperial Baths when in London:

> One night it was overrun with bishops. It must have coincided with some Church assembly, or perhaps it was Boat Race night, but it was full of Church dignitaries. I found them an impressive body of men.
>
> Turkish baths are great levellers, and it takes something to look a bishop without staff or mitre and, indeed, without any clothes on at all.[45]

The Imperial Turkish Baths have been described so fully because, after the Jermyn Street Hammam, they were the most important and imposing baths to be built in the capital. No one who has used them can ever forget them—or forgive the cultural barbarism of allowing them to be demolished.

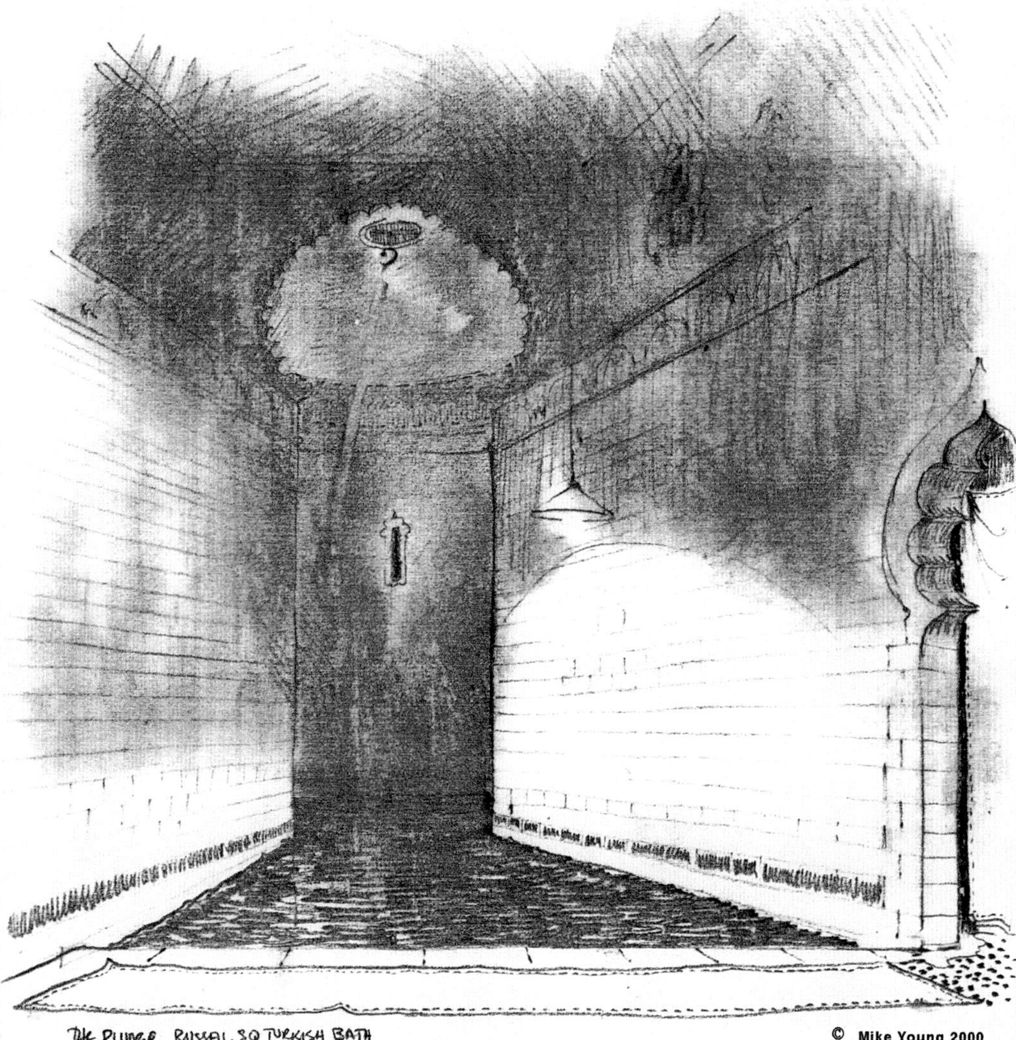

THE PLUNGE RUSSELL SQ TURKISH BATH
© Mike Young 2000

Fig 20.23
Mike Young's remembrance of the Russian bath's own plunge pool.
(Illustration © Mike Young, 2000, reproduced by kind permission of the artist)

Fig 20.24 (overleaf)
Front cover of a folded four-page leaflet detailing hours and charges.
Bodleian Library, University of Oxford, John Johnson Collection: Trade Cards 2 106)

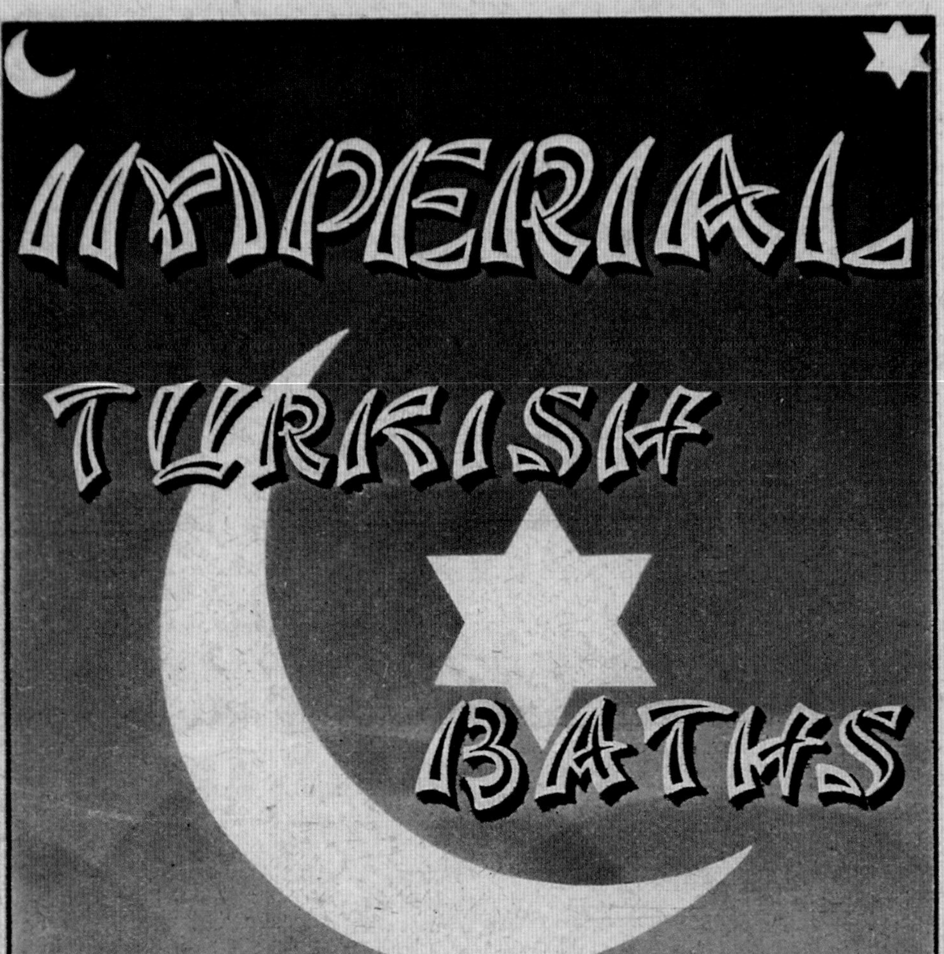

RUSSELL SQUARE
LONDON - W-C-1
TEL-TERMINUS 3655
LADIES - EXTN 102
GENTLEMENS " 103

21

Turkish baths for 'Members only' clubs

There do not appear to have been any private members' clubs set up solely to provide Turkish baths for their members. Those clubs which did provide them can be divided into two types, each with slightly different aims, according to whether they were in England or Scotland.

English clubs such as Prince's Racquets and Tennis Club were essentially sporting clubs where Turkish baths were just one of many services available to their members.

However, the Scottish clubs were established as limited liability companies specifically to finance the building of swimming pools for their members. Five of these were in Glasgow—two of them opening in 1878 before the city's first municipal pool—and two were in Edinburgh.

Even after other public baths opened in Scotland, the clubs were seen as catering for professional and business people who enjoyed swimming and Turkish baths but who didn't wish to use the 'invariably dirty' public pools where 'the spittoons were never clean' and their changing rooms overcrowded.[1]

By contrast, club pools were quieter and they all included, or later added, facilities such as Turkish baths, recreation areas, and reading rooms.

London's Bath Club in Dover Street, founded in 1894, was open to both sexes; none of the other English clubs initially allowed women members.[2]

Prince's Racquets and Tennis Club, London

Although the Prince of Wales was a member of this exclusive sporting club, it was actually named after its founders, George and James Prince, who opened it some time in the 1850s. Its original premises, next to Hans Place in Knightsbridge, included racquets and tennis courts, and a cricket pitch which was, for a time, the home of the MCC (Marylebone Cricket Club).

The Prince brothers were interested in racing and it seems likely that it was through Admiral Rous, who advocated the use of Turkish baths in the training of racehorses (see Chapter 25, page 270), that they decided to build a 'handsome and commodious' Turkish bath at their club.[3] Nothing more is known about this bath, except that Thomas Gibson Bowles, who later became a director of the London Hammam, was a club member and probably bathed there.

More is known about their second bath. The club had closed in 1885 on the expiry of its lease, but was reconstituted the following year when it moved into Humphrey's Hall, opposite Hyde Park Barracks. The Hall was converted into a clubhouse and sports centre by Peto Brothers, to the design of architect Edward Herbert Bourchier (*fl* 1881–1926), and opened by the Prince of Wales on 18 May 1889.

The 'elegantly constructed' Turkish bath was decorated by the Sicilian artist Emilio Marolda and a team of Italian artists. There was also a Russian vapour bath, sitz bath, needle shower, and hot and cold water baths. The plunge pool was lined with blue mosaic finished with a brass capping, and—for use by the Prince of Wales—there was a private bath constructed 'entirely of marble'. The fittings were supplied by John Smeaton, Son, & Co who specialised in furnishing the better class Turkish baths of the day (Fig 21.1).[4]

Prince's Club survived until just before World War II, when its building was requisitioned for the war effort. It was later demolished.

The Royal Automobile Club, London

In July 1911, thirteen years after its formation, the Royal Automobile Club (originally just The

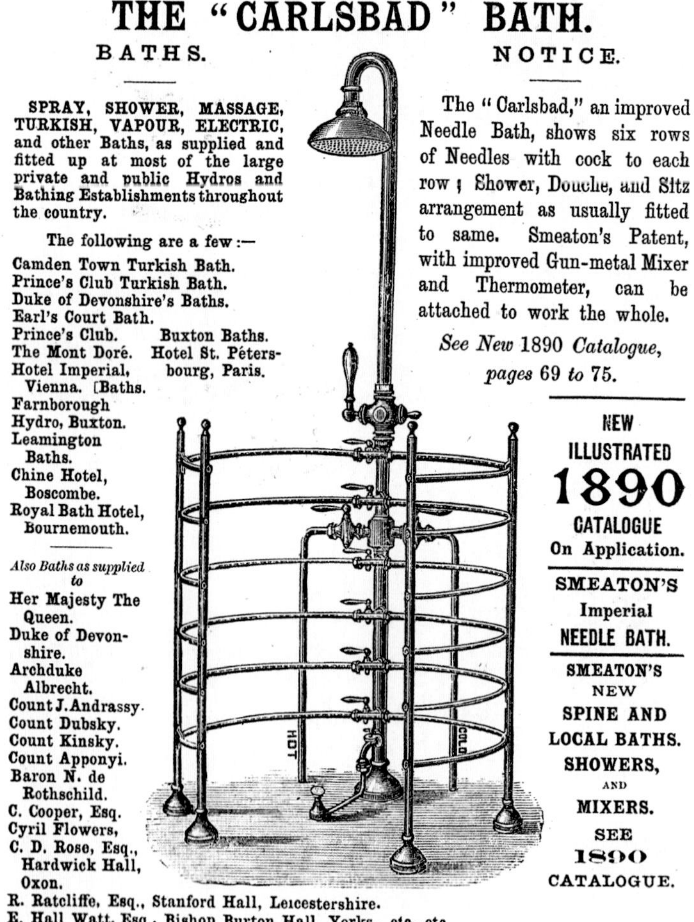

John Smeaton, Son, & Co.,
HEATING, SANITARY, DRAINAGE, AND VENTILATING ENGINEERS,
TURKISH BATH SPECIALISTS,
56, GREAT QUEEN STREET, LINCOLN'S INN FIELDS, LONDON, W.C.
THE "CARLSBAD" BATH.
BATHS.
SPRAY, SHOWER, MASSAGE, TURKISH, VAPOUR, ELECTRIC, and other Baths, as supplied and fitted up at most of the large private and public Hydros and Bathing Establishments throughout the country.
The following are a few:—
Camden Town Turkish Bath.
Prince's Club Turkish Bath.
Duke of Devonshire's Baths.
Earl's Court Bath.
Prince's Club.
The Mont Doré.
Hotel Imperial, Vienna.
Buxton Baths.
Hotel St. Pétersbourg, Paris.
Farnborough Baths.
Hydro, Buxton.
Leamington Baths.
Chine Hotel, Boscombe.
Royal Bath Hotel, Bournemouth.
Also Baths as supplied to
Her Majesty The Queen.
Duke of Devonshire.
Archduke Albrecht.
Count J. Andrassy.
Count Dubsky.
Count Kinsky.
Count Apponyi.
Baron N. de Rothschild.
C. Cooper, Esq.
Cyril Flowers,
C. D. Rose, Esq., Hardwick Hall, Oxon.
R. Ratcliffe, Esq., Stanford Hall, Leicestershire.
E. Hall Watt, Esq., Bishop Burton Hall, Yorks., etc., etc.
NOTICE.
The "Carlsbad," an improved Needle Bath, shows six rows of Needles with cock to each row; Shower, Douche, and Sitz arrangement as usually fitted to same. Smeaton's Patent, with improved Gun-metal Mixer and Thermometer, can be attached to work the whole.
See New 1890 Catalogue, pages 69 to 75.
NEW ILLUSTRATED 1890 CATALOGUE On Application.
SMEATON'S Imperial NEEDLE BATH.
SMEATON'S NEW SPINE AND LOCAL BATHS. SHOWERS, AND MIXERS. SEE 1890 CATALOGUE.
HOT
COLD
PLANS and DRAWINGS on application. ESTIMATES FREE.
SEE OTHER ADVERTISEMENT.

Fig 21.1
Advertisement for one of the needle showers popular with Turkish bath planners. (Robert Owen Allsop, The Turkish bath*, Spon, 1890)*

Automobile Club), moved from Piccadilly to Pall Mall, where its new clubhouse, the largest in London's clubland, had just been completed.

When it opened, a perceptive correspondent in *The Times*, who could not, of course, have known that around 90 years later, each of the club's 12,000 members would receive a £34,000 share of the proceeds from the sale of its motoring services section, wrote:

> It is to be hoped that the RAC will not forget amidst its splendours that it is essentially an organization to protect automobilists and encourage motoring in all forms. There is always the danger of the Club's losing its moral, though not its legal, hold upon the movement it was founded to support; and marble halls must not be allowed to displace altogether the study of mechanical traffic.[5]

Attitudes change over time, and a fierce controversy erupted at the end of the 1990s, when there was a move to redevelop the club's unique Edwardian Turkish bath.

The building was designed in the Beaux-Arts tradition by the Anglo-French partnership of Charles Mewès (1858–1914) and the Englishman, Arthur Joseph Davis (1878–1951)—whose hotel, The Ritz, had opened in nearby Piccadilly five years earlier. There was also some design input from E Keynes Purchase, an architect member of the club's committee.

Looking at the building as it was when first opened, the top four floors housed accommodation for members and staff; below these, on the first floor, was the members' dining room, committee room, associates' room, billiard room and library, and below this, the restaurant and reception rooms on the ground floor. All the sporting facilities were in the basement. These included a gymnasium, three racquets courts, an extravagantly designed swimming pool decorated in Pompeian style,[6] and the Turkish baths suite.

The entrance to the baths (Fig 21.2) is down a wide passageway leading from the main vestibule into the large irregularly shaped spacious *frigidarium* (Fig 21.3). Its marble-clad walls, its squat fluted Doric columns, and its two large semi-circular alcoves (Fig 21.4), give the room a vaguely Grecian appearance, encouraged by the design of its furniture, especially some of its chairs (Fig 21.5).[7] Curtained changing cubicles, with couches for relaxation, originally lined the long sides of the room. If the total effect does not quite work, it has to be said that Edwardian bathers would have found it very comfortable, and compared with most baths of the period, it was clean and luxurious.

Even looked at from an early 20th-century perspective, it is surprising to find that the only way from the *frigidarium* to the *tepidarium* (Fig 21.6) is through the alcove set aside for smokers—though state-of-the art air-conditioning throughout the building may have helped relieve any discomfort felt by non-smokers. A three-panel glass screen at the far end of the *tepidarium* originally allowed bathers to observe fellow members in the main swimming pool.[8]

From the *tepidarium*, bathers could progress either to the *caldarium* and *laconicum*

Fig 21.2 (far left)
Entrance to the Turkish bath at the members-only Royal Automobile Club, Pall Mall. (© Malcolm Shifrin)

Fig 21.3 (near left)
The frigidarium *shortly after the club opened in 1911. (The Royal Automobile Club, Pall Mall, London, SW1Y 5HS)*

Fig 21.4 (below)
The frigidarium *in 2001 before refurbishment. (© Malcolm Shifrin)*

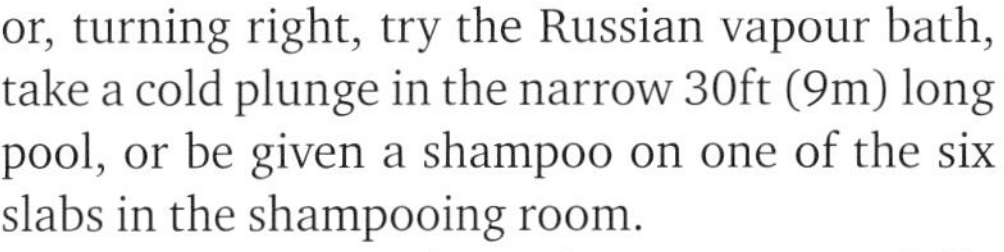

or, turning right, try the Russian vapour bath, take a cold plunge in the narrow 30ft (9m) long pool, or be given a shampoo on one of the six slabs in the shampooing room.

Temperatures and ventilation were carefully controlled (Table 21.1). The rooms were heated by passing clean filtered air over high pressure steam tubes, raising it to the required temperature. The usual method, where the hot air then passed through each room in turn, cooling on its way, was considered objectionable. Here, each room had its own fresh-air inlet near the ceiling (Fig 21.7), and an extraction grating on the opposite wall near the floor.[9]

Towards the end of the 1914–18 war, the club was requisitioned to provide workspace for government office workers involved in the war effort. Patriotic though the club's members were, it was difficult for them to have to surrender their expensive new building so soon after it opened.

The club fought a rearguard action, pointing out that at the beginning of the war it had offered honorary membership to all overseas

Table 21.1 Ventilation and temperatures

	Number of air changes per hour	*Max. temperature (°F)*
Laconicum	6	260 (127°C)
Caldarium	4	180 (82°C)
Tepidarium	6	120 (49°C)
Frigidarium	4	75 (24°C)
Shampooing room	4	75 (24°C)
Plunge pool room	2	75 (24°C)
Russian bath	1	n/a

Fig 21.5 (above)
Distinctive chairs in the frigidarium *in 2001. (© Malcolm Shifrin)*

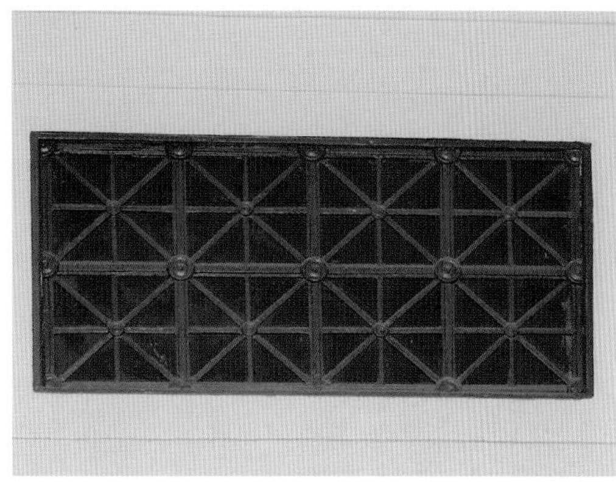

Fig 21.6 (near right)
The tepidarium *shortly after the club opened.*
(The Royal Automobile Club, Pall Mall, London, SW1Y 5HS)
Fig 21.7 (far right)
One of the warm air inlets in the frigidarium.
(© Malcolm Shifrin)

officers. This had been widely taken up, and it was argued that requisitioning the club would 'seriously dislocate a large amount of business of national importance.'

Notwithstanding, the order stood, although after hearing that the Turkish bath was chiefly used by officers, Sir Alfred Mondsaid agreed that,

> 'if the space taken up by the bath could not be utilized for office work, he would be prepared to consider whether the bath could not be reserved for the use of officers home on short leave.'[10]

In addition to contributing its considerable motoring expertise to the war effort, the club organised dances and concerts for the overseas officers, and served over 1,380,000 meals. The Turkish baths remained open day and night and over 74,000 baths were taken, officers knowing that 'when they could not find a bed anywhere, they could always come to the Turkish bath at the Club.'[11]

At the end of the 1990s, the Royal Automobile Club—now totally divorced from RAC Motoring Services and, of course, open only to its own members—undertook a major refurbishment of its building. In the basement, the gymnasium and the women's changing room (the latter originally designed for members' guests) both needed enlarging, in part because membership was now open to women in their own right.

At one stage there was a suggestion that a large corridor should, in effect, cut the Turkish bath in two and a number of normally staid members went public with their protests, to the vicarious enjoyment of the readers of London's popular press.

Happily, wiser counsel prevailed when the chief engineer suggested that additional space could be provided by removing a boiler room and internal chimney stack, made redundant by modern heating methods.

As a result, the baths have been most sensitively refurbished and, with one or two exceptions, look little different from how they appeared when first opened. Behind the scenes, though, changes have been far-reaching, with pool equipment, drainage, and heating systems all utilising modern technology.

More visibly changed is the plunge pool (Fig 21.8) with its modern sauna and adjacent shower. In the *frigidarium*, three walls are now lined with relaxation cubicles instead of the original two, and much of the earlier furniture and fittings survive. The smoking area in the *tepidarium* (Fig 21.9) has, of course, disappeared and the once transparent panels at the near end of the room are now of frosted glass, so there is no longer a view over the swimming pool.

Temperatures in Turkish baths today are generally cooler that those aimed for in Victorian times. Here the original *laconicum* temperature of 260°F (127°C) has been reduced, according to its literature, to a maximum of 145°F (63°C).

The other major difference between 1911 and 2014, is that instead of the Turkish baths

Fig 21.8
The cold plunge pool after refurbishment.
(© Malcolm Shifrin)

Fig 21.9
Part of the refurbished tepidarium*—without the smoking area.*
(© Malcolm Shifrin)

being a male-only preserve, men and women each have one day in the week for single-sex bathing. The other days are mixed sessions and, in a welcome following of continental practice, costumes are optional, except in the *frigidarium*, where they are mandatory.

The Scottish baths clubs

Seven Scottish clubs were founded between 1870 and 1886 (Table 21.2).

Considering the facilities they wished to provide, all were under-capitalised. Each was beset at some time by financial problems. But what is remarkable is that four of these clubs are still open, even if only two retain their Turkish baths.

Although the Warrender Club closed after barely 19 years, their baths were bought by Edinburgh Corporation, which refurbished them and added a Russian steam bath. They were re-opened as public baths on 27 December 1907[12] and, some time around 1915, the corporation advertised for tenders to construct a plunge pool.[13] The Turkish baths remained open until at least 1929 when, on the evening of 8 October, 'a sudden failure of the electric light' left bathers in the dark.[14]

Two of the other clubs, the Arlington and the Western, seriously considered merging in 1972, though this never came to fruition.[15]

The Dennistoun Club remained open for almost a century, yet very little is known about it, except that the Turkish baths had a plunge pool, and that the building is still in existence, though now used for other purposes.

The Arlington Baths Club, Glasgow

There were earlier swimming clubs in Britain, but the Arlington was the first in Scotland specifically set up to build a pool and clubhouse for its members, claiming that it was 'the first club of its kind in the Kingdom.' Its stylish single-storey building, designed by architect John Burnet (1814–1901) and opened in 1871, housed a swimming pool, slipper baths, and a small reading room. However,

> the want of a Turkish Bath was soon felt, and one of a very primitive character was arranged for in the basement, which did duty for some time and was largely taken advantage of.[16]

This was so successful that in 1875 the club opened the first of its four extensions to the building, a T-shaped Turkish bath suite. At the top left of the 'T' was the *frigidarium*, with benches and couches lining the walls, and loose-covered easy chairs in the centre. To its right, double doors and a short curtained

Table 21.2 Scottish baths clubs

Club founded	*Club*	*Location*	*Turkish bath opened*	*Turkish bath closed*
1870	Arlington	Glasgow: Arlington Street	1 Aug 1871	Still open in 2013
1875	Victoria	Glasgow: Butterbuggins Road	1876	1942
1875	Western	Glasgow: West George Street	29 Apr 1878	Still open in 2013
1882	Drumsheugh	Edinburgh: Old Queensferry Road	1884	1970s *
1883	Pollokshields	Glasgow: Leslie Street	20 Mar 1885	1937
1884	Dennistoun	Glasgow: Craigpark Street	1885 [?]	1983
1886	Warrender	Edinburgh: Thirlestane Street	17 Dec 1887	1929 [?] *

* Indicates that the club itself was still open in 2013

Fig 21.10
The tepidarium *at the Arlington today: 'Arlington Baths—Turkish Sunlight'*
(30 × 32 in, oil on board)
Painting by Lesley Banks.
(© 2000 Lesley Banks www.lesleybanks.com)

passage led into the large *tepidarium* (Fig 21.10), nearly 30ft (9.1m) square with, at the centre of its tiled floor, a shallow octagonal pool fed by a small decorative fountain. With a 20ft (6m) high domed ceiling, pierced with multiple Moorish star-shaped stained-glass openings, set round a small square window, it must have surprised and delighted its first members.

Opposite the *tepidarium* entrance, a wall comprising three large arches and a doorway led to the *caldarium*. The lower portion only of each arch was filled with plate glass which, in the central arch, was pivoted so that it could be opened.

Also leading off the entrance to the *tepidarium*, double doors led to the shampooing room in the vertical portion of the 'T'. Further on was the washing room, with a small plunge pool leading, through an opening in the wall, directly into the main swimming pond, or pool.

Above the water, the opening was covered with plate glass, the upper part of which could be opened. This allowed bathers to swim underneath from one area to the other, while maintaining the necessary air flow at the top.[17]

Apart from the *frigidarium*, all areas of the Turkish bath opened off each other. Fresh air, drawn through grilles into the basement, passed over the heating surface of a Constantine's Convoluted Stove. It then entered the *caldarium* through a grating directly above the stove, before continuing through the open tops of the arches into the *tepidarium*, cooling as it went.

While this was, by now, a standard method of heating Turkish baths, its use here is especially significant because the original clubhouse was already heated by hot air circulating through underfloor ducts, rather like the Roman-style hypocaust used in the earliest Victorian Turkish baths.

In practice, the single stove proved to be inadequate. Although the *frigidarium* had its own fireplace, the temperatures in the hot rooms were difficult to maintain, and members found the washing and shampooing rooms to be too cool.[18]

In 1877, a second Convoluted Stove was added and this effectively solved the problem. So much so that when, soon afterwards, local architect John Leck Bruce (1850–1921) compared the heating system with that at the nearby Victoria Baths Club, the Arlington was found to be much more efficient.[19]

Bruce found that the temperature in the Arlington *caldarium* was 210°F (99°C), (though this could be increased to 230F (210°C) by closing the swivelling portion of the central arch), while the temperature in the *tepidarium* was about 144° (62°C).

The stoves continued in use for a further 19 years when new ones were installed at a cost of £149.[20] Not until 1950 were the coke-burning stoves replaced by 'the most modern system of steam heating.'[21]

Today there is no plunge pool, though the massage room (Fig 21.11) survives, and the arches enclosing the *caldarium* are now fully glazed, and none swivels.[22] Otherwise, apart from the stoves and the fountain (which was at some stage replaced by a drinking fountain), the baths remain largely as they were when built, though the rooms are now maintained at lower temperatures, and the club has had women members for many years.

The Victoria and Western Baths Clubs, Glasgow

In March 1876, the Victoria Baths Company announced a competition for plans, 'in Moorish or oriental style', for a clubhouse with swimming and Turkish baths. It was won by Thomas Lennox Watson (1850–1929), who had the good fortune to have just finished designing the Gothic style hydro which was soon to dominate the Kilmalcolm landscape.

The Turkish baths comprised a series of rooms (one of which was the *frigidarium*) placed on four sides of a central, hexagonal *caldarium*. Its opposing walls were 24ft (7.3m) apart, and it had a 17ft (5.2m) high groined ceiling, pierced by a double-glazed circular stained-glass window. A triangular *laconicum*, a shampooing room and a washing-room, opened off other sides of the hexagon.[23]

The baths were somewhat idiosyncratically heated, with the shampooing room kept at

Fig 21.11
The massage room and its unique massage slab. (© Patis Paton Photography www.patispatonphotography.com)

115°F (46°C) by a 4in (102mm) steam pipe, and the two hot rooms each relying on a Pennycook Patent Caloric Multitubular Stove.

Apart from the swimming pond and a Russian bath, there was also a reading room and facilities for billiards and snooker.

The club remained open for over 60 years, closing in May 1942 'for the duration of the war.' A committee was formed to 'ensure the reopening of the baths' afterwards, but they remained closed[24] and the building was later demolished.

The Western Baths Club in Hillhead, however, which opened a year after the Victoria, not only managed to remain open during the war, but is still open, though the club itself is the successor of the original one.

In the 1870s, Hillhead was still an autonomous Scottish burgh, not yet a suburb of Glasgow. Development was taking place, however, with the area being favoured by wealthier Glaswegians building homes suited to their monied status. In 1876, finding that the Arlington was now too far away for regular swimming, a number of members broke away to form the Western Baths Club Company Ltd (Fig 21.12) in order to build a new club nearer home. Among them were such well-known names as Adam Teacher of the whisky company and J A and W G Blackie of the publishing house.[25]

Possibly influenced by the fact that architect George Bell was a shareholder, the club

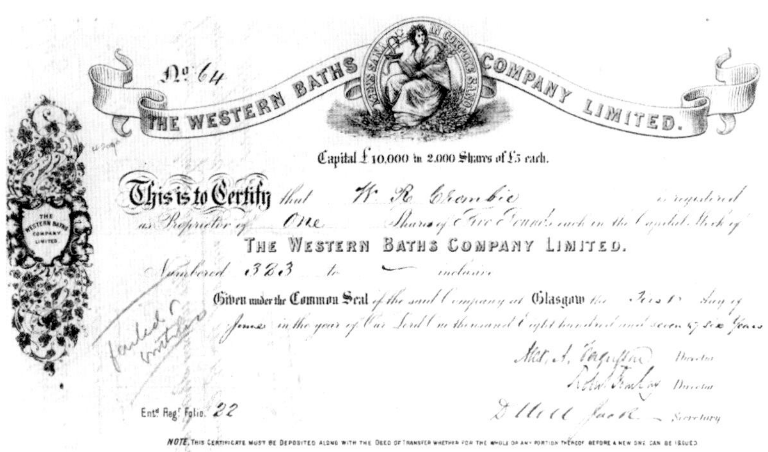

No. 64

THE WESTERN BATHS COMPANY LIMITED.

Capital £10,000 in 2,000 Shares of £5 each.

This is to Certify that W. R. Crombie is registered as Proprietor of One Shares of Five Pounds each in the Capital Stock of THE WESTERN BATHS COMPANY LIMITED. Numbered 323 to — inclusive

Given under the Common Seal of the said Company at Glasgow the First day of June in the year of Our Lord One thousand Eight hundred and seventy six Years

Director

Director

Secretary

Entd Regr Folio. 22

NOTE. This Certificate must be Deposited along with the Deed of Transfer whether for the whole or any portion thereof before a new one can be issued.

Fig 21.12
Certificate for one £5 share in the Western Baths Club Company Ltd.
(W M Mann, 1876 The baths: the story of the Western Baths…, *The club, 1993, p.19. Kind permission of W M Mann)*

appointed Clarke & Bell (1841–1903) to design their new clubhouse (Fig 21.13), a central three-storey block flanked by a pair of two-storey wings, looking virtually the same today as when it was built. At the rear of the centre and right-hand sections lies the swimming pond, for 20 years the largest indoor swimming pool in Scotland.[26] The Turkish baths suite (Fig 21.14) occupies the left-hand section, effectively one third of the ground floor area of the building.

Down a small flight of steps in the entrance hall, double swing doors on the left led into the shoe room where members exchanged their outdoor footwear for club slippers. Here, members chose whether to continue on through a second pair of doors opening into the cooling-room, or along a corridor on the left leading to a number of slipper baths (unaccountably labelled 'plunge baths' on the plan), and a vapour bath.

The cooling-room (Fig 21.15), 42ft × 22ft (12.8m × 6.7m), was furnished with easy chairs, settees and even a *causeuse*, or circular three-seat sofa, and around the room were a number of curtained dressing cubicles, some with couches. On one side, a door allowed access to the Russian bath, while on the other, a wide passageway with a central marble plunge pool (Fig 21.16), 5ft (1.5m) deep, led to the hot room. The shampooing room was on one side of the pool, and the washing-room, with three needle showers and a wave douche, was on the other.

The hot room, little smaller than the cooling-room, was unusually large and would have been very expensive to keep at the required temperature. Decoratively dominating the room was an octagonal-based dome of stained glass which took the height of the room at its apex to 23ft (7m). Similar domes lit the plunge pool and cooling-room.

The neighbourhood may have been fashionable and the residents wealthy, but the financial situation in Glasgow and the surrounding area in 1878 was extremely difficult after the City of Glasgow Bank crashed. Added to this, it appears that the building may have suffered subsidence and needed major repairs. The upshot was that at the beginning of 1884 the company was unable to continue. It went into liquidation and all its shareholders lost their money.

A second Western Baths Company was formed, and the building was bought from the liquidator for £6,000 by a Mr James Muirhead on the new company's behalf. But it was two years before the baths reopened. It remained

Fig 21.13
The Western Baths Club, Glasgow, with the Turkish baths on the left.
(W M Mann, 1876 The baths: the story of the Western Baths…, *The club, 1993, p.27. Kind permission of W M Mann)*

empty in the meantime, suffering the fate of most empty buildings—broken windows and structural neglect.

The poet Robert Service described how, when he was about 10 years old, he was with a couple of friends when they found a window which could be pushed open. The following day, more adventurous than the others, he went in alone to explore.

> Furtively I pushed open a door. Beyond was the room where the Turkish bathers reposed. Under a glass cupola that grudgingly yielded a pallid light were two lines of velvet couches. They were mouldy and gutted, and some rats scurried over them. Then I was conscious of a dreadful stench. I was shrinking back when suddenly I gasped with horror. Lying on a couch was the body of a man. His head was lower than his feet. I saw a black hole for a mouth and empty eyes. Through a mat of hair his face was the white of a shark's belly. His arms and legs sprawled wide, while one hand trailed on the rotted carpet. I had a feeling as if lice were creeping under my skin, and panting with fear I fled.[27]

The subscribers and directors of the new company showed courage which must have seemed foolhardy to many, but within a year nearly 600 shares of £5 each had been taken up by 32 shareholders, most of whom were directors of their own large companies.[28] The club reopened in October 1886 and started to recover, weathering financial ups and downs, and the occasional crisis.

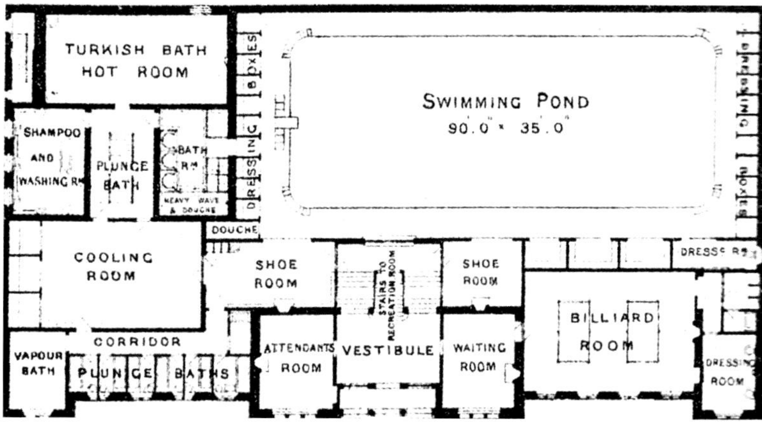

Fig 21.14
Ground floor plan of the Turkish baths and swimming pond.
(The Architect, 12 November 1881)

On the afternoon of 22 December 1905, part of the Turkish baths caught fire. A temporary roof was installed but, barely a week later, a second fire broke out in the same place causing much further damage. As part of their insurance settlement, the company agreed to rebuild the bath using fireproof blocks. At the same time, to help reduce heating costs, it was regretfully decided not to replace the three stained-glass domes.

Eighty-five years later, however, in 1990, the club decided to celebrate Glasgow's year as European City of Culture by reinstating the dome over the hot room (Fig 21.17), wisely choosing a completely modern design, to great effect.[29] Other changes have also been made. Significantly, the over-large hot room has been divided into three, to give two smaller rooms at

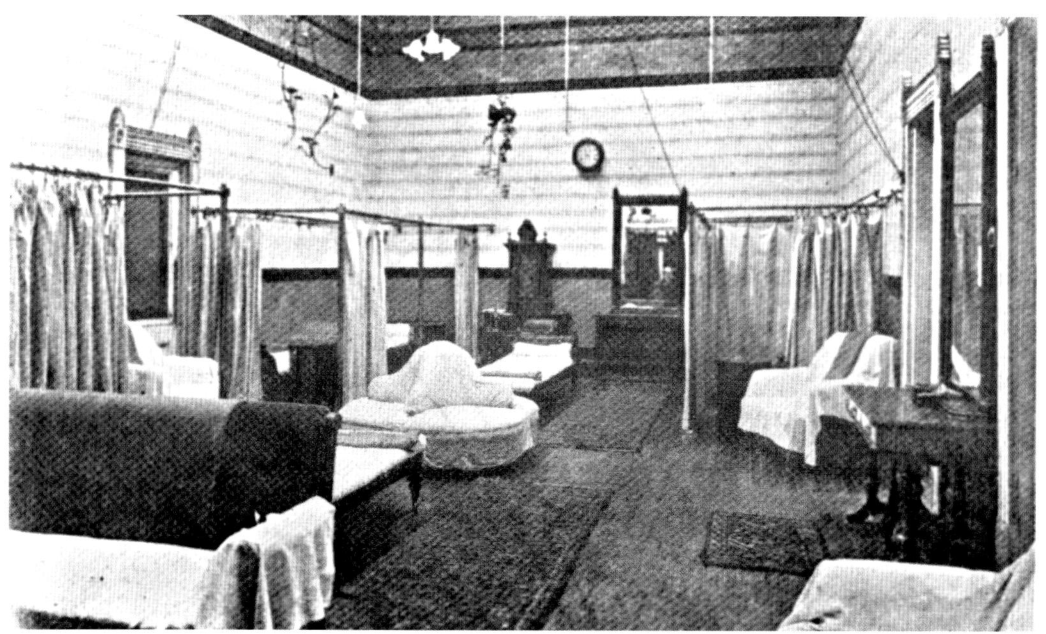

Fig 21.15
The cooling-room with changing cubicles, c 1900.
(W M Mann, 1876 The baths: the story of the Western Baths…, *The club, 1993, p.22. Kind permission of W M Mann)*

Fig 21.16
The cold plunge pool, c 1905.
(W M Mann, 1876 The baths: the story of the Western Baths…, *The club, 1993, p.35. Kind permission of W M Mann)*
Fig 21.17
The hot room at the Western baths with its new dome. (Kind permission of W M Mann www.thewesternbaths.co.uk)

different temperatures, together with a modern Russian steam room.[30]

Gradually, the club's future, and—as a consequence—that of its Turkish baths, became more secure. Today the company augments its income by letting out its facilities to a number of swimming and water polo clubs. Its membership is not only larger, but more representative of its community. For as recently as the late 1950s, membership was closed to black Glaswegians. Prospective members were required to state their religion, and new Jewish or Catholic members were only admitted when another one left.[31]

Drumsheugh Baths Club, Edinburgh

The Drumsheugh Swimming and Turkish Baths Company Limited was incorporated in 1882 with the aim of building a swimming pool and Turkish baths in Edinburgh.

Its prospectus, offering 2,400 shares of £5, was designed to raise a capital of £12,000. The club site, on steeply sloping ground, was to cost £2,500 and a further £8,500 would be needed to cover the erection and furnishing of the baths.[32]

Sir John James Burnet (1857–1938), son of the Arlington's architect, was commissioned to design a building in 'Saracenic style', to be erected in Dean Village. Nowhere near the necessary capital was raised, and the plans were cut back so as to omit the club rooms planned for a fourth storey.[33]

The Scotsman did not like the façade (Fig 21.18), writing:

> Externally, the building is of little architectural account—its only characteristic features being a series of Turkish lantern ventilators; but the interior is unique in its way—a certain Oriental feeling pervading all its parts.[34]

For example, there was a gallery on each of the long sides of the swimming pond hall: one of these was the gymnasium, but the other, which housed the Turkish baths, had a glazed gilded lattice-work screen, or *mashrabiyya,* through which the swimmers could be watched. At night, the rooms were lit by antique Turkish lamps.

The Turkish baths comprised four rooms leading off each other: the *frigidarium*, 40ft × 50ft (12m × 15m); the *tepidarium*, 36ft × 21ft (11m × 6.4m); an outer *caldarium*, 20ft × 12ft (6m × 3.7m); and a crescent-shaped inner *laconicum*, 18ft × 12ft (5.5m × 3.7m).

A long narrow plunge pool passed under a glass-covered arch connecting the *frigidarium* and the *tepidarium*, which was in turn separated from the *caldarium* by a *mashrabiyya*. A heavily curtained opening led on to the *laconicum*. Also leading off the *tepidarium* was the shampooing room, with its showers and marble slabs.

The rooms were heated by steam coils designed to maintain the two hottest rooms at 200°F (93°C) and 220°F (104°C), though it is impossible to tell whether these temperatures

Fig 21.18
The Drumsheugh Baths Club, Edinburgh. (Photo: Paul McClure, Washington, DC)

were actually achieved. In addition there was also a Russian steam bath.

The club opened on 26 December 1884, with William Cameron as manager. From the start, women (Fig 21.19) were able to use the baths for several hours on three days in the week.

John Sweetman, in his 1988 book on Islamic influences on British and American art and architecture, wrote that the building's 'arched main interior remains the most impressive "Saracenic" example in Scotland' adding, in a footnote, that the baths 'still exist, though some features are now missing',[35] and in 1995, Miles Danby, in *Moorish style*, praised the elegance and sensitivity of the building.[36]

However, neither writer mentions that the object of their praise was not Burnet's original building, but a later copy of it. For the original was completely destroyed by fire on the night of 6 February 1892. The flames spread to a mission hall behind the baths and to the sculptor D W Stevenson's studio, severely damaging both.[37]

Burnet's company, Burnet, Son & Campbell, was responsible for reconstructing the baths on the original site, at an estimated cost of £6,000. The Moorish style building was to be, as the journal *Building News* laconically put it, 'Similar in almost every respect to the old one, but fireproof.'[38]

The fire explains Sweetman's footnote about features that were now missing. The rebuilt Turkish bath was not as large as the original, the main difference being that, in addition to the *frigidarium*, there were only two hot rooms instead of three.

But the elegance and stylishness of the replacement building, with its façade broken by 'horseshoe arched windows shuttered with Moorish metal grilles (Fig 21.20) bearing the

Fig 21.19
Daisy and Polly Duncan painted in the Drumsheugh Baths Club cooling-room on a women's day in 1890. The artist is believed to be a member of the Balfour Kinner family (Courtesy of Doug Corrance)

Fig 21.20
The decorative gates at the Drumsheugh Baths Club. (Photo: Paul McClure, Washington, DC)

title 'DRUMSHEUGH SWIMMING AND TURKISH BATHS COMPANY L^{D}'[39] is in no way diminished. The Turkish suite was built in brick and stone, with plain blue-green glazed tiles in the hot rooms, and a domed *frigidarium*.[40]

How many architects must secretly yearn to have a similar opportunity to rebuild an earlier design, and take advantage of the experience gained during the construction of the original?

Shortly after the baths were rebuilt, the company found the financial strain too great and went into liquidation. A new company, the Drumsheugh Baths Club Limited, was formed, which then acquired the building from the liquidator for £4,500, to include all fixtures and fittings.[41]

The suggestion, in *Building News*, that the rebuilt baths were fireproof proved to be incorrect when the building again caught fire on the afternoon of 17 June 1920. This time, however, the fire was less serious and the fire brigade soon had the blaze under control. Not, however, before the roof of the Turkish baths had been partially destroyed.[42]

During World War II, the club played its part in the war effort by inviting 'all Officers of HM Forces and all ranks Women's Services (if wearing uniform) to the Swimming, Shower, Plunge, Turkish and Russian Baths, on special guest terms.'[43] We can only assume that they were allowed to remove their uniforms once inside.

A refurbishment in 1967 saw the conversion of the Turkish baths into a learners' pool. A new timber floor, more appropriate for a gym, was installed, probably in 1977. But the Victorian swimming pool (with rings and a trapeze over the water), was still 'lit by cupolas in an open timbered roof and a tall arched window', the roof being 'supported by Moorish arches on slender cast-iron columns'.[44]

The Pollokshields Baths Club, Glasgow

As befits a baths company based in a 'well-to-do district' like Pollokshields, its baths were designed by an architect chosen by open competition. This was won by James Hamilton (*c* 1826–94) who had previously designed at least four Scottish hydropathic establishments, as well as baths within Taymouth Castle.

The two-storey building, now demolished, had accommodation for the bathmaster in part of the upper floor, with furnaces, laundry, and a drying area in the basement. In addition to the swimming pond there were rooms for billiards, cards, and reading.[45]

Apart from the cooling-room, the Turkish bath had two hot rooms: a *tepidarium* kept at 130°F (55°C) and a *sudatorium* (*caldarium*) where the temperature could be varied between 160°F (71°C) and 220°F (104°C). A shampooing room, and a washing-room with wave douche and a variety of showers, were also included. All rooms had mosaic paved floors, and inner domed ceilings. These had coloured, star-shaped lights in the *tepidarium*, and tinted glass cupolas in the others.

A complementary Russian vapour bath had seating on three levels, offering bathers a choice of temperatures.

The baths closed in 1937, probably unnecessarily, due to overt antisemitism. The *Glasgow Herald* cited financial difficulties, but it appears that this was due to 'the dwindling in Pollokshields of that type of household which used to frequent the Baths.'[46] This, according to W M Mann, referred to the changing demographic of Pollokshields. The resultant increase in the number of Jewish members 'was resented and objected to by the Gentile members, many of whom resigned, causing the club to close.'

Rallying round the new homeless members, the remaining Glasgow baths clubs, who had probably—like the Western—severely limited their Jewish membership, decided that any former Pollokshields member would be admitted to their clubs without needing to pay an entry fee.

The prejudiced attitude of the Pollokshields members was, in fact, no different from that prevalent in most clubs at the time. It is not unknown even today in other types of club, though now, perhaps, disguised rather more carefully.

Turkish baths and naturism

Naturist clubs are different from those already discussed in this chapter in that none owns a Turkish bath, though many have their own grounds, often with swimming pool and sauna.

Over 50 clubs around Britain organise regular swimming and sauna sessions at their local public baths, most of them under the auspices of British Naturism (BN, formerly the Central Council for British Naturism). BN clubs follow a child and vulnerable adult safeguarding policy produced in association with the NSPCC, and BN provides a training and assessment programme for its member clubs.

§Four of these clubs in England are located in areas where they are able to hire the local public Turkish baths (Fig 21.21), and one Scottish club hires those belonging to one of the private members' clubs.

Fig 21.21
At one of the weekly naturist sessions at the Arlington Club's Turkish baths in Glasgow.
(Courtesy of The Scottish Outdoor Club at www.scotnaturist.freeservers.com Photo: © Alan Oliver at www.alanoliverphoto.com)

Since Britain's remaining baths are increasingly operated on behalf of local authorities, rather than by them, there has been a consequent banning of the traditionally permitted naked bathing (even in single-sex sessions) and the naturist clubs are a last bastion of sanity.

The whole point of a Turkish bath, sauna, or steam room is to allow the hot air to reach a bather's skin. Covering it in a costume totally negates the purpose of the bath. You might just as well try skating on an ice rink with roller skates; it's possible, but hardly satisfactory. Sweating in a costume is also unhygienic because the normal quick shower before a swim—which removes sweat from the naked body—leaves most of it soaked into any costume being worn. For this reason, many spas and saunas in Germany and Holland—mixed and single sex—wisely ban costumes altogether.

We should remember that any Victorians who were averse to nakedness in the Turkish bath, covered themselves with a towel loosely wrapped round themselves, or wore a loose light robe. Constricting costumes are a 20th-century nonsense.

22

Turkish baths in private houses

Several of those involved in the introduction of the Victorian Turkish bath into England were wealthy enough to have baths in their own homes. With the exception of David Urquhart's bath at Riverside and George Crawshay's second bath at Haughton Castle (Fig 22.1), most of them were simple adaptations of existing rooms and were quite small.

The earliest private Turkish baths in England

In 1856, when Crawshay visited Urquhart at St Ann's in an attempt to sort out the future of the *Sheffield Free Press*, he was much impressed by what he saw of the first experimental Turkish bath, and on his return home decided to build one at his Tyneside home.

Fig 22.1 (below) Ambrotype of a hot room in a very early private bath, possibly George Crawshay's second bath. This is probably one of the earliest photographs taken inside a Turkish bath, and it is thought that the photographer was Robert Crawshay. (V & A Museum, Ambrotype Neg. No. HJ1905)

Fig 22.2 (above right) Preston Cottage, where Henry Wilson built his Turkish bath in 1857. (© Jane Nesbitt)

The following year he returned to St Ann's, this time with local artist and architect James Shotton (1824–96),[1] and employed him to design a bath for him. Built at the side of his house, [2] this was the 'the first Turkish bath to be built in England since the days of the Romans.'[3] However, unlike William Potter's bath, built in Manchester a few months later, it was not open to the public.

Soon afterwards, *The Builder* published an article describing a private bath constructed at South Preston Cottage, North Road, in North Shields (Fig 22.2). The house, built around 1809 by John Plummer, was the oldest and largest in Preston Village. In 1857, it was owned by Henry Wilson, a grocer and flower dealer who was living there with his wife Alice, and their family.[4] Wilson added the bath behind his vinery, and the bathing procedure described in the article shows that he was an experienced bather.

The 8ft (2.4m) high bath was about 16ft long by 6ft wide (4.9m × 1.8), and divided into two rooms. A 10in × 12in (254mm × 305mm) flue from an outside furnace ran beneath the red tiled floor. The walls were fitted with ventilators, and a small aperture in the chimney removed the stale air.

Such a building would have cost between £10 and £20, and fuel to feed the furnace for two to three hours cost 4d. This enabled the inner room to be kept at 120–150°F (49–66°C) and the outer one at 80–90°F (27–32°C) for much longer than the two hours needed for a bath.[5]

Urquhart thought the article should be read by anyone commissioned to design or build Turkish baths, and sent copies to his friends, including Sir John Fife.

Urquhart's bath at his Riverside home near Rickmansworth

There were actually two Turkish baths at Riverside. The first, 'a mere case, about seven feet cube, enclosing a boiler, erected in an outhouse' was built for use by the outdoor servants. But it was also used by the Urquharts while the larger bath was being constructed (and also later when the main bath was being improved). Though small, it worked effectively and Urquhart invited others to see it in action.

'This Oriental luxury', he wrote, 'may be obtained by any one for the sum of £5, and is within the reach of any one who possesses a coal-box.'[6]

The second bath (Fig 22.3) was altogether grander, occupying an area 30ft × 20ft (9m × 6m) and with two levels, 25ft (7.6m) high overall. Daylight was filtered through a roof light of coloured glass.[7]

Erasmus Wilson, wrote a description of the bath in nine-and-a-half pages of florid prose, beginning,

> We arrive at the door of the *Frigidarium*; we loosen the latchets of our shoes, and we leave them behind the lintel; the portal opens, and we enter. The apartment is small, but it is sunny and bright; through the glass doors we see a balcony festooned with the tendrils of the rose, now leafless and out of bloom, for it is early winter ... [8]

But even described in plainer language, the Riverside baths were impressive, especially since in 1860 there were still very few public Turkish baths in the country.

The hottest 'room', in effect a sort of four-poster divan enclosed in scarlet hangings, was built directly over the hypocaust so that its customary temperature of 240–250°F (116–121°C) was economically maintained. The second 'hot room', a perfumed area with an ordinary divan, was still close enough to the source of heat to enable it to be kept at 170°F (77°C). Four steps further down, by the plunge pool, a third divan was provided, as the temperature there, 150°F (66°C) was raised by means of warm air entering directly from the furnace through a decorative grating.

Fig 22.3
David Urquhart's world-famous Turkish bath at Riverside, near Rickmansworth, Hertfordshire.
*(*The manual of the Turkish bath*, ed John Fife, Churchill, 1865)*

Cushions were placed around the room, to make sitting on the marble floors more comfortable. Opposite the 'hot room' was a curtained recess, with a step down to a sloping floor where the bather could wash before venturing into the plunge pool. There, water, to a depth of 4–5 ft (1.2–1.5m) was pumped up from the adjacent river and, during the summer, kept cold with blocks of ice.

The Riverside bath was a most effective weapon in Urquhart's campaign to encourage the widespread building of Turkish baths throughout the country. Several letters survive from visitors. One dated 14 July 1860, from Richard Summers of Pimlico, seems typical:

> I write this to state that I have been severely afflicted upwards of 32 months during which time I have tryed a very many medicins prescribed by the first Doctors which were all to no use. I am very happy to say that after having 7 baths at your house I can walk much better the Pains are leaving me. I have great faith that after a few more Baths I shall be able to give you a statement of perfect cure.[9]

Urquhart did not set himself up as a doctor. However, he saw no valid reason why he should not recommend what we might call an alternative therapy, which he had himself found so beneficial. And Dr Thudichum was one of several doctors who sought the benefits of Riverside for their patients. Agnes Robertson was one of them, and he personally accompanied her there, arranging for her to be admitted daily for several weeks in 1861.

That she was not an altogether willing patient is clear from her letter thanking Urquhart for his help in her cure, and for putting up with her initial unwillingness to follow his rules.

> I may as well mention that for the first month I felt attendance on the Bath as irksome & only a duty, now I experience all the pleasurable sensations described by so many.[10]

Thudichum was one of the group of Urquhart's friends who regularly met at Riverside. Several of them later became directors of the London & Provincial Turkish Bath Company, which was probably first mooted there. Others used Riverside to further their cause. George Witt wrote asking Urquhart whether he could bring Miss Rothschild's architect, Mr (later Sir) George Gilbert Scott, to encourage her to include a Turkish bath in the establishment she was thinking of donating to §Lewes.[11] Dr Arthur Leared of the Brompton Consumptive Hospital[12] and Dr R H Goolden of St Thomas's Hospital[13] have already been mentioned.

Later, the bathing procedures at the Jermyn Street Hammam were based on those followed by his Riverside guests. Strictly adhered to, they began:

> The two baths at Riverside, are open for the use of persons suffering from disease, only on the following conditions: –
>
> The bath being the practice of a cleanly and polite people, the habits of cleanliness and politeness must be observed. Visitors, therefore, must seek to learn from the attendants how to conduct themselves.[14]

There followed eight regulations covering such matters as the removal of shoes before entering, and washing in water taken *from* a basin and not *in* the basin. These rules were important to Urquhart, and several were still being issued, unaltered, to Jermyn Street bathers as late as 1929.[15]

Rolland, Witt and Wilson build baths

By 1860, when the London & Provincial was being set up, two of Urquhart's long-time friends and supporters, Stewart Erskine Rolland and (before their unfortunate quarrel) Dr George Witt, both built Turkish baths in their London homes. Both invited friends to bathe and used such opportunities to gain support for the bath and the new company.

Rolland's bath in Victoria Street was converted from a third-floor kitchen 15ft (4.6m) long by 9ft (2.7m) wide. We know about its construction because, in response to readers' requests, *The Field* published a brief account of it, together with a quotation from T Allen of 7 Great Smith Street for the work involved.

This included replacing the existing floor, constructing a furnace with flues round the walls, and encasing them so as to support seating. The floor was to be covered in perforated tiles and the walls doubled for insulation. Allen asked £20 17s 0d for the bath, and £19 0s 0d for the felt lining, battening, lathing, and plastering.

Rolland kept the furnace burning day and night at a cost of about 10d for coal.[16] According to Erasmus Wilson, the temperature was 160°F (71°C) and the wooden couches were covered with soft Turkish sheets. In the adjoining *lavatorium* there was a douche, alternating hot and cold water, the sensation of which, he wrote, 'is beyond anything delicious'.[17]

George Witt had a larger ground floor room (Fig 22.4), 12ft (3.7m) high, at his house at 22 Princes Terrace (later renamed and renumbered as 40 Ennismore Gardens).

This was paved with ornamental tiles and divided into two smaller rooms, the larger of which was twice the length of the other. The ceiling and the double wall partition were both filled with sawdust for insulation, with two doors leading from the larger *frigidarium*, (which doubled as a changing room) to the *caldarium*.

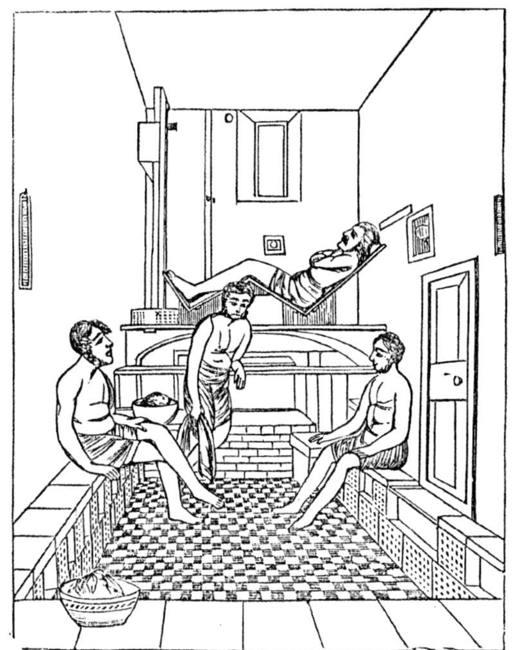

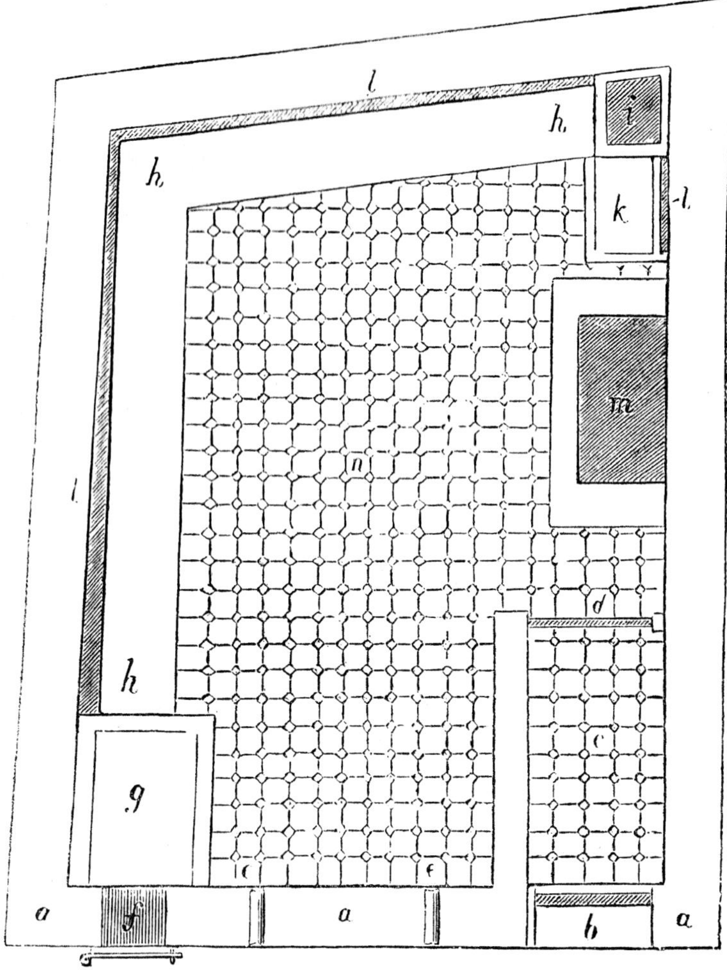

This was arranged at two levels so as to provide, in effect, a *laconicum*, furnished with a specially manufactured dureta.[18] An exterior furnace heated the air which circulated round the room in flues supporting the seating. The temperature was normally 135–140°F (60°C), though this could be raised if desired.[19]

The bath comfortably held six or seven bathers, and many doctors were granted invitations to use it, to familiarise themselves with its therapeutic possibilities.[20]

Erasmus Wilson had a two-room bath (Fig 22.5) at his Richmond Hill house. With an emphasis on retaining heat within the *caldarium*, there were insulating gaps between its double external walls, and a vestibule with doors at either end to create a heat barrier between it and the *frigidarium*.

An internal furnace obtained its fresh air from outside, and the heated air passed through flues around the inside of the two external walls, on its way out through the chimney. The seating was supported by the flue casing, as seems to have been normal at that time.[21]

Advantages of the smaller Turkish bath

In 1861, Urquhart moved from Riverside, probably for financial reasons, to Montagu Cottage, a 'snug little house' in Worthing.[22] Here he immediately built a Turkish bath, for it was by now, as a treatment for his neuralgia, an essential part of his life.

The expensive Turkish bath at Riverside was a showpiece used for converting the medical fraternity and gaining financial support for the Jermyn Street baths; but the small inexpensive one at Worthing was no less important in gaining support. For Urquhart found that Riverside often discouraged others from building a bath, as it concentrated their minds on the cost rather than the advantages.[23]

At Worthing he was able to repeat the kind of advice he had given when briefly living at Lytham St Anne's, before moving to Rickmansworth. He had invited some of the Stalybridge Foreign Affairs Committee, with its secretary, B Greenwood, to try the first Manchester Turkish bath. Replying to their letter of thanks, Urquhart told them that the best way of thanking him was to build their own bath. Although

Fig 22.4 (above left) George Witt's bath at Princes Terrace (later renamed Ennismore Gardens), London. (Spencer Wells, 'Lecture on the revival of the Turkish, or ancient Roman bath', Medical Times & Gazette, *3 November 1860, pp.423–7. Wellcome Library, London)*

Fig 22.5 (above right) Erasmus Wilson's bath at Richmond Hill. (Erasmus Wilson, The eastern, or, Turkish bath, *Churchill, 1865)*

the Manchester bath 'has cost some money', he wrote,

> the bath I have constructed in this [Lytham] house has cost next to nothing. It was constructed in half a day; the expense 27s. It is capable of holding three at once. When raised to the highest temperature, twenty minutes, or even ten, are amply sufficient; so that such a bath could bathe one hundred persons in twelve hours at an expense of not more than twopence for fuel.[24]

Urquhart was fond of this type of extrapolation—that if one person took x minutes to bathe, then y baths could be taken in z hours. He used it, as we saw, in his business plan for the Jermyn Street baths four years later, with unfortunate consequences which were predictable.

The L-shaped Worthing bath (Fig 22.6) had a freestanding radiating stove with an iron pipe to remove the smoke, so there were no flues. There were two couches, one of which was placed against the wall. In the foot of the L was a small pool 3ft (0.9m) deep, about 3ft by 4ft (0.9m × 1.2m) in area. The tap and waste pipe were 2½in (64mm) in diameter to allow a quick change of water, and the tap was high enough to allow bathers to cool their heads under the stream. Two sheets of gap-separated glass formed a window to help retain the heat, and three ventilation plugs could be opened if required.

Urquhart used coke instead of coal at a cost of 2d per day and 'all the heat was used since it warmed the house as well.' The temperature of the bath ranged between 180–230°F (82–110°C). The total cost of the bath, water fittings, building three of the walls and a plain cement covered floor, was £37 0s 0d.[25]

Urquhart's stated bath temperatures were higher than those of Rolland, Witt, or Wilson. This was no exaggeration; an entry for 15 April 1863 in Major Robert Poore's diary read, 'Called on Urquharts at Montagu Cottage. Went to his bath, 220 degrees [104°C].'[26]

Similar fairly simple Turkish baths continued to be built in private houses until at least the turn of the century. In the early 1860s, some of those connected with the Turkish Bath Movement were already building their second baths. George Crawshay, for example, built a bigger one when he moved to Haughton Castle in Hexham.

Isaac Ironside, early owner of the *Sheffield Free Press*, built his first bath as soon as he returned from his stay at St Ann's in 1857; later, in 1864, he built a smaller one. After reading about Urquhart's Worthing bath, he wrote to John Johnson to say that he had constructed a similar one at his Carr's Road house in Walkley, so that he could be independent of his servants.

He lay the fire before retiring at night, lighting it at around five or six o'clock the following morning. He then entered the bath, the heat reaching about 180°F (82°C) in an hour, and rising later to 230°F (110°C). He normally went in and out about six times, usually taking about three hours, though sometimes longer. He claimed to be able to tell when the heat reached 200°F from the effect on his body without needing a thermometer.[27]

We do not know whether the liberal statesman John Bright ever used the Pioneers' co-operative bath, but in 1872 he had one built at One Ash, his Rochdale home. It was almost taken for granted by then that Constantine's Convoluted Stoves were ideally suited for heating private homes. They were easily tailored in the factory, by varying the number of convolutes so as to produce the right amount of heat needed in houses of any size. 'The stove acts admirably', Bright wrote, thanking Constantine. 'On Friday the bath was heated up to one hundred and sixty degrees.'[28]

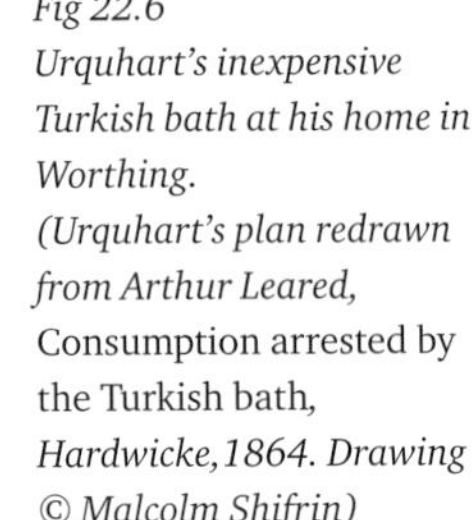

Fig 22.6
Urquhart's inexpensive Turkish bath at his home in Worthing.
(Urquhart's plan redrawn from Arthur Leared, Consumption arrested by the Turkish bath, *Hardwicke, 1864. Drawing © Malcolm Shifrin)*

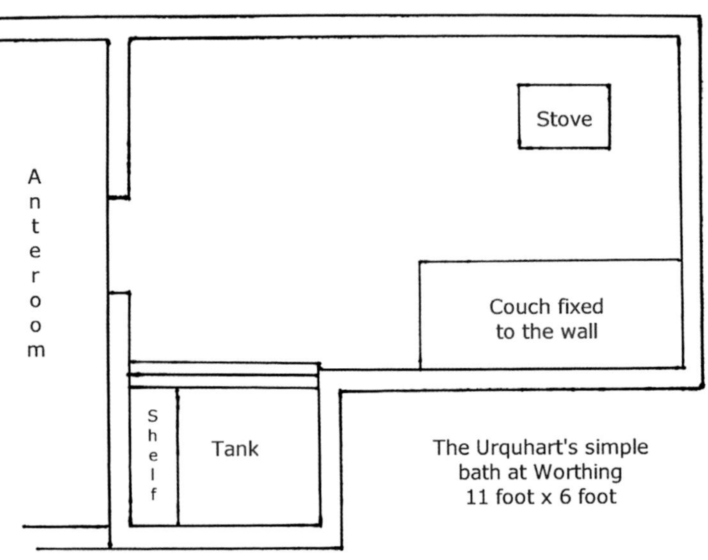

Private Turkish baths for the wealthy

With the wider general acceptance of the bath, it became almost fashionable for those with larger properties to have an architect-designed bath built within their homes, or as an extension to them.

At the same time as Bright's Turkish bath was being constructed, architect James Boucher (1826–1906) included a rather more expensive bath in the house he designed at 22 Park Circus, Glasgow, for Walter Macfarlane, proprietor of the Saracen Ironworks. This was lavishly decorated. The frieze in the *caldarium*, for example, was painted in sepia, with tropical plants sketched from a display—specially arranged for the Spode artist Charles Ferdinand Hürten—in the Duke and Duchess of Devonshire's conservatories at Chatsworth.[29]

With a grant from Historic Scotland in the early 1990s, the house was restored and, until recently, the former *caldarium*, now panelled with carved wood and silk, could be hired for private weddings with just the couple and two witnesses.[30]

Another of Constantine's successful installations was at Hall Barn, Beaconsfield, for Sir Edward Lawson (Lord Burnham), owner of the *Daily Telegraph*. Here bathed the renowned and the wealthy, as pictured by T P O'Connor,

> The bath—complete, beautiful, cosy—is in charge of a personal servant, named Nelson—quite a character in his way—who is extremely popular; has been the guide, philosopher, and friend of every one of the many illustrious persons who have passed through the bath and through his own strong hands. He is the best masseur in England. His visitors' book is quite a valuable curiosity. It has autobiography, sketches, verses, compliments from almost every notable person in the country. The Prince of Wales has twice expressed his warm gratitude ...[31]

Constantine was not slow to advertise his successes. In 1888, he wrote a letter to the editor of *Building News*, which was then publishing Robert Owen Allsop's series of articles on the bath.[32]

It was simple, Constantine claimed, to build a Turkish bath in a private house, because a Convoluted Stove was capable of heating the whole house as well. Reinforcing his claim, he attached a plan of Alston Lodge, the house built for local magistrate Thomas Craig and his wife, Annie, at Chellow Dean.

Thomas Owen builds his own bath

Another 'great believer in the efficacy of the Turkish bath, of which he, with characteristic thoroughness, made a special study', was Thomas Owen, a vice-president of the Vegetarian Society.[33]

He gained much from 'an extensive correspondence' with Urquhart, building his first small bath in 1873, followed by a larger one when he moved to Fernbank in Mount Road, Oswestry. By then he was also advising friends on how to build baths, even producing a small booklet on the subject.[34]

The Fernbank bath had a hot room, cooling-room and washing-room, and was 'built with hollow brick walls, sand-packed ceilings, and cemented floors to retain the heat.' This radiated from the furnace and a flue which passed through the rooms. The heat ranged 'from 150°F to 250°F [66–121°C], and even greater heat, up to 300°F [149°C], can be produced if required.'

In common with several other Turkish bath advocates, Owen was also, perhaps unwisely, tempted to put his thoughts into verse. An excerpt will more than suffice.

> VERSES COMPOSED AT MIDNIGHT, IN 200° FAHRENHEIT, FEBRUARY, 1912.
>
> Night after night, at boiling point,
> My radiant chamber glows.
> No limb or nerve resents the heat,
> Save finger-tips and toes.
> While resting thus on wooden couch,
> The skin begins to ooze,
> Till streamlets join and rivers form,
> As heated rays diffuse.
> At intervals the surface hot
> With water cool is laved.
> And by degrees the skin is rid
> Of cuticle depraved.

Lord Armstrong's bath at Cragside

As a member of the House Committee of the Newcastle-on-Tyne Infirmary, William George Armstrong (Lord Armstrong), will have been well aware of the bath's therapeutic value. So it is significant that he decided to build one at his Rothbury home, Cragside, soon after he became a member of the committee.

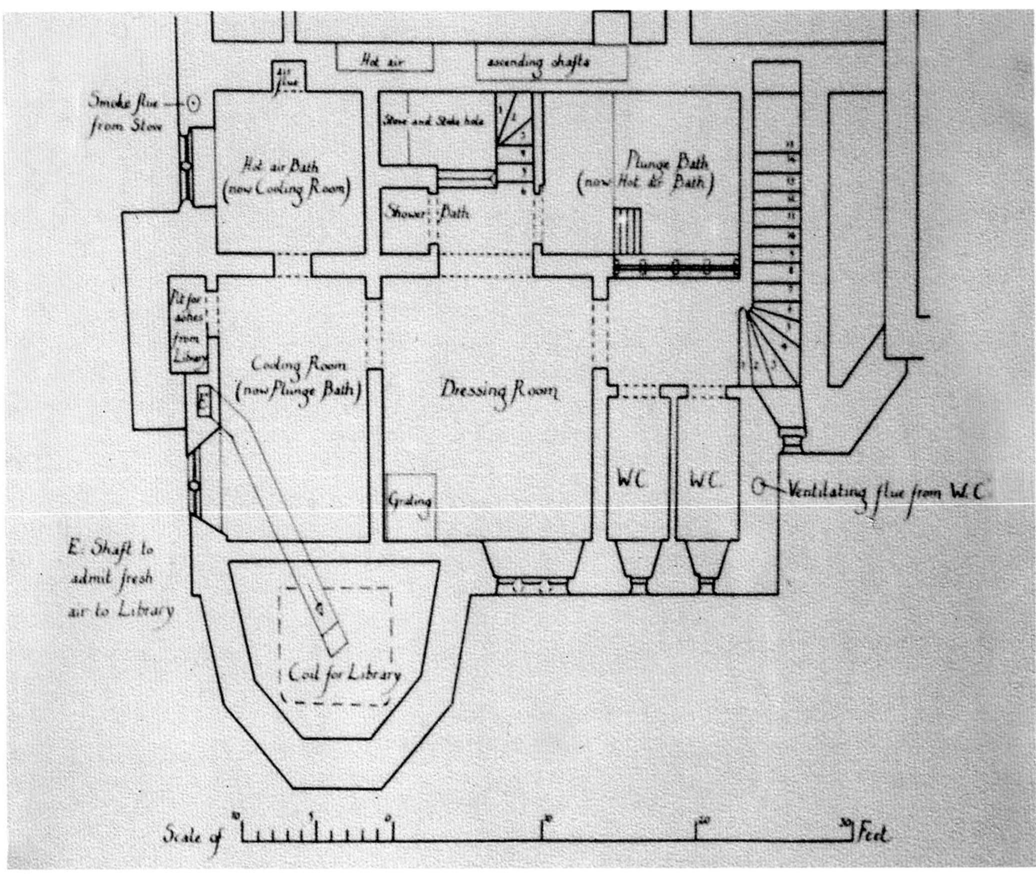

Fig 22.7
A (slightly distorted) copy of Norman Shaw's original design for the baths at Cragside, changed during their construction.
(Photo © Malcolm Shifrin)

The house was originally built to the design of an unknown architect early in the 1860s. It was much enlarged and reconstructed at the end of the decade by Richard Norman Shaw (1831–1912). The plans for a Turkish bath suite under the library (Fig 22.7) are dated 5 May 1870, but the baths which were built show that at some stage the positioning of the rooms was completely changed.

Shaw is not known to have previously built a Turkish bath, and it may be that Armstrong himself advised on the actual layout, or that advice was sought from the Tyneside architect, James Shotton, with whose work Armstrong would certainly have been familiar.

They may even have known each other personally. A few years earlier, Shotton had designed Crawshay's first bath and then, in 1869, the Cecil Street baths for the North Shields Turkish Baths Company, in which Crawshay, together with Addison Potter and Robert Spence Watson, both closely related to Armstrong, were all shareholders.[35] (In 1874, Shotton went on to design the Pilgrim Street Baths for the Newcastle-upon-Tyne Turkish Bath Company, in which three other relatives of Armstrong also had shares.[36])

The Cragside Turkish bath was ready for use on 4 November 1870.[37] In addition to the hot room, there was a cooling/dressing room (Fig 22.8), a drench shower (Fig 22.9), and a plunge pool 'lined with blue and white Delftware tiles in a floral pattern' (Fig 22.10), with a top border of tiles featuring a number of different horsemen.[38]

Armstrong, a famous inventor in the fields of engineering and armaments, designed a central heating system for the whole house, and hot air entered the *caldarium* through a grating in the floor (Fig 22.11).

He also designed a hydroelectric powerhouse so that, in 1880, Cragside became the first house in the world to be lit by hydroelectricity, and the first to be lit by Joseph Swan's newly invented incandescent light bulbs.[39]

A decade after it was built, therefore, the Cragside Turkish bath became the first to be lit by electricity. This must surely have influenced the decision, a couple of years later, to use electricity and Swan's bulbs in the new Turkish baths at Whitehaven, situated just 100 miles

to the south-west. Opened four years later in 1894, these were the first commercial Turkish baths in the country to use electric lighting—a year ahead of architect Charles John Phipps (1839–97), whose Savoy Hill Turkish Baths were the first such baths in London.

Cragside is now owned by the National Trust, and the bath—once used by the then Prince of Wales, the Shah of Persia, and the King of Siam (Thailand)—is among the rooms open to view.

Isaac Holden's bath at Oakworth House

Like Armstrong, Isaac Holden was also an inventor. His achievements included the Lucifer (striking) match—from which he made nothing as he omitted to patent it—and wool combing machinery—from which he made a fortune. He was a Liberal MP for 30 years from 1865, was made a baronet in 1893, and died in 1899.

Figs 22.8–22.11
Features at Cragside
Top left: The wardrobe.
Top right: The drench shower.
Bottom left: The Turkish bath plunge pool.
Bottom right: A hot-air grating in the hot room.
(© Malcolm Shifrin)

Fig 22.12 (right) Oakworth House, West Yorkshire, home of Sir Isaac Holden. (Courtesy of Stephen Sharp)

Oakworth House (Fig 22.12) was built in stages between 1864 and 1875, on the site of an earlier house owned by his second wife, Sarah Sugden.[40] In July 1877, Holden wrote to Joseph Constantine, asking him for advice on improving its heating and installing a Turkish bath.[41]

Holden was unaware that as a young lad Constantine had been a hand-comber at Holden's mill, and had lost his job after the invention of the new machinery. But, as he later told Mrs Holden, it was the best thing that could have happened to him because he then became a bathman in Keighley, and in 1850 opened his own vapour bath establishment in Manchester. He dedicated two of his books to Holden in gratitude.[42]

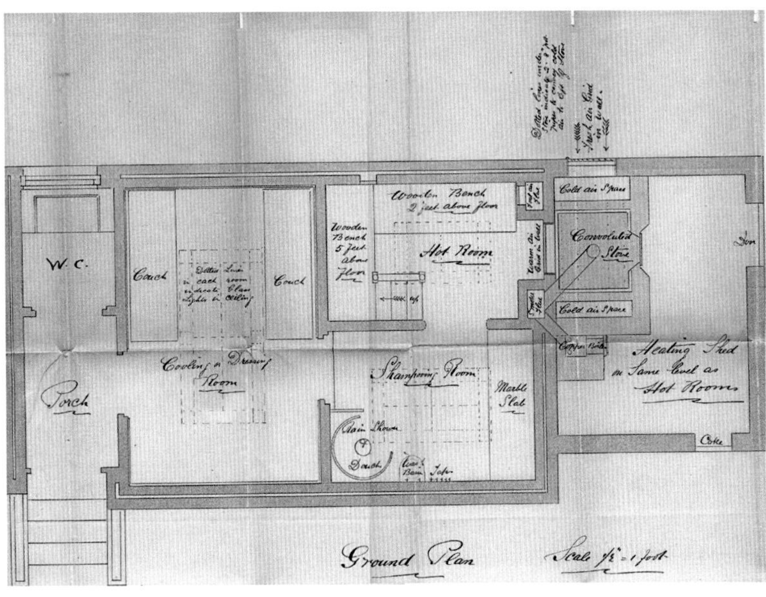

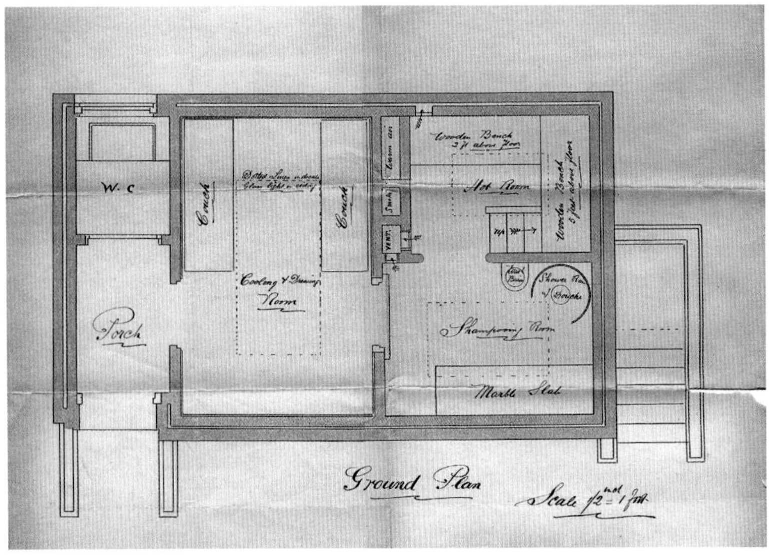

Figs 22.13 and 22.14 (below) Top: Constantine's single storey proposal for the Oakworth Turkish bath. Bottom: Constantine's alternative proposal with the boiler house below the bath. (The Papers of Sir Isaac Holden and Family, Special Collections, University of Bradford.)

Constantine submitted two versions of a spacious well-equipped building, for siting close to the house.[43] The first (Fig 22.13) was on a single level, with the furnace room placed next to the bath; the second (Fig 22.14) was on two levels, with the furnace room in a basement. The layouts of the hot room and shampooing room were slightly rearranged, so that the flues would be in the most appropriate position, but the facilities in each were the same.

They comprised an entrance porch with adjacent toilet, a large cooling and dressing room, a hot room with two benches—one of which was raised 5ft (1.5m) above the floor—and a shampooing room with marble slab, circular needle douche, and washbasin.

Constantine's detailed quotation (Fig 22.15) was itemised, and at a total cost of £101 13s 0d does not seem over-expensive for a wealthy man's Turkish bath in a house which was to cost £80,000.

Yet the auction catalogue produced for the sale of the house after Holden's death, described a smaller, very different Turkish bath. In a plan (Fig 22.16) in the papers of Steve Sharp, a descendant of the family of builders who were involved in the construction of the house,[44] the bath was shown sandwiched between a billiard room on one side, and a dynamo house and a potting house on the other, all within a small building close by the main house.

Unusually, the Turkish bath could only be reached from the billiard room. A door led into a vestibule at the end of which was a toilet which could be used by billiard players or bathers. Also opening off the vestibule were, at either end, the hot room (11ft × 13ft [3.4m ×4m]) and the cooling-room (10ft × 11ft [3m ×3.4m]), while between them was the shampooing room (11ft × 12ft [3.4m × 3.7m]) with shower.

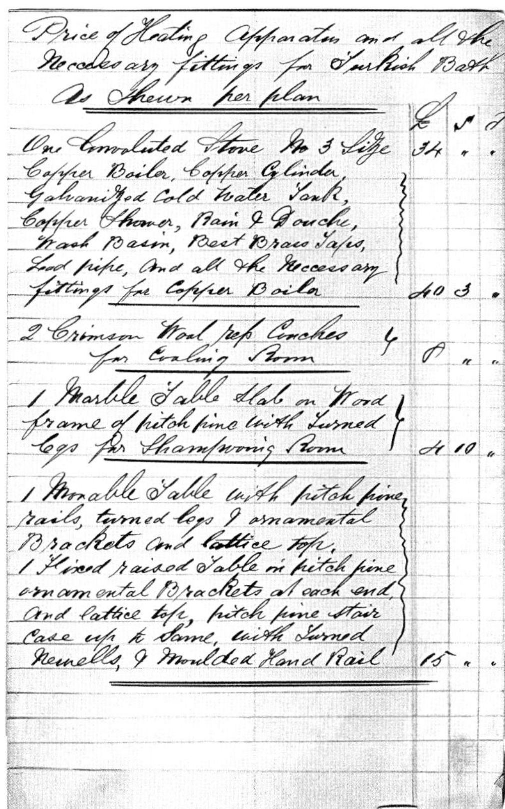

Price of Heating Apparatus and all the Necessary fittings for Turkish Bath As Shewn per plan

	£	s	d
One Convoluted Stove No 3 Size	34	"	"
Copper Boiler, Copper Cylinder, Galvanized Cold Water Tank, Copper Shower, Rain & Douche, Wash Basin, Best Brass Taps, Lead pipe, And all the Necessary fittings for Copper Boiler	40	3	"
2 Crimson Wool rep Couches for Cooling Room	8	"	"
1 Marble Table Slab on Wood frame of pitch pine with Turned legs for Shampooing Room	4	10	"
1 Movable Table with pitch pine rails, turned legs & ornamental Brackets and lattice top, 1 Fixed raised Table in pitch pine ornamental Brackets at each end, And lattice top, pitch pine Stair Case up to Same, with Turned Newells, & Moulded Hand Rail	15	"	"

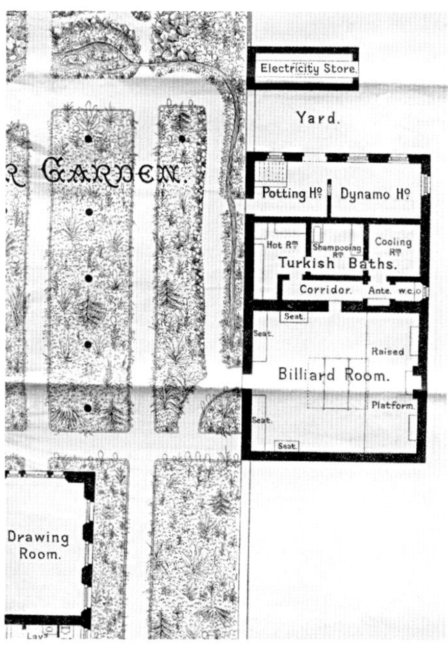

Fig 22.15 (far left)
Constantine's estimate for the heating apparatus and furniture.
(The Papers of Sir Isaac Holden and Family, Special Collections, University of Bradford.)
Fig 22.16 (left)
The Turkish bath which was actually built at Oakworth House.
(Courtesy of Stephen Sharp)

According to Constantine, Holden was an extremely health-conscious person and a great believer in exercise. Even at the age of 83 he walked regularly for one-and-a-half hours daily and on his return,

> He went into his private Turkish bath, which is always kept warm, took a warm and cold shower and changed his underclothing … He takes one Turkish bath a week, and if the least out of sorts two or three.[45]

Holden's bath was destroyed when Oakworth House burnt down in 1909. Its layout and style seems to have been rather similar to that which Constantine designed and fitted out 10 years later for Theodore Mander at Wightwick Manor, Wolverhampton. Holden's bath led directly off a billiard room; Mander's bath was located adjoining one. In both cases, the Convoluted Stove also kept the billiard room warm.

Theodore Mander's bath at Wightwick Manor

Wightwick (pronounced *wittick*) was built in 1887 for Theodore Mander who, with his brother Charles, was joint owner of the family paint and varnish firm, Mander Brothers. Theodore was also a local councillor, alderman, magistrate and, briefly, Mayor of Wolverhampton. Within six years the house was already being altered and considerably enlarged.

Edward Ould (1852–1909), of the Chester and Liverpool firm of Grayson and Ould, was the architect of the original house and its 1893 extension. It is not known if he had any previous experience of designing Turkish baths, but his ground floor plan of the original building clearly shows a Turkish baths suite (Fig 22.17).

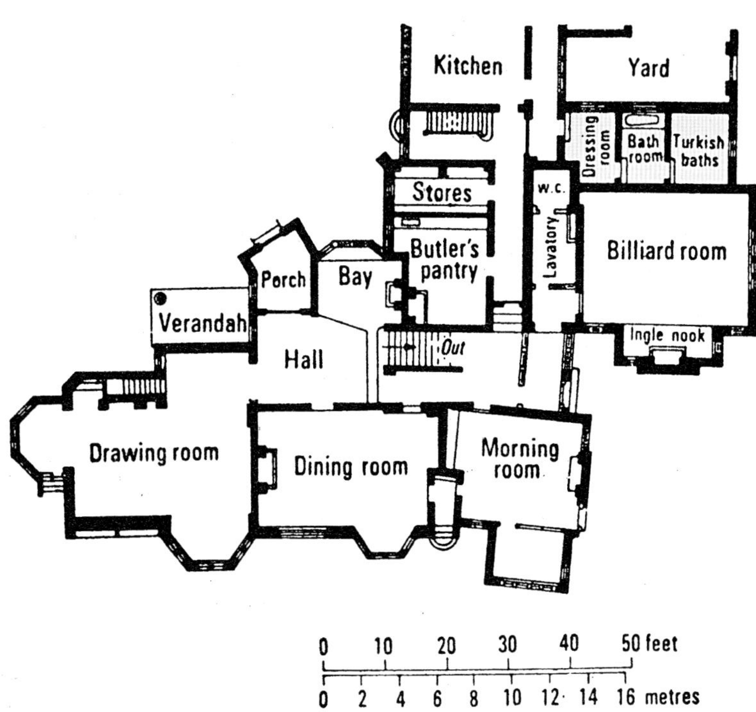

Fig 22.17
Ground floor plan of Wightwick Manor (detail).
(Historic England Archive DP172005, Building News *24 May 1889)*

What is unusual is the designation of the middle room (Fig 22.18) as a bathroom, and the inclusion in the plan of a slipper bath. In fact, there seems to be no evidence to show that a bath was ever installed, and a recent examination of the room showed no remains of any water feed or outlet drain. Neither is it mentioned in the article which appeared in *The Architect* shortly after the original house was finished.

> The building, which is of brick, consists of three rooms—two hot-rooms and a cooling-room. The centre one answers as 'tepidarium' and shampooing-room ... The cavity in the walls is made use of for ventilating the bath, and is useful as a non-conductor from the cold air outside. The inside walls are of glazed bricks in various colours, designed in good taste. These walls form the best surface for hot-rooms; they are easily washed. The ceilings are concrete, and the floor neatly tiled.
>
> The bath is effectually heated by Messrs J Constantine & Son's (Manchester) Convoluted Stove. The size of warm-air flue is 2 feet 9 inches [.84m). The air to be heated is drawn from outside through flues of equal dimensions.[46]

The plan of the Turkish bath reproduced in one of Constantine's books (Fig 22.19) differs from the architect's original drawing in a number of respects—although it still includes a slipper bath.[47]

All we know for certain is that the stove was installed in the basement and that clean heated air was fed into the hot room by means of a tiled duct (Fig 22.20), topped with a grille (Fig 22.21) about 3ft 6in (1.1m) above floor level.

It seems unlikely that we shall ever know exactly how the Turkish bath was originally built. Patricia Pegg found that the records of Grayson and Ould were destroyed in an air raid during World War II, and that there is a gap in the family archive for the period between 1887 and 1893 when Mander was involved in planning, building and extending Wightwick Manor. So 'there are none of the letters one might expect to find from Edward Ould, with suggestions and inquiries about the design of the new house ... '[48]

The 1893 extension, as large as the original house, was added to the east side of the building. It was during this work that the original billiard room was demolished and the Turkish bath cooling-room removed to make space for a larger corridor leading from the kitchen to a new dining room.

The two remaining rooms in the Turkish bath have been 'restored' by the National Trust, which acquired the house in 1937. They are now open for public viewing, but it is difficult to determine how authentic the restoration has been and a number of questions remain unanswered:

Fig 22.18
The 'bathroom' in the Turkish bath in the 1990s—but see text.
(© Malcolm Shifrin)

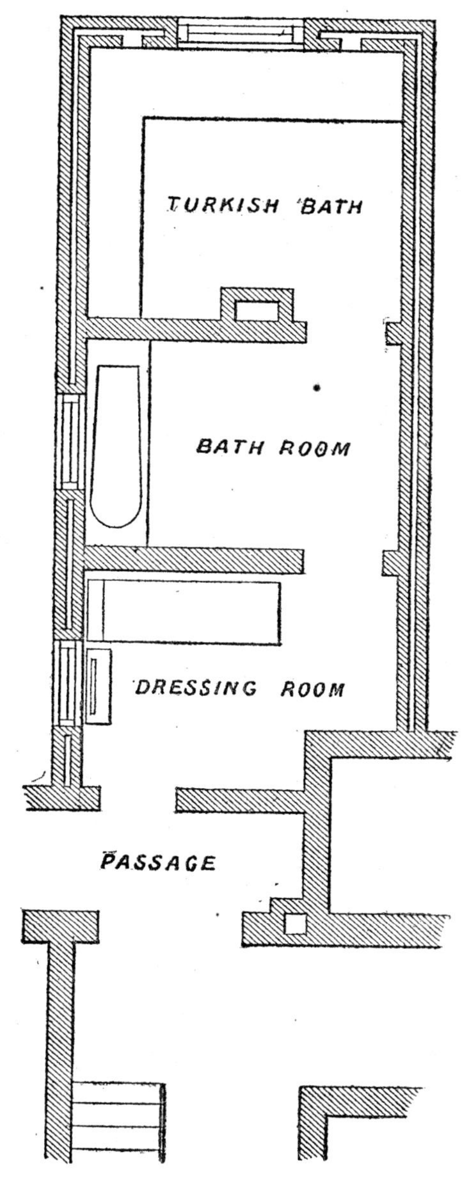

Fig 22.19 (top left) Constantine's plan of the Turkish bath at Wightwick Manor. (Joseph Constantine, Fifty years of the water cure, *2nd ed, Manchester: Heywood, 1893)*
Fig 22.20 (top right) The hot-air duct in the hot room at Wightwick Manor. (© Malcolm Shifrin)
Fig 22.21 (bottom right) The top of the duct with the hot-air grille. (© Malcolm Shifrin)

First, the arched opening between the hot room and the cooling-room has been fitted with a polished wooden-framed door similar to that between the new cooling-room and the enlarged corridor.

As one would expect, Constantine's plan does not show doors separating the rooms. These would have stopped the necessary free flow of hot air between the rooms, cooling as it progressed.

Second, each of the rooms has a window which is not included in the original plan, and there seems to be no evidence as to when they were added. External windows were sometimes found in Turkish baths, but the type currently in place would not have conserved the heat, and would have added considerably to the fuel costs. And the building of the extension does not in itself seem to have required any windows to be moved, yet even the one in the hot room is not positioned as shown on Constantine's plan.

Third, no steps appear either on the architect's original plan, or on Constantine's. So when the 1893 extension (with its new dining room) was built, the floor levels were changed. Either those in the two extant rooms were lowered, or those of the cooling-room and corridor raised. The now necessary steps were added, built of plain concrete.

Finally, in Turkish baths which were not heated by a hypocaust, it would have been normal for bathers to walk directly on a tiled floor, or on matting, rather than on the slatted duckboards currently covering the floor. These, like the slatted wooden seating, would have been unusual in a Victorian Turkish bath. Perhaps this part of the restoration has been influenced by modern sauna practice.

If the restoration is authentic, it is puzzling that—in a house of such distinction—steps intended for use by the master of the house would not have been tiled to match the floors within the baths, and that the seating was not of marble, which was to be found even in local authority Turkish baths.

Nevertheless, we are fortunate still to be able to see at least part of one of the few Turkish baths remaining in an English country house.

Colonel North's bath at Avery Hill

Unfortunately, enemy bombing in World War II destroyed what was probably one of the most exotic of the private Turkish baths, that at Colonel North's house at Avery Hill (Fig 22.22) in what is now the London Borough of Greenwich.

John Thomas North, universally known as Colonel North, the Nitrate King, was the self-made son of a coal merchant. He made the first of his fortunes in Chile during and after the Great Pacific War between Chile and her two northern neighbours, Bolivia and Peru. He returned to England in 1882, and the following year took out a 10-year lease on an empty house at Avery Hill in Eltham, at that time in Kent.

North bought the house in 1888 and, though it was by no means small, he decided to enlarge it in order to build, amongst other things, painting and sculpture galleries to house his art collection.

Before leaving for a visit to Chile in 1889, North commissioned the architect Thomas William Cutler (1842–1909) to make £40,000 worth of alterations and additions to the house. When North returned he discovered that the architect had actually commissioned £100,000 worth of work. North dismissed him and appointed Cutler's assistant, J O Cooke, to replace him.

By the time the house was completed, North had also added a fernery, conservatory and a huge dome-covered Winter Garden. The separate stable block, like the mansion itself, was centrally heated, and lit by electricity generated in an engine room to the west of the main building.

Fig 22.22
Postcard: Colonel North's home at Avery Hill, Eltham. (Author's collection)

Fig 22.23 (opposite top)
Plan of the Turkish bath at Avery Hill.
(Historic England Archive DP172004, The Builder *26 November 1892)*
Fig 22.24 (opposite bottom)
The square tepidarium *with its octagonal ceiling.*
(Historic England Archive DP172003, The Builder *26 November 1892)*

Upstairs was a corridor,

> eighty-foot long and hung with crimson velvet and lit by windows with stained glass panels. Opening off it were the sixteen principal bedrooms and dressing rooms.
>
> Exceeding them all in sheer extravagance was the three-roomed Turkish bath which caught the attention of architectural correspondents in the 1890s.[49]

The entrance was through a lobby—a very short passage with a door at either end—to help retain the heat within the Turkish bath area (Fig 22.23). This led into the largest room of the three, more a *lavatorium* than a *frigidarium*. To the right of the entrance was a toilet and a large walk-in cupboard for towels and, if necessary, bathers' clothes, and on the opposite wall was a bath and washbasin.[50]

Opposite the lobby was the door leading into the marble-floored *tepidarium* (Fig 22.24). Although the *tepidarium* was square in shape, the ceiling was octagonal, supported by arcading. On the right, a horseshoe arched window overlooked a courtyard and white marble benches lined two of the walls. On the left was the arched opening to the *caldarium.*

The rectangular *caldarium* had an arched window opposite the entrance, and below this was a lattice-covered compartment through which hot air entered the bath. The windows in both hot rooms consisted of two panes of glass with a heat insulation gap between them. The other two walls had white marble benches, partly positioned within high arched niches. A contemporary postcard (Fig 22.25) shows the view from the *caldarium* to the *tepidarium*

All the walls, ceilings, and arcadings were covered in Burmantofts faïence in shades of white, red, blue, green, and grey.[51] At present, however, there are conflicting views as to which colours were used in each room. All the rooms had decorative marble floors, and the impact of the baths on a first-time visitor must have been overwhelming.

North lived in his completed house for just a little over five years.[52] He died suddenly in his City office on 5 May 1896. The house remained empty for around ten years and was bought by the London County Council for its first residential training college for women teachers.

It would be pleasing to know that, for once, a trophy Turkish bath built for the nouveau riche was now freely used by the college staff and

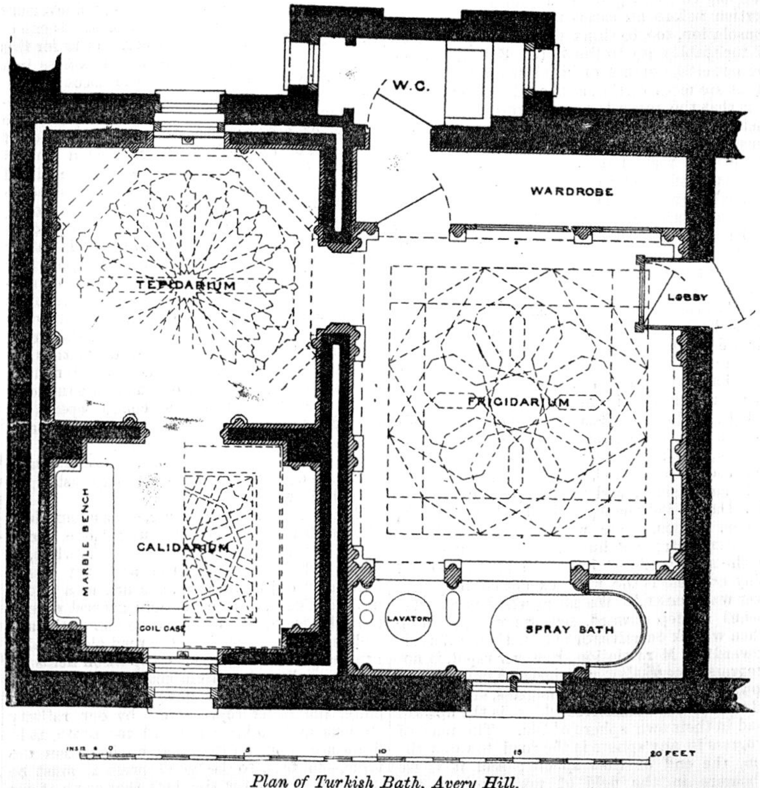

Plan of Turkish Bath, Avery Hill.

Published by A. Dale Sheppard, Broadway, Eltham.
Avery Hill—Turkish Bath

Fig 22.25
Postcard: Looking into the tepidarium *from the* caldarium.
(Author's collection)

students who followed. But a postcard similar to that illustrated here, briefly glimpsed on eBay, and sent shortly after the college opened, suggests otherwise.

An unknown correspondent, Sheila, writes asking her Ian whether he would like a bath in them. 'They are all marble. Of course no one uses them.' Seemingly not even members of staff. Why? Shyness? Propriety? Or, perhaps, just expense?

23

The Turkish bath at sea

The White Star Line pioneered the provision of Turkish baths (and also, incidentally, swimming pools) on the great, early 20th century ocean liners. In doing so, they set a precedent not only for their own ships, but also for those of other British shipping lines such as Cunard, with which it merged in 1934. Foreign shipping lines, including the Hamburg Amerikanische Packetfahrt Actien Gesellschaft (HAPAG), also followed suit.

White Star was proud of its 'notable innovations', and made special mention of the Turkish baths in most of its publicity. Their liners have been widely studied, so we know more about their Turkish baths than those of other lines.

The *SS Adriatic*

The last of the Big Four class, the *SS Adriatic*, was the first ocean liner to provide a Turkish bath for the use of its passengers. The suite included hot, temperate and cooling-rooms (Fig 23.1), a plunge bath and massage couches. There were also three electric baths (Fig 23.2), though these were apparently little used.

Mark Chirnside's plans of the various areas of the bath show that they were well laid out, so it must be assumed that advice had been sought from an experienced Turkish bath designer (Fig 23.3). The arrangement of the facilities on the later *Titanic* and *Olympic* liners was not as satisfactory, and it may be that by this time the company felt it no longer needed such advice, without realising that layout is critical to the optimal effectiveness of a Turkish bath.

That the original 1907 design *was* successful may be deduced from the fact that there were so few changes made when the ship was refurbished after the 1914–18 war (Fig 23.4), or when it was converted to cabin class in 1928 (Fig 23.5). One of the three electric bath rooms was replaced by a dressing room, and a second

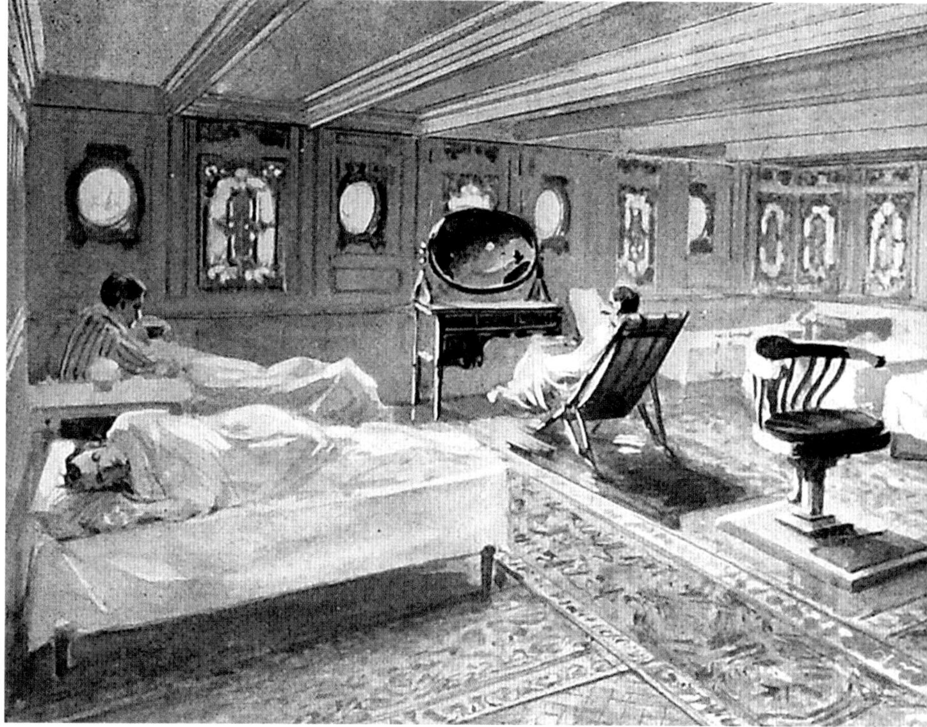

Fig 23.1 (above)
The original cooling-room on the SS Adriatic
(Mark Chirnside Collection)

Fig 23.2 (left)
One of the three original electric bath rooms on the SS Adriatic*—this was the only one with portholes.*
(Courtesy of Christopher Jones Collection)

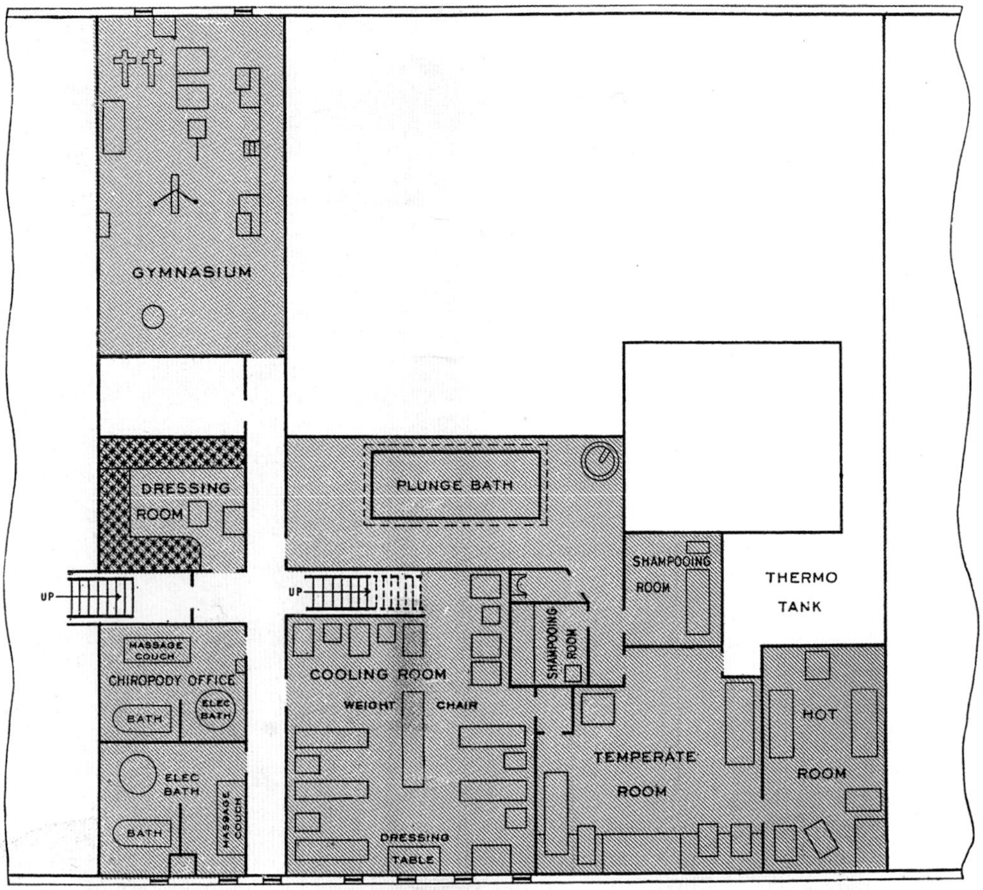

Fig 23.3
1931 plan of the Turkish baths on the SS Adriatic*, after the liner was converted to cabin class in 1928. (Mark Chirnside Collection)*

one partitioned to provide space for a chiropodist. Otherwise, apart from the addition of curtains round some of the loungers, a more sophisticated weighing chair (enabling bathers to check their weight before and after a Turkish bath), and a larger dressing table, all that can be detected are a few minor rearrangements of the furniture.

The Turkish bath was not only publicised in the company's brochures but also on their souvenirs. Passengers could, for example, purchase a tin of biscuits made by the long-established

Fig 23.4 (below)
The refurbished cooling-room on the SS Adriatic *with the weighing chair centre front of image.*
© National Museums Northern Ireland. Collection Harland & Wolff, HOYFM.HW.H1007, Ulster Folk & Transport Museum)

Fig 23.5 (below right)
The cooling-room after the 1928 conversion to cabin class.
(White Star Line Boston–New York Service: Cabin accommodation, c1930, p.5. Author's collection)

Fig 23.6
The cooling-room—one of a number of images of the liner decorating a Carr's biscuit tin.
(Photo: © Historic England, DP166128)

firm of Carr & Co Ltd of Carlisle. This was decorated with a large picture of the ship on the lid and, displayed round the edge, were four vignettes of scenes on board (Fig 23.6).

Tickets for the Turkish or electric baths had to be purchased at the ship's enquiry desk. Either type of bath cost 4s or $1, a price which remained constant throughout the life of the liner.[1]

It is interesting to see what changes were made after the liner was converted to cabin class, enabling less wealthy passengers (considered slightly 'lower class', perhaps) to use the baths.

The provision of curtains round some of the loungers in the cooling-room has already been mentioned. The hours set aside for use by men and women also changed. When the boat first sailed, men were able to use the Turkish baths early in the morning, from six till eight, and then again in the afternoon from two till six—a total of six hours per day. The afternoons from two till six were set aside for women—allowing them only four hours per day.

But after the liner was converted, the early-morning bath was no longer available. Women used the baths for three hours in the morning, and men for five hours in the afternoon and early evening. What we do not know is whether the new hours reflected experience of past usage, or whether they were designed to save money on staffing.

What is beyond doubt is that in pioneering the provision of Turkish baths on the *Adriatic*, the White Star Line created a model for the future provision of sauna, steam room, and health spa on today's cruise liners worldwide.

RMS Olympic and *RMS Titanic*

There was considerable rivalry between Cunard and White Star before the two lines merged. So when Cunard introduced the *Lusitania* and *Mauretania* on their transatlantic route, White Star followed almost immediately with their *Olympic* and *Titanic* counterparts.

Both were designed to provide the ultimate in luxury travel, and both had virtually identical swimming pools with adjacent Turkish baths suites. The midsummer issue of *The Shipbuilder*[2] was a special number devoted to the sister ships which were, at the time, considered to be the peak of British shipbuilding achievement. The journal's description of the Turkish baths applied, in all but the smallest detail, to both ships, though most of the images which survive are actually of the *Olympic* (Fig 23.7).

On the other hand, Bruce Beveridge's plan of F Deck (Middle Deck) (Fig 23.8) is based on the March 1912 version of the First Class Plan of Passenger Accommodation for the *Titanic*.[3]

The swimming bath was located on the starboard side of F Deck, just forward of the Turkish bath which conveniently adjoined the main companionway. In addition to the hot, temperate, and cooling-rooms, there were two shampooing rooms, a steam room and a single electric bath.

By all published accounts, the cooling-room was one of the most extraordinary rooms in the ship, and was decorated in the 'Arabian' style of

Fig 23.7
Postcard showing the cooling-room on the RMS Olympic.
(Author's collection)

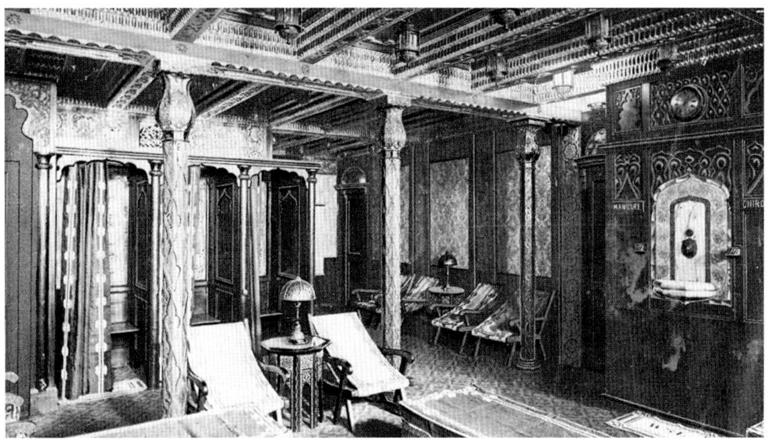

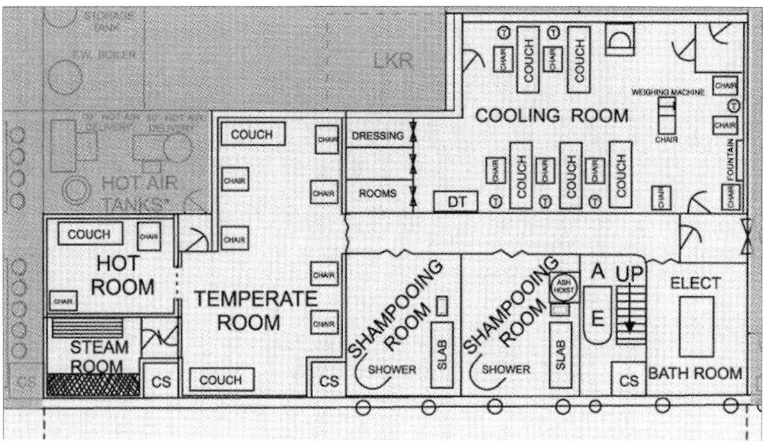

Fig 23.8
Bruce Beveridge's plan of the Turkish baths on the RMS Titanic.
(Bruce Beveridge, and others, Titanic: the ship magnificent, *Vol.2, History Pr, 2008. Courtesy Bruce Beveridge)*

the 17th century (Fig 23.9). James Cameron's 2012 dive to the wreck lying on the ocean bed brought back images which even now show that, for once, the publicity material did justice to its subject (Fig 23.10).

> The portholes are concealed by an elaborately carved Cairo curtain, through which the light fitfully reveals something of the grandeur of the mysterious East. The walls from the dado to the cornice are completely tiled in large panels of blue and green, surrounded by a broad band of tiles in a bolder and deeper hue. The ceiling cornice and beams are gilt, with the intervening panels picked out in dull red. From the panels are suspended bronze Arab lamps. A warm coloured teak has been adopted for the dado, doors, and panelling, and forms a perfect setting to the gorgeous effect of the [floor] tiles and ceiling. The stanchions, also cased in teak, are carved all over with an intricate Moorish pattern, surmounted by a carved cap. Over the doors are small gilt domes, semi-circular in plan, with their *soffits carved in low relief geometrical pattern. Low couches are placed around the walls with an inlaid Damascus table between each, upon which coffee and cigarettes or books may be placed. On one side is a handsome marble drinking fountain, set in a frame of tiles. A teak dressing table and mirror, with all its accessories, and a locker for valuables are also provided, while placed around the room are a number of canvas chairs.[4]

Fig 23.9
Although there are several photographs of the cooling-room in the Olympic, *this is the only one taken of that in the* Titanic; *the motif was the same but the layout was different.*
(Ken Marschall Collection)

The high decorative standard of the two English liners, and the facilities provided for First Class passengers—perceived as exemplifying the ultimate in luxury—were far superior to those on the German liner *Imperator* launched three years later.

Suppliers of goods to the *Titanic* were not slow to advertise the fact, rather as those patronised by the royal family still boast their 'By Appointment' logos. An advertisement for Vinolia Otto Toilet Soap appeared in the *Illustrated London News* on 10 April 1912, just days before the fatal disaster. The vignette of the Turkish bath appearing in this advertisement is exactly the same as that used in an earlier one for the *Olympic*.[5] Even today the Turkish bath is shown on items such as commemorative plates.

Since the Turkish baths were adjacent to the swimming pool which was restricted to first-class passengers, it must be assumed that the Turkish baths were similarly restricted. On the *Olympic* they were reserved for the use of Ladies from 10 am to 1 pm, and for Gentlemen from 2 pm to 7 pm, and a ticket, as on the *Adriatic*, cost 4s or $1.[6]

Because of the tragic history of the *Titanic*, almost anything to do with the ship is avidly sought by collectors and, although quite a few tickets survive, they fetch staggering prices. Ticket no 657, for example, fetched £900 at Onslow's sale in 1990.[7]

Passengers on the *Titanic*, having paid their dollar, were well looked after by a team of five staff, three men: J B Crosbie, W Ennis, and L Taylor—none of whom was to survive the voyage—and two women: Annie Caton and Mrs Maud Slocombe, both of whom were more fortunate.[8]

But in spite of such care and attention, not all passengers enjoyed their Turkish bath on board. Another survivor, Mrs Frederic Oakley Spedden, wrote in her diary for 11 April,

> I took a Turkish bath this morning. It was my first and will be my last, I hope, for I never disliked anything in my life so before, though I enjoyed the final plunge in the pool.[9]

Fig 23.10
The Titanic's *Turkish baths were recorded underwater during James Cameron's 2012 expedition. This mosaic image was laboriously assembled from numerous individual closer views to create a fuller, wide view by Ken Marschall. (© James Cameron, 2005; enhancement and mosaic by Ken Marschall)*

Nevertheless, it is fair to say that most passengers who took Turkish baths in these liners enjoyed them, leading to the inclusion of similar suites on both the *Queen Mary* and the *Queen Elizabeth*.

The *RMS Berengaria*

The *Berengaria* had its origins as the German-built *Imperator*. It was transferred to the White Star Line after World War I as compensation for the sinking of the *Lusitania*, beginning its new life in 1919.

The Turkish bath supervisor and its first masseur was probably Arthur Mason. His young assistant during 1935 was fifteen-year-old John Dempsey who, many years later, wrote about his work there.[10]

The Turkish bath suite comprised at least two hot rooms, with parquet floors and tiled with small Italian mosaic designs. There was also a cooling-room, called a rest room, which adjoined the swimming pool. Since there was a direct connection to the swimming pool, most bathers arrived in their dressing gowns, and it was part of Dempsey's job to show them to the changing cubicles and take them to the first hot room. Each bather was provided with a towel, a jug of drinking water and a glass. After about 20 minutes in the hot rooms, the perspiring bathers were taken to a table where raffia brushes were used to exfoliate dead skin.

Next to the hot rooms was the shower with its hosepipes. Stimulating and therapeutic, the jets were sprayed onto the passengers following their Turkish bath, after which they were helped to dry off and returned to their cubicle, covered with towels, and told to relax prior to their massage.

The shampooing room had a central table and raffia brushes were used to soap the bathers before their massage. Mason, a professional masseur, used a massage lotion made to his own recipe, which he taught his young assistant:

> Slivers were shaved off a bar of Knights Castile soap into a large bottle. Hot water and '365' Eau-de-Cologne were added along with a dash of olive oil. The bottles had to be kept hot in a basin of water to prevent the solution solidifying. The concoction, which was quite pliable and pleasant to use, became a lifetime standard for me and I never used anything else. An alcohol rub or '365' Cologne was also patted onto the body in the cubicle. It had a satisfying smell but its main purpose was to close the pores to prevent a chill setting in.

Many well-known male passengers, including the Prince of Wales,[11] took advantage of the facilities on the *Berengaria*. Others included Johnny Weismuller (the screen Tarzan), comedian Phil Silvers, actor George Arliss, Nöel Coward, and H G Wells. There was no Turkish bath for women passengers.

White Star considered the inclusion of Turkish baths on their liners to be a success, so it was only to be expected that the company would provide them on their new liner, No 534, to be known as the *Queen Mary*.

The *RMS Queen Mary*

When the *Queen Mary* left on her maiden voyage, the Turkish baths were being run by Arthur Mason, who had been specially transferred from the *Berengaria*. His first assistant was a young boxer named Eddie Vincent. However, after a few return trips, Mason asked for him to be replaced by his previous assistant, John Dempsey. The Turkish baths proved to be very popular with passengers and, after a short time, another assistant, Harry Leather, had to be appointed.[12]

The Turkish baths were situated on C Deck. Their main entrance was opposite the First Class dining room, and a second, smaller one, led off the balcony of the two-deck-high swimming pool. The company had allowed for a probable cost of £5,800.[13]

Seven companies tendered quotations for constructing the Turkish baths suite. They included such well-known names as Hampton & Sons, and Waring & Gillow, with quotations ranging from £3,845 to £5,150, excluding the costs of the electric bath, massage slabs, and scales. It was decided to accept the tender of Trollope & Sons, even though it was £205 above the lowest quote. They had already won the tender for the adjacent swimming pool and it was hoped that being able to build both facilities would simplify the construction process.

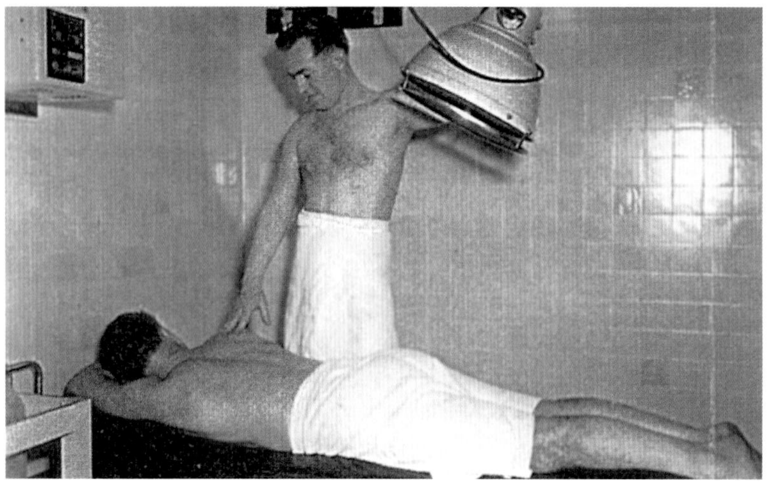

Fig 23.11
A variety of treatments was also available in the Queen Mary's *Turkish baths suite. (John Dempsey,* I've seen them all naked, *Waterfront, 1992, p.1)*

The *frigidarium* had eight cubicles with large plush curtains which could be pulled across for privacy. Each was fitted with a relaxation bench and a locker with hangers. A ninth cubicle housed an electric bath—here, a large box through which only the bather's head protruded—similar to the cabinet baths designed for home use at the end of the 19th century, but heated by electricity.

From the *frigidarium*, a long corridor with a drinking fountain led to the *tepidarium*, which was fitted with two slabs for resting on, and a Russian steam bath.[14] There followed the *caldarium* and, at the end, the smallest and hottest of the three hot rooms, roughly 7ft (2.1m) square, the *laconicum*.[15] All the hot rooms had artificial pearl ceilings, and glass windows in their doors so that attendants could check if anyone seemed unwell. Room temperatures ranged from 80°F to 200°F (27°C to 93°C).

Initially, there had been complaints that the freshness of the hot air in the earlier liner, *Olympic*, was not all it should have been, but considerable advances had been made in heating technology in the decades which followed, and the equipment installed by Richard Crittall & Co was much better.

Clean vapour was supplied to the Queen Mary steam room through a specially designed stainless steel diffusion pipe. In the *caldarium* and *laconicum*, the patent hot-air heaters were supplemented by radiant heat panels, and the maintenance of the correct temperatures was ensured by electrically operated magnetic valves and thermostats.[16]

The shampooing room had two Pilkington armour plated glass massage slabs, together with washbasins and a shower. Completing the suite was an office for the attendant, and a further room in which bathers could obtain ultraviolet (Fig 23.11), infrared, or *diathermy treatments under the supervision of the nursing sister or dispenser.

During World War II, the *Queen Mary* was requisitioned as a troop carrier. By that time, the Turkish baths had already been patronised by many famous Cunard White Star passengers, including the Czech Foreign Minister, Jan Masaryk; Viennese operatic tenor Richard Tauber; Errol Flynn, Sam Goldwyn, Louis B Mayer, Gabriel Pascal, Robert Taylor and Jack Warner from the film world; and boxers Joe Baski, Kid Berg and Tommy Farr.

Following the practice now prevailing on other liners with Turkish baths, there were separate sessions for male and female passengers

(Fig 23.12). But, as in public baths, the hours were not evenly distributed.

For some years after the post-war refit and relaunch in 1946, it seemed as though things would soon be back to normal. Indeed, the 1950s have been described as the golden years for Cunard. But by the 1960s, the liner's usage figures were being examined very closely indeed as travellers increasingly considered the advantages of speedy air travel.

Fig 23.12
Opening hours on the Queen Mary *shown on a wooden board with space for (the missing) Gentlemen / Ladies indicator at the bottom.*
(Courtesy of Joe Johnston)

The *RMS Queen Elizabeth*

The *Queen Elizabeth* spent her first years as a troop carrier during World War II. She was refitted in 1946, and both Harry Leather and John Dempsey, who before the war had worked on the *Queen Mary*, were appointed to the new liner, together with a young boy, Tommy McDonald, as assistant. The liner was in no condition for luxury cruising.

> There was dirt, dust and workmen everywhere: joiners, carpenters, fitters … Nobody knew where the Turkish bath was but we eventually found it under the first class restaurant. We cleaned and scrubbed the place until it began to look something like a Turkish bath. Whatever we needed for stores had to be ordered … the same Knights Castile soap, '365' Cologne for alcohol rubs and bottles of olive oil.[17]

The facilities provided were, in general, similar to those on the earlier Queen, though the furnishings were, perhaps, a little softer. John Dempsey describes the Turkish bath suite as consisting of

> a long corridor with various rooms on either side. The first door on the right opened into the electric therapy room with radiant heat and ultraviolet. The door opposite led to the swimming pool. On the right of the corridor was our locker room and lavatory and to the left were eight cubicles with curtains, beds and lockers …

This part of the corridor (Fig 23.13), some 25ft long and 10ft wide (7.6m × 3m), acted as the *frigidarium*—a far more utilitarian space than the lavishly furnished rooms in the *Olympic* and the *Titanic*.[18]

There was also an electric bath, although this was so little used that it was soon converted into a linen store, and three showers with jets of ice cold or hot water.

The shampooing room had two up-to-date tables with chrome surrounds and a two-inch armoured glass surface. This made it extremely easy to remove any surplus massage oil which might seep through the clean towels on which the bathers lay.

The Turkish baths suite comprised three hot rooms: the *tepidarium* at 150°F (66°C) and *caldarium* at 175°F (79°C), each 14ft × 10ft 6in (4.3m × 3.2m), and the much hotter *laconicum* at 200°F (93°C) which was only 7ft 6in × 10ft 6in (2.3m × 3.2m). Finally, next to these was a Russian steam bath.

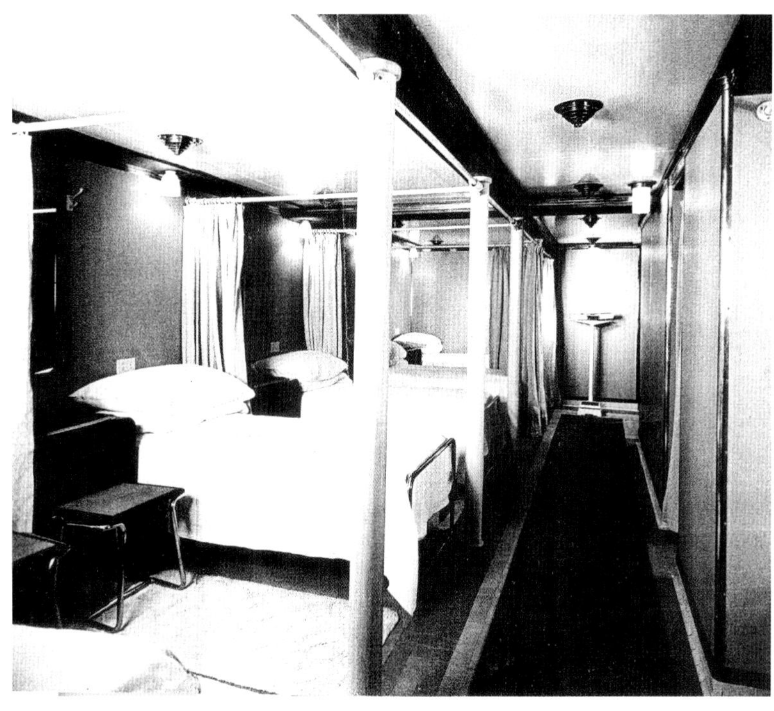

Fig 23.13
The Queen Elizabeth *cooling-room.*
(By courtesy of the University of Liverpool Library, D42/PR1/19/100, The Cunard Archive)

> The [whole] place was completely tiled in magnolia and we had plenty of wonderful soft carpeting which was easy on the feet. It was a very light colour so shoes were banned and we didn't like people coming straight in from the swimming pool …

The baths were open each day from 7 am till 10 am, and from 2 pm till 7 pm for the male passengers, and from 10 am till 2 pm, under the direction of Mrs Wilson (the masseuse) for female passengers. The return trip took from 11 to 13 days, and each crew member would work five consecutive trips with the sixth taken as leave.

Once passengers had enjoyed a Turkish bath on board, they tended to return, encouraged also by the reduced rate for tickets valid for the whole voyage. According to Dempsey:

> Passengers usually booked the Turkish bath for the whole voyage and, most often, at the same time every day. They didn't come down because they wanted to lose weight or were suffering from some ailment or muscle disorder but because it formed part of their entertainment aboard ship. We were well known for our stories and general bonhomie (Fig 23.14). It was an opportunity for them to leave their cabins and the upper decks filled with lounges, smokerooms and restaurants to let their hair down for a while. They usually told a few stories and had a pint of beer with us. Occasionally they came down just for a snooze in one of our cubicles. It was fun.

John Dempsey was to work on the *Queen Elizabeth* for 14 years before he decided to move to Bermuda where he had been asked to run the Turkish bath in a newly built hotel.

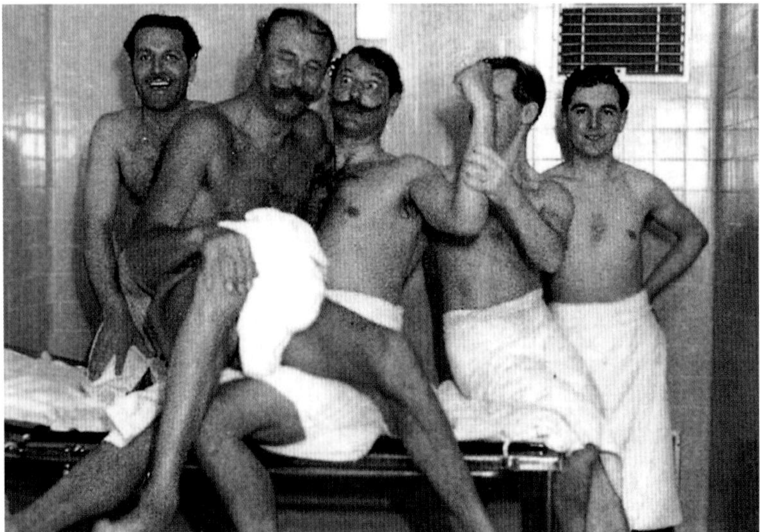

Fig 23.14
For passengers on the Queen Elizabeth, *the Turkish bath 'formed part of their entertainment aboard ship'. (John Dempsey,* I've seen them all naked, *Waterfront, 1992, p.34)*

Difficult decisions

By the beginning of the 1960s, the 'golden age' of the liners was in decline. The concept of a leisurely crossing of the Atlantic by sea was increasingly affected by the growing popularity of jet air travel. Passenger numbers fell, and Cunard began seriously to examine the costs of every aspect of their liner operation.

The financial return on the provision of Turkish baths on the *Caronia* and the two Queens made dismal reading.

On the *Queen Mary*, a Turkish bath with an alcohol rub cost 10s. A bath and rub on each of the three full days of the voyage could be taken for a ticket costing only £1 5s 0d.[19]

A memorandum from the Cunard general manager's office, dated 6 May 1963, noted that on the *Queen Mary*, the cost of the Turkish baths staff (two males, one female, and a boy) exceeded the receipts by £2,298 5s 0d. This was a considerable loss, and more than the £1,971 5s 0d loss (with the same complement of staff) being made on the slightly newer *Queen Elizabeth*.[20]

An analysis of the previous year's voyage receipts showed that on the *Queen Mary*, able to accommodate 776 cabin class passengers, the average number of 'treatments' given per sailing day was only 10.7, or three less per day than the *Queen Elizabeth* with its 823 first-class passengers. Even here, the average number of 13.7 daily 'treatments' was still painfully low.

The writer of the memorandum, Mr T Laird, asked whether any overtime was being worked, and suggested that if the staffing could be reduced by one person, and the charges to the passengers raised, then the service 'might be put on a profitable basis'.

A statement of receipts from Turkish baths taken for the periods April to July 1963 and 1964, was sent to Cunard's head office in October 1964, and the decline in overall takings was shown to have continued.[21]

It is not known whether any changes were actually made to the level of staffing or to the basic price of a Turkish bath, but by this time Cunard must already have been considering whether to continue the liners in service.

The *Queen Mary*'s last passenger voyage was in 1967, and the *Queen Elizabeth*'s was in 1968, a year before the maiden voyage of its replacement, the QE2.

24

The portable Turkish bath

> I do so hope that your Cold is better,—as well as your husband's—& that you have both boiled yourselves over the Turkish Bath.

So wrote the painter Philip (later Sir Philip) Burne-Jones, son of the better known pre-Raphaelite painter Sir Edward Burne-Jones, writing in 1890 to a Mrs Hamilton, to ask whether he might bring a friend to visit and, undoubtedly, charming her with his delightful sketch (Fig 24.1).[1]

whether you would mind
our invading you.
If you would let us
come, do you think
you would add to your
kindness by letting me
know when?
I do so hope your
Cold is better, — as
well as your husband's —
& that you have both
boiled yourselves
over the Turkish Bath.
And how is Miss Melville?

Always yours very sincerely
Philip Burne-Jones

The cabinet bath in hospitals

The bath drawn by Burne-Jones was one of several types developed 30 years earlier, when Mr W R Gore, an Irish surgeon, described the construction of a simple hot-air bath for use in hospitals. He wrote in a local medical journal that he had introduced it into the City of Limerick Hospital and, after a period of successful use, hoped that the design would be taken up by other hospitals.[2]

The bath was designed so that the height of the seat could be adjusted (Fig 24.2). The front of the cabinet opened to allow the patient to enter. A footrest was provided and the patient sat with his or her head outside the cabinet, a position achieved by the use of a somewhat terrifying device reminiscent of a horizontal guillotine. A small flap at the side of the cabinet allowed a hand to be extended, to enable an attendant to take the patient's pulse, and a thermometer was attached to the bath. The author claimed that the bath could easily be constructed for about £2.

The air was heated by one of three recommended methods. The first utilised a special candle heater known as the Laconicum (Fig 24.3), manufactured by Price's Patent Candle Company, a company which still successfully sells candles today.

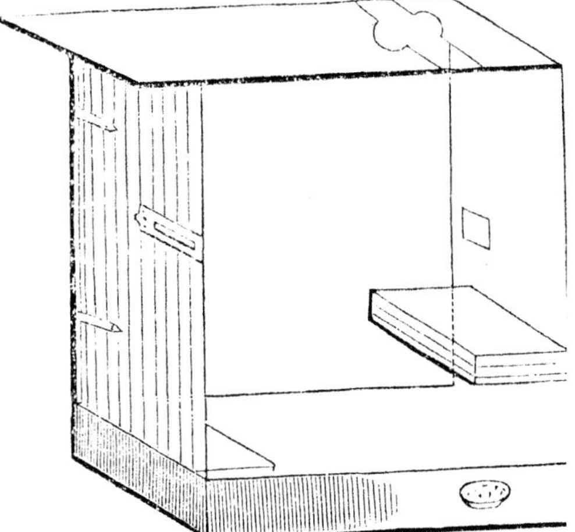

Fig 24.1 (above)
Part of a letter from Philip Burne-Jones with a sketch of a 'crinoline' bath.
(Author's collection)
Fig 24.2 (left)
Simple hot-air bath introduced into the City of Limerick Hospital by Irish surgeon, W R Gore.
(Dublin Medical Press, 23 May 1860.
Author's collection)

More common though, was a methylated spirits lamp, where the length of wick determined the amount of heat produced. In either case the heater was usually placed on a small tile at the base of the cabinet.

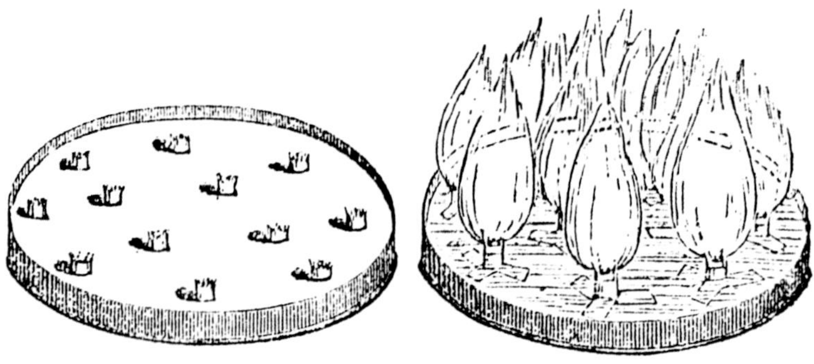

Fig 24.3
The 'Laconicum' Air Bath Heater, unlit and lit, manufactured by Price's Patent Candle Company. (Medical Times & Gazette, *11 February 1860, p.156. Wellcome Library, London)*

If a gas supply was available, a small heater with a number of gas burners and a control tap was placed outside the cabinet, and was the cheapest means of heating the air.

Gore advocated his bath for use in army hospitals, and even suggested that its portability might have a secondary value as a packing box for hospital stores.

Ewart's Hot Air Bath (Fig 24.4) was a commercially developed version of this design. Health and safety regulations being non-existent, one can only agree with Lawrence Wright's view that the closeted bather, 'could hardly escape from this pillory in a hurry, and to overfill or overset the spirit lamp would be to invite a dreadful scene'.[3]

In 1873, the *British Medical Journal*'s column describing new inventions included a new portable Turkish bath designed for hospital use (Fig 24.5). This bath could be taken to the patient, rather than the patient being required to go to the bath.[4]

Its portability was enhanced by its ability to be turned round completely in a space little more than its own length. The patient's head remained outside the bath, which could be raised or lowered to enable it to be at the same level as the patient's bed.

Perhaps most important of all in a busy hospital, the enclosed dry air could be heated to 180°F (82°C) in less than 10 minutes, and to the full temperature of 220°F (104°C) in 15. Additionally, when prescribed, the bath could be used with plain or medicated vapour, and there was,

> every facility for shampooing ... A shower-head is attached, by means of which a copious discharge of tepid or cold water can be suddenly or gradually, at the pleasure of the bather, or attendant, as the case may be, be made to flow.

The bath was invented, patented, and manufactured by William Patch Wyatt and David Jones of Islington, London, and on 19 August 1874, the Patent Turkish Baths Company

Fig 24.4
Ewart's Hot Air Bath was a more sophisticated version of Gore's hospital bath. (Used with the agreement of David Ewart)

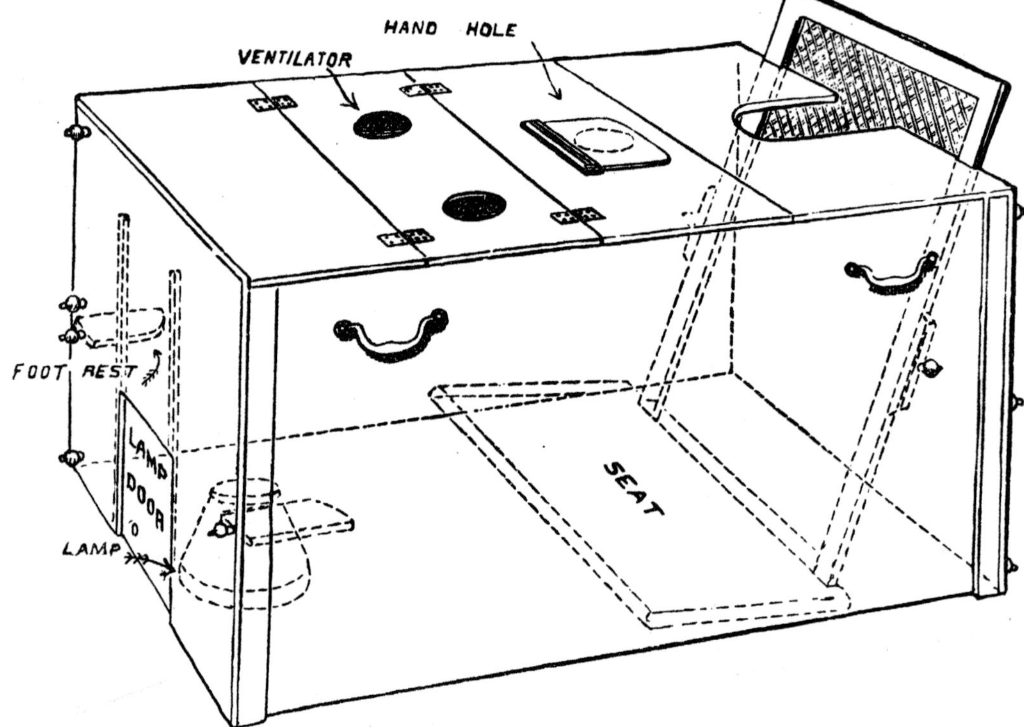

Fig 24.5 *(opposite top left) Portable Turkish bath with shower incorporated.* (British Medical Journal, *21 June 1873)*

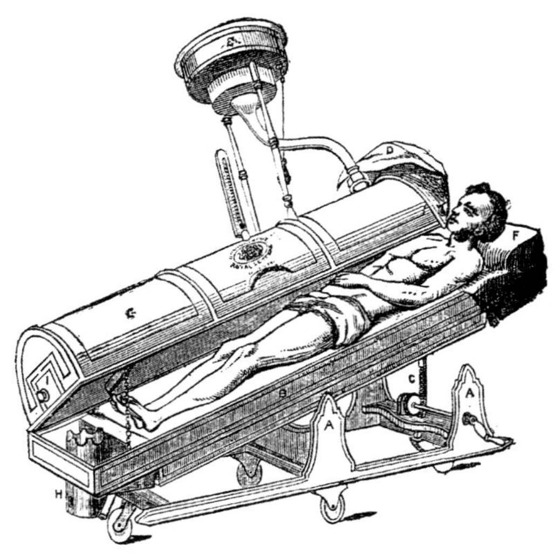

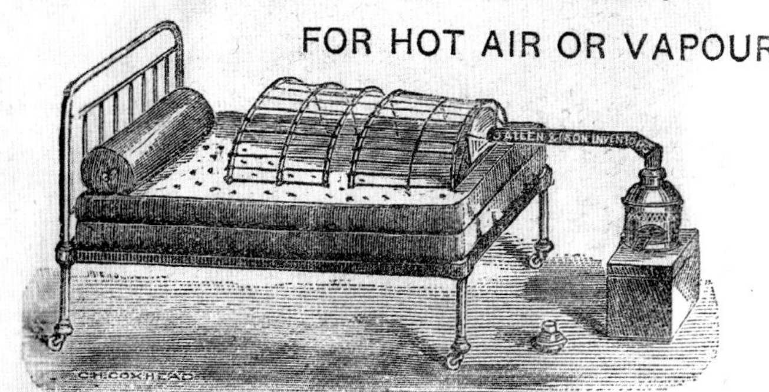
JAMES ALLEN & SON'S
PORTABLE TURKISH BATH
AS APPLIED TO THE BED.
FOR HOT AIR OR VAPOUR.
Apparatus complete, in wood box, with pair of wicker frames and foot-plate .... £2 5 0.

Fig 24.6 (top right)
A Turkish bath for use in bed. (W Gordon Stables, Turkish and other baths, *Dean, 1883, p.80)*

Fig 24.7 (above)
Foot's portable Turkish bath, with its lamp, snuffers and wick, medicator, and spirit measure. (Author's collection)

Limited was set up, with premises at the Weavers' Hall, Basinghall Street, to acquire their patents and manufacturing business.[5]

As with many such inventions, it is difficult to tell how successful or widely used this particular device was. There is a suggestion that there was also a Turkish bath establishment on the premises, which might have helped keep the company afloat. Benjamin Bell owned the Wool Exchange Turkish Baths there in 1883, but it is not known if he opened them himself, or bought an existing establishment. Bell's baths remained open until 1938, but the Patent Turkish Baths Company was dissolved in 1885, soon after the sale of its premises.

A Turkish bath for the bedridden

The purchase of such a portable bath would have been too expensive for many hospitals, and it is probable that most of them used a far simpler device (Fig 24.6) similar to those used in the mid-1870s at London's Whitechapel Hospital. This comprised a simple wicker support frame resting on the patient's bed. When enclosed by an easily removable material, an air chamber was formed around the patient. Hot air was fed in through a tube attached to one of the many external heaters available from a number of manufacturers (Fig 24.7).

Such a heater was extremely adaptable, because hot air could easily be directed either over the whole body, or locally if heat was needed on, for example, a single arm or leg (Fig 24.8). The device could be used to provide hot dry air (for a Turkish bath) or, with the addition of a specially designed water container or medicator, steam for a plain or medicated vapour bath.

One version, with two frames for the bed, was made by James Allen, of Marylebone Lane. It came in a strong wooden box and, at the beginning of the 20th century, still sold for £2 5s 0d in best quality tin, or £3 5s 0d in strong copper. Published testimonials, from satisfied customers at home, such as Lady Crawford of Aberdeen, also included others from further afield. One was from a Lieutenant H E Belfield,

Fig 24.8
Localised Turkish bath, here used for the feet.
(Arnold & Sons Catalogue of surgical instruments and appliances, *c 1885, p.545)*

who had his bath sent to him in Malta where he was stationed.[6]

While the Allens clearly claimed (on the heater itself) that they were its inventors and manufacturers, the same device, suitably rebadged, could be found for the same price in other catalogues, such as those of Arnold & Sons, and Maw & Son.

The heater comprised a cylindrical air compartment, with an opening at the front. Above this was a tightly fitting domed top, with a right-angled tube and two tapered extensions which, fitted together, acted as a heated air duct. Underneath, a separate methylated spirits lamp with three wicks was placed.

These were the portable Turkish baths which, though originally designed for hospital use, were later to be heavily advertised for use in the home—and they were increasingly popular amongst those who could afford them.

Cabinet baths in the home

Cabinets were upright with an inbuilt seat or, more usually, were designed to enclose a chair provided by the purchaser.

Two forms of enclosure predominated, the first being a type of crinoline worn, cloak-like, by the bather (Fig 24.9). The second utilised a 'crinoline frame' which was attached to the bather's own chair, and was similar to that used in the hospital hot-air bed bath (Fig 24.10).

This was sold by James Allen & Son *c* 1910 for £2 10s 0d in tin, and £3 10s 0d in copper. The spirit lamp was still the favoured heater for this type of bath, but it was now a little safer, being supplied with a spirit measure (to avoid overfilling) and an extinguisher, or snuffer (to ensure that the wick did not re-ignite after use).

More comfortable, was the Gem Quaker box-framed enclosure, which was usually a metal framework covered with flexible material (Fig 24.11). Being light in weight at under 20lb (9kg), this was considered especially suitable for use by women.

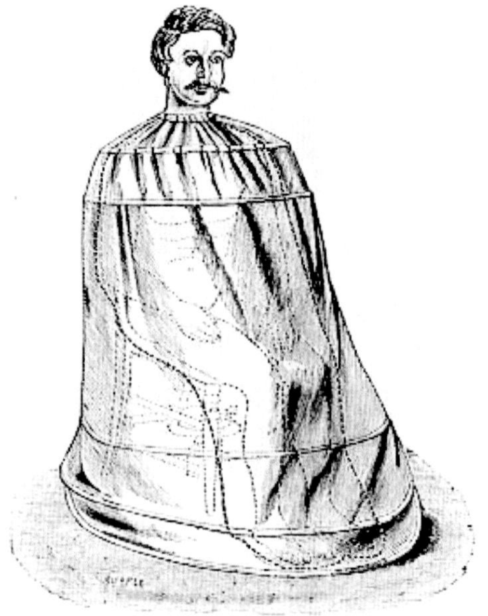

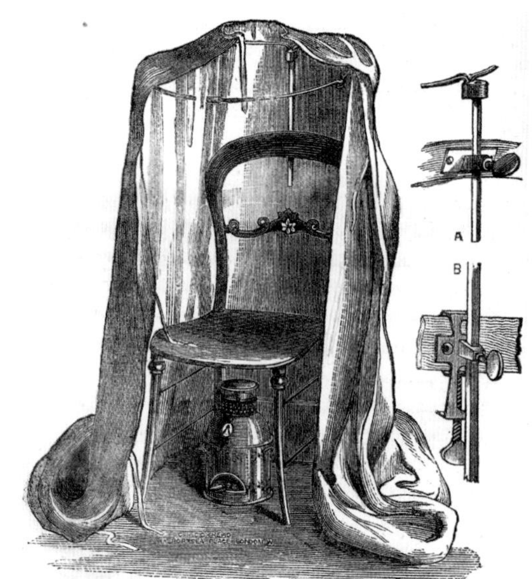

Fig 24.9 (right)
The 'Crinoline' bath worn cloak-like by the bather.
(J L Milton, On the modified Turkish and vapour bath…, *Hardwicke, 1874)*
Fig 24.10 (far right)
James Allen & Son's 'Cloak bath' attached to a chair.
(W Gordon Stables, Turkish and other baths, *Dean, 1883, p.44)*

Fig 24.11
The Gem Quaker easy-to-carry lightweight enclosure.
(The Gem Quaker Turkish bath cabinets *[catalogue], The company, 191?)*

Several companies targeted their advertising at women, emphasising the bath's ability to 'clear the complexion' 'leaving it clean and soft as velvet' and, less accurately, as an aid which 'REDUCES SURPLUS FLESH'. The price of such portable Turkish baths started at 25s, including the spirit heater. It was claimed that in less than half an hour, the air temperature could be raised to 170°F (77°C).

Phebe Lankester, writing under the pseudonym 'Penelope' in her syndicated newspaper feature for women called 'Our ladies' column, by one of themselves', wrote that she had recently been presented with such a bath.

> [N]ow, when the wind blows bitterly through my windows … and … all the world seems dark and dreary … when life ceases to be interesting, and I feel rigid and miserable, I shall get into my Cabinet Turkish Bath and set my skin at work instead of my brain … After sitting in it for half an hour, a tepid cold sponge bath and brisk rubbing with rough towels should follow, and the sensation of relief and comfort is experienced which only those who attend to their skins, as important factors in good health, can realise. My cabinet bath was bought in London, but I suppose I must not say where.[7]

Spirit and gas lamps were still the favoured form of heater, though by now all but the least expensive models placed the heater outside the enclosure, the hot air being funnelled through a duct into the space beneath the bather's chair. Gas heaters were considered the most convenient, since it was easier to control the temperature and the cabinet warmed up more speedily.

At this time, better-class homes were lit by gas, and among the many Turkish bath cabinets manufactured by the Gem company was one that plugged into the light socket. Their 'No.1 Bath, with Gas Outside Stove' (Fig 24.12) cost 60s, to which had to be added extra tubing 'with push-on ends to connect the tube to the bather's own gas jet. 4ft [1.2m] and 6ft [1.8m] lengths cost 2/6d and 4/- respectively'.[8]

A strong advocate of the home Turkish bath was Gordon Stables, well known to parents as 'Medicus', who advised their children on health matters in the *Boys' Own* and *Girls' Own* papers. He wrote a book on Turkish baths which seems to have been published at his own expense. He was also the author of innumerable adventure stories for boys, a fact which can, perhaps, be deduced from his extraordinary account of the arrival, from the local railway station, of his cabinet bath.

Fig 24.12
The Gem Quaker outside gas stove and cabinet.
(The Gem Quaker Turkish bath cabinets *[catalogue], The company, 191?)*

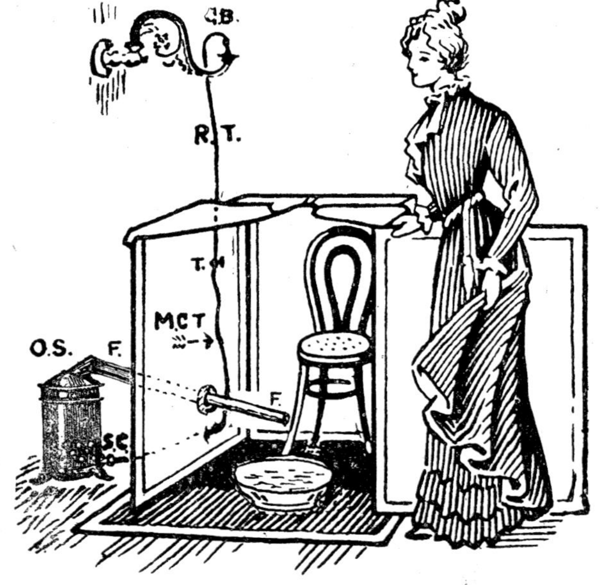
Gem Outside Gas Stove.
G.B.
R.T.
T.
MCT
O.S.
F.
F.
S.C.
O.S., outside stove; G.B., gas bracket; R.T., rubber tubing, which conveys gas to the stove; T., tap, inside bath, by which the bather controls gas supply; M.C.T., metal-covered tube, from tap to stove; F.F., funnel which conveys the hot air, or vapour, from stove into the bath.

Fig 24.13
The Tourist's or Traveller's Bath.
(W Gordon Stables, Turkish and other baths, *Dean, 1883, p.51)*

> A box! Whatever could it be, we wondered. It was not the season for sending anything particular from the country. Christmas was a long way ahead, and grouse shooting had not begun. We undid the outer covering and exposed it to view. It was shaped like a spirit-case, but it could not be that. 'That box may contain' we mused, as we gazed on it, 'untold luxury in the shape of tea, or a new patent photographic apparatus, or a magic lantern, or an English concertina, or—yes—or—or—or a land torpedo sent by a Fenian, that will explode when we lift the lid, blow the roof off the house, and send us sailing away skywards, accompanied by the furniture and things.
>
> We clapped a cautious ear to the lid and listened. There was no suspicious ticking audible within, so we summoned up courage and—opened the box, and lo! and behold, Allen's portable Turkish bath.[9]

Another variant of the portable Turkish was the Tourist's or Traveller's Bath (Fig 24.13). This comprised a stove which was used with, for example, one's host's chair and towel, and which was small enough for a cyclist to take in his bag. (Stables also wrote guide books for the touring cyclist.) But the Tourist's bath had other uses as well and could boil water to make tea or coffee. Furthermore, in conjunction with the outside cover of the apparatus, it could be 'used for frying Bacon, Chop, Steak, or cooking Omelettes, etc. It has an extra thick plate to prevent burning'.

Accidents and safety

Given the methods used to heat the air in the cabinet bath, it would be surprising if there were no records of fatal accidents. In 1885, *Swimming Notes* published a letter from a Mr G A Roberts, advising readers with less safety consciousness than we should expect today, that you do not need to do without a Turkish bath just because the local council will not build one.

> A spirit lamp (which can be purchased for one shilling) is placed under a cane-bottomed chair, upon which the bather sits, denuded of all clothing save a gown or wrapper made for the purpose (a large heavy blanket will do), which fits closely round the neck, falling over the knees and leg, enveloping the entire chair except the back, near the floor, left open for the escape of fumes and admission of air ... The cost of the bath is one penny, that being the price of the spirit.[10]

Almost immediately a reader must have alerted the editor to the dangerous nature of this type of bath, by drawing his attention to the recent death of Dr W B Carpenter. This leading London physician had himself been in the habit of regularly taking such a bath in his own home. Two weeks after printing Mr Roberts' letter, the editor followed up by referring to Dr Carpenter's death.

> ... The bath that had for so long cost him but a penny per day, at last cost him his life. We therefore trust that those of our readers who may use a similar bath will take every possible precaution to avoid accidents, fatal or otherwise. In the event of the spirit-lamp being upset, it will be well to promptly divest ourselves of the blanket in which we are wrapped, and by covering the flames with it, exclude the air which is as necessary to the spread of fire as breathing is to our existence.[11]

Although wood-panelled Turkish bath cabinets (Fig 24.14) were more expensive than those discussed so far, they had a number of advantages. Sturdiness was an obvious factor. Constantine's Turkish Baths in Oxford Street, Manchester, sold simple wooden cabinet baths in the mid-1880s for £4, with the spirit heater costing an additional 8s.[12] Was Constantine so

certain of the inferiority of cabinet baths that he knew his customers would quickly return to his own establishment, to be looked after by his well-trained staff?

The solid construction of some of these baths made them more transportable than portable (Fig 24.15). But the major advantage was safety, since it was easier to use an external heating apparatus which could be firmly attached to the cabinet.

In the 1890s, the Gem Wood Bath Cabinet, was 'Absolutely the Safest, Most Complete, Effective, Durable, and Handsome Bath Cabinet in the World', cost eleven guineas, complete with choice of gas or spirit external heater in copper, adjustable seat, bookrest, and a book of directions.[13]

Nevertheless, many of the early chair-supported frame baths were still in use at the end of the 19th century; even, as we discovered from Philip Burne-Jones's sketch of the Hamiltons' bath, in families where expense would not have been a primary consideration.

Although the 1939 Army & Navy Stores catalogue, for example, was still offering the No 2 Gem Special Cabinet at £6 5s 6d including an external tin heater, or for £7 1s 6d with an external copper heater, cabinet baths had rapidly declined in popularity after the end of World War I.[14]

Fig 24.14
The Gem Wood Cabinet cost £11 11s with heater, bookrest and water glass holder.
(The Gem Quaker Turkish bath cabinets *[catalogue], The company, 191?)*

Fig 24.15
Ellis's beautiful 1870s bath, from the Oxfordshire Museum's Dew Collection. (Photo © Malcolm Shifrin Courtesy of the Oxfordshire Museum)

25

Turkish baths for animals

St Ann's Hydropathic Establishment, already prosperous by the mid-1850s, largely relied on its own home farm to provide fresh local produce for its patients and staff.

It was, therefore, almost predictable that Dr Barter should build a Turkish bath for his cattle (Fig 25.1) soon after he began using one to treat his patients. He saw no reason why the therapeutic potential of the bath should not be just as effective with animals. He believed that just as it was good for 'affections of the lungs, the bronchi, and congested conditions of the human body', so it should be good for 'pleuro-pneumonia, and other distempers to which cattle are subject.'[1]

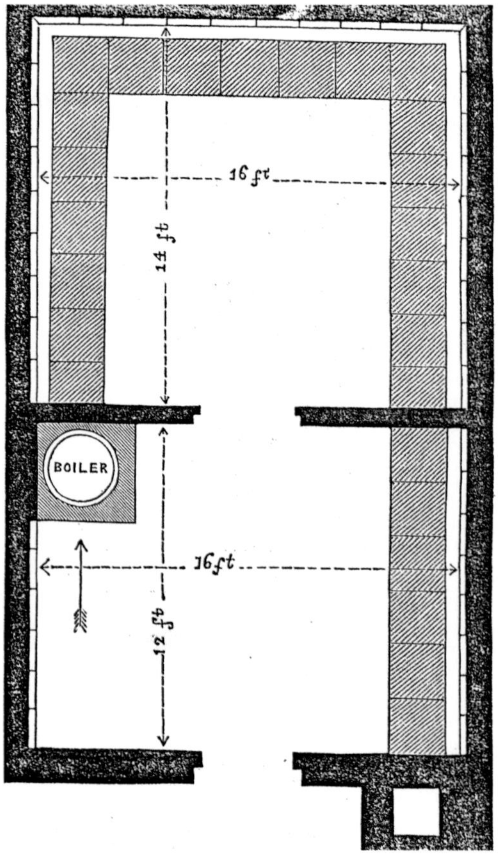

BOILER

16 ft

14 ft

16 ft

12 ft

Fig 25.1
Dr Barter's Turkish bath for the cattle on this farm at St Ann's.
(Wade, Robert C, 'Report [on] the utility of the Turkish bath…' Edinburgh veterinary review, *vol.2; no.8; October 1860. Wellcome Library, London)*

Turkish baths for farm animals

He seems to have had positive results. In one test, seven out of eight cows with pleuro-pneumonia were cured, while only one died—a much lower death rate than usual.[2]

Barter also believed in preventative medicine, and cows were given Turkish baths for several days before calving. It is interesting to note, in this context, that in the Finnish countryside, women often chose to give birth in the family sauna,[3] although it seems unlikely that Barter was aware of this.

John Enraght Scriven claimed to have been the first to use the cattle bath for a sick horse.[4] He happened to be staying at St Ann's at the time, and he looked after it himself for five days because his grooms were too 'ignorantly prejudiced' to enter the bath themselves.[5]

When Dr Robert Wollaston visited St Ann's in 1859, he reported that the cattle bath was also being used for any horses or dogs on the farm who were unwell.

> It is curious to observe with what patience and apparent satisfaction they endure the process of sudorification. Various diseases incidental to domestic animals, besides the distemper and epidemics, have been cured by the hot-air Bath; and I witnessed the curious spectacle of seeing two horses submitted to the process, with the perspiration rolling off their bodies, afterwards washed with tepid water, and then groomed or rubbed down with brushes steeped in cold water.[6]

By the end of 1859, similar baths had been erected in neighbouring farms. In nearby Cork, cattle baths were provided at two veterinary establishments. And when, the following year, Barter opened his Turkish baths in Dublin's

Lincoln Place, there was an adjoining bath for horses and other animals—this at a time when London still had no Turkish bath for people.

There were, of course, doubters. One architectural correspondent found it a source of great amusement, writing,

> Possibly we may hear by-and-by of elderly maiden ladies availing themselves of the system in restoring to convalescence their pet 'tabbies' and 'poodles',[7]

and suggesting that the eastern pipe and shampooing process might prove something of a novelty.

That same year, 1860, the Council of the Royal Agricultural Society of Ireland set up a sub-committee to report on 'the efficacy of the Turkish bath as a remedy for distemper in horned animals'.[8]

Its members visited Turkish baths for cattle at four farms, including St Ann's, and concluded:

1. the proportion of deaths to recoveries from distemper in cattle was much lower with use of the bath;
2. the animals' constitution was not adversely affected by it, their milk returning almost immediately after relief from disease;
3. with lesser animals also, treatment was very favourable, especially of inflammatory diseases of the internal organs.

At St Ann's, for example, out of three pigs with malignant black distemper, a disease considered virtually incurable, two recovered after use of the bath.

With such a small survey, the results were not statistically significant and some observations were contested. Mr St John Jefferyes of Blarney Castle, at a meeting of the Royal Agricultural Society in Cork, explained how a tenant of his had claimed some success in curing distemper in cattle by the use of a Turkish bath. While he was himself absent, his clerk had, without his authority, erected a bath at a cost of £26, and this had been inspected by Mr Ball and Mr Wade, who had been brought there by Dr Barter.

There was one part of their report, he claimed, which was so surprising that he did not know how the visitors could have swallowed it,

> namely, that a cow which was put in the bath sick, would be well next day, and would be turned out. His experience of the Turkish Bath for three or four months was this: He had several cows attacked with distemper during the time. Four or five of those recovered without going near the baths; three or four died in the bath; and he had not a single recovery in the bath; consequently it was impossible to call it a remedy for lung distemper.[9]

He continued that Mr Forrest, a tenant of his, had sent two of his cattle into the bath and both had died. The Turkish bath as a cure for pleuro-pneumonia was a 'perfect sham', and if all his cows were ill he would not send a single one there if it were right next door.

But John Enraght Scriven (who had first treated a horse using the bath) wrote, in an article 'Four years' experience of the bath on an Irish farm', that he now treated horses, sheep, pigs, dogs, cats, hens and chickens in it.

The fire was permanently lit, the floor above was tiled so that the bath acted also as a kiln for drying grain, and the furnace gave a constant supply of hot water. The total cost for fuel, working, and repairs was £30 per year, including the attendant's wages.[10]

Articles like this, and the widespread publicity arising from the report in the *Edinburgh Veterinary Review*, undoubtedly encouraged the spread of Turkish baths for animals. This was not confined to Irish farming circles, but also impacted abroad.

In 1866, for example, Charles Hamilton Macknight built a Turkish bath—the structure of which still survives (Fig 25.2)—on his

Fig 25.2 Charles Hamilton Macknight's Turkish bath for his merino sheep. (Photo [1983] by courtesy of Professor Campbell Macknight, great-grandson of Charles Hamilton Macknight)

Fig 25.3
Admiral Henry John Rous (1795–1877)—'arbiter of matters equine'.
*(*Vanity Fair*, 7 May 1870. Author's collection)*

property, Dunmore, in the Western District of Victoria, Australia. Macknight's great interest at that time was the breeding of merino sheep, despite the locality making them prone to attacks of fluke. But on 7 October 1867, he wrote in his journal that he had successfully run sheep through the bath, and 'effectively killed the ticks at 180°F [82°C]'.[11]

Turkish baths for racehorses

Back on mainland Britain, it was the horse-racing fraternity, rather than gentlemen farmers, who initially adopted the Turkish bath to protect their investment in stock, though again, not without controversy. Just as the bath was advocated as a panacea for all human ills, so it was with horse diseases.

In a seminal article, 'The Turkish bath as a means of training', published in *The Field* in 1860 and widely reprinted, Admiral Henry John Rous (Fig 25.3) argued that the traditional practice of sweating racehorses, to remove unwanted fat by means of heavily clothed four or five mile gallops, was unnecessary (Fig 25.4).[12]

It left the horse exhausted, fit the following day only for a walk, and frequently resulted in accidents injuring the horse's legs. But sweating in a Turkish bath was far more effective, and left the horse lively and in peak condition. Furthermore, there was a great improvement in the horse's general health.

Rous's views were listened to with respect. As Frank Siltzer wrote in the 1920s:

> [His] position as the sole arbiter of matters equine at Newmarket and elsewhere is without parallel in the history of the turf.[13]

But, as so often with proselytisers, he overstated his case. It appeared to many that he was advocating the use of the Turkish bath instead of ordinary exercise, whereas the bath might have been more readily acceptable if recommended as a complement to exercise.

It was claimed that Thormanby, winner of the 1860 Oaks, and Kettledrum, winner of the 1861 Derby, were both trained using the Turkish bath.

However, two strong advocates of the Turkish bath brought some much needed reality to bear.

Sir Thomas Spencer Wells, surgeon to Queen Victoria's household and specialist in ovarian diseases, had checked, and found that Thormanby had only taken the bath once, when suffering from a cold. 'A useful institution', he said, 'should not be brought into ridicule by over-praise'.[14]

Erasmus Wilson argued that like the prize-fighter, runner, or rower, 'the racehorse must still have his muscles trained by exercise' though the baths would 'amply and sufficiently provide' for the removal of fat.[15]

It was probably due to the influence of Rous that the London & Provincial received a letter from a Mr Isaacson, asking about the possibility

Fig 25.4
The traditional manner of sweating a race horse in the early 19th Century.
Sweating a race horse,
J Wheble, 1816.
Author's collection)

of their building a Turkish bath at Newmarket.[16] Rolland went there with Somers Clarke to discuss the matter, but the company, then in the midst of obtaining and finding the finance for its own bath, wrote afterwards declining the project.[17]

By 1861 several training stables had installed Turkish baths, while in Melton Mowbray, there was one for horses trained for hunting.

A simple bath, such as the one at Brackley, Northamptonshire, comprised a loose box (in the form of an enclosed and covered stall in which an animal can be comfortably confined), a flue passing round the wall from an adjacent stove, insulation placed beneath the horse's feet, good ventilation, and drinking water. The temperature ranged from 120° (49°C) to 140°F (60°C). Some horses went into the bath three or four times a week, others every day except Sunday.[18]

But there were also more elaborate facilities, such as the two-room bath illustrated in Walsh's 1862 manual, *The Horse, in stable and field* (Fig 25.5).[19]

'The use of the Turkish bath for racers', *The Field* had written a little earlier, 'is spreading far and wide, the local prejudices of trainers succumbing to the manifest instances of its efficacy.'[20]

But not all trainers, and not for all purposes, as Journeyman laconically notes in his appraisal of the racehorse Ben Jonson, in George Moore's *Esther Waters*:[21]

> A nailing good horse once … But there's no use in thinking of him. They've been trying for years to train him. Didn't they used to get the flesh off him in a Turkish bath? …[Fulton] used to say that it didn't matter 'ow you got the flesh off so long as

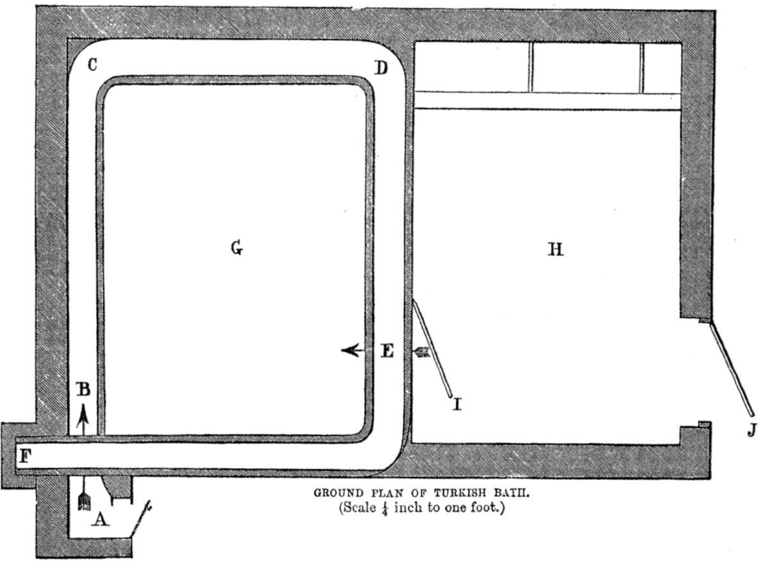

Fig 25.5
A two-room Turkish bath for horses.
(Walsh, J H, The horse, in the stable and the field, *Routledge, 1862)*

you got it off ... But the Turkish bath trained horses came to the post limp as old rags. If a 'orse 'asn't the legs you can't train him.

The consensus seems to have followed W J Miles who, after quoting and critiquing Rous at length in *Modern practical farriery*, concluded that,

the hot-air bath will be found in practice rather a remedial application for abnormal states of the horse's condition, or a direct agent for the removal of disease, than a systematic adjunct to ordinary training processes.[22]

If Turkish baths appeared in mainland racing stables before they did on farms, their later agricultural use was not without some success.

The *Scottish Farmer* reported in 1862 that Lord Kinnaird, a reformer who helped ease the conditions of the working class, was using a Turkish bath for cattle at a much higher temperature than was usual in Ireland. He argued that, in cases of pneumonia, the temperature needed to be 'very great—up to 200° to 212°—boiling point, in fact' otherwise no curative effect was apparent. Regularly used at this heat, he claimed that it helped to prevent acute disease, and more speedily relieve it, if it was chronic.[23]

The surgeon, Sir John Fife, in what may have been early praise for natural farming methods, wrote that he saw the pig benefiting most from the bath:

It is not only its maladies, more injurious to man than those of all other animals combined, to which an end is put at once; but the sweetening of its flesh, the facilitating of the formation of that flesh, the restoration of its dimensions, and the whole at a greatly reduced expenditure of food.[24]

We may not be able to discover how long the Turkish bath survived in the countryside, but its use with working horses in the urban environment lasted well into the 20th century.

Turkish baths for urban workhorses

In the north, Turkish baths for town horses are known to have been provided in 1860 by Clement Stephenson, 'the best vet in Newcastle'. An article in *The Field* quotes a private letter dated 27 May from G[eorge] Crawshay to a Mr R [probably Stewart Rolland]:

I went ... and found the fire on and the bath heating, the whole contrived most cheaply and simply. A horse had been in on Friday, and had had a sweat with excellent results.[25]

Further south, another vet, James Moore, opened a bath in London's Upper Berkeley Street in 1862. Together with Joseph Walton, Moore applied for a patent for improving the ventilation of such baths.

Floor traps (Fig 25.6) ensured that,

the evacuations and other offensive or unhealthy matters can be washed and carried away without producing any steam or vapour.[26]

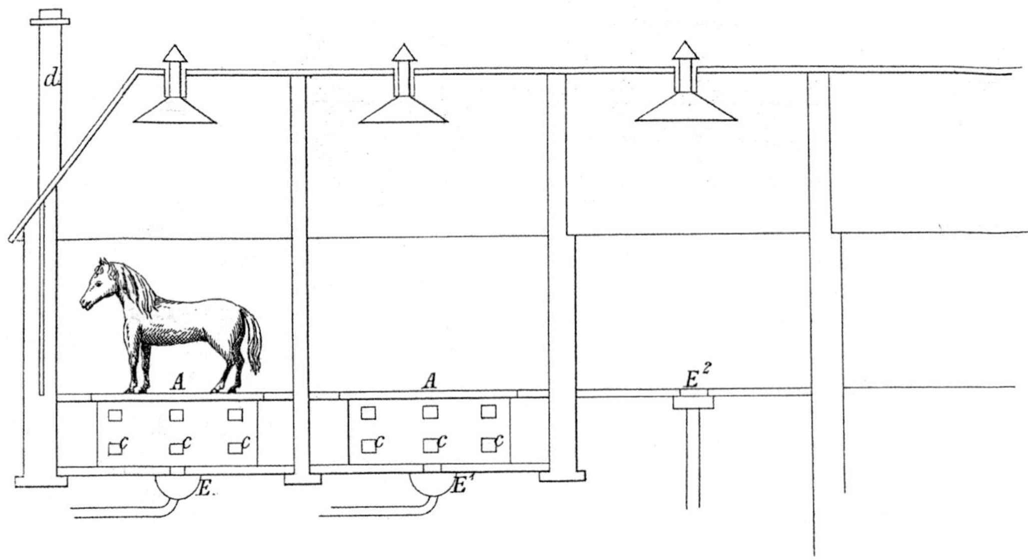

Fig 25.6
Ventilating Turkish baths for horses.
(Walton, Joseph and Moore, James, Improvements in the mode of ventilating and heating rooms, Turkish baths..., *Letters Patent: 1862; no.2127*
Author's collection)

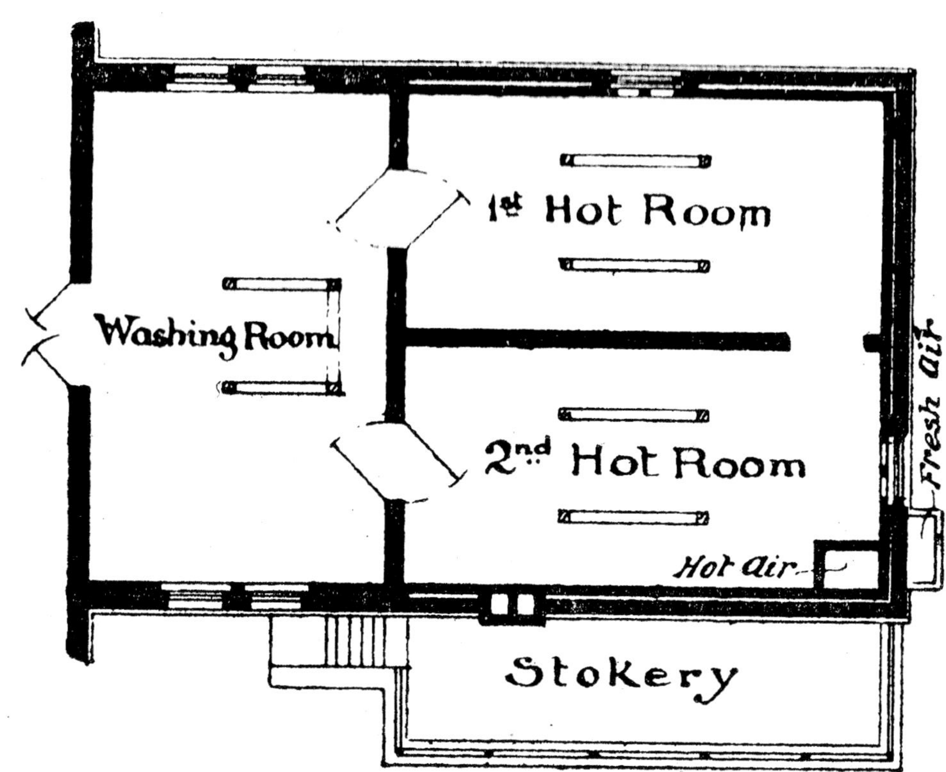

Fig 25.7
Plan of the Turkish bath at the Great Northern Railway's hospital for horses at Totteridge.
(Robert Owen Allsop, The Turkish bath, *Spon, 1890 p.142)*

With the rapid growth of the railway companies, it is easy to forget how important horses still were in the Victorian era. It has been estimated, for example, that in 1893 there were about 300,000 working horses in London alone.[27] Pickfords, the carriers, and the Great Northern Railway Company both owned facilities which cared for their horses. But it is probable that there were other smaller facilities, not to mention those outside the capital.

In 1872, Pickfords, the carriers, built a Turkish bath for horses at their large Finchley depot.[28] The company would have found this method of sweating their horses especially beneficial, as five-mile gallops would have been a non-starter.

By 1919 Pickfords had nearly 1,900 horse-drawn vehicles, and 1,580 horses to draw them, even though they already had 46 motor vehicles. And as late as 1946 they still had 300 horse vans.[29]

Their Turkish bath was heated by the 'industry standard' furnace, Constantine's Convoluted Stove. Three years after it was installed, Joseph Constantine wrote to ask if his stove was still performing well and a Mr Hayward replied,

> We use it regularly three days per week, and sometimes oftener. Never less than twenty horses per week are put into it, undergoing sweating, washing, and drying again in an outroom ... [30]

In 1884, 12 years after its installation, Constantine wrote again. This time a Mr Brett assured him that they still used his bath, and found it 'useful and beneficial to the horses', but for how much longer is unknown.

The second of these major facilities was the hospital for horses in Totteridge (Fig 25.7), which the Great Northern Railway opened in 1884.[31] This included a Turkish baths suite with three interconnected rooms in which, again, the air was heated by one of Constantine's stoves.

Inside, there was a large wash, or grooming room, slightly heated, with a hot and cold water supply. From there, the horse entered the first hot room, or *tepidarium*, maintained at between 140°F (60°C) and 150°F (66°C). After being thoroughly acclimatised, it could then, if necessary, pass on to the hottest room, or *caldarium*, maintained between 160°F (71°C) and 170°F (77°C). Finally, without any need to turn round, the horse returned again to the grooming and washing room.

In 1900, 16 years after the Totteridge baths were built, George Wade wrote that at King's Cross Station, the company's London terminus, up to 1,000 heavy horses would be working at the same time. Another 300 would be off duty, and resting in the stables which had been built under the goods platform. A further 185 horses worked in the passenger parcels department, and 40 on railway omnibus duties and in the adjoining yard.[32]

The horses, which cost about £60 each, worked 12 hours per day for four or five days per week, with a working life of about four years. Taking the company's other stations and goods depots into consideration, it is clear that much time and money was spent in housing and feeding them, and the Turkish baths would have helped keep them in good condition.

Victorian carriages, buses, and trams also relied on animal horse power. In 1893, the London General Omnibus Company had about 10,000 horses drawing a thousand buses.[33] We do not yet know if their horse infirmary had a Turkish bath, though a company in New York, with more than 2,000 horses running their buses, opened one in 1882. The hospital's Dr Hough said, 'The Third-Avenue Company takes good care of its horses, and it pays'.[34] He also claimed to have invented the Turkish bath for horses. This was clearly incorrect, but he may have been referring to the steam baths which the hospital also used.

It is probably impossible to determine when Turkish baths for animals went out of use, but advice on how to build them was still being published at the end of the 19th century.

Robert Owen Allsop's book *The Turkish bath: its design and construction*, published in 1890, included a chapter on the subject. Allsop drily acknowledged that,

> Animals of many kinds, including horses, dogs, cows, sheep, and pigs, have been experimented upon with regard to the bath, and with much success. But for practical purposes all we need here consider is the design of the bath for horses, since a bath for a horse will evidently be suitable for a cow, and might not be wholly beneath the dignity of a pig.[35]

PART V

The world of the bather

26

Victorian women and the Turkish bath

If any aspect of the Victorian Turkish bath is going to be difficult to examine as part of a general survey it is, predictably, the impact of the bath on women, and of women on the bath. One obvious approach would be to summarise the results of studies already undertaken.

But if such studies exist, they are well hidden—even more so than the data on which they might be based. So, here, I must be content merely to indicate what we already know, and signpost those areas where it would be interesting to probe further.

Of the 600 or so Turkish baths which we have been considering, at least 370 were baths for the general public which opened during Queen Victoria's reign; just over 100 of them provided, to a greater or lesser degree, facilities for women (Fig 26.1).

For convenience, in this chapter only, I have referred to these as 'the women's baths.' The term is, of course, quite inaccurate, but I have used it in order to avoid constant repetition of necessarily lengthy qualifications.

Irrespective of whether women were offered bathing facilities in a specific establishment, women were actually involved in almost all of them—as shareholders, proprietors, or managers, and as receptionists, attendants, or shampooers.

This, then, is a first impression of the Turkish baths which Victorian women bathed in, and those they worked in—a tentative look at facilities, availability, admission charges, and the wages paid.

Early attitudes

When Victorian Turkish baths were introduced, it was taken for granted that they should be used by both men and women. But it was not long before women's use of the bath was belittled as being somehow less important.

Fig 26.1
Women were able to relax and enjoy each other's company in the Turkish bath, just as the men did in the Queen Elizabeth*'s bath (see page 260).*
(Courtesy Ruth Corney)

Although Dr Barter's first bath, at St Ann's hydro, was built as a therapeutic facility, by 1872 an anonymous leader in the Manchester *Critic* was advising that,

> If ladies only knew what a real and lasting beautifier the Turkish Bath is, they would abandon all agitation for 'Women's Rights,' &c, and at once build a Turkish Bath for their own special use. By using it, they would thereby render themselves so fascinating and beautiful, that there would be no resisting any appeals they might make to the weaker sex.[1]

By the late 1880s, although the health benefits were rarely completely omitted, the promise of softer skin and beautiful hair was still one of the most common approaches to women as potential bathers. Here, in an advertisement rather more balanced than most in this respect, is Lillie Langtry's puff for the Pilgrim Street Turkish Baths in Newcastle-upon-Tyne:

> I write a line to tell you how much pleased I have been with the way you manage the Ladies' Bath. I attribute my perfect health entirely to the Turkish bath which I take twice a-week regularly. I find it keeps my skin in excellent condition, notwithstanding the pigments one is unfortunately obliged to use on the stage, and I think for all

> small ailments the Turkish Baths is the best Doctor to fly to.[2]

Some writers, like Dr Thomas Lewen Marsden, had a more patronising attitude to women and Turkish baths:

> To show the delightful influence of the Turkish Bath, suppose a man comes home ill-natured, jaded, and weary with the affairs of the world, cross with his wife, and quarrelling even with his dinner; let the good wives who hear me take my advice, and tell their husbands to go wash in a Turkish Bath, and they will throw off their ill-humours—mental and bodily—and then return delighted, as I am sure they will be, in spirit, happy with their wives, contented with their dinners, and playful with their children.[3]

Barter, of course, did not subscribe to such views, providing Turkish baths for all his patients and, as we have seen, for his farm workers and their families also.

Similarly, William Potter's original bath in Manchester was open for women two mornings per week, supervised by his wife Elizabeth, yet his example was not followed, even as a minimal provision, by all later Turkish baths.[4]

The ownership of Victorian Turkish baths by women

It is difficult to analyse women's ownership of Turkish baths with any degree of accuracy as information is not easy to find in any methodical way. We can never know how many Turkish baths there actually were, so I have probably underestimated the total number open to women.

Turkish baths were considered perfectly respectable and their growing popularity coincided with the rise of the joint stock company. So it is worth noting that women were among the shareholders in many of the 100 or so companies whose records survive.

But—although this might be a slight underestimate—I found only 21 women who were proprietors of baths open to women, of whom 18 were widows or legatees of male proprietors.[5]

And two women were appointed manager of an establishment. One of them, Emma Clarborough, was manager of the Norfolk Street Turkish Baths in Sheffield, between the early 1880s and 1898.[6] She was then promoted, becoming company secretary of the Sheffield Turkish and Public Baths Co Ltd, which owned the baths until 1903.[7]

I have not been able to find accurate information in any *consistent* manner because data for each establishment is not available continuously, but only at randomly available points in time. Furthermore, even the information which *is* available frequently comes from inaccurate sources such as directory entries. As the digitisation of local newspapers progresses, future researchers should find it easier to find more information and, with a greater number of sources, be able to ensure greater accuracy.

Women's access to Victorian Turkish baths

Of our 100-plus women's baths, 38 provided totally separate facilities, in the same building, but with separate entrances, and 64 provided separate sessions for women on specific days, or at stated times.

Only two Turkish baths not adjoining a men's bath are known to have catered solely for women. The first was opened by Bradford Corporation in 1883 at Lister Terrace, and remained open for 13 years (see Chapter 15, page 155).[8]

The second, only mentioned once, in 1883, was at 8 Osnaburgh Street, just outside London's Regent's Park. There is no evidence to suggest that these remained open for very long. At the cost of 3s 6d for a bath, or 5s 0d for a private one, it was expensive, even for this part of town.[9]

Even when women could afford the baths, class got in the way. It seems typically Victorian that the Keighley Board of Health decided to build separate first- and second-class baths—for men and women to use on different days—instead of one bath for men, and another for women, both of which could then be used every day.[10]

In the Turkish baths open to the general public, women were almost invariably at a disadvantage. Where facilities were shared, only one, Richardshaw Lane in Leeds, allowed women equal access (Table 26.1).

Of the 51 establishments for which occasional figures are available, over half limited women to the equivalent of one day per week, while the remainder divided roughly equally between one-and-a-half days, and two days.

Table 26.1 Shared use of Turkish baths by women

Baths	Female: male ½-days/wk	Female: male hrs/day
2	1:11	—
27	2:10	—
8	3:9	—
10	4:8	—
1	6:6	—
1	—	2:8
2	—	4:8

Times were available for 51 baths only. The table is designed to give a general impression only, using the limited data available.

In 1858, a letter to the editor of a local paper about the Leeds Road establishment in Bradford read:

> I know it is not orthodox for ladies to be newspaper correspondents. This however is a subject in which our sex has equal interest with the gentlemen ... The ladies ought to have at least three nights in the week. On the two nights of the week the rooms are inconveniently crowded, and even sometimes during the afternoons.[11]

Such complaints were not unusual. Women were told their days were not sufficiently patronised. One company chairman, apologising for the provision of just one day per week, said they had found,

> wherever they had enquired that the ladies had not taken advantage of those baths, and, however much they might desire to be gallant to them, they wanted to see their funds first.[12]

James Forder Neville put it more bluntly, saying that they tried to open a separate bath in Paddington but 'Paddington women won't take Turkish baths.'[13]

Probably Dr Baxter Langley was closer to the mark when he argued that it was the high prices which kept women away, and that public baths should make special provision for them.[14] But providing publicly funded Turkish baths was (perhaps conveniently) thought to be of doubtful legality at that time, and none was built in London till after Victoria's reign.

Wealthier women were easily able to take Turkish baths in hotels or fashionable hydropathic establishments (Fig 26.2). We know that women visited hydros on their own because, from 1888, St Ann's Hydro was served by its own railway station—St Ann's Hill on the Cork and Muskerry Light Railway—and five years later it was found necessary to add a separate Ladies' Waiting Room to meet their needs.[15]

Fig 26.2
The women's cooling-room at Smedley's Hydro in Matlock.
(Smedley's Hydropathic Establishment, *Matlock: the hydro, 1920s. Author's collection)*

Although some Turkish bath companies restricted the times when their baths were available to women on the basis that they were underused, others were not averse to making arrangements for special groups of women, if there was the possibility of making a profit.

In 1882, when the Oriental and General Bath Company of Leeds refurbished its 16-year-old baths in Cookridge Street, it was decided to build a separate Turkish bath suite for women, and to include a mikveh.

> A special feature of this establishment is the Jewesses' baths, comprising first and second class, built at the request of the Jewish community, from plans supplied by the Chief Rabbi, and used exclusively by Hebrews ... [16]

The *mikveh* (a ritual bath which requires running water) is used by Jews on special occasions, but particularly by women after childbirth or menstruation. The Oriental was one of a number of companies which made such provision as part of their women's Turkish baths suite. Later, the practice was followed by a number of local authorities, as at Nottingham in 1896, and as recently as 1937 in the Pier Approach Baths at Bournemouth (Fig 26.3).

Advertisements for separate women's facilities, perhaps surprisingly, often emphasised that they were 'under the supervision of Females'[17] or, if shared, that 'none but females (specially instructed) are in attendance.'[18]

We might take this as understood, but Victorian proprietors may have felt it necessary to distance their baths from the disreputable bagnios and 'hummums' of the recent past, which were often no more than brothels (Fig 26.4). They may also have wished to stress that the therapeutic Turkish bath would be a comfortable experience; that women had no cause to fear the intrusions on their privacy often suffered during visits to their male doctors (Fig 26.5).

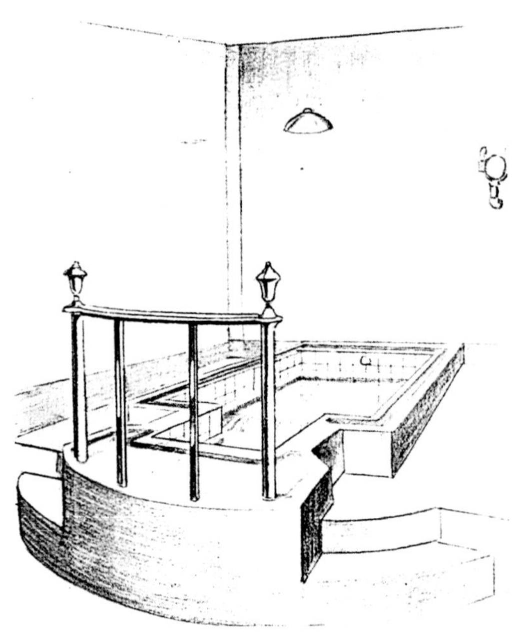

Fig 26.3 (right)
The mikveh at the Pier Approach Baths in Bournemouth.
*(*Bournemouth Pier Approach Baths, *The Corporation, 1937. Reproduced by permission of Bournemouth Libraries)*

Fig 26.4 (below)
The caricaturist Thomas Rowlandson visits a bagnio at the start of the 19th century.
(Thomas Rowlandson, A diver, *Ackerman, 6 April 1803. Author's collection)*

Admission charges and employees' wages

Before 1881, the cheapest Turkish baths most frequently found ranged from 6d to 1s. By the end of the century, 1s was the more common price.

Although the lower price was usually for a second- or third-class bath, this did not mean that it would necessarily be inferior to one which was first class. There were a few instances where there might be two hot rooms instead of three, but the lower price usually meant that the same baths were used at a different time of the day, or that bathers had to bring their own towels.

But personal cleanliness was almost impossible for those who were too poor to afford even sixpence for a Turkish bath. And although women were usually charged the same as men, very few women had any disposable income of their own, and subsidised entrance voucher schemes, such as that run by the Cardiff branch of the Ladies' Sanitary Association (see Chapter 16, page 175), were extremely rare, and might have been unique.

Even bath charges as low as 6d or 1s take on a different perspective when compared with what a woman could earn by working in the baths.

For example, in 1891, Gloucester Corporation charged 2s 0d for a first-class Turkish bath including a private dressing cubicle, plunge bath, shampoo, and use of the lounge, and 1s 6d for a second-class bath after 6 pm.

In the same year, at the same baths, a young woman was appointed at 12s 0d per week to issue tickets, and a Mrs Turner was engaged as a female shampooer 'she to attend when required and to be paid 4s 0d for each day she attends.'[19]

She was still there in 1921 when the Corporation presented her with a 'purse and contents as a token of appreciation', though we are not told the value of the contents.[20]

Histoire générale du toucher.
PL. XXIX.
Toucher, la femme debout

Fig 26.5
The 'aversion of eye contact' during a gynaecological examination.
(Jacques-Paul, Maygrier, Nouvelles demonstrations d'accouchemens, *Paris, 1822. Wellcome Library, London)*

In 1896, as part of Charles Booth's *Life and labour of the people in London*, George Duckworth interviewed James Forder Neville about his shampooers.[21] At that time there were around 40 Turkish baths in London, and Neville suggested that between them they employed around 100 male, and 20 female, shampooers.

Nevill's Aldgate establishment had baths for women (entered from Commercial Road) and for men (entered from Whitechapel High Street round the corner). Both were open for the same number of hours each day.

The standard wage of a London shampooer was 20s (£1) per week; Nevill's paid 22s simply to be able to say that 'Nevill's pays more than anyone else'. But this rate did not apply to all his employees; women shampooers were paid only 14s per week (Table 26.2).

Table 26.2 Shampooers' wages at Nevill's Baths in 1896

Men's annual wage	£57 4s 0d
Men's annual tips	£143 0s 0d
Men's annual income	£200 4s 0d
Women's annual wage	£36 8s 0d
Women's annual tips	£26 0s 0d
Women's annual income	£62 8s 0d

The facilities and appearance of the women's baths

Many establishments, even those open to both sexes, were quite simple—a converted house or a shop; but a few were purpose-built, and rather more luxurious.

The §Brighton Hammam, for example, was lavishly fitted inside with marble, coloured tiles, and fine woodwork. Its Alhambric hall was entered through red curtained Moorish triple arches, and furnished with divans 'pillowed in damask and silk'.[22]

The women's baths on the first floor were smaller, had a separate entrance, and a large cooling-room, which was elaborately decorated and furnished, 'feminine taste and elegance of disposition being, of course, considered and provided for.' As in most women-only baths, there was no plunge pool.

And elsewhere, pretty curtains and a dressing table were often intended to divert attention from the smaller size of the women's baths, and the fact that not all the men's facilities were matched in the women's baths (Fig 26.6).

Women's areas were generally smaller, or else they were the same as the men's second-class baths, as in Cookridge Street, Leeds.[23] Even a quick glance at the plans of Nevill's Northumberland Avenue baths (Fig 26.7) shows that the difference could be considerable.[24] Even so, when author Dollie Radford visited Nevill's with her friend Eleanor (Tussy) Marx, she wrote, 'They are regal! I enjoyed myself there ever so much, & longed to stay for ever.'[25]

Fig 26.6
'Pretty curtains and a dressing table' at Nottingham.
*(*Baths and bathing, *Nottingham: The Hammam, 1898. Courtesy Nottingham Local Studies Library)*

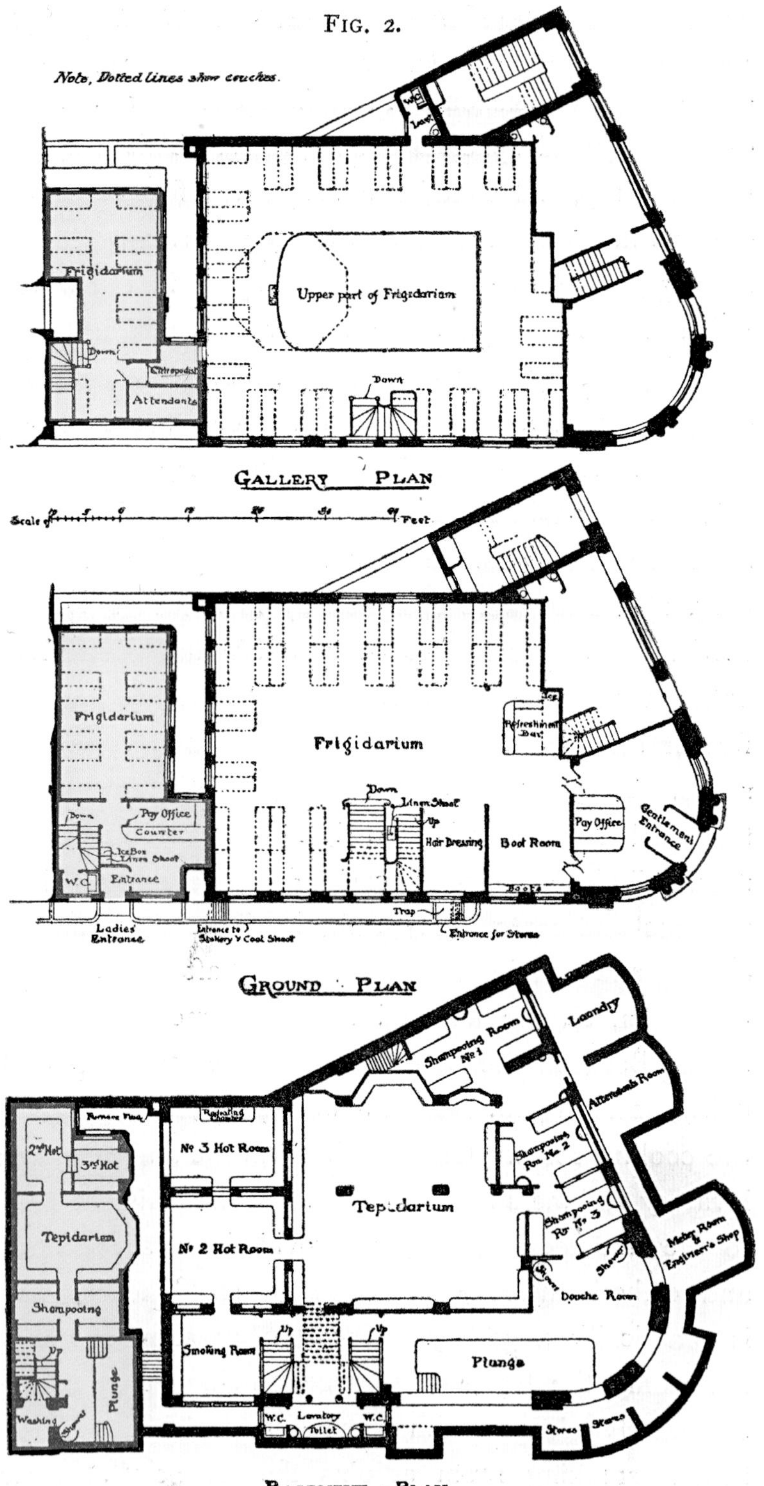

Fig 26.7
The men's and women's baths at Nevill's, Northumberland Avenue. (R O Allsop, The Turkish bath, *Spon, 1890, p.24. Enhancement © the author)*

Air temperatures varied from establishment to establishment. Men's hot rooms ranged from 120°F (49°C) to 230°F (110°C). This might seem high, but the body can easily cope, provided the air is dry. Matilda Ellrington, a young servant who looked after the Urquhart children, testified on oath at the inquest on baby William that she had happily spent half an hour at 180°F (82°C) in the Turkish bath at his Riverside home.[26]

Most women seemed to prefer slightly lower temperatures, but we do not know why. Amongst men, there may have been a certain macho competitiveness to see who could bear the hottest room for the longest time—the least beneficial approach to determining the best temperature.

Women bathers were more concerned with privacy than men, preferring individual changing cubicles to undressing with others in a cooling-room. 'Penelope' suggested in 'Our ladies' column' that,

> there is something contrary to feminine instinct in the gregarious nature of a public Turkish bath. We like such things best at home, or at all events at some bathing establishment where we may be residing for a time ...[27]

Robert Owen Allsop understood that many British women, unlike their French counterparts at spas such as Aix-les-bains, preferred not to get undressed or take showers in communal areas (Fig 26.8).

'In ladies' baths', he wrote, 'more privacy must be observed. Each lady bather should have a private dressing and reposing room, even if only formed by dwarf wooden partitions',[28] and 'private shampooing recesses' should be formed with partitions of wood and 'obscure glass.'[29]

Nevertheless, when there was a plunge pool, perhaps some women swam naked just as the men did. For although there are numerous references to 'full loose robes',[30] or 'a kind of toga ... descending from the shoulders',[31] no other garments are ever mentioned, however detailed the description of the bathing process.

But in suggesting that 'a plain, circular bath with steps around' would be appropriate because in 'ladies' baths ... the true dive does not pertain',[32] Allsop was clearly unaware of the active female membership of the burgeoning mid-1880s swimming clubs.[33]

Attitudes and benefits

The typical male view was still that ladies, as distinct from women in the 'labouring classes', should never undertake physical exercise or exert themselves in any way. As the pseudonymous author of a booklet espousing the bath

Fig 26.8
Postcard: showering in the open at Aix-les-bains in France.
(Author's collection)

declared in 1858, 'to ladies, to invalids, and men of business, whose sedentary occupations preclude the possibility of healthful exercise', the Turkish bath was 'an inestimable boon.'[34]

Proprietors reinforced such attitudes, unimaginatively parroting each other. In 1895, Joseph Constantine reprinted advice already written several years earlier 'by a medical man'.[35] Incredibly, this was printed yet again, almost word for word, nearly 80 years after it was first written, in a booklet published by Derby Council in 1964—the so-called Swinging Sixties:

> LADIES need these baths even more than gentlemen, and are more benefited by them, owing to their being usually more confined indoors, having less exercise, etc.[36]

In a classic example of the medical profession attempting social control, women of all ages were linked with 'all who have any kind of constitutional weakness, and all persons over thirty-five years of age'—all of whom should 'ask medical advice before taking their first Turkish bath.'[37]

While some doctors openly disliked the Turkish bath, seeing themselves being deprived of work, others, including Dr Elizabeth Blackwell, the first woman doctor to be admitted to the General Medical Council's register, sought a professional excuse for cutting down on its use, advising that it should only be given under medical supervision.[38]

While bath proprietors did not wish to offend their local doctors and risk the loss of their patients, they most certainly knew that the bath itself was not harmful to women. Indeed, those women who worked long hours as masseuses in the heat of the baths not only came to no harm, but frequently lived longer than those persuaded to avoid exercise.

As early as 1859, William Potter somewhat coyly advertised the arrangements made at his bath 'for the special accommodation of ladies', few of whom were yet, it seemed,

> conscious of its power to mitigate the natural ills and inconveniences to which nature and an artificial mode of life have subjected them. This portion of the subject can, however, only be slightly touched upon, but a word to the wise will be sufficient.[39]

The Turkish bath was later reported to have had a beneficial effect in connection with

Fig 26.9
Maud and her friends visit a Turkish bath in London.
*(*Maud: the diaries of Maud Berkeley, *adapted by Flora Fraser, Secker, 1985, p.125)*

irregular menstruation and, as we have seen, mention of this was made in accounts of its use in Victorian asylums.

While the Turkish bath was undoubtedly less harmful than most patent medicines, some proprietors did make extravagant claims, suggesting, for example, that it 'removes the cause of barrenness';[40] others, more sensibly, advised women that it would not harm them while pregnant or nursing,[41] a view not held by all doctors, even today.

Charles Bartholomew boasted numerous testimonials claiming relief from pain in a wide range of illnesses, including many for which there was then no known cure. About a third of those he published were from women.[42]

But apart from testimonials, which were often solicited, there are few personal accounts of the use of the Turkish bath written by women. We only exceptionally find out how Victorian women felt before, during, and after the bath. And there are even fewer accounts of younger women going to the baths in a group solely to enjoy themselves, as Maud Berkeley and her friends did on Wednesday 30 March 1892, and as Maud so delightfully illustrated (Fig 26.9) and described.[43]

> The fancy has taken us to have a Turkish bath. Ethel was first recommended to take this unusual type of exercise by her doctor in India, when she complained of lassitude. Apparently, it invigorates the cells of the skin and promotes well-being. We decided we were all in need of this aid to health.
>
> Very charming baths, tiled in turquoise. Expected a Turkish pasha to leap out at any moment and entice us into his harem. Ethel poured scorn on these fancies.
>
> Felt very strange and defenceless, wrapped in towels...Hoped that the attendant might bring us Turkish sweetmeats as we lay on our couches, but she only brought more and more towels.

Who *were* the women bathers? How did they travel to the baths? Did they usually go singly or with friends? How did they finance their visits? Were women able to use male approval of the Turkish bath to facilitate the management of such visits for their own enjoyment? Was there a social change between the 1850s and 1880s which made it acceptable to 'pamper' oneself without the need to justify the bath as a medical necessity?

We have much still to learn.

27

Victorian Turkish baths: 'sites of sex and sociability'?

In this chapter I discuss activity of a sexual nature which takes place, took place, or is reputed to have taken place within a number of Victorian Turkish baths. We will look briefly at how attitudes and behaviour have changed over the life of the bath, and the passing centuries.[1]

In discussing the first of these periods, the latter part of the 19th century, we come across Anthony Trollope's short story *The Turkish bath*, which is set in the Jermyn Street Hammam. Two short case studies consider how this story has been treated: first, by literary critics suggesting what might have been in Trollope's mind when he wrote it; second, by queer theorists attempting to use it as evidence for hidden history. These studies are followed by some rare evidence of how things might actually have been.

London and New York in the early 1900s

In a chapter on London's Turkish baths in his meticulously researched book *Queer London: perils and pleasures in the sexual metropolis, 1918–1957*, Matt Houlbrook refers to London's Turkish baths as affirmative 'sites of sex and sociability'.[2]

The book focuses on the period between the end of World War I and the publication of the influential report on homosexual offences and prostitution, chaired by John (later Lord) Wolfenden.[3] The Wolfenden Report, as it was generally known, led—but only after a further 10 years—to the decriminalising of homosexual behaviour between consenting adults in private, though it had no relevance to their behaviour within public spaces such as Turkish baths.

Houlbrook's chapter, 'The Baths', is based on a wide range of sources including biographical material, law reports, committee minutes, guide books, newspaper reports, and excerpts from interviews with a number of gay men.

He concludes that during this period, gay men began to feel increasingly secure, and more or less safe from prosecution in several of London's commercial Turkish baths, and even in some of those run by local authorities. In such surroundings many men who were worried or uncertain about their sexuality were able to discover that they were not unique, and that there was a lively community to which they could belong.

Matt Cook, in his equally well-researched *London and the culture of homosexuality, 1885–1914*,[4] deals with the period immediately before Houlbrook's, yet there are only two references to Turkish baths in his index, and neither refers to a Turkish bath in London—indeed, one is in Paris.

This lack of information might seem surprising, since in New York, according to George Chauncey, this period, just after the turn of the century, was the time when many of that city's Turkish baths first became more gay-friendly, and increasingly tolerated overt sexual activity.[5] This led, around the 1920s and 1930s, to the appearance of the first exclusively gay bathhouses—most of which were actually Russian steam baths. Consequently, the word bathhouse came to have a more sexual connotation in the United States than it has in Britain, where it is now less frequently heard in general use.

Chauncey's chapter on New York's gay bathhouses presents an informed and highly readable view of how the bathhouse moved from a time when it was intermittently raided by the police to a time when it became more widely accepted as part of the New York scene.

Why, then, is there no similar London scenario described in that part of Cook's study which deals with the same period?

Available and unavailable evidence

One undoubted reason is that it is difficult to find any real evidence to show how any similar transformation might have taken place, either in London or elsewhere in the British Isles. This is only to be expected of a way of life which was not only illegal at the time, but was subject to extremely harsh punishment when defendants were unsuccessful in court.

Matt Houlbrook, referring to the period between 1918 and 1957, writes that for an institution which occupies such 'a prominent place in the contemporary queer imagination ... [the baths] have left relatively few traces in the historical record.' He continues,

> The legal sources on which much of my work draws are scant in this respect since the baths were simply beyond the knowledge of most Londoners—including the [Metropolitan Police and the London County Council] for long periods of time. This is, in itself, a remarkable testament to the security the baths offered: this was a commercial space in which men felt safe enough to have sex relatively openly—a public space which was, in effect, private.[6]

As a result of his research, Houlbrook manages to paint a remarkably detailed picture of the gay scene in some of London's Turkish baths at that time. But it is, by design, a picture of the first half of the 20th century.

We know almost nothing about the situation in the Victorian era, except that in any group of people, at any time, there will generally be a relatively small but highly significant proportion of people who prefer sexual activity with a person of the same sex.

So it would be nonsensical to suggest that, even in the early Victorian Turkish baths (where the sexes were invariably separated), there were not some bathers who enjoyed looking at the bodies of others, exchanging meaningful glances, feeling attraction, or even desiring physical contact. But that is quite different from suggesting that there was overt sexual activity, and that this was generally accepted.

In these first early baths, located in hydropathic establishments, or run by Urquhart's committees, where the Turkish bath was so new that its users saw themselves as harbingers and proselytisers on its behalf, physical contact of a sexual nature would not have been tolerated, either by the majority of bathers, or by the management.

The lack of any perceptible evidence as to the existence of such overt activity at this time has led some scholars to adopt a fresh research approach.

Reading the early Victorian Turkish baths

In a general work such as this, it is not appropriate to examine in any detail the important work on sexuality which was begun nearly 40 years ago by a new generation of historians—historians whose research, like that of Houlbrook and Cook, is unencumbered by secrecy or the baggage of the past. Yet as soon as one examines the history of the Turkish bath prior to the beginning of the twentieth century, these new approaches inescapably demand our attention because of this absence of clearly perceptible evidence.

Especially is this so in the light of research inspired by that part of the work of Michel Foucault which asks what it is that has made us believe that sex is something which needs to be hidden, and about which we must be silent.[7]

'Answering, or re-posing this question is the principal theme' of *Nameless offences: homosexual desire in the 19th century* by H G Cocks. In his introduction, Cocks refers to another of Foucault's ideas—that when authority seeks to identify objects for investigation and control, the result is not repression or censorship, but the emergence of new ways of representing them.

> While the law, and its language, has been the focus of historians, queer theorists and literary scholars have devoted themselves to disinterring the hidden meanings and evasions of Victorian literature. Queer theory in particular has encouraged practices of reading which seek to draw out the homosexual undercurrent in texts which, because of their historical location, could not explicitly identify or name their desire. Therefore this body of work adopts the suggestion that silence about sex does not produce an absence, but merely incites other, richer languages of description.[8]

Clearly, when the texts being examined are, for example, contemporary histories or factual travel writing, such an approach can be a powerful tool.

But great rigour is required when deriving 'evidence' from fiction in order to substantiate an intuited theory, whether in literary criticism, or in revealing previously hidden history.

For, even when the setting of a narrative is stated to be an identifiable, named location, there is a real danger that, in teasing out hidden meanings, there can be a failure to distinguish clearly between actuality and artistic licence.

The London Hammam at 76 Jermyn Street

1. As a literary case study

A relevant example of artistic licence in fiction can be found in Neil Bartlett's stylish *Mr Clive & Mr Page* (published in the United States as *The house on Brooke Street*).[9] Mr Page is said to meet Mr Clive outside the Jermyn Street baths referred to in the book as 'the London and Provincial at number seventy-six'.[10]

But the actual location which Bartlett had in mind was further down Jermyn Street—the baths 'where Rock Hudson was thrown out for importuning in 1952'.[11] These were the Savoy Turkish baths, opened in 1910, at 92 Jermyn Street. This all-male establishment was one of three London baths which were open all night, and were widely known to be much frequented by gays (Fig 27.1).

Nevertheless, Bartlett explained, 'the name "London and Provincial" felt exactly right for the sort of place a queen like my Mr Page would go [to]', even though it was actually the name of the company which had owned The Hammam at number 76.

By the time of the Rock Hudson incident at the Savoy, The Hammam had been closed for 12 years. But this has not stopped one writer from linking it to some of the later incidents in Bartlett's novel, and commenting that it 'offered steam rooms, plunge pools and massage parlours.'[12]

Fig 27.1
The Savoy Turkish Baths at 92 Jermyn Street—the last of the Savoy chain. (Unknown photographer)

Quite apart from artistic licence in works of fiction, the mere existence of two separate Turkish baths in Jermyn Street has caused much confusion, even in such standard reference works as *The Survey of London*, where §three of the seven references to Turkish baths have factual errors.

There are several works of fiction which do have scenes set in the baths at 76 Jermyn Street. The most significant is Anthony Trollope's short story *The Turkish bath* (Fig 27.2), first published in the monthly *St Paul's Magazine* in 1869, seven years after the baths opened, and later published with other stories in his book *An editor's tales*.

The Turkish bath tells of how a magazine editor is fooled into reading a manuscript written by a man who has followed him into the baths. Wrapped only in towels, the editor allows himself to be engaged in conversation with someone whose clothing and general appearance,

Fig 27.2
Anthony Trollope—as editor—seated with Molloy (right), in Trollope's short story set in the Jermyn Street Hammam. (Wood engraving by Joan Hassall from The Folio Society edition of Mary Gresley and Other Stories *by Anthony Trollope, courtesy of Simon Lawrence)*

away from the baths, would have warned against such an encounter.

In the first part of the story Trollope describes the baths and the bathing procedure, combining straightforward description with gentle tongue-in-cheek humour, for example, when describing the ritual of the towels,[13] the clapping of the hands (see page 297), the hardness of the marble, and the avoidance of conversation. The second part relates the actual encounter in the baths, and the third brings the story to a close in the home of the would-be author.

Mark Turner, in a ground-breaking analysis, suggests that the stories in *An editor's tales* use 'some of the conventions of porn (coded for a male reader) and so approach a veiled form of pornography intended to appeal to his male audience', [14] or, as one critic summarised part of Turner's argument, *The Turkish bath* is a 'soft-porn story of gay cruising.'[15]

Not being a work of literary criticism, this chapter is no place for an in-depth discussion of the validity of Turner's interpretation of Trollope's underlying meaning. It is, of course, impossible to determine what was going on in Trollope's mind when he wrote the story, or to be absolutely certain about his intentions. But Turner's arguments are the result of intensive study and have been well received by other scholars.

What should concern us here is that while critics are entitled to use any part of a text, or even the teased-out meaning of a text, in a critical analysis of a work of literature, they need constantly to bear in mind that their analysis *is of a work of fiction*. So even though a setting might be specifically identified with a real place, this does not necessarily mean that every single part of that description is totally factual, or was ever intended to be.

Trollope himself remarked, referring to this and other stories from *St Paul's Magazine*,

> I do not think there is a single incident in [*An editor's tales*] which could bring back to any one concerned the memory of a past event. And yet there is not an incident in the outline of which was not presented to my mind by remembrance of some fact ...[16]

Turner is well aware of this, commenting,

> The stories were not intended to be exact memories, and Trollope admits to condensing and constructing a number of editorial experiences in particular stories. But fiction is not fact and it is at least problematic to criticize it as such.[17]

Turner's analysis of what was in Trollope's mind is not materially affected by his taking the author's description of the baths as being wholly accurate. Yet even a scholar as careful as Turner cannot resist an occasional embellishment when his argument could be made just as effectively by simply analysing the action. He writes, for example,

> ... the nature of Trollope's Turkish Bath seems intended to arouse by teasingly positing the possibility of a homosexual encounter to male readers. The young, oriental boys, the heat, the steam, the nudity, the silence, the tension about etiquette, the supply of men: this is the stuff of cruising.[18]

While the phrase 'young, oriental boys' may perhaps sound sexually suggestive, the phrase 'oriental boys', young or otherwise, does not appear in the story. Trollope uses 'young' only to describe the men lying on a sofa: Walker of the treasury, and the editor's friends.

He actually uses the phrase 'eastern boys' rather than 'oriental boys'—and then only once. But apart from an office boy, there is no mention in the company's minutes of any youths being employed, and it seems much more likely that, in the context of the baths, Trollope is using 'boy', as most frequenters of St James would do at that time, to indicate a servant, the first meaning of the word given in the *Oxford English Dictionary*.

Here, 'eastern boy' would probably indicate that the attendant was not white, and might have previously been employed in a *hammam* in North Africa or France. This suggestion is supported by a Charles Keene caricature in *Punch* which appeared on 26 January 1866, just three years before Trollope's story was published, which purports to show a West End Turkish bath in a fictitious 'Latherington Street' (Fig 27.3).

More telling is Turner's use of the word 'steam' which does not appear anywhere in Trollope's story either. Why should it when there was no steam room in The Hammam? But in modern bathhouses, of course, the steam room is frequently the most usual place for initial sexual overtures. And, except in the plunge pool (strangely, not mentioned by Trollope), there was no open nudity in The Hammam at that time, bathers being swathed in at least two towels. Even in the pool, it was underwater nudity in dim light.

Finally, Turner implies—and in a later treatment states—that the baths were 'men-only'.[19] In fact The Hammam did provide women's

Fig 27.3
Charles Keene's imaginary Turkish bath at Latherington Street, W. (Punch, *20 January 1866, p.26. Author's collection)*

Turkish baths which only closed two years after Trollope wrote his story. Of course, this does not alter the all-male environment of the men's baths, but it does mean that it was possible for a woman, possibly a friend, to see a bather leaving the baths with an inappropriate companion.

If these might be considered minor points in an otherwise careful analysis, not all who followed Turner were as wary. Kate Flint, in her chapter 'Queer Trollope' in the Cambridge companion to the author, interprets Trollope as saying that the story 'was closely based on fact.'[20]

Flint loses no time in attuning the reader's mind to her thesis. In Trollope's story, she explains, a man starts up a conversation with the editor 'in the all-male Jermyn Street Turkish Baths. This is a queer setting indeed ...' Her juxtaposition of 'all-male', 'Turkish baths', and 'queer' can hardly be accidental. 'All-male' already seems to have become part of the history of the baths. And her use of the phrase 'clothes disappear completely' does not immediately signify that everyone was draped in towels—though she does clarify this later.

In justification for the attribute 'queer', Flint refers to phrases highlighted by Turner, such as 'very skilled eastern boys.' She also notes Trollope's description of how the narrator, adopting the editorial 'we',

> divested ourselves of our ordinary trappings beneath the gaze of five or six young men lying on surrounding sofas ...

a quotation which, in the story, continues,

> – among whom we recognised young Walker of the Treasury, and hereby testify on his behalf that he looks almost as fine a fellow without his clothes as with them.[21]

Yet at the time when Trollope was writing, it would have been almost impossible to have seen anyone naked in The Hammam.

Bathers undressed in compartments—cubicles with couches for reclining after the bath (Fig 27.4). These were situated, slightly raised, on the ground floor. Two of them were fitted with curtains for those who required total privacy.[22] The remainder had decorative screens well over 3ft 6in (1.1m) high placed between them and the main cooling-room, with even higher screens between cubicles.

A person undressing could not normally be seen by anyone lying on one of the four sofas

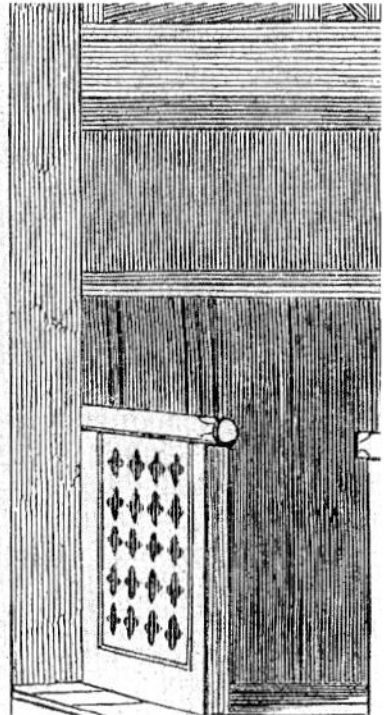

Fig 27.4
Partitioned changing and relaxation cubicles at The Hammam (detail from Fig 8.5, see page 72). (Illustrated London News, *26 July 1862. Author's collection)*

placed in pairs on each side of the pool; nor was it possible, for that matter, from any of the easy chairs which were placed, some years later, with their backs to the cubicles (Fig 27.5).

There was, besides, a strict puritanical attitude to nudity. The view of Erasmus Wilson, one of the founders of the London and Provincial company, that bathing with others without a costume was 'an evil', has already been noted.

Though bathers were naked in the cold plunge pool, as soon as they reached the pool steps they were surrounded by a 'gigantic crinoline of towels suspended from the roof to serve the ends of modesty while occupied with the friendly towel' (Fig 27.6), before being seen in the cooling-room.[23]

If we accept that Turner's interpretation of the story is valid, what might have been the source of those parts of Trollope's description which, though fictional, nevertheless seem to ring true? Were they imaginary details Trollope added to emphasise the hidden story—another example of artistic licence? Or has Trollope drawn his description of the baths from more than one establishment, in the same way that authors, including Trollope, sometimes base a character on aspects of more than one person?

It would be easy to hypothesise such a scenario, taking note of the fact that, between 1859 and 1867, Trollope worked for the Post Office in St Martin's-le-Grand. He could not fail to have been familiar with the Post Office Turkish Baths in the same road at No 19, owned between 1861 and 1864 by Major Richard Culverwell. Apart from a women's day on Tuesdays, these baths were for men only, and admission on Saturdays and Sundays was, at 1s, much cheaper than at The Hammam.[24]

Perhaps Walker of the Treasury was really a 'Mr Smith' of the Post Office? Could these baths, before they closed, have been the first recruiting ground for the fifteen-year-olds who later moved on to Cleveland Street—scene of the scandal in 1889 involving several aristocratic clients and male prostitutes, some of whom were employed as Post Office telegraph boys? [25] Of course, this is fanciful conjecture, but it is, at least, based on realistic possibilities.

Issues such as these are necessarily important to those researching the history of The Hammam but, as noted earlier, they do not necessarily affect critiques of the story as a work of literature. But if, on the other hand, an aspect of queer theory, or a history of gay appropriation of public spaces, for example, is to be supported to any extent by a work of fiction, the historian must first take great care in determining which parts of the text being mined are based on fact, and which on artistic licence.

2. As a case study in history

Since Victorian Turkish baths have not, until recently, received much scholarly attention, John Potvin's 'Vapour and steam: the Victorian Turkish bath, homosocial health, and male bodies on display' has been much cited, though a more inappropriate use of the words vapour and steam in the title of an article about the Jermyn Street Hammam it would be difficult to find.[26]

More or less the same material forms the basis of Potvin's two chapters, 'Steamy boundaries: Turkish baths, homosocial health and male bodies on display' [27] and 'Hot by design: the secret life of a Turkish bath in Victorian

Fig 27.5
The easy chairs with their backs to the changing cubicles (detail from Fig 9.11, see page 83). (Wiltshire and Swindon Archives WSA 1915/220)

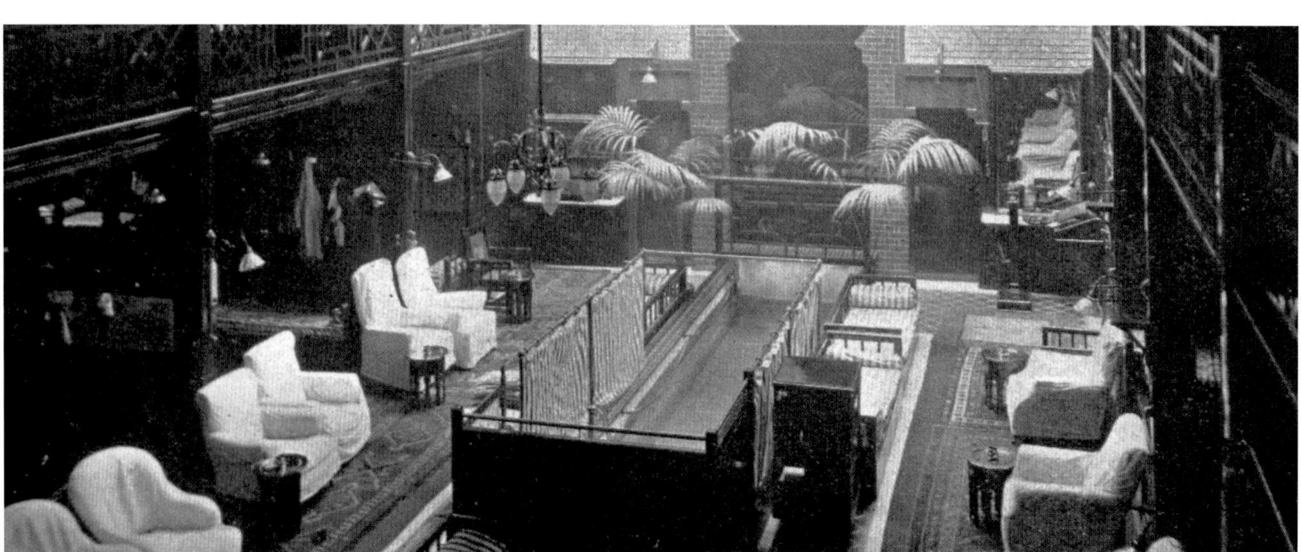

London',[28] the latter aptly described by one reviewer as,

> positively dripping with suggestive language from the description of the hot room as the 'climax of the homosocial ritual' to the supposition that the baths are 'spaces in which masculinity and sexuality are as slippery as the soapy passageways of the baths themselves.'[29]

Unfortunately, all three versions contain a number of errors and misunderstandings. Here, I take issue with the author's basing so much of his main thesis on the supposed existence of steam in The Hammam.

The inclusion of the words 'vapour' and 'steam' in the titles of two of his treatments is nonsensical when the whole object of the Victorian Turkish bath was to enable the body to sweat profusely by means of hot *dry* air. There was no steam at The Hammam until a Russian bath was added as part of the 1907–08 refurbishment (see page 83).[30]

There were, of course, *separate* steam baths in England even before the arrival of the Turkish bath. The second edition of Mathias Roth's book on the Russian bath, with an image of his own establishment in Old Cavendish Street, was published two years before the first Turkish bath opened in Britain.[31]

But only one of the important architect-designed Turkish baths of that period had steam rooms: not Burton's (1861) in the Euston Road designed by James Schofield; not the Camden Town Baths in Kentish Town Road (1878) designed by H H Bridgman; not Nevill's flagship baths in Northumberland Avenue (1884) designed by Robert Walker; not the Savoy Baths in Savoy Hill (1885) designed by C J Phipps; and not even the Wimbledon Theatre Turkish baths (built as late as 1910). The only exception around that time was Elphick's New Broad Street baths for the Nevilles.

This general absence of steam is confirmed when the standard book on the design of the Turkish bath by Robert Owen Allsop, published in 1890, has no mention of the provision of a steam bath.[32] He did include a chapter on vapour and Russian baths in his book *The hydropathic establishment and its baths* published the following year, but he also included douche rooms, electrical treatment, the pine cure and the *sun bath, as was to be expected in a book written for a different clientele.[33]

Only as late as 1906, was a chapter on the steam bath to be found in the standard British work on public baths by Alfred Cross.[34] By this time an increasing number of local authorities were adding Russian baths to their swimming pools, though in some cases, as with Liverpool Corporation, this was instead of the Turkish bath because of its lower cost.

Fig 27.6
Right of centre, the suspended towel 'crinoline' allowed bathers, after emerging naked from the plunge pool, to dry themselves modestly while an attendant waits with a fresh dry towel.
(Sims, G, Living London *Cassell, 1902, Vol II, p.369)*

Potvin argues that being with others in the all-male environment of the Jermyn Street Hammam, participating in its sweating, bathing, and relaxing activities, gave rise to a pleasurable bodily reaction,

> which enlivened a distinctly illicit homoerotic gaze and subsequent queer appropriation of its space, despite its best attempts to keep things clean and pure.[35]

The theory initially looks plausible, concerning, as it does, an early Victorian establishment which survived for 30 years after homosexual activity is known to have taken place in at least three other Turkish baths in London. How else to explain the progression from absence to tolerance? But Potvin is not painting a general picture here. The Hammam is specifically included:

> By examining the design and male culture of the Jermyn Street Hammam, this article attempts to tease out how a queer constituency gradually appropriated this and other Turkish baths as a destination for clandestine sex and community.[36]

But he produces no evidence for such activity in The Hammam. He seems to lack any understanding of how the steaminess and humidity of the *hammams* in Morocco and Turkey

Fig 27.7
Interaction between bathers in the cooling-room at The Hammam.
(An eye for architecture, *Tulane University Library, 1984.* Author's collection)

(described by Urquhart in *The Pillars of Hercules*) differed from the Victorian Turkish bath as exemplified by the London Hammam.

Neither does he seem to have any knowledge of how or why the baths company was set up, or of the people who set it up and ran it, imagining that,

> Urquhart sought out professionals to employ in his establishments [sic] in London and procured most of the attendants and shampooers directly from Turkey, namely from Istanbul.'[37]

In fact, apart from an unconfirmed specialist in coffee-making from Istanbul,[38] the only foreigner appointed by Urquhart was the Armenian Chief Shampooer, Youssouf Hieronymus, and it is not known whether even he was 'brought over directly from Turkey'.

Any writer needing to describe a building which no longer exists has to turn to contemporary building journals to get at the facts. But Potvin uses the journals in an attempt to tease out what he wants to find. For although each of his three treatments includes a plan of The Hammam,[39] he does not appear to notice that it has no steam room or, for that matter, any passageways—soapy or otherwise.

An intuitive conviction that The Hammam was appropriated as a gay space very soon after it opened should not lead to the invention of steam and vapour.

Potvin also draws conclusions about the interaction between bathers, and the manner in which their bodies related to each other spatially, from pictures (see page 72) published in the weekly *Illustrated London News* on 26 July 1862.[40]

But this was two days before the baths actually opened, at 10 am the following Monday.[41] So either the drawings were artist's impressions executed beforehand, possibly after sight of one of George Daniel Stevenson's presentation illustrations for Somers Clarke (Fig 27.7), or, more likely, they were drawn at the special pre-opening session held on 16 July[42] for company directors and their friends. Most of these bathers already knew each other and would, therefore, be standing and chatting in groups, quite differently from individual bathers using the bath once it was open to the public.

Potvin moves seamlessly back and forth in time, to and fro between different baths, without immediately indicating the dates of the opinions he quotes. So unless readers check the endnotes as they read, it is possible to assume that everything refers to the London Hammam.

It is important to emphasise that I do not contest that Potvin's scenario *might* be applicable after, say, the 1890s—though it would be much likelier in other baths—merely that none of his arguments offers any 'teased out' evidence of such activity in The Hammam at any time. By the mid-1880s the Paddington Hammam (Fig 27.8) at 8 Harrow Road was already open, and this seems a much more likely location for a gradual queer appropriation.

3. Perhaps, after all?

By 1884, 20 years after Urquhart retired for health reasons to the warmer climates of France and Switzerland, and seven years after his death, Thomas Gibson Bowles wrote to his fellow directors about what he saw as falling standards at The Hammam. If there had been any signs of creeping appropriation, it would certainly have been included amongst Bowles's highly critical list of things to be rectified, one of which was that, by then, the shampooers lacked the necessary skills.[43]

In fact there is no specific mention of improper behaviour within the baths anywhere in the company's surviving minute book. This covers the years till the early 1890s, when the minutes were detailed enough to record a complaint (discussed at the same meeting as Bowles's letter) that one of the bathers had been 'blowing his nose into his fingers in the washing room'.

However, six years earlier, there had been a recorded incident when David Urquhart Junior, managing director at the time, 'referred to an evil that was showing itself of bathers being advised by some of the shampooers to be rubbed [rubbing being no more than a contemporary synonym for massage] at their own homes instead of coming to the bath.'[44]

If the word 'serious' had been used instead of 'evil', it would be natural to assume that this practice worried the company because of lost revenue. But the only use of the word evil in nearly 30 years' minutes suggests an implied and understood sexual connotation. By providing massage at a bather's house, the shampooer was not only able to pocket the fee and the gratuity, but would be able to offer sexual services at a much higher rate.

But this does not support Potvin's claim of 'queer appropriation'; it argues against it. The main reason for offering massage at home would surely have been because it was considered too risky to give improper massage at The Hammam, and probably too risky even to suggest it to someone who had not already agreed to be massaged at home.

Fig 27.8
Mike Young's remembrance of the balcony at the Paddington Hammam. (Illustration © Mike Young, 2000, reproduced by kind permission of the artist)

Further, although Bowles had a lot to say about the services of the shampooers in his letter to the directors six years later, neither the letter nor the discussion which followed mentioned the earlier 'evil' which would have been dealt with as soon as the matter was raised.

The 20th century

Unlike most of the cubicles at The Hammam, those in the majority of later Turkish baths were curtained, and so were considered more or less private. This was true whether in commercial open-all-night establishments, such as the Imperial Hotel, the Jermyn Street Savoy, and the Harrow Road baths, or in local authority baths such as Bermondsey and Greenwich in London, or Leeds and Sheffield in the provinces.

But, as Houlbrook notes—quoting from an account of visits to London's baths around 1900 by an American writer, Edward Stevenson—even as late as the beginning of the 20th-century, sexual activity in the baths was still limited to gazing at bodies and arranging later meetings elsewhere.[45]

By the end of World War I, the situation was quite different, and Houlbrook's account of the relationship between gays and the London Turkish baths between 1918 and the end of the 1950s cannot be bettered.

When Houlbrook writes that for long periods the activities within the baths were 'simply beyond the knowledge' of the Metropolitan police,[46] this could often mean beyond their *official* knowledge, since the baths were used by men from a wide spectrum of occupations, not excluding those connected with the law.

In 2000, when Bob H. was 78, he remembered being at Greenwich Turkish baths in the mid-1960s, writing that it was a friendly place,

> where very pleasant sex and conversation was often [had] with a middle aged big chested man, who days later almost floored me by having seen several of us shoppers across Regent Street, bent down to my ear to ask if I would be 'there' on the Saturday, my friend being a London Policeman! [47]

In local authority baths, gays tended to meet at the same times on the same days, becoming what Bob called a Turkish 'Male Club'. First names were the order of the day and no one ever asked what anyone did for a living. On one occasion, though, he was told by another regular that,

> the chubby kindly man in his 50s had some time ago sent a pal of his 'down for seven years' at the local assizes, which was a bit of an eye-opener. 'Of course I don't mention it to him when we're at it', my friend added!

Not everyone who used the all-night baths was gay; nor was everyone who used the baths during the daytime necessarily heterosexual. Overt sexual activity was accepted, as we have seen, in some Turkish baths at a time when homosexual practices were illegal even in private. There was often a natural sympathy for those persecuted in law for consensual behaviour concerning which the law had no right to be involved.

And while there were exceptions, most bathers seem to have been mutually tolerant—perhaps an indication of widely changing attitudes which reflected a growing acceptance that there was urgent need for the repeal of a law relating to the private behaviour of such a significant proportion of the population.

By the end of 1975, all London's commercial Turkish baths had closed. There was still sexual activity in some of the local authority baths, such as that noted at Greenwich, but behaviour in most of them was, and usually remains, more circumspect.

Sexual activity was also known to have taken place at Turkish baths in Swindon, Leeds and Glasgow, noted here as randomly chosen cities merely to indicate that it was not confined to the capital. It also took place at the Victoria Baths in Manchester, where management decided, some time around the 1980s, to place an 'internal window between our Russian bath and the Shampooing Room' so as to 'make the steam room less private ...'[48]

Similar activity has not been found to have taken place in women's baths, though negatives are often impossible to prove.

Numerous lesbian, gay, bisexual, and transgender (LGBT) groups were questioned about this, but the general view was expressed by Anne, a correspondent who wrote,

> I have been around the gay scene now for forty years and had many many friends, some no longer with us. I have heard many male friends talk about Turkish Baths, usually in a jocular fashion over dinner, again many years ago. I have never ever heard any women who have had any visits to Turkish Baths for any similar reason.[49]

In this context, there has never been a need for Turkish baths to become safe havens for women, as lesbian love was not legislated against. And as Anne also suggested, women seem to approach other women differently.

The 21st century

So is sexual activity between gay men acceptable in Turkish baths today? In most of Britain, LGBT people currently have virtually the same rights as non-LGBT people, and are on the road towards full equal rights in law also. So the question is no longer relevant as it stands. Whatever is acceptable behaviour for heterosexuals in public Turkish baths is acceptable for gays; whatever is generally considered inappropriate or unacceptable also similarly applies to all.

These laws ensure that there is no longer any legal obstacle standing in the way of gay bars, gay saunas, or gay steam baths, and managements are free to make whatever house rules they wish. Bathing facilities are now available for all of us, according to our individual preferences.

28

Inside the Victorian Turkish bath

Although many Victorians appreciated the value of the Turkish bath as a cleansing agent or as a reliever of pain, it was increasingly used, as it still is, for relaxation and de-stressing oneself (Fig 28.1).

After the bath, the body may indeed be left, as Urquhart wrote, 'shining like alabaster, fragrant as the cistus, sleek as satin, and soft as velvet',[1] but later writers, such as Franklen Evans, pointed out that the bath was also,

> exceedingly quiet, and the warmth and tranquillity together have a most soothing effect upon the nervous system, and render the bather for a time completely oblivious of the cares of the outer world.[2]

Earlier, Dr Balbirnie, a fervent advocate of the bath, also praised it as an aid to relaxation, and felt it necessary to indicate how this was to be achieved.

> Calm and repose of mind and body, is the first essential rule of conduct in the Bath. All distracting thoughts and passions, therefore, should be left at the door, or laid aside with one's garments. Even to talk is more or less to excite the brain, and should be avoided as much as possible.[3]

The unquiet baths

But in the real world, it is not always easy to find places which are 'exceedingly quiet,' and disturbances of one sort or another are just as likely to occur in the bath as anywhere else. One such incident was related by George Elson, one of the very few people to have written about working in a Turkish bath.

At the age of 10 he was apprenticed to a chimney sweep as a climbing boy—one of the last—continuing as boy, journeyman, and finally master chimney sweep, for nearly 30 years.

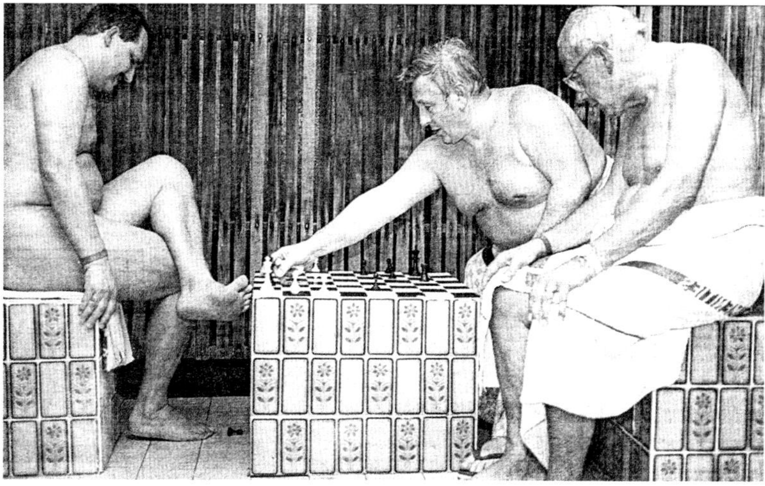

Fig 28.1
Three regulars at the Stockton-on-Tees Turkish Baths enjoy a game of chess. The baths were closed and demolished in 1998. (Photograph © Mike Urwin Neg. 98/05/542)

In the early 1870s, although he had never been in a Turkish bath before, he became a shampooer at the Sansome Walk Baths in Worcester, his wife soon being persuaded to supervise the women bathers. After three years he moved to Leamington and described in his autobiography some of the bathers he looked after in the 1880s.

> One night, while sitting in a hot room registering a hundred and sixty degrees of heat, two bathers commenced discussing that much-debated question—the 'Tichborne Claimant.'[4]
>
> Both being well posted upon every tittle of evidence which supported their side, not a moment was lost, as at it they went hammer and tongs, neither allowing the other to finish a sentence, and in their vehemence perspiring profusely all the while, and all the more by reason of their excited arguments, till half an hour, then three-quarters passed by, and as neither appeared on the point of giving in, but rather were waxing hotter and hotter in their arguments and temperature, feeling their health was likely to suffer, I was obliged to urgently request, and then to insist, on one of them coming to be shampooed, and very reluctantly one gave way.'[5]

It was not just the men who declined to remain silent. Women bathers liked to chat. While there are no records of anything as wild as some of the hen parties held in today's saunas, the idea is not new. The phrase 'hen party' itself was first used in print in 1887.

A Mrs Charles II Raymond of New York was the originator of the Turkish Bath Party (or TB party) in the 1890s. She advised that, if possible, a really 'swell' hostess hire the entire baths for the party.

> It is the proper thing to have your TB party in the evening and after all the minutiæ of the bath have been gone through with and the ladies have lounged around in the perfect freedom from clothes necessitated by the nature of a Turkish bath, and exchanged all the tidbits of gossip, they don their clothes, and are conveyed by carriages to a fashionable clubhouse, where they are met by the husband, brother or father of the hostess and her friends, who have been enjoying a TB or other diversions, and they end up the evening with a supper.[6]

Women's wish to have time apart from their men has not diminished with time. 'This is my day for myself', says Amy, a 1990s home help who once discharged herself from hospital so as not to miss her weekly bath at Lewisham's Ladywell Baths.

> It's an unwinding session. You've got no hassle here: no phone ringing, no one knocking at the door, no one shouting at you to make them a cup of tea. Today they fend for themselves at home while I pamper myself.

The same women had been meeting there for years; and though they claimed that they wouldn't recognise each other with their clothes on, they knew all the ins and outs of each other's lives. As one of the regulars put it: 'You bare your body and you bare your soul down here.'[7]

That many Turkish baths have a number of bathers who visit *their* baths on a regular basis is well known. Whenever a Turkish bath is threatened with closure, they usually form the backbone of any resistance.

The 1980s Porchester Turkish Bath Supporters Club was slightly different. They came together, not when their own comfort was threatened, but to help others in less fortunate circumstances than their own, on one occasion

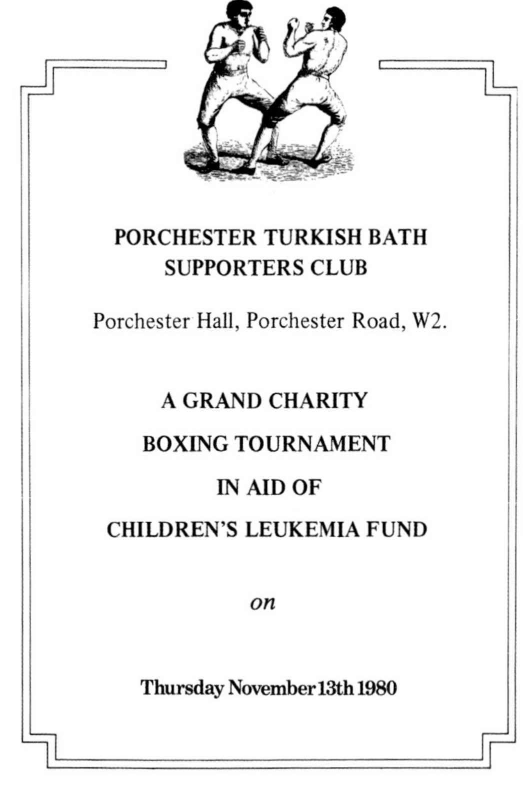
PORCHESTER TURKISH BATH
SUPPORTERS CLUB

Porchester Hall, Porchester Road, W2.

A GRAND CHARITY
BOXING TOURNAMENT
IN AID OF
CHILDREN'S LEUKEMIA FUND

on

Thursday November 13th 1980

Fig 28.2
Programme from a charity event organised by the Porchester Turkish Bath Supporters Club. (Author's collection)

organising a 'Grand Charity Boxing Tournament in aid of Children's Leukemia Fund' (Fig 28.2).

Not all help afforded by bathers was planned in advance. In 1870, Australian newspapers reported an incident which took place in the Hobart Turkish Baths in Tasmania shortly after they opened. It seems that,

> on the ladies' day at the Turkish baths, while some ladies, who are in the habit of attending there, were as usual enjoying the luxury of the bath, they were joined by a young girl whose bashful appearance and evident ignorance of the bathing process induced the more experienced ladies to proffer both advice and assistance. The one was implicitly followed, and the other gratefully received: but by-and-bye their aid was required in a manner they had not calculated on. The result was that before the young lady left the bath-room there was a visitor there who had not paid for admission, and Hobart Town had an addition made to its population.[8]

Most of those taking Turkish baths had a more uneventful bathing experience—one that would, with few differences, be recognised by any bather who had 'taken a Turkish' during the past 150 years.

Bathers' first Turkish baths

Every bather has to have visited a Turkish bath for the first time. To the uninitiated, this often seems a strange ritual to be endured rather than enjoyed.

Indeed, a certain type of aficionado will always attempt to make a ritual out of a simple practical necessity. In his story *The Turkish bath*, discussed earlier, Trollope gently pokes fun at what a later generation would call one-upmanship.

> Very much will depend on the manner in which [the bather] claps his hands, and the hollowness of the voice in which he calls for water. There should, we think, be two blows of the palms. One is very weak and proclaims its own futility. Even to dull London ears it seems at once to want the eastern tone. We have heard three given effectively, but we think that it requires much practice; and even when it is perfect, the result is that of western impatience rather than of eastern gravity. No word should be pronounced, beyond that one word,—Water. The effect should be as though the whole mind were so devoted to the sudorific process as to admit of no extraneous idea. There should seem to be almost an agony in the effort,—as though the man enduring it, conscious that with success he would come forth a god, was aware that being as yet but mortal he may perish in the attempt. Two claps of the hand and a call for water, and that repeated with an interval of ten minutes, are all the external signs of life that the young Turkish bather may allow to himself while he is stretched upon his marble couch.[9]

But this was not, of course, intended as a serious guide for the newcomer.

In 1933, when admission to Harrogate's Royal Baths still cost only 4s, an article appeared describing a Yorkshireman's first visit. Lengthy and laboured by today's standards, the adventures and misunderstandings of the novice were described, from sitting fully dressed in his changing cubicle wondering why he hadn't started to sweat, through the hot rooms and a steam bath, to his turn with the shampooer.

> ... So, first, he warmed t' slab wi' a bucket of 'ot water. Then 'e says, 'Sit dahn here, sir.' So Ah sat dahn. An' 'e got hold of my arms—first one, then t' other—an' rubbed them up an' dahn. Then he did t' same wi' my legs. Then 'e says 'Lie on yer back, please.' An' he started an' pummelled me wi' his fingers an' thumbs, right from my neck dahn ter my feet. Then he says 'Turn over, please.' An' 'e'd got mi 'ed in a sort o' wooden block, which mi neck just fitted in. An' Ah began ti think of t' guillotine. But t' shampooer said 'You're all right,' an' 'e 'elped me to turn over, so as Ah shouldn't slip off t' slab like. Then 'e started pummellin' and rubbin' me again, right from mi neck to mi feet. 'My word,' he says, 'it's coming out of you.'[10]

And so on, through the showers and cooling-room, to a final summing up: 'But Ah wor well satisfied wi' my "turkish". And, my word, you do feel grand after it!'

Throughout the life of the bath there were many similar articles, the writer almost invariably feeling it mandatory to attempt a humorous approach—the words pummelling, torture, and the phrase 'boiled alive' occurring only too frequently.

To find out how the Victorian Turkish bath really felt to a first timer one has to go to unpublished sources, such as Wendy Stacey's recent account of her visit to the Imperial Hotel Baths (see page 221), or this one by 'RLO', remembering a night spent at the Savoy Turkish Baths at 92 Jermyn Street in 1967, when he was not much older than 16.[11]

RLO's account is included in full for its detail, and also because these baths were often thought of as being an entirely gay establishment, which it could never have been at that time.

> When I entered Jermyn Street, the first thing I saw was a lit-up frosted glass sign with Savoy Turkish baths on it. The entrance to the baths was shared with another shop with both doors at a 45 degree angle on to the street. On entering, there was a long wooden-panelled counter on the left, with small safe deposit boxes behind it and I think that there was a glass screen on the left half of the counter. There was a sign showing 21s 6d entrance fee and for this you were given a black and white chequered cotton towel which you would wear and a large white towel to dry yourself with.
>
> You handed over your valuables, which were locked in one of the safe deposit boxes, and the key was given to you. It had a leather strap which you put around your wrist. I was also asked to hand over my shoes to the man behind the counter and when I joked was it to stop me running off without paying the extras, he just smiled at me.
>
> You turned right and walked down the stairs to a lower level. Someone was lying on a towel-covered couch. A masseur was rubbing oil into his client's back, while someone else was frying bacon and eggs on a gas stove in a small kitchen nearby. You could get a basic fry up, sandwich and drink at almost any time of the night.

Turning to the left led you into the area where the cubicles and beds were and where you changed. With the chequered towel around your waist and carrying the white towel, you descended down to the next level, taking the stairs by the kitchen. At the bottom to the right was the steam room with its large white marble steps against one wall where you sat and let the steam open up the pores of your skin.

After the steam room you had to shower, then jump into a small ice-cold rectangular pool which was up to your chest, then climb out up a wooden ladder. Turning left, you came to the first hot room, which was like a sauna to make you sweat. Once you grew accustomed to its heat, you would then go into the next room. This was smaller and hotter with wooden slats keeping your backside off the hot marble slab seat. You could then go into the last hot room, which was even smaller and so hot you had to be careful not to burn yourself on the hot marble, even with the wooden slats. Also the heat took your breath away.

There was a massage area, which I think was near the steam room, but I cannot be certain. It had a couple of marble slabs large enough for a man to lie on, so that he could have a massage with soap. I used to prefer soap as it was easy to shower off, unlike oil. There was not a set price. You just gave what you felt was a fair fee, which was about 10s old money. Remember that in 1967 the average wage was about £16 a week. After a while, you got to know the various masseurs and you had your favourite who suited you.

By then you felt very relaxed and ready for a sleep, even though the light was left on in the room where the cubicles were. Others came in through the night: gamblers, men out on the town like me and some who had just come in for a massage. I never remember any trouble there but it was a long time ago.

Accidents and death in the baths

Accidents happen everywhere, but when the bath was new, anything untoward was picked up and used as ammunition by those physicians who saw it as a threat. If someone died while at the bath, from whatever cause, it was usually reported, as one would expect, with headlines such as DEATH IN THE TURKISH BATH, but always with the implication that the death was caused by the bath.

§One of the most tragic cases was the death of William, the Urquharts' own 13-month-old son. Teething and in pain, he had been left for five minutes in his cot on the floor of the Riverside cooling-room at 95°F (35°C) when he suffered a fit. He was taken out of the bath and his parents tried to revive him, but he died before the doctor arrived.

At the end of a three-day inquest, despite the doctor's testimony that the bath was not responsible, the jury's conclusion, as reported in the local paper, was that 'the evidence is unsatisfactory as to the cause of death', and that 'The jury highly censured the treatment of deceased.'[12] The behaviour of the jury throughout the trial, their unusual censure of two bereaved parents who were actually shown to have cared deeply for their children, and the manner in which all this was reported, led Urquhart to take the reporter to the High Court where he was finally able to clear his name.[13]

In public baths, the most common type of accident seems to have been when a bather tripped or slipped onto a hot floor heated by a hypocaust. This might not have been all that unusual in practice, but only came to light when an older bather, or one who was unwell, was unable get up again quickly enough and was severely injured or died. This would usually be recorded as death by misadventure, but sometimes accompanied by remarks implying, for example, that a bather should never be left alone in a hot room.

If a bather had a heart attack in the bath, or sometimes even after returning home, there was often the suggestion that this was caused by the bath. But repeatedly, coroners would conclude that the bather's general health was such that he could have died at any time, and that the bath had no specific impact.

As Dr J L W Thudichum said in his lecture to the Royal Society of Medicine in 1861,

> As the bath becomes a common agent employed by the mass of the people, accidents and deaths in the bath, and illness apparently dating from its use, will, perhaps, now and then occur. People often die in their beds, and yet we do not think it dangerous to lie in them.[14]

Fires

Fires were a frequent occurrence in the 19th-century town, and Turkish baths were often damaged. Some, such as the Camden Town baths (Fig 28.3), designed by Henry Hewitt Bridgman (1845–98), were sufficiently damaged to preclude their reopening. Others, such as those at Dalston, were completely destroyed by fire.

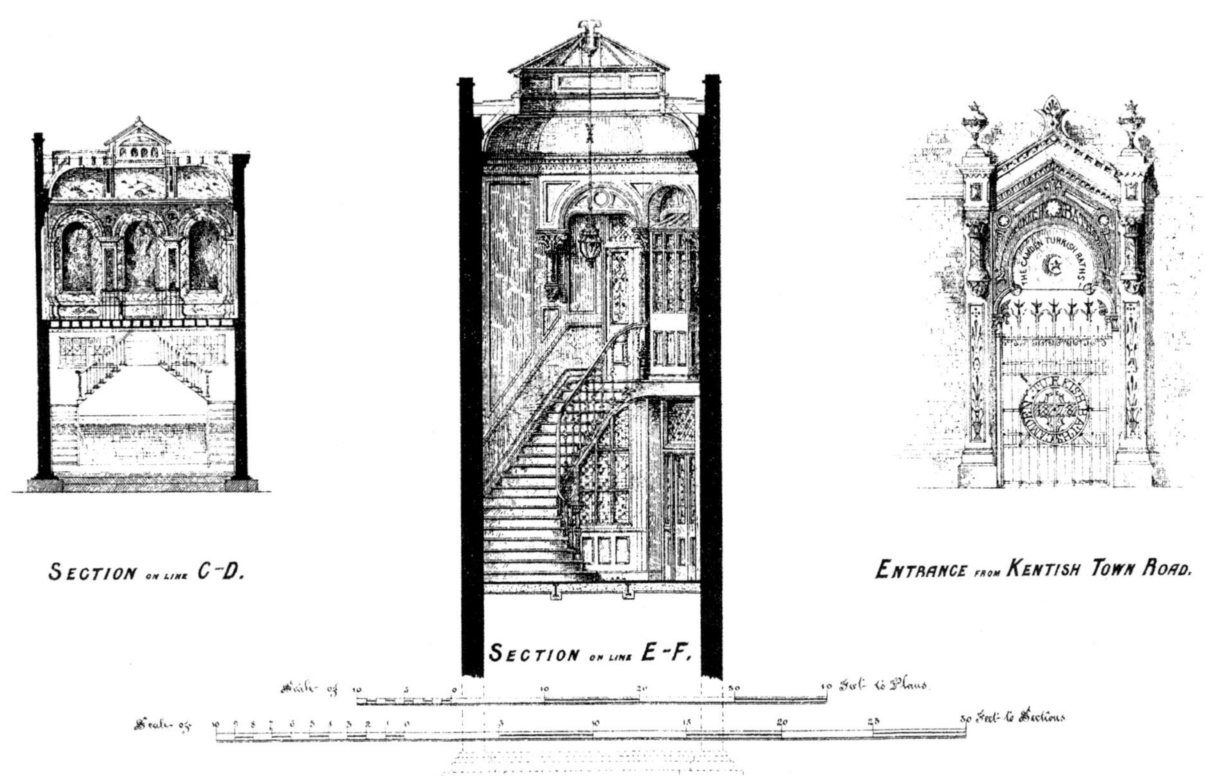

Fortunately, most baths caught fire when the premises were empty, and the owner's main concern was whether there was enough insurance cover. Newspaper reports usually ended by indicating whether the proprietor was covered for fire, presumably as a lesson to others. Even when the building was insured, this did not always help the proprietor.

At one o'clock in the morning of 2 April 1888, Fleming's Turkish Baths at 90 Princes Street, Edinburgh (Fig 28.4), caught fire and in spite of the Fire Brigade's valiant efforts with three separate sources of water, the fire was not extinguished for several hours.[15] By this time,

> the entire roof of the back portion of the premises was destroyed, while the furnishings of the bathroom proper, as well as of the smaller rooms, were also greatly damaged—smoke and water having completed the work of the flames so far as the internal fittings were concerned.[16]

It is thought that the fire originated in one of the hot rooms and was caused by the heating apparatus. The damage was estimated at about £1,000. Although the owner of the building was insured for his share of the damage, Fleming had not insured his share as tenant, and this seems to have marked the end of his career

FIRST CLASS TURKISH BATH

ENTRANCE - 90 PRINCES STREET. EDINBURGH.

ON THE MODEL OF JERMYN STREET BATH, LONDON.

OPEN DAILY FROM 8 A.M. UNTIL 9 P.M.

TURKISH, RAIN, DOUCHE,

AND

SWIMMING BATHS,

(FIRST CLASS,)

90 PRINCES STREET, EDINBURGH,

Three Doors West of New Club.

TERMS FOR TURKISH BATHS.

Admittance Daily from 8 A.M. until 9 P.M., . .	2s. 6d
After 6 P.M., ...	1s. 6d.
Other Baths, ...	1s.
Course of 12 Baths, from 8 A.M. to 6 P.M., .	£1, 5s. 0d.
Course of 12 Baths, after 6 P.M., . . .	15s. 0d.

Available for Three Months.

LADIES.—A Bath Suite, for which previous notice is required, may be had.

Fig 28.3 (above) Features of H H Bridgman's Camden Turkish Baths. (Building News, 29 November 1878. Author's collection)

Fig 28.4 (left) Advertisement for the Turkish, Rain, Douche, and Swimming Baths in Edinburgh's fashionable Princes Street. (Author's collection)

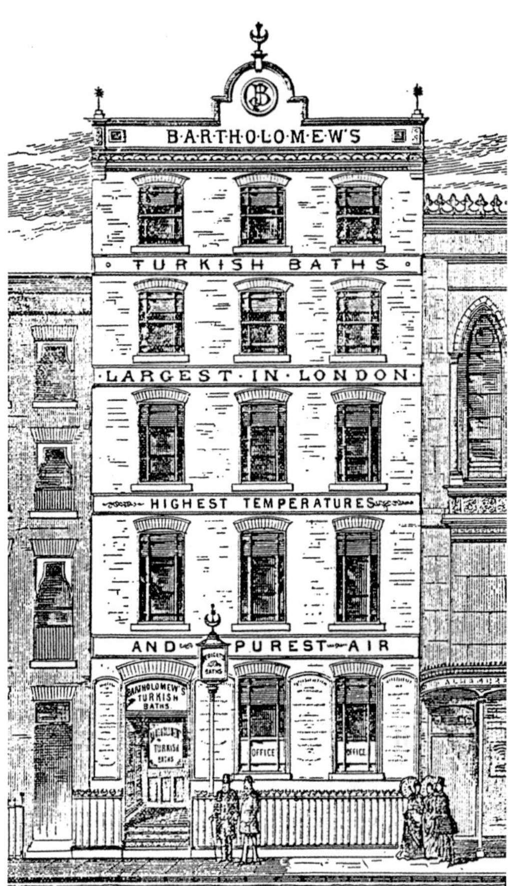

Fig 28.5 (right)
The original entrance to the Miller Arcade Turkish Baths, Preston.
(© Malcolm Shifrin)
Fig 28.6 (far right)
Bartholomew's Turkish Baths, 23 Leicester Square, London.
(Charles Bartholomew, Illustrated guide to the Turkish baths, *Marshall, 1887)*

as a Turkish baths proprietor. When the baths reopened, there was a new lessee, Alexander Hardie.

Towards the end of the century, increased attention was paid to the risk of fire. In 1901, when Alfred Arbury opened his Turkish baths in the Miller Arcade, Preston (Fig 28.5), he would have known that he had chosen a safe location. For the building, designed by architect Edwin Bush (1861–1918) and now Grade II Listed, had won a competition in 1895 for the 'best planned fire-proof arcade.' The baths closed in 1947 but a partially bricked up doorway marked 'Turkish Baths' can still be seen.

Such improved risk awareness did little to prevent fires in older buildings. In Britain, probably the worst of these happened in London's Leicester Square, on the night of 10 August 1930, at Bartholomew's Turkish Baths (Fig 28.6), owned since 1919 by Archibald Butler.

It was not the first time these baths had been on fire. They had caught alight, and were largely destroyed, when the Alhambra Theatre burned down in December 1882. It was Bartholomew who then bought and rebuilt them.

But the later fire was more serious because three of the staff lived on the premises. One was away at the time, but two had gone to bed at 11 o'clock. Firemen found the dead body of Miss Rachel Barker, the 62-year old cashier, on the fourth floor, while they were searching the building. Although suffering from severe burns and cuts, 70-year-old Elizabeth Evans fared better:

> Hundreds of people who were leaving the cafés and restaurants at the time of the outbreak, stopped to watch, and saw the rescue of Miss Evans. She had clung to the letter 'R' of the sign 'TURKISH BATHS' (Fig 28.7) until an escape was got up to her, and firemen carried her down to safety. Two firemen were taken to hospital suffering from the effects of smoke, but were able to leave after treatment.[17]

The building itself was severely damaged, part of its roof destroyed, and part of the rebuilt Alhambra next door was also slightly damaged.

The cause of the fire was never discovered. In what *The Times* had called 'A mysterious case', cash-boxes had been discovered empty, having been broken open by some instrument closely resembling a fireman's or salvage man's axe, suggesting to the coroner that someone had not been attending wholly to the fire. Neither was he happy with the work of the police, wanting to know how the fire advanced as far as it did,

Fig 28.7
Part of a postcard showing the sign which saved Miss Evans's life, with the Alhambra and its domes, stars, and crescents on the right.
(Author's collection)

so that someone lost her life, without the police noticing it at an earlier stage.

At the end of the three-day inquest, the jury's verdict left these questions, and a number of others, unanswered.[18] The baths remained permanently closed.

Thefts

It was not necessary for a bath to be on fire for a till to be robbed, or a bather's property stolen.

One optimist advertised in the *Irish Times* that his 'massive Gold Ring, shield pattern, blue and gold stone' was missing from his vest pocket while at the Dublin Hammam in Sackville Street, ending, 'The present possessor will please return it to its owner', followed by his address.[19]

At that time it was not altogether clear whether the bath proprietor was legally responsible for a bather's property. After another theft at the same baths, and within weeks of the earlier one, the Recorder awarded a Mr Robinson £10 as part of the value of a watch and chain lost while at the baths.

Robinson was not satisfied with this and took Mr Richard Barter to court, seeking to make him answerable on the principle that having a hotel annexed to the baths made him liable as innkeeper under common law. But Robinson lost his case because although Barter *was* in the position of an innkeeper, 'persons going in merely for the purpose of enjoying the baths' could not be considered hotel guests within the meaning of the law.[20]

The most common method of protecting a bather's property was the provision of small lockers in which any valuables could be placed. The key was either given to the bather to take into the baths, or left with the attendant at the ticket office. Neither option was totally satisfactory. In a number of cases the attendant handed the key to someone pretending to be its owner at a time when the baths were quite full. It was argued, with some justification, that it was not always possible to remember who had been given a particular key. In other cases, the key was stolen from the bather's clothes left within a changing cubicle.

In none of these cases was the proprietor deemed responsible because reasonable arrangements for the care of bathers' property had been put in place. The baths were legally considered to be *gratuitous bailees* and so were only liable if negligence could be proved.

At the High Street Turkish Baths in Birmingham, where such precautions had been successful for some time, valuables were nevertheless stolen from several bathers on the same evening, after which the thief quietly left the baths and was never caught.[21]

When details of the raid appeared in the papers, there were letters from bathers and proprietors full of ideas for improving the safety of bathers' belongings. One writer described a system seen in America, whereby the locker key is worn round the neck, which 'does not add picturesqueness to the bath room, but, at any rate, it acts as a "charm" against the bath thief.'[22] Such a system was also used in Britain, but the Borough of Dewsbury, among others, supplied a token for wearing round the neck. The token was later exchanged for the correct locker key (Fig 28.8).

Apart from such casual thefts, there were occasional robberies of a more serious nature which, if occurring in a film, would be considered far-fetched. In one such instance, £6,363 was stolen from the North Eastern Banking Company's branch in Sunderland. In a carefully planned operation, Mr Ralph Ord, son of the local bank manager, was taken to an unidentified Turkish bath in Newcastle-upon-Tyne, where the keys to the bank were taken from his pocket and casts made while he was bathing. On another occasion, Mr Kaines, the cashier, was similarly treated, in order to get casts of the strong room keys.[23]

Fig 28.8
Locker token used at the Dewsbury Turkish baths until they closed in 1972. (Author's collection)

In another case, three men held up the night cashier at the Savoy Turkish Baths in Jermyn Street, escaping in a car with £7. When the 54-year old cashier, Mr J Edwards, 'threw a stool at a masked man who threatened him with a gun the man fired two shots, one of which hit the ceiling of the baths.'[24]

But in the basement, where Franklen Evans would have been disappointed to find that 20th-century bathers were no longer 'exceedingly quiet', none of the 50 customers in the various hot rooms heard anything at all untoward.

29

Advertising the Victorian Turkish bath

Victorian Turkish Bath proprietors seem to have used advertisements for three main purposes: initially, to attract attention to the baths; second to provide information—what facilities were available, when they were open and how much they charged; and finally to bring patrons back again by reminding them of the bath when they were at work or back at home. In this they were probably little different from providers of any other goods or services during the Victorian era and just beyond.

Though the cinema, radio, television, and latterly the internet, all became widely available in the 20th century, such media were too expensive to be used by individual establishments. Local authority Turkish baths are, however, sometimes found on the internet, included as part of a page dealing with a health suite, or day spa.

So we are looking, in the main, at various types of printed advertisements, supplemented by exterior signs, usually inanimate, though occasionally human.

Very few Turkish bath signs seem to have survived the closure of the baths they advertised. Undoubtedly someone, somewhere, is probably collecting them, just as the relatively few printed items are, one hopes, being collected by members of The Ephemera Society, or one of the other national ephemera societies.[1]

It is extremely important that they should be collected, for ephemera, 'the minor transient documents of everyday life',[2] are often the only source of information we have about some baths, including some very important ones.

Attracting the bather into the baths

I have only ever come across two outdoor signs from Turkish baths which are no longer open. But one sign, possibly unique, is a magnificent vitreous enamel specimen (Fig 29.1). Hand-cut[3] in the shape of a life-size bather, it advertised William Cooper's Savoy Turkish baths in London, some time between 1910 and 1912 when he owned six baths.

Fig 29.1
Life-size enamel sign for the Turkish Baths in the Savoy chain.
(Author's collection)

THE MAN AND THE MOMENT.

Fig 29.2 (above) Postcard from the well-known London Life *series showing a billboard man advertising the Savoy Turkish Baths in Savoy Street. (Author's collection)*

*Fig 29.3 (above right) A Bert Thomas caricature of the Savoy billboard man. (*Punch*, 20 October 1909, p.279. Author's collection)*

As these closed, their addresses were painted over on the signs outside those which remained. We know this because the Metropolitan Museum of Art in New York has a photograph, taken by Bill Brandt in the 1930s, showing the sign outside the women's baths in Duke of York Street. By that time, these, and the men's baths round the corner at 92 Jermyn Street, were the only ones still open, and with their names not obliterated on the sign.[4]

Cooper also employed men clad in towels, more or less as shown on his sign, to carry double-sided billboards on their shoulders. We do not know how many there were, but there must have been several, because they were widely recognised by Londoners.

A photograph of one of them in Savoy Street (with Piccadilly in the background) was included in the *London Life* series of postcards, published around 1913 (Fig 29.2).

He was well known, and there were caricatures of him in, for example, *Punch* (Fig 29.3) and *London Opinion*, both published around the same time, the latter afterwards being reprinted as a colour postcard (Fig 29.4).

Cooper was not the first to use 'human directionals' (as they are called in the trade). Sandwich boards appear to have been utilised to advertise Turkish baths at least as early as 1862, as a caricature in that year's *Punch Almanac* confirms (Fig 29.5). Headed 'The use of advertisement', it has Mr Sweep saying, 'It's enuff to tempt one. He looks so jolly Clean hisself!'

One other unusual sign, most of which has survived, is that using mosaic tiles set into the pavement, advertising the Imperial Hotel Turkish Baths in Russell Square (Fig 29.6).

Such advertisements were relatively expensive, if long lasting. Most advertisements attempting to find new clients appeared in newspapers, magazines, and occasionally, if there was a bath nearby, in theatre programmes (Fig 29.7).

Most newspaper advertisements, especially in the national press, appeared in the classified

columns, often placed with others in a group of rival establishments. Usually they were two- or three-liners with just the name, address and, perhaps, a slogan. But in the less expensive local papers, small display advertisements were more affordable. Some were simple, announcing, for example, that Mr Thomas Shore was opening a new Turkish bath for horses at Exwick, near Bristol.[5]

More sophisticated were the advertisements of the eclectic William Cooper who always seemed to be running more than one type of business at a time. As a large manufacturer of garden sheds and portable buildings, he became one of the main contractors for erecting viewing stands for the 1911 coronation procession of King George V. Cooper's firm was reported to have built over 50 stands, capable of accommodating from 250 to 3,500 people in each.[6] He then became the booking agent for the seats, advertising his Turkish baths on the back of each ticket (Fig 29.8), and offering accommodation at the baths, at 10s per night, to those visiting London for the occasion.[7]

Others took advantage, sometimes in more senses than one, of whatever was concerning people at the time. 'IMPORTANT', headlined one advertisement for the Turkish Baths at Stephen's Green West in Dublin,

> In these times of threatened Epidemic, when there is so much alarm in every mind, it is an unspeakable comfort and relief to know that this dreadful Epidemic of Cholera can be certainly prevented by a continuous partaking of a really high-class Turkish Bath.[8]

There was, of course, no Trades Descriptions Act in the 19th century, and no control over how goods or services were advertised. Medical cure-all claims were the norm rather than the exception. Part of a typical classified advertisement—this one for Holman's Turkish Baths from an 1880 issue of the *Stockton Herald*—noted that:

Fig 29.4 (above left)
A postcard with the Savoy billboard man in the background.
(Author's collection)
Fig 29.5 (above)
Caricature (artist unknown) showing a sandwich board advertising a Turkish bath.
*(*Punch almanac, *1862 Author's collection)*
Fig 29.6 (below)
Mosaic set into Russell Square pavement.
(© Malcolm Shifrin)

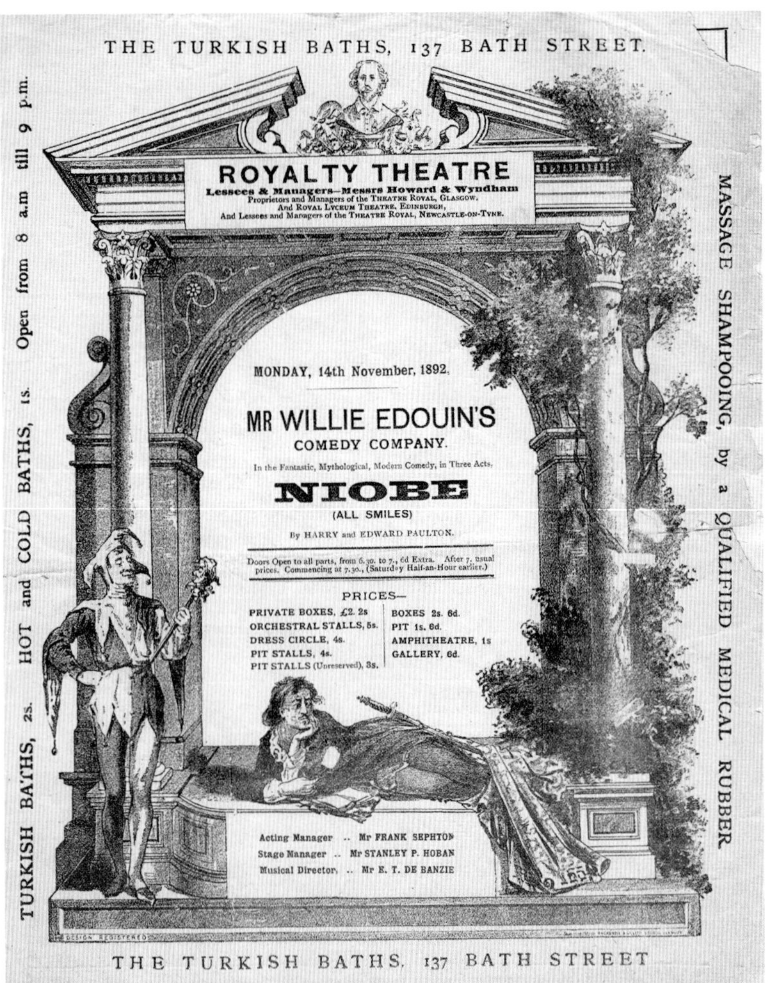

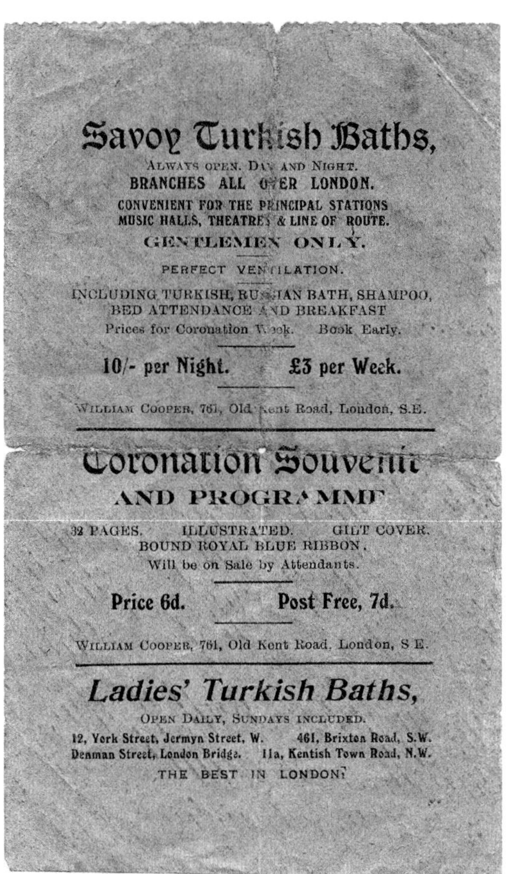

Fig 29.7 (above) Glasgow theatre programme with Turkish baths advertisement around the four edges of its cover. (Author's collection)

Fig 29.8 (above right) Reverse of 1911 coronation procession ticket for Seat No.32 in Block B1 St Clements Dane. (Author's collection)

SINCE the opening of the above Establishment several persons suffering from GOUT, CHRONIC RHEUMATISM, DROPSY, ENLARGEMENT OF THE LIVER, &c, have been sent by some of our principal Medical Gentlemen, who have in many cases declared the results to be marvellous. Nothing equals the Baths for colds when properly applied … N.B.—A course of Baths would produce the same effect as a month of Hydropathic treatment.[9]

By 1935, Bradford Corporation, for example, mentioned health only in the most general way when attempting to persuade its residents to use the Turkish bath regularly.[10]

> *Here's the way, if health you seek:*
> *Take a Turkish! Every week.*

While the 1992 leaflet produced by Civic Leisure Ltd, for the Turkish baths they operated for Westminster City Council, suggests the ultimate soft sell:

> Escape the hustle and bustle of everyday life and relax both mind and body.

Those concerned about their weight were frequently targeted by baths proprietors. Turkish baths were generally considered an easy way to lose a few pounds—and so they were, but for a very limited period. In the 1890s, *Punch* artist, Linley Sambourne, regularly recorded his weight before and after his bath, usually losing around two pounds each time, and almost as quickly putting them back on.

To encourage prospective clients who were staying at the Imperial Hotel, there was a WATCH YOUR WEIGHT card placed in each room (Fig 29.9). It showed the 'correct' weight for men and women of different heights and builds—no specific claims were made for the Turkish baths, just a brief mention of how to reach them.

When temporary weight loss was urgently required, the Turkish bath delivered, and it was widely used by boxers, who needed to be under a specified weight in order to qualify, or jockeys for whom every additional ounce was a liability. Sometimes they did this to excess, as did the 5ft 10in (1.8m) high best all-round jockey of his time, Fred Archer. So what better place to advertise baths for these people than on weighing machine tickets?

One inexpensive way of advertising your Turkish bath was to let your clients do it for you. A pile of picture postcards at the reception desk encouraged bathers who had enjoyed the baths to send a card to their friends. Surprisingly, very few baths here or in Ireland seem to have adopted this practice.

The only ones so far known to have been issued by commercial baths are those from Nevill's and the Savoy, some of whose cards are illustrated earlier in the book. Harrogate Council has long produced attractive postcards illustrating their Turkish baths. But while hydros and hotels have published a plethora of cards, very few have used them to illustrate their Turkish baths, most proprietors preferring to show the buildings or the grounds.

The situation in the United States was quite different, and though most of their cards illustrate the outside of a baths building (Fig 29.10), there have been others. The card from the Sultan Baths in San Francisco, for example, suggests that the lure of the 'oriental' did not pass by the USA (Fig 29.11). But seven floors of baths must surely have been worth a visit.

While it may be difficult to make the inside of a hot room look attractive in a photograph, there were many cooling-rooms which could have provided suitable subjects, yet few have been found.

The image in an advertisement is important and should be relevant. The message propounded by the man in the white coat on the card from the Times Square baths (Fig 29.12) is very similar to that on the Westminster Council leaflet: 'The best tonic is a weekly Turkish Bath. It improves the Skin and is good for the Nerves.' But the image suggests that the man could just

WATCH YOUR WEIGHT

MEN

HEIGHT		5' 2"	5' 3"	5' 4"	5' 5"	5' 6"	5' 7"	5' 8"	5' 9"	5' 10"	5' 11"	6' 0"	6' 1"	6' 2"
SMALL BUILD	LBS.	119-128	122-132	126-136	129-139	133-143	136-147	140-151	144-155	148-159	152-164	157-169	163-175	168-180
	ST.	8.7-9.2	8.10-9.6	9.0-9.10	9.3-9.13	9.7-10.3	9.10-10.7	10.0-10.11	10.4-11.1	10.8-11.5	10.12 11.10	11.3-12.1	11.9-12.7	12.0-12.12
MEDIUM BUILD	LBS.	127-136	130-140	134-144	137-147	141-151	145 156	149-160	153-164	157-168	161-173	166-178	171-184	176-189
	ST.	9.1-9.10	9.4-10.0	9.8-10.4	9.11-10.7	10.1-10.11	10.5-11.2	10.9-11.6	10.13-11.10	11.3-12.0	11.7-12.5	11.12-12.10	12.3-13.2	12.8-13.7
LARGE BUILD	LBS.	133-144	137-149	141-153	145-157	149-162	153-166	157-170	161-175	165-180	169-185	174-190	179-196	184-202
	ST.	9.7-10.4	9.11-10.9	10.1-10.13	10.5-11.3	10.9-11.8	10.13-11.12	11.3-12.2	11.7-12.7	11.11-12.12	12.1-13.3	12.6-13.8	12.11-14.0	13.2-14.6

WOMEN

HEIGHT		4' 9"	4' 10"	4' 11"	5' 0"	5' 1"	5' 2"	5' 3"	5' 4"	5' 5"	5' 6"	5' 7"	5' 8"	5' 9"
SMALL BUILD	LBS.	104-111	105-113	107-115	110-118	113-121	116-125	119-128	123-132	126-136	129-139	133-143	136-147	139-150
	ST.	7.6-7.13	7.7-8.1	7.9-8.3	7.12-8.6	8.1-8.9	8.4-8.13	8.7-9.2	8.11-9.6	9.0-9.10	9.3-9.13	9.7-10.3	9.10-10.7	9.13-10.10
MEDIUM BUILD	LBS.	110-118	112-120	114-122	117-125	120-128	124-132	127-135	130-140	134-144	137-147	141-151	145-155	148 158
	ST.	7.12-8.6	8 0-8.8	8.2-8 10	8.5-8.13	8.8-9.2	8.12-9.6	9.1-9.9	9.4-10.0	9.8-10.4	9.11-10.7	10.1-10.11	10.5-11.1	10.8-11.4
LARGE BUILD	LBS.	117-127	119-129	121-131	124-135	127-138	131-142	133-145	138-150	142-154	145-158	149-162	152-166	155-169
	ST.	8.5-9.1	8.7-9.3	8.9-9.5	8.12-9.9	9.1-9.12	9.5-10.2	9.7-10.5	9.12-10.10	10.2-11.0	10.5-11.4	10.9-11.8	10.12-11.12	11.1-12.1

IMPERIAL TURKISH BATHS
LADIES AND GENTLEMEN
Entrance through Hotel Lounge

Fig 29.9
Plasticised 'Watch Your Weight' card from the Imperial Hotel, London. (Author's collection, with thanks to an anonymous donor)

Turkish Baths Building, 55 Atlantic St., Norfolk, Va.
TURKISH BATHS & ROOMS

Figs 29.10 and 29.11
Two postcards, the first (left) depicting the exterior of the Turkish baths building on Atlantic Street, Newport, Virginia, and the second (right), advertising the Sultan Turkish Baths in San Francisco, California. (Author's collection)

"Guard Your Health!"

42ND STREET COR. 6TH AVENUE. NEW YORK

MODERN SANITARY CENTRAL

44-46 North Fitzhugh St., ROCHESTER, N. Y.
RATES $1.00 PER DAY INCLUDING PLUNGE AND SHOWER

Fig 29.12 (left)
Postcard advertising the Times Square De Luxe Turkish Baths.
(Author's collection)
Fig 29.13 (right)
One of a series of monthly postcard calendars advertising the New Turkish Baths Hotel in Rochester, NY.
(Author's collection)

as easily be advertising a toothpaste, or a quack medicine.

The calendar card from the New Turkish Bath Hotel (Fig 29.13) is one of a set published month by month, though it is not known for how long this continued. Designed for hanging over a desk, the card has a pre-punched hole at the top. But the message being conveyed by the image is unclear, for any thoughts of an enjoyable and unusual honeymoon are immediately dashed by the bottom line, which reads, ENTIRELY SEPARATE DEPARTMENT FOR WOMEN.

Satisfying enquirers

Experienced bathers, away from their usual bath and venturing into a different one, are usually satisfied with a flyer or card which lists facilities, hours, and charges. All this is given in a typical manner by Mr and Mrs Cook on their leaflet (Fig 29.14), adding for good measure that their bath in Toronto, which opened in 1874 and was to survive for 75 years, had 'The Largest Marble Plunge Bath on the Continent'.

In many cases, the basic information on such leaflets differed little from that on the rather more permanent rate cards. These were often folded to provide several 'pages'. Although there must have been many of these from different establishments, few seem to have survived, because it would have been natural to dispose of them when they became outdated, or the baths closed.

One of the more attractive survivors is a chromolithographed leaflet, with three folds and eight 'pages', issued by H H Bridgman's

TELEPHONE No. 1286.
KING STREET
TURKISH BATH
176 King Street West.
LADIES
Monday, Wednesday and Friday Mornings
From 10 a.m. to 1 p.m., $1, or
13 Tickets $10.
CLOSING AT 2 O'CLOCK.
GENTLEMEN.
Other Mornings and every afternoon, $1.00.
Evening from 6 to 9, 75c.
The Largest Marble Plunge Bath on the Continent.
Soap Wash, with Hot or Cold Shower and Plunge Bath, 50 Cents.
Mr. & Mrs. T. COOK
CHIROPODISTS.
Many years Proprietors of the Montreal Turkish Baths

Fig 29.14 (right)
Leaflet advertising the King Street Turkish Bath in Toronto, Canada.
(Courtesy of Toronto Public Library)
Fig 29.15 (opposite top)
Obverse of a leaflet from the Camden Turkish Baths, Kentish Town Road, London.
(Amoret Tanner Collection)
Fig 29.16 (opposite bottom)
Inside opening of the Savoy Turkish Baths rate card.
(Author's collection)

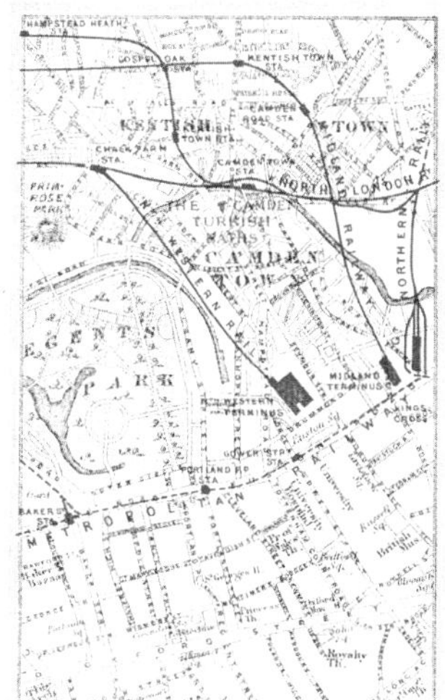

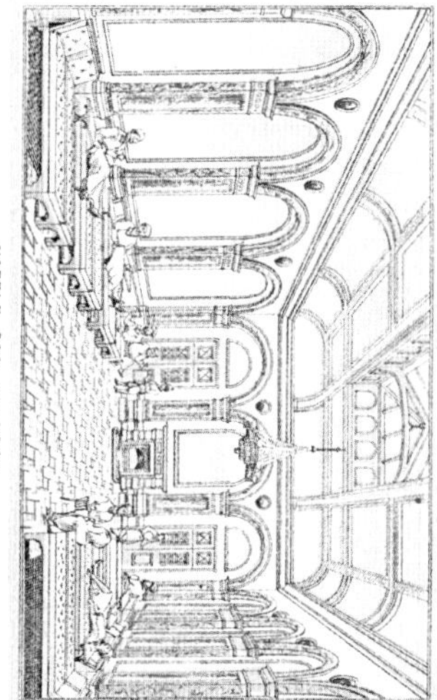

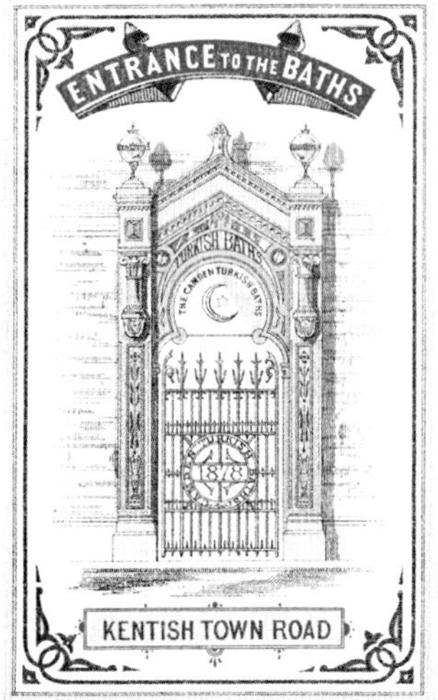

Turco Roman Baths (Fig 29.15). Situated next to Camden Town Station, and known as the Camden Turkish Baths, they closed following a fire in 1916, though parts of the building remain standing.[11]

The Savoy's four-sided folding card may have been kept as a souvenir because the baths were the first in London to be lit by electricity, and the whole-year calendar on the outer back page may also have encouraged the recipient to keep it. Unusually, but well judged, the inside of the folder included the temperatures of the hot rooms, in addition to sketches of the interior (Fig 29.16).

The card was issued in 1885, the year the baths opened and 17 years before William Cooper made it the flagship bath of his chain. It was built for the Savoy Turkish Baths Co Ltd, whose shareholders included many celebrities from the worlds of comic opera (François Arsène Cellier, George Grossmith and Rutland Barrington), the theatre (Michael Gunn, George Joseph Edwardes and Samuel French), and hotels and restaurants (Alphonse Romano and George Shield).

American trade cards were different from British ones in the 19th century. In the States, with the advent of chromolithography, printers would produce attractive sets of picture cards. The bath proprietor would chose a set, and the cards would then be overprinted with his name, address, opening hours and services. The idea was that bathers would return, and thereby add to their card collections.[12]

This resulted in there being little connection between the pictures used and the business being advertised, although in the case of

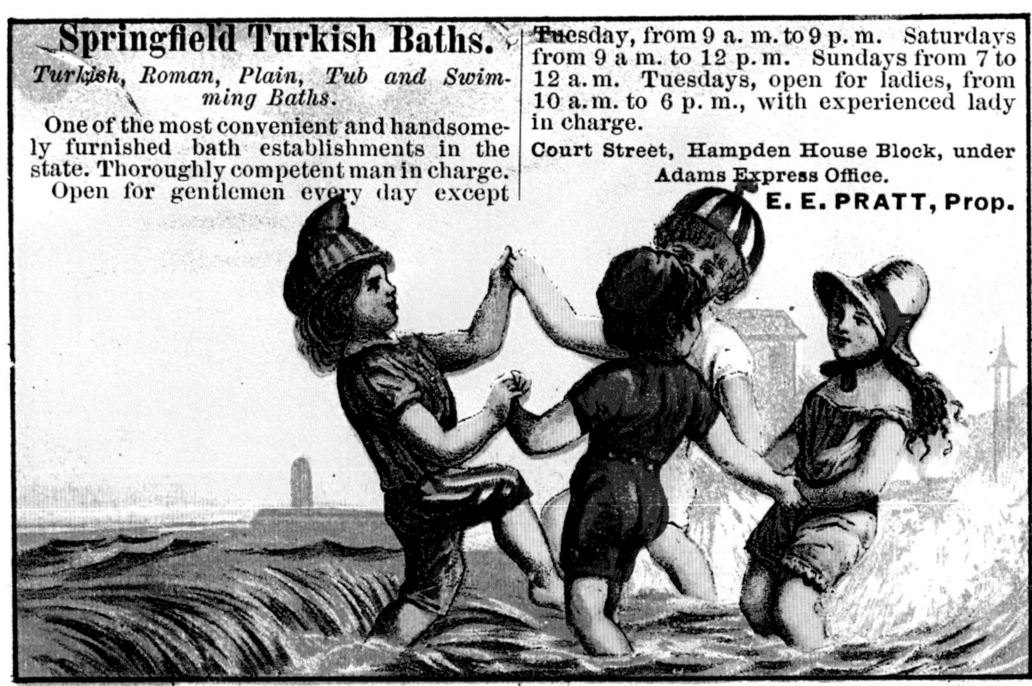

Fig 29.17
Trade card advertising the Springfield, Massachusetts, Turkish Baths. (Author's collection)

Fig 29.18
Trade card advertising Miller's Turkish Baths, New York, NY. (Author's collection)

Fig 29.19 (below)
Trade card advertising the Galt House Turkish Baths in Louisville, Kentucky. (Author's collection)

the Springfield baths there was at least a vague suggestion of some form of bathing (Fig 29.17).

The pictures on most of the cards, like those from Miller's Turkish baths in New York City (Fig 29.18), and the fan-shaped novelty card advertising the Galt House baths in Louisville, Kentucky (Fig 29.19), had no connection at all with the baths. But there was always the reverse of the card available for displaying opening hours and prices.

For some, a leaflet was considered too small to enable the proprietor to adequately sell his establishment, and a number of baths gave away small brochures of anything up to around 48 pages. But in practice these larger booklets often contained very little about the actual establishment which was publishing them.

This was to be expected when the Turkish bath was only one of several facilities, as in the mid-1930s Herriots Bath Club in the basement of Sunlight House (Fig 29.20). Designed by Joseph Sunlight (1889–1978) as Manchester's first skyscraper, it is now a Grade II listed building. The page describing the Turkish bath includes a sketch of the architect's art deco take on an ogee arch (Fig 29.21).

Other brochures with line drawings of Turkish baths included those advertising establishments in Grimsby and Blackburn, though there may well have been several others. But most of them merely rehashed the same excerpts

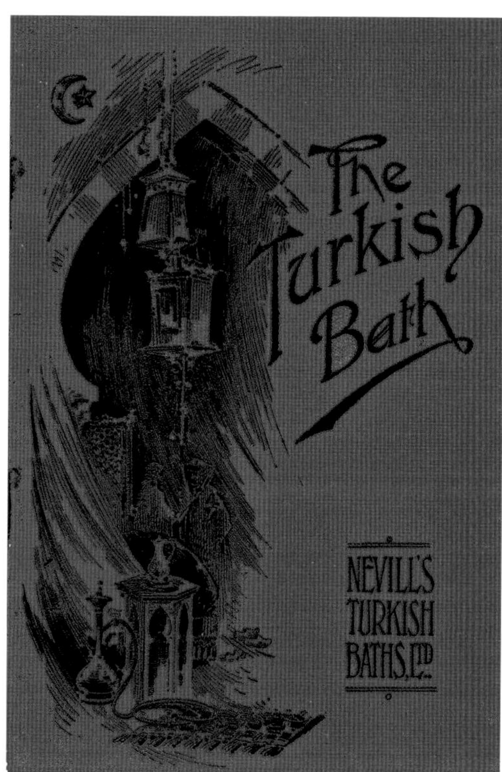

Clockwise from top left
Fig 29.20
Front cover of a booklet advertising the newly-opened Herriot's Bath Club in Manchester.
(Author's collection)
Fig 29.21
Inside page illustrating the hot rooms at Herriot's Bath Club.
(Author's collection)
Fig 29.22
One of the booklets published by Nevill's Turkish Baths.
(Author's collection)

from old books on the bath, or articles about its health benefits, together with solicited (and occasionally a few unsolicited) testimonials. Several of Charles Bartholomew's brochures included many pages of testimonials.

Nevill's produced a number of booklets over the years, but in the undated one shown here (Fig 29.22), for example, the only information specific to Nevill's is a list of their baths, and a couple of general paragraphs about their history on the inside of the back cover.

§Nevill's did not really need testimonials, solicited or unsolicited. For just as Trollope and Galsworthy[13] paid tribute to the Jermyn Street Hammam by including it in their books, so Nevill's Northumberland Avenue Turkish Baths featured in books by a number of authors with whom most of their potential clientele would have been familiar.

Probably the most well-known mention is in the opening of Conan Doyle's short story *The adventure of the illustrious client* which describes Sherlock Holmes and Dr Watson relaxing after their Turkish bath there (Fig 29.23).

> Both Holmes and I had a weakness for the Turkish bath. It was over a smoke in the pleasant lassitude of the drying-room that I have found him less reticent and more human than anywhere else. On the upper floor of the Northumberland Avenue establishment there is an isolated corner where two couches lie side by side, and it was on these that we lay upon September 3, 1902, the day when my narrative begins. I had asked him

Fig 29.23 (above) Watson and Sherlock Holmes relax at Nevill's Turkish Baths in Northumberland Avenue. (Arthur Conan Doyle, The Adventure of the illustrious client. *Howard K Elcock, illustrator)*

Fig 29.24 (above right) Booklet advertising the Earls Court Turkish Baths in the 1920s. (Author's collection)

whether anything was stirring, and for answer he had shot his long, thin, nervous arm out of the sheets which enveloped him and had drawn an envelope from the inside pocket of the coat which hung beside him.

Holmes and Watson were not the only patrons of these baths. They were also frequented by Bunny Manders and Raffles, the two characters on the other side of the law, created by Conan Doyle's brother-in-law, E W Hornung. And P G Wodehouse has his character Psmith follow his boss Bickersdyke into the same baths in *Psmith in the City*.

Conan Doyle's own first experience of Turkish baths may well have been at the Southsea Baths in Portsmouth (see Ch 13, page 138), very near to where he lived between 1882 and 1890 and where he had his only medical practice. He visited Southsea again for a few months in 1896 when a company was being formed to buy the baths, and his close friend, Dr James Watson, with whom he had probably been to the baths on many occasions, bought 100 shares, keeping them till 1906 when the baths were bought by their manager, F Brough Burden.

Why go away for a cure? a brochure published in the mid-1920s by Archibald Reynolds James, advertising his Earls Court Turkish Baths, is worthy of note (Fig 29.24). It includes photographs, artist's impressions, and a couple of images which could have been either. In addition to a description of the bath, and its opening hours and charges, it also includes general articles, a series of questions and answers descended from Bartholomew's Socratic dialogues, and a range of mostly solicited testimonials. Among these was one from the managing director of Barkers of Kensington, another from Mr Toms of Derry and Toms, and the almost mandatory batch from ministers of various Christian denominations.

Not all booklets were wholly serious. For a while, Nevill's gave away an illustrated booklet with an account of a visit to one of their baths by Terry (ie, Horace Thorogood), featuring caricatures by David Low, including one of Colonel Blimp, inspiration for Powell and Pressburger's famous World War II film, *The life and death of Colonel Blimp*.

Relying even more on humorous images, Benjamin Bell, advertising his baths at Buckingham Palace Road and Basinghall Street in the 1880s, produced a booklet consisting solely of eight amusing silhouettes of a newcomer being guided round the baths by his more experienced friend (Fig 29.25).

Fig 29.25
A silhouette caricature showing an old hand introducing his friend Jones to the hot room of Benjamin Bell's Turkish Baths. Eight of these drawings were stapled together to form a small booklet given to potential customers.
(Amoret Tanner Collection)

Encouraging repeat visits

Collectable American trade cards have already been mentioned as a way of encouraging return visits to the baths. Token gifts (today's freebies) seem to have been given by very few establishments, especially in Britain, where there was a preference for proselytising booklets—inherited, perhaps, from the religious tracts which were so common in the 19th century.

British items found have been limited to smoking accessories, lucifer boxes such as those given by Faulkner (Fig 29.26) and the Imperial Hotel baths, and bookmatches, which were also given away around the world.

In the United States, the matches were sometimes loose, held in a slightly more substantial holder (Fig 29.27). I have only found two non-smoking-related gifts. The first is a most impressive baseball scorer presented to bathers at the Oriental Turkish Baths in Columbus,

Fig 29.26
Upper and lower views of a hinged tin for lucifers (matches), with a striker panel on the outside of the base.
(Author's collection)

Fig 29.27 (right) Metal folding case for matches, from the Munro Hotel, Cincinnati, Ohio. (Author's collection)

Fig 29.28 (far right) Tip dish manufactured by Wood & Sons for the Imperial Hotel. (Author's collection)

Ohio, and the second is a pen from the Turkish bath in Mason City, Iowa.

In the days when smoking was not only permitted in public places but, by the provision of hotel and club smoking rooms, effectively encouraged, ashtrays seem always to have been treated as fair game by souvenir hunters, the name of the establishment being an advertisement rather than a claim to ownership.

Sometimes mistaken for them, however, were tip dishes, often very attractively produced by well-known firms such as Wood & Sons (Fig 29.28). These were much rarer, and unlike ashtrays, were not intended to be taken away, but provided as a receptacle for guests who wished to show their appreciation for good service by leaving a gratuity.

PART VI

Victorian Turkish baths in the 21st century

30

Victorian Turkish baths today and tomorrow

In 1990, when I first became interested in the history of Victorian Turkish baths, at least 34 baths built on the Victorian model were still open in the British Isles—although there were no longer any in Ireland where the bath started.

In November 1999, when the *Victorian Turkish Baths* website first went online, there were only 24 remaining, and the last one in Wales had closed.

Now, writing in May 2014, there are only 12 (Fig 30.1). Unfortunately, others are under threat, so the list of where you can still 'take a Turkish' appears only on the website.

Why has an institution like the Victorian Turkish bath, which spread round the country so quickly, almost as quickly contracted to the point of near extinction over a period of around 150 years?

The rapid spread of the bath: social factors

A number of factors helped make the mid-19th century ripe for such a development. Sanitary concerns resulting from the cholera epidemics of the previous decades were beginning to be acted on, even if it was in a relatively limited way. The provision of baths and washhouses was feasible in a way that providing running water to every dwelling was not, although the positive benefits to be obtained were minimised because the Baths and Wash-houses Acts were permissive rather than mandatory.

Lack of medical knowledge during the 19th century, and lack of even basic pain killers till the end of the century, encouraged people to try alternative methods of relief such as the

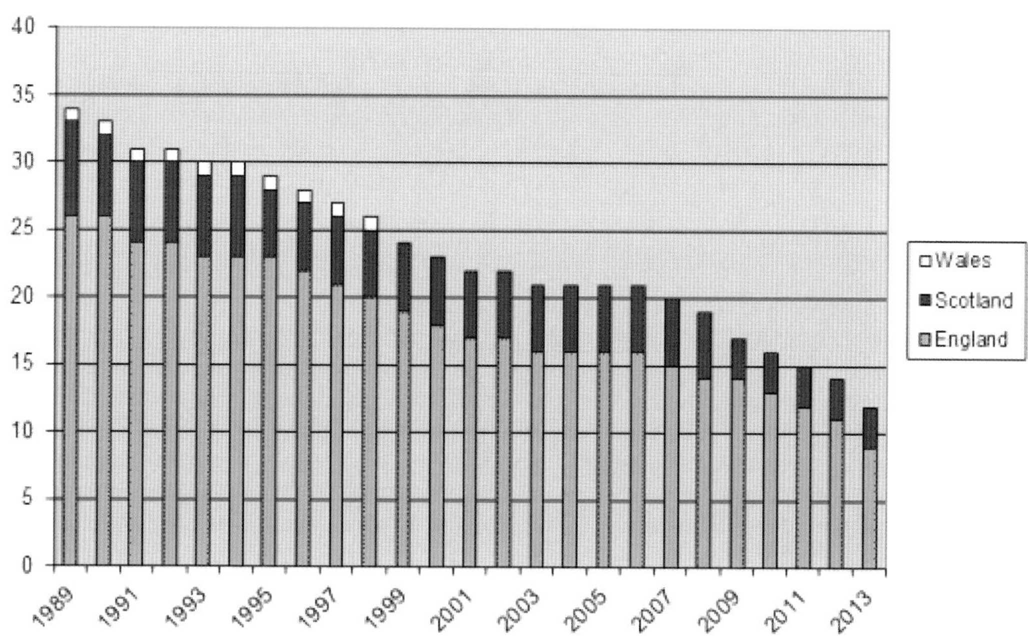

Fig 30.1
Graph showing the number of Victorian Turkish baths still open 1989–2013 (© Malcolm Shifrin)

Turkish bath (and also, of course, patent medicine and quack doctors).

The spread of the bath was encouraged in Ireland, for therapeutic and sanitary reasons, by a relatively wealthy medical advocate in the person of Dr Richard Barter, who was personally able to initiate the building of Turkish baths throughout the island; in England and south Wales, the initiative came from David Urquhart, many of whose political pressure groups built their own baths, and campaigned for others; while in Scotland, the initiative came largely from local hydropathists.

The use of the bath was also encouraged by members of social welfare organisations such as the Ladies' Sanitary Association, and by special interest groups such as the temperance societies. While for members of a less obvious special interest group, the leisured wealthy class, the bath became a fashionable pursuit.

Nevertheless, in real terms, only a very small minority of the population ever used Turkish baths, compared with those who used slipper baths, and those who availed themselves of the growing number of indoor and outdoor swimming pools.[1]

The rapid spread of the bath: economic factors

From the viewpoint of the entrepreneur, it was relatively cheap to provide and run a Turkish bath and, for an individual proprietor in the right location, it could be relatively easy to make an acceptable profit.

It was not difficult to start a small Turkish bath by inexpensively converting the basement of an existing house or shop, perhaps with the addition of part of the ground floor as a reception area.

Wages, for any work which the proprietor or members of the family did not wish to do themselves, were extremely low. Fuel also was still cheap, though this was soon to change. The 1867 annual report of the Manchester and Salford Baths and Laundries Company, for example, noted that 'the extraordinary rise in the price of coal has added more than £150 to the [annual] expenditure for coals.'[2] But, for a while, both these factors made for low running costs in the early baths.

Their proprietors also benefited because the Victorian Turkish bath really had no competition. For therapeutic use, hydropathy and the cold-water cure were expensive. They required lengthy stays at a hydropathic establishment, for a treatment which was hardly enjoyable and which most people could not afford.

For cleansing purposes, the steam or vapour baths which existed in the 19th century consisted of cabinet baths. These were not very comfortable and bathers were unable to move around and socialise, while the more spacious communal Finnish sauna was unknown in the British Isles at that time.

The gradual decline

As the 20th century approached, these advantages began to disappear. The rising cost of fuel has already been mentioned. Wages certainly rose between the mid-1860s and mid-1870s, putting up the cost of staffing the baths, but how this affected the cost of living of the various classes of bather is a moot point. During the following century, wages went down as well as up, and all one can deduce with any certainty is that wages would have formed a higher proportion of the running costs of a small establishment by the end of the 20th century than they did when the first baths opened.

But three factors were probably more important. The first was the rise (although initially slow) in the number of homes with hot and cold running water. This considerably reduced, and eventually completely removed, the use of the bath by people for whom it was basically a means of personal cleansing.

Second, the increasing effectiveness of drugs as painkillers and (following World War II) as curative agents, together with an exponential growth in medical knowledge, had virtually ended the use of the Turkish bath as a therapy.

Against this, however, should be set those sufferers from complaints such as rheumatism, for which there is still no cure, and who continue to find the bath a useful palliative. There has also been a growing realisation that it appears to help reduce tension and the stress of everyday life, and that it is pleasurable.

Enjoying the Turkish bath as a leisure activity is now completely accepted and there is no longer a need to justify its use by citing hygienic or medical purposes. Logically, this should

Fig 30.2 (left)
A modern glass-fronted, tiled Russian steam bath, designed for commercial use. (Nordic Sauna and Steam Ltd. www.nordic.co.uk)
Fig 30.3 (right)
A large modern sauna for use in hotels, clubs, and health spas. (Delmi Sauna for Nordic Sauna and Steam Ltd. www.nordic.co.uk)

have led to a greater use of Turkish baths rather than their near disappearance.

Here the third factor comes into play, for the Victorian Turkish bath is no longer without any competition. The arrival of the first saunas in London and Manchester at the end of 1959,[3] and their speedy adoption elsewhere, created a new generation of hot-air bathers. Steam rooms had been in existence since the beginning of the 20th century, sometimes added to an existing Turkish bath, sometimes (especially in local provision) instead of a Turkish bath. Though cheaper to build than a Turkish bath, they still had to be converted from an existing room, or built from scratch. Here, the game changer was the prefabricated plastic steam room with its compact electric steam generator.

To the baths proprietor and local authority provider alike, the advantages of these newer hot-air baths were significant: space, installation costs and heating costs.

For a large establishment three saunas could be fitted into the area taken up by a traditional Victorian Turkish bath. More important, outside peak usage hours, two of them could be switched off, thereby saving costs, whereas the heat in a Turkish bath has to be maintained throughout the day even if it is empty.

In a smaller establishment, if there are no customers, a steam room (Fig 30.2) can remain switched off, and yet be ready to use in the time taken for a customer to change and shower. Even a sauna can be ready for use in less than an hour.

The bathing experience in a Victorian Turkish bath is quite different from that in a sauna or steam room. But that is of little concern to local authorities who are increasingly short of cash, or to hotels, health clubs and individual proprietors who need to make a profit.

Nor is it of concern to most of their 21st-century customers, who have probably never used a Turkish bath. Even among Turkish bath aficionados, few would go so far as Eric Newby who, in the 1980s, complained that most Turkish baths in Britain had been 'knocked down and replaced by the sauna, which is about as much fun as being buried alive in a red-hot cigar box.'[4]

Jeffrey Bernard comes closer to the views of many when he writes that he finds the sauna

> 'claustrophobic and akin to a punishment box in which you sweat it out metaphorically, so to speak, as well as physically. The Turkish bath is by comparison, spacious. It's also nicely social.'[5]

To be fair, both these authors are writing about saunas in Britain; anyone familiar with the much larger ones frequently found in, for example, Holland and Germany, will know that they can be just as large and sociable as a Turkish bath (Fig 30.3).

The future of the Victorian Turkish bath

So ultimately we are likely to be left with perhaps a handful of usable Turkish baths retained, in the main, because their buildings are of historic importance in their own right. These include the Victorian baths in Scotland; Victorian and Edwardian baths such as those at Swindon, Harrogate and Carlisle; and a handful of later Victorian-style baths, such as those at Birmingham and Northampton in the provinces, and Porchester Hall in London.

We can only hope that planners have learnt from the unforgivable destruction of the Imperial Hotel Turkish baths.

Fig 30.4 (above)
The re-use of the cooling-room at Nevill's Bishopsgate Churchyard Turkish baths as part of a 1990s restaurant.
(© Malcolm Shifrin)
Fig 30.5 (below)
Manchester's Victoria Baths: winner of the first BBC2 Restoration Award.
(Courtesy Aidan O'Rourke)

The example of the refurbished baths at Harrogate shows that if done in a sympathetic manner, Turkish baths can again become popular, though the jury is still out on London's inter-war baths at York Hall and Ironmonger Row, which have been turned into expensive day spas with hot rooms.

Where architecturally important baths face closure, a caring planning committee and a watchful local community can help ensure that baths are reused rather than demolished, leaving us able to appreciate at least some of the visual delights of a decorative exterior, such as Elphick's baths in Bishopsgate Churchyard (Fig 30.4), or the unique baths in what was once part of the Wimbledon Theatre.

But most inspiring are the three local communities where bathers, originally protesting at the closure of a well-loved facility, stayed together afterwards. They formed strong vibrant groups determined to take over the baths buildings, energetically continue to raise funds to repair them, and work towards reopening the baths they grew up with and miss.

The Re-open Newcastle Turkish Baths & City Pool Group, the Govanhill Baths Community Trust in Glasgow, and the Victoria Baths Trust in Manchester (Fig 30.5)[6] deserve our admiration and also, wherever we live, our support. For they are working to preserve the heritage which belongs to all of us. If it disappears completely, it will not return.

NOTES AND REFERENCES

Abbreviations used in notes

BCDU Balliol College. Papers of David Urquhart
WS Wiltshire and Swindon Local History Centre
WS-GWR – Great Western Railway Company
WS-MFS – – Medical Fund Society
WS-Poore – Poore Papers
WS-LPTB – – London & Provincial Turkish Bath Co Ltd
TNA The National Archives
WL Wellcome Library, London

Preface

1 After this preface was written, I was delighted to learn that Charlotte Jones has just completed (March 2015) *An historical geography of Turkish baths in Victorian Britain* for submission as a PhD thesis to University College London—the first on Victorian Turkish baths.

Glossary

1 Nielsen, Inge *Thermae et balnea: the architecture and cultural history of Roman public baths*. 2nd edn (Aarhus Univ Pr, 1993) p.3

2 Personal communication from Kathryn Ferry. March 2014

1 Introduction

1 Davies, D S *Public health* (Bristol: British Association, 1898)

2 Urquhart, David *The Pillars of Hercules, or, a narrative of travels in Spain and Morocco in 1848* (Bentley, 1850)

2 Early communal hot-air baths

1 Pliny the Elder *The natural history*. Book 11. Chap. 96; translated by John Bostock and H T Riley (Available online from the Perseus Digital Library at http://www.perseus.tufts.edu/hopper/text?doc=Plin.+Nat.)

2 Grilli, Peter *Pleasures of the Japanese bath* (New York: Weatherhill, 1992)

3 Konya, Allan *The modern sauna and related facilities* (Reading: Archimedia, 2012)

4 Yegül, Fikret *Baths and bathing in classical antiquity* (Cambridge, (Mass); London: MIT Press, 1992)

5 Rook, Tony *Roman baths in Britain* (Oxford: Shire, 2002)

6 Meunier, Pascal *Hammams* (Paris: Dakota, 2005)

7 Avcıoğlu, Nebahat 'Identity-as-form: the mosque in the West' *Cultural Analysis* (Univ California, 6; 2007) pp.91–112

3 The British 'discovery' of the hot-air bath

1 Montagu, Mary Wortley *Letters of the Right Honourable Lady M-y W-y M-e: written, during her travels in Europe, Asia and Africa, etc* (Homer, 1764)

2 Madden, Richard Robert *Travels in Turkey, Egypt, Nubia, and Palestine in 1824–27* (Whittaker, 1829)

3 Lane, Edward William *An account of the manners and customs of the modern Egyptians, written in Egypt during the years 1833–35, etc* (1836)

4 Thackeray, William Makepeace *Notes of a journey from Cornhill to Grand Cairo…* (Chapman and Hall, 1846) p.104

5 Urquhart, David *The spirit of the East: illustrated in a journal of travels through Roumeli during an eventful period* (Henry Colburn, 1838) vol.2; p.47

6 Avcıoğlu, Nebahat 'David Urquhart and the role of travel literature in the introduction of Turkish baths to Victorian England' **In:** *Interpreting the orient: travellers in Egypt and the Near East* Paul and Janet Starkey (eds) (New York: Ithaca Pr, 2001) p.70

7 Said, Edward W *Orientalism* (Routledge, 1978)

8 *Strictures on the personal cleanliness of the English with a description of the hamams of the Turks and an attempt to shew their conformity with the baths of the antient Romans, etc* (Pisa: printed by N. Capurro, 1828)

9 Carlile, Richard 'Strictures on the personal cleanliness of the English' *The Lion* (31 Oct 1828) p.576

10 *Strictures on the personal cleanliness of the English with a description of the hamams of the Turks and an attempt to shew their conformity with the baths of the antient Romans, etc* (Pisa: printed by N. Capurro, 1828) pp.117–22

11 Ibid, p.35

12 Urquhart, David *The Pillars of Hercules, or, a narrative of travels in Spain & Morocco in 1848* (Richard Bentley, 1850) vol.2; p.38

13 Ibid, vol.2; p.32

14 Ibid, vol.2; pp.38–42

15 Beamish, Richard *The functions of the skin, and the value of the bath, with special reference to the improved Turkish bath* (Bailliere, 1859)

4 The birth of the Roman-Irish or Victorian Turkish bath

1 *Recollections of the late Dr Barter*, by the author of *Simple questions and sanitary facts* (Dublin: McGee, 1875). The book's author was Mrs C G Donovan who wrote pamphlets on hygiene, etc, and helped fund the building in Cork, in 1863, of Barter's Turkish Baths for the Destitute Poor.

2 *Recollections of the late Dr Barter*, by the author of *Simple questions and sanitary facts* (Dublin: McGee, 1875) **Quoted in:** Metcalfe, Richard *The rise and progress of hydropathy in England and Scotland*. 2nd edn (Simkin, Marshall, 1906) pp.123–3

3 The spelling of the name of Dr Richard Barter's Hydropathic Establishment, and its location at St Ann(e)'s Hill, varies in contemporary documents, including those published by the hydro itself. I have attempted to be consistent by using St Ann's (rather than St Anne's) except when quoting directly from a document which uses the latter.

4 Claridge, R T *Hydropathy; or, the cold water cure, as practised by Vincent Priessnitz, at Gräefenberg, Silesia, Austria* (Madden, 1842)

5 Metcalfe, Richard *The rise and progress of hydropathy in England and Scotland*. 2nd edn (Simkin, Marshall, 1912) p.126 Metcalfe also wrote one of the two standard English works on Vincent Preissnitz, the other being by Captain Claridge.

6 Drake, Francis *The Anglo-Roman or 'Turkish bath': its history, proper construction, present status and various uses* (Ward & Lock, 1862)

7 *Recollections of the late Dr Barter*, by the author of *Simple questions and sanitary facts* (Dublin: McGee, 1875) p.17

8 Metcalfe, Richard *The rise and progress of hydropathy in England and Scotland*. 2nd edn (Simkin, Marshall, 1912) p.128
9 Ibid, p.129
10 Urquhart, David *The Turkish bath, with a view to its introduction into the British dominions* [Extracts from *The Pillars of Hercules*; edited by Richard Barter] (Bryce, 1856)
11 'Testimonial to R Barter, Esq' *Cork Constitution* (7 Jun 1856)
12 'Medical treatment at St Anne's' *Free Press* (9 Mar 1856)
13 Wollaston, Robert 'The Turkish bath' *Limerick Chronicle* (1 Oct 1859)
14 *Recollections of the late Dr Barter*, by the author of *Simple questions and sanitary facts* (Dublin: McGee, 1875) p.16
15 Metcalfe, Richard *The rise and progress of hydropathy in England and Scotland.* 2nd edn (Simkin, Marshall, 1912) p.131
16 Dunlop, Durham *The philosophy of the bath*. 4th edn (Kent, 1889) p.171
17 Some sources refer to the architect and sculptor as the doctor's son, but the doctor's son, Richard (later Sir Richard), was a farmer. Others refer to him as the doctor's nephew, the relationship I favoured until recently. However, after reading the sculptor-architect's obituary, in which he is only referred to as the doctor's namesake, I now take the view that the similarity of names is only a coincidence. See: Crosbie, Thomas 'Necrology: Richard Barter, Sculptor' *Journal of the Cork Historical and Archæological Society* (1896) pp.85–8
18 'Introduction of the Turkish bath into Ireland' *Free Press* (21 Jun 1856) p.1
19 **Quoted in:** 'The Turkish Bath Movement' *Free Press* (30 Aug 1856) p.24
20 'Fête at St Anne's Hill, Blarney' *Free Press* (17 Sep 1856) pp.50–51
21 Urquhart, David. Letter. 1 Sep 1856 to the editor of the *Cork Herald* **Reprinted in:** 'The Turkish Bath Movement' *Free Press* (20 Sep 1856) pp.47–8
22 'Fete at St Anne's Hill' *Cork Examiner* (1 Jul 1857) p.2 **Reprinted in:** 'The Turkish bath' *Manchester Examiner* (21 Jul 1857)
23 Barter, Richard. Letter. 28 Feb 1858 to Mr Wrenfordsley **Reprinted in:** *Bradford Advertiser* (10 Apr 1858) p.4
24 Barter, Richard *Heating and ventilating buildings, &c* (Letters Patent: 1859; no.208)
25 [Invitation card] (11 May 1858) Cork City and County Archives; U140 C 263
26 Barter, Richard *The Turkish bath: being a lecture delivered in the Mechanic's Institute, Bradford, on Tuesday evening, July 8th, 1858* (Bradford: Printed by J M Jowett, 1858)

5 David Urquhart, his Foreign Affairs Committees, and their baths

1 Marx, Karl *Karl Marx, Frederick Engels: collected works.* vol.12 (Lawrence & Wishart, 1975-) p.477
2 Taylor, Miles 'Urquhart, David (1805–1877)' *Oxford dictionary of national biography* (Oxford: OUP, 2004) http://www.oxforddnb.com/view/article/28017 Accessed 31 Jan 2013
3 In this book, I do not discuss any of the historical events which led to Urquhart's campaigning activities nor, except *en passant*, any of the political activities which the Foreign Affairs Committees undertook in the hope of influencing the actions of their government. These have been well covered in, for example: Bolsover, G H 'David Urquhart and the Eastern Question, 1833–37: a study in publicity and diplomacy' *Journal of Modern History* (Dec 1936); Briggs, Asa 'David Urquhart and the West Riding Foreign Affairs Committees' *The Bradford Antiquary* (1962) pp.197–207; Gleason, John Howes *The genesis of Russophobia in Great Britain: a study of the interaction of policy and opinion* (Cambridge (Mass.): Harvard Univ Pr, 1950); Salt, John 'Local manifestations of the Urquhartite movement' *International Review of Social History* (1968) p.365; Shannon, Richard 'David Urquhart and the Foreign Affairs Committees' **In:** *Pressure from without in early Victorian England* Patricia Hollis (ed) (Edward Arnold, 1974); Taylor, A J P *The trouble makers: dissent over foreign policy, 1792–1939: The Ford Lectures, Oxford, 1956* (Hamish Hamilton, 1957); Taylor, Miles 'The old radicalism and the new: David Urquhart and the politics of opposition, 1832–1867' **In:** *Currents of radicalism: popular radicalism, organised labour and party politics in Britain, 1850–1914* Eugenio F Biagini and Alastair J Reid (eds) (Cambridge: CUP, 1991)
Much useful information, used by most later writers, is to be found in Margaret H Jenks's unpublished PhD thesis: *The activities and influence of David Urquhart, 1837–56, with special reference to the affairs of the Near East* (University of London, 1964)
4 Bolsover, G H 'David Urquhart and the Eastern Question, 1833–37: a study in publicity and diplomacy' *Journal of Modern History* (Dec 1936) p.444
5 Marx, Karl *Karl Marx, Frederick Engels: collected works.* vol.39 (Lawrence & Wishart, 1975-) p.395
6 Anderson, Olive *A Liberal state at war: English politics and economics during the Crimean War* (Macmillan, 1967) p.146
7 Constantine, Joseph *Fifty years of the water cure, with autobiographical notes* (Manchester: John Heywood, 1892) pp.34–5
8 Bailey, Cyril *Francis Fortescue Urquhart: a memoir* (Macmillan, 1936) p.7
9 Robinson, Gertrude *David Urquhart: some chapters in the life of a Victorian knight-errant of justice and liberty* (Oxford: Basil Blackwell, 1920) p.251
10 Briggs, Asa 'David Urquhart and the West Riding Foreign Affairs Committees' *The Bradford Antiquary* (1962) pp.206–7 (referring to a meeting at Crossroads described in BCDU. I G10, John Waddington. Letter to John Johnson, 17 Feb 1858)
11 Briggs, Asa 'David Urquhart and the West Riding Foreign Affairs Committees' *The Bradford Antiquary* (1962) p.205; note 16
12 Morley, John *Life of Cobden* (Fisher Unwin, 1881) p.101
13 *Dictionary of national biography.* vol.20; Leslie Stephen (ed) (Smith, Elder, 1885–1903) pp.43–5
14 Holyoake, George Jacob *Bygones worth remembering* (Fisher Unwin, 1905) vol.2; p.267
15 BCDU, Box 6, David Urquhart (Jnr). Letter to Gertrude Robinson, 3 May 1920
16 Currie, Mary Montgomerie 'The feast of kébôbs: a reminiscence' *Blackwood's Edinburgh Magazine* (Apr 1904) p.472
17 BCDU, I J9.11a iv, Ahmed Khan. Letter to David Urquhart, translated for him by Charles Wells [1863]
18 BCDU, I J9.11b, Hassan of Circassia. Letter to David Urquhart, translated for him by Charles Wells [1863?]
19 Jenks, Margaret H. Unpublished PhD Thesis. *The activities and influence of David Urquhart, 1837–56, with special reference to the affairs of the Near East* (University of London, 1964) p.312
20 Bishop, Maria Catherine *A memoir of Mrs Urquhart* (Kegan Paul, 1897) pp.123–4
21 BCDU, I G15, Stewart Rolland. Letter to unknown correspondent, 29 Dec [1858]
22 BCDU, I G24.3, John Johnson. Letter to Miss Curtis, 1 Jul 1862
23 TNA BT31 30704/2070
24 *…and Mr Fortescue: a selection from the diaries from 1851 to 1862 of Chichester Fortescue, Lord Carlingford;* Osbert Wyndham Hewett (ed) (John Murray, [1958]) p.16
25 Ibid, p.54
26 Ibid, p.75
27 Bishop, Maria Catherine *A memoir of Mrs Urquhart* (Kegan Paul, 1897) p.2

28 BCDU, I 10.6, Benjamin Morrell. Letter to David Urquhart, 19 Feb 1861
29 BCDU, I 7, David Scott. Letter to [John Johnson], 12 Apr 1861
30 BCDU, I G1.a, Thomas Dean. Letter to Harriet Urquhart, 6 Jul 1874
31 Bishop, Maria Catherine *A memoir of Mrs Urquhart* (Kegan Paul, 1897) p.196
32 'The Baths at Riverside' *St Albans Times* (May 1860)
33 Johnson's letter to an overseas enquirer is quoted in: *Is the Turkish bath injurious? Fly-sheet no.14* **Reprinted in:** *The Hammam of the Turks: collected fly-sheets* (The Hammam, 1867)
34 BCDU, I G1.a, John Harlow. Letter to Harriet Urquhart, 28 Nov 1859
35 Jenks, Margaret H Unpublished PhD thesis. *The activities and influence of David Urquhart, 1837–56, with special reference to the affairs of the Near East* (University of London, 1964) pp.335–6
36 Briggs, Asa 'David Urquhart and the West Riding Foreign Affairs Committees' *The Bradford Antiquary* (1962) p.199
37 These included David Ross of Bladensberg (together with whom he had fought in the Greek War of Independence, and through whom he was later to meet his wife), Robert Monteith of Carstairs (also much involved in the temperance movement), and Charles Attwood (a brother of Thomas Attwood, campaigner for the 1832 Reform Act and the People's Charter).
38 Maehl, William H, Jnr, 'David Urquhart' **In:** *Biographical dictionary of modern British radicals;* Joseph O Baylen and Norbert J Gossman (eds) (Brighton: Harvester Pr, 1984) p.510
39 Marx, Karl. Letter to Ferdinand Lassalle 1860. **Cited in:** *Karl Marx, Frederick Engels: collected works.* vol.41 (Lawrence & Wishart, 1975-) p.153
40 'Isaac Ironside, 1808–1870' **In:** Farley, M Foster *Biographical dictionary of modern British radicals* (Brighton: Harvester Pr, 1984) pp.258–61
41 Claeys, Gregory *Citizens and saints: politics and anti-politics in early British socialism* (Cambridge: CUP, 1989) p.239
42 *Sheffield Times* (14 Jan 1854) p.6 **Cited in:** Salt, John 'Experiments in anarchism, 1850–1854' *Transactions of the Hunter Archaeological Society* (1971) p.359
43 Merson, Allan *The Free Press, 1851–66* (*c* 1976) p.4 (Unpublished typescript in the Leeds Local & Family History Library)
44 Salt, John 'Experiments in anarchism, 1850–1854' *Transactions of the Hunter Archaeological Society* (1971) pp.358–9
45 The identities of the various owners and editors of the *Sheffield Free Press* and its London-based successor are still not fully known and are discussed more fully on the *Victorian Turkish Baths* website.
46 Robinson, Gertrude *David Urquhart: some chapters in the life of a Victorian knight-errant of justice and liberty* (Oxford: Basil Blackwell, 1920) pp.310–311
47 BCDU, I G20 Stafford, John Shalcross. Letter to John Johnson, Undated
48 BCDU, I G7 Dundee, David Scott. Letter to [?] John Johnson, 12 Apr 1861
49 BCDU, I G19 North Shields, Thomas Woodruff. Letter to Urquhart, 19 Feb 1861
50 BCDU, I G11 Leeds, John Waddington. Letter to John Johnson, 25 Jul 1858
51 Shannon, Richard 'David Urquhart and the Foreign Affairs Committees' **In:** *Pressure from without in early Victorian England* Patricia Hollis (ed) (Edward Arnold, 1974) p.257
52 BCDU, I G19 North Shields, Thomas Woodruff. Letter to Urquhart, 23 Jun 1861
53 'Turkish baths' *North and South Shields Gazette* (4 Sep 1862) p.1
54 *Kelly's Post Office directory of Newcastle*
55 Jenks, Margaret H Unpublished PhD thesis. *The activities and influence of David Urquhart, 1837–56, with special reference to the affairs of the Near East* (University of London, 1964) p.335
56 Charles Bartholomew's will (26 Jun 1883), Somerset House, M26
57 Bartholomew, Charles *Mr Bartholomew's evidence before a committee of medical men on the prevention and cure of disease by the use of Turkish and oxygen baths: the symposium held at the Bristol Athenaeum 11–12 June 1866* (Bristol: Taylor, 1866)
58 Metcalfe, Richard *The water cure: a plea for hydropathic dispensaries* (Tweedie, 1878) p.30
59 Turner, E S *Taking the cure* (Michael Joseph, 1967) p.228
60 'Physic v. Turkish baths' *Daily Bristol Times and Mirror* (12 Jun 1866)
61 Personal interview with the late Leonard Park. June 1991
62 'Drugs v. Turkish baths' *Daily Bristol Times and Mirror* (13 Jun 1866)
63 'Introduction of the Turkish bath into Ireland' *Sheffield Free Press* (21 Jun 1856) p.1
64 Holyoake, George Jacob *Sixty years of an agitator's life* (Fisher Unwin, 1906) vol.1; p.280
65 Merson, Allan *The Free Press, 1851–66* (*c* 1976) p.6 (Unpublished typescript in the Leeds Local & Family History Library)
66 Wilson, Erasmus *The eastern, or Turkish bath: its history, revival in Britain and application to the purpose of health* (John Churchill, 1861) pp.93–103
67 Ironside, Isaac 'The Turkish bath' *Sheffield Free Press* (24 Jan 1857) p.6
68 'Introduction of the Turkish bath into Ireland' *Sheffield Free Press* (21 Jun 1856) p.1
69 'Medical treatment at St Annes' *Sheffield Free Press* (29 Mar 1856) p.4
70 'Introduction of the Turkish Bath into our towns and cities' *Sheffield Free Press* (5 Jul 1856) p.6
71 Prins, Gwyn 'Oral history' **In:** *New perspectives on historical writing* (Cambridge: Polity Pr, 1991) p.115
72 'Mr Urquhart: the apostle of the oriental baths' *Sheffield Free Press* (23 Aug 1856) p.5 **Reprinted from:** *Cork Herald* (18 Aug 1856)
73 'The Turkish bath' *Sheffield Free Press* (23 Aug 1856) p.6
74 'Turkish baths: public meeting in Cork' *Free Press* (2 Aug 1856) p.1
75 Bartholomew, Charles 'The Turkish Bath Movement' *Free Press* (23 Aug 1856) p.12
76 Attwood, Charles 'The Turkish Bath Movement' *Free Press* (30 Aug 1856) p.24
77 'The Turkish Bath Movement: fête at St Anne's Hill, Blarney' *Free press* (17 Sep 1856) pp.50–51
78 BCDU, I G14.7, Charles Bartholomew. Letter to David Urquhart, 26 Sep 1856
79 Bartholomew, Charles 'Correspondence' *Free Press* (11 Oct 1856) pp.70–71
80 'Transactions of the committees: Wakefield', *Free Press* (27 May 1857) p.344
81 Maxfield, John [the younger] *The Turkish bath* (Gloucester: the corporation, 1895) p.3
82 Maxfield, John [the elder] 'The Turkish bath' *Sheffield Free Press* (17 Jan 1857) p.6
83 Ironside, Isaac 'The Turkish bath' *Sheffield Free Press* (24 Jan 1857) p.6
84 See, for example: Bartholomew, Charles *The Turkish bath in health, sickness, convalescence: a popular hand-book for the robust & invalid* (Ward, Lock & Tyler, [1869]) pp.65–6
85 Potter, William 'The Turkish bath' *Sheffield Free Press* (18 Jul 1857) p.3; *Free Press* (22 Jul 1857) p.408
86 'The Turkish baths at Broughton Lane' [advertisement] *Halifax Courier* (24 Dec 1858) p.1
87 'Information about the Turkish bath' *The Reasoner* (26 Aug 1860) p.279
88 WL, *Western Ms.6236: Correspondence on Turkish baths; 13*, H K Mallen. Letter to David Urquhart, *c* 1858
89 *A Century of co-operation in Keighley: 1860–1960* (Keighley: Keighley Co-operative Society, 1960)
90 Rhodes, Joseph *Half a century of co-operation in Keighley, 1860–1910* (Keighley: Keighley Co-operative Society, 1911) p.19
91 'A Brief History of Inner Wheel' (Association of Inner Wheel Clubs in Great Britain & Ireland) http://home.btconnect.com/associationofinnerwheelclubs/Pages/Our_History_Page.htm (Accessed 1 Sep 2013)

92 Stropher, Thomas *History of Winchester streets* (Typed transcript of the unpublished manuscript in Winchester Libraries Local History Collection)
93 BCDU, Box 10: I G1.23, Henry Butcher. Letter to David Urquhart, Feb 1866
94 Label on the back of a photograph of 'Mrs Butcher who looked after the Turkish Baths'. (Hampshire Record Office, Winchester: 85M88/16 fol.26
95 BCDU, I G14 Manchester, John Johnson. Letter to David Urquhart, 6 Jun 1858
96 BCDU, I G14 Pt.2 Joseph Foden. Letter to John Johnson, 9 Jun 1860

6 Dr Richard Barter and the bath

1 'Improvements in Bray: lecture by Dr Barter' *Freeman's Journal* (14 Oct 1859)
2 'Turkish baths in Cork' *Cork Examiner* (18 May 1859) p.2 I am much indebted to Roger Herlihy for this reference.
3 [Advertisement] *Cork Examiner* (1 Jul 1859) p.1
4 *A guide to Cork City's historic plaques and signs* (Cork: City Council) http://www.heritagecouncil.i.e./fileadmin/user_upload/Publications/Architecture/PLAQUES_BROCHURE.pdf Accessed 1 July 2013 I am most grateful to Jezz Nicholson and Stephanie Jenkins for this reference.
5 'Improvements in Bray: the Turkish bath' *Freeman's Journal* (14 Oct 1859)
6 Morphy, John *Recollections of a visit to Great Britain and Ireland in the summer of 1862* (Palmer, 1863) p.25
7 Wollaston, Robert *The sanitary advantages of baths, especially the Turkish or Roman bath: a lecture delivered at … Cheltenham, on 15 November 1859* (Cheltenham: Henry Davies, 1860) pp.35–6
8 'The Queen at Killarney' *Morning Chronicle* (2 Sep 1861)
9 P.B. 'The Lakes of Killarney' *Gardener's Monthly* (May 1868) p.132
10 'Improvements in Bray: lecture by Dr Barter' *Freeman's Journal* (14 Oct 1859)
11 'Turkish baths at Bray' *Agricultural Review* (23 Aug 1859) p.3
12 Dargan's instruction: 'Improvements in Bray: lecture by Dr Barter' *Freeman's Journal* (14 Oct 1859); description of the baths: Wollaston, Robert *The sanitary advantages of baths, especially the Turkish or Roman bath: a lecture delivered at … Cheltenham, on 15 November 1859* (Cheltenham: Henry Davies, 1860) p.35
13 Powell, G R *The official railway handbook to Bray…* (Dublin: M'Glashan & Gill, 1860) p.87
14 'Improvements in Bray: lecture by Dr Barter' *Freeman's Journal* (14 Oct 1859)
15 WS-Poore, 1915/73. Diary, 10 Mar 1864
16 Davies, K Mary 'A lost Victorian treasure: Bray's Turkish baths' *Journal of the Bray Cualann Historical Society* (2004) p.16
17 Davies, [K] Mary *That favourite resort: the story of Bray, Co. Wicklow* (Bray: Wordwell, 2007) *passim*
18 'Improvements in Bray: lecture by Dr Barter' *Freeman's Journal* (14 Oct 1859)
19 Westrup, Thomas 'Death in a Turkish bath at Limerick' *The Lancet* (11 May 1861) p.471
20 'Limerick Turkish baths' *Limerick Chronicle* (5 Sep 1872)
21 'Safe and desirable investment' [advertisement] *Limerick Chronicle* (12 Apr 1890)
22 Wollaston, Robert *The sanitary advantages of baths, especially the Turkish or Roman bath: a lecture delivered at … Cheltenham, on 15 November 1859* (Cheltenham: Henry Davies, 1860) p.36
23 'Prospectus' [advertisement] *Freeman's Journal* (8 Jun 1861)
24 'The Turkish bath in Dublin' *Freeman's Journal* (3 Feb 1860) p.3
25 'The new baths, Lincoln-place' *Dublin Builder* (1 Jan 1860) p.176
26 Whammond, G K *Illustrated guide to Dublin & Wicklow* (Dublin: McGee, 1868)
27 'The new baths, Lincoln-place' *Dublin Builder* (1 Jan 1860) p.176
28 For example: O'Dwyer, Frederick *Lost Dublin* (Dublin: Gill & Macmillan, 1981 p.58
29 'A visit to a Turkish bath, by A Moist Man' *Bristol Times* (15 Dec 1860) p.6
30 'The new baths, Lincoln-place' *Dublin Builder* (1 Jan 1860) p.176
31 'Turkish Bath Company' [advertisement] *Irish Times* (9 Nov 1859) p.2
32 Mac Con Iomaire, Máirtín *The Emergence, development and influence of French* haute cuisine *on public dining in Dublin restaurants 1900–2000: an oral history*. vol 2: *From ancient Ireland to 21st century Dublin* (Dublin Institute of Technology PhD Thesis, 2009) p.95
33 'Turkish Baths, Lincoln Place' [advertisement] *Irish Times* (15 Oct 1867) p.1
34 Madden, Richard Robert *Travels in Turkey, Egypt, Nubia and Palestine in 1824–27* (Henry Colburn, 1829)
35 **Quoted in:** *The New Irish bath versus the old Turkish, or, pure air versus vapour: being an answer to the mis-statements of Drs Madden and Corrigan*; 'Photophilus' (ed) (Dublin: McGee, 1860) p.8
36 *The New Irish bath versus the old Turkish, or, pure air versus vapour: being an answer to the mis-statements of Drs Madden and Corrigan*; 'Photophilus' (ed) (Dublin: McGee, 1860) p.36; note
37 **Quoted in:** *The New Irish bath versus the old Turkish, or, pure air versus vapour: being an answer to the mis-statements of Drs Madden and Corrigan*; 'Photophilus' (ed) (Dublin: McGee, 1860) p.18
38 **Quoted in:** *The New Irish bath versus the old Turkish, or, pure air versus vapour: being an answer to the mis-statements of Drs Madden and Corrigan*; 'Photophilus' (ed) (Dublin: McGee, 1860) p.37
39 'The Turkish bath: a lecture by Dr Barter' *Freeman's Journal* (9 Feb 1860) p.ii
40 'Improvements in Bray: lecture by Dr Barter' *Freeman's Journal* (14 Oct 1859)
41 Metcalfe, Richard *Sanitas sanitatum et omnia sanitas* (Co-operative Printing Co, 1877) p.319
42 Wollaston, Robert *The sanitary advantages of baths, especially the Turkish or Roman bath: a lecture delivered at … Cheltenham, on 15 November 1859* (Cheltenham: Henry Davies, 1860) p.37
43 'Turkish baths for the poor' *Cork Examiner* (4 Feb 1863)
44 'Wanted immediately to lease or purchase' [advertisement] *Irish Times* (17 Jun 1868) p.2
45 'The Hammam, Dublin' *Hydropathic Record* (May 1869) p.126
46 'New Turkish baths' *Freeman's Journal* (15 Mar 1869)
47 'The "Hammam" Dublin' *Hydropathic Record* (May 1869) p.164
48 *Thom's official directory of the United Kingdom of Great Britain, 1868*
49 'New Turkish baths' *Freeman's Journal* (16 Jan 1871)
50 'The Hammam, Sackville-street' *Freeman's Journal* (15 Apr 1871)
51 'The Hammam Hotel and Turkish Baths' *Irish Times* (28 Nov 1881) p.1
52 *The Census of Ireland, 1911*
53 'The lighter side of the revolution' *Irish Times* (2 May 1916) p.3
54 'Hemming-in the end: "Nearing the end"' *The Times* (4 Jul 1922) p.10
55 'Shell and flame: incendiary bombs' *The Times* (6 Jul 1922) p.10
56 'Awards by the Recorder of Dublin' *Irish Times* (16 Feb 1924) p.8
57 'Destroyed area: Upper Sackville Street' *Irish Times* (23 Jul 1924) p.12
58 'Fermoy' *Hydropathic Record* (May 1869)
59 'A new Turkish bath at Blarney, Co. Cork' *Irish Builder* (1870) p.170
60 'The Turkish bath' *Irish Times* (7 Jul 1870) p.5; (8 Jul 1870) p.5
61 Barter, [Anna Madeline] 'Turkish bath and home for patients of the poorer classes…' **In:** *Woman's mission: a series of congress papers on the philanthropic work of women by eminent writers*; Angela Burdett-Coutts (ed) (Samson Low, 1893) p.450
62 O'Leary, Stephen 'St Anns Hydro' *Old Blarney: Journal of the Blarney and District Historical Society* (2000; 5) pp.3–31
63 'The Turkish bath' *The Field* (5 May 1860) pp.369–70

7 The Victorian Turkish bath travels overseas

1 'The Turkish bath is now open' [advertisement] *Bradford Advertiser* (10 Apr 1858) p.4
2 'Northern lectures, debates, and Turkish baths' *The Reasoner* (3 Oct 1858)
3 I am most grateful to Susan Aykut, with whom, some years ago, I enjoyably exchanged references and information about Victorian Turkish baths in Australia.
4 'The Turkish bath' *Sydney Morning Herald* (13 Oct 1859) p.4
5 'The improved Turkish bath' [advertisement] *Sydney Morning Herald* (28 Oct 1859) p.8
6 'Sydney Turkish Bath Company' [advertisement] *Sydney Morning Herald* (27 Jun 1860) p.2
7 WL, *Western Ms.6236: Correspondence on Turkish baths; 21*, John Le Gay Brereton. Letter to David Urquhart, 10 Jul 1860
8 'The Turkish Bath Company' *Sydney Morning Herald* (11 Jul 1860)
9 'The Turkish Bath Company' *Sydney Morning Herald* (21 Aug 1860) p.9
10 'Opening of the new Turkish Baths' *Sydney Morning Herald* (15 Mar 1861) p.8
11 'Notice' [advertisement] *Sydney Morning Herald* (28 Nov 1862) p.8
12 'Notice' [advertisement] *Sydney Morning Herald* (4 Dec 1862) p.1
13 [Turkish baths sold] *Sydney Morning Herald* (21 Feb 1863) p.3
14 'Addition to the Turkish bath' *Sydney Morning Herald* (6 Jun 1864) p.4
15 'New Turkish baths' *Sydney Morning Herald* (4 Mar 1884) p.5
16 'The Turkish Bath Company' *Sydney Morning Herald* (7 Mar 1887) p.8
17 'The Turkish Baths Company' *Sydney Morning Herald* (26 Apr 1890)
18 'Booth's Turkish Baths' [advertisement] *Sydney Morning Herald* (24 Feb 1906) p.2
19 [Many visitors to Sydney…] *Argus* (24 Nov 1922) p.8
20 'Preliminary announcement' [advertisement] *Sydney Morning Herald* (8 Aug 1923) p.5
21 'The Oriental Baths' *Argus* (24 July 1860)
22 [The Otago Turkish Bath Company] *Tuapeka Times* (21 Mar 1874) p.2
23 'The Otago Turkish baths' *Otago Witness* (2 Jan 1875) p.3
24 [It will be remembered…] *Otago Witness* (16 Dec 1876) p.15
25 [The annual report of the Dunedin Central Mission…] *Otago Witness* (1 Apr 1908)
26 http://www.manoir-victoria.com/index.php/en/hotel-history-picture-location/hotel-manoir-victoria-history Accessed 9 Feb 2012
27 For example: 'The Turkish bath' [advertisement] *Brooklyn Daily Eagle* (11 Sep 1863) p.3
28 'The Turkish bath' [advertisement] *Brooklyn Daily Eagle* (3 Oct 1863) p.2
29 Van Giesen, R E 'The History and therapeutic use of the Turkish bath' *Medical and Surgical Reporter, Pennsylvania* (26 Oct 1872) pp.381–387
30 'The Turkish bath' [advertisement] *Brooklyn Daily Eagle* (3 Oct 1863) p.2
31 This information comes from an as yet unidentified issue of the *Brooklyn Standard Union* published some time between September and December 1863
32 Shepard, Charles H *Turkish baths: no. 63 Columbia Street, Brooklyn Heights, N.Y.* (New York: the baths, [1863])
33 'The Turkish baths in Brooklyn' *Brooklyn Daily Eagle* (19 Oct 1863) p.3
34 D.H.J. 'The Turkish bath, as I found it' *Brooklyn Daily Eagle* (26 Sep 1864) p.2
35 'The Turkish bath establishment' *Brooklyn Daily Eagle* (10 Dec 1866) p.9
36 'The Hammam' *Brooklyn Daily Eagle* (3 Apr 1867) p.2
37 'Dr Shepard's Turkish bath: the first establishment in this country' *Brooklyn Daily Eagle* (14 Dec 1880) p.2
38 'A Luxurious institution: the new Turkish bathing establishment on Clinton Street' *Brooklyn Daily Eagle* (22 Apr 1880) p.2
39 Wood, A L and Woodruff, B C *The medical and surgical uses of electricity* (Brooklyn: The Brooklyn Turkish Bath Co, 1893)
40 'Dr Shepard's Turkish bath: the first establishment in this country' *Brooklyn Daily Eagle* (14 Dec 1880) p.2
41 Shepard, Charles H *Rheumatism and its treatment by Turkish baths* (New York: [the baths], 1892)
42 Shepard, Charles H 'Hydrophobia'. *Journal American Medical Association* (1897)
43 'Farewell to the grip' *Brooklyn Daily Eagle* (10 Feb 1899) p.2
44 Lancaster, Clay *Old Brooklyn Heights: New York's first suburb*. 2nd edn (New York: Dover, 1979) p.67
45 Avcıoğlu, Nebahat *Turquerie and the politics of representation, 1728–1876* (Farnham: Ashgate, 2011) pp.228–239
46 'Patrimoine' *Dunkerque Magazine* (Apr 2011) pp.28–31
47 *Baden-Baden and its environs* (Zurich: Orel Füssli, [1888] p.18

8 Building the Jermyn Street Hammam

1 'What is a Turkish bath?' *The Field* (2 Jun 1860)
2 'The Turkish bath' *The Field* (9 Jun 1860)
3 WL, *Western Ms.6236: Correspondence on Turkish baths; 39*, David Urquhart. Letter to John Louis William Thudichum, 7 Feb 1861
4 See: WL, *Western Ms.6236: Correspondence on Turkish baths; 20, 23–27, 36–39*
5 Wilson, Erasmus *The eastern or Turkish bath, its revival in Britain, and application to the purposes of health* (John Churchill, 1861)
6 WS-LPTB. *Minutes* (19 Nov 1860)
7 See, for example: WL, *Western Ms.6236: Correspondence on Turkish baths; 29*, George Witt. Letter to David Urquhart, 3 Dec 1860
8 WS-LPTB. *Minutes* (20 Nov 1860)
9 TNA BT31 30704/2070
10 WS-LPTB. *Minutes* (6 Dec 1860)
11 WL, *Western Ms.6236: Correspondence on Turkish baths; 29–31*, George Witt. Letter to David Urquhart, 3 Dec 1860; David Urquhart. Letter to George Witt, 7 Dec 1860; George Witt. Letter to David Urquhart, 8 Dec 1860.
12 WS-LPTB. *Minutes* (6 Dec 1860)
13 WL, *Western Ms.6236: Correspondence on Turkish baths; 34*, David Urquhart. Letter to Stewart Erskine Rolland, [17 Dec 1860]
14 WL, *Western Ms.6236: Correspondence on Turkish baths; 32*, David Urquhart. Letter to Stewart Erskine Rolland, 18 Dec [1860]
15 WS-LPTB. *Minutes* (18 Dec 1860)
16 'His last journey' *Scotsman* (27 Sep 1930) p.18
17 WS-LPTB. *Minutes* (28 Dec 1860)
18 WL, *Western Ms.6236: Correspondence on Turkish baths; 33*, Stewart Erskine Rolland. Letter to David Urquhart, 28 Dec 1860
19 Ibid, 35, Stewart Erskine Rolland. Letter to Harriet Urquhart, 19 Jan 1861
20 WS-LPTB. *Minutes* (22 Jan 1861)
21 Millingen, [J M] 'The eastern bath' *Free Press* (26 May 1858) pp.131–2
22 **Quoted in:** *Manual of the Turkish bath*; John Fife (ed) (Churchill, 1865) pp.216–8
23 This question is treated more comprehensively, and most persuasively, in: Avcıoğlu, Nebahat *Turquerie and the politics of representation, 1728–1876* (Farnham: Ashgate, 2011) pp.214–9
24 BCDU, I G 3, John Johnson. Letter to David Urquhart, 6 Feb 1861
25 WL, *Western Ms.6236: Correspondence on Turkish baths; 40*, David Urquhart. [Draft] Letter to [potential shareholders?], 9 Feb 1861
26 WS-LPTB. *Minutes* (19 Feb 1861)
27 Ibid, *Minutes* (9 Apr 1861)
28 Ibid, *Minutes* (16 Apr 1861)
29 Ibid, *Minutes* (23 Apr 1861)
30 Ibid, *Minutes* (30 Apr 1861)
31 Ibid, *Minutes* (1 May 1861)
32 WL, *Western Ms.6236: Correspondence on Turkish baths; 40*, David Urquhart. Letter to [Harriett Ann Curtis?], 9 Feb 1861
33 Avcıoğlu, Nebahat *Turquerie and the politics of representation, 1728–1876* (Farnham: Ashgate, 2011) p.212
34 WL, *Western Ms.6237: Notes on Turkish baths; 3*, An account of the Turkish bath in Golden Square: noting income and expenditure and numbers of bathers, 11 September-29 December 1860…Ms.
35 WS-LPTB. *Minutes* (11 Jun 1861)
36 *Manual of the Turkish bath*; John Fife (ed) (Churchill, 1865) pp.259–79

37 WS-LPTB. *Minutes* (17 Dec 1861)
38 Ibid, *Minutes* (15 Apr 1862)
39 Ibid, *Minutes* (18 Dec 1862)
40 Ibid, *Minutes* (13 May 1862)
41 BCDU, I G 3, John Johnson. Letter to Harriett Urquhart, 24 May 1862
42 'Turkish baths' *Standard* (10 Apr 1863) p.6
43 WS-LPTB. *Minutes* (17 Jun 1862)
44 BCDU, I G 3, John Johnson. Letter to Harriett Ann Curtis, 1 Jul 1862
45 'The new Turkish Hammam, Jermyn Street, St James's' *Building News* (4 Jul 1862) pp.11–12
46 This description of the inside of the Hammam is compiled from accounts in: 'The new Turkish Hammam, Jermyn Street, St James's' *Building News* (4 Jul 1862) pp.11–12; 'The Hammam, or Turkish bath' *Illustrated London News* (26 July 1862) p.96 & p.111; 'Turkish baths, Jermyn Street, St James's' *Building News* (13 Mar 1863) pp.199–202; 'Turkish baths' *Standard* (10 Apr 1863) p.6
47 'The new Turkish Hammam, Jermyn Street, St James's' *Building News* (4 Jul 1862) p.12
48 'The Hammam' [advertisement] *Morning Post* (25 Jul 1862) p.1

9 The Jermyn Street Hammam, 1862–1941

1 WS-LPTB. *Minutes* (11 Aug 1862)
2 Ibid, *Minutes* (29 Aug 1862)
3 BCDU, I G 3, John Johnson. Letter to David Urquhart, [End of 1862?]
4 BCDU, I G 21, Abel Andrew. Letter to John Johnson, 16 Dec1862
5 WS-LPTB. *Minutes* (4 Aug 1862)
6 Ibid, *Minutes* (13 Jan 1863)
7 Ibid, *Minutes* (22 Jan 1862)
8 Ibid, *Minutes* (1 Jun 1876)
9 Ibid, *Minutes* (9 Dec 1867)
10 Ibid, *Minutes* (30 Nov 1872)
11 Ibid, *Minutes* (18 Nov 1871)
12 Ibid, *Minutes* (? 1885)
13 WS-Poore, 1915/73. Diary 12 Sep, 16, 17, 18, 20, 21 Oct 1862
14 BCDU, I K2, Robert Poore. Letter to Lord Denbigh, 2 Apr 1869
15 WS-Poore, 228. Robert Poore. Letter to Nina Poore, 4 Oct 1910
16 WS-Poore, 1915/73. Diary 8, 16 Nov 1862
17 WS-LPTB. *Minutes* (9 Feb 1863)
18 WS-Poore, 1915/73. Diary 19, 25 Feb 1863
19 TNA BT31 30704/2070
20 WS-LPTB. *Minutes* (26 Jan 1863)
21 'Marlborough-Street' *The Times* (16 Mar 1863) p.11
22 'The Turkish Bath Company…' *Freeman's Journal* (8 Dec 1863) p.4
23 Bishop, Maria Catherine *A memoir of Mrs Urquhart* (Kegan Paul, 1897) p.187
24 'Court of Exchequer' *The Times* (8 Dec 1863) p.11
25 WS-LPTB. *Minutes* (11 Dec 1863)
26 Ibid, *Minutes* (27 Feb 1864)
27 Ibid, *Minutes* (22 Mar 1864)
28 Ibid, *Minutes* (12 Apr 1864)
29 Ibid, *Minutes* (19 Apr 1864)
30 'Prince Napoleon…' *Daily News* (30 Sep 1863)
31 'The Prince of Wales in the bath' *Caledonian Mercury* (20 Feb 1865)
32 'The Court Chronicle…' *Huddersfield Chronicle* (4 Mar 1865) p.3
33 'Turkish baths' [advertisement] *Morning Post* (29 Oct 1866) p.1
34 'Turkish bath, Jermyn-street, St. James' *Standard* (19 Dec 1866) p.3
35 WS-LPTB. *Minutes* (20 May 1868)
36 'Turkish baths, no.76 Jermyn-street' *Building news* (3 Nov 1871) I am grateful to Paul Clerkin and his Archiseek website for this reference.
37 WS-LPTB. *Minutes* (28 Jun 1861; 18 Mar 1872)
38 Ibid, *Minutes* (30 May 1873)
39 Ibid, *Minutes* (1 Dec 1873)
40 Ibid, *Minutes* (15 May 1874)
41 *Walter Penhaligon* (Royal Warrant Holders Association, 1907)
42 BCDU, I N 1, Cheshire and Lancashire FACs. Letter to Harriett Urquhart, 17 Jun 1877
43 'We have repeatedly pointed out…' The *Lancet* (26 Feb 1881); 'The Jermyn Street Hammam' *British Medical Journal* (12 Mar 1881)
44 Allsop, Robert Owen *The Turkish bath: its design and construction* (Spon, 1890) p.19
45 WS-LPTB. *Minutes* (22 Nov 1881)
46 WL, *Western Ms.6238: Correspondence of Harriet Angelina Urquhart 28*, Francis Francis [Jnr]. Letter to [E B] Neill, [1884]
47 WS-LPTB. *Minutes* (22 May 1884) include a copy of the letter from Bowles dated 9 May
48 Ibid, *Minutes* (4 Dec 1883)
49 Ibid, *Minutes* (22 Nov 1887); Gloucester City Council. Baths Committee. *Minutes* (18 Nov 1898)
50 'Guildford Turkish Bath' [advertisement] *Andrew's Guildford almanac* (1874); 'The Guildford Turkish Bath' [advertisement] *Guildford almanac* (1894)
51 *Kelly's directory of Hampshire*
52 Bolton, Gambier 'Pictures on the human skin' *Strand Magazine* (1897) pp.425–434. I am most indebted to James Bradley for this reference.
53 TNA BT31 30704/2070
54 'Society jottings' *Manchester Times* (20 Jul 1889)
55 'No. 76, Jermyn-street' [advertisement] *The Times* (17 Feb 1891) p.15; *The Times* (11 May 1892) p.14
56 Sims, George Robert *Living London: its work and its play* … vol.2 (Cassell, 1902) p.367
57 *The Hammam Turkish bath* (The Hammam, [*c* 1929])
58 TNA CRES 35/2108 – No 76 (and additional premises in rear)
59 'A Turkish bath is a necessity of modern life' [advertisement] *Observer* (10 May 1908) p.1
60 'A new Turkish bath house' [advertisement] *The Winning Post Summer Annual 1908* (Winning Post, 1908) p.xiii
61 TNA BT31 30704/2070
62 WS-Poore, 1915/220 Letter to shareholders (13 Dec 1940)
63 City of Westminster *Air damage report. District: Mayfair; Incident No.1327* (18 Apr 1941)
64 TNA BT31 30704/2070

10 Early problems and controversies

1 Mahomed, Sake Deen *Shampooing, or, benefits resulting from the use of the Indian medicated vapour bath…* 3rd edn (Brighton: William Fleet, 1838)
2 Roth, Mathias *The Russian bath* (Groombridge, 1852)
3 Bolton, John Adams *An improved apparatus for heating Turkish baths, public and private buildings…* Letters Patent: 1861; no.689
4 'A visit to the Turkish bath in Leicester' *Leicester Advertiser* (25 May 1861)
5 'Turkish baths on new principles' [advertisement] *The Times* (10 Apr 1861) p.3
6 Drake, Francis *The Anglo-Roman or 'Turkish bath'* (Ward & Lock, 1862)
7 For example: *Bristol Mercury* (13 Apr 1861); *The Times* (2 May 1861)
8 Banham, Peter Reynam *The architecture of the well-tempered environment* (Architectural Press, 1969) p.53
9 Drake, Francis *The Anglo-Roman or 'Turkish bath'* (Ward & Lock, 1862)
10 Haughton, Edward 'Turkish baths' *Medical Times & Gazette* (30 Nov 1861) p.567
11 Bernan, Walter (ie, Robert Stuart Meikleham) *On the history and art of warming and ventilating rooms and buildings* (Bell, 1845) (See: Essay XIII: vol.2; pp.207–229)
12 Whitaker, Thomas and Constantine, Joseph UK *Improvements in the construction of stoves…* Letters Patent: 1866; no. 2448
13 'The warming and ventilating of buildings' *Builder* (2 Nov 1867) p.807
14 'The Turkish bath' *Kidderminster Shuttle* (18 Feb 1871)
15 Bruce, J L 'On the heating and ventilation of Turkish baths' *Proceedings of the Glasgow Philosophical Society* (1878) pp.493–506
16 'The heating and ventilation of Turkish baths' *Builder* (30 Aug 1879) p.981

17 Bruce, J L 'On the heating and ventilation of Turkish baths' *Proceedings of the Glasgow Philosophical Society* (1878) pp.493–506
18 See, for example, the letters in *The Lancet* during January and February 1861.
19 Haughton, Edward 'On the oriental bath' *Dublin Hospital Gazette* (15 Sep 1857) pp.280–82
20 Wollaston, Robert 'The Turkish bath' *British Medical Journal* (23 Feb 1861) pp.211–2
21 Wyld, George *The Turkish bath or hot-air bath* (Leath & Rose, 1860)
22 Barter, Richard *The rise and progress of the 'Turkish bath'* (Dublin: McGee, 1861)
23 Barter, Richard UK *Heating and ventilating buildings, &c* (Letters Patent: 1859; no.208)
24 Urquhart, David *The Turkish bath, with a view to its introduction in the British Dominions*; edited by Richard Barter (Bryce, 1856)
25 Thudichum, J L W 'The Turkish bath' *Transactions of the Royal Medical Society* (1861) p.40
26 'The Roman bath' *The Lancet* (5 Jan 1861)
27 Allsop, Robert Owen *The Turkish bath: its design and construction* (Spon, 1890) pp.78–9
28 'Public baths and washhouses; report of paper read by Hessell Tiltman (6 Feb 1899)' *Building News* (10 Feb 1899) pp.188–190
29 Cross, Alfred W S *Public baths and wash-houses: a treatise on their planning, design, arrangement, and fitting…* (Batsford, 1906) Chapter 15

11 19th-century attitudes to the Victorian Turkish bath

1 *Slater's general and classified directory and street register [for] Manchester (1858)* Adverts p.14
2 Laurie, James *The Roman or Turkish baths* (Edinburgh: MacLachlan & Stewart, 1864) Laurie actually attributed the saying to an un-named American medical writer.
3 Dunlop, Durham *The philosophy of the bath: or air and water in health and disease* (Simpkin, Marshall, 1868)
4 Bartholomew, Charles *A lecture on Turkish baths, delivered before the members of the Balloon Society…26 March 1886* (Marshall, 1886)
5 'The Turkish bath in disease' *The Lancet* (13 Dec 1862)
6 Haigh, William 'Turkish baths' *Medical Times & Gazette* (14 Dec 1861) p.627
7 'Medico-legal and medico-ethical' *British Medical Journal* (29 Feb 1896) p.568
8 TNA BT31 30704/2070
9 TNA BT31 531/2134
10 'Turkish baths: public meeting in Cork' *Cork Examiner* (23 Jul 1856) p.iv
11 'The City Turkish Bath' *Littell's Living Age; third series* (vol.13; Apr-Jun 1861) pp.743–5
12 Jeaffreson, Samuel 'President's address' *British Medical Journal* (5 Aug 1865) pp.107–115
13 Jagger, J *The Turkish bath* (Barker: [1860])
14 Quoted on the pamphlet, probably from an item in Holyoake's paper *The Reasoner* which was very pro Turkish baths
15 'The Turkish Bath Movement' *Free Press* (20 Sep 1856) pp.47–8
16 'Turkish baths' *The Times* (28 Oct 1862) p.10; col.4
17 'The Turkish bath in Leeds Road' *Bradford Advertiser* (20 Feb 1858) p.4
18 J.A. [ie, John Abel] *The Turkish bath: an antidote for the cravings of the drunkard* (Dublin: Webb, 1859) (*Tracts on the drink question; no.1*)
19 This quote, and the one following, are from letters replying to the author's questionnaire transcribed in: Metcalfe, Richard *Sanitas sanitatum et omnia sanitas* (Co-operative Printing Co, 1877)
20 Lemon, James *Reminiscences of public life in Southampton, from 1866 to 1900* (Southampton: Gilbert, 1911) p.253
21 *The City of Birmingham Baths Department* (Birmingham: The Council, 1951) p.50
22 Booth, Charles *Descriptive map of London poverty 1889* (London Topographical Society, 1984)
23 J.W.A. 'Opening baths on Sundays' *Bury Times* (26 Nov 1864) p.8
24 Cooper, William 'Opening baths on Sundays' *Bury Times* (19 Nov 1864)
25 Thomas, Peter 'William Bishop and the Putney Baths' *Wandsworth Historian* (1986)
26 *Programme of opening ceremony of Turkish Baths at the Old Kent Road Public Baths* (Camberwell Borough Council, 1905)
27 See, for example: Richardson, B W 'The Hot-air bath' *British Medical Journal* (2 Feb 1861) pp.114–5
28 Thudichum, J L W 'The Turkish bath' *Transactions of the Medical Society* (1861) pp.39–52
29 Garlike, Thomas W 'The Turkish bath' *The Lancet* (2 Mar 1861) pp.225–6
30 'The Turkish-Roman bath: what are its right uses?' *British Medical Journal* (2 Mar 1861) pp.231–2
31 Robertson, C Lockhart 'A review of Erasmus Wilson's *The eastern or Turkish bath*' *Journal of Mental Science* (1861) pp.210–231
32 Thomson, Spencer *A dictionary of domestic medicine*. 38th edn (Griffin, 1906)
33 Kiallmark, Henry Walter 'The Turkish bath' *The Lancet* (19 Jan 1861) p.70
34 Haughton, Edward 'Turkish Baths' *Medical Times & Gazette* (30 Nov 1861) p.567
35 'Abuse of massage' *Journal of Balneology & Climatology* (Apr 1897) pp.185–7
36 Wilson, Erasmus *The eastern, or Turkish bath: its history, revival in Britain and application to the purpose of health* (John Churchill, 1861) p.103
37 Jagger, J *The Turkish bath* (Barker: [1860])
38 'The hot-air bath' *British Medical Journal* (2 Feb 1861) pp.114–5)

12 Ownership

1 Winstanley, Michael J *The shopkeeper's world, 1830–1914* (Manchester: Univ Pr, 1983) p.42
2 'Re Edwin Wellington Simkin' *Birmingham Daily Post* (13 Feb 1892)
3 TNA BT31 10625/80400
4 *Post Office Glasgow directory*; *Slater's directory of Ireland*; *Slater's royal national directory of Scotland*
5 'Tobacco cultivation at home' *Birmingham Daily Post* (29 Dec 1886) p.7
6 Bartholomew, Charles. Letter to William Park, 18 Nov 1886. I am grateful to the late Leonard Park for access to this letter.
7 Personal interview with the late Leonard Park, June 1991
8 Baker, Alfred *The life of Sir Isaac Pitman (inventor of phonography)* (Pitman, 1908) p.195
9 Metcalfe, Richard *Sanitas sanitatum et omnia sanitas* (Co-operative Printing Co, 1877) p.312
10 Birmingham Corporation. Baths and Parks Committee. *Minutes* (17 Jul 1877)
11 Metcalfe, Richard *Sanitas sanitatum et omnia sanitas* (Co-operative Printing Co, 1877) p.313
12 I am especially indebted to Norman Ashfield for his information on the members of the Hunt family, of which he is one of the last survivors, and on the running of their baths.
13 R.E.J.F. 'It's heatwave weather all the time in this job!' *Bath Evening Chronicle* (4 Jun 1955)
14 'Notes' *Darlington & Stockton Times* (19 Sep 1891)
15 TNA BT31 3171/18404
16 *Slater's directory of Cumberland*
17 **Quoted in:** Scarr, R 'Turkish baths became headquarters of Darlington YMCA' *Darlington & Stockton Times* (13 Oct 1956)
18 *London Gazette* (8 Dec 1882)
19 TNA BT31 3171/18404
20 McCormick *The Peases & the S&D Railway* (Newton Aycliffe: Bermac Publ, 2008)
21 Beirne, Peter 'The Ennis Turkish baths, 1869–1878' *The Other Clare* (2008) pp.12–17 Also available online from the Clare County Library website at: http://www.clarelibrary.i.e./eolas/coclare/history/ennis_turkish_baths.htm
Beirne's included quotation is from:

Becker, Bernard H *Disturbed Ireland: being the letters written during the winter of 1880–81* (Macmillan, 1881) p.160
22 TNA BT31 1699/6111
23 TNA BT31 581/2409
24 'Laying the foundation stone of the Brighton "Turkish Bath"' *Freemasons Magazine and Masonic Mirror* (21 Mar 1868) pp.239–240
25 Foley, Ronan *Healing waters: therapeutic landscapes in historic and contemporary Ireland* (Farnham: Ashgate, 2010) p.102
26 BCDU, I G14.7, Charles Bartholomew. Letter to David Urquhart, 26 Sep 1856
27 'WANTED' [advertisement] *Western Daily Press* (17 Dec 1860)
28 See, for example, *Bristol Mercury* (22 Dec 1860) p.1
29 'The Turkish bath' *Bristol Mercury* (29 Dec 1860) p.8
30 Bartholomew, Charles *Mr Bartholomew's evidence before a committee of medical men…* 6th edn (Bristol: the author, [1870])
31 'Turkish baths!!' [advertisement] *Bristol Mercury* (8 Jun 1861)
32 'Mr C Bartholomew…' *Bristol Mercury* (30 Nov 1861)
33 'The Turkish Baths' [advertisement] *Webster's directory of Bristol and Glamorganshire* (1865) Adverts p.21
34 'Neath New Gas Company' *Cambrian* (29 Jun 1866)
35 Balbirnie, John *The sweating cure: the physiological basis and curative effects of the Turkish bath* (Job Caudwell, 1864)
36 'Opening of the Turkish baths' *Cambrian* (15 Apr 1864)
37 'Neath New Gas Company' *Cambrian* (29 Jun 1866)
38 *Wilson's trades directory of Wales, 1885*
39 TNA BT 31/1291/3262
40 Davis, Dorothy *A history of shopping* (Routledge, 1966) p.288
41 *Wilts and Gloucestershire Standard* (22 Feb 1868)
42 Winstanley, Michael J *The shopkeeper's world, 1830–1914* (Manchester: Univ Pr, 1983) p.37
43 Bartholomew, Charles *A lecture on Turkish baths: twenty-seven years' experience of the physiological action of the Turkish bath in health and disease* (Marshall, 1886) Rear cover
44 Personal communication from John Cooper, William Cooper's grandson, 17 Jan 2008
45 Jermyn Street Turkish Baths Ltd, Re, [1971] 1 *WLR* 1042: 27, 35 The case relates to the oppression of minority shareholders. I am most grateful to Nick Fox for this reference.
46 The unidentified cutting is in: WL, *Western Ms.6237: Notes and press cuttings on Turkish baths; Item 1*
47 Urquhart, David 'Construction of a bath for medical purposes' **In:** Leared, Arthur *Consumption arrested by the Turkish bath: reprint of Dr. Leared's report in* The Lancet (Robert Hardwicke, 1864)
48 'Rochdale' *Free Press* (25 Mar 1857) p.262
49 BCDU, Box I G 14, John Johnson. Letter to David Urquhart, 9 Dec 1858
50 'Local Turkish bath' *Rochdale Observer* (19 Mar 1859)
51 'Subscribers Turkish baths' *Rochdale Observer* (2 Jul 1859)
52 'Turkish baths' *Rochdale Observer* (30 Jul 1859)
53 'Subscription Turkish baths' *Rochdale Observer* (19 Nov 1859)
54 Firth, Joseph 'A visit to Rochdale' *The Reasoner* (5 May 1861) pp.259–61
55 Royle, Edward *Victorian infidels: the origins of the British Secularist Movement, 1791–1866* (Manchester: University Press, 1974) pp.227–8
56 'Rochdale Subscription Turkish Bath' *Rochdale Observer* (3 Dec 1859)
57 'Turkish baths, Church Cottage' *Rochdale Observer* (5 Mar 1881)
58 'Turkish Baths turned into a limited company' *Rochdale Observer* (2 April 1881) p.6
59 'Turkish Baths turned into a limited company' *Rochdale Observer* (2 April 1881) p.1)

13 Housing the Victorian Turkish bath

1 'Doncaster Oriental Chambers and Turkish Bath Company' *Doncaster Gazette* (4 Mar 1899) p.6
2 *London Gazette* (21 May 1965) p.5005
3 Page, Thomas *Page's handbook to Brighton and its vicinity* (Hall, 1871) **Quoted in:** Musgrave, Clifford *Life in Brighton from the earliest times to the present.* Rev edn (Chatham: John Hallewell, 1981) p.205
4 Fisher, David *Directory of cinemas in Brighton and Hove* http://www.brightonfilm.com/Academy.htm Accessed 14 Aug 2013
5 Fletcher, Geoffrey S *London overlooked* (Hutchinson, 1964) p.78
6 [The new Turkish baths…] *Builder* (9 Feb 1895) p.98; 'New Turkish Bath' *Building News* (8 Feb 1895) p.191
7 I am grateful to Roger Bowdler for a copy of his unpublished notes (14 April 1992) on the Gallipoli Restaurant which occupied the building for a while.
8 These same interlocking tiles were also used at the entrances to the Brighton Dome and the Brighton Museum and Art Gallery, where they can still be seen.
9 'The Royal Baths at Harrogate' *Journal of Balneology & Climatology* (Jul 1897)
10 Pearson, Lynn *Tile gazetteer: a guide to British tile and architectural ceramics locations* (Shepton Beauchamp: Richard Dennis, 2005) p.383
11 *Recollections of the late Dr Barter*, by the author of *Simple questions and sanitary facts* (Dublin: McGee, 1875) p.36
12 'Bermondsey's new £150,000 palace of baths' *Daily Mirror* (26 Sep 1927) p.1
13 City of Carlisle. Baths Sub-Committee. *Minutes* (2 Sep 1908; 7 Oct 1908)
14 Dickens, Marie K *Changing the face of Carlisle: the life and times of Percy Dalton, City Engineer and Surveyor, 1926–1949* (South Stainmore: Hayloft, 2002)
15 Pearson, Lynn *Tile gazetteer: a guide to British tile and architectural ceramics locations* (Shepton Beauchamp: Richard Dennis, 2005) p.61
16 Danby, Miles *Moorish style* (Phaidon, 1995) pp.174–5
17 'Carnegie baths and gymnasium' *Dunfermline Press* (25 Mar 1905) p.5
18 Gordon, Ian and Inglis, Simon *Great lengths: the historic indoor swimming pools of Britain* (Swindon: English Heritage, 2009) p.135
19 Personal communication from Andrew Stewart, Area Leisure Manager, 25 June 2013
20 Herbert, Tony 'Baths, washhouses and toilets' **In:** Pearson, Lynn *Tile gazetteer: a guide to British tile and architectural ceramics locations* (Shepton Beauchamp: Richard Dennis, 2005) p.23
21 English Heritage Listed Building: 1278714
22 Wilkins, Rachel *Turrets, towels and taps* (Birmingham: City Museum and Art Gallery, 1984) p.13
23 'Sheffield: new Turkish baths' *Building News* (23 Nov 1877) p.524
24 Williams, Prue *Victoria Baths: Manchester's water palace* (Reading: Spire Books, with the Friends of Victoria Baths, 2004)
25 *Souvenir to commemorate the opening of the City Hall and Northumberland Baths* (Newcastle-on-Tyne: The Council, 1928)
26 *Opening of the Central Swimming Baths…* (Middlesbrough: the County Borough Council, 1933) p.14
27 *Official opening of Remedial Suite and Sports Hall at Victoria Leisure Centre* (Nottingham: The Council, 1975)
28 'New leisure centre opened' *Nottingham Arrow* (Oct 1975)
29 Ryan, P J 'The Volunteers: the 1916 Rising and its aftermath' *Old Limerick Journal* (Winter 2003) p.4
30 *Kelly's directory of Hampshire for 1885; Chamberlain's Portsmouth directory, 1887*
31 'Diffusion of Turkish baths' *The Reasoner* (2 Apr 1861) p.234
32 '…we were aware of the importance of the baths largely due to your excellent website, and my field team have been clutching a

print-out of Potter's plan throughout the duration of the excavation!'(Personal communication from Ian Miller, Senior Project Manager, Oxford Archaeology North)

33 See, for example: Bodington, G F 'The Turkish bath' *The Lancet* (26 Jan 1861); Drake, Francis 'The Anglo-Roman or Turkish bath' *Builder* (8 Jun 1861)

34 Avcıoğlu, Nebahat 'Constructions of Turkish baths as a social reform for Victorian society: the case of the Jermyn Street Hammam' **In:** *The hidden iceberg of architectural history* (Society of Architectural Historians of Great Britain, 1998) p.68

35 Hay, W H 'Liverpool Architectural Society: lecture on Turkish baths' *Builder* (16 Feb 1861) p.106

36 For example: *Cambridge Independent Press* (21 Feb 1863) p.1

14 Commercial Turkish baths

1 Shifrin, Malcolm *Victorian Turkish Baths* http://www.victorianturkishbath.org

2 Wilson, Erasmus *The eastern, or Turkish bath* (Churchill, 1861) p.99

3 Wells, Spencer *Lecture on the revival of the Turkish, or ancient Roman bath* (John Lane, 1860); 'Turkish baths in London' *The Reasoner* (3 Feb 1861) p.69; Sheppard, Edgar *Bathing: how to do it, when to do it, and where to do it.* 2nd ed. (Robert Hardwicke, 1866)

4 Holyoake, George Jacob 'Northern lectures, debates, and Turkish baths' *The Reasoner* (3 Oct 1858) pp.1–2

5 BCDU, Box 10: I G6, A E Robinson. Letter to David Urquhart, 1 May 1858

6 'The Turkish bath' *Halifax Courier* (1 May 1858) p.5

7 'Turkish Baths, Northgate' [advertisement] *Halifax Guardian* (8 May 1858)

8 'The Turkish baths at Broughton Lane' [advertisement] *Halifax Courier* (24 Dec 1858)

9 'A seasonable act of kindness' *Bradford Observer* (24 Jun 1858) p.5

10 Burland, John Hugh *Annals of Burnley.* I am most grateful to Mr Hepworth for this information.

11 *Kelly's directory of Leeds*

12 Constantine, Joseph *Handy book on hydropathy, practical and domestic, with a concise introduction to the principles of the science …* (Whitaker, 1860) 'The opening of Constantine's New Turkish, Russian, And Hydropathic Baths…' [advertisement] *Manchester Times*

13 Constantine's New Hydropathic Baths are now open' [advertisement] *Manchester Guardian* (6 Jun 1861) p.1

14 'The opening of Constantine's New Turkish, Russian, And Hydropathic Baths…' *Manchester Times* (31 Aug 1861)

15 TNA BT31 532/2139

16 'Opening of the new Turkish baths' *Liverpool Mercury* (6 Aug 1861)

17 Haughton, Edward 'Short description of the process gone through at The Oriental Baths' [Attached to paper delivered 17 April 1861] *Proc Liverpool Architectural & Archaeological Society*

18 'Oriental Bath Company of Liverpool (Limited)' [advertisement] *Liverpool Mercury* (12 Oct 1861)

19 'Alteration of the Turkish baths, Mulberry-Street' *Liverpool Mercury* (6 Oct 1862)

20 English Heritage The National Heritage List for England ID.1290277

21 'The pencil and gold pen manufactory, Birmingham' *Building News* (21 Aug 1863) p.650

22 'Opening of Mr Wiley's Turkish baths' *Birmingham Daily Post* (13 Feb 1863) p.3

23 *Jones' mercantile directory of Birmingham* (1865)

24 'The new Turkish baths' *Birmingham Daily Post* (24 Dec 1862)

25 'Turkish Baths, Frederick Street' [advertisement] *Birmingham Daily Post* (5 Mar 1863)

26 TNA BT31 330/1171

27 'To bath managers and others' [advertisement] *Bradford Observer* (24 Mar 1859)

28 'Scarborough Public Bath Company, Limited' [advertisement] *Scarborough Gazette* (2 Jul 1863) p.1

29 Smith, Janet *Liquid assets: the lidos and open air swimming pools of Britain* (Swindon: English Heritage, 2005) p.47

30 Berryman, B 'Bland's Cliff Baths' *Scarborough Mercury* (27 Feb 1971)

31 'Scarborough Public Bath Company, Limited' [advertisement] *Scarborough Gazette* (2 Jul 1863) p.1

32 'Scarborough Public Bath Company, (Limited)' [advertisement] *Scarborough Gazette* (18 Jun 1864) p.1

33 Berryman, B 'Bland's Cliff Baths' *Scarborough Mercury* (27 Feb 1971)

34 Curl, James Stevens *Victorian architecture: diversity & invention* (Reading: Spire, 2007) p.171

35 Brodrick, Cuthbert *Design for the Oriental Baths, Cookridge Street, Leeds* RIBA Library Drawings Collection RIBA12126

36 Linstrum, Derek *Towers and colonnades: the architecture of Cuthbert Brodrick* (Leeds: Philosophical and Literary Society, 1999) p.112

37 'New buildings in Leeds' *Leeds Mercury* (11 Nov 1881)

38 'Opening of Oriental Baths in Leeds' *Leeds Mercury* (1 May 1882)

39 B., Frank 'In a Turkish bath' *Leeds Mercury* (4 Feb 1888)

40 'The Cookridge Street Baths' *Leeds Evening Express* (11 Feb 1898)

41 'Public baths in Leeds' *Leeds Standard* (29 Jan 1898)

42 'Purchase of Cookridge-Street Baths by the Leeds Corporation' *Leeds Standard* (12 Feb 1898)

43 'Turkish baths in Leeds' *Yorkshire Evening Post* (7 Jan 1901) p.3

15 Municipal Turkish baths

1 [New Turkish baths] *Irish Times* (7 Apr 1873) p.2

2 *Baths in Nottingham* (Nottingham: Public Baths and Washhouses Committee, 1944) p.13

3 Nottingham Corporation. Public Baths and Washhouses Committee. *Minutes* (19 Apr 1859)

4 Ibid, *Minutes* (28 Sep 1860)

5 Ibid, *Minutes* (4 Feb 1861)

6 Ibid, *Minutes* (9 Sep 1861)

7 Ibid, *Minutes* (23 Sep 1861)

8 Ibid, *Minutes* (3 Jun 1862)

9 *Baths in Nottingham* (Nottingham: Public Baths and Washhouses Committee, 1944) p.13

10 'Public baths' [advertisement] *Nottingham Magazine* (Jul 1862)

11 TNA BT31 15637/48534

12 *Wright's directory of Nottingham for 1903*

13 Nottingham Corporation. Baths and Washhouses Committee. *Minutes* (1916, 1917)

14 Nottingham City Council. *Minutes* (13 Nov 1939)

15 Ibid, *Minutes* (15 Dec 1939)

16 *Opening of the [new] Turkish bath* (Bury: The Council, 1898) p.5

17 *Ibid*, p.10

18 Baines, Thomas *Yorkshire, past and present* vol.2; pt.1 (s.l.: Mackenzie, s.d.) p.316

19 Bradford Corporation. Sanitary, Baths and Cemetery Committee. *Minutes* (1865) pp.20–21

20 During the period 1883–1900, the committee responsible for Bradford's baths and wash-houses changed its name almost as frequently as its annual reports, starting as the Hackney Carriage and Cleansing Committee, passing en route through the Baths, Tramways and Team Labour Committee, until finally becoming the Baths Committee. This information comes from these annual reports.

21 *Opening of the new Central Baths* (Bradford: The Council, 1905) p.3

22 Ibid, pp.13–14

23 Personal interview with the late Leonard Park. June 1991

24 Robertson, William *Rochdale past and present: a history and guide* (Rochester, Schofield and Hoblyn, 1875) pp.49–9

25 'Portobello' *Scotsman* (9 Feb 1898)

26 'Baths, Newport (Mon)' *Builder* (28 Jun 1890) p.478

27 *Public baths* (Newport: The Council, [*c* 1935])
28 Newport County Borough. Baths Sub-committee. *Minutes* (3 Feb 1890)
29 Ibid, *Minutes* (24 Feb 1890)
30 Ibid, *Minutes* (28 Apr 1890)
31 *Public baths* (Newport: The Council, [*c* 1935])
32 *Butcher's Cardiff directory* (1880)
33 Evans, Franklen G *The Turkish bath in health and disease, with special reference to the establishment in Cardiff* (Cardiff: The Guardian Office, 1868) pp.5–6
34 *The Empire Swimming Pool, Cardiff, Wales* The film can be viewed at the National Library of Wales, though a watermarked timed version can be viewed online at: https://www.youtube.com/watch?v=RzW-DfFtZd0
35 *Taking the plunge* [motion picture] 18 min. (Cardiff City Council, [*c* 1968] Available for viewing at: http://www.youtube.com/watch?v=RzW-DfFtZd0
36 Gordon, Ian and Inglis, Simon *Great lengths: the historic indoor swimming pools of Britain* (Swindon: English Heritage, 2009) p.51
37 'Opening of the Stalybridge public baths' *Manchester Guardian* (9 May 1870) p.3
38 *Borough of Stalybridge centenary booklet, 1857–1957* (Stalybridge: The Council, 1957) p.97
39 'Ashton-under-Lyne baths being erected' *Builder* (2 Jul 1870) p.524
40 *Ashton-under-Lyne Reporter* (12 March 1928) **Quoted in:** *Sport and the working class in modern Britain*; edited by Richard Holt (Manchester: University Press, 1990) p.95
41 'Ashton-under-Lyne foam baths' *Baths and Bath Engineering* (Mar 1938) p.50
42 'Opening of the Carnegie Baths at Dunfermline' *Dundee Courier* (13 Jul 1877)
43 'An example for Edinburgh' [Letter to the editor] *Scotsman* (9 Mar 1916) p.6
44 'Opening of Alloa Public Baths & Gymnasium' *Alloa Journal* (30 Apr 1898)
45 Gordon, Ian and Inglis, Simon *Great lengths: the historic indoor swimming pools of Britain* (English Heritage, 2009) p.97
46 Metcalfe, Richard *Sanitas sanitatum et omnia sanitas* (Co-operative Printing Co, 1877)
47 Ibid, p.151
48 Ibid, p.273
49 This section of the chapter is based on Dover Town Clerk's questionnaire and the replies he received, held at East Kent Archives Centre: DO/CA/11/14
50 'Dover Corporation Turkish Baths' *Dover Express* (5 Jun 1903)
51 *Souvenir of the opening of the public baths...* (Camberwell Borough Council, 1905)
52 The Ironmonger Row Baths were built in two phases. The main baths, opened in 1931, were designed by Alfred William Stephens Cross and his son, Kenneth Mervyn Baskerville Cross. Alfred died shortly after its completion and the 1938 extension with the Turkish baths was designed by Kenneth.
53 Shifrin, Malcolm '"A dream to keep you happy for a week": the Dalston Turkish baths—and two that never happened' *Hackney History* (Friends of Hackney Archives, 2008) pp.38–49

16 Turkish baths for the working classes

1 'Lochhead Hydropathic Establishment' *Aberdeen Journal* (2 Jan 1861)
2 J.A. [ie, John Abel] *The Turkish bath: an antidote for the cravings of the drunkard* (Dublin: Webb, 1859)
3 Haughton, Edward *Facts and fallacies of the Turkish bath question* (Dublin: Robertson, 1860)
4 *Irish Times* (23 Mar 1860) p.4
5 'The Belfast Turkish Baths' *Irish Times* (11 Mar 1861) p.3
6 'The Improved Turkish baths' [advertisement] *Belfast News-letter* (28 Sep 1860)
7 'The Improved Turkish baths' [advertisement] *Belfast News-letter* (30 Oct 1860)
8 'The Turkish baths' *Belfast News-letter* (12 Jul 1861)
9 Metcalfe, Richard *Sanitas sanitatum et omnia sanitas* (Co-operative Printing Co, 1877) p.319
10 'Turkish baths and the working-classes' *Belfast News-letter* (19 Apr 1872)
11 'Turkish baths for sale' [advertisement] *Irish Times* (26 Jul 1881) p.8
12 'New Turkish baths' [advertisement] *Belfast News-letter* (5 Oct 1893)
13 'The improved Turkish or Roman baths for the poor' [advertisement] *Cork mercantile directory* (1862) pp.72–3
14 *Recollections of the late Dr Barter*, by the author of *Simple questions and sanitary facts* (Dublin: McGee, 1875)
15 I am indebted to John S Gordon for this information from Dickens's letters
16 'Turkish baths for the working classes, by An Irishwoman' *Irish Times* (8 Mar 1872) p.6
17 Metcalfe, Richard *Sanitas sanitatum et omnia sanitas* (Co-operative Printing Co, 1877) p.164
18 'Turkish baths for the poor' *Cork Examiner* (24 Feb 1863)
19 '[A correspondent...]' *Irish Times* (11 Nov 1871) p.2
20 *Chat upon health: Pat Dennehy visits Mrs Magrath* (Burns, 1875) p.16
21 Goad plans. Map 8 drawn 1897.
22 *Irish Times* (30 Oct 1871) p.3
23 'Turkish baths for the working classes' *Irish Times* (8 Mar 1872) p.6
24 'People's Turkish baths' *Irish Times* (17 Nov 1871) p.2
25 [Turkish baths] *Irish Times* (8 Apr 1872) p.2
26 'A Turkish bath for the working classes' *Irish Times* (13 Nov 1871) p.6
27 'The People's Turkish Baths' *Freeman's Journal* (25 May 1872)
28 Metcalfe, Richard *Sanitas sanitatum et omnia sanitas* (Co-operative Printing Co, 1877) p.146
29 Cale, Michelle 'Mary Bayley' **In:** *Oxford dictionary of national biography*, http://www.oxforddnb.com/view/article/50730 Accessed 25 Jan 2012
30 Metcalfe, Richard *The water cure: a plea for hydropathic dispensaries* (Tweedie, 1878)
31 Solly, Henry *Working men's social clubs and educational institutes* (Working Men's Club and Institute Union, 1867) p.94
32 'Working men's clubs' *Daily News* (19 Oct 1863)
33 'Public baths' *Cambrian* (4 Dec 1863)
34 Dowling, William Charles *The Ladies' Sanitary Association and the origins of the health visiting services* University of London. Unpublished MA thesis (University of London, 1963)
35 Evans, Franklen G *The Turkish bath in health and disease, with special reference to the establishment in Cardiff* (Cardiff: The Guardian Office, 1868) p.7
36 Cattell, John and Falconer, Keith *Swindon: the legacy of a railway town* (Swindon: HMSO, for English Heritage, 1995)
37 Darwin, Bernard *A century of medical service: the story of the Great Western Railway Medical Fund Society, 1847–1947* (Swindon: the society, 1947)
38 '[Perhaps the most interesting lecture...]' *Free Press* (26 May 1858) pp.132–3
39 Cattell, John and Falconer, Keith *Swindon: the legacy of a railway town* (Swindon: HMSO, for English Heritage, 1995) p.80; fig 85
40 WS-MFS. *Minutes* (5 Nov 1860)
41 Ibid, (9 Jul 1861)
42 Ibid, (13 Feb 1864)
43 *Kelly's directory of Wiltshire* (1867)
44 WS-MFS. *Minutes* (2 Sep 1867)
45 Ibid, (30 Nov 1867)
46 Ibid, (7 Sep 1868)
47 Ibid, (21 Sep 1869)
48 *Rate Book* (1869)
49 Darwin, Bernard *A century of medical service: the story of the Great Western Railway Medical Fund Society, 1847–1947* (Swindon: The Society, 1947) p.28
50 Cattell, John and Falconer, Keith *Swindon: the legacy of a railway town* (Swindon: HMSO, for English Heritage, 1995) p.113

51 WS-MFS. *Minutes* (29 Jan 1878)
52 WS-MFS. *Minutes* (1 Jul 1878)
53 WS-MFS. Rules 1878
54 WS-MFS. *Minutes* (3 Jul 1882)
55 Ibid, (31 Jul 1888)
56 WS-GWR. Drawing 2515/409/1262
57 Drawing RAIL 258/411 The National Archives
58 WS-GWR. Drawing 2515/404/1288
59 McCallum, Andrew 'It's hot but in the end it's a real Turkish delight' *Swindon Evening Advertiser* (18 Apr 1958)
60 Personal interview with Ray Parry, at his home. 10 Jan 1992
61 *The Jubilee of Crewe: containing a brief history of the rise and progress of the borough, from 1837 to 1887...* (Crewe: Printed at the Guardian Office, [1887] p.14
62 *Eardley's Crewe almanack* (1874)
63 Chaloner, W H *The social and economic development of Crewe, 1780–1923* (Manchester: Univ Pr, 1950) p.53
64 *Eardley's Crewe almanack* (1896)
65 *Change at Crewe* ([Chester]: Cheshire Libraries, 1984)
66 *Eardley's Crewe almanack* (1892)
67 Billups, Barbara *Crewe swimming baths: an architectural and social history* (Nantwich: Printed by Johnsons, 1984) p.8
68 For background information on Salt and Saltaire I am much indebted to Roger Clarke, Andrée Freeman, David King, Craig McHugh, Sandi Moore, Dave Shaw, Ian Watson, and Julie Woodward
69 Balgarnie, Robert *Sir Titus Salt, Baronet* (Hodder, 1877)
70 'Titus Salt: baths & washouses: Saltaire; 43' [plans] West Yorkshire Archive Service, Bradford.
71 Holroyd, Abraham *A life of Sir Titus Salt, with an account of Saltaire* (Saltaire: The Author, 1871) p.15
72 'The improved condition of the poor, by A Peripatetic' *London Society* (1870) p.90
73 Dickens, Charles [Jnr] 'A Yorkshire colony' *All the Year Round* (21 Jan 1871) p.1
74 'Public baths and washhouses in Leeds' *Leeds Mercury* (6 Aug 1878)
75 *White's directory of Bradford, Halifax...* (1887)
76 Holroyd, Abraham *A life of Sir Titus Salt, with an account of Saltaire* (Saltaire: the author, 1871) p.15
77 'The Wimbledon Theatre' *Wimbledon and District Gazette* (24 Dec 1910)
78 Parton, Helen 'Turkish delight' *Intra* (Aug 2002) p.48
79 'The Corporation Baths: coming of age' *Southampton and District Pictorial* (12 Mar 1913) p.7

17 The Turkish bath in the workhouse

1 'Turkish bath in the workhouse' *Cork Constitution* (24 Jun 1859) p.3
2 Barter, Richard *The rise and progress of the Turkish bath* (Dublin: McGee, 1861)
3 Reports and minutes of the Board of Guardians of the Fermoy Poor Law Union, held at Cork City and County Archives.
4 'Lismore' *Waterford News. Supplement* (26 Mar 1892) p.1; col.6
5 Ibid, (30 Jul 1892) p.4; col.2
6 'Turkish baths' *Otago Witness* (11 Oct 1867) p.7
7 *Lunatic asylums (Cork &c Counties)* (House of Commons, 1870)
8 'Reports on the nursing and administration of Irish workhouses and infirmaries. VI: Clones Union, Co. Monaghan' *British Medical Journal* (2 Nov 1895)
9 'Turkish bath'*Scotsman* (2 Sep 1873) p.3
10 Richardson, B W 'The medical history of England: the medical history of Lynn. Part 2' *The Medical Times & Gazette* (13 Feb 1864) p.181

18 The Turkish bath in asylums

1 'The Turkish bath as a cure for insanity' *Daily Southern Cross* (17 Nov 1862) p.4
2 Barter, Richard *The rise and progress of the 'Turkish bath'...* (Dublin: Wm McGee, 1861)
3 'Serious accident in a Turkish bath' *British Medical Journal* (22 Jun 1889) p.1421
4 '[At the meeting of the Cork District Lunatic Asylum...]' *The Times* (11 May 1861) p.12
5 'The Turkish bath for the insane' *The Lancet* (18 May 1861) p.490
6 '[One would, naturally, have expected to hear...]' *British Medical Journal* (11 May 1861) p.503
7 'Turkish baths in lunatic asylums' *Medical Times and Gazette* (18 May 1861) p.540
8 'The Turkish bath in insanity' *The Lancet* (10 May 1862) p.494
9 'The Turkish bath as a cure for insanity' *Daily Southern Cross* (17 Nov 1862) p.4
10 'The Turkish bath in insanity' *The Lancet* (10 May 1862) p.494
11 *The fortieth report (with appendices) of the Inspectors of Lunatics (Ireland)* (Dublin: HMSO, 1891) p.126
12 'The Turkish bath' *Sydney Morning Herald* (18 Oct 1862) p.5
13 Robertson, C Lockhart 'A review of Erasmus Wilson's *The eastern or Turkish bath*' *Journal of Mental Science* (1861) pp.210–231
14 Robertson, C Lockhart. Letter to David Urquhart. Feb 1863. Transcribed in *Manual of the Turkish bath* John Fife (ed) (Churchill, 1865) pp.347–51
15 Robertson, C L 'A case of mania, with albuminuria, cured by the Roman bath' *British Medical Journal* (27 Feb 1864) pp.229–30
16 Robertson, Charles Lockhart. Letter to David Urquhart. Feb 1863. Transcribed in *Manual of the Turkish bath* John Fife (ed) (Churchill, 1865) pp.347–51
17 Digby, Anne *Madness, morality and medicine: a study of the York Retreat, 1796–1914* (CUP, 1985) pp.134–5
18 Urquhart, David. Letter to John Fife. 3 Nov 1863. Transcribed in *Consumption arrested by the Turkish bath* (Hardwicke, 1864) pp.1–2
19 'The Turkish bath' *Freeman's Journal* (22 Sep 1863)
20 'The Turkish bath' *Freeman's Journal* (13 Oct 1863)
21 Metcalfe, Richard *The rise and progress of hydropathy in England and Scotland* (Simkin, Marshall, 1906) pp.139–40
22 WS-Poore, 1915/73. Diary, 16 May 1864
23 Letter. David Urquhart to Edgar Sheppard. 23 May 1864. Transcribed in *Manual of the Turkish bath* John Fife (ed) (Churchill, 1865) pp.353–6
24 Letter. Edgar Sheppard to David Urquhart. 13 October 1864. Transcribed in *Manual of the Turkish bath* John Fife (ed) (Churchill, 1865) p.412
25 Letter. David Urquhart to Edgar Sheppard. 23 May 1864. Transcribed in *Manual of the Turkish bath* John Fife (ed) (Churchill, 1865) pp.353–6
26 County Lunatic Asylum at Colney Hatch. *Annual report 1864* (Harrison, 1865) p.48
27 Ibid, *1865 (*Harrison, 1866) p.5
28 Hunter, Richard and Macalpine, Ida *Psychiatry for the poor: 1851 Colney Hatch Asylum—Friern Hospital 1973: a medical and social history* (Dawsons, 1974) p.146
29 County Lunatic Asylum at Colney Hatch *Annual report 1866* (Harrison, 1867) p.52
30 Ibid, *1866* (Harrison, 1867) p.75
31 Ibid, *1868* (Harrison, 1869) p.31
32 Ibid, *1868* (Harrison, 1869) p.15
33 Hunter, Richard and Macalpine, Ida *Psychiatry for the poor: 1851 Colney Hatch Asylum—Friern Hospital 1973: a medical and social history* (Dawsons, 1974) p.85
34 North Wales Counties Lunatic Asylum *Annual report 1869* (Denbigh: the asylum, 1870) p.10
35 Ibid, *1870* (Denbigh: the asylum, 1871) pp.10–11
36 'The Turkish bath in the treatment of insanity' *The Lancet* (11 Feb 1871) pp.199–200
37 North Wales Counties Lunatic Asylum *Annual report 1871* (Denbigh: the asylum, 1872) p.13

38 The Retreat, York *Papers on future expansion and the building of the new Gentlemen's Lodge (July 1874)* University of York. Borthwick Institute RET 2/2/7/1
39 Digby, Anne 'Quantitative and qualitative perspectives on the asylum' **In:** *Problems and methods in the history of medicine* Roy Porter and Andrew Weir (eds) (Beckenham: Croom Helm, 1987) p.154
40 The Retreat, York *Papers on future expansion and the building of the new Gentlemen's Lodge (July 1874)* University of York. Borthwick Institute RET 2/2/7/1
41 The Retreat, York. Committee of Management. *Minutes 13 May 1873–19 Mar 1889.* (15 Dec 1874) University of York. Borthwick Institute RET 1/1/4/4
42 Ibid, (16 Feb 1875)
43 Ibid, (25 Mar 1875)
44 The Retreat, York. *Proposed lodge buildings [Plan]* University of York. Borthwick Institute RET 2/1/13/7
45 Baker, Robert 'Notes of ten years' experience in the use of the Turkish bath in the treatment of mental ill-health' *Journal of Mental Science* (Jul 1889) p.184 plate
46 The Retreat, York. *Proposed lodge buildings [Plan]* University of York. Borthwick Institute RET 2/1/13/7
47 Baker, Robert 'Notes of ten years' experience in the use of the Turkish bath in the treatment of mental ill-health' *Journal of Mental Science* (Jul 1889) p.184 plate
48 'Lunacy and mental deficiency' *British Medical Journal* (26 Sep 1925) pp.571–2
49 Baker, Robert 'Notes of ten years' experience in the use of the Turkish bath in the treatment of mental ill-health' *Journal of Mental Science* (Jul 1889) p.185
50 *Draft note on the opening times and charges for the new baths attached to the Retreat* [Undated *c* 1876] University of York. Borthwick Institute RET 5/7/7/2
51 'The Turkish baths question in York: letter to the editor' *York Herald* (17 Sep 1877) p.7
52 Baker, Robert 'Notes of ten years' experience in the use of the Turkish bath in the treatment of mental ill-health' *Journal of Mental Science* (Jul 1889) pp.185–9
53 Borsay, Anne and Shapely, Peter *Medicine, charity and mutual aid: the consumption of health and welfare in Britain, c.1550–1950* (Farnham: Ashgate, 2007) p.169
54 'Proposed lunatic asylum, St Ann's Heath, Virginia Water' *Builder* (24 Aug 1872) p.665
55 Elliott, John *Palaces, patronage and oils: Thomas Holloway—his sanatorium, college and picture gallery* (Egham: RHUL, 1996)
56 West Riding Pauper Asylum *Annual report for 1871* (Wakefield: the asylum, 1872)
57 Personal phone conversation with Eric H Pryor
58 'A mental reception hospital: opening ceremony at Northampton' *British Medical Journal* (22 Oct 1927) p.749
59 'Letter to the editor' *Birmingham Daily Post* (6 Mar 1863)
60 'Serious accident in a Turkish bath' *British Medical Journal* (22 Jun 1889) p.1421
61 Michael, Pamela and Hirst, David 'Recording the many faces of death at the Denbigh Asylum, 1848–1938' *History of Psychiatry* (March 2012)
62 Baker, Robert 'Notes of ten years' experience in the use of the Turkish bath in the treatment of mental ill-health' *Journal of Mental Science* (Jul 1889) pp.189

19 The Turkish bath in hospitals

1 Haughton, Edward *Facts and fallacies of the Turkish bath question* (Dublin: Robertson, 1860)
2 *Annual report of the Infirmary. 109th report* (Newcastle-on-Tyne: The Infirmary, 1860) Back cover
3 Dunlop, Durham *The philosophy of the bath*. 4th edn (Kent, 1880) pp. 416–7
4 Bishop, M C *A memoir of Mrs Urquhart* (Kegan Paul, 1897)
5 **Quoted in:** 'Roman hypocaust and sweating bath' *Free Press* (16 Dec 1857) p.572
6 *Annual report of the Infirmary. 109th report* (Newcastle-on-Tyne: The Infirmary, 1860) p.12
7 Enever, G *The History of the Newcastle Infirmary, 1751 to 2001* http://research.ncl.ac.uk/nsa/tl3.htm Accessed July 2011
8 *Annual report of the Infirmary. 109th report* (Newcastle-on-Tyne: The Infirmary, 1860) p.12
9 **Quoted in:** 'The Turkish bath' *Freeman's Journal* (22 Oct 1859)
10 'Remedial effects of the Turkish baths' *Medical Times and Gazette* (23 Nov 1861) pp.544–5
11 'The Turkish, or Roman bath, in Leicester' (*Leicester Journal*, 1861) p.8
12 *Annual report of the Infirmary. 113th report* (Newcastle-on-Tyne: The Infirmary, 1864) p.12
13 TNA BT31 1752/6521
14 *Annual report of the Infirmary* (Newcastle-on-Tyne: The Infirmary) Reports for the years 1884–8 and 1892–7
15 Ward's directory of Newcastle and district 1897
16 'The Turkish bath: letter from Dr Goolden' *The Lancet* (26 Jan 1861) pp.95–7
17 [Editorial] *The Lancet* (26 Jan 1861) pp.91–2
18 Leared, Arthur 'On the treatment of phthisis by the hot-air bath' *The Lancet* (21 Nov 1863) pp.587–8
19 'Annual meeting of the subscribers to the Denbighshire Infirmary' *North Wales Chronicle* (11 Feb 1871)
20 'Annual meeting at the Denbighshire Infirmary' *North Wales Chronicle* (3 Feb 1872)
21 'Hospital for consumption' *Builder* (22 Nov 1879)
22 [Editorial] *The Lancet* (26 Jan 1861) p.91
23 'The Turkish bath: letter from Dr Goolden' *The Lancet* (26 Jan 1861) pp.95–7
24 London Metropolitan Archives: H01/ST/A/114/044
25 Goolden, R H. 'St Thomas's Hospital: case of diabetes treated by the use of the Turkish bath' *British Medical Journal* (12 Sep 1863) p.279
26 Metcalfe, Richard *Sanitas sanitatum et omnia sanitas* (Co-operative Printing Co, 1877) p.316
27 'The Southport Convalescent Hospital' *Liverpool Mercury* (3 Feb 1888)
28 For example: [advertisement] *Huddersfield Daily Chronicle* (2 Oct 1885) p.1
29 *A Brief history of Huddersfield Royal Infirmary* (Huddersfield: The Infirmary, 1922) p.37
30 *Annual report* (Huddersfield: Royal Infirmary, 1912) p.72
31 'Turkish baths hope fades' *Huddersfield Examiner* (21 Apr 1951)
32 'Edinburgh Royal Infirmary' *Scotsman* (14 Jul 1896) p.7
33 'Edinburgh Royal Infirmary' *British Medical Journal* (3 Nov 1900) p.1338

20 The Turkish bath in hydros and hotels

1 Durie, Alastair J *Water is best: the hydros and health tourism in Scotland, 1840–1940* (Edinburgh: John Donald, 2006) Chapter 1: Hydropathy makes its entrance
2 'To contractors' [advertisement] *Bradford Observer* (13 Jan 1859) p.1
3 *Ben Rhydding: the principles of hydropathy and the compressed-air bath, together with a chapter on the improved Roman or Turkish bath, by a graduate of the Edinburgh University* (Simpkin, Marshall, 1859)
4 Baird, James *Ben Rhydding: its amenities, hygiene, and therapeutics* (Dennant, 1871) p.74
5 Macleod, William *Directory of Ben-Rhydding, with a chapter on the water cure and homoeopathy* (London, 1852)
6 'Matlock Bank Hydro' [advertisement] *Post Office directory of Birmingham for 1863*
7 Metcalfe, Richard *The Rise and progress of hydropathy in England and Scotland* (Simpkin, Marshall, 1912) p.104
8 *Cork constitution* (12 Jun 1838) **Quoted in:** O'Mahony, Colman *The Maritime Gateway to Cork: a history of the outports of Passage West and Monkstown from 1734–1942* (Cork: Tower Books, 1986)

9 *Cork constitution* (25 May 1839) **Quoted in:** O'Mahony, Colman *The Maritime Gateway to Cork: a history of the outports of Passage West and Monkstown from 1734–1942* (Cork: Tower Books, 1986)
10 O'Mahony, Colman *The Maritime Gateway to Cork: a history of the outports of Passage West and Monkstown from 1734–1942* (Cork: Tower Books, 1986) p.70
11 I am most grateful to Marie Gethins and Neil Hegarty for several helpful references to the hotel baths at Glenbrook.
12 'Monkstown baths and hotel' *Cork Examiner* (11 Jun 1858) p.2
13 'Monkstown baths and hotel' *Cork Examiner* (11 Jun 1858) p.3
14 **Quoted in:** O'Mahony, Colman *The Maritime Gateway to Cork: a history of the outports of Passage West and Monkstown from 1734–1942* (Cork: Tower Books, 1986)
15 'Royal Victoria Hotel' *Cork Examiner* (6 Jul 1858) p.2
16 'Turkish bath at Carrigmahon' *Cork Examiner* (11 Jun 1858) p.3
17 **Quoted in:** O'Mahony, Colman *The Maritime Gateway to Cork: a history of the outports of Passage West and Monkstown from 1734–1942* (Cork: Tower Books, 1986)
18 From May 1859, Curtin ran a series of advertisements in the *Cork Examiner* indicating that Curtin's Baths were the 'Best Hydropathic Baths' and included a Turkish Bath.
19 O'Mahony, Colman *The Maritime Gateway to Cork: a history of the outports of Passage West and Monkstown from 1734–1942* (Cork: Tower Books, 1986) p.71
20 Gibson, Charles Bernard *The History of the county and city of Cork* (Cork: Newby, 1861) p.406
21 Jones, Robert Watkin *Heating and ventilating Turkish baths* (Eyre & Spottiswoode, 1861) (Letters Patent: 1861; no.2120)
22 'The oriental hamaam' [advertisement] *Cork Examiner* (30 Jul 1861) p.1
23 **Quoted in:** O'Mahony, Colman *The Maritime Gateway to Cork: a history of the outports of Passage West and Monkstown from 1734–1942* (Cork: Tower Books, 1986)
24 Barter, Richard '[Letter to the Editor]' *Irish Times* (7 Nov 1868) p.4
25 Gibson, Charles Bernard *The History of the county and city of Cork* (Cork: Newby, 1861) p.406
26 'Seaside residences at Carrigmahon, County Cork' *Irish Builder* (1879) p.318
27 Allsop, Robert Owen *The Turkish bath: its design and construction* (Spon, 1890) p.135. The only other book wholly about the Victorian Turkish bath was written mainly for the professional plumber. This was: Cosgrove, J J *Design of the Turkish bath* (Pittsburgh: Standard Sanitary Mfg, 1913)
28 Allsop, Robert Owen *The Hydropathic establishment and its baths* (Spon, 1891) p.56
29 *War Poets Collection* http://www2.napier.ac.uk/warpoets/ Accessed 17.12.2012
30 'Shipwreck off Blackpool' *Preston Guardian* (21 May 1881)
31 Blaker, Catriona *Edward Pugin and Kent: his life and work within the county.* 2nd edn (Ramsgate: The Pugin Society, 2012) pp.44–7
32 *View book and guide to Brighton* (Bright, c1895) p.64
33 Taylor, Nicholas 'Doll's palace: demolition of the Imperial Hotel and Turkish baths' *Architectural Review* (Dec 1966)
34 TNA BT31 36887/115439
35 'The Imperial London Hotels, Ltd: prospectus' *Irish Times* (2 May 1911) p.9
36 London Metropolitan Archives. GLC/AR/BR/19/0175
37 McHardy, George *Reception at the Imperial Hotel.* The Victorian Society (Unpublished typescript, 18 February 1966)
38 MacCarthy, Fiona 'Imperial demolition' *Manchester Guardian* (1 Nov 1966)
39 I am most grateful to Mike Young for his description of the hot rooms and other areas of the Imperial baths. We both used them in our time, but he has a prodigious memory where I have a sieve—and he is an artist.
40 London Metropolitan Archives. GLC/AR/BR/19/0175
41 I am especially grateful to Wendy Stacey for allowing me to use her description of a visit with her friend to the Imperial Turkish baths.
42 Routh, Jonathan *The Good loo guide: where to go in London* (Wolfe, 1965) p.36
43 London Metropolitan Archives. GLC/AR/BR/19/0175
44 I am again indebted to Mike Young for his description of the Russian bath which fills in the details not apparent on the plan itself, and yet again for his evocative illustration of the new plunge pool.
45 Bermant, Chaim 'The Schwitzers' *Jewish Chronicle* (14 Nov 1969)

21 The Turkish bath in 'members only' clubs

1 Mann, W M *1876 The baths: the story of the Western Baths, Hillhead, from 1876 to 1990* (Glasgow: the club, [1991] p.11
2 I am grateful to Sally Mitchell for leading me to the online version of *The Englishwoman's Year Book for 1901* which lists contemporary women's clubs. The first club for both men and women was the Albermarle which opened in 1874; the first for women only was the Alexandra, which opened ten years later, but neither had a swimming pool or Turkish baths.
3 Rous, Henry John 'The Turkish bath as a means of training' *The Field* (12 May 1860) pp.381–2
4 'Sporting Intelligence: Prince's Club' *The Times* (20 May 1889) p.10
5 'Automobilism: the Royal Automobile Club's new home' *The Times* (28 Mar 1911) p.15
6 For further information about the swimming pool, see: Gordon, Ian and Inglis, Simon *Great lengths: the historic indoor swimming pools of Britain* (Swindon: English Heritage, 2009) pp.162–3
7 Bowdler, Roger *The RAC Club, Pall Mall, Westminster: the swimming pool and Turkish baths. HART reports and papers; 31* (Swindon: English Heritage, 2000)
8 Trotter, H M and others *Report of a deputation appointed on 16th Feb and confirmed on 27 Nov 1911 for the purpose of obtaining information with reference to the proposed annexe at the Central Baths, Morley Street* (Bradford: The Council, 1912) p.11 I am extremely grateful to Susan Caton of the Bradford City Libraries for bringing this document to my attention.
9 Ibid, p.12
10 'Automobile Club' *The Times* (1 Feb 1917)
11 'War service' *Scotsman* (12 Jun 1919)
12 'Opening of Warrender Public Baths' *Scotsman* (27 Dec 1907) p.9
13 'City of Edinburgh' [advertisement] *Scotsman* (24 Jun 1915) p.1
14 'Lights that failed' *Scotsman* (9 Oct 1929) p.11
15 Mann, W M *1876 The baths: the story of the Western Baths, Hillhead, from 1876 to 1990* (Glasgow: the club, [1991] p.77
16 Arlington Baths Company Limited *1st Annual report [for 1871]* (Glasgow: the company, 1872)
17 Bruce, J L 'On the heating and ventilation of Turkish baths' *Proceedings of the Glasgow Philosophical Society* (1878) pp.493–506
18 Arlington Baths Company Limited *7th Annual report [for 1877]* (Glasgow: the company, 1878)
19 Bruce, J L 'On the heating and ventilation of Turkish baths' *Proceedings of the Glasgow Philosophical Society* (1878) pp.493–506
20 Arlington Baths Company Limited *26th Annual report [for 1895–6]* (Glasgow: the company, 1897)
21 Arlington Baths Company Limited *80th Annual report [for 1949–50]* (Glasgow: the company, 1950)
22 I am most grateful to Anne Steer, at that time Administrator at the Arlington Baths Club, for help on several occasions.

23 Bruce, J L 'On the heating and ventilation of Turkish baths' *Proceedings of the Glasgow Philosophical Society* (1878) pp.493–506
24 'Victoria Baths, Glasgow' *Glasgow Herald* (4 May 1942) p.6
25 Mann, W M *1876 The baths: the story of the Western Baths, Hillhead, from 1876 to 1990* (Glasgow: the club, [1991]) pp.9, 14
26 Gordon, Ian and Inglis, Simon *Great lengths: the historic indoor swimming pools of Britain* (Swindon: English Heritage, 2009) p.74
27 Service, Robert *Ploughman of the moon: an adventure into memory* (New York: Dodd, Mead, 1945) pp.54–6 (Quoted in W M Mann's history of the baths)
28 Mann, W M *1876 The baths: the story of the Western Baths, Hillhead, from 1876 to 1990* (Glasgow: the club, [1991]) p.23
29 Ibid, pp.33, 35
30 Personal communication from Mr W M Mann, the club's Honorary Secretary
31 Mann, W M *1876 The baths: the story of the Western Baths, Hillhead, from 1876 to 1990* (Glasgow: the club, [1991]) p.66
32 'The prospectus is issued…' *Scotsman* (8 Mar 1882) p.4
33 'Drumsheugh Baths Company Limited' *Scotsman* (28 Aug 1885) p.2
34 'The Drumsheugh Baths' *Scotsman* (22 Dec 1884) p.12
35 Sweetman, John *Oriental obsession: Islamic inspiration in British and American art and architecture, 1500–1920* (Cambridge: CUP, 1988) p.292; note 67
36 Danby, Miles *Moorish style* (Phaidon, 1995) pp.173–4
37 'Fires' *The Times* (8 Feb 1892) p.6c
38 'Edinburgh' *Building News* (1 Jul 1892) p.30
39 Burrell, Kirsty 'Drumsheugh Baths Club' *Homes & Interiors Scotland* (No.31; Sept/ Oct 2003) pp.108–114
40 Danby, Miles *Moorish style* (Phaidon, 1995) pp.173–4
41 Drumsheugh Baths Club website http://www.drumsheughbaths.com/ history.asp Accessed 9 Nov 2010
42 'Fire at Drumsheugh Baths' *Scotsman* (18 Jun 1920) p.4
43 *Edinburgh war time guide 1942* (Edinburgh: City of Edinburgh Council of Social Service Citizen's Advice Bureau, 1942)
44 *Edinburgh Evening News* (18 Oct 1967) and Burrell, Kirsty 'Drumsheugh Baths Club' *Homes & Interiors Scotland* (no.31; Sept/ Oct 2003) pp.108–114
45 'Pollokshields Baths' *Glasgow Herald* (21 Mar 1885) p.6
46 'Glasgow baths closed' *Glasgow Herald* **Quoted in:** Mann, W M *1876 The baths: the story of the Western Baths, Hillhead, from 1876 to 1990* (Glasgow: The Club, [1991]) p.57

22 Turkish baths in private houses

1 'The Turkish bath in Tyneside' *Newcastle Journal* (7 Mar 1857) p.5
2 Adamson, Horatio A 'Tynemouth House' *Shields Daily News* (13 Jul 1893) p.3
3 *Newcastle Daily Journal. Supplement* (22 Jan 1861) **Cited in:** Barter, Richard *The Rise and progress of the 'Turkish bath', as first introduced into and patented in the UK by Dr Barter* (Dublin: Wm McGee, 1856) p.5
4 Personal communication from Jane Nesbitt, great-great-granddaughter of Ralph Nesbitt who lived next door in the Fox Hunter Inn.
5 'The construction and use of the Turkish bath' *Builder* (24 Oct 1857) p.615
6 'The baths at Riverside' *Free Press* (26 May 1858) p.130; col.3 [An unattributed letter to the editor, possibly from Harriet Urquhart]
7 'The baths at Riverside' *Free Press* (26 May 1858) p.130; col.2 [An unattributed letter to the editor, possibly from Harriet Urquhart]
8 'The eastern, or Turkish bath' **In:** *Manual of the Turkish bath* John Fife (ed) (John Churchill, 1865) pp.121–2
9 WL, *Western Ms.6236: Correspondence on Turkish baths; 22*, Richard Summers. Letter to David Urquhart, 14 Jul 1860
10 BCDU, I G 24 Misc – 5, Agnes Robertson. Letter to David Urquhart, 28 Aug 1861
11 WL, *Western Ms.6236: Correspondence on Turkish baths; 18*, George Witt. Letter to David Urquhart, 22 Apr 1860
12 Leared, Arthur 'The treatment of Phthisis by the Turkish bath' **In:** *Manual of the Turkish bath* John Fife (ed) (John Churchill, 1865) pp.121–2
13 Goolden, R H 'The Turkish bath' *The Lancet* (26 Jan 1861) pp.95–7
14 *Manual of the Turkish bath* John Fife (ed) (John Churchill, 1865) p.129
15 *Hammam Turkish bath* (The Hammam, 1929) pp.12–14
16 'The Turkish bath' *The Field* (16 Jun 1860) p.503
17 Wilson, Erasmus 'Thermo-therapeia (the heat cure)' *British Medical Journal* (13 Oct 1860) pp.789–794
18 Wilson, Erasmus *The eastern, or Turkish bath* (Churchill, 1861) pp.93–5
19 Wilson, Erasmus 'On the revival of the eastern bath in Britain, and its application to sanitary purposes' *Transactions of the National Association for the Promotion of Social Science* (1861) p.706
20 Rayner, T *A voice from the thermae* 2nd edn (Dublin: Porter, 1861) p.21
21 Wilson, Erasmus *The eastern, or Turkish bath* (Churchill, 1861) pp.88–9
22 *…and Mr Fortescue: a selection from the diaries from 1851 to 1862 of Chichester Fortescue, Lord Carlingford* Osbert Wyndham Hewett (ed) (Murray, [1958]) p.198
23 *Consumption arrested by the Turkish bath* (Hardwicke, 1864)
24 Urquhart, David. Letter to B Greenwood. [November 1857] Transcribed in *The Free Press* (16 Dec 1857)
25 Urquhart, David. Letter to John Fife. 13 Jan 1864. Transcribed in *Consumption arrested by the Turkish bath* (Hardwicke, 1864)
26 WS-Poore, 1915/73. Diary, 15 April 1863
27 Ironside's letter is quoted in: *The importance of radiating heat: fly-sheet no.13* **Reprinted in:** *The Hammam of the Turks: collected fly-sheets* (The Hammam, 1867)
28 Constantine, Joseph *Hydropathy in city and town* (Heywood, 1905) Appendix p.xxviii
29 *Art Journal* (1875)
30 Gillie, Oliver 'Brides restore romance to palace of dreams' *Independent* (17 May 1994) p.9
31 O'Connor, T P [One of the pleasantest…] (*MAP*, 2 Jul 1898) p.53
32 Constantine, Joseph 'Private Turkish baths' *Building News* (3 Aug 1888) p.161
33 'The Late Mr T Owen of Oswestry' *Border Counties Advertiser* (31 May 1916)
34 Owen, Thomas *How I came to build a Turkish bath* (Oswestry: Commercial Circular, 1912) pp.12–13
35 TNA: BT31 1424/4142
36 TNA: BT31 1752/6521
37 *Cragside: Northumberland* (The National Trust, 1992)
38 http://www.tilesoc.org.uk/tile-gazetteer/ northumberland.html#20r Accessed 18 Jan 2012
39 *Cragside: Northumberland* (The National Trust, 1992)
40 Personal communication from Steve Sharp. 22 Sep 2002
41 Constantine, Joseph *Fifty years of the water cure, with biographical notes* 2nd edn (John Heywood, 1893) p.38–9
42 Constantine, Joseph *Hydropathy at home: the domestic practice of the water cure…* 3rd edn revised and enlarged (Simpkin Marshall, 1884); *Hydropathy, health, and longevity* (Manchester: Heywood, 1895)
43 *Papers of Sir Isaac Holden (1807–1897) and Family, West Riding wool combers*. J B Priestley Library. University of Bradford. I am most grateful to Alison Cullingford, Special Collections Librarian at the J.B. Priestley Library for her help in finding these plans and Constantine's estimate for the work to be done.
44 Personal communication from Steve Sharp. 28 Sep 2002

45 Constantine, Joseph *Health and activity in middle and later life* (Simpkin, Marshall, 1890) pp.64–5
46 **Quoted in:** Constantine, Joseph *Health and activity in middle and later life* (Simpkin, Marshall, 1890) pp.73–4
47 Constantine, Joseph *Health and activity in middle and later life* (Simpkin, Marshall, 1890) p.74
48 Pegg, Patricia *A very private heritage* (Malvern: Images, 1996) pp.183–4
49 Shorney, David *A brief history of the mansion at Avery Hill*. Rev edn (Thames Polytechnic, 1990)
50 'Interior of Turkish bath, Avery Hill' *Builder* (26 Nov 1892)
51 http://www.tilesoc.org.uk/tile-gazetteer/greenwich.html#2r Accessed 18 Jan 2012
52 Shorney, David *A brief history of the mansion at Avery Hill*. Rev edn (Thames Polytechnic, 1990)

23 The Turkish bath at sea

1 *Boston-New York Service cabin accommodation* (White Star Line, 1929); From the website of the Immigrant Ships Transcribers Guild http://www.immigrantships.net/
2 '*Olympic* and *Titanic*: the White Star triple screw Atlantic liners' *Shipbuilder* (Midsummer 1911) pp.81–2, 84
3 Beveridge, Bruce and others *Titanic: the ship magnificent*. vol.2: *interior design & fitting out* (Stroud: History Pr, 2008) p.418
4 '*Olympic* and *Titanic*: the White Star triple screw Atlantic liners' *Shipbuilder* (Midsummer 1911) pp.81–2, 84
5 The earlier advertisement for Vinolia Toilet Soap appeared in, for example, *Ladies' Field* (10 Jun 1911) p.xcvi
6 *White Star Line: Royal and United States Mail Steamers* (Liverpool: The company, 1913)
7 Checkland, Sarah Jane 'Questions on sale of *Lusitania* document' *The Times* (12 Apr 1990) p.3
8 McMillan, Beverly and Lehrer, Stanley Titanic*: fortune & fate: catalogue from The Mariners' Museum Exhibition* (New York: Simon & Schuster, 1998) pp.173–88
9 © 2004 Coleman/Spedden Family Archives, Courtesy of Leighton H. Coleman III
10 Dempsey, John *I've seen them all naked* (Poole: Waterfront Publ,1992) pp.4–11
11 'Sports on the *Berengaria*' *Scotsman* (26 Aug 1924) p.4
12 Dempsey, John *I've seen them all naked* (Poole: Waterfront Publ,1992) p.12
13 *Memo on the quotations for building the Turkish baths* **In:** The Cunard Archive, Sydney Jones Library, University of Liverpool. D42/C3/389 (Nov 1931) p.8
14 Dempsey, John *I've seen them all naked* (Poole: Waterfront Publ,1992) p.12
15 'Swimming pools in the *RMS Queen Mary*' *Baths and Bath Engineering* (Jun 1936) pp.110–111
16 'The Cunard White Star, North Atlantic quadruple-screw, geared-turbine, express passenger steamship: *Queen Mary*' *Shipbuilder and Marine Engine-builder* (June 1936) pp.171, 173
17 Dempsey, John *I've seen them all naked* (Poole: Waterfront Publ,1992) pp.27–34
18 Room sizes are taken from Messrs Trollope & Sons winning quotation for fitting out the Turkish baths suite. **In:** The Cunard Archive, Sydney Jones Library, University of Liverpool. D42/C3/208 B18
19 Winter, Ron Queen Mary*: her early years recalled* (Wellingborough: Stephens, 1986)
20 *Memo*. Cunard General Manager's Office to the Chief Catering Superintendent, 6 May 1963. **In:** The Cunard Archive, Sydney Jones Library, University of Liverpool. D42/C3/208 B18
21 'Queen Mary*: receipts for Turkish bath services during the period April-July 1963 and for the same period in 1964* Typescript (21 Oct1964). **In:** The Cunard Archive, Sydney Jones Library, University of Liverpool. D42/C3/208 B18

24 The portable Turkish bath

1 Burne-Jones, Philip. Letter to Mrs Hamilton, 30 October 1890 (Author's collection)
2 Gore, W R 'The hospital hot-air bath, for administering hot air, vapour, medicated air and gases' *Dublin Medical Press* (23 May 1860) pp.393–4
3 Wright, Lawrence *Clean and decent: the fascinating history of the bathroom & the water closet…* (Routledge, 1960) p.113
4 'The patent portable Turkish bath' *British Medical Journal* (21 June 1873) p.704
5 TNA BT31 2009/8670
6 Stables, W Gordon *Turkish and other baths: a guide to good health and longevity* (Dean, [1883]) p.80
7 'A Private hot-air bath, by Penelope' *Rochdale Times* (2 Apr 1881) p.6
8 *The Gem Quaker Turkish Bath Cabinets* (Gem Supplies Co) [s.d.] p.10
9 Stables, W Gordon *Turkish and other baths: a guide to good health and longevity* (Dean, [1883]) pp.46–7
10 'You don't have to do without a Turkish bath' *Swimming Notes* (7 Nov 1885)
11 'It was described…' *Swimming Notes* (21 Nov 1885)
12 Constantine, Joseph *Hydropathy at home: the domestic practice of the water cure …* 3rd edn revised and enlarged (Simkin, Marshall, 1884) p.185
13 *The Gem Quaker Turkish Bath Cabinets* (Gem Supplies Co) [s.d.] pp.14–15
14 *The Army & Navy Stores Ltd General price list, 1939–40* (the store, 1939)

25 Turkish baths for animals

1 Dunlop, Durham *The philosophy of the bath, or air and water in health and disease* (Simpkin Marshall, 1868) p.419
2 Wade, Robert C 'Report of the committee appointed to inquire into the utility of the Turkish bath, erected by Dr Barter, at St Ann's, Blarney, for the cure of distemper in cattle' *Edinburgh Veterinary Review* (Oct 1860) pp.389–94
3 Korhonen, Nina 'The sauna: a sacred place' *Universitas Helsingiensis* (4/1998)
4 'Par ci—par lá: at the bath, by "The Wanderer"' *Echoes from the Clubs* (20 Nov 1867) pp.37–9
5 Scriven, J E 'Four years experience of the bath on an Irish farm' **Reprinted in:** *Manual of the Turkish bath: heat a mode of cure and a source of strength for men and animals, from the writings of Mr Urquhart* John Fife (ed) (Churchill, 1865) pp.389–404
6 Wollaston, Robert 'The Turkish bath' **Quoted in:** *Aberdeen Water Cure Journal* vol.1; pp.274–5
7 'New baths, Lincoln-Place' *Dublin Builder* (1 Jan 1860) p.176
8 Wade, Robert C 'Report of the committee appointed to inquire into the utility of the Turkish bath, erected by Dr Barter, at St Ann's, Blarney, for the cure of distemper in cattle' *Edinburgh Veterinary Review* (Oct 1860) pp.389–94
9 **Quoted in:** Haughton, Edward *Facts and fallacies of the Turkish bath, or, what kind of bath should we have?* (Dublin: William Robertson, 1860) p.39
10 Scriven, J E 'Four years experience of the bath on an Irish farm' **Reprinted in:** *Manual of the Turkish bath: heat a mode of cure and a source of strength for men and animals, from the writings of Mr Urquhart* John Fife (ed) (Churchill, 1865) pp.389–404
11 'Charles Hamilton Macknight' *The Dunmore Journal* (vol.3: 1 Jan 1866–5 Mar 1873) Collection State Library of Victoria MS 8999 **Quoted in:** Aykut, Susan 'Washing from the inside out: Turkish baths down under' *TASA Review* (vol.16; no.1) pp.10–12
12 Scriven, J E 'Four years experience of the bath on an Irish farm' **Reprinted in:** *Manual of the Turkish bath: heat a mode of cure and a source of strength for men and animals, from the writings of Mr Urquhart* John Fife (ed) (Churchill, 1865) pp.389–404
13 Siltzer, Frank *Newmarket: its sport and personalities* (Cassell, 1923)

14 Wells, T Spencer 'Lecture on the revival of the Turkish, or ancient Roman bath' *Medical Times & Gazette* (3 Nov 1860) pp.423–7
15 Wilson, Erasmus *The eastern, or Turkish bath: its history, revival in Britain and application to the purpose of health* (Churchill, 1861) pp.153–9
16 WS-LPTB. *Minutes* (12 Mar 1861)
17 Ibid, *Minutes* (19 Mar 1861)
18 Rous, Henry John 'The Turkish bath as a means of training' *The Field* (12 May 1860) pp.381–2
19 Walsh, J H *The horse, in the stable and the field: his varieties, management in health and disease, anatomy, physiology, etc* (Routledge, 1862) pp.266–9
20 'The Turf' *The Field* (23 Feb 1861) p.150
21 Moore, George *Esther Waters* (Scott, 1894)
22 Miles, W J *Modern practical farriery: a complete guide to all that relates to the horse* (MacKenzie, [*c* 1870])
23 'A Turkish bath for cattle' *Scottish Farmer* (10 Sep 1862) **Quoted in:** *The Hammam of the Turks: collected fly-sheets* (London Hammam, 1867) p.7
24 *Manual of the Turkish bath: heat a mode of cure and a source of strength for men and animals, from the writings of Mr Urquhart* John Fife (ed) (Churchill, 1865) pp.385
25 'What is the Turkish bath?' *The Field* (2 Jun 1860)
26 Walton, Joseph and Moore, James *Improvements in the mode of ventilating and heating rooms, Turkish baths, hothouses, and buildings of all kinds* (Letters Patent: 1862; No.2127)
27 Gordon, William John *The horse-world of London* (Religious Tract Society, 1893)
28 'Turkish baths for horses' *Builder* (31 May 1884)
29 http://pickfords.co.uk/html/about/aboutpickfords_history2.htm Accessed August 2007
30 Constantine, Joseph *Hydropathy, health and longevity* (Manchester: Heywood, 1895) pp.373–4
31 Ibid, pp.374–6
32 Article by George Wade in the July 1900 issue of *Railway Magazine* **Quoted in:** Child, Sally 'The Horse in the city' *The Victorian Society Annual* (The Society, 1996) p.10
33 Gordon, William John *The horse-world of London* (Religious Tract Society, 1893)
34 'A novel horse hospital: Turkish, Russian, and electric baths' *New York Times* (13 Mar 1882)
35 Allsop, Robert Owen *The Turkish bath: its design and construction* (Spon, 1890)

26 Victorian women and the Turkish bath

1 'The Turkish bath' *Critic* (17 Feb 1872) p.124
2 Coley, Frederic Collins *The Turkish bath* (Walter Scott, 1887) p.10, and widely used elsewhere in advertisements
3 Marsden, Thomas Lewen *The Turkish bath, or patriarchal regenerator by hot air: a lecture delivered in the Town Hall, Southport* (Southport: Haigh's Turkish Baths, [1861]) p.20
4 'The Turkish baths at Broughton Lane' [advertisement] *Halifax Courier* (24 Dec 1858)
5 Shifrin, Malcolm *'The ladies ought to have at least three nights in the week': women and Victorian Turkish baths.* 12th Annual Conference of the Women's History Network. King's College, University of Aberdeen, Scotland, 14 September 2003 *Contested terrains: gendered knowledge, landscapes, and narratives*
6 *Kelly's directory of Leeds*
7 *Kelly's directory of the West Riding of Yorkshire*
8 *Opening of the Central Baths: 13 September 1905* (Bradford: The Council, 1905) p.3
9 'Turkish bath for ladies' [advertisement] *Morning Post* (15 Mar 1883) p.1
10 'Keighley Baths' *Keighley News* (25 Jul 1868)
11 L.E.P. 'The Turkish bath [letter to the editor]' *Bradford Advertiser* (27 Feb 1858) p.4
12 'Opening of the Northampton Turkish bath this day' *Northampton Daily Chronicle* (17 May 1892)
13 Booth, Charles *Life and labour of the people in London...* 2nd edn (Macmillan, 1902–1903) The notes for the interviews are in the Charles Booth Archive at the London School of Economics. This interview is from Group B, vol.161, p.12 recto
14 Metcalfe, Richard *Sanitas sanitatum et omnia sanitas* (the author, 1877) p.298
15 Newham, Alan T *The Cork and Muskerry Light Railway* (Oxford: Oakwood Pr, 1968)
16 *Industries of Yorkshire* (Historical Publ Co, 1888) p.168
17 Barker, S and Henderson, S *Thermo-therapeutics* (Henry Renshaw, 1861)
18 'The Turkish bath is now open!' [advertisement] *Bradford Advertiser* (10 Apr 1858) p.4
19 Gloucester Corporation. Baths Committee. *Minutes* (17 August 1891)
20 Gloucester Corporation. Market, Quay and Baths Committee. *Minutes* (15 July 1921)
21 Booth, Charles *Life and labour of the people in London...* 2nd edn (Macmillan, 1902–1903) The notes for the interviews are in the Charles Booth Archive at the London School of Economics. This interview is from Group B, vol.161, pp.11–12
22 'Opening of Turkish baths in Brighton' *Builder* (24 Oct 1868) p.786
23 *Industries of Yorkshire* (Historical Publ Co, 1888) p.168
24 Allsop, Robert Owen *The Turkish bath: its design and construction* (Spon, 1890) p.24
25 Radford, Dollie *Diary, 1883–1889* p.198 UC Southern Regional Library Preservation Microfilming Services: William Andrew Clark Memorial Library/ UCLA: 26–7. I am most grateful to Hadeel J Azhar for sending me this reference, taken from her current research on *Dollie Radford and female friendships* for her PhD thesis at Edinburgh Napier University.
26 'Adjourned inquest: second day' *Buckinghamshire Advertiser* (13 Feb 1858) p.4
27 Penelope [pseud.] 'Turkish baths' *Rochdale Times* (2 Apr 1881) p.6
28 Allsop, Robert Owen *The Turkish bath: its design and construction* (Spon, 1890) p.14
29 Ibid, p.44
30 Barter, Richard *The Turkish bath: being a lecture delivered in the Mechanics' Institute, Bradford on 8 July 1858* (Bradford: Jowett, 1858) p.24
31 Haughton, Edward 'A short description of the process gone through at The Oriental Baths, Mulberry Street, Liverpool' *Liverpool: Architectural & Archaeological Society proceedings* (1860)
32 Allsop, Robert Owen *The Turkish bath: its design and construction* (Spon, 1890) p.111
33 'What is this I hear?' *Swimming Notes* (8 Mar 1884) p.4
34 Diogenes [pseud.] *Life in a tub.* 3rd edn (Dublin: McGee, 1858) p.50
35 Constantine, Joseph *Hydropathy, health and longevity* (Manchester: John Heywood, 1895) p.169
36 *Swim and keep fit: Derby Baths and Entertainments official guide* (Derby: The Council, 1964) p.18
37 Coley, Frederic Collins *The Turkish bath* (Scott, 1887) p.42
38 Blackwell, Elizabeth. Letter to Richard Metcalfe, *c* 1873. **Reprinted in:** Metcalfe, Richard *Sanitas sanitatum et omnia sanitas* (the author, 1877) p.290
39 Potter, William *The Roman or Turkish bath: its hygienic and curative properties* (Simkin & Marshall, 1859)
40 Bartholomew, Charles *Mr Bartholomew's evidence before a committee of medical men on the prevention and cure of disease.* 6th edn (Bristol: Marshall, 1870) p.20
41 *A chat upon health: Pat Dennehy visits Mrs Magrath* (T Burns, 1875) p.9
42 For example: Bartholomew, Charles *Mr Bartholomew's evidence before a committee of medical men on the prevention and cure of disease.* 6th edn (Bristol: Marshall, 1870) pp.76–80, 119–122
43 *Maud: the diaries of Maud Berkeley;* adapted by Flora Fraser (Secker & Warburg, 1985) p.125

27 Victorian Turkish baths: 'sites of sex and sociability'

1 I am especially grateful to Deborah Morse, Professor, English at The College of William & Mary, and to Matt Houlbrook, Senior Lecturer in Modern British History, University of Birmingham, who commented most helpfully on an early draft of this chapter. They are in no way responsible for any errors which remain, neither do they necessarily agree with the views I have expressed.
2 Houlbrook, Matt *Queer London: perils and pleasures in the sexual metropolis, 1918–1957* (Chicago: Univ Pr, 2005) p.108
3 *Report of the Committee on homosexual offences and prostitution* (HMSO, 1957)
4 Cook, Matt *London and the culture of homosexuality, 1885–1914* (CUP, 2003)
5 Chauncey, George *Gay New York: the making of the gay male world, 1890–1940* (Flamingo, 1995) Chapter 8: The social world of the baths
6 Houlbrook, Matt *Queer London: perils and pleasures in the sexual metropolis, 1918–1957* (Chicago: Univ Pr, 2005) p.94
7 Foucault, Michel *The history of sexuality*. vol.1: *An introduction;* translated by Robert Hurley (Allen Lane, 1979) p.9 **Glossed in:** Cocks, H G *Nameless offences: homosexual desire in the nineteenth century* (Tauris, 2003) p.2
8 Cocks, H G *Nameless offences: homosexual desire in the nineteenth century* (Tauris, 2003) p.3
9 Bartlett, Neil *Mr Clive & Mr Page* (Serpent's Tail, 1996)
10 Ibid, p.16
11 Personal communication. Neil Bartlett. 19 April 2009
12 Cleminson, Julie *Walking in London: the fiction of Neil Bartlett, Sarah Waters and Alan Hollinghurst: writing missing voices of sexuality, class and gender back into history through re-imagining the city space.* Ph D Thesis Brunel University 2009 http://bura.brunel.ac.uk/bitstream/2438/4356/1/Fulltext%28Thesis%29.pdf Accessed 20 May 2012
13 For a recent study of Trollope's account of the towel ritual, see: Spooner, Catherine *Modes of wearing the towel: masculinity, insanity and clothing in Trollope's Turkish bath* **In:** *Bodies and things in nineteenth-century literature and culture;* Katharina Boehm (ed) (New York: Palgrave Macmillan, 2012)
14 Turner, Mark W *Trollope and the magazines: gendered issues in mid-Victorian Britain* (Basingstoke: Palgrave Macmillan, 1999) Chapter 5: The editor as predator in *Saint Pauls*. This particular quotation is from page 198, but the whole chapter is well worth reading, even by the non-specialist.
15 Markwick, Margaret 'Out of the closet: homoerotics in Trollope's novels' **In:** *The politics of gender in Anthony Trollope's novels: new readings for the twenty-first century* Margaret Markwick, Deborah Morse, and Regenia Gagnier (eds) (Farnham: Ashgate, 2009) p.66
16 Trollope, Anthony *An autobiography* (Edinburgh: Blackwood, 1883) p.337
17 Turner, Mark W *Trollope and the magazines: gendered issues in mid-Victorian Britain* (Basingstoke: Palgrave Macmillan, 1999) p.192
18 Ibid, p.204
19 Turner, Mark W *Backward glances: cruising the queer streets of New York and London* (Reaktion, 2001) p.74
20 Flint, Kate 'Queer Trollope' **In:** *The Cambridge companion to Anthony Trollope* Carolyn Dever and Lisa Niles (eds) (CUP, 2010) p. 109
21 Trollope, Anthony 'The Turkish bath' *St Paul's Magazine* (Oct 1869) p.113
22 'Metropolitan improvements; ix: Turkish baths' *Standard* (10 Apr 1863) p.6
23 'Turkish baths' *Standard* (10 Apr 1863) p.6
24 'Dr Culverwell's Ladies' Turkish Baths' [advertisement] *Anglo-American Times* (6 Oct 1866)
25 The scandal at Cleveland Street, Fitzrovia, involved several aristocratic clients (said by some American newspapers to include the eldest son of the Prince of Wales) and male prostitutes, some of whom were fifteen-year-olds employed as Post Office telegraph boys. See, *eg*, Hyde, H Montgomery *The Cleveland Street scandal* (Allen, 1976)
26 Potvin, John 'Vapour and steam: the Victorian Turkish bath, homosocial health, and male bodies on display' *Journal of Design History* (vol.18; no.4) pp.319–333
27 Potvin, John *Material and visual cultures beyond male bonding, 1870–1914: bodies, boundaries and intimacy* (Farnham: Ashgate, 2007) Chapter 4
28 Potvin, John 'Hot by design: the secret life of a Turkish bath in Victorian London' **In:** *Craft, space and interior design, 1855–2005* Sandra Alfoldy and Janice Helland (eds) (Farnham: Ashgate, 2008)
29 Partington, Matthew 'Review: Craft, Space and Interior Design 1855–2005' *Journal of Design History* (2009; vol.22; no.1) pp.79–80
30 TNA CRES 35/2108 – No 76 (and additional premises in rear)
31 Roth, Mathias *The Russian bath, published with a view to recommending its introduction into England for hygienic as well as curative purposes*. 2nd edn (Groombridge,1855)
32 Allsop, Robert Owen *The Turkish bath: its design and construction* (Spon, 1890)
33 Allsop, Robert Owen *The hydropathic establishment and its baths* (Spon, 1891)
34 Cross, Alfred W S *Public baths and wash houses* (Batsford, 1906)
35 Potvin, John 'Vapour and steam: the Victorian Turkish bath, homosocial health, and male bodies on display' *Journal of design history* (vol.18; no4) p.319
36 Ibid, p.320
37 Potvin, John *Material and visual cultures beyond male bonding, 1870–1914: bodies, boundaries and intimacy* (Farnham: Ashgate, 2007) p.93
38 'The new Turkish Hammam, Jermyn Street, St James's' *Building News* (4 Jul 1862) p.12
39 Urquhart, David 'On the art of constructing Turkish baths: and their economy as a means of cleanliness' *Journal of the Society of Arts* (28 Feb 1862) p.227
40 'The Hammam, or Turkish bath' *Illustrated London News* (26 Jul 1862) p.96 + p.iii
41 'The Hammam' [advertisement] *Morning Post* (25 Jul 1862) p.1
42 WS-LPTB. *Minutes* (8 Jul 1862)
43 Ibid, *Minutes* (20 Mar 1890)
44 Ibid, *Minutes* (11 Jun 1887)
45 Houlbrook, Matt *Queer London: perils and pleasures in the sexual metropolis, 1918–1957* (Chicago: Univ Pr, 2005) p.97
46 Ibid, p.94
47 Personal communication. Bob H. (16 Sep 2000)
48 Personal communication. Gill Wright (21 Jan 2013)
49 Personal communication. Anne (25 Apr 2013)

28 Inside the Victorian Turkish bath

1 Urquhart, David *The Pillars of Hercules, or, a narrative of travels in Spain and Morocco in 1848* (Bentley, 1850) vol.2; p.37
2 Evans, Frenklen *The Turkish bath in health and disease…* (Cardiff: The Guardian, 1868)
3 Balbirnie, John *The sweating cure.* 2nd edn (Southport: the author, 1864) p.31
4 The Tichborne case was a legal *cause célèbre* that enthralled Victorian England in the 1860s and 1870s. It concerned the claim by Thomas Castro (sometimes called Arthur Orton, but usually referred to as 'the Claimant') to be the missing heir to the Tichborne baronetcy. He failed to convince the courts, and served a long prison sentence for perjury.
5 Elson, George *The last of the climbing boys* (John Long, 1900) pp.271–2
6 'Turkish bath parties' *Baltimore Sunday Herald* (24 May 1893)
7 Longwell, Ann 'Steam baths' *Sunday Times Colour Supplement* (31 Jan 1991)

8 'Child-birth in a Turkish bath' *Dundee Courier & Argus* (19 Apr 1870)
9 Trollope, Anthony *The Turkish bath* (Strahan, 1870)
10 'A Yorkshireman takes his first Turkish bath' *Harrogate Herald* (8 Mar 1933)
11 I am most grateful to 'Harry' for allowing me to publish this remembrance of his first visit to the Savoy Baths.
12 'The adjourned inquest: third day' *Buckinghamshire Advertiser* (16 Feb 1858) p.4 William's death and the inquest, about which Marx wrote to Engels, are more fully covered in my article 'The Turkish-bath baby-death mystery' *Hertfordshire's Past* (Autumn 1998) pp.24–31 and on the *Victorian Turkish Baths* website.
13 'The amendment of the law of libel …' *Bucks Herald* (8 May 1858) p.4
14 Thudichum, J L W 'The Turkish bath' *Transactions of the Medical Society* (1861) pp.39–52
15 'Fire at the Turkish baths in Princes' Street' *Scotsman* (2 Apr 1888) p.7
16 'Serious fire in Edinburgh' *Scotsman* (3 Apr 1888) p.4
17 'Fire at Turkish baths' *The Times* (11 Aug 1930) p.10
18 'Leicester-square fire' *The Times* (16 Aug 1930) p.7; (22 Aug 1930) p,7; (2 Sep 1930) p.9
19 'Missed…' [advertisement] *Irish Times* (21 Feb 1873) p.1
20 'Consolidated Nisi Prius Court' *Irish Times* (26 Apr 1873) p.5
21 'Daring robberies at the High Street Baths' *Birmingham Daily Post* (24 Oct 1887) p.5
22 E. E. 'Robbery at the Turkish baths' [letter] *Birmingham Daily Post* (25 Oct 1887) p.4
23 'The Sunderland bank robbery' *Pall Mall Gazette* (30 Jun 1897)
24 'Shots in Turkish bath' *The Times* (10 Oct 1955) p.8

29 Advertising the Victorian Turkish bath

1 The Ephemera Society, The Ephemera Society of America, and The Ephemera Society of Australia, all have websites and welcome new members.
2 Maurice Rickards, founder of The Ephemera Society.
3 I am indebted to Paul Atterbury of the *BBC Antiques Roadshow* for this information.
4 I am grateful to Meredith Friedman, Collections Manager at the Metropolitan Museum of Art's Department of Photographs, for the information about the painted-out addresses.
5 'Turkish baths for horses' [advertisement] *Western Times* (25 May 1861) p.8
6 'Building the stands' *Dominion* (21 Jun 1911) p.8
7 'Coronation procession' [advertisement] *London Standard* (7 Jun 1911) p.7
8 'Important' [advertisement] *Irish Times* (21 Sep 1892) p.1
9 'Curative Turkish baths' [advertisement] *Stockton Herald* (8 May 1880) p.4
10 *Facilities and tariffs relating to medicated, electrical, Turkish, swimming baths and public wash-houses* (Bradford: The Corporation, 1935)
11 *Camden Town Conservation Area Appraisal and Management Strategy* [Camden Council, April 2014]
12 Rickards, Maurice *The encyclopedia of ephemera* (British Library, 2000) p.335
13 In John Galsworthy's *In Chancery*, part of his *Forsyte saga*, a stressed Soames Forsyte pays an unplanned visit to The Hammam.

30 Victorian Turkish baths today and tomorrow

1 Campbell, Agnes *Report on public baths and wash-houses in the United Kingdom* (Edinburgh: Carnegie UK Trust, 1918) Appendix I
2 Manchester and Salford Baths and Laundries Company Limited *Annual report for 1867* (Manchester: The Company, 1868)
3 Frayn, Michael 'Water torture: Manchester's first sauna' *Guardian* (19 Nov 1959)
4 Newby, Eric *On the shores of the Mediterranean* (Pan, 1985) pp.192–3
5 Barnard, Jeffrey *Low life* (Duckworth, 1986) p.61
6 Williams, Prue *Victoria Baths: Manchester's water palace* (Reading: Spire, 2004)

RESOURCES CITED, AND SELECT BIBLIOGRAPHY

Libraries and archives

I am deeply indebted to the staff of the five national libraries of Ireland and the United Kingdom, the Library of the University of Cambridge, and the public libraries in most of the major towns of both countries over a period of twenty or so years. Without their help, writing this book would have been impossible to contemplate.

I have also particularly benefited from the help received in locating documents found in the following collections and archives:

City of Westminster Archives
Cork City & County Archives
Hampshire Archives and Local Studies
Leeds Local History Library
London Metropolitan Archives
National Art Library
RIBA Library Drawings & Archives Collection
The National Archives
University of Bradford, J B Priestley Archive (Papers of Sir Isaac Holden, 1807-1897, and Family)
University of Liverpool, Sydney Jones Library (Cunard Archive)
University of London LSE (Charles Booth Archive)
University of Oxford, Balliol College (Papers of David Urquhart)
University of Oxford, Bodleian Libraries, John Johnson Collection of Ephemera
University of York, Borthwick Institute for Archives (York Retreat Collection)
Wellcome Library, London (Western Manuscripts Collection)
West Yorkshire Archive Service
Wiltshire & Swindon History Centre (The Poore Papers, and the Great Western Railway Company (GWR) Archive)

Primary sources

Directories

United Kingdom of Great Britain. *Thom's official directory*

Cumberland. *Slater's directory*
Hampshire. *Kelly's directory*
West Riding of Yorkshire. *Kelly's directory*
Wiltshire. *Kelly's directory*

Birmingham. *Jones' mercantile directory*
Birmingham. *Post Office directory*
Bradford, Halifax. *White's directory*
Bristol and Glamorganshire. *Webster's directory*
Crewe. *Eardley's Crewe almanack*
Guildford. *Andrew's almanac*
Leeds. *Kelly's directory*
Manchester. *Slater's directory*
Newcastle and District. *Ward's directory*
Newcastle-on-Tyne. *Kelly's directory*
Nottingham. *Wright's directory*
Portsmouth. *Chamberlain's directory*

Ireland. *Slater's directory*
Cork. *Mercantile directory*

Scotland. *Slater's royal national directory*
Glasgow. *Post Office directory*

Wales. *Wilson's trades directory*
Cardiff. *Butcher's directory*

Canada. *Lovell's Montreal directory*

Annual Reports

Denbigh. North Wales Counties Lunatic Asylum
Dublin. Inspectors of Lunatics (Ireland)
London. County Lunatic Asylum at Colney Hatch
West Riding of Yorkshire. West Riding Pauper Asylum

Fermoy. Board of Guardians of the Fermoy Poor Law Union

Huddersfield. Royal Infirmary
Newcastle-on-Tyne. Infirmary

Glasgow. Arlington Baths Co Ltd
Manchester. Manchester and Salford Baths and Laundries Co Ltd

Minutes

Birmingham Corporation. Baths and Parks Committee
Bradford Corporation. Sanitary, Baths and Cemetery Committee
Carlisle. Baths Sub-Committee
Gloucester Corporation. Baths Committee
Gloucester Corporation. Market, Quay and Baths Committee
Newport County Borough. Baths Sub-committee
Nottingham City Council
Nottingham Corporation. Baths and Washhouses Committee
Nottingham Corporation. Public Baths and Washhouses Committee

London. London & Provincial Turkish Baths Co Ltd
Swindon. Great Western Railway Company Medical Fund Society

Patents

Barter, Richard *Heating and ventilating buildings, &c* (Letters Patent: 1859; no.208)
Bolton, John Adams *An improved apparatus for heating Turkish baths, public and private buildings…* (Letters Patent: 1861; no.689)
Jones, Robert Watkin *Heating and ventilating Turkish baths* (Letters Patent: 1861; no.2120)
Walton, Joseph and Moore, James *Improvements in the mode of ventilating and heating rooms, Turkish baths, hothouses, and buildings of all kinds* (Letters Patent: 1862; no.2127)
Whitaker, Thomas and Constantine, Joseph *Improvements in the construction of stoves…* (Letters Patent: 1866; no.2448)

Journals and magazines

Aberdeen Journal
Aberdeen Water Cure Journal
Agricultural Review
All the Year Round
Alloa Journal
Anglo-American Times
Baths and Bath Engineering
Blackwood's Edinburgh Magazine
British Medical Journal
Builder
Building News
Critic
Dominion
Dublin Builder
Dublin Hospital Gazette
Dublin Medical Press
Echoes From the Clubs
Edinburgh Veterinary Review
Free Press
Hydropathic Record
Illustrated London News
Journal of Balneology & Climatology
Journal of Mental Science
Journal of the Society of Arts
Ladies' Field
Leicester Journal
London Society
MAP
Medical and Surgical Reporter, Pennsylvania
Medical Times & Gazette
Proc. Glasgow Philosophical Society
Proc. Liverpool Architectural & Archaeological Society
Punch
Sheffield Free Press
Shipbuilder
Southampton and District Pictorial
St Albans Times
St Paul's Magazine
Strand Magazine
Swimming Notes
The Field
The Lancet
The Reasoner
Trans. Medical Society
Trans. National Association for the Promotion of Social Science
Universitas Helsingiensis
Vanity Fair
Victorian Society Annual
Waterford News
Winning Post

Newspapers

Argus
Baltimore Sunday Herald
Bath Evening Chronicle
Belfast News-Letter
Birmingham Daily Post
Border Counties Advertiser
Bradford Advertiser
Bradford Observer
Bristol Mercury
Bristol Times
Brooklyn Daily Eagle
Brooklyn Standard Union
Buckinghamshire Advertiser
Bucks Herald
Bury Times
Caledonian Mercury
Cambrian
Cambridge Independent Press
Cork Constitution
Cork Examiner
Cork Herald
Daily Bristol Times and Mirror
Daily Mirror
Daily News
Daily Southern Cross
Darlington & Stockton Times
Doncaster Gazette
Dover Express
Dundee Courier & Argus
Dunfermline Press
Freeman's Journal
Glasgow Herald
Halifax Courier
Halifax Guardian
Harrogate Herald
Huddersfield Chronicle
Huddersfield Daily Chronicle
Huddersfield Examiner
Illustrated Melbourne Post
Irish Times
Keighley News
Kidderminster Shuttle
Leeds Evening Express
Leeds Mercury
Leeds Standard
Leicester Advertiser
Limerick Chronicle
Liverpool Mercury
London Gazette
London Standard
Manchester Guardian
Manchester Times
Morning Chronicle
Morning Post
New York Times
Newcastle Journal
North and South Shields Gazette
North Wales Chronicle
Northampton Daily Chronicle
Nottingham Arrow
Observer
Otago Witness
Pall Mall Gazette
Preston Guardian
Rochdale Observer
Rochdale Times
Scarborough Gazette
Scarborough Mercury
Scotsman
Shields Daily News
Stockton Herald
Swindon Evening Advertiser
Sydney Morning Herald
The Times
Tuapeka Times
Western Daily Press
Western Times
Wilts and Gloucestershire Standard

Wimbledon and District Gazette
York Herald

Books

Allsop, Robert Owen *The hydropathic establishment and its baths* (Spon, 1891)

—*The Turkish bath: its design and construction* (Spon, 1890)

Baden-Baden and its environs (Zurich: Orel Füssli, [1888]

Baines, Thomas *Yorkshire, past and present.* vol.2; pt.1 ([s.l.]: Mackenzie, [s.d.])

Baird, James *Ben Rhydding: its amenities, hygiene, and therapeutics* (Dennant, 1871)

Balbirnie, John *The sweating cure: the physiological basis and curative effects of the Turkish bath* (Job Caudwell, 1864)

Balgarnie, Robert *Sir Titus Salt, Baronet* (Hodder, 1877)

Barker, S and Henderson, S *Thermo-therapeutics* (Henry Renshaw, 1861)

Barter, Richard *The rise and progress of the 'Turkish bath'…* (Dublin: McGee, 1861)

—*The Turkish bath: being a lecture delivered in the Mechanic's Institute, Bradford…* (Bradford: J M Jowett, 1858)

Bartholomew, Charles *Illustrated guide to the Turkish baths* (Marshall, 1887)

—*Lecture on Turkish baths: twenty-seven years' experience of the physiological action of the Turkish bath in health and disease* (Marshall, 1886)

—*Mr Bartholomew's evidence before a committee of medical men on the prevention and cure of disease.* 6th edn (Bristol: Marshall, 1870)

—*The Turkish bath in health, sickness, convalescence, etc* (Ward, Lock, [1869])

Baths and bathing (Nottingham: The Nottingham Hammam, [1898])

Beamish, Richard *The functions of the skin, and the value of the bath, with special reference to the improved Turkish bath* (Bailliere, 1859)

Ben Rhydding: *the principles of hydropathy and the compressed-air bath, together with a chapter on the improved Roman or Turkish bath, by a graduate of the Edinburgh University* (Simpkin, Marshall, 1859)

Bishop, Maria Catherine *A memoir of Mrs Urquhart* (Kegan Paul, 1897)

Campbell, Agnes *Report on public baths and wash-houses in the United Kingdom* (Edinburgh: Carnegie UK Trust, 1918)

Chat upon health: Pat Dennehy visits Mrs Magrath (T Burns, 1875)

Claridge, R T *Hydropathy; or, the cold water cure, as practised by Vincent Priessnitz, at Gräefenberg, Silesia, Austria* (Madden, 1842)

Coley, Frederic Collins *The Turkish bath* (Walter Scott, 1887)

Constantine, Joseph *Fifty years of the water cure, with autobiographical notes* (Manchester: John Heywood, 1892)

—*Health and activity in middle and later life* (Simpkin, Marshall, 1890)

—*Hydropathy at home: the domestic practice of the water cure …* 3rd edn (Simpkin Marshall, 1884)

—*Hydropathy in city and town* (Heywood, 1905)

—*Hydropathy, health and longevity* (Manchester: Heywood, 1895)

Cosgrove, J J *Design of the Turkish bath* (Pittsburgh: Standard Sanitary Mfg, 1913)

Cross, Alfred W S *Public baths and wash-houses: a treatise on their planning, design, arrangement, and fitting…* (Batsford, 1906)

Davies, D S *Public health* (Bristol: British Association, 1898)

Descriptive notice of the rise and progress of the Irish Graffenberg… (Printed by Levey, Robinson and Franklyn, 1858)

Drake, Francis *The Anglo-Roman or 'Turkish bath': its history, proper construction, present status and various uses* (Ward & Lock, 1862)

Diogenes [pseud.] *Life in a tub.* 3rd edn (Dublin : McGee, 1858)

Dunlop, Durham *The philosophy of the bath: or air and water in health and disease* (Simpkin, Marshall, 1868)

Elson, George *The last of the climbing boys* (John Long, 1900)

Evans, Frenklen *The Turkish bath in health and disease…* (Cardiff: The Guardian, 1868)

Gibson, Charles Bernard *The history of the county and city of Cork* (Cork: Newby, 1861)

Glimpse of Saint Ann's… (St Ann's: Sweeney, 1869)

Gordon, William John *The horse-world of London* (Religious Tract Society, 1893)

Hammam of the Turks: collected fly-sheets (The Hammam, 1867)

Hammam Turkish bath (The Hammam, 1929)

Haughton, Edward *Facts and fallacies of the Turkish bath, or, what kind of bath should we have?* (Dublin: William Robertson, 1860)

Hedley, W S *The hydro-electric method in medicine* (Lewis, 1894)

Holroyd, Abraham *A life of Sir Titus Salt, with an account of Saltaire* (Saltaire: the author, 1871)

Holyoake, George Jacob *Bygones worth remembering* (Fisher Unwin, 1905)

—*Sixty years of an agitator's life* (Fisher Unwin, 1906)

Industries of Yorkshire (Historical Publ Co, 1888)

J.A. [ie, John Abel] *The Turkish bath: an antidote for the cravings of the drunkard.* (Dublin: Webb, 1859) (*Tracts on the drink question: no.1*)

Jagger, J *The Turkish bath* (Barker: [1860])

Jubilee of Crewe: containing a brief history of the rise and progress of the borough, from 1837 to 1887… (Crewe : Printed at the Guardian Office, [1887]

Lane, Edward William *An account of the manners and customs of the modern Egyptians…* (1836)

Laurie, James *The Roman or Turkish baths* (Edinburgh: MacLachlan & Stewart, 1864)

Leared, Arthur *Consumption arrested by the Turkish bath…* (Hardwicke,1864)

Lemon, James *Reminiscences of public life in Southampton, from 1866 to 1900* (Southampton: Gilbert, 1911)

Macleod, William *Directory of Ben-Rhydding, with a chapter on the water cure and homoeopathy* (Charles Gilpin, 1852)

Madden, Richard Robert *Travels in Turkey, Egypt, Nubia and Palestine in 1824-27* (Henry Colburn, 1829)

Mahomed, Sake Deen *Shampooing, or, benefits resulting from the use of the Indian medicated vapour bath...* 3rd edn (Brighton: William Fleet, 1838)

Manual of the Turkish bath: heat a mode of cure and a source of strength for men and animals, from the writings of Mr Urquhart; John Fife (ed) (Churchill, 1865)

Marsden, Thomas Lewen *The Turkish bath, or patriarchal regenerator by hot air: a lecture* (Southport: Haigh's Turkish Baths, 1861)

Maxfield, John [the younger] *The Turkish bath* (Gloucester: The Corporation, 1895)

Maygrier, Jacques-Paul *Nouvelles demonstrations d'accouchemens* (Paris, 1822)

Metcalfe, Richard *Sanitas sanitatum et omnia sanitas* (Co-operative Printing Co, 1877)

—*The rise and progress of hydropathy in England and Scotland* (Simkin, Marshall, 1906)

—*The water cure: a plea for hydropathic dispensaries* (Tweedie, 1878)

Miles, W J *Modern practical farriery: a complete guide to all that relates to the horse* (MacKenzie, [c 1870])

Milton, J L *On the modified Turkish and vapour bath...* (Hardwicke, [1874])

Montagu, Mary Wortley *Letters of the Right Honourable Lady M-y W-y M-e...* (Homer, 1764)

Moore, George *Esther Waters* (Scott, 1894)

Morley, John *Life of Cobden* (Fisher Unwin, 1881)

Morphy, John *Recollections of a visit to Great Britain and Ireland in the summer of 1862* (Palmer, 1863)

New Irish bath versus the old Turkish, or, pure air versus vapour: being an answer to the mis-statements of Drs Madden and Corrigan; 'Photophilus' (ed) (Dublin: McGee, 1860)

Opening of the [new] Turkish bath (Bury: The Council, 1898)

Opening of the Central Baths: 13 September 1905 (Bradford: The Council, 1905)

Opening of the Central Swimming Baths... (Middlesbrough: the County Borough Council, 1933)

Owen, Thomas *How I came to build a Turkish bath* (Oswestry: Commercial Circular, 1912)

Pictorial & descriptive guide to Dublin (Ward Lock, 1919)

Pliny the Elder *The natural history.* Book 11. Chap. 96; translated by John Bostock and H T Riley. http://www.perseus.tufts.edu/

Potter, William *The Roman or Turkish bath: its hygienic and curative properties* (Simkin & Marshall, 1859)

Powell, G R *The official railway handbook to Bray...* (Dublin: M'Glashan & Gill, 1860)

Principles and practice of modern house-construction; G Lister Sutcliffe (ed) (Blackie, 1898-9)

Programme of opening ceremony of Turkish Baths at the Old Kent Road Public Baths (Camberwell Borough Council, 1905)

Rayner, T *A voice from the thermae* 2nd edn (Dublin: Porter, 1861)

Recollections of the late Dr Barter, by the author of *Simple questions and sanitary facts* (Dublin: McGee, 1875)

Rhodes, Joseph *Half a century of co-operation in Keighley, 1860-1910* (Keighley: Keighley Co-operative Society, 1911)

Robertson, William *Rochdale past and present: a history and guide* (Rochester: Schofield and Hoblyn, 1875)

Robinson, Charles M and Shepherd, Charles H *Philosophy of health and beauty* ([s.n.], [s.d.])

Roth, Mathias *The Russian bath* (Groombridge, 1852)

Shepard, Charles H *Rheumatism and its treatment by Turkish baths* (New York: [the baths], 1892)

—*Turkish baths: no. 63 Columbia Street, Brooklyn Heights, N.Y.* (New York: the baths, [1863])

Sims, G *Living London* vol.2 (Cassell, 1902)

Smedley, John *Practical hydropathy* 12th edn (Kent, 1870)

Solly, Henry *Working men's social clubs and educational institutes* (Working Men's Club and Institute Union, 1867)

Souvenir of the opening of the public baths... (Camberwell Borough Council, 1905)

Souvenir to commemorate the opening of the City Hall and Northumberland Baths (Newcastle-on-Tyne: The Council, 1928)

Stables, W Gordon *Turkish and other baths: a guide to good health and longevity* (Dean, [1883])

Strictures on the personal cleanliness of the English with a description of the hamams of the Turks... (Pisa: printed by N. Capurro, 1828)

Swim and keep fit: Derby Baths and Entertainments official guide (Derby: The Council, 1964)

Tasmanian scenery (Melbourne: Fergusson & Mitchell, [188?])

Thackeray, William Makepeace *Notes of a journey from Cornhill to Grand Cairo...* (Chapman and Hall, 1846)

Thomson, Spencer *A dictionary of domestic medicine.* 38th edn (Griffin, 1906)

Trollope, Anthony *An autobiography* (Edinburgh: Blackwood, 1883)

Trotter, H M and others *Report of a deputation appointed on 16th Feb and confirmed on 27 Nov 1911 for the purpose of obtaining information with reference to the proposed annexe at the Central Baths, Morley Street* (Bradford: The Council, 1912)

Urquhart, David *The Pillars of Hercules, or, a narrative of travels in Spain and Morocco in 1848* (Bentley, 1850)

—*The spirit of the East: illustrated in a journal of travels through Roumeli during an eventful period* (Henry Colburn, 1838)

—*The Turkish bath, with a view to its introduction into the British dominions* (Bryce, 1856)

View book and guide to Brighton (Bright, c 1895)

Walsh, J H *The horse, in the stable and the field: his varieties, management in health and disease, anatomy, physiology, etc* (Routledge, 1862)

Walter Penhaligon (Royal Warrant Holders Association, 1907)

Whammond, G K *Illustrated guide to Dublin & Wicklow* (Dublin: McGee, 1868)

White Star Line: Royal and United States Mail Steamers (Liverpool: The Company, 1913)

Wilson, Erasmus *The eastern, or Turkish bath: its history, revival in Britain and application to the purpose of health* (John Churchill, 1861)

Wollaston, Robert *The sanitary advantages of baths, especially the Turkish or Roman bath* (Cheltenham: Henry Davies, 1860)

Woman's mission : a series of congress papers on the philanthropic work of women by eminent writers; Angela Burdett-Coutts (ed) (Samson Low, 1893)

Wood, A L and Woodruff, B C *The medical and surgical uses of electricity* (Brooklyn: The Brooklyn Turkish Bath Co, 1893)

Wyld, George *The Turkish bath or hot-air bath* (Leath & Rose, 1860)

Secondary sources

Theses

Cleminson, Julie *Walking in London: the fiction of Neil Bartlett, Sarah Waters and Alan Hollinghurst: writing missing voices of sexuality, class and gender back into history through re-imagining the city space.* PhD thesis (Brunel University, 2009) http://bura.brunel.ac.uk/bitstream/2438/4356/1/Fulltext%28Thesis%29.pdf

Dowling, William Charles *The Ladies' Sanitary Association and the origins of the health visiting services.* MA thesis (University of London, 1963)

Jenks, Margaret H *The activities and influence of David Urquhart, 1837-56, with special reference to the affairs of the Near East.* PhD thesis (University of London, 1964)

Mac Con Iomaire, Máirtín *The emergence, development and influence of French* haute cuisine *on public dining in Dublin restaurants 1900-2000: an oral history.*vol.2: *From ancient Ireland to 21st century Dublin.* PhD thesis (Dublin Institute of Technology, 2009)

Periodicals

Architectural Review
Art Journal
Bradford Antiquary
Cultural Analysis
Dunkerque Magazine
Dunmore Journal
Gardener's Monthly
Hackney History
Hertfordshire's Past
History of Psychiatry
Homes & Interiors Scotland
International Review of Social History
Intra
Jewish Chronicle
Journal American Medical Association
Journal of Design History
Journal of Modern History
Journal of the Bray Cualann Historical Society
Nottingham Magazine
Old Blarney
Old Limerick Journal
Other Clare
Trans. The Hunter Archaeological Society
Universitas Helsingiensis
Victorian Society Annual
Wandsworth Historian
Waterford Historian

Newspapers

Independent
Sunday Times Colour Supplement

Books

...and Mr Fortescue: a selection from the diaries from 1851 to 1862 of Chichester Fortescue, Lord Carlingford; Osbert Wyndham Hewett (ed) (Murray, [1958])

Adams, Carol *Ordinary lives* (Virago, 1982)

Anderson, Olive *A Liberal state at war: English politics and economics during the Crimean War* (Macmillan, 1967)

Avcıoğlu, Nebahat *Turquerie and the politics of representation,1728–1876* (Farnham: Ashgate, 2011)

Bailey, Cyril *Francis Fortescue Urquhart: a memoir* (Macmillan, 1936)

Baker, Alfred *The life of Sir Isaac Pitman (inventor of phonography)* (Pitman, 1908)

Banham, Peter Reynam *The architecture of the well-tempered environment* (Architectural Press, 1969)

Barnard, Jeffrey *Low life* (Duckworth, 1986)

Bartlett, Neil *Mr Clive & Mr Page* (Serpent's Tail, 1996) (Published in the USA as *The house on Brooke Street*)

Beveridge, Bruce and others *Titanic: the ship magnificent.* vol.2: *interior design & fitting out* (Stroud: History Pr, 2008)

Billups, Barbara *Crewe swimming baths: an architectural and social history* (Nantwich: Printed by Johnsons, 1984)

Biographical dictionary of modern British radicals; Joseph O Baylen and Norbert J Gossman (eds) (Brighton: Harvester Pr, 1984)

Blaker, Catriona *Edward Pugin and Kent: his life and work within the county*. 2nd edn (Ramsgate: The Pugin Society, 2012)

Bodies and things in nineteenth-century literature and culture; Katharina Boehm (ed) (New York: Palgrave Macmillan, 2012)

Boggs, Richard *Hammaming in the Sham* (Garnet, 2010)

Booth, Charles *Descriptive map of London poverty 1889* (London Topographical Society, 1984)

Borough of Stalybridge centenary booklet, 1857-1957 (Stalybridge: The Council, 1957)

Borsay, Anne and Shapely, Peter *Medicine, charity and mutual aid: the consumption of health and welfare in Britain, c.1550-1950* (Farnham: Ashgate, 2007)

Bowdler, Roger *The RAC Club, Pall Mall, Westminster: the swimming pool and Turkish baths: HART reports and papers; 31* (English Heritage, 2000)

Brief history of Huddersfield Royal Infirmary (Huddersfield: The Infirmary, 1922)

Brief history of Inner Wheel (Association of Inner Wheel Clubs in Great Britain & Ireland) http://home.btconnect.com/associationofinnerwheelclubs/Pages/Our_History_Page.htm (Accessed 1 Sep 2013)

Cambridge companion to Anthony Trollope; Carolyn Dever and Lisa Niles (eds) (CUP, 2010)

Camden Town Conservation Area Appraisal and Management Strategy [Camden Council, April 2014]

Cattell, John and Falconer, Keith *Swindon: the legacy of a railway town* (Swindon: HMSO, for English Heritage, 1995)

A Century of co-operation in Keighley: 1860-1960 (Keighley: Keighley Co-operative Society, 1960)

Chaloner, W H *The social and economic development of Crewe, 1780-1923* (Manchester: Univ Pr, 1950)

Change at Crewe ([Chester]: Cheshire Libraries, 1984)

Chauncey, George *Gay New York: the making of the gay male world, 1890-1940* (Flamingo, 1995)

City of Birmingham Baths Department (Birmingham: The Council, 1951)

Claeys, Gregory *Citizens and saints: politics and anti-politics in early British socialism* (Cambridge: CUP, 1989)

Cocks, H G *Nameless offences: homosexual desire in the nineteenth century* (Tauris, 2003)

Colclough, Bernard *Waterford or thereabouts* (Waterford: [the author],1993)

Cook, Matt *London and the culture of homosexuality, 1885-1914* (CUP, 2003)

Craft, space and interior design, 1855-2005; Sandra Alfoldy and Janice Helland (eds) (Farnham: Ashgate, 2008)

Cragside: Northumberland (The National Trust, 1992)

Curl, James Stevens *Victorian architecture: diversity & invention* (Reading: Spire, 2007)

Currents of radicalism: popular radicalism, organised labour and party politics in Britain, 1850-1914 Eugenio F Biagini and Alastair J Reid (eds) (Cambridge: CUP, 1991)

Danby, Miles *Moorish style* (Phaidon, 1995)

Darwin, Bernard *A century of medical service: the story of the Great Western Railway Medical Fund Society, 1847-1947* (Swindon: The Society, 1947)

Davies, K Mary *That favourite resort: the story of Bray, Co. Wicklow* (Bray: Wordwell, 2007)

Davis, Dorothy *A history of shopping* (Routledge, 1966)

Dempsey, John *I've seen them all naked* (Poole: Waterfront Publ,1992)

Dickens, Marie K *Changing the face of Carlisle: the life and times of Percy Dalton, City Engineer and Surveyor, 1926-1949* (South Stainmore: Hayloft, 2002)

Dictionary of national biography; Leslie Stephen (ed) (Smith, Elder, 1885-1903)

Digby, Anne *Madness, morality and medicine: a study of the York Retreat, 1796-1914* (CUP, 1985)

Durie, Alastair J *Water is best: the hydros and health tourism in Scotland, 1840-1940* (Edinburgh: John Donald, 2006)

Edinburgh war time guide 1942 (Edinburgh: City of Edinburgh Council of Social Service Citizen's Advice Bureau, 1942)

Elliott, John *Palaces, patronage and oils: Thomas Holloway—his sanatorium, college and picture gallery* (Egham: RHUL, 1996)

Enever, G *The history of the Newcastle Infirmary, 1751 to 2001* http://research.ncl.ac.uk/nsa/tl3.htm

Eye for architecture (Tulane University Library, 1984)

Facilities and tariffs relating to medicated, electrical, turkish, swimming baths and public wash-houses (Bradford: The Corporation, 1935)

Farley, M Foster *Biographical dictionary of modern British radicals* (Brighton: Harvester Pr, 1984) pp.258-61

Fisher, David *Directory of cinemas in Brighton and Hove* http://www.brightonfilm.com/Academy.htm

Fletcher, Geoffrey S *London overlooked* (Hutchinson, 1964)

Foley, Ronan *Healing waters: therapeutic landscapes in historic and contemporary Ireland* (Farnham: Ashgate, 2010)

General price list, 1939-40 (The Army & Navy Stores Ltd, 1939)

Gleason, John Howes *The Genesis of Russophobia in Great Britain: a study of the interaction of policy and opinion* (Cambridge (Mass.): Harvard Univ Pr, 1950

Gordon, Ian and Inglis, Simon *Great lengths: the historic indoor swimming pools of Britain* (Swindon: English Heritage, 2009)

Grilli, Peter *Pleasures of the Japanese bath* (New York: Weatherhill, 1992)

Guide to Cork City's historic plaques and signs (Cork: City Council) http://www.heritagecouncil.ie/

Hammam Turkish bath (The [London] Hammam, 1929)

Hidden iceberg of architectural history (Society of Architectural Historians of Great Britain, 1998)

Houlbrook, Matt *Queer London: perils and pleasures in the sexual metropolis, 1918-1957* (Chicago: Univ Pr, 2005)

Hunter, Richard and Macalpine, Ida *Psychiatry for the poor: 1851 Colney Hatch Asylum—Friern Hospital 1973...* (Dawsons, 1974)

Interpreting the orient: travellers in Egypt and the Near East; Paul and Janet Starkey (eds) (New York: Ithaca Pr, 2001)

Konya, Allan *The modern sauna and related facilities* (Reading: Archimedia, 2012)

Lancaster, Clay *Old Brooklyn Heights: New York's first suburb.* 2nd edn (New York: Dover, 1979)

Linstrum, Derek *Towers and colonnades: the architecture of Cuthbert Brodrick* (Leeds: Philosophical and Literary Society, 1999)

Mann, W M *1876 The baths: the story of the Western Baths, Hillhead, from 1876 to 1990* (Glasgow: The Club, [1991]

Marx, Karl *Karl Marx, Frederick Engels: collected works.* vol.12 (Lawrence & Wishart, 1975-)

Maud: the diaries of Maud Berkeley; adapted by Flora Fraser (Secker & Warburg, 1985)

McCormick *The Peases & the S&D Railway* (Newton Aycliffe: Bermac Publ, 2008)

McHardy, George *Reception at the Imperial Hotel.* The Victorian Society (Unpublished typescript, 18 February 1966)

McMillan, Beverly and Lehrer, Stanley *Titanic: fortune & fate* (New York: Simon & Schuster, 1998)

Meunier, Pascal *Hammams* (Paris: Dakota, 2005)

Musgrave, Clifford *Life in Brighton from the earliest times to the present.* Rev edn (Chatham: John Hallewell, 1981)

New perspectives on historical writing (Cambridge: Polity Pr, 1991)

Newby, Eric *On the shores of the Mediterranean* (Pan, 1985)

Newham, Alan T *The Cork and Muskerry Light Railway* (Oxford: Oakwood Pr, 1968)

Nielsen, Inge *Thermae et balnea: the architecture and cultural history of Roman public baths.* 2nd edn (Aarhus Univ Pr, 1993)

O'Dwyer, Frederick *Lost Dublin* (Dublin: Gill & Macmillan, 1981

O'Mahony, Colman *The Maritime Gateway to Cork: a history of the outports of Passage West and Monkstown from 1734-1942* (Cork: Tower Books, 1986)

Official opening of Remedial Suite and Sports Hall at Victoria Leisure Centre (Nottingham: The Council, 1975)

Oxford dictionary of national biography http://www.oxforddnb.com/

Pearson, Lynn *Tile gazetteer: a guide to British tile and architectural ceramics locations* (Shepton Beauchamp: Richard Dennis, 2005)

Pegg, Patricia *A very private heritage* (Malvern: Images, 1996)

Politics of gender in Anthony Trollope's novels: new readings for the twenty-first century; Margaret Markwick, Deborah Morse, and Regenia Gagnier (Eds) (Farnham: Ashgate, 2009)

Potvin, John *Material and visual cultures beyond male bonding, 1870–1914: bodies, boundaries and intimacy* (Farnham: Ashgate, 2007)

Pressure from without in early Victorian England; Patricia Hollis (ed) (Edward Arnold, 1974)

Problems and methods in the history of medicine; Roy Porter and Andrew Weir (eds) (Beckenham: Croom Helm, 1987)

Public baths (Newport: The Council, [c 1935])

Report of the Committee on Homosexual Offences and Prostitution [Chairman Sir John Wolfenden] (HMSO, 1957)

Rickards, Maurice *The encyclopedia of ephemera* (British Library, 2000)

Robinson, Gertrude *David Urquhart: some chapters in the life of a Victorian knight-errant of justice and liberty* (Oxford: Basil Blackwell, 1920)

Rook, Tony *Roman baths in Britain* (Oxford: Shire, 2002)

Routh, Jonathan *The good loo guide: where to go in London* (Wolfe, 1965)

Royle, Edward *Victorian infidels: the origins of the British Secularist Movement, 1791-1866* (Manchester: Univ Pr, 1974)

Said, Edward W *Orientalism* (Routledge, 1978)

Service, Robert *Ploughman of the moon: an adventure into memory* (New York: Dodd, Mead, 1945)

Shifrin, Malcolm *Victorian Turkish Baths* http://www.victorianturkishbath.org

Shorney, David *A brief history of the mansion at Avery Hill.* Rev ed. (Thames Polytechnic, 1990)

Siltzer, Frank *Newmarket: its sport and personalities* (Cassell, 1923)

Sims, George Robert *Living London: its work and its play*...vol.2 (Cassell, 1902)

Smith, Janet *Liquid assets: the lidos and open air swimming pools of Britain* (Swindon: English Heritage, 2005)

Sport and the working class in modern Britain; edited by Richard Holt (Manchester: Univ Pr, 1990)

Sweetman, John *Oriental obsession: Islamic inspiration in British and American art and architecture, 1500-1920* (Cambridge: CUP, 1988)

Taylor, A J P *The trouble makers: dissent over foreign policy, 1792-1939: The Ford Lectures, Oxford, 1956* (Hamish Hamilton, 1957)

Turner, E S *Taking the cure* (Michael Joseph, 1967)

Turner, Mark W *Backward glances: cruising the queer streets of New York and London* (Reaktion, 2001)

—*Trollope and the magazines: gendered issues in mid-Victorian Britain* (Basingstoke: Macmillan, 1999)

Victorian catalogue of household furnishings (Studio Edns, 1994)

War Poets Collection http://www2.napier.ac.uk/warpoets

Whammond, G K *Illustrated guide to Dublin & Wicklow* (Dublin: McGee, 1868)

Wilkins, Rachel *Turrets, towels and taps* (Birmingham: City Museum and Art Gallery, 1984)

Williams, Prue *Victoria Baths: Manchester's water palace* (Reading: Spire, 2004)

ACKNOWLEDGEMENTS

This book is the result of twenty-five years research into the history of the Victorian Turkish bath. During that period I have received help and encouragement from hundreds of people, in libraries, archives, and by letter and email.

For many of those years I had no idea that I would eventually write a book and so, especially in the beginning, when few librarians wore name badges and I was too shy to ask, I did not note down the names of these extremely knowledgeable and helpful professionals. And even if I had done so, many will now be working elsewhere, or may have changed their names.

As a retired librarian myself, I know that the smile, or an on-the-spot 'thank you' which I received after finding some elusive information for an enquirer, were what helped make librarianship so rewarding. So I hope that those who helped me in the same way will have felt the same, and will forgive my not naming them individually.

I feel that it would be invidious to list those with whom I have corresponded in any artificial 'order of importance', so I have chosen to thank them more or less in the order that I encountered them.

So I must first thank Norman Ashfield who was with me when I first discovered Charles Bartholomew's monogram (p. 6). He told me about his family connection with the baths, encouraged me to find out more about them and, later, gave me photographs and a nineteenth century ticket to the Leicester Square baths. And his off-the-cuff sketches enrich my section on the family-run Turkish bath in Chapter 12.

Norman also led me, indirectly, to 92-year-old Leonard Park, who agreed to be interviewed, gave me a wonderful mental picture of Bartholomew's baths in Worcester, and lent me documents about his father's connection with Bartholomew.

Others who agreed to be interviewed were Ray Parry about his time at Swindon, and Michael Birkett about the last years of two important companies, Nevill's and the Savoy. I was also able to speak by phone with Eric Pryor about the Claybury Asylum baths.

After a few years, I realised that my research was becoming serious and that I needed to learn how professional historians worked. I was fortunate in being able to read for an MA in Penelope Corfield's *Modern history: power, culture, society* at Royal Holloway, University of London, in 1996–7, and I gained much from the course, and from her comments—and those of her colleagues Gregory Claeys and Mary Ann Elston—on essays which later became the basis of several parts of the book and which are duly acknowledged in the endnotes.

Stumbling upon a postcard depicting a Turkish bath led me to join the Ephemera Society, and at one of their ephemera fairs I met Amoret Tanner who first suggested that I should write a book on the bath. In the event, I decided to compile a website instead. But over the years I have learned much from her about the value of ephemera in historical research, and from her fellow members, Michael Twyman, Rob Barham, and Malcolm Warrington, who will probably not have realised how much I have learned from them and their society's journal *The Ephemerist*.

It was coming across my website which first led John Hudson, Head of Publishing at what was then part of English Heritage, to write and ask if I would like to work with them on a book. His support and encouragement throughout has eased my work and, like his dry sense of humour, is much appreciated.

I am especially grateful to Kathryn Ferry who read an early draft of the book and whose comments greatly improved it. Special thanks are also due to two extremely busy academics, Deborah Denenholz Morse and Matt Houlbrook, who nevertheless most kindly found time to read early drafts of parts of Chapter 27, and whose valuable comments helped me avoid errors in areas where I was but a wandering stranger. I owe a special debt of gratitude to the publishing team at Historic England, especially my ever-patient and understanding editor Robin Taylor, their indefatigable Sales & Publicity Manager Clare Blick, and designer and layout manipulator extraordinaire, John Duggan of Sparks Publishing Services, Oxford. I am also extremely grateful to my wife, Devra Wiseman, whose copy-editing has improved the book beyond measure. In all these cases, any remaining errors or infelicities are, of course, my own.

Thanks are due to my daughter, Tash Shifrin, for visualising and creating the five special maps, and to Mike Young for his wonderfully evocative drawings of the Harrow Road and Imperial Hotel baths, and for our correspondence about them.

Others, with whom I have corresponded over lengthy periods, and who have helped interpret source documents and provide helpful information include Nebahat Avcıoğlu, Alastair Durie, Mary Davies, Ronan Foley, David Ritarose,

Susan Aykut, and Peter W Beirne. Other long-term correspondents include Gill Wright, Maurice Logan-Salton and Chris Brady.

I would also like to thank Neill Bartlett, John Cooper, Wendy Stacey, 'Anne', 'George', and 'R.L.O' who all gave me permission to quote from their correspondence with me.

I have also corresponded over the years with Charlotte Jones who has been working on the first PhD thesis to be written on the subject of the Victorian Turkish bath. I am especially grateful that one of her questions made me go back over my own research and detect a statement made without any supporting evidence because, like many other researchers, I had wanted it to be so. I am grateful also to Hadeel J Azhar, another PhD student, who most kindly allowed me to use information from the thesis on Dollie Radford which she is currently writing.

I am by no means the first author to thank Patrick Leary for his labour of love, the interdisciplinary mailing list *VICTORIA: 19th-Century British Culture & Society* hosted by Indiana University. I have subscribed to this for well over a decade and, as an independent researcher without access to institutional resources, it has been indispensable. It has also enabled me—and I know of others also—to feel part of the wider academic community, despite our independent status; its members have always been unstinting in helping us to locate information and understand concepts from areas beyond our own. That the following list of those who have helped during the course of my research includes so many of Patrick's listees is in itself an indication of my debt to him.

Those who have allowed me to use their images are thanked in individual credits so, finally, I would like to thank the following correspondents (some of whom, inevitably, are no longer with us) whose input has contributed in some way to the book: Mikkel Aaland, Steve Adams, Christine Alfano, Peter Allanson, Sian Anthony, Helen Arkwright, Michelle Ashmore, Chris Baggs, Jeff Behary, Andrew Bethune, Steve Betts, Bruce E Beveridge, Tarquin Blake, Catriona Blaker, Anne Boddaert, Andrew Bolton, Robert Bolton, Andrew Bond, Tom G A Bowles, James Bradley, John Bradley, Penelope Bullock, Joanne Burke, Heather Burns, Miriam Burstein, Philip Bye, Ion Castro, Susan Caton, Mark Chirnside, Ruth Corney, Doug Corrance, Ruth Cotton, Etta Cowman, Christine Crumblehulme, Alison Cullingford, Gill Culver, Eileen Curran, Rod Currie, Marcia D'Alton, Roger Darke, Mark David, Mark Davis, Arjan de Haan, Dennis Denisoff, Virginia Dodier, Ruth Doherty, Steven Done, Harriet Eaton, Ron Edwards, Michelle Elleray, Carl Evans, David Ewart, Michelle Faber, Helen Farrar, Malcolm Farrar, Judith Flanders, Paula Fleming, Jane Fletcher, Nick Fox, Andree Freeman, Martina Fuseli, David Gardiner-Hill, Marie Gethins, Donna Goldthwaite, John S Gordon, Alison Goss, George A Goulty, James Gregory, Lesley Hall, Anneliese Harmon, Philip Harper, Val Harrison, Jane Helliwell, Ronnie Herlihy, Dave Hewitt, Peter Higginbotham, Yvonne Hillyard, Ruth Hobbins, Andrew Hobbs, Chris Hobbs, Steven Hobbs, Mark Hodson, Alison Holmes, Dee Hoole, Christian Horvath, Philip Howard, David Howells, Susan Hoyle, Maggie Humberston, Helen Jackson, Lee Jackson, Heather James, Barry Johnson, Christopher Jones, Ellen Jordan, Angela Kale, Leslie Katz, Susan Kemp, David King, Daniel Klistorner, Heike Kronenwatt, Marie-Lena Kuttruff, James Lamantia, Julie-Anne Lambert, David Latané, Alan Leonard, Paul Lewis, Matt Lodder, Marc J Loost, Cammwy MacDonald, Campbell Macknight, Mike Maguire, Bill Mann, Ken Marschall, Eithne Massey, Eve McAulay, Andrew McGilp, Craig McHugh, Helen McNamara, Mary Millar, Ian Miller, Margaret Molyneux, Ellen Moody, Chris Moore, Sandi Moore, Tracy Moroney, Dave Morris, Frank Murray, Jane Nesbitt, Katherine Newey, Mariam Nicolson, Richard Norman, Kostya Novoselov, Sue Nzilani, Jon Oates, Liz Oldham, Joe O'Leary, Alan Oliver, Michael Oppler, Tijen O'Reilly, Bruce E Osborne, David Oswald, Karen Palmer, Suzy Payne, Lynn Pearson, M Jeanne Peterson, Stephen Phillips, Louise Pressley, Janet Priest, Barbara Reader, Robert Redfern-West, Chris Richardson, Ruth Richardson, Bennery Rickard, Elinor Robinson, Peter W Robinson, Will Robley, Tony Rook, David Rose, Bruce Rosen, Stuart Rosenblatt, Alex Sakula, Toby Salisbury, Anna Sander, Brian Scott, Richard Scully, Frank Sharman, Steve Sharp, Dave Shaw, David Shaw, Maureen Shettle, Gary Simons, Kathleen Sims, Noël Siver, Amy Smith, Louise Smith, Monty Smith, Theodore Sourkes, Anne Steer, Parks Stephenson, Andrew Stewart, Timothy Stunt, Christopher Suggs, Charlotte Swire, Paul Taylor, Phillip Taylor, Hannah Thomas, Tracey Townsend, Vicky Traino, Shanta Trusewich, Hans van Lemmen, Larry Walsh, Miriam Ward, Ian Watson, Stephen Wildman, Chris Willis, Paul Windley, Helena Wojtczak, Michael Wolff, Dave Woodcock, Irene Wynne, Tony Zimnoch.

To those whose names I have accidentally omitted, I apologise, for I am no less grateful to you, and if you contact me, I will add your name to the complementary website page, together with any other omissions or corrections.

INDEX 1
TURKISH BATHS OPEN TO THE PUBLIC

Note: page numbers in *italics* refer to illustrations; page numbers in **bold** refer to illustrations with accompanying text

(C) refers to commercial establishments
(M) refers to municipal establishments, or those taken over by them (F) denotes an establishment started by a member of one of the Foreign Affairs Committees

Members of the public may on occasion have used baths designed for special users (eg, hydros) included in **Index 2.** These baths are not included in the present index as their main purpose was to provide baths for the special users.

INDEX 2

TURKISH BATHS FOR SPECIAL CLASSES OF USER

Note: page numbers in *italics* refer to illustrations; page numbers in **bold** refer to illustrations with accompanying text

INDEX 3
PEOPLE

Note: page numbers in *italics* refer to illustrations; page numbers in **bold** refer to illustrations with accompanying text

(F) denotes a member of one of the Foreign Affairs Committees, or someone very close to them

INDEX 4
SUBJECT INDEX

Note: page numbers in *italics* refer to illustrations; page numbers in **bold** refer to illustrations with accompanying text